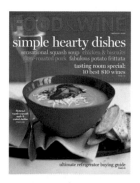

FOOD & WINE

annual cookbook 2008

an entire year of recipes

FOOD & WINE ANNUAL COOKBOOK 2008

EDITOR **Kate Heddings**
ART DIRECTOR **Patricia Sanchez**
DESIGNER **James Maikowski**
SENIOR EDITOR **Zoe Singer**
ASSISTANT FOOD EDITOR **Melissa Rubel**
COPY EDITOR **Lisa Leventer**
EDITORIAL ASSISTANT **Cecilia Knutsson**
PRODUCTION **Christine DeLorenzo**
PHOTO COORDINATOR **Lisa S. Kim**

PRESIDENT/C.E.O. **Ed Kelly**
SENIOR VICE PRESIDENT, CHIEF MARKETING OFFICER **Mark V. Stanich**
C.F.O./S.V.P./CORPORATE DEVELOPMENT & OPERATIONS **Paul B. Francis**
VICE PRESIDENT, BOOKS AND PRODUCTS **Marshall Corey**
SENIOR MARKETING MANAGER **Bruce Spanier**
ASSISTANT MARKETING MANAGER **Sarah H. Ross**
BUSINESS MANAGER **Thomas Noonan**
CORPORATE PRODUCTION MANAGER **Stuart N. Handelman**
DIRECTOR OF FULFILLMENT **Phil Black**
MANAGER OF CUSTOMER EXPERIENCE AND PRODUCT DEVELOPMENT **Charles Graver**
ASSISTANT FULFILLMENT AND OPERATIONS MANAGER **Rene O'Connell**
PRODUCTION DIRECTOR **Rosalie Abatemarco Samat**

FRONT COVER
Orecchiette with Sautéed Greens and Scallion Sauce, p. 180
PHOTOGRAPH BY Quentin Bacon
FOOD STYLING BY Jee Levin
PROP STYLING BY Dani Fisher

BACK COVER
PHOTOGRAPH (O-HURRICANE) BY Victoria Pearson
FOOD STYLING (O-HURRICANE) BY Rori Trovato
PHOTOGRAPH (CHICKEN) BY Yunhee Kim
PHOTOGRAPH (SQUASH) BY John Kernick
PHOTOGRAPH (CHURROS) BY Tina Rupp
FOOD STYLING (CHICKEN, SQUASH, CHURROS) BY Jee Levin

FLAP PHOTOGRAPHS
DANA COWIN PORTRAIT BY Andrew French
KATE HEDDINGS PORTRAIT BY Andrew French

AMERICAN EXPRESS PUBLISHING CORPORATION

ISBN 1-932624-24-4
ISSN 1097-1564

Published by American Express Publishing Corporation
1120 Avenue of the Americas, New York, New York 10036

Manufactured in the United States of America

FOOD & WINE MAGAZINE

VICE PRESIDENT/EDITOR IN CHIEF **Dana Cowin**
CREATIVE DIRECTOR **Stephen Scoble**
MANAGING EDITOR **Mary Ellen Ward**
EXECUTIVE EDITOR **Pamela Kaufman**
EXECUTIVE FOOD EDITOR **Tina Ujlaki**
EXECUTIVE WINE EDITOR **Lettie Teague**

FEATURES
FEATURES EDITOR **Michelle Shih**
TRAVEL EDITOR **Salma Abdelnour**
SENIOR EDITORS **Ray Isle, Kate Krader**
ASSOCIATE EDITOR **Jen Murphy**
ASSISTANT EDITOR **Ratha Tep**
ASSISTANT HOME & STYLE EDITOR **Jessica Romm**
EDITORIAL ASSISTANTS **Alessandra Bulow, Megan Krigbaum**

FOOD
SENIOR EDITOR **Kate Heddings**
SENIOR ASSOCIATE EDITOR **Nick Fauchald**
ASSOCIATE EDITOR **Emily Kaiser**
EDITORIAL ASSISTANT **Kristin Donnelly**
TEST KITCHEN SUPERVISOR **Marcia Kiesel**
SENIOR TEST KITCHEN ASSOCIATE **Grace Parisi**
TEST KITCHEN ASSOCIATE **Melissa Rubel**
KITCHEN ASSISTANT **Chris Fletcher**

ART
ART DIRECTOR **Patricia Sanchez**
SENIOR DESIGNER **Courtney Waddell**
DESIGNER **Michael Patti**
DESIGNER (BOOKS) **James Maikowski**

PHOTO
DIRECTOR OF PHOTOGRAPHY **Fredrika Stjärne**
DEPUTY PHOTO EDITOR **Joni Noe**
PHOTO ASSISTANT **Rebecca Jacobs**

PRODUCTION
ASSISTANT MANAGING EDITOR **Christine Quinlan**
PRODUCTION MANAGER **Matt Carson**
DESIGN/PRODUCTION ASSISTANT **Carl Hesler**

COPY & RESEARCH
COPY CHIEF **Michele Berkover Petry**
SENIOR COPY EDITOR **Ann Lien**
ASSISTANT RESEARCH EDITORS **Emily McKenna, Kelly Snowden, Emery Van Hook**

EDITORIAL BUSINESS COORDINATOR **Kerianne Hansen**

FOOD & WINE

annual cookbook

an entire year
of recipes

2008

American Express Publishing Corporation, New York

FOOD & WINE
BOOKS

contents

foreword **7**   wine pairings **380**   recipe index **392**   contributors **418**

P. 104

winter

starters & drinks
10

main courses
32

side dishes
68

desserts & brunch
88

spring

starters & drinks
116

main courses
130

side dishes
174

desserts & brunch
190

P. 264

P. 314

summer

starters & drinks
206

main courses
220

side dishes
258

desserts & brunch
270

autumn

starters & drinks
286

main courses
302

side dishes
340

desserts & brunch
358

A stylishly homespun meal at Swanson
Vineyards features recipes from chef
Thomas Keller, including Lemon-Brined
Fried Chicken (P. 313).

foreword

Every year at FOOD & WINE, we're on the lookout for what's next, whether it's a new ingredient, an up-and-coming chef or a little-known wine that's a perfect match with food. Those trends are reflected in the recipes gathered in our annual cookbook. This year, excited by the rising appreciation of seasonality and the growing importance of farmers' markets all around the country, we've organized the recipes in this book into four sections: winter, spring, summer and autumn. Look for your favorites in each section, and check out the menus for entertaining (page 388), which showcase the best each season has to offer.

There's also year-round inspiration in the fantastic recipes from our Tasting & Testing column, in which Grace Parisi, F&W's senior test kitchen associate, develops the very best version of a classic recipe and then provides super-useful and amazingly delicious variations. Our favorites: tomato sauce, burgers and fruit pies. You'll also find easy guides to mastering the grill, putting together the perfect American cheese plate and selecting a great steak. As always, we've noted simple wine pairings throughout the book, and included an essential wine glossary that suggests affordable and accessible choices.

We love tasting all of these recipes in our Test Kitchen, and we love even more when we know that you've re-created them at home.

Dana Cowin
Editor in Chief
FOOD & WINE Magazine

Kate Heddings
Editor
FOOD & WINE Cookbooks

Lachlan Mackinnon Patterson and Bobby Stuckey, co-owners of Frasca Food and Wine in Boulder, Colorado, make smoky Grilled Capon with Salsa Verde (P. 41).

winter

starters & drinks 10

main courses 32

side dishes 68

desserts & brunch 88

starters & drinks

starters

Caramelized Onion and Toasted Bread Soup

TOTAL: 50 MIN

8 SERVINGS ● ○ ●

- 3 slices of white sandwich bread, cut into 1-inch squares
- 3 tablespoons unsalted butter
- 2 large white onions, thinly sliced
- 1½ cups water, plus more for deglazing
- 4½ cups whole milk

Salt and freshly ground pepper

Crème fraîche and snipped chives
        or ¼ cup Herbed Crème Fraîche
        Dip (p. 15), for garnish

1. Preheat the oven to 350°. Spread the bread squares on a baking sheet and toast for about 10 minutes, until golden.

2. Meanwhile, melt the butter in a large skillet. Add the onions, cover and cook over moderate heat, stirring, until softened, about 5 minutes. Reduce the heat to moderately low and cook uncovered until the onions are deeply golden, 30 minutes. Stir in 2 to 3 tablespoons of water a few times during cooking to deglaze the pan.

3. Add the toasted bread, the milk and the 1½ cups of water to the skillet and bring to a boil, scraping up any browned bits. Simmer over very low heat just until the bread is very soft, about 5 minutes. Transfer to a blender and puree until smooth.

4. Transfer the soup to a saucepan and bring to a simmer. Season with salt and pepper and pour into bowls. Garnish with crème fraîche and chives and serve.
—*Pim Techamuanvivit*

MAKE AHEAD The onion and bread soup can be refrigerated overnight.

WINE Complex, aromatic Chenin Blanc.

Passatelli in Brodo

ACTIVE: 45 MIN; TOTAL: 3 HR 45 MIN

6 SERVINGS

One 4-pound chicken

- 3 quarts water
- 1 quart low-sodium chicken broth
- 1 onion, halved
- 1 carrot, halved
- 1 celery rib, halved
- 1 bay leaf
- 1 teaspoon whole black peppercorns

One 4-ounce Parmigiano-
        Reggiano rind

Kosher salt

- 2 ounces mortadella, cut into ½-inch pieces
- 4 large eggs
- 1 large egg yolk
- 1 teaspoon finely grated lemon zest

Pinch of freshly grated nutmeg

- 1¼ cups plain dried bread crumbs
- ¼ cup freshly grated Parmigiano-Reggiano, plus more for serving
- 2 tablespoons unsalted butter, cut into 6 pats

1. In a soup pot, bring the chicken, water, broth, onion, carrot, celery, bay leaf and peppercorns to a boil. Simmer over low heat for 2 hours. Add the cheese rind and simmer for 1 hour. Strain the broth and discard the solids. Skim well and season with salt. You should have 10 cups.

2. Meanwhile, in a mini food processor, pulse the mortadella until finely chopped. Add the eggs, egg yolk, lemon zest and nutmeg and process to a loose paste. Transfer the mixture to a medium bowl and stir in the bread crumbs, the ¼ cup of grated cheese and ½ tablespoon of kosher salt; the dough will be stiff. Knead the dough with your hands until the ingredients are evenly combined.

3. In a large saucepan, bring 4 cups of the broth to a gentle boil. Working in 3 batches, transfer ½ cup of the dough at a time to a potato ricer with large ¼-inch holes. Squeeze 2-inch lengths of the dough into the simmering broth, cutting the dumplings with a paring knife. Repeat immediately with another ½ cup of dough. Stir and cook gently just until the *passatelli* float to the surface and are tender, about 2 minutes. Using a skimmer, transfer the *passatelli* to a large bowl. Repeat with the remaining dough. Save the broth in the saucepan for another use.

4. Bring the remaining 6 cups of broth to a simmer. Spoon the *passatelli* into 6 bowls and top with the pats of butter. Pour the hot broth on top and serve right away, passing grated cheese at the table.
—*Paul Bartolotta*

MAKE AHEAD The dough can be refrigerated overnight. Bring to room temperature before using. The broth can be refrigerated for 5 days or frozen for 2 months.

WINE Cherry-inflected, earthy Sangiovese.

Chicken Soup with Rosemary Matzo Balls

ACTIVE: 1 HR; TOTAL: 5 HR 45 MIN
8 SERVINGS ●

STOCK

- 5 pounds chicken wings
- 2 tablespoons vegetable oil
- 4 large onions, finely chopped
- 7 pounds chicken backs, necks and feet
- 6 carrots—4 finely diced, 2 sliced ½ inch thick
- 2 celery ribs, finely diced
- 5 bay leaves
- 2 heads of garlic, halved crosswise
- 5 large thyme sprigs
- 2 rosemary sprigs
- 2 teaspoons black peppercorns
- ¼ cup sherry vinegar
Salt

MATZO BALLS

- 4 large eggs
- ¼ cup reserved chicken fat or unsalted butter
- ¼ cup club soda
- 2 scallions, white and tender green parts only, sliced paper-thin
- ½ teaspoon very finely chopped rosemary leaves
- ½ teaspoon salt
- ½ cup plus 4 teaspoons matzo meal

SOUP

- 2 leeks, white and tender green parts only, very thinly sliced
- 2 skinless, boneless chicken breast halves, cut into ¾-inch dice (about 1¼ pounds)
- 2 skinless, boneless chicken thighs, cut into ¾-inch dice (about 10 ounces)

1. MAKE THE STOCK: Preheat the oven to 425°. Spread the chicken wings in a large roasting pan and roast for about 30 minutes, until golden brown.

2. Meanwhile, in a large stockpot, heat the vegetable oil. Add the onions, cover and cook over moderately high heat, stirring occasionally, until softened, about 5 minutes. Uncover and cook, stirring frequently, until the onions are lightly browned, about 5 minutes longer. Add the chicken backs, necks and feet, the diced carrots, celery, bay leaves, garlic, thyme, rosemary, peppercorns and 8 quarts of water and bring to a light boil, skimming any scum that rises to the surface.

3. Add the roasted chicken wings to the stockpot. Place the roasting pan over 2 burners, add the vinegar and 2 cups of water and simmer over high heat, scraping up any browned bits. Add the liquid to the pot and simmer gently over moderate heat for 2½ hours. Carefully strain the stock

into another large pot and discard the solids, including the wings. You should have about 8 quarts of liquid. Let the stock cool, then spoon off as much of the chicken fat as possible and reserve it for making the matzo balls. Season the chicken stock lightly with salt.

4. MAKE THE MATZO BALLS: In a medium bowl, whisk the eggs with the reserved chicken fat, club soda, sliced scallions, chopped rosemary leaves and salt. Whisk in the matzo meal. Cover the bowl and refrigerate for 1 hour, until the mixture is slightly firm.

5. MAKE THE SOUP: Bring a small saucepan of salted water to a boil. Add the sliced carrot and leeks and cook over high heat until tender, about 7 minutes; drain. In a saucepan, bring 2 cups of the stock to a simmer. Add the diced chicken breast and thighs and cook over moderately low heat until just white throughout, about 6 minutes. Transfer the chicken to a plate; reserve the broth for another use (see Note).

6. Bring a large saucepan of the chicken stock to a simmer. Scoop rounded tablespoons of the matzo mixture into balls (about 2 dozen balls) and add them to the simmering stock. Cover and cook over very low heat until the matzo balls are tender, fluffed and cooked through, about 25 minutes. Using a slotted spoon, transfer the matzo balls to a clean pot. Add the chicken, carrots and leeks and 8 cups of the stock and bring to a simmer. Ladle the soup and matzo balls into bowls and serve.
—*Dan Barber*

NOTE The broth gets cloudy from cooking the chicken and matzo balls, but it's perfectly delicious. Save it to use as the base for another soup.

MAKE AHEAD The stock can be refrigerated for 5 days or frozen for 2 months; skim off the fat after it's chilled. The cooked matzo balls can be refrigerated in an airtight container for up to 2 days.

WINE Rich, complex white Burgundy.

Butternut Squash Soup with Apple and Smoked Cheddar

ACTIVE: 35 MIN; TOTAL: 1 HR 25 MIN

4 SERVINGS ●

- 2 tablespoons extra-virgin olive oil
- 1 medium onion, halved and thinly sliced
- ¾ cup apple cider

One 1¾-pound butternut squash— peeled, seeded and cut into 1-inch dice (5¼ cups)

- 4½ cups chicken stock or low-sodium broth
- ½ cup heavy cream

Salt and freshly ground pepper

- 2 tablespoons unsalted butter
- 1 McIntosh apple, cut into ½-inch dice
- ⅓ cup coarsely shredded smoked cheddar cheese (2 ounces)

1-inch pieces of chives or thinly sliced sage leaves, for garnish

1. In a large saucepan, heat the olive oil. Add the onion and cook over moderately high heat, stirring occasionally, until golden, about 8 minutes. Add the apple cider and cook until syrupy, about 3 minutes. Add the butternut squash and chicken stock and bring to a boil. Cover and simmer until the squash is very tender, about 40 minutes.

2. In a blender, puree the soup in batches. Return the soup to the saucepan and stir in the cream. Season with salt and pepper and keep warm.

3. Heat a medium skillet. Add the butter and diced apple and cook over high heat until the apple is tender and golden around the edges, about 2 minutes. Remove the skillet from the heat. Season lightly with salt and pepper.

4. Ladle the soup into warmed bowls, garnish with the cheddar, sautéed apples and chives and serve. —*Jeremy Silansky*

MAKE AHEAD The soup can be refrigerated for up to 2 days.

WINE Lush, fragrant Viognier.

Chestnut and Celery Root Soup with Chorizo and Scallops

ACTIVE: 35 MIN; TOTAL: 1 HR

4 SERVINGS ●

- 2 chestnuts, scored
- ⅓ cup peeled and diced celery root
- 1½ cups water
- 2 tablespoons heavy cream

Salt

Freshly ground white pepper

- 4 baguette slices
- 1 teaspoon extra-virgin olive oil, plus more for brushing
- 1 dry chorizo link (3 ounces), cut into 1-inch matchsticks
- 8 sea scallops (¾ pound)

1. Preheat the oven to 400°. Boil the chestnuts in salted water until just tender, about 5 minutes. Take 1 chestnut out of the water at a time, and while still hot, hold it with a kitchen towel and peel with a paring knife. Crumble the chestnuts.

2. In a small saucepan, cover the chestnuts and celery root with the 1½ cups of water and the cream, add a pinch of salt and bring to a boil. Simmer over moderate heat until the celery root is very tender, about 25 minutes. Transfer the mixture to a blender and puree until silky. Pour the soup into a small saucepan and season with salt and white pepper.

3. Brush the baguette slices with oil and bake until crisp, about 5 minutes. In a small skillet, heat the 1 teaspoon of oil. Add the chorizo and cook over moderate heat until sizzling, about 1 minute.

4. Remove the small white muscle from the side of each scallop. Slice the scallops crosswise ⅛ inch thick. Arrange the slices in 4 shallow bowls and season with salt and pepper. Scatter half the chorizo on top. Bring the soup to a simmer and pour over the scallops. Top with the remaining chorizo and serve with the baguette toasts. —*Yves Camdeborde*

WINE Ripe, luxurious Chardonnay.

Spinach and Egg-Drop Pasta Soup

TOTAL: 30 MIN

10 SERVINGS ●

"In our house, *stracciatella* was a catch-all," says Tom Valenti, chef and owner of Ouest in New York City. The name, from the Italian *stracciatto* ("torn apart"), refers to the strands of egg beaten into the simmering broth. "We always started with good homemade stock and then added whatever was around: beans, leftover sausage, shredded chicken." With a few truffle shavings, this simple, rustic soup can be dressed up for a holiday dinner party.

- ½ pound *tubetti, ditali* or other small pasta
- 2 quarts chicken stock
- 4 garlic cloves, thinly sliced
- 5 ounces baby spinach

Salt and freshly ground black pepper

- 4 large eggs, beaten
- ½ cup freshly grated Parmigiano-Reggiano cheese, plus more for serving

Extra-virgin olive oil, for drizzling

Lemon wedges, for serving

1. Bring a large pot of salted water to a boil over high heat. Add the pasta and cook until al dente. Drain well.

2. In a medium saucepan, combine the stock and sliced garlic and bring to a simmer over moderate heat; simmer for 3 minutes. Add the drained pasta and baby spinach and continue to simmer over moderate heat until the spinach wilts. Season the soup with salt and pepper. Gently stir in the beaten eggs, breaking them into long strands. Gently simmer the soup until the eggs are just firm, about 1 minute. Stir in the ½ cup of grated Parmigiano-Reggiano cheese. Ladle the soup into bowls, drizzle with olive oil and serve, passing lemon wedges and more Parmigiano-Reggiano on the side. —*Tom Valenti*

WINE Fresh, lively Soave.

SPINACH AND EGG-DROP PASTA
SOUP (P. 12) AND HAM,
SOPPRESSATA AND TWO-CHEESE
STROMBOLI (P. 67)

Eggs with Brown Butter and Salmon Caviar

TOTAL: 40 MIN
12 SERVINGS

Instead of preparing the usual deviled eggs, F&W's Grace Parisi tops hard-boiled eggs with julienned radish, salmon caviar and brown butter for a refined but tempting hors d'oeuvre. She was inspired by an appetizer of radish, caviar and brown butter at Manhattan's Prune restaurant.

- 1 dozen large eggs
- 3 large radishes, finely julienned
- 2 tablespoons crème fraîche or sour cream
- ½ teaspoon finely grated lemon zest

Salt and freshly ground pepper

- 1 ounce salmon caviar
- 2 tablespoons unsalted butter

1. Put the eggs in a large saucepan, cover with cold water and bring to a rolling boil over high heat. Cover the saucepan tightly and remove from the heat. Let stand, covered, for 12 minutes.

2. Fill a medium bowl with ice water. Pour out the water from the saucepan and shake the pan gently to crack the egg shells. Transfer the eggs to the ice water to cool, then pat the eggs dry. Peel the eggs and halve each one lengthwise. Slice a thin sliver from the bottom of each egg half to keep it steady.

3. In a small bowl, combine the julienned radishes with the crème fraîche, grated lemon zest and a pinch each of salt and pepper. Spoon the radish mixture on top of the eggs and top each with a small dollop of salmon caviar.

4. In a small skillet, cook the butter over moderate heat until lightly browned and fragrant, about 5 minutes. Season with salt and spoon a small drizzle over the caviar. Serve right away. —*Grace Parisi*

MAKE AHEAD The unpeeled hard-boiled eggs can be refrigerated for up to 3 days.

WINE Dry, rich Champagne.

Chicken Liver Pâté with Pistachios

ACTIVE: 1 HR; TOTAL: 3 HR 20 MIN
MAKES ABOUT 5 CUPS

This pâté makes an elegant holiday gift presented in a pretty porcelain ramekin with crackers or crispy wafers, like Margaret's Artisan Flatbread. The buttery, earthy pâté can be spread on crostini, stuffed into Cognac-poached prunes or shaped into small balls and deep-fried with sage leaves.

- 2 sticks softened unsalted butter, plus 4 tablespoons melted
- 3 large shallots, very thinly sliced (1 cup)
- 2 pounds chicken livers, trimmed

Salt and freshly ground black pepper

- ¾ cup dry Marsala
- ½ cup chicken stock
- 1¼ cups salted roasted pistachios, ½ cup chopped
- ¼ cup chopped parsley
- 1 teaspoon chopped thyme

1. In a large skillet, melt 4 tablespoons of the softened butter. Add the shallots and cook over moderately low heat, stirring occasionally, until softened, about 8 minutes. Add the chicken livers, season with salt and black pepper and cook over moderate heat, turning a few times, until the livers are firm, about 4 minutes. Pour in the Marsala and simmer for 2 minutes, stirring a few times. Pour in the chicken stock and simmer, turning the livers a few times, until the livers are light pink in the center, about 6 minutes. Remove the pan from the heat and let the mixture cool for 5 minutes.

2. Transfer 10 of the livers to a plate. Transfer the contents of the skillet to a blender and puree. Cut the remaining 1½ sticks of softened butter into tablespoons. With the machine on, add the butter and blend until it is completely incorporated.

3. Scrape the puree into a large bowl. Cut the reserved 10 livers into ½-inch pieces

and fold them in, along with the whole pistachios, the parsley and the thyme. Generously season the pâté with salt and pepper. Spoon the pâté into four 1½-cup ramekins, cover with plastic wrap and refrigerate until firm, about 2 hours.

4. Pour 1 tablespoon of the melted butter over each pâté to seal it, then garnish with the chopped pistachios. Cover the ramekins and refrigerate until the butter is firm, about 20 minutes. —*Marcia Kiesel*

SERVE WITH Toast or crackers.

MAKE AHEAD The pâté can be refrigerated for up to 2 weeks.

WINE Dry, earthy sparkling wine.

Mini Brioche Lobster Rolls

TOTAL: 30 MIN
MAKES 12 ROLLS ●

- ¾ pound cooked lobster meat, crabmeat or shrimp, coarsely chopped
- ¼ cup plus 2 tablespoons mayonnaise
- 1 teaspoon chopped tarragon
- ½ teaspoon finely grated lemon zest

Salt and freshly ground black pepper

- 12 mini brioche or Parker House rolls (about 2½ inches)

Snipped chives, for garnish

1. In a food processor, combine the lobster meat with the mayonnaise, chopped tarragon and grated lemon zest and pulse to a chunky paste. Season with salt and black pepper.

2. Using a paring knife, cut a 1½-inch-round plug out of the top of each roll, leaving a ½-inch border all around. Using a small spoon, carefully hollow out the rolls. Spoon the lobster filling into the rolls and garnish with the chives. —*Grace Parisi*

MAKE AHEAD The lobster salad can be refrigerated for up to 2 days. The mini lobster rolls can be refrigerated in an airtight container for up to 3 hours.

WINE Ripe, luxurious Chardonnay.

CHICKEN LIVER PÂTÉ WITH PISTACHIOS

MINI BRIOCHE LOBSTER ROLLS

Herbed Crème Fraîche Dip with Crudités

 **TOTAL: 15 MIN**
8 SERVINGS ● ○

1 cup crème fraîche
3 tablespoons minced parsley
3 tablespoons snipped chives
2 tablespoons finely chopped
   tarragon
1½ tablespoons fresh lemon juice
Kosher salt
2 pounds asparagus, peeled if thick
1 bunch of small radishes

1. In a bowl, whisk the crème fraîche with the parsley, chives and tarragon. Whisk in the lemon juice and season well with salt.
2. Bring a large, deep skillet of salted water to a boil over high heat and fill a bowl with ice water. Cook the asparagus in the boiling water until tender, about 5 minutes. Drain and immediately transfer to the ice water to cool. Drain and pat dry.

3. Arrange the asparagus and radishes on a large serving platter and serve with the Herbed Crème Fraîche Dip.
—*Pim Techamuanvivit*

MAKE AHEAD The crème fraîche dip and the asparagus and radishes can be refrigerated for up to 8 hours.
WINE Dry, light Champagne.

Warm Leek and Goat Cheese Dip

 **TOTAL: 30 MIN**
12 SERVINGS ● ○

4 tablespoons unsalted butter
8 small leeks (about 2 pounds),
   white and tender green
   parts only, cut into
   ⅓-inch rings
1 pound fresh goat cheese,
   at room temperature
½ pound cream cheese, at
   room temperature

Salt and freshly ground pepper
2 tablespoons snipped chives
Flatbreads, pita crisps, crackers,
   crusty bread or raw vegetables,
   for serving

Melt the butter in a large, deep skillet. Add the leeks and stir to coat. Cover and cook over high heat until just beginning to soften, about 3 minutes. Uncover and cook over moderate heat, stirring frequently, until tender and lightly browned in spots, about 8 minutes. Remove from the heat. Stir in the goat cheese and cream cheese until completely melted and season with salt and pepper. Transfer to a warmed serving dish, sprinkle with the snipped chives and serve immediately, with flatbreads.
—*Grace Parisi*

MAKE AHEAD The dip can be refrigerated overnight; reheat in a 325° oven for 15 to 20 minutes, until hot.
WINE Dry, rich Champagne.

●HEALTHY ●MAKE AHEAD ·VEGETARIAN ●STAFF FAVORITE

15

THREE-CHEESE MINI MACS

Pimento Cheese

TOTAL: 25 MIN PLUS 1 HR CHILLING
MAKES 3 CUPS ● ○ ○

- 1 cup mayonnaise
- ¼ small Vidalia onion, finely chopped
- ½ teaspoon hot sauce
- 1 pound sharp cheddar cheese, coarsely shredded
- ½ cup diced drained pimientos (from one 7-ounce jar)

In a food processor, blend the mayonnaise, onion and hot sauce. Add the cheese and pulse until finely chopped. Add the pimientos and pulse until combined. Transfer to a bowl. Refrigerate until firm, at least 1 hour. —*Angie Mosier*

SERVE WITH Crackers or vegetables.

MAKE AHEAD The Pimento Cheese can be refrigerated for up to 3 days.

WINE Fresh, fruity rosé.

Bagel Chips with Ricotta, Chive Puree and Prosciutto

 TOTAL: 30 MIN
MAKES 48 CANAPÉS ●

- ½ cup snipped chives
- ¼ cup extra-virgin olive oil
- 2 tablespoons marcona almonds
- Salt
- 1 cup fresh ricotta cheese
- 48 small plain bagel chips (1½ inches)
- 12 thin slices of prosciutto (about 4 ounces), cut into 3-inch-wide strips

1. In a blender or mini food chopper, pulse the chives, oil, almonds and a pinch of salt to a coarse puree.

2. Lightly season the ricotta with salt and spread about 1 teaspoon onto each bagel chip. Top each with a little chive puree and a loosely rolled prosciutto slice. Transfer to a platter and serve. —*Grace Parisi*

MAKE AHEAD The hors d'oeuvres can be kept at room temperature for up to 1 hour.

WINE Fresh, lively Soave.

Three-Cheese Mini Macs

 TOTAL: 45 MIN
MAKES 48 MINI MACS ● ○ ○

Anything big made small is ultrafun for cocktail parties, and these quick one-bite macaroni and cheeses are the ultimate example. Assembled in mini muffin pans, they can be baked just as guests arrive.

- ½ pound elbow macaroni
- 1½ tablespoons unsalted butter, plus more for brushing
- ¼ cup freshly grated Parmigiano-Reggiano cheese
- 2 tablespoons all-purpose flour
- ¾ cup milk
- 4 ounces cheddar cheese, shredded (1 packed cup)
- 4 ounces deli-sliced American cheese, chopped
- 1 large egg yolk
- ¼ teaspoon smoked Spanish paprika

1. Preheat the oven to 425°. Bring a large saucepan of salted water to a boil over high heat. Add the macaroni and boil until al dente, about 5 minutes. Drain, shaking off the excess water.

2. Brush four 12-cup nonstick mini muffin tins with butter. Sprinkle with 2 tablespoons of the grated Parmigiano-Reggiano; tap out the excess.

3. In a large saucepan, melt the 1½ tablespoons of butter. Whisk in the flour over moderate heat; continue whisking for 2 minutes. Whisk in the milk and cook, whisking, until the mixture comes to a boil, about 5 minutes. Add the cheddar and American cheeses and whisk until they are smoothly melted. Take the saucepan off the heat and whisk in the egg yolk and smoked paprika. Fold in the cooked and drained macaroni.

4. Spoon slightly rounded tablespoons of the macaroni and cheese mixture into the prepared muffin cups, packing them gently. Sprinkle the remaining 2 tablespoons of grated Parmigiano-Reggiano evenly over the tops.

5. Bake in the upper and middle thirds of the oven for about 10 minutes, until golden and sizzling. Let cool for 5 minutes. Using a small spoon, carefully loosen the mini macs, transfer to a large serving platter and serve immediately. —*Grace Parisi*

WINE Fruity, low-oak Chardonnay.

Spanish Devils

TOTAL: 30 MIN
MAKES 48 PIECES ●

These warm, gooey stuffed dates are a riff on the classic "devils on horseback," almond-stuffed prunes wrapped in bacon, then broiled.

- 24 Medjool dates
- 2 ounces dry chorizo, skinned and finely chopped (⅓ cup)
- 3 ounces Italian Fontina cheese, shredded (½ cup)

Preheat the oven to 350°. Make a small slash in each date and remove the pits, keeping the fruit as intact as possible. Fill each date with chorizo and Fontina, pinch them closed and set them on a baking sheet. Bake for about 12 minutes, until the cheese is melted. Cut each date in half crosswise, transfer to a platter and serve warm. —*Grace Parisi*

MAKE AHEAD The stuffed dates can be refrigerated overnight. Bake them just before serving.

WINE Earthy, medium-bodied Tempranillo.

SUPERFAST

stuffed dates

Originally from Morocco, dried Medjool dates are a particularly large, moist variety with slightly wrinkled brown skin and sticky, caramel-flavored flesh. For a quick bite to serve with cocktails, replace their pits with almonds or pieces of Parmigiano-Reggiano.

Chilled Shrimp with Remoulade

ACTIVE: 30 MIN; TOTAL: 1 HR

12 SERVINGS ● ●

Shrimp remoulade is a classic part of a Réveillon menu, the traditional Christmas meal in New Orleans. Chef John Besh, a Louisiana native, makes it every year.

REMOULADE

- 1 cup mayonnaise
- ¼ cup Dijon mustard
- 2 tablespoons prepared horseradish
- 2 tablespoons chopped flat-leaf parsley
- 1 small shallot, minced
- 1 medium garlic clove, very finely chopped
- 1 tablespoon white wine vinegar
- 1 teaspoon fresh lemon juice
- 1 teaspoon hot sauce
- ½ teaspoon paprika
- ¼ teaspoon cayenne pepper
- ¼ teaspoon garlic powder

Salt

SHRIMP

- 1 gallon water
- ½ cup kosher salt
- ¼ cup sweet paprika
- 1 teaspoon cayenne pepper
- 1 teaspoon garlic powder
- ¼ cup fresh lemon juice
- 4 bay leaves
- 1 small onion, sliced ¼ inch thick
- 1 head of garlic, halved crosswise
- 1 large thyme sprig
- 1 tablespoon black peppercorns
- 1 tablespoon ground coriander
- 24 jumbo shrimp, shells cut down the back and veins removed
- 6 cups baby arugula or mâche

1. MAKE THE REMOULADE: In a bowl, stir together all of the remoulade ingredients.

2. PREPARE THE SHRIMP: In a large pot, combine all of the ingredients except the shrimp and arugula; bring to a boil. Cover and simmer over moderate heat for 5 minutes. Uncover, add the shrimp and bring back to a simmer. Cover, remove the pot from the heat and let stand until the shrimp are just cooked through, 10 minutes.

3. Drain the shrimp; transfer to a baking sheet to cool. Refrigerate until chilled.

4. Peel the shrimp. Line a platter with the arugula and top with the shrimp. Serve with the remoulade. —*John Besh*

WINE Rich, complex white Burgundy.

Oyster Tartlets

TOTAL: 50 MIN

12 SERVINGS

Oysters are a prominent part of many Gulf Coast holiday meals. As a child, New Orleans chef John Besh loved when a family friend made little puff pastry cups and filled them with oysters in cream sauce. In this version, Besh places the oysters in mini tart shells, then tops them with a creamy horseradish sauce and crispy bread crumbs.

- 1 tablespoon unsalted butter
- 2 tablespoons all-purpose flour
- ½ cup milk
- 1 tablespoon minced onion
- 1 bay leaf
- 1½ teaspoons prepared horseradish

Salt and freshly ground pepper

- ¾ cup *panko* (Japanese bread crumbs)
- ½ cup freshly grated Parmigiano-Reggiano cheese
- 2 tablespoons extra-virgin olive oil
- 24 prebaked mini phyllo shells
- 24 small shucked oysters

1. Preheat the oven to 400°. In a small saucepan, melt the butter over moderately high heat. Stir in the flour, then whisk in the milk until smooth. Bring to a simmer, whisking. Stir in the onion and bay leaf and simmer over low heat, whisking, until no floury taste remains, 10 minutes. Pass through a coarse strainer set over a small bowl; discard the bay leaf. Stir in the horseradish and season with salt and pepper. Press a piece of plastic wrap onto the sauce.

2. In a small bowl, combine the *panko* and cheese and stir in the olive oil. Arrange the phyllo shells on a rimmed baking sheet. Place an oyster in each shell. Spoon about 1 teaspoon of the horseradish sauce into each shell and sprinkle some of the *panko* mixture on top. Bake in the upper third of the oven for about 10 minutes, until the tartlets are hot throughout and crisp on top. Serve right away. —*John Besh*

WINE Creamy, supple Pinot Blanc.

Ricotta-Stuffed Arancini

ACTIVE: 1 HR; TOTAL: 1 HR 40 MIN

MAKES 20 ARANCINI ● ●

Arancini means "little oranges," referring to the golden color of these fried rice balls and to their usual round shape. A popular Italian snack, *arancini* are often filled with meat, cheese or vegetables.

- 2 tablespoons extra-virgin olive oil, plus more for frying
- ½ small onion, minced
- 1¼ cups arborio rice
- ¼ cup dry white wine
- 4 cups water
- 2 teaspoons chopped thyme

Finely grated zest of ½ lemon

Salt and freshly ground pepper

- ½ cup fresh ricotta cheese
- 1 tablespoon freshly grated Parmigiano-Reggiano cheese

All-purpose flour, for dredging

- 2 large eggs, beaten
- 1 cup fine dried bread crumbs

1. In a medium saucepan, heat the 2 tablespoons of olive oil. Add the onion and cook over moderately low heat until softened. Add the rice; stir over moderately high heat until coated with oil and sizzling, about 2 minutes. Stir in the wine and simmer until evaporated, 3 minutes. Add the water and bring to a boil. Simmer over moderately low heat, stirring occasionally, until the water has been absorbed and the rice is tender, about 20 minutes. Transfer the rice to a bowl and let cool to room temperature.

CRISPY POTATO LATKES

A guest ready for a delicious potluck dinner.

2. Stir the thyme and lemon zest into the rice and season with salt and pepper. In a small bowl, blend the ricotta with the Parmigiano and season with salt and pepper. Put 2 tablespoons of the rice mixture in your moistened palm. Make an indentation in the center of the mound and fill it with about 1 teaspoon of the ricotta mixture. Fold the rice around the filling to enclose it and pat the rice into an oval. Repeat with the remaining rice and ricotta.

3. In a medium saucepan, heat 2 inches of olive oil to 300°. Set a rack over a large baking sheet. Put the flour, eggs and bread crumbs in 3 shallow bowls. Dredge the rice ovals in the flour, shaking off any excess. Dip the ovals in the egg, then coat with the bread crumbs. Deep-fry 5 ovals at a time until golden brown, about 2 minutes. With a slotted spoon, transfer the *arancini* to the rack to drain while you fry the rest. Serve hot or warm. —*Palma D'Orazio*

MAKE AHEAD The uncooked breaded rice balls can be refrigerated overnight. Bring to room temperature before frying. The fried arancini can be refrigerated overnight and reheated in a 350° oven.
WINE Fresh, fruity rosé.

Crispy Potato Latkes
TOTAL: 1 HR
8 SERVINGS ● ○

Writer Periel Aschenbrand got this recipe for onion-sweetened potato pancakes from her late grandmother, who fled Lithuania during the Holocaust and settled in Tel Aviv before moving to the U.S.

    2 **pounds Yukon Gold potatoes,
       peeled**
    2 **medium onions**
    2 **large eggs, lightly beaten**
    ¼ **cup all-purpose flour**
    1 **tablespoon kosher salt**
Vegetable oil, for frying

1. Using a food processor or a box grater, coarsely shred the potatoes and onions. Transfer them to a colander and squeeze dry. In a large bowl, mix the potatoes and onions with the eggs, flour and salt.
2. In a 10-inch cast-iron skillet, heat ¼ inch of oil until shimmering. Working in batches, drop rounded tablespoons of the potato mixture into the skillet, pressing lightly to flatten them. Cook over moderately high heat, turning once, until browned, about 5 minutes. Reduce the heat if the latkes brown too quickly. Drain the latkes on paper towels, transfer to a warmed plate and serve right away.
—*Periel Aschenbrand*
SERVE WITH Applesauce.
MAKE AHEAD The fried potato latkes can be held at room temperature for up to 3 hours. Reheat on a large rimmed baking sheet in a 350° oven before serving.
WINE Creamy, supple Pinot Blanc.

Caramelized Onion Tart with Whole Wheat Crust

ACTIVE: 50 MIN; TOTAL: 1 HR 35 MIN

8 SERVINGS ● ●

1½   cups whole wheat flour, plus
       more for dusting

Salt

1   stick plus 1 tablespoon cold
     unsalted butter, cut into
     ½-inch dice

¼   cup cold water

3   tablespoons extra-virgin olive oil

4   medium onions, halved and
     thinly sliced (about 1½ pounds)

2   teaspoons coarsely chopped
     fresh thyme

Freshly ground pepper

3   ounces creamy blue cheese,
     crumbled (about ¾ cup)

1. In a food processor, pulse the 1½ cups of flour with ½ teaspoon salt. Add the butter and pulse until it's the size of small peas. Sprinkle in the cold water and pulse until the dough begins to come together. Scrape onto a sheet of plastic wrap and pat into a disk. Wrap the dough and refrigerate until firm, at least 1 hour.

TIP

best foodie websites

jbprince.com Chefs adore the wide selection of tools, including sprayers for applying thin layers of chocolate.

gustiamo.com This well-designed site allows users to search food products by region for 20 regions in Italy.

amazon.com Seattle chef Tom Douglas's most extravagant purchases: signed first editions of Jacques Pépin's cookbooks.

2. Preheat the oven to 400°. Meanwhile, in a large skillet, heat the oil. Add the onions and cook over moderate heat until soft and lightly golden, 25 minutes. Reduce the heat to low and continue to cook until golden, about 15 minutes. Stir in the thyme and season with salt and pepper. Let cool.

3. On a lightly floured work surface, roll out the dough to a 12-inch round. Wrap around the rolling pin and transfer to a 10-inch fluted tart pan with a removable bottom. Press the dough into the pan and trim off any excess. Use the scraps to patch any cracks. Prick holes all over the bottom of the crust with a fork. Bake until the crust is lightly browned, about 20 minutes.

4. Spread the onions in the tart shell and sprinkle with the blue cheese. Bake until the cheese is melted and the onions are warm, about 5 minutes. Cut the tart into wedges and serve. —*Dede Sampson*

WINE Fruity, light-bodied Beaujolais.

Dan Dan Noodles

 TOTAL: 35 MIN

4 SERVINGS ● ●

¼   cup peanut oil

½   cup raw peanuts

1   small jalapeño, minced

1   small garlic clove, halved

One ¼-inch slice of fresh ginger,
       peeled and chopped

2½   tablespoons soy sauce

2   tablespoons water

1½   tablespoons rice vinegar

1   tablespoon Sriracha chile sauce

1   tablespoon sugar

1   teaspoon Asian sesame oil

Kosher salt

12   ounces chow mein noodles

Cucumber matchsticks, sliced
       scallions, chopped cilantro,
       sesame seeds and lime halves,
       for garnish

1. In a large skillet, heat the oil. Add the peanuts and fry over moderate heat until golden, 8 minutes; cool slightly. Transfer

to a food processor. Add the jalapeño, garlic and ginger and process until minced. Add the soy sauce, water, rice vinegar, Sriracha, sugar and sesame oil and process until smooth. Season well with salt.

2. In a large pot of boiling, salted water, cook the noodles until al dente. Drain and rinse under cold water, then pat dry. Toss with the dressing, top with the garnishes and serve. —*Joanne Chang*

WINE Full-bodied, minerally Riesling.

Red Curry Buffalo Wings

 TOTAL: 45 MIN

12 SERVINGS ●

1   tablespoon Thai red curry paste

¼   cup vegetable oil

4   pounds chicken drumettes (upper
     portion of the chicken wing)

Salt and freshly ground pepper

1   cup unsweetened coconut milk

1½   tablespoons Asian fish sauce

1½   tablespoons dark brown sugar

Lime wedges, for serving

1. Preheat the oven to 450° and position a rack nearest the top. In a large bowl, whisk ½ teaspoon of the red curry paste with the oil. Add the chicken, season with salt and pepper and toss to coat. Spread the chicken on a large rimmed baking sheet and bake for 25 minutes, turning once, until cooked through and starting to brown. Remove from the oven; preheat the broiler.

2. Meanwhile, in a medium saucepan, combine the coconut milk, fish sauce, brown sugar and the remaining 2½ teaspoons of red curry paste and bring to a boil. Cook over high heat, stirring occasionally, until slightly thickened, 3 minutes.

3. Transfer the chicken to a large bowl, pour in the coconut-curry sauce and toss well. Pour off any excess fat on the baking sheet. Return the chicken and sauce to the baking sheet. Broil for 5 minutes, turning once, until browned. Serve with lime wedges. —*Grace Parisi*

WINE Intense, fruity Zinfandel.

Lachlan Mackinnon Patterson and Bobby Stuckey of Frasca Food and Wine host a winter grilling party.

Ginger Beef and Pork Toasts

TOTAL: 30 MIN

MAKES 32 TOASTS

These crispy hors d'oeuvres are similar to Asian shrimp toasts (flavored shrimp paste spread on bread and fried), except they're made with a succulent combination of beef and pork.

Butter, for the baking sheet
- ½ pound ground pork
- ½ pound ground beef chuck
- 1 tablespoon minced fresh ginger
- 1 large garlic clove, minced
- 2 tablespoons chopped cilantro
- 2 teaspoons cornstarch
- ¾ teaspoon salt
- 1 egg white
- 8 slices of white sandwich bread
- 1 teaspoon Asian sesame oil, plus more for brushing
- 1 tablespoon sesame seeds
- 2 tablespoons soy sauce
- 2 tablespoons rice vinegar

1. Preheat the oven to 425°. Lightly butter a large baking sheet. In a bowl, combine the ground meats, ginger, garlic, cilantro, cornstarch, salt and egg white and knead until blended.

2. Arrange the bread on a work surface. Divide the meat mixture among the bread slices and spread it roughly into a 3-inch square on each slice. Brush lightly with sesame oil and sprinkle with the sesame seeds. Trim the bread into 3-inch squares, then cut each square into quarters. Transfer to the baking sheet.

3. Bake for 10 minutes, until the meat is cooked through. Turn on the broiler. Broil the toasts for 2 minutes, until they are lightly browned.

4. Meanwhile, in a small bowl, combine the soy sauce, rice vinegar and the 1 teaspoon of sesame oil. Transfer the toasts to a platter and serve warm or at room temperature with the dipping sauce. —*Grace Parisi*

WINE Rich Alsace Gewürztraminer.

Eggplant Caponata Crostini

ACTIVE: 40 MIN; TOTAL: 1 HR 40 MIN

MAKES 40 CROSTINI ● ● ○

One 1½-pound eggplant

Kosher salt
- 3 tablespoons extra-virgin olive oil
- 1 small red onion, sliced
- 1 tablespoon drained capers
- 1 tablespoon chopped kalamata olives
- 1 tablespoon aged balsamic vinegar
- ½ cup tomato sauce or puree

Freshly ground pepper
- 40 thin toasted baguette slices, for serving
- 1 tablespoon chopped basil

1. Quarter the eggplant lengthwise. Scoop out the very seedy parts and discard. Cut the remaining eggplant into ½-inch dice. In a colander set in the sink, lightly salt the eggplant cubes and toss well. Top with a sturdy plate weighed down with a heavy can and let drain for 1 hour. Rinse the eggplant cubes and pat dry.

2. In a large skillet, heat 1 tablespoon of the oil. Add the eggplant and cook over moderately high heat, stirring occasionally, until tender, about 5 minutes. Transfer the eggplant to a bowl.

3. Add the onion and the remaining 2 tablespoons of oil to the skillet and cook over moderately low heat until the onion is tender, about 6 minutes. Return the eggplant to the skillet. Stir in the capers, olives and balsamic vinegar and cook until the vinegar has evaporated. Add the tomato sauce and cook over low heat, stirring, until thickened, about 2 minutes. Season with salt and pepper and transfer to a bowl to cool.

4. Shortly before serving, spread the caponata on the baguette toasts and garnish with the basil. —*Elena Bisestri*

MAKE AHEAD The caponata can be refrigerated for up to 3 days.

WINE Lively, fruity Merlot.

Watercress Salad with Beets and Roasted-Garlic Crostini

ACTIVE: 35 MIN; TOTAL: 1 HR 45 MIN

4 SERVINGS ○

Jeremy Silansky, chef de cuisine at American Flatbread in Waitsfield, Vermont, is able to get local watercress year-round from a friend who cultivates the spicy winter green in a pond behind her house. Silansky pairs watercress with the classic combination of sweet roasted beets and tangy goat cheese, which he buys from Vermont Butter & Cheese Company.

- ¾ pound medium red and golden beets
- 1 head of garlic
- ¼ cup plus 2 teaspoons extra-virgin olive oil, plus more for drizzling

Salt and freshly ground pepper
- 1 tablespoon very finely chopped shallot
- 1 tablespoon fresh orange juice
- 1 tablespoon fresh lemon juice
- 1 tablespoon white wine vinegar
- ½ tablespoon honey

Eight ½-inch-thick baguette slices
- ½ pound watercress, large stems trimmed
- ½ cup peeled and diced celery root
- 4 ounces fresh goat cheese, crumbled

1. Preheat the oven to 350°. Place the beets in a small baking dish and cover it with foil. Cut off the top third of the head of garlic and set it on a sheet of foil. Drizzle the garlic with olive oil and wrap it in the foil. Bake the beets and garlic until tender, about 1 hour.

2. Peel the beets and cut into wedges. Squeeze the garlic cloves into a bowl and mash with a fork. Stir in 2 teaspoons of olive oil and season with salt and pepper.

3. In a bowl, whisk the shallot, orange and lemon juices and vinegar. Stir in the honey until dissolved. Whisk in the remaining ¼ cup of oil. Season with salt and pepper.

4. Place the baguette slices on a large baking sheet and drizzle them lightly with olive oil. Bake until the slices are crisp, about 7 minutes. Spread the baguette slices with the mashed garlic.

5. In a large bowl, toss the watercress with the celery root and roasted beets. Add the dressing and toss well. Mound the salad on plates and sprinkle with the crumbled goat cheese. Serve the salad right away, with the roasted-garlic crostini.
—Jeremy Silansky

MAKE AHEAD The roasted and peeled beets can be refrigerated for up to 2 days.
WINE Minerally, complex Sauvignon Blanc.

Fried Baby Artichokes
TOTAL: 50 MIN

10 SERVINGS ●

This recipe is based on a preparation that originated in Rome's Jewish ghetto. It is one of Palma D'Orazio's most requested dishes at her New York City restaurant, Palma. Frying brings out the artichokes' sweetness.

20 baby artichokes (about
      4 ounces each)
Extra-virgin olive oil, for frying
Salt and freshly ground pepper
¼ cup freshly grated Parmigiano-
      Reggiano cheese
¼ cup finely chopped
      flat-leaf parsley

1. With a small, sharp knife, cut off the artichoke stems. Snap off the leaves until you reach the inner leaves. Cut off the top third of the artichokes and trim any tough parts. Quarter the artichokes lengthwise.
2. In a medium saucepan, heat 2 inches of olive oil to 300°. Fry the artichokes in the hot oil in batches until richly browned and crisp, about 2 minutes per batch. Transfer the artichokes to a paper towel–lined plate to drain and season with salt and pepper. Transfer the artichokes to small plates or a shallow serving bowl, sprinkle with the cheese and parsley and serve. *—Palma D'Orazio*

EGGPLANT CAPONATA CROSTINI

FRIED BABY ARTICHOKES

Greek Salad Skewers with Anchovy Aioli

TOTAL: 30 MIN

MAKES 36 SKEWERS ●●

2 oil-packed anchovy fillets, drained and chopped

1 garlic clove, mashed

2 tablespoons red wine vinegar

½ cup mayonnaise

2 tablespoons extra-virgin olive oil

1 small seedless English cucumber (about ¾ pound)—peeled, quartered lengthwise and sliced ½ inch thick

½ pound feta cheese, preferably French, cut into ¾-inch cubes

36 whole tiny cherry tomatoes or 18 halved grape tomatoes

1. In a small bowl, using a spoon, mash the anchovies and garlic to a paste. Whisk in the vinegar, followed by the mayonnaise. Gradually whisk in the olive oil and transfer the aioli to a small bowl.

2. Arrange the cucumbers on a work surface. Top each with a cube of feta, followed by a tomato. Poke a 4-inch skewer or toothpick through each stack and transfer to a platter. Serve the skewers along with the aioli. —*Grace Parisi*

MAKE AHEAD The skewers can be covered and refrigerated for up to 4 hours.

WINE Zesty, fresh Vinho Verde.

SUPERFAST

creamy blue cheese dip

Blue cheese makes an addictive dip: Combine ¼ cup each crumbled blue cheese, sour cream and mayonnaise. Fold in 2 teaspoons chopped chives and serve with sliced apple and fennel.

Chicory Salad with Quince and Pecans

TOTAL: 40 MIN

12 SERVINGS ●●○

New Orleans chef John Besh considers the combination of a bitter green with a sweet fruit and a strong cheese a personal favorite. This version features fresh quince, a winter fruit that's like a cross between an apple and a pear. If fresh quince is unavailable in the produce section, try preserved quince from a jar.

2 cups water

¼ cup cider vinegar

3 tablespoons light brown sugar

1 jalapeño, seeded and very finely chopped

1 teaspoon finely grated fresh ginger

½ teaspoon ground coriander

½ cinnamon stick

Salt

2 quinces—peeled, cored and thinly sliced

1½ cups pecan halves (6 ounces)

2 tablespoons sherry vinegar

2 tablespoons red wine vinegar

¼ cup vegetable oil

¼ cup walnut oil

1 teaspoon sugar

Freshly ground pepper

1½ pounds chicory, stems discarded and leaves torn into bite-size pieces (16 cups)

1 cup crumbled blue cheese (4 ounces)

1. Preheat the oven to 350°. In a large saucepan, combine the water with the cider vinegar, brown sugar, jalapeño, ginger, coriander, cinnamon stick and a pinch of salt and bring to a boil. Add the sliced quince, cover and simmer over low heat until they are tender, about 15 minutes. With a slotted spoon, transfer the poached quince to a small bowl. Discard the quince poaching liquid.

2. Meanwhile, spread the pecan halves on a rimmed baking sheet and sprinkle with salt. Bake for about 7 minutes, until the pecans are toasted.

3. In a small bowl, combine the sherry and red wine vinegars with the vegetable oil, walnut oil and sugar. Whisk well until smoothly combined; season the vinaigrette with salt and pepper.

4. In a large salad bowl, toss the chicory with the poached quince, pecans and blue cheese. Pour the dressing over the salad and toss well. Serve right away.
—*John Besh*

MAKE AHEAD The recipe can be prepared through Step 3 up to 1 day ahead. Refrigerate the poached quince and vinaigrette separately, and bring them to room temperature before tossing the salad. The toasted pecan halves can be stored in an airtight container at room temperature.

WINE Light, fresh Pinot Grigio.

Italian Tuna, Green Olive and Tangerine Salad on Grilled Bread

TOTAL: 25 MIN

8 SERVINGS ●●

At Frasca Food and Wine in Boulder, Colorado, chef Lachlan Mackinnon Patterson preserves his own tuna in olive oil to make this terrific tuna salad, which is brightened with tangerine and green olives and served on garlicky grilled bread.

1 medium tangerine

One 8-ounce jar Italian tuna in olive oil, drained and lightly flaked

¼ cup mayonnaise

16 pitted Picholine olives, coarsely chopped

2 tablespoons very finely chopped chives

1 tablespoon minced shallot

Salt and freshly ground pepper

1 baguette, split lengthwise

Extra-virgin olive oil, for brushing

1 large garlic clove, peeled

CHICORY SALAD WITH QUINCE AND PECANS

GREEK SALAD SKEWERS WITH ANCHOVY AIOLI

1. Light a grill. Peel the tangerine, removing the white pith. Using a small, sharp knife, cut between the membranes to release the sections onto a plate. Cut the sections into ½-inch pieces; discard any seeds.

2. In a large bowl, mix the tuna with the tangerine, mayonnaise, olives, chives and shallot and season with salt and pepper.

3. Brush the cut sides of the baguette with olive oil. Grill cut side down over high heat for 2 to 3 minutes, or until browned and crisp. Turn and grill until lightly browned on the second side, about 30 seconds longer. Rub the cut sides of the baguette with the garlic. Mound the salad on the baguette, cut into 8 pieces and serve.
—*Lachlan Mackinnon Patterson*

MAKE AHEAD The tuna salad minus the tangerines can be refrigerated overnight. Fold in the fruit and grill the bread just before serving.

WINE Fresh, fruity rosé.

Green Salad with Goat Cheese and Pistachios

TOTAL: 25 MIN
4 SERVINGS ● ●

Chef Pino Maffeo of Boston Public in Boston uses red verjus (a tart juice made primarily from grapes) to dress a long list of ingredients, including fennel, cucumber, bell pepper, carrots, bean sprouts and oven-dried tomatoes. For this simplified version, the verjus is dropped and the ingredients list is pared down to include only the most important flavors.

½ small shallot, minced
2 tablespoons red wine vinegar
¼ cup extra-virgin olive oil
Salt and freshly ground pepper
One 5-ounce bag mesclun greens
½ small fennel bulb, cored and thinly sliced
½ seedless cucumber, peeled and thinly sliced
½ red bell pepper, cored and thinly sliced
¼ small red onion, thinly sliced
1 avocado—peeled, pitted and thinly sliced
2 ounces crumbled fresh goat cheese
¼ cup roasted shelled pistachios

In a large bowl, combine the minced shallot with the red wine vinegar and olive oil and whisk until smoothly incorporated. Season with salt and pepper. Add the mesclun greens and sliced fennel, cucumber, bell pepper and onion. Toss the ingredients until well combined. Add the avocado slices and crumbled goat cheese, season with salt and pepper and gently toss the salad again. Sprinkle the pistachios on the salad, mound the salad onto 4 plates and serve immediately.
—*Pino Maffeo*

WINE Lively, tart Sauvignon Blanc.

Green Salad with Nutty Vinaigrette

TOTAL: 15 MIN

8 SERVINGS ● ○

Created by chef David Kinch of Manresa in Los Gatos, California, this simple salad has a nicely nutty dressing made with both walnut and hazelnut oils. When tatsoi (an Asian green) is flowering in Kinch's garden, he garnishes the crisp greens with the delightfully spicy yellow blossoms.

- 1 teaspoon Dijon mustard
- 2 tablespoons sherry vinegar
- 3 tablespoons extra-virgin olive oil
- 2 tablespoons walnut oil
- 1 tablespoon hazelnut oil

Salt and freshly ground
  black pepper

- ¾ pound baby greens, such as baby lolla rossa (12 cups)
- 1 ounce edible flowers, such as tatsoi, nasturtiums or marigolds (optional)

In a large salad bowl, whisk together the Dijon mustard and sherry vinegar. Gradually whisk in the olive oil, followed by the walnut and hazelnut oils. Season with salt and black pepper. Add the baby greens and flowers, toss gently and serve.
—*David Kinch*

WINE Fresh, minerally Vermentino.

Cheese Crisps

ACTIVE: 30 MIN; TOTAL: 1 HR 30 MIN
MAKES 4 DOZEN CRACKERS ● ○
These terrific cheddary wafers get their pleasing crackle from a secret ingredient: Rice Krispies.

- 1½ sticks unsalted butter, softened
- 1 pound cheddar cheese, shredded
- 2 cups all-purpose flour
- ½ teaspoon cayenne pepper
- ½ teaspoon salt
- 2 cups crispy rice cereal

1. Preheat the oven to 350°. Position racks in the middle and lower thirds of the oven. In a bowl, beat the butter and cheddar at medium speed until combined. Add the flour, cayenne and salt and beat until a crumbly dough forms. Add the rice cereal and beat briefly to combine.

2. Form level tablespoons of dough into balls; place on 4 large baking sheets. With a fork, press a crosshatch pattern into the balls, pressing them into 2-inch rounds.

3. Bake the crisps 2 sheets at a time for about 25 minutes, until they are lightly browned; shift the pans from top to bottom and front to back halfway through baking for even cooking. Let cool completely.
—*Courtney Waddell*

MAKE AHEAD The crisps can be stored in an airtight container for up to 1 week.
WINE Dry, fruity sparkling wine.

Crispy Frico with Soppressata

TOTAL: 50 MIN

8 SERVINGS ●

Frico are Italian cheese crisps made by melting and frying grated cheese.

- 2¾ cups coarsely grated montasio or Parmigiano-Reggiano cheese (11 ounces)
- 1¼ cups coarsely grated Piave or Parmigiano-Reggiano cheese (5 ounces)
- ½ pound thinly sliced soppressata

1. Preheat the oven to 350°. In a large bowl, toss the grated cheeses together. In the corner of a large nonstick baking sheet, sprinkle ¼ cup of the grated cheese in a 4-inch round. Repeat to make 3 more rounds on the baking sheet, leaving about 2 inches between the rounds.

2. Bake the *frico* for 5 minutes, or until the cheese is slightly melted and golden brown. Let cool on the sheet for 2 minutes to firm up. Using a metal spatula, transfer the *frico* to a platter to cool completely; they'll crisp as they cool. Repeat with the remaining cheese. Arrange the *frico* and soppressata on the platter and serve.
—*Lachlan Mackinnon Patterson*

WINE Juicy, fresh Dolcetto.

Cheddar-and-Cayenne Crackers

ACTIVE: 30 MIN; TOTAL: 3 HR 30 MIN
MAKES ABOUT 10 DOZEN
CRACKERS ● ● ○
A deep cheesy flavor and a crispy, blistery texture make these cheddar crackers delectable, and a touch of cayenne pepper gives them an addictive kick.

- 1 stick unsalted butter, at room temperature
- 1 pound sharp cheddar cheese, coarsely shredded
- 1 teaspoon salt
- ¼ teaspoon cayenne pepper

Dash of hot sauce

- 1½ cups all-purpose flour, plus more for rolling

1. In a standing electric mixer fitted with a paddle, beat the butter with the cheese, salt, cayenne and hot sauce at medium speed until blended. Add the 1½ cups of flour and beat at low speed, scraping the side and bottom of the bowl, until a soft dough forms. (Alternatively, mix the dough with a handheld mixer.) Pat the dough into 2 disks, wrap in plastic and refrigerate until chilled, at least 2 hours.

2. Preheat the oven to 350°. Line 2 baking sheets with parchment paper. Work with 1 disk of dough at a time; keep the second one refrigerated: On a lightly floured work surface, roll out the dough to a 12-by-10-inch rectangle. Cut the dough into 2-by-1-inch strips. Transfer the strips to the baking sheets. Bake for 25 minutes, or until the crackers are lightly browned, shifting the baking sheets halfway through. Slide the paper onto racks and let the crackers cool. Repeat with the remaining dough.
—*Natalie Chanin*

MAKE AHEAD The cracker dough can be refrigerated for up to 2 days. The baked crackers can be stored at room temperature in an airtight container for up to 3 days. Recrisp in a warm oven.
WINE Lively, fruity Merlot.

Crisp Salami Cocktail Mix

TOTAL: 30 MIN
12 SERVINGS ●●

F&W's Grace Parisi quickly fries salami, then crisps chickpeas and rosemary in the same delicious cooking oil. Make twice as much as you think you'll need—this cocktail mix is irresistible.

3 cups vegetable oil,
    for frying
½ pound thinly sliced
    Genoa salami, cut into
    ½-inch-wide strips
One 19-ounce can chickpeas,
    drained and patted dry
3 tablespoons cornstarch
3 large rosemary sprigs
1 cup roasted and salted
    shelled pistachios

1. In a large saucepan, heat the oil to 350° (a strip of salami dropped in should sizzle). Line a large rack with several layers of paper towels. Fry the salami strips in 3 or 4 batches over moderate heat, until crisp and lightly browned, stirring to separate the slices, about 2 minutes per batch. Using a slotted spoon, transfer the salami to the paper towels to drain; the salami will firm up as it cools. Transfer the cooled salami to a large bowl.

2. In a medium bowl, toss the chickpeas with the cornstarch. Add the chickpeas to the hot oil and fry over moderate heat, stirring occasionally, until deeply golden, 5 to 6 minutes. Using a slotted spoon, transfer the chickpeas to the paper towels to drain; let cool slightly. Add the chickpeas to the bowl with the salami.

3. Add the rosemary to the hot oil and fry, stirring occasionally, until crisp and fragrant, about 1 minute. Drain on the paper towels and let cool. Strip the rosemary needles from the stem and add to the bowl. Add the pistachios, toss gently and serve.
—*Grace Parisi*

MAKE AHEAD The mix can be made up to 4 hours ahead.

Spiced Pecans

TOTAL: 30 MIN
MAKES 5 CUPS ●○

2 teaspoons kosher salt
¾ teaspoon freshly ground
    black pepper
Scant ½ teaspoon cayenne pepper
1½ teaspoons cinnamon
1½ tablespoons light brown sugar
5 cups pecan halves (18 ounces)
4 tablespoons unsalted
    butter, melted

Preheat the oven to 350°. In a small bowl, combine the salt, black pepper, cayenne, cinnamon and brown sugar. Spread the pecans on a large rimmed baking sheet and toast for 10 minutes, until fragrant. Transfer the pecans to a large bowl and toss with the butter. Add the spices and toss to coat. Return to the baking sheet and toast for 3 to 4 minutes longer, until fragrant. Let cool. —*Angie Mosier*

MAKE AHEAD The spiced pecans can be stored in an airtight container for 3 days.

Rosemary-Maple Cashews

ACTIVE: 10 MIN; TOTAL: 40 MIN
MAKES 8 CUPS ●○

8 cups raw cashews
5 tablespoons pure maple syrup
2½ tablespoons extra-virgin
    olive oil
1 tablespoon minced
    fresh rosemary
¼ teaspoon cayenne pepper
Kosher salt and freshly
    ground black pepper

1. Preheat the oven to 375°. In a large bowl, toss the cashews with the maple syrup, olive oil, rosemary and cayenne.

2. Spread the nuts on a large rimmed baking sheet and toast for 30 minutes, stirring occasionally, until browned. Immediately season with salt and black pepper; let cool, tossing occasionally. —*Melissa Rubel*

MAKE AHEAD The cashews can be stored in an airtight container for up to 2 weeks.

drinks

Middle Eastern Yogurt Coolers

TOTAL: 15 MIN
MAKES 8 DRINKS ●●○

Growing up in Jal El Dib, Lebanon, fashion consultant Rita Nakouzi would drink *ayran,* lightly salted yogurt over ice.

6 cups plain whole-milk yogurt
3 cups water
Salt
Ice
8 mint sprigs, for garnish

In a pitcher, whisk the yogurt with the water and season lightly with salt. Fill tall glasses with ice. Pour in the yogurt drink, garnish with the mint sprigs and serve.
—*Rita Nakouzi*

Bluegrass Cobbler

TOTAL: 15 MIN
MAKES 1 DRINK ●○

For this drink, cocktail consultant Tony Abou-Ganim likes Blanton's, a caramelly, easy-drinking bourbon, but any smooth bourbon you have on hand will be fine.

2 orange slices
2 fresh pineapple sticks
2 brandied cherries
Ice
2 ounces Blanton's Original
    Bourbon
½ ounce maraschino liqueur
¾ ounce fresh lemon juice
½ ounce simple syrup (see Note)
1 fresh cherry, for garnish

In a cocktail shaker, muddle 1 orange slice, 1 pineapple stick and the brandied cherries. Fill with ice, then add the bourbon, maraschino liqueur, lemon juice and simple syrup. Shake well and strain into a rocks glass filled with ice. Garnish with the remaining orange slice and pineapple stick and a fresh cherry.
—*Tony Abou-Ganim*

NOTE To make simple syrup, dissolve 1 part sugar in 1 part simmering water. Let cool.

Santa's Little Helper

TOTAL: 15 MIN PLUS 2 HR CHILLING

MAKES 10 DRINKS ●●

One 750-ml bottle Zinfandel

1 cup apple brandy

1 cup fresh orange juice

½ cup simple syrup (see Note)

¼ cup cinnamon schnapps

Ice

Orange wheels, for garnish

In a pitcher, combine the wine, brandy, orange juice, simple syrup and schnapps. Cover and refrigerate until chilled, about 2 hours. Stir and pour into 10 ice-filled rocks glasses. Garnish each drink with an orange wheel. —*Nick Fauchald*

NOTE Dissolve ½ cup of sugar in ½ cup of simmering water. Let cool.

Frost Nip

 TOTAL: 15 MIN

MAKES 8 DRINKS ●

Ice

2 cups Sauvignon Blanc

1 cup gin

¾ cup fresh grapefruit juice

¼ cup maraschino liqueur

¼ cup simple syrup (see Note)

8 lemon twists, for garnish

Fill a pitcher with ice. Add the wine, gin, juice, liqueur and simple syrup. Stir well and strain into 8 chilled cocktail glasses. Garnish each drink with a lemon twist.
—*Nick Fauchald*

NOTE Dissolve ¼ cup of sugar in ¼ cup of simmering water. Let cool.

Champagne Mojitos

 TOTAL: 45 MIN

MAKES 12 DRINKS ●●

¾ cup simple syrup (see Note)

1½ cups packed mint leaves, plus 12 mint sprigs for garnish

6 limes, cut into wedges

2 cups light rum

Cracked ice

3 cups Champagne

1. In a large pitcher, combine the simple syrup with the mint leaves and lime and muddle well with a wooden spoon. Add the rum and stir. Strain into another pitcher.
2. Fill tall glasses with cracked ice and pour in the drink, filling them about two-thirds full. Top with Champagne, garnish with the mint sprigs and serve.
—*John Besh*

NOTE Dissolve ¾ cup of sugar in ¾ cup of simmering water. Let cool.

MAKE AHEAD The mojitos can be prepared through Step 1 and refrigerated in the pitcher overnight.

Hot Spiced Wine

 TOTAL: 15 MIN

MAKES 12 DRINKS ●●

Red wine and kirsch are the base for this delicious seasonal drink, which is laced with warming spices like cinnamon, cardamom and black peppercorns.

2 bottles light-bodied red wine

1¼ cups sugar

Zest of 1 orange, removed with a vegetable peeler

Zest of 1 lemon, removed with a vegetable peeler

3 black peppercorns, crushed

2 cardamom pods, crushed

One 3-inch cinnamon stick, crushed

1 clove, crushed

½ cup kirsch

In a large saucepan, combine the red wine with the sugar and the orange and lemon zests. Put the spices in a tea ball and add to the saucepan. Bring the wine to a very slow simmer over moderate heat, stirring to dissolve the sugar. Remove from the heat, discard the tea ball and stir in the kirsch. Ladle the spiced wine into heat-proof glasses and serve at once.
—*John Besh*

MAKE AHEAD The spiced wine can be kept overnight at room temperature. Reheat before serving.

Le Demon Vert

 TOTAL: 15 MIN

MAKES 1 DRINK ●

The Art of the Bar, from San Francisco institution Absinthe Brasserie & Bar, is one of several recent recipe books from great bars. Published in 2006, it includes this drink, a potent concoction built around the anise-flavored spirit Absente.

Ice

1½ ounces Broker's gin

½ ounce Absente

½ ounce Velvet Falernum

½ ounce fresh lime juice

1 black licorice stick, for garnish

In an ice-filled shaker, combine the gin, Absente, Velvet Falernum and fresh lime juice and shake until cold. Strain into a chilled cocktail glass and garnish with a black licorice stick.
—*Jeff Hollinger and Rob Schwartz*

The Thoroughbred

TOTAL: 15 MIN PLUS 2 TO 5 DAYS FOR INFUSING

MAKES 6 DRINKS ●

Bartenders have been infusing vodka for years; now they're joyfully infusing bourbon with everything from black cherries to bacon. Chris Beveridge, formerly at 12 Baltimore in Kansas City, Missouri, favors apples, cinnamon and vanilla.

One 750-milliliter bottle Woodford Reserve bourbon

3 medium Granny Smith apples, cored and quartered

4 cinnamon sticks

2 vanilla beans

Ice

In a large glass jar, combine the bourbon, apple, cinnamon and vanilla. Cover, shake and refrigerate for 2 to 5 days, shaking the jar and tasting the infusion daily. Strain through a fine sieve into another jar. Serve the infused bourbon on the rocks, or shake with ice and strain into a chilled cocktail glass. —*Chris Beveridge*

MOCK GIN AND PICKLED
PEARL ONIONS

Paprika Punch

TOTAL: 30 MIN

MAKES 4 DRINKS ● ●

½ cup sugar

1 cup water

1 red bell pepper, coarsely chopped

1 cup fresh lemon juice

1¼ cups white rum

Ice

1. In a saucepan, combine the sugar and ½ cup of water and simmer over low heat just until the sugar is dissolved. Let cool.
2. Puree the pepper in a blender until smooth. Strain the puree through a fine sieve set over a small bowl.
3. In a pitcher, combine the lemon juice with the sugar syrup, 3 tablespoons of the bell pepper juice and the remaining ½ cup of water. Stir in the rum and serve in tall glasses over ice. —*Eben Freeman*

Sticky Toffee Pudding Eggnog

ACTIVE: 15 MIN; TOTAL: 2 HR 15 MIN
PLUS 2 DAYS FOR INFUSING

12 SERVINGS ● ●

1 quart heavy cream

10 ounces store-bought sticky toffee pudding (see Note)

6 eggs, separated

½ cup sugar

½ cup plus 2 tablespoons Cognac

½ cup plus 2 tablespoons dark rum

½ teaspoon salt

1. In a container with a tight lid, pour the cream over the sticky toffee pudding. Cover and refrigerate for 2 days.
2. In a large bowl, beat the egg yolks with the sugar. Stir in the Cognac and rum.
3. Strain the cream through a fine sieve, pressing on the solids. Whip 3 cups of the cream until stiff. Fold in the yolk mixture. In a clean bowl, beat the egg whites with the salt on high speed to stiff peaks, then fold into the whipped cream. Refrigerate until chilled, 2 hours. —*Eben Freeman*
NOTE Sticky toffee pudding is available at Whole Foods and specialty food shops.

Mock Gin

TOTAL: 15 MIN PLUS 6 HR STEEPING

MAKES ABOUT 4 QUARTS ● ●

No bathtubs are required to make this aromatic ersatz gin. F&W's Nick Fauchald simply infuses vodka with the botanicals that professional distillers use, including juniper berries and dried orange peel. The fragrant, amber-colored (and lawful) result is delicious in martinis and other gin-based cocktails.

3½ liters plus 350 milliliters neutral-tasting vodka, such as Smirnoff

½ cup juniper berries

⅓ cup dried orange peel

1 tablespoon grains of paradise (see Note)

1 tablespoon cardamom seeds

One 1-inch piece of dried ginger root (see Note)

1 teaspoon coriander seeds

1 teaspoon orris root (see Note)

1. In a small saucepan, combine the 350 milliliters of vodka with the juniper berries, dried orange peel, grains of paradise, cardamom seeds, dried ginger root, coriander seeds and orris root. Bring the mixture to a simmer, cover and cook over moderately low heat for 10 minutes. Remove from the heat and let steep for at least 6 hours or overnight.
2. Strain the essence through a double layer of cheesecloth into a large pitcher. Add the 3½ liters of vodka and stir to combine. Pour the gin into bottles and seal. —*Nick Fauchald*

SERVE WITH Pickled Pearl Onions (recipe follows).

NOTE Grains of paradise are small reddish-brown seeds from a West African plant in the ginger family. Dried ginger root, unlike ground ginger, is the whole root dried. Orris root, an antiquated term for "iris root," is the aromatic root of several iris species, used in gin and perfumes.

All three ingredients can be found at specialty food stores and Kalustyan's (212-685-3451; kalustyans.com).

MAKE AHEAD The Mock Gin can be kept in a capped bottle at room temperature for up to 1 month.

PICKLED PEARL ONIONS

TOTAL: 45 MIN PLUS 3 WEEKS
FOR PICKLING

MAKES FOUR ½-PINT JARS ● ● ●

An avid gardener, F&W's Marcia Kiesel loves mini vegetables and often pickles gherkins and pearl onions as gifts. Her lemon-and-clove-spiked onions are crunchier and less sweet than commercial brands. Perfect for martinis, they can also be sliced and tossed in a salad, stir-fried or tucked inside sandwiches.

1¼ pounds pearl onions, trimmed

8 cloves

1 teaspoon yellow mustard seeds

Eight ½-inch-wide strips of lemon zest

1¼ cups water

1¼ cups white vinegar

3 tablespoons sugar

2 teaspoons kosher salt

1. Bring a medium saucepan of water to a boil over high heat. Add the onions and boil over high heat for 4 minutes. Drain the onions and let cool slightly. When the onions are cool enough to handle, slip off their skins.
2. Pack the onions into four ½-pint jars. Add 2 of the cloves, ¼ teaspoon of the mustard seeds and 2 strips of lemon zest to each jar.
3. In a small saucepan, combine the water, white vinegar, sugar and salt and bring to a boil over high heat, stirring to dissolve the sugar. Pour the brine over the onions to cover. Let cool completely, then seal the jars and refrigerate the onions for at least 3 weeks and up to 1 year. —*Marcia Kiesel*

main courses

Battered Cod with Marie Rose Sauce

 TOTAL: 45 MIN
6 SERVINGS

At his restaurant Eamonn's A Dublin Chipper, Dublin-born Cathal Armstrong brings the fish-and-chips tradition to Alexandria, Virginia. Marie Rose sauce is one of Armstrong's seven "secret" sauces.

- ½   cup mayonnaise
- 2   tablespoons ketchup
- 1   tablespoon fresh lemon juice
- 1   teaspoon Tabasco
- 1¾ cups water
- 2   cups all-purpose flour, plus more for dusting

Salt
- ¼   teaspoon baking soda
- 1   quart vegetable oil, for frying
- 2   pounds skinless cod fillets, cut into 4-inch pieces

1. In a bowl, whisk the mayonnaise with the ketchup, lemon juice and Tabasco.
2. Pour the water into a large bowl. Using a handheld electric mixer at low speed, beat in the 2 cups of flour, ½ teaspoon of salt and the baking soda. Strain the batter into another bowl.

3. In a large saucepan, heat the oil to 360°. Line a rack with paper towels. Dust 5 pieces of cod with flour, then tap off the excess. Dip the cod in the batter, scraping the pieces lightly against the side of the bowl to remove excess batter, and add to the hot oil. Fry over moderate heat until golden and crisp, about 7 minutes. Using a slotted spoon, transfer the fish to the rack. Repeat with the remaining fish and batter. Sprinkle with salt and serve at once, with the sauce. —*Cathal Armstrong*
WINE Fruity, soft Chenin Blanc.

Salt-Baked Branzino with Citrus, Fennel and Herbs

ACTIVE: 1 HR; TOTAL: 1 HR 45 MIN
8 SERVINGS ●

- 6   pounds kosher salt, plus more for seasoning
- 12 parsley sprigs, plus ¾ cup finely chopped leaves
- 12 cilantro sprigs, plus ¾ cup finely chopped leaves
- 12 rosemary sprigs, plus ¾ cup finely chopped leaves
- 16 large egg whites (2 cups)

Four 1½-pound whole sea bass, such as branzino, cleaned
- 1   lemon, thinly sliced, plus lemon wedges for serving
- 1   orange, thinly sliced
- 1   fennel bulb, thinly sliced

1. Preheat the oven to 350°. In a large bowl, mix the 6 pounds of kosher salt with the chopped parsley, cilantro and rosemary. Add the egg whites and stir until the salt is evenly moistened.
2. Season the sea bass cavities with salt and fill them with the herb sprigs and the sliced lemon, orange and fennel.
3. Using half of the herbed salt mixture, form 2 mounds on each of 2 large rimmed baking sheets. Pat each mound into a rectangular bed about ½ inch thick and the length and width of the fish. Set each fish on a salt bed and cover with the remaining herbed salt, patting to enclose the fish completely.
4. Bake for 45 minutes, or until an instant-read thermometer inserted behind the head registers 135°.
5. Using a wooden spoon, tap the salt to crack it; lift off the crusts in large pieces. Remove the fish skin and lift the fillets from the bones. Transfer to a platter and serve with lemon wedges. —*Artan Gjoni*
WINE Fresh, minerally Vermentino.

SALT-BAKED BRANZINO
WITH CITRUS, FENNEL AND HERBS

REDFISH ON THE HALF SHELL

ROASTED SALMON WITH TOMATO JAM

Redfish on the Half Shell

TOTAL: 25 MIN
6 SERVINGS ●

Donald Link, chef and owner of Cochon and Herbsaint in New Orleans, suggests grilling or roasting this fish, then serving it in its hardened skin ("on the half shell"). You can also use a large, flexible spatula to slide the fillets off the skin and onto a platter, discarding the skin, for a more elegant presentation. Redfish—a white-fleshed fish with big scales that are hard to remove—is an ideal choice, but striped bass is great, too. You'll have to buy the fish directly from a fishmonger; ask him to leave the scales on the fillets.

¼ cup plus 2 tablespoons
   extra-virgin olive oil, plus
   more for brushing
2 redfish or striped bass
   fillets with scales still on
   (about 2½ pounds) and
   pin bones removed
½ teaspoon crushed red pepper
Salt and freshly ground
   black pepper
¼ cup very finely chopped
   flat-leaf parsley
2 medium garlic cloves,
   very finely chopped
Lemon wedges, for serving

1. Preheat the oven to 475°. Lightly oil a large rimmed baking sheet. Lay the redfish fillets skin side down on the baking sheet and brush them with 2 tablespoons of the olive oil. Sprinkle with the crushed red pepper and season with salt and black pepper. Roast on the bottom rack of the oven for about 20 minutes, or until the flesh flakes with a fork.

2. Meanwhile, in a small bowl, mix the parsley and garlic with the remaining ¼ cup of olive oil and season with salt and black pepper. Transfer the fish to a platter, drizzle with the parsley-garlic oil and serve with lemon wedges. —*Donald Link*
WINE Dry, fruity sparkling wine.

Roasted Salmon with Tomato Jam

TOTAL: 1 HR

4 SERVINGS ●

At his restaurant Boston Public, chef Pino Maffeo makes this flavorful noodle salad with dried shrimp and a tomato jam of fresh tomatoes and Thai chiles. In this easy take on the dish, Asian fish sauce replaces the dried shrimp, and the tomato jam is a quick combo of canned tomatoes, rice vinegar and sugar.

- 4 ounces rice vermicelli
- ¼ cup plus 1 tablespoon canola oil
- 1 large jalapeño, seeded and very finely chopped
- 1 medium garlic clove, very finely chopped
- ¼ cup minced fresh ginger
- 1 large shallot, thinly sliced
- ½ teaspoon Madras curry powder
- 2 tablespoons Asian fish sauce
- 2 tablespoons fresh lime juice, plus lime wedges for serving
- 1 small red bell pepper, very thinly sliced
- 3 tablespoons chopped cilantro, plus leaves for garnish
- 1 small onion, very finely chopped

One 14-ounce can diced tomatoes, drained
- ½ teaspoon crushed red pepper
- 2 tablespoons light brown sugar
- 2 tablespoons rice vinegar

Salt and freshly ground black pepper

Four 6-ounce center-cut salmon fillets with skin

1. Preheat the oven to 375°. Add the vermicelli to a saucepan of boiling water. Let stand off the heat for 10 minutes, until softened.

2. Meanwhile, in a small skillet over moderately low heat, warm 2 tablespoons of the canola oil. Add the chopped jalapeño, garlic and 2 tablespoons of the minced ginger and cook over moderately low heat until fragrant, about 4 minutes. Add the shallot and cook, stirring, until softened, 5 minutes. Stir in the curry powder and remove the skillet from the heat. Add the fish sauce and lime juice, scraping up any bits stuck to the pan.

3. Drain the vermicelli and shake dry. Cut into 4-inch lengths and transfer to a medium bowl. Add the curry sauce, sliced red bell pepper and chopped cilantro and toss well.

4. In a small saucepan, heat 2 tablespoons of the canola oil. Add the remaining 2 tablespoons of minced ginger and the chopped onion and cook over moderate heat until softened, about 4 minutes. Add the diced tomatoes, crushed red pepper, brown sugar and rice vinegar and cook over moderate heat, mashing and stirring occasionally, until the mixture is thick and jamlike, about 10 minutes. Season the jam with salt and black pepper.

5. In an ovenproof skillet, heat the remaining 1 tablespoon of canola oil. Season the salmon fillets with salt and black pepper, then add them to the skillet skin side down. Cook over high heat for 3 minutes. Transfer the skillet to the oven and roast until nearly cooked through, 10 minutes.

6. Spoon the vermicelli salad onto 4 plates and top each with a piece of roasted salmon. Spoon some tomato jam over the salmon pieces, garnish with the cilantro leaves and serve with the lime wedges. —*Pino Maffeo*

WINE Fruity, light-bodied Beaujolais.

Steamed Dungeness Crab with Meyer Lemon Aioli

TOTAL: 10 MIN

4 SERVINGS ● ●

To locavores—people who eat and cook only ingredients that are grown locally—condiments present one of the biggest challenges. "Just to make a simple salad dressing, you have to find some local vinegars and mustard," says Dede Sampson, a chef and food buyer in the Berkeley, California, school district. Sampson relies on farm-fresh eggs, local McEvoy Ranch olive oil and seasonal Meyer lemons to make this bright aioli. Instead of preparing the mayonnaise yourself, you can add the lemon juice and garlic to ⅔ cup of store-bought mayonnaise.

- 2 large egg yolks
- ½ teaspoon Dijon mustard
- ½ cup extra-virgin olive oil
- 1 garlic clove, minced
- 1 tablespoon fresh Meyer lemon juice or regular lemon juice

Salt and freshly ground black pepper
- 2 large cooked Dungeness crabs, halved

In a medium bowl, whisk the egg yolks with the mustard. Slowly drizzle in the olive oil, whisking constantly, until a thick mayonnaise forms. Whisk in the minced garlic and lemon juice and season with salt and black pepper. Serve the steamed crab with the lemon aioli. —*Dede Sampson*

MAKE AHEAD The lemon aioli can be made up to 1 day ahead and stored, covered, in the refrigerator.

WINE Dry, rich Champagne.

SUPERFAST

cold shellfish platter

The lemon aioli above is perfect with steamed, chilled shrimp, crab and lobster. Place a bowl of aioli in the center of a platter filled with ice and arrange the seafood around it.

Supercrispy Pan-Fried Chicken

TOTAL: 1 HR 15 MIN PLUS 8 HR MARINATING

12 TO 16 SERVINGS ●●

Instead of deep-frying chicken in a vat of oil, Atlanta-based baker Angie Mosier prefers pan-frying, which creates delightfully crunchy and moist chicken without requiring quite so much oil. "For a covered-dish dinner, there's nothing better than a tray of drumsticks, which are easy to eat standing up," she says.

- 16 pieces of chicken (preferably drumsticks and thighs)
- 6 cups buttermilk
- 3 cups all-purpose flour
- 4 teaspoons salt
- 2 teaspoons freshly ground black pepper
- 1 teaspoon cayenne pepper
- 1½ quarts vegetable oil, for frying

1. In a large bowl, toss the chicken pieces with the buttermilk. Cover with plastic wrap and refrigerate the chicken for at least 8 hours or overnight.

2. In a large resealable plastic bag, combine the flour, salt, black pepper and cayenne. Set 2 large wire racks over rimmed baking sheets. Working in batches, drain the chicken, scraping off most of the buttermilk against the side of the bowl. Add the chicken to the bag a few pieces at a time and shake to coat completely. Transfer the chicken to the racks, pressing the flour to help it adhere as you remove the chicken from the bag.

3. Pour 1 inch of vegetable oil into each of 2 large cast-iron skillets and heat to 350°. Carefully add about half of the chicken to the oil, being sure not to crowd the skillet. Fry, turning a few times, over moderate heat until the chicken is golden and crisp all over and cooked through, 20 to 25 minutes; an instant-read thermometer should register 165° for thighs or drumsticks and 160° for breasts. As they're cooked, spread the fried chicken pieces out on paper towel–lined cooling racks to drain. Continue frying the chicken in batches, being sure to adjust the heat so that the oil temperature stays at 325° during frying (you may need to pause briefly between batches to adjust the heat). Transfer the chicken to a large serving platter and serve warm or at room temperature.

—*Angie Mosier*

MAKE AHEAD The fried chicken can be kept at room temperature for up to 4 hours. Serve at room temperature or reheat in a low oven before serving.

WINE Light, crisp white Burgundy.

Green-Chile Chicken Thighs with Arugula Salad

ACTIVE: 45 MIN; TOTAL: 2 HR 15 MIN

6 SERVINGS ●

Adam Perry Lang, chef and owner of Daisy May's BBQ USA in New York City, tasted New Mexican Hatch green-chile powder for the first time last year during one of his "flavor recon missions," he says. "I was absolutely amazed by the color, fruitiness and bright, floral taste. The powder isn't a substitute for fresh chiles; it's a whole different flavor experience." It took Perry Lang nearly two months to track down a purveyor, dagiftbasket.com ("my best-kept secret"); now he uses the powder to season grilled corn, pork and poultry, including these delightful, crisp chicken thighs. Perry Lang's Creamy Grits are the perfect side dish to serve with the chicken and arugula salad.

- 2 tablespoons unsalted butter
- 3 tablespoons New Mexican Hatch green-chile powder or other mild green-chile powder
- 1 teaspoon ground coriander
- 1 teaspoon dried oregano, preferably Mexican

Salt and freshly ground black pepper

- 12 chicken thighs on the bone, trimmed of excess skin
- 2 tablespoons coarsely chopped flat-leaf parsley
- 2 tablespoons fresh lemon juice
- 2 tablespoons extra-virgin olive oil
- 4 ounces baby arugula
- 2 tablespoons cilantro leaves
- ½ pound *queso fresco* or farmer cheese, crumbled (2 cups; see Note)

Creamy Grits (p. 85), for serving

1. Preheat the oven to 325°. Spread the butter in a medium roasting pan. In a small bowl, combine the green-chile powder, ground coriander and dried oregano with a generous pinch of salt and black pepper. Sprinkle the seasonings generously all over the chicken thighs, pressing to help them adhere.

2. Transfer the chicken to the roasting pan skin side down. Cover the chicken with foil and roast for 1 hour. Turn the chicken thighs and roast, uncovered, for 25 minutes longer, until they are cooked through and the pan juices are slightly reduced.

3. Light the broiler. Broil the chicken thighs 6 inches from the heat for about 2 to 3 minutes, until the skin is golden and crisp. Pour the pan juices into a gravy boat and stir in the chopped parsley and 1 tablespoon of the fresh lemon juice. Season the pan juices with salt and black pepper.

4. In a medium bowl, whisk the remaining 1 tablespoon of lemon juice with the olive oil and season with salt and pepper. Add the arugula, cilantro and *queso fresco* and season with salt and black pepper. Spoon the Creamy Grits into shallow bowls and top with the chicken thighs. Mound the arugula salad alongside, drizzle the pan juices all around and serve.

—*Adam Perry Lang*

NOTE *Queso fresco* is a crumbly fresh white Mexican cow's-milk cheese. Look for it at Mexican markets.

WINE Full-bodied, minerally Riesling.

Alabama artist Butch Anthony digs into Supercrispy Pan-Fried Chicken.

rubs for chicken

step 1: *pick your favorite flavors*

Jamaican

4 SERVINGS ●

F&W's Marcia Kiesel says Scotch bonnets and habaneros have a taste like no other chile: They are wonderfully fruity, sweet and blasting hot. Habanero hot sauce and allspice give this fiery rub great Caribbean flavor in the style of Jamaican jerk sauce.

SERVE WITH Tomato and shredded cabbage salad with garlic vinaigrette.

- ¼ cup plus 2 tablespoons Scotch bonnet or habanero hot sauce
- 3 scallions, minced
- 2 tablespoons vegetable oil
- 2 teaspoons ground allspice
- 2 teaspoons kosher salt
- 1 teaspoon cinnamon

Spanish

4 SERVINGS ●

To get the most out of a quick Spanish-inspired rub, Marcia Kiesel turns to pimentón de la Vera, which adds a smoky kick to roasted chicken.

SERVE WITH Roasted potatoes.

- 2 tablespoons extra-virgin olive oil
- 2 tablespoons chopped parsley
- 2 tablespoons dry sherry
- 2 garlic cloves, minced
- 2 teaspoons pimentón de la Vera (Spanish smoked paprika)
- 2 teaspoons kosher salt
- ½ small red onion, minced
- ½ teaspoon fennel seeds, chopped

Indian

4 SERVINGS ●

A good, complex curry powder is the key ingredient in the fragrant rub here, says Marcia Kiesel. The rub also gets an appealing touch of sweetness from minced onion.

SERVE WITH Chilled sliced cucumbers tossed with sour cream and mint.

NOTE For an outstanding selection of high-quality curry powders and other spices, go to kalustyans.com.

- 2 tablespoons vegetable oil
- 2 garlic cloves, minced
- 2 teaspoons kosher salt
- 2 tablespoons minced onion
- 1 tablespoon curry powder
- 1 jalapeño, seeded and minced

step 2: *mix all ingredients to a paste*

step 3: *roast in the oven*

4 SKIN-ON, BONE-IN BREASTS *12 ounces each*	**40 MIN AT 425°** Make 2 slashes in each breast. Rub the paste over the skin and into the slashes.
8 SKIN-ON, BONE-IN THIGHS *6 ounces each*	**45 MIN AT 425°** Make 2 slashes in each thigh. Rub the paste over the skin and into the slashes.
8 LEGS *4 ounces each*	**45 MIN AT 425°** Make 2 slashes in each leg. Rub the paste over the skin and into the slashes.
1 WHOLE CHICKEN *4 pounds*	**90 MIN AT 350°** Loosen the skin. Rub the paste under and over the skin.

Vegetable and Chicken Stir-Fry

TOTAL: 30 MIN
4 SERVINGS ●

¼ cup canola oil
1 medium onion, halved and very thinly sliced
½ pound skinless, boneless chicken thighs, cut into thin strips
1 tablespoon Asian fish sauce
1 small head of broccoli, cut into 1-inch florets
1 celery rib, thinly sliced
4 ounces snow peas (1½ cups)
1 garlic clove, thinly sliced
1 tablespoon very finely chopped fresh ginger
1 teaspoon *sambal oelek* or Chinese chile-garlic sauce
1 tablespoon hoisin sauce
1 tablespoon oyster sauce
1 cup mung bean sprouts
2 tablespoons shredded basil leaves
1 tablespoon fresh lime juice
Steamed jasmine rice, for serving

1. Heat a wok until very hot. Add 2 tablespoons of the canola oil, and when it is nearly smoking, add the sliced onion and chicken strips. Stir-fry over high heat until the chicken is lightly browned in spots but not cooked through, about 3 minutes. Add the fish sauce and stir-fry for 10 seconds. Scrape the chicken and onion onto a medium plate and wipe out the wok.

2. Heat the remaining 2 tablespoons of oil in the wok. Add the broccoli, celery, snow peas, garlic and ginger and stir-fry over high heat until crisp-tender, 3 to 4 minutes. Return the chicken and onion to the wok along with any accumulated juices. Add the *sambal* and hoisin and oyster sauces and stir-fry just until the chicken is cooked through, 3 to 4 minutes longer. Add the bean sprouts, basil and lime juice and toss well. Transfer to a bowl and serve right away, with jasmine rice. —*Pino Maffeo*
WINE Fresh, minerally Vermentino.

Ginger Duck Salad with Green Tea Dressing

ACTIVE: 30 MIN; TOTAL: 2 HR 30 MIN
6 SERVINGS ●

4 duck legs (about 1 pound each)
½ cup mushroom soy sauce (see Note)
¼ cup low-sodium soy sauce
3 tablespoons Chinese black vinegar or unseasoned rice vinegar
3 tablespoons sake
⅓ cup sugar
½ small onion, thinly sliced crosswise
½ star anise pod, broken
1 tablespoon minced fresh ginger
1 large garlic clove, smashed
1 tablespoon unseasoned rice vinegar
2 tablespoons canola oil
¼ teaspoon powdered green tea (*matcha*), plus more for dusting
Salt
1 Asian pear or Bosc pear, cored and cut into thin wedges
3 ounces mizuna or mesclun greens (3 cups)
1 cup finely shredded napa cabbage

1. Preheat the oven to 325°. Put the duck legs in a medium enameled cast-iron casserole. Add both soy sauces, the black vinegar, sake, sugar, onion, star anise, ginger and garlic. Add enough water to just cover and bring to a boil. Cover the casserole and transfer it to the oven. Braise the duck for 1½ hours, or until it is very tender. Remove the duck legs from the liquid and let cool. Discard the duck skin and braising liquid. Pull the meat from the bones in large shreds.

2. In a bowl, whisk the rice vinegar with the oil and the ¼ teaspoon of green tea. Season with salt. Add the Asian pear, mizuna and cabbage and toss. Transfer to plates, top with the shredded duck, sprinkle with green tea powder and serve. —*Hiro Sone*
NOTE Mushroom soy sauce is dark soy sauce flavored with straw mushrooms. Look for it in Asian markets.
MAKE AHEAD The duck can be refrigerated in the cooking liquid for up to 3 days.
WINE Full-bodied, minerally Riesling.

CHEF'S CHOICE

favorite stoves

MOLTENI There are fewer than 50 of these custom-designed stoves (above) in the U.S. (molteni.com).

VIKING These stoves have superprecise burner controls (vikingrange.com).

WOLF "It lights quickly with a strong, direct flame," says chef Ming Tsai of Blue Ginger in Wellesley, Massachusetts (wolfappliance.com).

ELECTROLUX Its S90 professional stoves have add-on options like an electric fryer (electrolux.com).

● HEALTHY ● MAKE AHEAD ○ VEGETARIAN ● STAFF FAVORITE

CHICKEN AND CHEESE ENCHILADAS VERDES

BASQUE CHICKEN WITH SWEET PEPPERS AND TOMATOES

Chicken and Cheese Enchiladas Verdes

ACTIVE: 45 MIN; TOTAL: 1 HR 15 MIN

4 TO 6 SERVINGS

Following her Mexican grandmother's enchilada recipe, cooking show host Marie Hejl first dips tortillas in a fresh tomatillo sauce, then fries them in oil. Here, to avoid spattering, the tortillas are first fried in oil, then coated with sauce.

- 2½ **pounds tomatillos, husked**
- 1 **large jalapeño, halved**
- ¼ **cup extra-virgin olive oil, plus more for frying**

Salt and freshly ground pepper

- 16 **corn tortillas**
- 3 **cups shredded cooked rotisserie chicken**
- 1½ **cups shredded sharp cheddar cheese (6 ounces)**
- ½ **cup crumbled** *queso fresco,* **plus more for serving**

Sour cream, lime wedges and chopped cilantro, onion and tomatoes, for serving

1. Preheat the oven to 350°. In a large, deep skillet of boiling water, cook the husked tomatillos and jalapeño over moderately high heat until softened, about 10 minutes. Drain the tomatillos and jalapeño, then transfer them to a blender and puree until the salsa verde is smooth.

2. Wipe out the skillet and heat the ¼ cup of olive oil in it. Add the salsa and bring to a boil over moderately high heat. Season with salt and pepper. Spoon a few tablespoons of the salsa into each of 2 shallow 5-by-10-inch baking dishes.

3. In a medium skillet, heat ¼ inch of olive oil until shimmering. Using tongs, dip a tortilla in the hot oil until coated and cook over medium heat, turning once, until pliable, about 10 seconds. With the tongs, carefully lift the tortilla out of the oil and dip it into the hot salsa verde, making sure to coat both sides. Transfer the salsa-coated fried tortilla to a large plate. Repeat with the remaining tortillas, stacking them on the plate.

4. Arrange 8 of the tortillas on a work surface and spoon shredded chicken in the center of each; season with salt and pepper. Roll the tortillas into loose cylinders and transfer them to one of the prepared baking dishes, seam side down. Repeat with the remaining tortillas, filling them with the shredded cheddar cheese. Spoon the remaining salsa verde over the enchiladas and sprinkle them with the ½ cup of crumbled *queso fresco.* Bake for about 30 minutes, until the enchiladas are hot and the salsa is bubbling. Serve the enchiladas with sour cream, lime wedges, cilantro, onion, tomatoes and additional *queso fresco* on the side. —*Marie Hejl*

WINE Rustic, peppery Malbec.

Grilled Capon with Salsa Verde

ACTIVE: 1 HR; TOTAL: 2 HR 15 MIN

8 SERVINGS ●

One 8-pound capon, cut into 4 pieces
    (see Note), wings, neck and
    carcass bones reserved

  1 leek, white and tender green
      parts only, thickly sliced

  1 medium onion, quartered

  1 carrot, thickly sliced

  1 celery rib, thickly sliced

  4 large parsley sprigs

  2 thyme sprigs

  1 bay leaf

Kosher salt

  1 gallon water

Vegetable oil, for coating

Freshly ground pepper

Salsa Verde (recipe follows)

1. Put the capon wings, neck and carcass bones in a large pot. Add the leek, onion, carrot, celery, parsley, thyme, bay leaf and 1 tablespoon of salt. Add the water and bring to a boil. Cover and simmer over low heat for 15 minutes.

2. Carefully add the capon legs followed by the breast pieces to the hot liquid in the pot and bring to a simmer. Reduce the heat to low and simmer until the capon breast pieces are just cooked through, about 20 minutes; transfer the breast pieces to a large rimmed baking sheet with tongs, being careful not to break the skin. Continue poaching the capon legs until cooked through, about 35 minutes longer; transfer to the baking sheet. Let the capon pieces cool to room temperature, then rub them all over with vegetable oil. Strain and reserve the poaching broth (use in the Grilled Cauliflower Salad with Raisin-Almond Dressing on p. 71, if desired).

3. Light a grill. Season the capon pieces with salt and pepper and grill skin side down over moderately high heat for about 5 minutes, or until the skin is crisp and lightly charred. Turn the capon pieces and grill for 5 minutes longer, or until they're browned and heated through; let cool slightly. Thickly slice the breast and thigh meat. Arrange the capon on a platter and serve with the Salsa Verde.

—*Lachlan Mackinnon Patterson*

NOTE Have your butcher cut up the capon for you: You should have 2 whole legs and 2 boneless breast halves (with skin) with the first joint of the wing attached. Keep the bones for the poaching liquid.

WINE Bright, tart Barbera.

SALSA VERDE

 TOTAL: 25 MIN

MAKES 3 CUPS ● ○

  2 cups basil leaves

  3 cups flat-leaf parsley leaves

 ¼ cup plus 2 tablespoons
      chopped cornichons

  2 tablespoons drained capers

  1 medium shallot, chopped

  1 tablespoon chopped garlic

  2 tablespoons fresh lemon juice

  1 cup extra-virgin olive oil

 ¾ cup vegetable oil

Salt and freshly ground pepper

In a food processor, combine all of the ingredients except the salt and pepper. Puree until smooth. Scrape the salsa into a bowl and season with salt and pepper.
—*L.M.P.*

MAKE AHEAD The Salsa Verde can be refrigerated overnight.

Basque Chicken with Sweet Peppers and Tomatoes

ACTIVE: 20 MIN; TOTAL: 1 HR 10 MIN

4 SERVINGS ●

Yves Camdeborde, chef at Le Comptoir in Paris, is from the Béarn, the southwestern French region bordering Basque Country, and he grew up eating Basque dishes like this. Camdeborde updated the recipe and shortened the usual cooking time so that the vegetables keep more of their texture and flavor. He sometimes adds potatoes to the dish.

  2 tablespoons extra-virgin
      olive oil

  4 chicken drumsticks

  4 chicken thighs

Salt and freshly ground pepper

  1 large onion, thinly sliced

 ½ red bell pepper, thinly sliced

 ½ green bell pepper, thinly sliced

  2 large garlic cloves, thinly sliced

20 cherry tomatoes, halved

  4 jarred piquillo peppers, drained

  1 teaspoon chopped thyme

  1 cup dry white wine

  1 cup water

  2 ounces serrano ham or prosciutto,
      sliced ¹⁄₁₆ inch thick and cut into
      thin strips

1. Preheat the oven to 400°. In a large, deep ovenproof skillet, heat the oil. Season the chicken with salt and pepper and add to the skillet, skin side down. Cook over moderately high heat until richly browned, about 4 minutes per side. Transfer the chicken to a large plate, skin side up.

2. Add the onion, red and green bell peppers and garlic to the skillet and cook over moderately low heat, stirring occasionally, until softened, about 10 minutes. Add the cherry tomatoes, piquillo peppers and thyme; once the tomatoes are hot, pour in the wine and simmer over moderately high heat for 1 minute. Stir in the water and bring to a boil. Return the chicken to the skillet, skin side up. Cover tightly and braise in the oven for about 20 minutes, until the chicken is cooked through.

3. Transfer the chicken to a shallow serving dish. With a slotted spoon, transfer the vegetables in the skillet to the serving dish and cover with foil to keep warm. Boil the cooking juices over high heat until reduced to 1 cup, about 10 minutes. Add the serrano ham and bring to a simmer. Remove from the heat and season with salt and pepper. Pour the juices over the chicken and vegetables and serve. —*Yves Camdeborde*

WINE Cherry-inflected, earthy Sangiovese.

Thai Chicken Stew with Potato-Chive Dumplings

 TOTAL: 45 MIN
4 SERVINGS ●●

Boston chef Pino Maffeo serves his vibrant, spicy, warming stew with *gai lan* (Chinese broccoli). Sautéed garlic chives stud his plump potato dumplings. In this delicious spin on Maffeo's recipe, baby bok choy, an easy-to-find Chinese green, replaces the *gai lan,* while regular chives stand in for the more obscure garlic chives.

- ½ pound baking potatoes, peeled and cut into 1-inch chunks
- 2 tablespoons canola oil
- 1 pound skinless, boneless chicken thighs, cut into 1-inch pieces
- 1 large onion, very finely chopped
- 1 large jalapeño—halved, seeded and thinly sliced
- ¼ cup Asian fish sauce
- 3 cups chicken stock or low-sodium broth
- 2 tablespoons all-purpose flour, plus more for rolling
- 1 large egg yolk
- 2 tablespoons very finely chopped chives

Salt

- 1 pound baby bok choy, cut into 1-inch pieces
- 1 tablespoon cornstarch dissolved in 1 tablespoon water
- 2 tablespoons shredded basil leaves

Lime wedges, for serving

1. Put the potato chunks in a medium saucepan and cover with hot water. Bring the water to a boil over high heat and boil until the potatoes are completely tender, about 12 minutes. Do not pour off the potato cooking water.

2. Meanwhile, heat the canola oil in a large, heavy casserole. Add the chicken pieces and cook them over high heat, stirring a few times, until lightly browned all over, about 4 minutes. Add the chopped onion and sliced jalapeño and cook, stirring, until the onion is softened, 4 minutes. Add 3 tablespoons of the fish sauce and the chicken stock and bring to a boil over high heat. Cover and cook over moderate heat until the chicken is just cooked through, about 10 minutes.

3. Using a slotted spoon, transfer the potatoes to a ricer and press into a bowl. (Alternatively, mash the potatoes.) Reserve the potato water. Add the 2 tablespoons of flour, egg yolk, chives and ½ teaspoon of salt to the potatoes and stir until a stiff dough forms. Turn the dough out onto a heavily floured board and divide it in half. Roll each piece into a ½-inch-thick rope. Cut the ropes into 1-inch pieces.

4. Add the bok choy to the stew and cook until crisp-tender, about 5 minutes. Add the cornstarch mixture and cook, stirring, until thickened, 1 minute.

5. Return the potato water to a boil and add the dumplings. Cook over high heat until they rise to the surface, then simmer for 2 minutes. Using a slotted spoon, transfer the dumplings to the chicken stew. Add the basil and the remaining 1 tablespoon of fish sauce and simmer the stew for 2 to 3 minutes. Serve with lime wedges. —*Pino Maffeo*
WINE Light, crisp white Burgundy.

Asian-Glazed Pork Shoulder

ACTIVE: 15 MIN; TOTAL: 1 HR 15 MIN
8 SERVINGS ●●

Ming Tsai, chef at Blue Ginger in Wellesley, Massachusetts, and host of *Simply Ming* on PBS, experienced the power of the pressure cooker during a taping of *Iron Chef America* a few years ago. Using the device, he was able to make one of his favorite childhood dishes, slow-braised pork shoulder, in just an hour. "At a restaurant you have all day to braise," Tsai says. "That's not true on *Iron Chef.*" Now he's always looking for new ways to exploit his cooker, making duck legs, chicken thighs and spareribs as well as the juicy glazed pork shoulder he's eaten his whole life.

- 3 cups soy sauce
- 1½ cups dry red wine
- 1½ cups water
- ¾ cup balsamic vinegar
- 1 pound dark brown sugar
- 6 scallions, white and light green parts cut into 2-inch lengths, dark green parts thinly sliced
- 3 small dried red Thai chiles
- One 4-inch piece of fresh ginger, thinly sliced
- 1 head of garlic, halved crosswise
- 1 medium orange, quartered
- One 4-inch cinnamon stick
- One 4-pound piece of boneless pork shoulder, quartered

Freshly ground pepper

1. In an 8-quart pressure cooker, combine the soy sauce, wine, water, vinegar, sugar, scallion lengths, chiles, ginger, garlic, orange and cinnamon stick. Cook over moderately high heat, stirring, until the sugar is dissolved. Season the pork with pepper; add it to the pressure cooker. Close and lock the cooker and bring to full pressure over high heat. Adjust the heat to maintain full pressure; cook for 1 hour, or until the pork is very tender. Slowly release the pressure and open the cooker. Transfer the pork to a cutting board; cover with foil.

2. Strain 1 cup of the cooking liquid into a small saucepan; discard the remaining liquid. Boil over high heat until the liquid is reduced by two-thirds and thick, about 5 minutes. Brush a light coating of the sauce over each piece of pork to glaze it. Thinly slice the pork, garnish with the dark green scallion slices and serve. —*Ming Tsai*
SERVE WITH Steamed Chinese broccoli.
MAKE AHEAD The cooked pork can be refrigerated in the liquid overnight.
WINE Round, deep-flavored Shiraz.

THAI CHICKEN STEW
WITH POTATO-CHIVE DUMPLINGS

Pork and Wild Mushroom Daube

ACTIVE: 2 HR; TOTAL: 6 HR PLUS
2 DAYS OF CHILLING
4 TO 6 SERVINGS

PORK

3 pounds boneless pork shoulder, cut into 2½-inch pieces

One 750-milliliter bottle Viognier

1 medium onion, thinly sliced

1 medium carrot

Bouquet garni: 6 sprigs each of parsley, thyme and winter savory plus 2 bay leaves and 1 leafy celery top, tied with twine

Spice bundle: ½ teaspoon lavender flowers, 12 crushed peppercorns and 10 crushed juniper berries, tied in cheesecloth

1½ tablespoons extra-virgin olive oil

DAUBE

1½ ounces dried porcini (1 cup)

3 tablespoons extra-virgin olive oil

Salt and freshly ground pepper

1 tablespoon all-purpose flour

2½ tablespoons brandy

1 large onion, thinly sliced

1 large carrot, cut into ½-inch dice

4 ounces pork skin with a thin layer of fat, cut into 2-by-½-inch strips

1 head of garlic, separated into cloves but not peeled

10 crushed juniper berries

Reserved bouquet garni

GARNISH

3 tablespoons extra-virgin olive oil

1½ pounds oyster and cremini mushrooms, halved if large

Salt and freshly ground pepper

4 garlic cloves, minced

⅓ cup finely chopped parsley

1 teaspoon red wine vinegar

1. MARINATE THE PORK: Put the pork in a large bowl. Add the wine, onion, carrot, bouquet garni, spice bundle and olive oil. Cover and refrigerate overnight.

2. Pour the pork into a colander set over a bowl. Discard the onion and carrot. Squeeze the spice bundle over the meat; discard. Reserve the bouquet garni and marinade.

3. MAKE THE DAUBE: In a bowl, soak the porcini in 1 cup of hot water until soft, about 20 minutes. In a large skillet, heat 2 tablespoons of the oil. Season the pork with salt and pepper. Brown in 2 batches over moderately high heat; transfer to a plate.

4. Return the pork to the skillet and sprinkle with the flour. Stir over moderate heat until the flour dissolves, 1 minute. Add the brandy and carefully ignite it with a long match; shake the skillet until the flames die down. Return the pork to the plate. Add the remaining 1 tablespoon of oil to the skillet with the onion and carrot. Season

with salt and cook over moderately low heat until lightly browned, 10 minutes.

5. Lift the porcini from the soaking liquid and coarsely chop them; reserve the soaking liquid. Add the porcini to the skillet and cook for 3 minutes, stirring.

6. Preheat the oven to 250°. Line the bottom of a 4½-quart enameled cast-iron casserole with the pork skin, fat side down. Spoon ⅓ of the pork over the skin followed by ⅓ of the vegetable mixture and ⅓ of the garlic cloves. Season with salt and pepper and sprinkle with some of the juniper berries. Repeat this layering 2 more times.

7. Return the skillet to moderately high heat. Pour in the porcini liquid, stopping short of the grit at the bottom. Add the reserved marinade; simmer, scraping up the browned bits from the bottom, until reduced to 2 cups. Pour over the daube.

8. Tuck the reserved bouquet garni into the daube. Add enough water to just cover the meat and bring to a boil over moderately high heat. Place a round of parchment paper on the surface of the meat and cover with the lid. Bake the casserole in the oven until the meat is tender, about 2½ hours. Let cool. Discard the parchment, bouquet garni and any bits of juniper. Refrigerate overnight.

9. MAKE THE GARNISH: Preheat the oven to 250°. In a large skillet, heat 2 tablespoons of the oil until shimmering. Add the mushrooms and season with salt and pepper. Cover and cook over moderate heat until softened, 5 minutes. Remove the lid. Continue cooking until the liquid evaporates and the mushrooms start to brown, 4 minutes. Add the remaining 1 tablespoon of oil and the garlic and cook, stirring, until fragrant, 3 minutes. Stir in the parsley.

10. Skim the fat from the daube. Add the mushrooms and bring to a simmer, stirring. Bake for about 1½ hours, uncovered, until the liquid is slightly reduced and the meat is very tender. Stir in the vinegar and season with salt and pepper. —*Paula Wolfert*
WINE Lush, fragrant Viognier.

WHO'S YOUR FANTASY COOKING TEACHER?

❝ Paula Wolfert. She's *appassionata* about all food in the Mediterranean. **❞** —*Mario Batali*

FRANÇOIS PAYARD *wants a class with* → MARIO BATALI *wants a class with* → PAULA WOLFERT

PORK AND WILD MUSHROOM DAUBE

Tuscan Pork Stew with Polenta

ACTIVE: 1 HR 30 MIN; TOTAL: 2 HR
30 MIN PLUS 6 HR MARINATING
6 SERVINGS ●

Wild boar is indigenous to Tuscany, where rock star Sting has an estate. Sting's chef, Joe Sponzo, cooks boar in a rustic, wine-based stew to serve over polenta. For cooks who don't have easy access to this "gamey beast," as Sponzo calls it, pork shoulder is a good substitute.

PORK

- 1 bottle dry red wine
- 4 rosemary sprigs
- 4 sage sprigs
- 1 red onion, coarsely chopped
- 1 celery rib, coarsely chopped
- 1 carrot, coarsely chopped
- 3 bay leaves
- 1 tablespoon black peppercorns
- 1 tablespoon juniper berries
- 2 teaspoons whole cloves
- 3 pounds boneless pork shoulder, cut into 2-inch cubes

STEW AND POLENTA

- ¼ cup extra-virgin olive oil
- 1 celery rib, very finely chopped
- 1 carrot, finely chopped
- 1 small red onion, finely chopped
- 1 large garlic clove, thinly sliced
- 1 tablespoon very finely chopped sage
- 1½ teaspoons very finely chopped rosemary
- Salt
- Crushed red pepper
- 1 cup dry red wine
- ¼ cup tomato paste
- 3 cups chicken stock or low-sodium broth

- 2 whole cloves, 8 juniper berries, 2 bay leaves and 4 peppercorns, tied in cheesecloth
- 8 cups water
- 2 cups polenta (not instant)
- 2 tablespoons unsalted butter
- 2 tablespoons chopped flat-leaf parsley

1. MARINATE THE PORK: In a large resealable plastic bag, combine the red wine, rosemary and sage sprigs, chopped red onion, celery and carrot, bay leaves, black peppercorns, juniper berries and whole cloves. Add the pork cubes and seal the bag, pressing out the air and making sure the ingredients are well combined. Refrigerate the pork in the marinade for at least 6 hours or overnight.

2. MAKE THE STEW AND POLENTA: Rinse off the pork cubes in a colander and discard the marinade. In a medium enameled cast-iron casserole, cover the pork cubes with 2 inches of water and bring to a boil. Simmer for 10 minutes, then drain. Pat the pork dry with paper towels.

3. Wipe out the casserole, add the olive oil and heat until the oil is shimmering. Add the pork cubes, chopped celery, carrot and red onion and sliced garlic and cook over moderate heat, stirring occasionally, until the meat and vegetables are lightly browned, about 10 minutes. Add the chopped sage and rosemary, season with salt and a pinch of crushed red pepper and cook for 1 minute. Pour in the red wine and bring to a simmer. Cook over moderate heat until the wine is nearly evaporated, about 10 minutes. Stir in the tomato paste. Add the chicken stock and spice bundle and bring to a boil.

4. Partially cover the casserole and cook the stew over very low heat until the meat is very tender and the liquid has reduced by half, about 1 hour and 45 minutes.

5. Meanwhile, bring the 8 cups of water to a boil in a large saucepan. Whisk in the polenta in a thin stream. Cook the polenta over low heat, whisking constantly, until it begins to thicken, about 5 minutes. Continue cooking over low heat, stirring frequently with a wooden spoon, until the polenta is very thick and no longer tastes gritty, about 30 minutes. Stir in the butter and season the polenta with salt.

6. Use a wide spoon to skim the fat from the stew. Remove and discard the spice bundle. Stir in the chopped parsley and season the stew with salt. Spoon the polenta into 6 shallow bowls, spoon the pork stew on top and serve piping hot.
—*Joe Sponzo*

WINE Cherry-inflected, earthy Sangiovese.

Baked Beans with Pork Belly and Quince

ACTIVE: 45 MIN; TOTAL: 3 HR PLUS
OVERNIGHT SOAKING
10 SERVINGS ●

Michel Nischan likes to modernize classic New England recipes for the menu of Dressing Room, his restaurant in Westport, Connecticut, which serves what he calls "updated heritage cuisine." Here he puts a spin on traditional baked beans by swapping bacon with fresh pork belly and replacing the usual molasses with fresh quince, which sweetens the beans while also thickening the sauce.

- 1 tablespoon extra-virgin olive oil
- 2½ pounds pork belly, skin discarded, belly sliced 1 inch thick and cut into 1-inch dice
- 1 large onion, very finely chopped
- 4 cups dried Tarbais or cannellini beans (26 ounces), soaked overnight and drained
- One 28-ounce can diced tomatoes, drained
- 6 thyme sprigs

2   bay leaves

2   quarts Ham Hock Stock
    (p. 159), chicken stock or
    canned low-sodium
    chicken broth

2   pounds quince (about 4)—
    peeled, cored and
    cut into ½-inch dice

Salt and freshly ground
    black pepper

¼   cup snipped chives

1. Heat the olive oil in a large enameled cast-iron casserole. Add half the diced pork belly and cook over moderate heat, stirring occasionally, until lightly browned on all sides, about 10 minutes. Use a slotted spoon to transfer the pork belly to a plate. Repeat, browning the remaining diced pork belly and transferring it to the plate. Add the chopped onion to the casserole and cook over moderate heat, stirring, until softened, about 5 minutes. Return all the diced pork belly to the casserole and add the soaked beans, diced tomatoes, thyme sprigs and bay leaves. Add the Ham Hock Stock and bring to a boil over high heat. Partially cover the casserole, reduce the heat and simmer over low heat until the beans are almost tender, about 45 minutes. Use a ladle to skim off the fat from the surface.

2. Add the diced quince to the beans, stir and season with salt and black pepper. Partially cover the casserole and continue to cook over low heat until the pork, beans and quince are all completely tender, about 45 minutes longer.

3. Preheat the oven to 425°. Transfer the contents of the casserole to one 3-quart or two 1½-quart baking dishes and bake until the surface of the beans is lightly browned, about 30 minutes. Sprinkle with the snipped chives and serve.
—*Michel Nischan*

MAKE AHEAD The baked beans can be refrigerated overnight. Rewarm over low heat or in a 375° oven.

WINE Intense, fruity Zinfandel.

Pork-and-Ricotta Meatballs in Tomato Sauce

ACTIVE: 30 MIN; TOTAL: 3 HR

8 SERVINGS ● ●

Chef Nate Appleman of A16 in San Francisco occasionally uses ground lamb, beef or veal in his tender, golf ball–size meatballs, which he bakes in a hearty tomato sauce. But this all-pork version, a weekly special, follows the restaurant's classic recipe, and it's hard to beat. "Sometimes you can almost feel the excitement at the tables when the servers announce, 'And of course, since it's Monday. . . we have meatballs,' " says A16's wine director, Shelley Lindgren.

Vegetable oil, for the pan

½   pound sliced white bread,
    crusts removed and bread
    cut into ½-inch dice
    (4 cups)

1½ pounds lean ground pork

3   ounces thickly sliced
    pancetta, very finely
    chopped

3   large eggs, lightly beaten

⅔   cup fresh ricotta cheese
    (5 ounces)

¼   cup finely chopped
    flat-leaf parsley

1   teaspoon dried
    oregano, crumbled

½   teaspoon fennel
    seeds, chopped

¼   teaspoon crushed
    red pepper

Kosher salt

Two 28-ounce cans peeled
    Italian tomatoes, crushed

Freshly ground black pepper

2   tablespoons finely shredded
    basil leaves

½   cup freshly grated Pecorino
    Romano cheese

1. Preheat the oven to 400°. Brush the bottom and sides of a medium roasting pan with vegetable oil. In the bowl of a food processor, pulse the diced bread to coarse crumbs. Transfer the crumbs to a large bowl and add the ground pork, chopped pancetta, beaten eggs, ricotta cheese, chopped parsley, crumbled oregano, chopped fennel seeds, crushed red pepper and 1½ teaspoons of kosher salt. Mix well. Shape the mixture into 24 meatballs, using about 3 rounded tablespoons of the mixture for each. Transfer the meatballs to the prepared roasting pan.

2. Roast the meatballs in the oven for about 30 minutes, or until firm and just beginning to brown. Using a spatula, loosen the meatballs from the bottom of the pan. Add the crushed tomatoes to the pan and season with salt and black pepper. Lower the oven temperature to 325° and cook uncovered for about 2 hours, or until the sauce is very thick and the meatballs are very tender; turn the meatballs once or twice during cooking.

3. Transfer the meatballs and tomato sauce to a large platter. Garnish with the shredded basil and grated Pecorino Romano cheese and serve immediately.
—*Nate Appleman*

MAKE AHEAD The cooked meatballs can be refrigerated for up to 2 days. Reheat and garnish with the shredded basil and grated Pecorino Romano cheese just before serving.

WINE Lively, fruity Merlot.

SUPERFAST

pork & apples

Season two 1-inch pork chops; sauté in 1 tablespoon of olive oil over high heat for 5 minutes per side. Remove to a plate. Add 1 peeled, sliced green apple and ¼ cup of cider to the skillet and simmer until soft. Melt in 1 tablespoon of butter and spoon over the chops.

Slow-Roasted Pork

ACTIVE: 20 MIN; TOTAL: 5 HR 30 MIN
12 SERVINGS ●

Metal artist and hunter Audwin McGee is a big fan of slow-cooked meats: "You just can't mess up a big hunk of pork. I like to use a bone-in Boston butt or shoulder with good fat content, so it doesn't dry up." His pork is smothered in a garlic-rosemary paste, then cooked at a low temperature for several hours until it's supertender.

- 3 garlic cloves, mashed to a paste
- 1 teaspoon very finely chopped rosemary leaves
- ½ teaspoon cayenne pepper
- ¼ cup extra-virgin olive oil
- Salt and freshly ground pepper
- One 9-pound fresh bone-in Boston butt or picnic ham with skin, at room temperature
- 2 pounds cipollini onions, peeled
- 6 thyme sprigs

1. Preheat the oven to 325°. In a small bowl, mash the garlic paste with the rosemary, cayenne, 2 tablespoons of the olive oil and 1 teaspoon each of salt and pepper.
2. Using a sharp paring knife, make 1-inch-deep slits all over the meat. Press as much of the spice paste into the slits as you can and spread the rest all over the skin. Set the pork in a large roasting pan and cover tightly with foil. Roast for 3 hours. Remove the foil and roast for about 1 hour and 45 minutes longer, until an instant-read thermometer inserted in the thickest part of the meat registers 165°.
3. Meanwhile, in a medium baking dish, toss the onions with the remaining 2 tablespoons of olive oil and the thyme sprigs and season with salt and pepper. Roast for 1 hour and 15 minutes, until the onions are tender and browned in spots.
4. Let the pork rest for 20 minutes. Remove the skin. Slice the meat as thinly as possible and serve with the onions.
—Audwin McGee

WINE Intense, fruity Zinfandel.

Red Wine–Braised Lamb Shanks

ACTIVE: 40 MIN; TOTAL: 2 HR 40 MIN
4 SERVINGS ●

- 2 tablespoons extra-virgin olive oil
- Four 1-pound lamb shanks
- Salt and freshly ground pepper
- 5 garlic cloves, peeled
- 4 medium carrots, sliced ¼ inch thick
- 4 medium celery ribs, sliced ¼ inch thick
- 1 large onion, coarsely chopped
- One 750-milliliter bottle dry red wine
- 1 cup water
- 3 bay leaves
- 12 peppercorns

1. Preheat the oven to 325°. In a large enameled cast-iron casserole, heat the olive oil. Season the lamb shanks with salt and pepper and brown them on 3 sides over moderately high heat, about 4 minutes per side. Add the garlic, carrots, celery and onion to the casserole. Add the red wine and boil for 3 minutes. Add the water and bring to a simmer. Add the bay leaves and peppercorns. Cover the casserole tightly and transfer to the oven. Braise the lamb shanks, turning once, for about 1½ hours, or until very tender.
2. Transfer the lamb shanks to an ovenproof serving dish. Using a fine sieve, strain the braising liquid into a medium saucepan, pressing on the solids. Boil the braising liquid over high heat until reduced to 1½ cups, about 20 minutes. Season the sauce with salt and pepper and pour about ½ cup over the lamb shanks; keep the remaining sauce warm. Cover the lamb shanks with foil and reheat in the oven for about 10 minutes. Serve the lamb shanks with the remaining sauce.
—Jeremy Silansky

SERVE WITH Maple-Glazed Root Vegetables (p. 78) and Braised Red Cabbage (p. 76).

WINE Intense, spicy Syrah.

Rack of Lamb with Rosemary Butter

ACTIVE: 15 MIN; TOTAL: 1 HR
8 SERVINGS

- 2 racks of lamb, 8 bones each, chine bones removed and rib bones frenched
- Salt and freshly ground pepper
- 2 tablespoons unsalted butter
- 2 tablespoons extra-virgin olive oil
- 5 large rosemary sprigs
- 1 teaspoon finely chopped thyme leaves
- 1 teaspoon finely chopped mint
- 1 tablespoon finely chopped flat-leaf parsley

1. Light a grill or preheat the oven to 375°. Season the lamb with salt and pepper.
2. If grilling: Melt the butter in the olive oil in a small saucepan. When the coals are covered in white ash, grill the lamb over low heat for about 40 minutes, turning every 2 to 3 minutes and brushing the racks with the rosemary sprigs dipped in the butter mixture. The lamb is done when an instant-read thermometer inserted in the thickest part of the meat registers 125° for rare.
3. If pan-roasting the lamb: Melt 1 tablespoon of the butter in 1 tablespoon of the oil in a large ovenproof skillet. Add the lamb racks fat side down and cook over moderately high heat until browned all over, about 5 minutes. Add the rosemary and the remaining 1 tablespoon each of butter and oil. Spoon some of the fat over the lamb. Transfer the skillet to the oven and roast for about 30 minutes, basting once or twice with the rosemary and fat and turning the racks halfway through. The lamb is done when an instant-read thermometer registers 125° for rare.
4. Transfer the lamb to a cutting board and let rest for 10 minutes. Carve the racks into chops. Sprinkle with the chopped thyme, mint and parsley and serve.
—David Kinch

WINE Firm, complex Cabernet Sauvignon.

Chef David Kinch seasons Rack of Lamb with Rosemary Butter.

TASTE TEST

grass-fed steak

All beef cattle are raised on grass; most are fattened with grain or corn for several months before slaughter. But a growing number of ranchers are raising cattle exclusively on grass. They say it's better for the environment, the animal and the person who eats the beef. Grass-fed (or "grass-finished") steaks are leaner; they're also higher in heart-healthy omega-3 fatty acids. In an F&W taste test of grass-fed rib eyes, we found that the flavor can vary, from pleasantly herbal to unappealingly gamey. Our favorites:

U.S. WELLNESS MEATS
$19 plus shipping for a thick 15 oz rib eye (877-383-0051 or grasslandbeef.com).

AMERICAN GRASS FED BEEF
$69 with shipping for four 8 oz rib eyes (866-255-5002 or americangrassfedbeef.com).

LASATER GRASSLANDS BEEF
$56 plus shipping for four 12 oz rib eyes (866-454-2333 or lgbeef.com).

All-American Hamburgers with Red Onion Compote

ACTIVE: 35 MIN; TOTAL: 1 HR 35 MIN
4 SERVINGS ●

A great burger starts with great ground beef, says David Walzog, executive chef at SW Steakhouse in the Wynn Las Vegas. He advocates ground-to-order beef with at least 20 percent fat content, seasoned generously with salt and pepper. "After that, it doesn't need much else," he says—just a sturdy bun and sauce that won't overpower the beef, like this sweet-and-sour red onion compote. To make the juiciest hamburger possible, Walzog says to shape the patty gently and then make a small indentation in the center; this ensures even cooking.

RED ONION COMPOTE

- 2 tablespoons vegetable oil
- 1 tablespoon ground coriander
- 3 medium red onions, finely diced (3 cups)
- 2 cups dry red wine
- 1 cup sugar
- 2 bay leaves
- 1 teaspoon finely grated orange zest
- ¾ teaspoon ground juniper berries
- 1 teaspoon chopped thyme
- 1 cup fresh orange juice

Salt

BURGERS

- 2 pounds ground chuck

Salt and freshly ground pepper

- 4 kaiser or brioche rolls, split and toasted

Lettuce leaves (optional)

1. MAKE THE RED ONION COMPOTE: In a medium saucepan, heat the vegetable oil. Add the coriander and cook over moderate heat for 30 seconds. Add the red onions, wine, sugar, bay leaves, orange zest, juniper berries, thyme and orange juice and bring to a boil. Simmer over moderate heat, stirring occasionally, until the mixture has thickened and reduced

to 2 cups, about 1 hour. Let the compote cool to room temperature. Discard the bay leaves and season with salt.

2. MAKE THE BURGERS: Heat a large cast-iron skillet. Gently form the ground chuck into four 4-inch patties about 1½ inches thick. Make a ½-inch indentation in the center of each patty and season generously with salt and pepper. When the skillet is hot, add the patties and cook over moderately high heat until browned, 4 to 5 minutes per side for medium-rare. Transfer to a large plate and let rest for 5 minutes.

3. Place the hamburgers on the toasted brioche buns, top with the compote, garnish with lettuce and serve.

—David Walzog

MAKE AHEAD The red onion compote can be refrigerated for up to 5 days. Bring to room temperature before serving.

WINE Lively, fruity Merlot.

Grilled Strip Steaks with Sweet Potato Hash Browns

ACTIVE: 35 MIN; TOTAL: 1 HR 15 MIN
4 SERVINGS

- 4 sweet potatoes (1¾ pounds), peeled and cut into 1-inch chunks
- 2 tablespoons extra-virgin olive oil
- 6 ounces lean slab bacon, sliced ¼ inch thick and cut into ½-inch pieces
- 1 pound Vidalia or other sweet onions, cut into ½-inch dice
- 2 tablespoons chopped parsley
- 2 tablespoons minced chives
- 1 teaspoon chopped thyme

Salt and freshly ground pepper
Four 12-ounce bone-in strip or shell steaks (see Note)

1. Light a grill. In a medium saucepan of salted boiling water, blanch the sweet potatoes for 3 minutes; drain well.

2. In a large skillet, heat the oil. Add the bacon and cook over moderate heat until crisp, 4 to 5 minutes. With a slotted spoon, transfer the bacon to paper towels to drain.

ALL-AMERICAN HAMBURGER WITH RED ONION COMPOTE   GRILLED STRIP STEAK WITH SWEET POTATO HASH BROWNS

Add the onions to the skillet and cook over moderate heat until browned, about 12 minutes. Add the sweet potatoes and cook over moderate heat, stirring occasionally, until just tender, about 15 minutes. Increase the heat to high and cook without stirring until browned on the bottom, about 2 minutes. Stir in the bacon, parsley, chives and thyme; season with salt and pepper.

3. Meanwhile, season the steaks generously with salt and pepper and grill over high heat until nicely browned outside and medium-rare within, about 4 minutes per side. Let rest for 5 minutes, then serve with the sweet potatoes. —*Frank Stitt*

NOTE If you want to cook 2-inch-thick steaks like the one pictured, grill over medium-high heat, turning every 5 minutes, until the meat is browned outside and an instant-read thermometer inserted into the center registers 130° for medium-rare, about 25 minutes total.

MAKE AHEAD The hash browns can be prepared up to 2 hours ahead.
WINE Rich, ripe Cabernet Sauvignon.

Thai Grilled Beef Salad

TOTAL: 30 MIN
4 SERVINGS ●

Four 4-ounce beef tenderloin steaks
  1 **tablespoon canola oil**
Salt and freshly ground pepper
  ¼ **cup water**
  2 **tablespoons sugar**
  1 **garlic clove, minced**
  3 **tablespoons Asian fish sauce**
  3 **tablespoons fresh lime juice, plus lime wedges for serving**
  1 **teaspoon** *sambal oelek* **or Chinese chile-garlic sauce**
  1 **seedless cucumber—peeled, halved and thinly sliced**
  ¼ **small red onion, thinly sliced**

  1 **cup mung bean sprouts**
  ½ **cup shredded mint leaves**
  2 **tablespoons salted dry-roasted peanuts, chopped**

1. Preheat a grill pan. Rub the steaks with the oil and season with salt and pepper. Grill over high heat, turning once, until an instant-read thermometer inserted in the thickest part of one steak registers 125°, about 12 minutes. Let rest for 10 minutes before slicing thinly.

2. Meanwhile, in a small skillet, heat the water with the sugar, stirring until dissolved. Transfer to a large bowl. Add the garlic, fish sauce, lime juice and *sambal* and let cool. Add the cucumber, onion, bean sprouts, mint and sliced steak and toss well. Sprinkle with the peanuts and serve right away, with lime wedges.
—*Pino Maffeo*

WINE Intense, fruity Zinfandel.

12
key terms for choosing beef

F&W's **Kristin Donnelly** demystifies the language you need to know when reading a steak house menu or talking to the butcher.

1 *angus*
Red and Black Angus produce consistently well-marbled beef. The best Black Angus meat can be labeled "Certified Angus Beef."

2 *chianina*
Originally from Tuscany, these lean, muscular steers are now raised at a small number of U.S. ranches.

3 *hereford*
Like the Angus breed, Hereford cattle are hardy, but they produce leaner steaks.

4 *wagyu*
Wagyu literally means "Japanese cattle." There are several breeds. Prized for its melt-in-the mouth marbling, it's so rich that it's often sold by the ounce. True Japanese 100 percent wagyu beef is now coming to the United States, after a ban was lifted in 2006.

5 *kobe*
True Kobe beef, famed for its incredible marbling, is from Japan's Hyogo prefecture (Kobe is the capital). A very limited amount of Kobe is exported to the United States. The "American Kobe" that appears on some menus is usually a cross between wagyu and Angus.

6 *piedmontese*
A boutique breed from Italy that is also raised (often grass-fed) by U.S. farmers, it is lean but still tender and flavorful.

7 *usda prime*
The USDA's top level, awarded to beef with the most marbling. About 2 percent of beef is graded prime; most goes to restaurants. Choice, which is sold at supermarkets, is the next best level.

8 *japanese grade 12*
Japan grades its beef on a scale of 1 to 12; the most densely marbled meat receives a 12. Most USDA prime cuts would rate between 4 and 6 in that system.

9 *natural*
Also referred to as "all-natural," the beef cannot contain artificial ingredients, like added colors, flavors or preservatives. The label does not refer to how the cattle are raised or slaughtered.

10 *certified organic*
Cattle feed must be vegetarian and grown without chemical pesticides or fertilizers. The steers must have access to the outdoors, including fresh air and pasture, and are not allowed to be given hormones or antibiotics. Organic certification is authorized by a USDA-approved agent.

11 *certified humane*
Cattle have access to clean food and water, sufficient protection from harsh elements and enough space to move around naturally. They receive antibiotics only when sick and are never given hormones. The certification is authorized by Humane Farm Animal Care, a consortium of animal welfare organizations.

12 *wet- vs. dry-aging*
Wet-aged beef is vacuum-sealed and aged for as long as several weeks, which helps tenderize it. Dry-aged beef is hung in a cold, moderately humid space to tenderize it and concentrate its flavor; because the beef loses weight through evaporation as it hangs, it's more expensive. At most steak houses, 21 days of dry-aging is standard.

Malabar Spice–Crusted Hanger Steaks with Gingered Carrot Puree

**ACTIVE: 35 MIN; TOTAL: 1 HR 10 MIN
PLUS 4 HR MARINATING**

4 SERVINGS

Bruce Sherman, chef at Chicago's North Pond, spent more than three years living in India. He uses spices from the Malabar Coast, a region in the southwestern part of the country, to form the crispy crust for his hanger steaks. "On the Malabar Coast, ginger, coconut and cinnamon all grow near each other, so the flavors naturally complement one another," he says.

- **2 tablespoons unsweetened, shredded coconut**
- **1½ tablespoons cinnamon**
- **⅛ teaspoon ground cloves**
- **1 tablespoon plus 1 teaspoon ground coriander**
- **1½ teaspoons freshly ground pepper**
- **Kosher salt**
- **Four 8-ounce hanger steaks, trimmed**
- **2 tablespoons vegetable oil**
- **1 teaspoon extra-virgin olive oil**
- **2 tablespoons minced onion**
- **½ teaspoon finely grated fresh ginger**
- **3 medium carrots, sliced ⅛ inch thick (1 cup)**
- **⅔ cup low-sodium chicken broth**
- **¼ cup fresh orange juice**
- **1 tablespoon cold unsalted butter**

1. In a small bowl, combine the coconut, cinnamon, cloves, 1 tablespoon of the coriander, the pepper and ½ teaspoon of salt and blend well. Set the steaks on a platter and sprinkle with the spice mixture. Gently coat the steaks with the vegetable oil. Cover and refrigerate for 4 to 6 hours. Bring to room temperature before grilling.

2. In a medium saucepan, heat the olive oil. Add the onion and ginger and cook over moderate heat until the onion is softened, about 2 minutes. Add the carrots and the remaining 1 teaspoon of coriander and cook, stirring, until the carrots start to soften, about 3 minutes. Add the broth and bring to a boil. Cover and cook over moderate heat until the carrots are tender, about 10 minutes. Uncover and continue cooking until about 2 tablespoons of liquid remain, about 3 minutes longer. Transfer the carrots to a blender and add the orange juice. Puree until smooth. Transfer the puree to a small saucepan.

3. Heat a large, lightly oiled grill pan. Season the steaks with salt and cook over high heat until browned, about 6 minutes per side for medium-rare. Transfer the steaks to a cutting board; let rest for 10 minutes.

4. Reheat the carrot puree and season with salt, then remove from the heat and whisk in the butter. Thinly slice the steaks across the grain. Arrange the sliced steak on plates and serve with the carrot puree.
—*Bruce Sherman*

WINE Ripe, juicy Pinot Noir.

Bone-In Rib Eye Steaks with Chanterelles

TOTAL: 1 HR

4 SERVINGS

"Bone-in rib eyes give you the most bang for your buck," says Thom Fox, chef de cuisine at San Francisco's Acme Chophouse. That's due to the cut's significant marbling (which makes it extra tender) and robust flavors. He tops his steaks with a pile of chanterelle mushrooms flavored with Dijon mustard and sweet Banyuls vinegar for a tangy kick.

- **1 cup beef broth**
- **6 tablespoons extra-virgin olive oil**
- **1 pound chanterelle mushrooms, quartered if large**
- **Salt and freshly ground pepper**
- **6 fresh or 3 dried bay leaves**
- **3 medium shallots, minced**
- **1 garlic clove, minced**
- **1 thyme sprig**
- **1½ tablespoons Banyuls vinegar or other red wine vinegar**
- **1 teaspoon Dijon mustard**
- **2 bone-in rib eye steaks (about 1¼ inches thick), at room temperature**

1. Light a grill. In a small saucepan, boil the broth over high heat until reduced to ½ cup, 7 minutes. Remove from the heat.

2. In a large skillet, heat 2 tablespoons of the oil. Add the chanterelles, season with salt and pepper and cook over moderately high heat until the liquid they release has evaporated, about 4 minutes. Continue cooking, stirring, until the mushrooms begin to brown, about 5 minutes longer. Add the remaining 4 tablespoons of oil, the bay leaves, shallots, garlic and thyme and cook over low heat, stirring, until the mushrooms are tender, 7 minutes. Add the reduced broth and simmer for 1 minute. Remove from the heat and stir in the vinegar and mustard. Season with salt and pepper and remove from the heat.

3. Season the steaks well with salt and pepper and grill over high heat until nicely browned and an instant-read thermometer inserted in the center registers 130° for medium-rare, about 6 minutes per side. Transfer the steaks to a cutting board and let rest for 10 minutes. Reheat the chanterelles and discard the bay leaves and thyme sprig. Thickly slice the steaks and serve with the mushrooms. —*Thom Fox*
WINE Firm, complex Cabernet Sauvignon.

TECHNIQUE

making flavored butter

Combine 1 stick softened butter with 1 tablespoon each chopped parsley, chives and shallots. Form into a log, wrap, chill and slice. Melt a pat of this tasty butter over broiled steak or fish.

Pepper-Crusted Prime Rib Roast with Mushroom-Armagnac Sauce

ACTIVE: 1 HR; TOTAL: 4 HR

4 TO 6 SERVINGS ●

To keep this prime rib extra juicy, ask your butcher to leave the fat cap on before tying the beef. Roasting the prime rib in a bath of butter, a common chef's trick, also helps.

PRIME RIB

1½ tablespoons Szechuan peppercorns
1½ tablespoons black peppercorns
1½ tablespoons white peppercorns
One 6-pound prime rib roast (2 bones)
Salt
1 tablespoon vegetable oil
1 stick unsalted butter, cut into tablespoons
6 thyme sprigs
4 bay leaves
4 marjoram or oregano sprigs
5 garlic cloves, smashed
4 large shallots, sliced ¼ inch thick

SAUCE

2 ounces dried porcini mushrooms (2 cups)
1½ cups boiling water
2 tablespoons extra-virgin olive oil
¾ pound white mushrooms, thinly sliced
2 medium shallots, thinly sliced
2 garlic cloves, smashed
3 thyme sprigs
1 cup Armagnac
½ cup dry white wine
2 cups low-sodium beef broth
2 tablespoons cold unsalted butter
Salt and freshly ground pepper

1. PREPARE THE PRIME RIB: Preheat the oven to 325°. In a pepper grinder or a spice mill, coarsely grind all of the peppercorns. Transfer to a small bowl. Season the roast with salt and the pepper mixture.

2. In a large ovenproof skillet, heat the oil until shimmering. Add the roast fat side down and cook over moderate heat until browned, about 5 minutes. Turn the roast and brown it on each of the other sides, about 13 minutes longer. Turn the roast fat side up and add the butter. When the butter is melted, baste the roast all over. Add the thyme, bay leaves and marjoram and roast in the oven for 1 hour.

3. Add the garlic and shallots to the skillet and continue roasting the meat until an instant-read thermometer inserted in the center registers 130° for medium-rare, about 45 minutes longer.

4. MEANWHILE, MAKE THE SAUCE: In a heatproof bowl, cover the porcini with the boiling water and let soak until softened, about 20 minutes. In a large skillet, heat the olive oil. Add the white mushrooms, shallots, garlic and thyme and cook over moderately high heat, stirring occasionally, until the mushrooms and shallots are browned, 8 minutes. Add the Armagnac and wine and boil over moderately high heat until reduced by half, 5 minutes.

5. Lift the porcini from their soaking liquid; reserve the liquid. Rinse the porcini and cut any large pieces in half. Carefully pour the porcini soaking liquid into the skillet, stopping before you reach the grit at the bottom. Boil the sauce until reduced by three-fourths, about 8 minutes. Add the beef broth and boil until reduced to 1½ cups, about 8 minutes. Strain the sauce through a fine sieve into a small saucepan, pressing on the solids; add the porcini.

6. When the roast is done, transfer it to a carving board and let rest for 20 minutes. With a slotted spoon, transfer the shallots and garlic to a plate. Bring the sauce to a simmer, remove from the heat and whisk in the butter 1 tablespoon at a time; season with salt and pepper. Carve the roast into slices. Scatter the shallots and garlic on top and serve with the porcini sauce.
—*Melissa Perello*

MAKE AHEAD The porcini sauce can be prepared through Step 5 and refrigerated overnight. Reheat gently and whisk in the butter before serving.

WINE Intense, fruity Zinfandel.

Horseradish-and-Herb-Crusted Beef Rib Roast

ACTIVE: 20 MIN; TOTAL: 4 HR 15 MIN

12 SERVINGS

The inspiration for this delicious roast comes from New Orleans chef John Besh's father-in-law, Pat Berrigan, who serves it every Christmas with horseradish sauce on the side. Besh opts to smear the roast with a horseradish, garlic and herb butter, which bakes to form an irresistible crust.

2 sticks unsalted butter, softened
1 head of garlic, cloves coarsely chopped
1 cup prepared horseradish
¼ cup plus 2 tablespoons chopped thyme
3 tablespoons chopped rosemary
3 tablespoons chopped sage
One 16-pound rib roast of beef
Salt and freshly ground pepper

1. Preheat the oven to 325°. In a food processor, combine the butter with the garlic, horseradish, thyme, rosemary and sage and process to a paste.

2. Stand the roast in a very large roasting pan. Season generously all over with salt and pepper and set it fatty side up. Spread the horseradish-herb butter all over the top. Bake for about 3½ hours, until an instant-read thermometer inserted in the center registers 125° for medium-rare. Transfer the roast to a carving board to rest for at least 20 minutes or for up to 1 hour before serving. —*John Besh*

NOTE If you like, reserve 3 tablespoons of the beef fat from the roasting pan to make Pat's Popovers (p. 110).

MAKE AHEAD The horseradish-herb butter can be refrigerated overnight.

WINE Rustic, peppery Malbec.

HORSERADISH-AND-HERB-CRUSTED BEEF RIB ROAST (P. 54) WITH ROOT VEGETABLE, PEAR AND CHESTNUT RAGOUT (P. 68), BRAISED KALE (P. 77) AND OYSTER DRESSING "GRAND-MÈRE" (P. 84)

Red Wine–Braised Chuck Roast

ACTIVE: 1 HR; TOTAL: 3 HR 30 MIN

4 SERVINGS ●

  2 tablespoons vegetable oil
One 3-pound beef chuck roast, tied
Salt and freshly ground black pepper
  1 cup dry red wine, such as Barbera
  2 cups beef broth
  3 cups water
  1 medium onion, halved and
    stuck with 2 whole cloves
  6 large garlic cloves
  4 large carrots, halved crosswise
  2 medium fennel bulbs, quartered
  1 bay leaf

1. Preheat the oven to 325°. In a skillet, heat the vegetable oil. Season the roast with salt and black pepper and sear on all sides over moderately high heat, 15 minutes; transfer the meat to a roasting pan.

2. Carefully add the red wine to the skillet and bring to a boil over high heat. Boil for about 3 minutes, scraping up the browned bits. Add the wine, broth and water to the roasting pan and bring to a boil. Add the onion, garlic, carrots, fennel and bay leaf. Cover and braise in the oven until the fennel is tender, about 1 hour; transfer the fennel to a baking dish and cover.

3. Return the roast to the oven; cook until the roast is tender and an instant-read thermometer inserted in the thickest part registers 180°, about 1 hour longer.

4. Discard the onion and bay leaf. Transfer the roast and carrots to the baking dish with the fennel. Cover and keep warm in the oven. Strain the cooking liquid into a saucepan, pressing to mash the garlic. Boil until reduced to 1½ cups, about 25 minutes. Season with salt and pepper.

5. Transfer the roast to a carving board and remove the strings. Cut into 4 thick slices and transfer to plates with the carrots and fennel. Pass the sauce at the table. —*Marcia Kiesel*

WINE Fruity, luscious Shiraz.

Adobo-Rubbed Beef Tenderloin

ACTIVE: 45 MIN; TOTAL: 2 HR PLUS OVERNIGHT MARINATING

4 TO 6 SERVINGS

Jeff Jackson, chef at the Lodge at Torrey Pines in La Jolla, California, rubs this beef tenderloin with a complex adobo paste made from three kinds of dried chiles: the spicy *guajillo*, the raisiny ancho and the smoky chipotle.

  2 large dried *guajillo* chiles
    (see Note)
  1 large dried ancho chile
    (see Note)
  1 small dried chipotle chile
    (see Note)
Boiling water
  3 garlic cloves, unpeeled
  1 medium tomato, cored
  2 tablespoons minced onion
  ¼ teaspoon dried oregano
  ¼ teaspoon ground cumin
  ¼ teaspoon dried thyme
Pinch of ground cloves
  1 tablespoon cider vinegar
Freshly ground black pepper
  2 tablespoons vegetable oil
One 2-pound center-cut beef
    tenderloin roast
Salt

1. Preheat the broiler. Break open all of the dried chiles and discard the seeds, stems and membranes. Heat a cast-iron skillet over moderate heat. Add the chiles skin side down and toast until their skins are blistered, about 4 minutes. Transfer the chiles to a medium heatproof bowl and cover with boiling water; set aside until the chiles are softened.

2. Add the garlic cloves to the cast-iron skillet and cook over moderately low heat until softened, about 10 minutes per side; peel and finely chop the cloves. Add the tomato cored side down and cook over moderately low heat, turning once, until charred, about 5 minutes per side; peel and coarsely chop the tomato.

3. Drain the chiles and transfer to a blender. Add the garlic, tomato, onion, oregano, cumin, thyme, cloves, vinegar and ¼ teaspoon of black pepper; puree until smooth. In a medium skillet, heat 1 tablespoon of the oil. Add the adobo puree and cook over moderately high heat, stirring often, until thickened, about 4 minutes; remove the skillet from the heat and let the adobo mixture cool completely.

4. Place the tenderloin in a large, shallow dish and season with salt and pepper. Coat the tenderloin with the adobo paste, cover and refrigerate overnight. Bring to room temperature before roasting.

5. Preheat the oven to 400°. In a large ovenproof skillet, heat the remaining 1 tablespoon of oil until shimmering. Wipe most of the marinade from the tenderloin, leaving a thin coat. Add the tenderloin to the skillet and brown on all sides over moderately high heat, 15 minutes. Transfer the skillet to the oven and roast the tenderloin for about 25 minutes, or until an instant-read thermometer inserted in the center registers 130° for medium-rare; transfer to a carving board and let rest for 10 minutes. Carve into 1-inch slices and serve. —*Jeff Jackson*

NOTE Dried *guajillo,* ancho and chipotle chiles are available at penzeys.com.

WINE Rustic, peppery Malbec.

Beef Brisket Pot Roast

ACTIVE: 45 MIN; TOTAL: 4 HR 30 MIN

6 TO 8 SERVINGS ●

At Five Points in New York City, the last thing chef and owner Marc Meyer cooks every night is the next day's pot roast. "We spread out the coals in the wood-burning oven and braise the roast overnight," he says. "The kitchen smells like caramelized beef and wine in the morning. That's a great aroma to start the day with." Rather than using a beef rump or chuck roast, Meyer opts for brisket with a nice layer of fat on top.

One 4-pound beef brisket with
    a ⅓-inch layer of fat
Salt and freshly ground pepper
 ¼ cup extra-virgin olive oil
 5 garlic cloves, smashed
 2 onions, coarsely chopped
 2 carrots, coarsely chopped
 1 celery rib, coarsely chopped
 3 bay leaves
 2 rosemary sprigs
 2 small dried red chiles
 2 cups dry red wine
One 14-ounce can whole plum
    tomatoes, drained
 3 cups low-sodium chicken broth

1. Preheat the oven to 325°. Season the brisket with salt and pepper. In a large skillet, heat the oil. Add the brisket fat side down and cook over moderately high heat until richly browned, 5 minutes. Turn and brown on the other side, 5 minutes longer. Transfer the meat fat side up to a roasting pan.

2. Add the garlic, onions, carrots and celery to the skillet and cook over moderate heat until softened, 10 minutes. Add the bay leaves, rosemary and chiles and cook, stirring, for 2 minutes. Add the wine and boil until reduced by half, 6 minutes. Add the tomatoes and simmer over low heat for 15 minutes. Pour over the brisket.

3. Add the broth to the skillet and bring to a simmer over high heat. Pour the broth around the brisket. Cover the pan with foil, transfer to the oven and braise until very tender, about 3 hours. Transfer the brisket to a platter and cover with foil.

4. Strain the contents of the roasting pan through a coarse strainer set over a large saucepan, pushing the vegetables through as much as possible. Boil the sauce over high heat until reduced to 3¼ cups, about 20 minutes; season with salt and pepper. Carve the brisket into ⅓-inch slices. Pour some of the sauce over the brisket to keep it moist and serve, passing the rest of the sauce at the table. —*Marc Meyer*
WINE Deep, velvety Merlot.

Sherry-Braised Short Ribs with Potato-Apple "Risotto"

**ACTIVE: 50 MIN; TOTAL: 3 HR 25 MIN
PLUS OVERNIGHT SALTING**
4 SERVINGS

Meltingly tender short ribs are paired here with an ersatz risotto made of diced potatoes and apples (instead of rice).

 8 meaty beef short ribs (6 pounds)
Kosher salt
 ¼ cup vegetable oil
 2 medium onions, coarsely chopped
 2 Granny Smith apples, cored
    and coarsely chopped
 1 head of garlic, cloves
    peeled and smashed
 1 carrot, coarsely chopped
 1 celery rib, coarsely chopped
 1 cup dry sherry
 1 cup tomato puree
 4 bay leaves
 3 cups low-sodium chicken broth
Freshly ground pepper
Potato-Apple "Risotto" (recipe
    follows), for serving

1. Generously season the short ribs with salt, cover with plastic and refrigerate overnight. Bring the ribs to room temperature before cooking.

2. Preheat the oven to 325°. In a large skillet, heat the oil until shimmering. Add 4 of the short ribs and cook over moderately high heat until browned on all sides, about 15 minutes. Transfer to a roasting pan. Repeat with the remaining short ribs.

3. Add the onions, apples, garlic, carrot and celery to the skillet; cook over moderate heat, stirring occasionally, until softened, 8 minutes. Scrape the vegetables into the roasting pan. Add the sherry to the skillet and bring to a boil over high heat, scraping up any browned bits. Add the tomato puree, bay leaves and chicken broth and bring to a boil. Pour the mixture over the short ribs. Cover the roasting pan with foil and bake for about 1 hour and 45 minutes, until the meat is very tender.

4. Transfer the ribs to a platter and cover with foil. Strain the cooking liquid through a coarse sieve set over a large saucepan, pressing on the solids and pushing the vegetables through as much as possible. Skim the fat. Boil the sauce over high heat until reduced to 3 cups, about 20 minutes. Season with salt and pepper. Set 2 short ribs on each plate and coat with sauce. Serve the Potato-Apple "Risotto" alongside. —*Scott Dolich*
WINE Fruity, light-bodied Beaujolais.

POTATO-APPLE "RISOTTO"
TOTAL: 1 HR 10 MIN
4 SERVINGS

 2 baking potatoes (1 pound), peeled
 2 Granny Smith apples,
    peeled and cored
 3 tablespoons unsalted butter
 4 garlic cloves, minced
 1 small onion, minced
 ¼ cup dry white wine
2½ cups low-sodium chicken broth
Salt and freshly ground pepper
 ½ cup freshly grated
    Parmesan cheese

1. Using a mandoline, cut the potatoes and apples into ⅛-inch slices. Stack the slices and cut them into ⅛-inch sticks, then cut the sticks into ⅛-inch cubes.

2. In a large skillet, melt 1 tablespoon of the butter. Add the garlic and onion and cook over moderate heat, stirring, until softened, about 4 minutes. Add the wine and simmer over moderate heat until almost evaporated, about 4 minutes. Add the potatoes, apples and chicken broth and bring to a boil over moderately high heat. Reduce the heat to moderate and simmer, stirring occasionally, until the potatoes are tender and the liquid has reduced to ¼ cup, about 25 minutes. Remove from the heat. Season with salt and pepper and stir in the remaining 2 tablespoons of butter until melted. Stir in the Parmesan and serve. —*S.D.*

GRILLED MEATBALLS WITH SCALLION
AND SHAVED CHEESE SALAD

Slow-Braised Osso Buco

ACTIVE: 1 HR; TOTAL: 4 HR 30 MIN

10 SERVINGS ●

The Italian *osso buco* translates as "hole in the bone," referring to the delectable marrow in the center of the veal shank bone. This Lombard specialty is ideal for entertaining because the flavor of the dish only improves if it's made in advance.

- **10 pieces of veal shank, about**
  ¾ pound each, tied
- **Salt and freshly ground pepper**
- **All-purpose flour, for dusting**
- **¼ cup extra-virgin olive oil**
- **6 medium carrots, cut into**
  ¼-inch dice
- **4 medium celery ribs,**
  cut into ¼-inch dice
- **2 large onions, cut into ¼-inch dice**
- **1½ cups dry white wine**
- **4 cups water**
- **¼ cup tomato paste**

1. Season the veal shanks with salt and pepper. Dust them with flour, shaking off the excess. In a large skillet, heat the olive oil. Add 5 of the veal shanks and cook over moderate heat until richly browned, about 4 minutes per side. Transfer the shanks to a roasting pan that's large enough to hold all 10 in a single layer without crowding. Repeat with the remaining shanks.

2. Preheat the oven to 300°. Add the carrots, celery and onions to the skillet. Cover and cook over moderate heat, stirring occasionally, until softened, about 12 minutes. Add the wine and boil uncovered over high heat until reduced to ⅓ cup, about 5 minutes. Stir in the water and tomato paste and bring to a boil. Pour the contents of the skillet over the shanks.

3. Cover the roasting pan with foil. Transfer the shanks to the oven and braise for 2 hours and 45 minutes, or until the meat is very tender. Transfer the shanks to a large rimmed baking sheet. Discard the strings and cover the shanks with foil. Increase the oven temperature to 350°.

4. Strain the liquid from the roasting pan into a large saucepan, reserving the vegetables. Boil the liquid over high heat until reduced to 4 cups, about 25 minutes. Return the vegetables to the sauce and season with salt and pepper.

5. Meanwhile, reheat the veal shanks in the oven until hot, about 7 minutes. Transfer the shanks to plates, ladle the sauce on top and serve. —*Palma D'Orazio*

MAKE AHEAD The shanks can be refrigerated in their sauce for up to 3 days. Add a little water to the pan before reheating.

WINE Complex, aromatic Nebbiolo.

Grilled Meatballs with Scallion and Shaved Cheese Salad

TOTAL: 1 HR 10 MIN

8 SERVINGS

Lachlan Mackinnon Patterson, chef at Frasca Food and Wine in Boulder, Colorado, makes his meatballs with a mixture of lamb, veal, bacon and a little ricotta cheese to keep everything moist. He serves them on an unconventional salad of grilled scallions with shaved Parmigiano-Reggiano.

- **2 pounds ground veal**
- **1 pound ground lamb**
- **3 large eggs, lightly beaten**
- **2 thick slices of lean bacon, minced**
- **¼ cup minced shallot**
- **¼ cup fine fresh bread crumbs**
- **¼ cup fresh ricotta cheese**
- **¼ cup freshly grated montasio or**
  Parmigiano-Reggiano cheese
- **Kosher salt**
- **3 cups chicken stock or**
  low-sodium broth
- **3 cups water**
- **1½ pounds thin scallions, trimmed**
- **Vegetable oil, for drizzling**
- **1 tablespoon olive oil**
- **One 3-ounce piece of Parmigiano-**
  Reggiano, shaved with a vegetable
  peeler into strips (about 1 cup)
- **1 preserved lemon, halved**
  (see Note)

1. Light a grill. In a large bowl, using your hands, mix the ground veal and lamb with the beaten eggs, minced bacon and shallot, fresh bread crumbs, fresh ricotta, grated montasio cheese and 2 teaspoons of salt. Shape the mixture into 40 golf ball–size meatballs.

2. In a wide saucepan, bring the chicken stock and water to a boil. Add half of the meatballs and simmer over moderately low heat until just cooked through, about 10 minutes. Using a slotted spoon, transfer the cooked meatballs to a rimmed baking sheet. Repeat the process with the remaining meatballs.

3. On another large rimmed baking sheet, drizzle the scallions with vegetable oil and season with salt. Working in 3 batches, grill the scallions over high heat for about 2 minutes, turning once, until charred on both sides; return the grilled scallions to the baking sheet. Gently toss the grilled scallions with the olive oil and Parmigiano-Reggiano shavings. Grill the preserved lemon halves cut side down over high heat for about 4 minutes, or until well charred. Squeeze the grilled lemon halves over the scallions and toss again. Arrange the grilled scallion salad in a large, shallow serving bowl.

4. Drizzle the meatballs lightly with vegetable oil and roll to coat. Grill the meatballs over high heat, rolling to turn them, until they are lightly charred all over and heated through, about 3 minutes total. Using tongs, arrange the meatballs on top of the grilled scallion salad and serve immediately.

—*Lachlan Mackinnon Patterson*

NOTE Preserved lemons, a staple of cooking in Morocco and Tunisia, are made by salt curing. They're available at specialty food stores and Middle Eastern markets.

MAKE AHEAD The poached meatballs can be refrigerated overnight. Bring to room temperature before grilling.

WINE Cherry-inflected, earthy Sangiovese.

Spicy Beef Chili

ACTIVE: 45 MIN; TOTAL: 2 HR

6 TO 8 SERVINGS ●●

- 2 tablespoons vegetable oil
- 2 pounds chuck steak, cut into ½-inch dice

Kosher salt and freshly ground pepper

- 1 pound hot Italian sausages, casings removed and meat broken into 1-inch pieces
- 1 large white onion, chopped
- 6 garlic cloves, minced
- 1 tablespoon chile powder
- 1 tablespoon sweet paprika
- 2 teaspoons ground cumin

One 28-ounce can diced tomatoes

- 1 cup water

One 15-ounce can pinto beans, drained

One 15-ounce can cannellini beans, drained

One 15-ounce can kidney beans, drained

Shredded cheddar cheese, chopped scallions, sour cream and chopped cilantro, for serving

1. In a large enameled cast-iron casserole, heat the oil. Season the chuck with salt and pepper and brown half over moderately high heat, 5 minutes. Using a slotted spoon, transfer the meat to a plate. Repeat with the remaining chuck. Add the sausage and brown, breaking it up with a spoon, 4 minutes. Add the sausage to the chuck.

2. Add the onion to the pot and cook over moderate heat until tender, 4 minutes. Add the garlic and cook for 2 minutes. Stir in the chile powder, paprika, cumin and the meats and their juices. Cook, stirring until fragrant, about 1 minute. Add the tomatoes and their juices and the water. Cover and simmer over moderately low heat for 1 hour.

3. Stir in the beans and simmer uncovered until thickened, about 15 minutes. Season with salt. Serve, passing the cheese, scallions, sour cream and cilantro on the side. —*Al Roker*

WINE Intense, fruity Zinfandel.

Meatballs with Tomato Sauce

TOTAL: 50 MIN

4 SERVINGS ●●

MEATBALLS

- 12 ounces leftover roast beef, veal or pork, coarsely chopped
- 3 tablespoons all-purpose flour
- 1 teaspoon baking powder
- 1 teaspoon salt
- ½ cup minced onion
- ¼ cup minced celery
- 1 garlic clove, minced
- ¼ teaspoon dried thyme
- ¼ teaspoon freshly ground black pepper
- 3 large eggs, beaten

Vegetable oil, for frying

SAUCE

- ¼ cup vegetable oil
- 3 garlic cloves, minced
- ½ cup minced onion
- ½ teaspoon dried thyme
- ½ teaspoon dried oregano

One 28-ounce can diced tomatoes with their liquid

- ⅓ cup pitted green olives, coarsely chopped

Salt and freshly ground pepper

1. **MAKE THE MEATBALLS:** Put the meat in a food processor and process until finely chopped. In a large bowl, mix the flour with the baking powder and salt. Add the meat, onion, celery, garlic, thyme, pepper and eggs and mix well with your hands. Form into 16 meatballs and flatten slightly.

2. In a large skillet, heat ¼ inch of oil until shimmering. Add the meatballs and cook over high heat until browned on the bottom. Turn the meatballs, reduce the heat to moderate and cook until browned on the second side, about 3 minutes. Transfer to a plate.

3. **MAKE THE SAUCE:** In a saucepan, heat the oil over moderate heat. Add the garlic, onion, thyme and oregano and cook until softened, 4 minutes. Add the tomatoes, cover and cook for 6 minutes. Roughly puree the sauce and return it to the pot.

4. In a small saucepan, cover the olives with water and bring to a boil over high heat; drain well. Add to the sauce, season with salt and pepper and bring to a simmer. Add the meatballs, simmer until heated through and serve. —*Jacques Pépin*

WINE Fruity, light-bodied Beaujolais.

Sicilian-Style Meatballs

ACTIVE: 1 HR; TOTAL: 1 HR 45 MIN

12 SERVINGS ●●

Two 28-ounce cans peeled Italian tomatoes

- ¼ cup extra-virgin olive oil

Kosher salt and freshly ground pepper

- 4 slices of white sandwich bread
- 4 large eggs, beaten
- 3 garlic cloves, minced
- ¼ cup chopped flat-leaf parsley
- 1 teaspoon minced marjoram
- 2 pounds ground beef chuck
- ½ cup dried currants
- ¼ cup pine nuts
- ¼ cup freshly grated Parmigiano-Reggiano cheese, plus more for serving
- ¼ cup plain dry bread crumbs
- 2 cups vegetable oil, for frying

1. Pour the tomatoes and their juices into a large enameled cast-iron casserole and crush them. Add the oil and season with salt and pepper. Bring to a boil over moderately high heat. Reduce the heat to low and gently simmer for 30 minutes.

2. Meanwhile, in a bowl, soak the bread in water until saturated. Squeeze out the water; transfer the bread to a large bowl. Mash to a paste and stir in the eggs, garlic, parsley, marjoram, 1 tablespoon of salt and ½ teaspoon of pepper. Mash until smooth. Add the chuck, currants, pine nuts and the ¼ cup of cheese and mix until combined. Add the bread crumbs 1 tablespoon at a time and knead until the mixture is firm enough to roll. Form the mixture into 36 meatballs (about 3 tablespoons each), tucking in the currants and pine nuts.

3. In a large nonstick skillet, heat the vegetable oil until shimmering. Add the meatballs in 2 batches and fry over moderate heat, turning, until browned and cooked through, about 12 minutes per batch. Using a slotted spoon, transfer the meatballs to a plate. Add the meatballs to the sauce and simmer for 30 minutes. Serve in bowls, passing more cheese at the table.
—*Frank Castronovo and Frank Falcinelli*
WINE Juicy, spicy Grenache.

Pasta Shells with Artichoke Cream and Smoked Chicken

TOTAL: 35 MIN
4 SERVINGS

One 8-ounce jar oil-packed
    artichoke bottoms, drained
    (see Note)
Salt and freshly ground pepper
  2 cups heavy cream
  1 tablespoon fresh lemon juice
  ½ pound medium pasta shells
  ¾ pound skinless smoked
    chicken breast, cut into
    1½-by-⅓-inch strips
 20 cherry tomatoes, quartered
  2 tablespoons minced chives

1. In a small saucepan, season the artichokes with salt and black pepper and simmer them in the cream over moderately low heat until they are very tender, about 12 minutes. Transfer the artichokes and cream to a blender and puree until smooth. Add the lemon juice and season with salt and pepper.

2. In a large saucepan of boiling salted water, cook the pasta until al dente. Drain the shells and return them to the pan. Add the artichoke cream, smoked chicken, tomatoes and chives; season with salt and pepper. Transfer to bowls and serve.
—*Yves Camdeborde*

NOTE Be sure not to use marinated artichokes; the tangy marinade will overwhelm the flavor of this dish.

WINE Fruity, soft Chenin Blanc.

SICILIAN-STYLE MEATBALLS

PASTA SHELLS WITH ARTICHOKE CREAM AND SMOKED CHICKEN

LASAGNA-STYLE BAKED PENNETTE WITH MEAT SAUCE

Lasagna-Style Baked Pennette with Meat Sauce

ACTIVE: 50 MIN; TOTAL: 1 HR 30 MIN

10 SERVINGS ●●

This hearty baked pasta is New York City chef Tom Valenti's ultimate make-ahead meal. "It's actually better the next day," he says. "I always make more than I think we'll need—and we always eat all of it."

- 1 pound *pennette* or *ditali*
- ¼ cup extra-virgin olive oil
- 1 large onion, very finely chopped
- 1 pound ground lamb
- 1 pound ground veal

One 28-ounce can diced tomatoes, drained
- 1 tablespoon tomato paste
- 2 teaspoons very finely chopped marjoram
- 2 tablespoons chopped flat-leaf parsley

Salt and freshly ground black pepper
- 1 stick unsalted butter
- ¾ cup all-purpose flour
- 1 quart whole milk
- 2 large egg yolks
- 1 cup freshly grated Parmigiano-Reggiano cheese

1. Preheat the oven to 350°. Bring a large pot of salted water to a boil over high heat. Add the *pennette* and cook the pasta until al dente. Drain well.

2. In a large, deep skillet, heat the olive oil. Add the chopped onion and cook over moderately high heat, stirring occasionally, until the onion is softened, about 4 minutes. Add the ground lamb and veal and cook, stirring to break up the lumps, until the meat is beginning to brown, about 10 minutes. Remove the skillet from the heat and stir in the drained diced tomatoes, tomato paste and chopped marjoram and parsley. Season with salt and black pepper. Transfer to a large bowl.

3. In a large saucepan, melt the butter. Add the flour and cook over moderate heat, whisking constantly, for 2 minutes. Gradually whisk in the milk and cook over moderately high heat, whisking constantly, until the sauce is very thick and boiling, 7 to 8 minutes. Remove the saucepan from the heat and whisk in the egg yolks and the grated Parmigiano-Reggiano cheese. Stir all but 1½ cups of the white sauce into the meat mixture along with the drained *pennette* and season with salt and black pepper. Spoon the pasta into a 3-quart baking dish. Spread the reserved 1½ cups of white sauce on top.

4. Bake the pasta in the center of the oven for about 30 minutes, until bubbling. Take the pan out of the oven and preheat the broiler. Broil the pasta 8 inches from the heat for about 2 minutes, until the top is browned and bubbling. Let rest for 10 minutes before serving. —*Tom Valenti*

SERVE WITH Escarole and radicchio salad.

MAKE AHEAD The recipe can be prepared through Step 3 and refrigerated overnight. An additional 30 minutes of cooking time may be necessary.

WINE Juicy, fresh Dolcetto.

Sizzled Clams with Udon Noodles and Watercress

TOTAL: 30 MIN

4 SERVINGS ●

At Boston Public, chef Pino Maffeo prepares this dish with thick, fresh egg noodles and hot chile oil, which are both house-made. Replacing the house-made noodles and hot chile oil with supermarket ingredients makes the dish as easy to prepare as it is delicious.

- 7 ounces dried udon noodles
- ¼ cup plus 1 teaspoon canola oil
- 2 dozen littleneck clams, scrubbed and rinsed
- 1 tablespoon very finely chopped fresh ginger
- 1 medium garlic clove, very thinly sliced
- 1 tablespoon very finely chopped flat-leaf parsley
- 1½ teaspoons Chinese black bean sauce
- ¼ cup sake
- 1 bunch watercress (6 ounces), thick stems discarded
- 1½ tablespoons oyster sauce
- 1 tablespoon unsalted butter
- 1 scallion, thinly sliced

Chile oil, for drizzling

1. Bring a medium saucepan of water to a boil over high heat. Add the udon and boil until tender, about 5 minutes. Drain the udon, transfer to a bowl and toss with 1 teaspoon of the canola oil.

2. Meanwhile, heat a wok over high heat until very hot. Add 2 tablespoons of the canola oil; when it starts smoking, carefully slide in the clams. Cover the wok and cook the clams undisturbed for 2 minutes. Uncover the wok and add the chopped ginger, garlic and parsley and the Chinese black bean sauce; stir-fry for 2 minutes. Carefully pour in the sake, cover the wok and cook until the clams open, about 5 minutes longer. Discard any clams that do not open. Pour the clams and their cooking liquid into a large serving bowl.

3. Return the wok to high heat and add the remaining 2 tablespoons of canola oil. Add the watercress and stir-fry until crisp-tender, about 2 minutes. Add the drained udon, oyster sauce and butter and stir-fry until the udon are evenly coated with the sauce. Return the clams and any accumulated juices to the wok and stir-fry just until all the ingredients are heated through and well combined. Transfer the udon and clams to the large serving bowl, garnish with the sliced scallion and drizzle with chile oil. Serve immediately. —*Pino Maffeo*

WINE Lively, tart Sauvignon Blanc.

Whole Wheat Linguine with Manila Clams and Baby Fennel

TOTAL: 30 MIN
4 SERVINGS ●

Dede Sampson, a Bay Area chef and locavore (someone who eats and cooks with ingredients that are grown locally), uses local farm-raised Manila clams year-round for this satisfying linguine. In other parts of the country, littleneck clams are easier to find in the winter. The juices of these small, quick-cooking clams enrich the anise-scented white wine broth here.

¾ pound whole wheat
   linguine or fettuccine
¼ cup extra-virgin
   olive oil
2 baby fennel bulbs or
   1 medium fennel bulb—
   halved, cored and cut
   into ¼-inch dice
2 garlic cloves, chopped
3 dozen Manila or littleneck
   clams, scrubbed and rinsed
⅔ cup dry white wine
¼ cup coarsely chopped
   flat-leaf parsley
Salt

1. Bring a large pot of salted water to a boil over high heat. Add the linguine and boil until the pasta is al dente; drain.

2. Meanwhile, in a large saucepan, heat the olive oil. Add the diced fennel and chopped garlic and cook over moderate heat, stirring frequently, until the fennel is softened, about 10 minutes. Add the clams and white wine, cover the saucepan and cook over moderately high heat until the clams open, about 5 minutes. Discard any clams that do not open.

3. Add the linguine to the saucepan and toss over moderate heat until the pasta is well coated, about 2 minutes. Sprinkle with the parsley and season with salt. Transfer to warm bowls and serve right away.
—*Dede Sampson*

WINE Tart, citrusy Riesling.

Crispy Tofu with Noodles

TOTAL: 35 MIN
4 SERVINGS ● ● ●

7 ounces dried udon noodles
½ cup plus 1 teaspoon canola oil
1 cup *panko* (Japanese
   bread crumbs)
6 ounces firm tofu, cut into
   1-inch squares
1 egg yolk
¾ pound mixed mushrooms,
   such as oyster, hen-of-the-woods
   and stemmed shiitake,
   thickly sliced
1 tablespoon very finely
   chopped fresh ginger
1 medium garlic clove, very
   finely chopped
¾ pound baby bok choy, cut
   into ¾-inch pieces
2 tablespoons oyster sauce
1½ tablespoons hoisin sauce

1. Bring a large saucepan of water to a boil over high heat. Add the udon and cook until tender, 5 minutes; drain. Toss with 1 teaspoon of the canola oil.

2. Meanwhile, put the *panko* in a large resealable plastic bag and crush into fine crumbs. In a shallow bowl, gently toss the tofu with the egg yolk. Transfer the tofu to the bag and coat with the *panko*.

3. Heat the remaining ½ cup of canola oil in a wok until just smoking. Add the breaded tofu squares and stir-fry over high heat until crisp, 2 to 3 minutes. Using a slotted spoon, transfer to a paper towel–lined plate to drain.

4. Pour off all but ¼ cup of the oil; return the wok to high heat. Add the mixed mushrooms and stir-fry until lightly browned, about 3 minutes. Add the chopped ginger, garlic and bok choy and stir-fry for 5 minutes. Add the drained udon and oyster and hoisin sauces and stir-fry for 2 minutes. Add the tofu and toss. Transfer to a large bowl and serve. —*Pino Maffeo*

WINE Lush, fragrant Viognier.

White Rice with Wild Mushrooms and Merguez

ACTIVE: 30 MIN; TOTAL: 1 HR 15 MIN
8 SERVINGS

Food blogger Pim Techamuanvivit cooks her rice in a clay pot from her native Thailand. This earthy baked rice, with mushrooms and chunks of the spicy lamb sausage merguez, is a terrific accompaniment to lamb dishes, but it's also hearty enough to eat on its own.

2 tablespoons extra-virgin olive oil
1½ cups Japanese short-grain rice
   (about 11 ounces)
3 cups mushroom broth, chicken
   stock or low-sodium broth
1 tablespoon soy sauce
1 pound wild mushrooms,
   such as oyster, thickly sliced
Salt and freshly ground
   black pepper
1 pound merguez sausage,
   casings removed

1. Preheat the oven to 350°. In a medium enameled cast-iron casserole, heat 1 tablespoon of the olive oil. Add the rice and cook over moderately high heat, stirring, until lightly toasted and well coated with oil, about 3 minutes. Add the mushroom broth and soy sauce and bring to a boil. Cover and cook over very low heat until the rice is tender and all of the liquid has been absorbed, about 20 minutes.

2. Meanwhile, in a large skillet, heat the remaining 1 tablespoon of olive oil. Add the mushrooms, season with salt and pepper and cook over moderately high heat, stirring occasionally, until lightly browned and tender, about 8 minutes. Transfer the mushrooms to a plate.

3. Add the merguez to the skillet and cook over moderately high heat, breaking up the sausage with a spoon, until cooked through and lightly browned in spots, 8 to 10 minutes. Return the mushrooms to the skillet and cook for 1 minute. Stir the merguez and mushrooms into the rice.

4. Bake the rice, covered, in the middle of the oven for 30 minutes. Remove the casserole from the oven and let stand for about 10 minutes; don't remove the lid. Fluff the rice with a spoon and serve.
—*Pim Techamuanvivit*

MAKE AHEAD The rice and merguez can be made through Step 3 and refrigerated overnight. Let return to room temperature before proceeding.

WINE Fresh, fruity rosé.

Pork Fried Rice

TOTAL: 25 MIN
4 SERVINGS ●

This fried rice was Chicago chef Takashi Yagihashi's favorite childhood after-school snack; it's also great for dinner.

   3   tablespoons soy sauce
   5   teaspoons rice vinegar
   1   tablespoon Asian sesame oil
   ¼   teaspoon sugar
   ¼   cup solid vegetable shortening
   ¾   pound Chinese barbecued pork, half cut into ½-inch dice and half sliced ⅓ inch thick
   ½   cup frozen peas, thawed
   2   large shiitake mushrooms, stems discarded and caps thinly sliced
   1   carrot, cut into ⅓-inch dice
   1   head baby bok choy, halved lengthwise and thinly sliced crosswise
   4   large eggs, lightly beaten
   6   cups cold cooked Japanese short-grain rice
   2   scallions, thinly sliced
Pinch of freshly ground black pepper
Kosher salt
   ¼   cup thinly sliced pickled ginger

1. In a small bowl, stir the soy sauce with the rice vinegar, sesame oil and sugar.
2. Heat a very large skillet. Add the shortening and let melt. Add the diced pork and stir-fry over high heat for 1 minute. Add the peas, shiitake, carrot and bok choy and stir-fry until tender. Add the eggs and scramble just until set.
3. Stir in the cooked rice, scallions, soy sauce mixture and black pepper and stir-fry until the rice is hot. Remove from the heat and season with salt. Spoon the fried rice into bowls, top with the sliced pork and pickled ginger and serve.
—*Takashi Yagihashi*

WINE Fruity, luscious Shiraz.

Carolina Gold Pilau with Shrimp

TOTAL: 1 HR
6 SERVINGS ●

Traditional Southern cooks make pilau by browning rice in oil, then simmering it in stock. But chef Anne Quatrano of Atlanta's Bacchanalia skips the browning and cooks delicate Carolina Gold rice with okra and shrimp for a satisfying main dish.

   2   slices of bacon
   1   tablespoon extra-virgin olive oil
   1   small sweet onion, finely diced
   2   garlic cloves, thinly sliced
   1   bay leaf
   1   thyme sprig
   ½   teaspoon crushed red pepper
   2   quarts chicken stock or low-sodium broth
Kosher salt
   2   cups Carolina Gold or other long-grain rice (14 ounces), rinsed (see Note)
   1   medium tomato—halved, seeded and diced
   ¼   pound okra, trimmed and sliced crosswise ¼ inch thick
   1   pound medium shrimp, shelled and deveined
   1   tablespoon minced parsley
   2   tablespoons cold unsalted butter, cut into cubes
Hot sauce, for serving

1. In a large, heavy casserole, cook the bacon in the oil over moderately high heat until crisp, 5 minutes. Remove the bacon with a slotted spoon and reserve for another use. Add the onion, garlic, bay leaf, thyme and red pepper to the pot and cook over moderately low heat, stirring, until the onion is softened, 5 minutes. Add the stock and 1½ teaspoons of salt and bring to a boil. Add the rice, return to a boil, stirring, and cover. Cook over low heat until the rice is barely tender, about 12 minutes.
2. Add the tomato and okra and cook until the rice is just tender, about 4 minutes. Add the shrimp and cook until pink and curled, 3 to 4 minutes; the rice should still be a little bit soupy. Discard the thyme and bay leaf and remove from the heat. Stir in the parsley and butter and serve, passing hot sauce on the side. —*Anne Quatrano*

NOTE Carolina Gold rice is available from ansonmills.com.

WINE Zesty, fresh Albariño.

SUPERFAST

party ideas

Duck Pâté Canapés Spread duck pâté on buttery toast points. Top with a dollop of grainy mustard and serve with cornichons.

Moroccan Lamb Chops Dust lamb chops with ground coriander and cumin. Sear on both sides and serve over couscous with chopped dates and nuts. Garnish with lemon wedges.

Broiled Salmon Mix mayonnaise with chopped parsley, dill and fresh lemon juice. Brush liberally over salmon fillets and broil.

Peas with Pancetta Sauté cubed pancetta until crispy and toss with blanched frozen peas. Sprinkle with grated Parmigiano-Reggiano and top with a squeeze of lemon.

Chef John Besh carves his Horseradish-and-Herb-Crusted Beef Rib Roast (p. 54) for Christmas dinner.

Buckwheat Crêpes with Roast Veal and Parmesan

TOTAL: 1 HR

4 SERVINGS ●

Many of Yves Camdeborde's customers at his Crêperie du Comptoir in Paris insist on ordering the traditional *complète*—a buckwheat crêpe with a fried egg, ham and cheese. Still, Camdeborde always hopes to change a few minds with unusual crêpes like this one, stuffed with roasted meat, arugula and Parmesan cheese.

- ½ cup buckwheat flour
- ¼ cup all-purpose flour
- Salt
- 1½ cups water
- 1 large egg, beaten
- Vegetable oil
- 8 thin slices of roast veal or pork
- 8 thin slices of Parmesan cheese (4 ounces)
- 1 bunch of arugula, stemmed
- Extra-virgin olive oil, for drizzling
- Freshly ground pepper

1. In a medium bowl, combine the buckwheat and all-purpose flours with 1 teaspoon of salt and whisk well. Add the water and egg and whisk until smooth. Cover the crêpe batter and let stand at room temperature for 30 minutes.

2. Preheat the oven to 400°. Heat a 10-inch cast-iron skillet over moderate heat until hot, about 4 minutes. Alternatively, heat a 10-inch nonstick skillet. Soak a paper towel with vegetable oil and carefully rub a thin film of oil in the skillet. Pour in ⅓ cup of the crêpe batter and immediately swirl the skillet to distribute the batter evenly over the bottom before it begins to set. Cook over moderately high heat until the crêpe is lightly browned on the bottom and the edge begins to curl, about 2 minutes. With a spatula, carefully flip the crêpe and cook on the second side for about 1 minute. Transfer the crêpe to a baking sheet. Repeat with the remaining batter to make 3 more crêpes.

3. Working on the baking sheet, fold the crêpes in half and then in half again to make triangles. Tuck the meat and cheese slices into the folds and bake the crêpes for about 4 minutes, until the cheese is melted. Open the crêpes and tuck a handful of arugula leaves in the center of each one. Drizzle with olive oil and season with salt and pepper. Close the crêpes and serve right away. —*Yves Camdeborde*

MAKE AHEAD The cooked crêpes can be refrigerated for 2 days.

WINE Bright, tart Barbera.

Ham, Soppressata and Two-Cheese Strombolis

ACTIVE: 30 MIN; TOTAL: 1 HR 30 MIN

10 TO 12 SERVINGS ● ●

As the child of Italian parents, New York City chef Tom Valenti recalls a refrigerator permanently stocked with *salume*, cheese and preserved vegetables like peperoncini, olives and roasted peppers. "My memory swept up all of those ingredients and rolled them up in pizza dough," he says. This hearty stromboli, stuffed with Italian meats and cheeses, is easy to reheat—or enjoy cold—for a late-night snack.

- All-purpose flour, for dusting
- Two 1-pound pieces of pizza dough
- ½ pound thinly sliced Black Forest ham
- ½ pound thinly sliced provolone cheese
- ½ pound thinly sliced hot or sweet soppressata
- ½ pound fresh mozzarella, cut into 4-by-¾-inch sticks
- 12 large basil leaves
- 8 ounces roasted red peppers from a jar, drained and cut into ½-inch strips
- 2 peperoncini, stemmed and finely chopped
- 1 large egg yolk beaten with 1 tablespoon water
- 2 tablespoons sesame seeds

1. Preheat the oven to 375°. On a lightly floured surface, roll out 1 piece of the pizza dough to a 14-by-10-inch rectangle about ¼ inch thick. With a long side facing you, layer half each of the ham, provolone and soppressata across the bottom half of the dough, leaving a ½-inch border on the bottom. Arrange half of the mozzarella strips across the soppressata. Top with half each of the basil leaves, roasted red pepper strips and chopped peperoncini. Loosely roll the dough around the filling and pinch the seams together to seal. Fold in the sides. Gently transfer the filled stromboli to a lightly oiled baking sheet, seam side down. Repeat with the remaining dough and fillings and carefully place the second filled stromboli on a second lightly oiled baking sheet.

2. Brush the strombolis with the egg wash and sprinkle with the sesame seeds. Make five 1-inch diagonal slashes across the top of each stromboli to allow steam to escape. Bake the strombolis for about 40 minutes, until the dough is golden. Transfer the baked strombolis to a rack and let cool for 20 minutes before slicing. Serve warm or at room temperature. —*Tom Valenti*

MAKE AHEAD The baked strombolis can be cooled, wrapped in foil and refrigerated overnight. Serve cold or rewarm the foil-wrapped strombolis in the oven.

WINE Cherry-inflected, earthy Sangiovese.

SUPERFAST

breakfast crêpes

For a festive holiday breakfast, double the buckwheat crêpe recipe at left; stack and wrap extras in foil. Reheat in the oven and serve with butter, jam and a dusting of confectioners' sugar.

side dishes

Root Vegetable, Pear and Chestnut Ragout

ACTIVE: 45 MIN; TOTAL: 1 HR 25 MIN

12 SERVINGS ●●

This ragout—slightly sweet and not too rich—is a wonderful mix of winter vegetables and fruit.

- 1½ pounds celery root, peeled and cut into 1-inch dice
- 1¼ pounds turnips, peeled and cut into 1-inch dice
- 4 Bosc pears (1½ pounds)— peeled, cored and cut into 1-inch dice
- 1¼ pounds baby golden or mixed beets, stems trimmed
- 2 tablespoons extra-virgin olive oil
- 3 garlic cloves, minced
- 1 large shallot, minced
- 1 tablespoon coarsely chopped thyme
- 1½ cups chicken stock or low-sodium broth
- 1 cup roasted peeled chestnuts from a jar (vacuum-packed)

Salt and freshly ground pepper

- 3 tablespoons unsalted butter, at room temperature

1. Bring a large pot of salted water to a boil. Add the celery root and boil until tender, about 6 minutes. With a slotted spoon, transfer to a large baking sheet. Add the turnips to the pot and cook until tender, about 5 minutes. Transfer to the baking sheet. Repeat with the pears, cooking them for 2 minutes and transferring them to the baking sheet. Add the beets to the pot and simmer for 15 minutes. Drain the beets and transfer to a large plate. Let cool slightly, then peel and quarter the beets.
2. Return the pot to the stove and add the olive oil. When it's hot, add the garlic, shallot and thyme and cook over moderate heat until softened, about 5 minutes. Add the stock and boil over high heat until reduced to 1 cup, about 5 minutes. Add the celery root, turnips and pears, cover and cook over moderately high heat, folding gently a few times, until heated through. Add the beets and chestnuts and season with salt and pepper. Cover and cook until heated through, about 3 minutes. Stir in the butter, transfer to a bowl and serve.
—*John Besh*

MAKE AHEAD The ragout (without the butter) can be refrigerated overnight. Reheat gently, then stir in the butter.

Crunchy Cabbage Salad

TOTAL: 15 MIN

6 TO 8 SERVINGS ●●

"Sometimes I make this simple salad with just one color of cabbage; sometimes I arrange it in alternating rows of color," says F&W contributing editor Jacques Pépin. He also likes the tangy-salty anchovy dressing on other crisp salad greens, such as escarole or chicory.

- 8 anchovy fillets, very finely chopped
- 4 garlic cloves, very finely chopped
- 2 tablespoons white wine vinegar
- ⅓ cup vegetable oil
- ¾ pound green cabbage, finely shredded (4½ cups)
- ¾ pound red cabbage, finely shredded (4½ cups)

Salt and freshly ground pepper

In a large bowl, mash the anchovies and garlic to a paste with a fork. Mash in the white wine vinegar, then slowly blend in the vegetable oil. Fold in the green and red cabbages and season with salt and pepper. Serve the cabbage salad at room temperature or slightly chilled.
—*Jacques Pépin*

ROOT VEGETABLE, PEAR AND
CHESTNUT RAGOUT

Citrus and Avocado Salad with Honey Vinaigrette

TOTAL: 35 MIN
6 SERVINGS ● ● ○

When chef Louis Lambert was growing up in West Texas, his grandmother served citrus and avocado salad to her bridge club. Today, Lambert embellishes her recipe with watercress and toasted pine nuts for crunch and goat cheese for tang.

- 2 tablespoons honey, preferably Tupelo
- 2 tablespoons fresh lime juice
- 2 tablespoons vegetable oil
- 1 tablespoon sour cream
- 1 tablespoon red wine vinegar
- 1 teaspoon poppy seeds
- Salt and freshly ground pepper
- 3 tablespoons pine nuts
- 2 red grapefruits
- 2 navel oranges
- 2 Hass avocados, cut into 1-inch dice
- 2 ounces fresh goat cheese, crumbled (optional)
- 2 bunches of watercress, thick stems discarded
- 2 tablespoons minced chives

1. In a small bowl, whisk the honey with the lime juice, oil, sour cream and vinegar. Stir in the poppy seeds and season with salt and pepper.

2. In a small skillet, toast the pine nuts over moderate heat, shaking the pan, until golden brown, about 2 minutes.

3. Using a sharp knife, peel the grapefruits and oranges, being sure to remove all of the bitter white pith. Working over a large bowl, cut in between the membranes to release the sections. Reserve the grapefruit and orange juices for another use. Pat the citrus sections dry with paper towels and return them to the bowl.

4. Add the avocados, goat cheese and watercress to the bowl; toss gently. Add the chives, pine nuts and dressing, toss again and serve. —*Louis Lambert*

Vegetable Salad with Curry Vinaigrette and Fresh Mozzarella

TOTAL: 35 MIN
4 SERVINGS ● ○

- 2 teaspoons vegetable oil
- ½ garlic clove, minced
- 1½ teaspoons curry powder
- 2 tablespoons extra-virgin olive oil
- 1 tablespoon French walnut oil
- 1½ tablespoons red wine vinegar
- Salt and freshly ground pepper
- 4 ounces snow peas
- 4 ounces haricots verts
- 4 ounces baby carrots
- 1 cup frozen peas
- 12 cherry tomatoes, halved
- 4 small hearts of romaine, quartered
- 2 tablespoons chopped basil
- 1 teaspoon minced tarragon
- ¼ pound salted fresh mozzarella, cut into ½-inch cubes

1. In a small skillet, heat the oil. Add the garlic and cook over low heat until golden, 30 seconds. Add the curry powder and cook until fragrant, 1 minute. Transfer to a bowl to cool. Whisk in the oils, then the vinegar. Season with salt and pepper.

2. In a saucepan of boiling salted water, blanch the snow peas until they are bright green, about 20 seconds. With a slotted spoon, transfer the snow peas to a baking sheet and spread them out to cool. Add the haricots verts to the boiling water and cook until crisp-tender, about 2 minutes. With a slotted spoon, transfer them to the baking sheet to cool. Repeat with the carrots, cooking until barely tender, 4 minutes; transfer to the baking sheet. Add the peas and cook until bright green, about 1 minute; transfer to the baking sheet.

3. In a large bowl, toss together all of the blanched vegetables, tomatoes, romaine, basil and tarragon. Add the mozzarella and curry vinaigrette, toss well and serve. —*Yves Camdeborde*

Roasted Carrot and Beet Salad with Oranges and Arugula

ACTIVE: 30 MIN; TOTAL: 1 HR 45 MIN
6 SERVINGS ● ●

When Joe Sponzo first started cooking for rock star Sting, he focused on creating elaborate meals. He quickly learned that when Sting and his wife ate at home, they preferred simple dishes made with seasonal ingredients, such as this vibrant salad of roasted vegetables with a citrusy vinaigrette. Although beets and blood oranges are more popular in southern Italy, Sponzo says that this salad is his simple variation of a traditional Tuscan root-vegetable salad.

- ¾ cup walnut halves (3 ounces)
- 8 carrots (1 pound), peeled and sliced on the diagonal ½ inch thick
- 3 beets (1 pound), scrubbed but not peeled
- Salt and freshly ground pepper
- ⅓ cup plus 1 tablespoon extra-virgin olive oil
- 1 rosemary sprig
- 2 thyme sprigs
- 2 garlic cloves
- 2 tablespoons fresh lemon juice
- 1 tablespoon balsamic vinegar
- 1 teaspoon finely grated orange zest
- 3 blood oranges or navel oranges
- 5 ounces baby arugula (6 loosely packed cups)
- 1 tablespoon snipped chives
- 2 teaspoons lemon thyme leaves

1. Preheat the oven to 400°. Spread the walnuts in a pie pan and toast until fragrant, about 8 minutes. Place the carrots and beets in separate pie pans. Season the carrots with salt and pepper and drizzle with 1 teaspoon of the olive oil. Season the beets with salt and pepper, drizzle with 2 teaspoons of the olive oil and add the rosemary, thyme and garlic cloves. Cover both pans tightly with foil and roast the vegetables until tender, about 30 minutes for the carrots and 1½ hours for the beets. Let cool. Discard the herbs and garlic.

2. Meanwhile, in a small bowl, whisk the lemon juice and balsamic vinegar with the remaining ⅓ cup of olive oil. Stir in the orange zest; season with salt and pepper.

3. Using a sharp knife, peel the oranges, making sure to remove all of the bitter white pith. Slice the oranges crosswise.

4. Peel the beets and thinly slice them crosswise. Arrange the beet slices around the edge of a large platter. Scatter the oranges and carrots over the beets. Drizzle ⅓ cup of the vinaigrette over the beets, carrots and oranges.

5. In a large bowl, toss the arugula with the remaining vinaigrette and season with salt and pepper. Mound the arugula in the center of the platter. Scatter the toasted walnuts, chives and lemon thyme around the platter and serve right away.

—*Joe Sponzo*

MAKE AHEAD The cooked vegetables and the citrus vinaigrette can be refrigerated overnight. Return to room temperature before serving.

Shredded Green Cabbage Salad with Lemon and Garlic

TOTAL: 15 MIN
8 SERVINGS ● ● ○

This light, tart salad could not be simpler: shredded green cabbage tossed with lemon juice, garlic, olive oil and salt. Wonderful with fish, the salad is also a popular accompaniment to *kaftah,* Middle Eastern braised ground beef.

- 1 garlic clove, peeled
- 2 tablespoons fresh lemon juice
- 2 tablespoons extra-virgin olive oil
- 2 pounds green cabbage, cored and finely shredded

Kosher salt

1. In a mortar, pound the garlic clove to a puree. Stir in the fresh lemon juice and olive oil.

2. In a large bowl, toss the shredded green cabbage with the dressing. Season with salt and toss again. Serve right away or slightly chilled. —*Samia Hojaiban*

Grilled Cauliflower Salad with Raisin-Almond Dressing

TOTAL: 50 MIN PLUS 2 HR MACERATING
8 SERVINGS ● ●

"There's a style of Italian cooking known as *exotico,*" says Lachlan Mackinnon Patterson, the chef at Frasca Food and Wine in Boulder, Colorado. "In Friuli it often refers to dishes from the port of Trieste, where spices and dried fruit are popular." This *exotico* cauliflower salad is tossed with two kinds of raisins and a dressing flavored with mustard seeds and cumin.

- 1 cup slivered blanched almonds
- 1 teaspoon yellow mustard seeds
- 1 teaspoon brown mustard seeds
- 1 teaspoon cumin seeds
- ¼ cup sugar
- 1 cup water
- 3 tablespoons white vinegar
- 1 cup golden raisins
- 1 cup dark raisins
- 1 cup dried cranberries

About 2 quarts chicken stock or low-sodium broth

- 3 heads of cauliflower, cored and separated into 4-inch-wide florets
- ¼ cup extra-virgin olive oil, plus more for tossing

Salt

- 2 tablespoons very finely chopped chives
- 1 tablespoon coarsely chopped flat-leaf parsley

1. Preheat the oven to 350°. Spread the slivered almonds in a pie plate. Toast the almonds in the oven, tossing halfway through, for about 4 minutes, or until lightly browned.

2. In a medium saucepan, toast the yellow and brown mustard seeds with the cumin seeds over high heat, shaking the pan frequently, until they are fragrant, about 20 seconds. Add the sugar, water and white vinegar and cook, stirring frequently, until the sugar is dissolved, about 2 minutes. Stir in both kinds of raisins and the cranberries, cover the saucepan and remove from the heat. Let the dressing stand, covered, for 2 hours.

3. Light a grill. In a large pot, bring the chicken stock to a simmer over moderate heat. Add the cauliflower florets, reduce the heat to moderately low and simmer until the cauliflower is just tender, about 10 minutes. Using a slotted spoon, transfer the cauliflower florets to a large baking sheet, spread in a single layer and let cool slightly. Toss the florets with olive oil and season with salt.

4. Transfer the cauliflower florets to the grill and cook over moderately high heat, stem end up, for 4 to 5 minutes, or until well-browned. Turn the cauliflower and grill for 2 minutes longer, or until tender; transfer the grilled cauliflower to a serving platter. Add the toasted slivered almonds, chopped chives and parsley and the ¼ cup of olive oil to the raisin dressing, stir well and season with salt. Spoon the raisin dressing over the grilled cauliflower florets and serve hot or at room temperature.

—*Lachlan Mackinnon Patterson*

MAKE AHEAD The poached cauliflower and the raisin dressing can be prepared through Step 3 and refrigerated in separate containers overnight; store the toasted almonds at room temperature. Let the cauliflower and the raisin dressing return to room temperature before grilling the cauliflower and finishing the dish.

italian imports

To find the best sun-dried tomatoes, instant polenta, artisanal pasta and other key Italian ingredients, the F&W staff tasted 76 imports. Here are our seven favorite jarred, boxed and bagged foods, plus superfast ways to use them.

product	*why we love it*	*superfast ideas*
1 *tuna in olive oil*	Callipo solid light yellowfin tuna from Calabria, a region along the southern coast of Italy, is pleasantly firm and lightly briny ($14 for 7 oz; igourmet.com).	Pile on ciabatta bread, top with cheese and broil for Italian Tuna Melts (P. 225).
2 *artisanal pasta*	**Martelli pasta is dried slowly over about two days to develop its sweet, wheaty flavor and rustic texture ($6.50 for 1.1 lb; zingermans.com).**	**Dress simply with raw tomatoes, minced garlic, torn basil and fruity olive oil.**
3 *instant polenta*	Dal Raccolto's polenta from Lombardy is appealingly smooth without seeming mushy and has true corn flavor ($2.50 for 13 oz; at specialty shops).	Slice cold cooked polenta, season with salt, then fry in butter until crisp for a side dish.
4 *sun-dried tomatoes*	**Masseria Maida's Pomodori Secchi are packed in olive oil next to the farm where they're grown ($19 for 6.4 oz; gustiamo.com).**	**Blend into Creamy Sun-Dried Tomato Soup (P. 206).**
5 *jarred chickpeas*	Radici of Tuscany's creamy chickpeas, seasoned with salt, olive oil and sage, are delicious enough to serve straight from the jar ($8.50 for 10 oz; cheftools.com).	Mash with a fork to serve as a dip or spread, adding olive oil for a thinner consistency.
6 *porcini mushrooms*	**A.G. Ferrari Foods' fragrant dried porcini from Valtellina, Italy's northern Alpine valley, taste earthy and buttery ($10 for 2 oz; agferrari.com).**	**Soak in warm water, then stir mushrooms and strained liquid into hot soups or stews.**
7 *salted capers*	Grown on Pantelleria, a tiny volcanic island between Sicily and Tunisia, La Nicchia Capperi Salati are floral and fruity ($15 for 5.3 oz; amazon.com).	Fry and toss with pasta for Spaghettini with Eggplant (P. 257).

Roasted Cauliflower with Ajvar Dressing

ACTIVE: 25 MIN; TOTAL: 50 MIN
4 SERVINGS ● ●

The Balkans are the source of a great condiment: *ajvar,* a red pepper and eggplant relish (available at kalustyans.com). Stir it into crème fraîche for a dip, or mix it into a vinaigrette, as in this recipe.

- 1 head of cauliflower (2¾ pounds), core trimmed, head quartered and sliced lengthwise ⅓ inch thick
- ½ cup extra-virgin olive oil
- Kosher salt and freshly ground black pepper
- 1 anchovy fillet, coarsely chopped
- 1 garlic clove, coarsely chopped
- 3 tablespoons mild or hot *ajvar*
- 1 tablespoon fresh lemon juice
- 1 tablespoon red wine vinegar
- 1 tablespoon chopped flat-leaf parsley
- 1½ tablespoons pine nuts, toasted

1. Preheat the oven to 425°. Heat a large rimmed baking sheet in the oven. In a bowl, toss the sliced cauliflower with 3 tablespoons of the olive oil and season with salt and black pepper. Spread the cauliflower on the preheated baking sheet and roast for 45 minutes, tossing halfway through, until tender and browned.

2. Meanwhile, heat the remaining 5 tablespoons of olive oil in a skillet. When the oil is hot, add the chopped anchovy; cook over moderate heat until it begins to dissolve. Add the chopped garlic and cook for about 30 seconds. Remove the skillet from the heat; let the oil cool for 5 minutes.

3. In a mini food processor, blend the oil from the skillet with the *ajvar,* lemon juice and vinegar. Add the parsley and pulse to combine. Season the *ajvar* dressing with salt and black pepper.

4. Transfer the cauliflower to a serving platter. Drizzle with the dressing and sprinkle with the toasted pine nuts. Serve warm. —*Melissa Rubel*

Roasted Cauliflower with Green Olives and Pine Nuts

 ACTIVE: 10 MIN; TOTAL: 40 MIN
4 SERVINGS ● ● ○

Roasting cauliflower caramelizes the florets, making them supersweet. Tossed with crunchy pine nuts and salty olives and capers, this dish is perfect with roasted chicken or steamed fish.

- 1 pound cauliflower, cut into 1-inch florets
- 2 tablespoons extra-virgin olive oil
- Salt and freshly ground pepper
- 2 tablespoons pine nuts
- ⅓ cup chopped pitted green olives
- 1 tablespoon chopped flat-leaf parsley
- 1 tablespoon drained capers

Preheat the oven to 425°. In a shallow 1½-quart baking dish, toss the cauliflower florets with the olive oil and season with salt and pepper. Roast for 20 minutes, or until the cauliflower is lightly browned in spots. Add the pine nuts, chopped olives and parsley and drained capers, toss well and roast for about 10 minutes longer, until the pine nuts are lightly toasted. Serve the cauliflower warm or at room temperature. —*Grace Parisi*

Hot, Buttered Cauliflower Puree

 TOTAL: 30 MIN
12 SERVINGS ● ● ●

New Orleans chef John Besh's three-year-old son loves this silky, luscious cauliflower puree, which is made with both cream and butter. Adjust the level of cayenne pepper to make the dish more or less spicy.

- Two 2-pound heads of cauliflower, cored and separated into 2-inch florets
- 2 cups heavy cream
- 1½ sticks unsalted butter
- Salt
- Cayenne pepper

1. Preheat the oven to 325°. In a large pot of boiling salted water, cook the cauliflower florets until tender, about 7 minutes. Drain well. Spread the cooked cauliflower on a large rimmed baking sheet and bake for about 5 minutes to dry it out.

2. In a small saucepan, combine the heavy cream with the butter and bring to a simmer over moderate heat just until the butter is melted.

3. Working in batches, puree the cauliflower in a blender with the warm cream mixture; transfer the puree to a medium microwave-safe bowl. Season with salt and cayenne. Just before serving, reheat the puree in the microwave in 1-minute intervals, stirring occasionally. —*John Besh*

MAKE AHEAD The puree can be refrigerated overnight. Reheat in a microwave.

Roasted Red Curry Carrots with Ginger and Garlic

ACTIVE: 15 MIN; TOTAL: 1 HR
6 SERVINGS ● ● ●

- 1 tablespoon vegetable oil
- 1 tablespoon unsalted butter, softened
- ½ teaspoon Thai red curry paste
- 1 pound carrots, cut crosswise on the diagonal ¼ inch thick
- 1 tablespoon julienned fresh ginger
- 1 large garlic clove, thinly sliced
- Salt
- ¼ cup water

Preheat the oven to 425°. In a 1½-quart shallow baking dish, combine the oil, butter and curry paste. Add the carrots, ginger and garlic, season with salt and toss to coat. Add the water and cover the dish tightly with foil. Roast the carrots for 30 minutes, or until just tender. Remove the foil and roast for 10 minutes longer, or until the carrots are browned in spots and the liquid in the dish has evaporated. Serve warm or at room temperature. —*Grace Parisi*

MAKE AHEAD The roasted carrots can be refrigerated overnight.

Stir-Fried Bok Choy with Miso

TOTAL: 15 MIN
6 SERVINGS ●

A dash of miso is great for adding quick flavor to mild vegetables like bok choy. Dried red chiles provide a touch of heat, but the dish is equally delicious without them.

- ½ cup low-sodium chicken broth
- 1 tablespoon white or red miso
- 1 tablespoon Chinese cooking wine or dry sherry
- 1½ teaspoons sugar
- 1 teaspoon cornstarch
- 1½ tablespoons vegetable oil
- 6 dried red chiles
- 3 medium garlic cloves, very finely chopped
- 2 pounds bok choy, cut into ¾-inch pieces

Salt

In a small bowl, whisk the broth with the miso, wine, sugar and cornstarch. Heat a large wok or skillet until very hot. Add the oil and chiles and cook over high heat until the chiles darken, 1 to 2 minutes. Add the garlic and cook for 10 seconds, stirring constantly. Add the bok choy, season with salt and stir-fry until the leaves are wilted and the stalks are crisp-tender, about 5 minutes. Stir the miso sauce, add it to the wok and stir-fry until it has thickened slightly, about 2 minutes longer.
—*Grace Parisi*

SUPERFAST

sweet carrot puree

Cook sliced carrots in 1 inch of water with a pinch of salt until soft. Transfer the carrots to a blender and reduce the cooking water to a honey-thick glaze. Puree the carrots with the glaze.

Minty Peas and Carrots

TOTAL: 20 MIN
6 SERVINGS ● ●

Cooked with shallots and butter, this easy side dish of peas and carrots tastes luxuriously rich. Mint adds a pleasant herbal freshness here; anise-scented tarragon would also be tasty.

- 1 tablespoon extra-virgin olive oil
- 4 carrots, cut into ½-inch dice
- 2 large shallots, halved and thinly sliced
- 1 pound frozen baby peas, thawed
- 2 tablespoons thinly sliced mint leaves
- 1½ tablespoons unsalted butter

Kosher salt and freshly ground pepper

Heat the olive oil in a large skillet. Add the carrots and shallots and cook over moderate heat, stirring frequently, until the carrots are just tender, about 8 minutes. Add the peas and cook, stirring, until the peas are heated through, about 3 minutes. Remove the skillet from the heat and stir in the sliced mint leaves and butter. Season with salt and pepper and serve.
—*Melissa Rubel*

Bay-Steamed Broccoli

ACTIVE: 10 MIN; TOTAL: 30 MIN
4 TO 6 SERVINGS ●

- 2 heads of broccoli (1½ pounds)
- 1½ cups water
- 4 fresh bay leaves
- 4 tablespoons unsalted butter
- ¾ teaspoon salt

Peel the broccoli stems. In a pot wide enough to hold the whole broccoli heads, bring the water, bay leaves, butter and salt to a boil. Add the broccoli and cover. Cook over moderate heat, turning once, until tender, 15 minutes. Transfer the broccoli to a warmed platter and cover with foil. Boil the cooking liquid until reduced to ¼ cup, 5 minutes. Pour the liquid over the broccoli, discard the bay leaves and serve.
—*Jeff Jackson*

Broccoli and Wild Mushroom Casserole

ACTIVE: 45 MIN; TOTAL: 2 HR
12 SERVINGS ●

Photographer and Alabamian Robert Rausch grew up eating casseroles based on vegetables—he and his mother are both vegetarians. The broccoli casserole his family loved is a step up from the standard church cookbook recipe, which calls for using canned mushroom soup: In place of that, Rausch uses wild mushrooms. He still relies on Ritz crackers, though, for the buttery topping.

- ¾ pound mixed wild mushrooms, such as cremini and shiitake, stemmed and quartered
- 1 stick unsalted butter, plus 1 tablespoon melted
- 1 large onion, minced
- 4 large celery ribs, finely diced
- 3 tablespoons all-purpose flour
- 1 cup chicken stock or low-sodium broth
- ¼ cup milk

Salt and freshly ground black pepper

- 1 cup mayonnaise
- 2½ pounds broccoli—heads cut into 1-inch florets, stems peeled and cut into ½-inch dice
- 1½ cups coarsely shredded sharp cheddar cheese (6 ounces)
- 1⅓ cups crumbled Ritz crackers (from 1 sleeve, about 35 crackers)

1. Preheat the oven to 350°. In a food processor, pulse the mushrooms until coarsely chopped. In a large saucepan, melt the stick of butter. Add the onion and celery and cook over moderately high heat, stirring, until softened, about 6 minutes. Add the mushrooms and cook, stirring, until their liquid evaporates and they begin to brown, about 6 minutes. Sprinkle the flour over the vegetables and cook, stirring, for 1 minute. Add the chicken stock and cook, scraping up any bits stuck to the pan, until

the mixture is very thick, about 3 minutes. Remove from the heat and stir in the milk. Season with salt and pepper. Transfer the mushroom mixture to a large bowl to let cool, then stir in the mayonnaise.

2. Arrange the broccoli florets and stems in a large steamer basket and steam until barely crisp-tender, about 3 minutes. Add the broccoli to the mushroom mixture and season with salt and pepper.

3. Butter a 13-by-9-inch baking dish. Add the broccoli-mushroom mixture, smoothing the surface. Sprinkle the cheese on top. In a bowl, toss the cracker crumbs with the melted butter and scatter them over the casserole. Cover with foil and bake for about 30 minutes, until bubbling. Remove the foil and bake for about 40 minutes longer, until the topping is golden and crisp. Serve the casserole warm or at room temperature. —*Robert Rausch*

MAKE AHEAD The casserole can be refrigerated overnight. Reheat before serving.

Broccoli-Cheddar Gratin with Chipotle

 TOTAL: 20 MIN
    8 SERVINGS ●

It's easy to love broccoli smothered in a cheesy sauce. Here, the gratin gets an addictive spicy kick from a bit of canned chipotle in adobo sauce.

2½ pounds broccoli,
    cut into spears
Salt
  2 tablespoons unsalted butter
  2 tablespoons all-purpose
     flour
  1 cup half-and-half
1½ cups shredded sharp cheddar
     cheese (6 ounces)
  1 teaspoon minced canned
     chipotle in adobo

1. Preheat the broiler and position a rack 8 inches from the heat. Set a steamer basket in a large, deep skillet filled with 1 inch of water and bring to a boil. Add the

broccoli spears, cover and steam over high heat until crisp-tender, about 5 minutes. Transfer the broccoli spears to a shallow 1½-quart baking dish, arrange them in a single layer and season with salt.

2. Meanwhile, in a medium saucepan, melt the butter. Add the flour and whisk over moderately high heat for 2 minutes. Add the half-and-half and cook, whisking constantly, until the sauce is thickened and bubbling, about 5 minutes. Remove from the heat and whisk in the shredded cheddar and minced chipotle.

3. Pour the cheese sauce over the broccoli in the baking dish. Broil for 5 minutes, reversing the position of the baking dish once halfway through to ensure even cooking, until the gratin is bubbling and the cheese sauce is browned in spots. —*Grace Parisi*

Broccoli Rabe with Garlic and Red Pepper

 TOTAL: 30 MIN
    10 SERVINGS ● ●

Broccoli rabe gets such a bad rap for its bitterness, which is a shame. Blanching the leafy stalks whole in boiling salted water for a few minutes mellows their flavor, and sautéing them in extra-virgin olive oil with garlic and a good pinch of crushed red pepper makes them one of the most delicious of all Italian vegetables.

  4 pounds broccoli rabe,
     thick stems discarded
 ⅓ cup extra-virgin olive oil
  6 garlic cloves, thinly sliced
  1 teaspoon crushed red pepper
Salt and freshly ground pepper

1. Bring a large pot of salted water to a boil. Add the broccoli rabe and cook until just tender but still bright green, about 3 minutes. Drain and coarsely chop.

2. In a large, deep skillet, heat the olive oil. Add the garlic and red pepper and cook over low heat until the garlic is golden, about 3 minutes. Add the broccoli rabe

and cook over moderately high heat, stirring, until hot, about 4 minutes. Season the broccoli rabe with salt and pepper and serve. —*Palma D'Orazio*

MAKE AHEAD The blanched broccoli rabe can be refrigerated overnight.

Swiss Chard with Poblanos and Hominy

 TOTAL: 40 MIN
    4 SERVINGS ● ●

Hominy turns roasted poblanos and Swiss chard into a hearty side dish. Wrapped in tortillas or served over rice, these greens are an excellent vegetarian main course.

  2 large poblano chiles
  3 tablespoons extra-virgin olive oil
  1 red onion, halved and
     sliced ½ inch thick
  1 pound Swiss chard—stems
     cut crosswise ½ inch thick,
     leaves cut into 1-inch ribbons
  2 large garlic cloves, very
     thinly sliced
One 15-ounce can hominy, drained
Kosher salt and freshly ground pepper
Lime wedges, for serving

1. Light a grill or preheat the broiler. Grill or broil the poblanos, turning frequently, until charred all over, 4 minutes. Transfer to a bowl, cover with plastic wrap and let stand for 15 minutes. Peel and seed the poblanos; cut into ½-inch-thick strips.

2. In a large skillet, heat the olive oil. Add the red onion slices and cook over moderately high heat until just softened, about 3 minutes. Add the Swiss chard stems and cook until crisp-tender, about 3 minutes. Stir in the garlic and poblanos and cook until the garlic is fragrant and the chiles are heated through, about 2 minutes. Add the chard leaves and cook, stirring occasionally, until tender, about 6 minutes. Add the hominy and cook until heated through, about 1 minute. Season with salt and pepper and transfer the stew to a bowl. Serve with lime wedges. —*Melissa Rubel*

Thin-Sliced Beans with Citrus Zest and Chives

TOTAL: 20 MIN
4 SERVINGS ● ●

To save time, use a food processor fitted with a slicing blade for the green beans.

- 2 **tablespoons extra-virgin olive oil**
- ¾ **pound green string beans and yellow wax beans, sliced diagonally ¼ inch thick**
- 2 **tablespoons water**
- **Salt and freshly ground pepper**
- ¼ **teaspoon finely grated lemon zest**
- ¼ **teaspoon finely grated lime zest**
- 2 **tablespoons snipped chives**
- 1 **tablespoon fresh lemon juice**

Heat the oil in a medium skillet. Add the beans and cook over moderately high heat, stirring, for 1 minute. Add the water; season with salt and pepper. Cover and cook the beans until crisp-tender, 2 minutes. Add the zest and chives and cook, stirring, until the beans are tender, 2 to 3 minutes longer. Stir in the lemon juice and serve. —*Heidi Swanson*

Braised Red Cabbage

TOTAL: 20 MIN
4 TO 6 SERVINGS ● ● ●

- ¼ **cup extra-virgin olive oil**
- **One 3-pound head of red cabbage, cored and sliced ¼ inch thick**
- 2 **tablespoons fresh lemon juice**
- **Pinch of crushed red pepper**
- **Salt and freshly ground black pepper**

In a medium enameled cast-iron casserole, heat the olive oil. Add the red cabbage and cook over moderately high heat, stirring, until sizzling, about 3 minutes. Cover tightly and cook over moderate heat, stirring occasionally, until just tender, about 6 minutes. Stir in the lemon juice and crushed red pepper. Season with salt and black pepper and serve. —*Jeremy Silansky*

MAKE AHEAD The braised cabbage can be made up to 4 hours ahead. Reheat gently.

Braised Green Beans with Tomatoes and Garlic

ACTIVE: 30 MIN; TOTAL: 1 HR 10 MIN
8 SERVINGS ● ●

Called *loobyeh* (LOO-beh), this comforting vegetable stew is a staple in Lebanon. Lebanese-born fashion consultant Rita Nakouzi's recipe is a combination of her mother's and aunt's versions; only as an adult was she finally able to add as much garlic as she wanted. After years of making what by her own admission was "a garlic attack," she says, "Now I've gotten better. It finally dawned on me: I don't think everyone else likes garlic as much as I do."

- 2 **tablespoons vegetable oil, preferably canola**
- 1 **large onion, thinly sliced**
- 12 **garlic cloves, 6 minced**
- 1½ **teaspoons sweet paprika**
- ¼ **teaspoon cayenne pepper**
- 1½ **pounds green beans**
- **One 16-ounce can diced tomatoes**
- **Salt and freshly ground black pepper**

1. In a large, deep skillet, heat the vegetable oil. Add the sliced onion and cook over moderate heat until translucent and softened, about 8 minutes. Add the minced garlic, paprika and cayenne pepper and cook, stirring, until fragrant, about 2 minutes. Add the green beans and 6 whole garlic cloves and cook for about 2 minutes, tossing to coat the beans.

2. Pour the diced tomatoes and their juices into the skillet and bring to a boil. Reduce the heat to low, cover the skillet and simmer, stirring occasionally, until the green beans are very tender, about 40 minutes. Season the braised green beans with salt and black pepper. Transfer to a platter and serve warm or at room temperature. —*Rita Nakouzi*

MAKE AHEAD The braised green beans can be refrigerated overnight. Reheat gently or bring to room temperature to serve.

Broken Lasagna with Walnut Pesto

TOTAL: 30 MIN
6 SERVINGS ● ● ●

"Whole-grain pasta is one of the easiest ways to sneak whole grains into your diet," says food blogger Heidi Swanson. Her lasagna, made with noodles broken into 1-inch pieces, features a healthy pesto made with walnuts and basil.

- 1 **cup walnut halves (4 ounces)**
- 2 **cups lightly packed basil leaves**
- 1 **large garlic clove, very thinly sliced**
- ¼ **cup extra-virgin olive oil**
- ¾ **cup freshly grated Parmigiano-Reggiano cheese**
- **Salt and freshly ground black pepper**
- 1 **pound whole wheat lasagna noodles, broken into 1-inch pieces**
- 6 **ounces watercress, arugula or other bitter greens, thick stems discarded and leaves coarsely chopped**
- **Sautéed mushrooms, for serving**

1. Preheat the oven to 350°. Bring a large pot of salted water to a boil over high heat. Spread the walnuts on a baking sheet and toast for 8 to 10 minutes, until they are fragrant and lightly browned. Let cool completely. Coarsely chop half of the toasted walnuts and set the remaining toasted walnuts aside.

2. In a food processor, pulse the remaining toasted walnuts with the basil leaves and sliced garlic until the walnuts are finely chopped. With the machine on, add the olive oil in a thin stream and process until the pesto is almost smooth. Add ½ cup of the grated Parmigiano-Reggiano cheese and pulse just until incorporated. Transfer the walnut pesto to a bowl and season it with salt and black pepper.

3. Add the broken whole wheat lasagna noodles to the boiling salted water and cook until al dente. Drain the pasta, reserving ½ cup of the pasta cooking water. Return the drained pasta to the pot. Add the watercress and walnut pesto and toss well to coat the noodles. Add the reserved pasta water and toss again until well coated. Transfer the pasta to bowls, garnish with the remaining ¼ cup of grated Parmigiano-Reggiano cheese, the chopped walnuts and sautéed mushrooms and serve the pasta immediately.
—*Heidi Swanson*

Braised Kale

TOTAL: 30 MIN
12 SERVINGS ● ●

This easy kale recipe—a simple braise of olive oil, garlic and chicken stock—is a terrific counterpoint to chef John Besh's rich Southern-style cooking.

- ⅓ cup extra-virgin olive oil
- 4 garlic cloves, very finely chopped
- 1½ cups chicken stock or low-sodium broth
- 3 pounds kale, stems and inner ribs discarded, leaves coarsely chopped

Salt and freshly ground pepper

1. In a very large soup pot, heat the olive oil. Add the garlic and cook over moderately high heat, stirring, just until fragrant, about 30 seconds. Add the chicken stock, then add the kale in large handfuls, letting it wilt slightly before adding more. Season with salt and pepper, cover and cook over moderate heat until the kale is tender, about 5 minutes.

2. Remove the lid and cook until the liquid has evaporated, about 3 minutes longer. Transfer to a bowl and serve.
—*John Besh*

MAKE AHEAD The braised kale can be covered and refrigerated overnight. Reheat before serving.

THIN-SLICED BEANS WITH CITRUS ZEST AND CHIVES

BROKEN LASAGNA WITH WALNUT PESTO

Butternut Squash with Homemade Harissa

ACTIVE: 25 MIN; TOTAL: 1 HR 40 MIN

6 SERVINGS ● ● ○

Harissa, a garlicky North African chile sauce, is usually served with couscous and stews. The homemade *harissa* featured here is supersimple to prepare, and any extra will keep in the refrigerator for up to a week, but jarred versions available at specialty markets make a fine substitute.

    3   garlic cloves, 2 thickly sliced
Kosher salt
    1   tablespoon tomato paste
    1   teaspoon freshly squeezed
        lemon juice
    1   tablespoon ancho chile powder
    1   tablespoon smoked paprika
    ¼   teaspoon cayenne pepper
    ¼   teaspoon ground cumin
    ¼   teaspoon caraway seeds,
        ground in a spice grinder
    ½   cup extra-virgin olive oil
    1½ pounds butternut squash—
        peeled, seeded and
        cut into 1½-inch chunks
    2   tablespoons water
Freshly ground black pepper

1. Preheat the oven to 375°. On a work surface, using the flat side of a chef's knife, mash the whole garlic clove to a paste with a pinch of salt. Scrape the garlic paste into a small bowl and stir in the tomato paste and fresh lemon juice. Add the ancho chile powder, smoked paprika, cayenne, cumin and caraway. Gradually stir in ¼ cup plus 2 tablespoons of the olive oil and season the *harissa* with salt.

2. In a bowl, toss the butternut squash and sliced garlic with 2 tablespoons of the *harissa,* the remaining 2 tablespoons of olive oil and the water and season with salt and pepper. Spread the squash in a single layer in an 8-inch square baking dish. Roast in the center of the oven for about 1 hour and 15 minutes, or until the squash is tender and browned in spots. —*Grace Parisi*

MAKE AHEAD The roasted squash can be refrigerated overnight. Rewarm in a 350° oven before serving.

Maple-Glazed Root Vegetables

ACTIVE: 25 MIN; TOTAL: 1 HR 10 MIN

4 SERVINGS ● ● ●

    2¼ pounds rutabagas, peeled and
        cut into 1-inch dice
    1½ pounds turnips, peeled and
        cut into 1-inch dice
    1   pound carrots, peeled and
        cut into 1-inch dice
    2   tablespoons extra-virgin olive oil
Salt and freshly ground pepper
    2   tablespoons sherry vinegar
    1   cup low-sodium chicken broth
    2   tablespoons pure maple syrup
    2   tablespoons unsalted butter

1. Preheat the oven to 400°. Divide the rutabagas, turnips and carrots between 2 large rimmed baking sheets. Drizzle 1 tablespoon of the oil over each sheet of vegetables and toss well to coat. Spread the root vegetables out in an even layer and season with salt and pepper. Roast until the vegetables are lightly browned and tender, about 40 minutes. Drizzle each pan with 1 tablespoon of the vinegar and toss until well coated. Roast until sizzling, about 3 minutes longer.

2. Meanwhile, in a small skillet, bring the chicken broth and maple syrup to a boil over high heat. Boil until reduced to ¼ cup, about 20 minutes. Remove from the heat and whisk in the butter.

3. Transfer the roasted root vegetables to a warmed bowl. Add the maple glaze and toss well. Serve right away.

—*Jeremy Silansky*

MAKE AHEAD The roasted root vegetables and maple glaze can be refrigerated separately for up to 1 day. Reheat the vegetables in a 350° oven for 10 minutes. Bring the glaze to a simmer before tossing with the root vegetables.

CHEF'S CHOICE

most useful pot or pan

SKILLET
Perfect for quick searing and stir-frying; Todd Gray of Equinox in Washington, DC, even uses it to "semi-deep-fry" chicken.

SAUCEPAN
"Straight sides let you cook sauces without burning the edges of the liquid," says Scott Dolich of Park Kitchen in Portland, Oregon.

DUTCH OVEN
"It's universal. You can roast a steak or make a vegetable ragout," says Josiah Citrin of Melisse in Santa Monica, California.

Baby Root Vegetable Stew with Black Tea Prunes

TOTAL: 1 HR 15 MIN

8 SERVINGS ●

This elegant vegetable recipe is a simplified version of a dish chef David Kinch serves at Manresa, his restaurant in Los Gatos, California. The stew combines tender carrots and turnips with black tea–soaked prunes in a flavorful soy broth.

- 4 ounces pitted prunes (1 cup)
- 2 cups strong brewed black tea
- 6 tablespoons unsalted butter
- ¾ pound baby carrots, quartered lengthwise
- 2 small turnips, peeled and cut into ½-inch wedges

Salt and freshly ground pepper

- ¾ pound radishes, quartered if large
- 2 cups chicken stock or low-sodium broth
- 3 tablespoons soy sauce
- ¾ pound fingerling potatoes, cut into ¾-inch pieces
- 1 small onion, finely chopped
- 1 large garlic clove, minced
- 1 large thyme sprig

Lemon wedges, for serving

1. In a small saucepan, cover the prunes with the tea and bring to a simmer. Remove from the heat, cover and let stand until the prunes are plump, about 1 hour. Drain the prunes and discard the tea.

2. Melt 4 tablespoons of the butter in a skillet. Add the carrots and turnips and season with salt and pepper. Cook over moderate heat, stirring, just until heated through, 2 minutes. Add enough water to cover the vegetables by 1 inch and bring to a boil. Simmer over moderate heat until tender, 7 minutes. Drain the vegetables.

3. In a medium saucepan, cover the radishes with the chicken stock and soy sauce and bring to a boil. Simmer over moderate heat until the radishes are tender, 10 minutes. Drain, reserving the cooking liquid.

4. In a large enameled cast-iron casserole, melt the remaining 2 tablespoons of butter. Add the potatoes and cook over moderate heat, stirring, until tender and golden, about 8 minutes. Add the onion and cook until softened, about 4 minutes. Stir in the garlic and cook until fragrant, 1 minute. Add the prunes, carrots, turnips and the radishes with their cooking liquid and season with salt and pepper. Add the thyme and bring to a simmer. Cook over moderately low heat, stirring, until the vegetables are tender and the liquid is slightly reduced, 8 minutes. Discard the thyme sprig. Serve with lemon wedges.

David Kinch

MAKE AHEAD The stew can be refrigerated overnight. Reheat gently.

Coal-Roasted Potatoes

ACTIVE: 15 MIN; TOTAL: 1 HR 45 MIN

8 SERVINGS ○

Slow-roasting Yukon Gold potatoes near the hot coals enhances their rich flavor. It also dries them out a little bit, which helps them soak up butter.

Eight ½-pound Yukon Gold potatoes, scrubbed

Vegetable oil, for brushing

Kosher salt

Unsalted butter, at room temperature, for serving

Salsa Verde (p. 41), for serving

Light a grill. Wrap each potato in a double layer of foil and arrange them around hot coals; the potatoes should be close to, but not touching, the coals. Roast the potatoes for about 1 hour and 15 minutes, until tender, turning them halfway through. Discard the foil, then brush the potatoes lightly with vegetable oil and season with salt. Grill the potatoes directly on the grate over moderately high heat for about 4 minutes per side, or until the skin is crisp. Split the potatoes in half crosswise and top with butter. Serve with the Salsa Verde alongside.

—Lachlan Mackinnon Patterson

Creamy Potatoes with Bacon

ACTIVE: 30 MIN; TOTAL: 1 HR

12 SERVINGS ●

Adding farmer cheese to creamy mashed potatoes gives them a nice tangy flavor; crunchy bits of bacon make this dish taste even better. New Orleans chef John Besh advises seeking out artisanally made bacon, like the kind from Tennessee's Benton's Smoky Mountain Country Hams (available at bentonshams.com). It's smoked in hickory wood, and Besh swears that it's the best bacon out there.

- 5 pounds Yukon Gold potatoes, peeled and cut into 3-inch chunks

Salt

- 1 pound thickly sliced bacon
- 2 sticks unsalted butter, softened
- 1 cup heavy cream, warmed
- ½ cup farmer cheese
- ½ cup minced chives

Salt and freshly ground black pepper

1. Put the potato chunks in a large pot and cover with water. Add salt and bring to a boil over high heat. Simmer over moderately high heat until the potatoes are tender, about 20 minutes.

2. Meanwhile, in a large skillet, cook the bacon in 2 batches over moderate heat, turning once, until crisp, 8 to 10 minutes per batch. Transfer the bacon to paper towels to drain, then coarsely chop.

3. Drain the potatoes and return them to the pot. Shake the pot over moderately high heat for about 20 seconds to dry the potatoes. Pass the potatoes through a ricer into a large pot. Add the butter, cream, cheese, chives and bacon and stir well. Season with salt and pepper and serve.

—John Besh

MAKE AHEAD The finished potatoes can be refrigerated overnight. Reheat in a microwave oven at high power at 1-minute intervals; stir the potatoes occasionally.

● HEALTHY ● MAKE AHEAD ○ VEGETARIAN ● STAFF FAVORITE

Japanese Frites

TOTAL: 25 MIN

6 SERVINGS ●

French fries have gone way beyond the prosaic russet potato—for example, there are the irresistible sweet potato fries created by chef Gene Kato for the Japonais restaurants. His *frites* are seasoned with a blend of Japanese flavorings, including nori flakes and the tingly spice mix *shichimi togarashi,* and served with a spicy mayonnnaise for dipping.

Vegetable oil, for frying

1 tablespoon nori flakes
   (see Note)

2 teaspoons *shichimi
   togarashi* (see Note)

2 teaspoons kosher salt

Pinch of freshly ground
   black pepper

1 cup mayonnaise

1 to 2 tablespoons *sambal
   oelek* or other Asian red
   chile sauce

1 tablespoon plus 1 teaspoon
   fresh lime juice

4 white or orange sweet
   potatoes, unpeeled and
   cut into ½-inch-thick
   sticks (3 pounds)

1. In a large pot, heat 3 inches of vegetable oil to 350°. Meanwhile, in a small bowl, mix the nori flakes with the *shichimi togarashi,* salt and black pepper. In another small bowl, mix the mayonnaise with the *sambal oelek* and fresh lime juice and stir until smoothly combined.

2. Working in batches, carefully add the sweet potato sticks to the hot oil and fry until they are tender and golden, about 7 minutes. Using a slotted spoon, transfer the sweet potato fries to paper towel–lined plates to drain. Generously sprinkle the hot fries with the nori-*togarashi* mixture and serve immediately, with the spicy mayonnaise on the side for dipping.

—*Gene Kato*

NOTE You can buy nori flakes (*aonori*) at Asian markets, or you can make your own: Toast a sheet of nori in a dry skillet for 1 minute, then finely grind it in a spice grinder. *Shichimi togarashi* is a Japanese seasoning blend that includes chiles, sesame seeds and orange peel.

Sweet Potato Gnocchi with Salsify, Chestnuts and Ham

ACTIVE: 1 HR 15 MIN;

TOTAL: 2 HR 30 MIN

10 SERVINGS ● ●

Connecticut chef Michel Nischan transforms a traditional Italian dish with local produce and country ham. "This satisfies people's yearning for pasta, but with a more American approach," he says.

2 pounds sweet potatoes, scrubbed

1 lemon, halved

1 pound salsify or parsnips

2 large eggs, beaten

Kosher salt

2 cups all-purpose flour, plus
   more for rolling

Freshly ground pepper

Pinch of freshly grated nutmeg

5 tablespoons unsalted butter

1 tablespoon vegetable oil

2 large shallots, minced

One 14-ounce jar vacuum-packed
   roasted chestnuts, halved

1¼ cups Ham Hock Stock
   (p. 159) or water

4 ounces thinly sliced country ham,
   cut into thin strips

¼ cup snipped chives

1. Preheat the oven to 375°. Pierce the sweet potatoes all over with a fork. Place the sweet potatoes on a rimmed baking sheet and bake for about 1 hour, until tender. Let cool slightly.

2. Meanwhile, fill a medium bowl with water and squeeze a lemon half into it. Peel the salsifies, adding them to the bowl as you go. Cut the salsifies into 1½-by-¼-inch sticks and return them to the water.

3. Peel the sweet potatoes and transfer them to a food processor. Puree until smooth. Transfer the puree to a large bowl and stir in the eggs and 1½ teaspoons of kosher salt. Add the 2 cups of flour, a generous pinch of pepper and the nutmeg and stir until a soft dough forms.

4. Transfer the dough to a heavily floured work surface and gently knead in more flour—as much as ½ cup—until the dough comes together but is still very soft. Divide the dough into 4 pieces and roll each piece into a 1-inch-thick rope. Cut the ropes into 1-inch lengths and dust each piece with flour. Roll each gnocchi against the tines of a floured fork to make small indentations. Transfer the gnocchi to a lightly floured baking sheet.

5. Bring a large pot of salted water to a boil. Add half of the sweet potato gnocchi and cook until they float to the surface, about 1 minute, then cook for 2 minutes longer. Using a slotted spoon, transfer the gnocchi to a large plate. Repeat with the remaining gnocchi.

6. Meanwhile, bring a medium saucepan of salted water to a boil. Drain the salsify sticks. Add the remaining lemon half and the drained salsify to the saucepan and cook over moderate heat until tender, about 15 minutes. Drain the salsify and discard the lemon half.

7. In a very large, deep skillet, melt 1 tablespoon of the butter in the oil. Add the shallots and cook over moderate heat until softened, about 2 minutes. Add the salsify, chestnuts and 1 cup of the Ham Hock Stock and simmer over moderate heat until slightly reduced, about 5 minutes. Add the gnocchi and the remaining ham stock and 4 tablespoons of butter and cook, stirring gently, until the gnocchi are hot and the sauce is thickened, about 3 minutes. Season with salt and pepper and transfer to a large platter. Sprinkle with the ham and chives and serve.

—*Michel Nischan*

JAPANESE FRITES

Golden Persian Rice

ACTIVE: 20 MIN; TOTAL: 2 HR

8 SERVINGS ●

Persian rice gets its extraordinary crust, or *tah dig,* as it slow-cooks in a thin layer of oil. The crust is bolstered here by crunchy triangles of pita bread. Tehran-born Alireza Sadeghzadeh, a software developer, learned the technique from his mother. "My mother did most of the cooking, and my father was her favorite critic," he recalls. "It definitely made eating together interesting as the two battled over the exact amount of salt or debated about whether the rice was over- or under-cooked."

- **3 cups long-grain white rice (1¼ pounds), rinsed**
- **Salt**
- **¼ cup vegetable oil**
- **Five 3-inch triangles of pita bread cut from the top layer of one 12- to 15-inch round**

1. Place the rice in a large nonstick saucepan with a rounded bottom. Cover the rice with 1 inch of water and bring to a boil over high heat. Boil over moderately high heat until the rice is softened but still very chewy, about 7 minutes. Drain in a colander and season the rice lightly with salt.

2. Wipe out the saucepan. Add the vegetable oil and heat until shimmering. Add the pita triangles, outer side down, and fry over moderately high heat until browned, about 1 minute. Transfer the browned pita triangles to a plate and remove the saucepan from the heat.

3. Using tongs, arrange the pita triangles evenly, browned side down, so that their short sides line up with the rim of the saucepan and their points meet in the center. Add half of the rice and press lightly, keeping the triangles in place. Add the remaining rice and press lightly to release any air pockets. Cover the rice with a clean folded kitchen towel and cover the saucepan with a lid.

4. Cook the rice over low heat for about 1½ hours, until the grains are tender and the moisture has evaporated. Remove the kitchen towel. Increase the heat to moderately high and cook, covered, for about 5 minutes, until the rice is browned on the bottom (you should hear sizzling and smell the rice toasting). Hold a larger serving platter over the top of the saucepan and invert the rice onto the platter in one fast motion. Serve immediately.

—*Alireza Sadeghzadeh*

Sweet Potato Casserole

ACTIVE: 45 MIN; TOTAL: 2 HR 30 MIN

12 SERVINGS ● ●

Alabama sculptor Sandi Stevens and her family eat locally grown sweet potatoes year-round. This casserole is a Stevens favorite: silky pureed sweet potatoes topped with a sweet and crunchy pecan-cornflake topping. If you don't have pecans or cornflakes on hand, Stevens says, make the topping with whatever nut or cereal happens to be in the cupboard.

- **5½ pounds sweet potatoes, peeled and cut into 2-inch chunks**
- **2 sticks unsalted butter, melted, plus more for the dish**
- **Salt**
- **1½ teaspoons freshly grated nutmeg**
- **1½ cups light brown sugar**
- **1 cup milk, warmed**
- **3 large eggs, beaten**
- **1 cup pecan halves (4 ounces)**
- **1 cup cornflakes**
- **½ teaspoon cinnamon**

1. Preheat the oven to 350°. Butter a 13-by-9-inch baking dish. Put the sweet potatoes in a large pot. Cover with cold water and bring to a boil. Cook over moderate heat until the sweet potatoes are tender, about 15 minutes. Drain well, shaking off the excess water. Transfer the sweet potatoes to a food processor (in batches, if necessary) and puree until smooth.

2. Scrape the sweet potato puree into a large bowl. Add half of the melted butter, 2 teaspoons of salt, 1 teaspoon of the nutmeg, ½ cup of the light brown sugar and the warmed milk and stir until thoroughly combined. Stir in the beaten eggs. Pour the mixture into the prepared baking dish and smooth the surface. Cover with foil and bake for 40 minutes.

3. Meanwhile, spread the pecans on a baking sheet and bake for 5 minutes, until lightly toasted. Let cool briefly, then transfer the pecans to a work surface and coarsely chop them. In a bowl, toss the toasted pecans with the cornflakes, cinnamon and the remaining melted butter, ½ teaspoon of nutmeg and 1 cup of light brown sugar. Season with salt.

4. Remove the foil from the sweet potato casserole. Spoon small clumps of the pecan-cornflake topping all over the top of the pureed sweet potato mixture. Continue to bake the sweet potatoes, uncovered, for about 40 minutes longer, until the pecan-cornflake topping is golden and sizzling. Let the sweet potatoes stand for 20 minutes before serving.

—*Sandi Stevens*

MAKE AHEAD The Sweet Potato Casserole can be baked up to 4 hours ahead and served warm or at room temperature.

SHORT-GRAIN is firm and sticky when cooked, making it ideal for dishes like sushi and rice pudding.

MEDIUM-GRAIN is moist and plump, so it's great in salads and risotto.

LONG-GRAIN has a dry, fluffy texture that's perfect in pilafs and soups.

GOLDEN PERSIAN RICE

INGREDIENT

whole grains

AMARANTH Loved by the Aztecs, this high-protein grain is mildly grassy, with a slight crunch. It can be cooked so it's thick like polenta or almost as fluffy as couscous. Stir it into soups or pop it like corn.

KAMUT Another high-protein ancient grain, this variety of modern durum wheat has a natural sweetness and a buttery quality. Its grains are twice the size of wheat berries; when cooked, they have a delightful chew that is ideal in grain salads and pilafs.

BUCKWHEAT Commonly regarded as a grain, buckwheat is actually a kind of herb with edible seeds. It's unrelated to wheat (despite the name) and has an earthy, nutty taste when toasted. The secret to preventing buckwheat from turning mushy: Toss with beaten egg white to coat before cooking.

Creamy Saffron Risotto

TOTAL: 40 MIN
10 SERVINGS

Risotto alla milanese is the traditional accompaniment to osso buco (see Palma D'Orazio's recipe for Slow-Braised Osso Buco, p. 59). The rice is flavored with saffron, deep red filaments that are the dried stigmas of a variety of crocus. Each crocus has three stigmas, and it takes more than 14,000 to make one ounce of saffron. Harvested exclusively by hand, saffron is the world's most expensive spice.

- 2½ **quarts light chicken stock or low-sodium broth**
- 4 **tablespoons unsalted butter**
- 1 **medium onion, very finely chopped**
- ½ **teaspoon saffron threads**
- 3¼ **cups arborio rice (1 pound 10 ounces)**
- 1½ **cups dry white wine**
- ½ **cup freshly grated Parmigiano-Reggiano cheese**

Salt and freshly ground black pepper

1. In a large saucepan, bring the chicken stock to a boil over high heat. Cover and keep hot over low heat.

2. In a heavy 6-quart pot or casserole, melt 2 tablespoons of the butter over moderate heat. Add the chopped onion and cook, stirring occasionally, until softened, about 6 minutes. Crumble in the saffron threads and cook for 1 minute, stirring. Add the arborio rice and stir to coat thoroughly with butter, about 2 minutes. Pour in the white wine and cook over moderately high heat, stirring, until the wine has evaporated. Add enough hot stock (about 1½ cups) to cover the rice and bring to a boil, stirring. Reduce the heat to moderate. Cook, stirring the rice constantly, until the stock has been absorbed. Continue adding the stock, 1½ cups at a time, and stirring until it is absorbed before adding more; the risotto is done when the rice is just tender and the liquid is thick, about 25 minutes total.

3. Remove the risotto from the heat and stir in the remaining 2 tablespoons of butter and the grated Parmigiano-Reggiano cheese. Season with salt and black pepper and serve immediately.
—*Palma D'Orazio*

MAKE AHEAD The risotto can be prepared through Step 2 (with all but the last 2 cups of stock added) and kept at room temperature for 1 hour. Bring the risotto to a simmer over moderately high heat, stirring constantly. Stir in the reserved 2 cups of stock and cook until the risotto is creamy before proceeding.

Oyster Dressing "Grand-Mère"

ACTIVE: 45 MIN; TOTAL: 1 HR 30 MIN
12 SERVINGS ● ●

According to New Orleans chef John Besh, "This is the only dish worthy of both Thanksgiving and Christmas dinner at our house." Why? Because it's unbelievably delicious—a bready dressing that's spicy, crispy and nicely briny.

- 2 **ounces slab bacon, cut into ¼-inch dice**
- 1 **stick unsalted butter**
- 1 **celery rib, cut into ¼-inch dice**
- ½ **green bell pepper, cut into ¼-inch dice**
- ½ **small onion, finely diced**
- 2 **large garlic cloves, minced**
- 2 **tablespoons sweet paprika**
- ½ **teaspoon garlic powder**
- ½ **teaspoon cayenne pepper**
- 2 **large baguettes (about 1 pound), cut into ½-inch dice (12 cups)**
- 4 **dozen shucked oysters plus 1 cup oyster liquor, oysters halved (2 cups)**
- 2 **scallions, very finely chopped**
- 2 **tablespoons chopped flat-leaf parsley**
- 4 **large eggs**
- 1 **teaspoon hot sauce**
- 1 **teaspoon kosher salt**

1. Preheat the oven to 350°. Butter a 10-by-14-inch shallow baking dish. In a large skillet, cook the bacon over moderate heat until crisp, about 5 minutes. Add the butter and let melt, then add the celery, green pepper, onion and minced garlic and cook until softened, about 8 minutes. Add the paprika, garlic powder and cayenne and cook for 3 minutes, stirring occasionally.

2. Put the diced baguettes in a large bowl. Spoon the bacon mixture on top. Add the oysters and their liquor along with the scallions and parsley.

3. In a small bowl, beat the eggs with the hot sauce and salt. Pour the eggs into the large bowl and combine. Scrape the dressing into the prepared baking dish and bake in the upper third of the oven for about 45 minutes, until heated through and crisp on top. Serve hot. —*John Besh*

MAKE AHEAD The baked dressing can be refrigerated overnight. Reheat the dressing in a 350° oven before serving.

Corn Bread with Scallions

ACTIVE: 10 MIN; TOTAL: 40 MIN
MAKES ONE 10-INCH LOAF ● ○

After cooking in Europe and writing and editing in New York, Paula Disbrowe packed her high heels and moved to Texas, where she spent three years as chef at Hart & Hind, a fitness retreat and cattle ranch. One result: her cookbook *Cowgirl Cuisine*, with updated chuckwagon recipes like this tender, lightly sweet corn bread.

1⅓ cups all-purpose flour
1 cup coarse stone-ground yellow cornmeal
2 teaspoons baking powder
1 teaspoon salt
Pinch of freshly ground pepper
1¼ cups low-fat milk
2 tablespoons honey
2 large eggs, beaten
⅓ cup plus 1 tablespoon corn oil
8 scallions, white and tender green parts only, thinly sliced

1. Preheat the oven to 400°. Place a 10-inch cast-iron skillet in the oven to heat. In a medium bowl, whisk the flour, cornmeal, baking powder, salt and pepper. In a small bowl, whisk the milk, honey, eggs and ⅓ cup of the oil. Add the wet ingredients to the cornmeal mixture and whisk just until combined. Stir in the scallions.

2. Add the remaining 1 tablespoon of oil to the hot skillet and swirl to coat. Pour the batter into the skillet and bake for about 30 minutes, until the top is golden and a toothpick inserted in the center comes out clean. Let cool slightly, then turn the corn bread out onto a plate. Invert it onto a rack to cool. Alternatively, serve the corn bread hot from the skillet.
—*Paula Disbrowe*

Cheesy Grits Casserole

ACTIVE: 45 MIN; TOTAL: 2 HR
12 SERVINGS ● ● ○

Alabama clothing designer Billy Reid says, "Folks in the South start eating grits young. You learn to love them as a kid and it never goes away." Old-fashioned stone-ground grits like those sold by McEwen & Sons in Wilsonville, Alabama (205-669-6605), give the casserole a better texture and flavor than quick-cooking grits.

8 cups water
2 cups coarse stone-ground white grits (12 ounces), rinsed
Salt and freshly ground pepper
1 stick unsalted butter, cut into chunks
½ pound sharp white cheddar cheese, coarsely shredded
3 large eggs, beaten

1. Preheat the oven to 350°. Butter a 13-by-9-inch baking dish. In a large, heavy pot, bring the water to a boil. Sprinkle the grits into the water, stirring constantly, and return to a boil. Cook over low heat, stirring frequently, until the grits are just tender, about 30 minutes. Season generously with

salt and pepper and cook, stirring, until the grits are very thick and tender, about 10 minutes longer. Off the heat, stir in the butter and shredded cheddar cheese, then stir in the beaten eggs.

2. Pour the mixture into the prepared dish and bake for 1 hour, until the grits are bubbling and the top is golden. Let cool for 20 minutes before serving. —*Billy Reid*

MAKE AHEAD The grits casserole can be refrigerated overnight. Reheat in a 350° oven before serving.

Creamy Grits

TOTAL: 40 MIN
6 SERVINGS ● ○

2 cups coarse stone-ground grits
Water
6 cups whole milk
Salt and freshly ground pepper
3 tablespoons unsalted butter
1 cup fresh or thawed frozen corn kernels

1. Put the grits in a medium bowl and cover with water. Stir a few times, then let stand for 1 minute. Tilt the bowl slightly, allowing the chaff to float to the top. Spoon off the chaff and drain the grits. Transfer the grits to a large, heavy saucepan. Add the milk and 2 cups of water and bring to a boil, stirring constantly. Cook over low heat, stirring occasionally, until the grains are just barely tender, about 15 minutes. Season with salt and pepper and continue cooking, stirring occasionally, until the grits are tender, about 10 minutes longer.

2. In a small skillet, melt 1 tablespoon of the butter. Add the corn and cook over high heat until crisp-tender, about 2 minutes. Stir the corn into the grits along with the remaining 2 tablespoons of butter. Serve warm. —*Adam Perry Lang*

MAKE AHEAD The grits can be kept at room temperature for up to 2 hours. Add a few tablespoons of warm water to thin the grits before reheating over moderate heat, stirring occasionally.

SAUTÉED CHICKPEAS WITH HAM AND KALE

Sautéed Chickpeas with Ham and Kale

TOTAL: 1 HR 10 MIN

6 SERVINGS ● ●

"I grew up in a ranching family in West Texas," says Austin pit master Louis Lambert, "and every summer when it was time to work cattle—branding and shipping—a camp cook would prepare three meals a day over an open fire for all of the cowboys." One of the cook's staple dishes was chickpeas simmered in a large Dutch oven with a smoked ham hock and lots of onion, garlic and chiles. Lambert's version also includes robust sautéed kale.

- 2 **tablespoons annatto seeds (achiote)**
- 6 **tablespoons extra-virgin olive oil**
- 1 **small onion, cut into 1-inch dice**
- 2 **plum tomatoes, cut into 1-inch dice**

One 4-ounce piece of smoked, cured ham, sliced ½ inch thick and cut into ½-inch dice

Salt and freshly ground black pepper

- 4 **garlic cloves, very finely chopped**

One 19-ounce can chickpeas, drained

- 2 **tablespoons pure ancho chile powder**
- 1 **teaspoon dried oregano**
- ½ **cup water**
- ½ **pound kale, stems discarded and leaves coarsely chopped**
- 2 **tablespoons fresh lemon juice**

1. In a small saucepan, cook the annato seeds in the olive oil over low heat for about 5 minutes. Remove the saucepan from the heat and let stand for 5 minutes. Strain the oil through a sieve set over a small bowl and discard the annatto seeds.

2. In a large skillet, heat 2 tablespoons of the annatto oil. Add the diced onion and cook over moderate heat, stirring occasionally, until the onion is starting to brown, about 8 minutes. Add the diced tomatoes and ham and season with salt and black pepper. Cook over high heat, stirring occasionally, until the tomatoes soften, about 3 minutes. Scrape the mixture into a medium bowl.

3. Wipe out the skillet. Add the remaining ¼ cup of annatto oil and the chopped garlic and cook over moderate heat, stirring, until golden, about 2 minutes. Add the drained chickpeas and cook over moderately high heat, stirring occasionally, until the chickpeas are starting to brown, about 3 minutes. Add the ancho chile powder and dried oregano and cook, stirring, until the seasonings are fragrant, about 1 minute. Add the reserved tomato-ham mixture and the water and bring to a boil. Lower the heat to moderate and add the chopped kale. Cover and cook, stirring occasionally, until the kale is just tender, about 5 minutes. Stir in the fresh lemon juice and season with salt and black pepper. Transfer the chickpeas and kale to a large serving bowl and serve immediately.

—*Louis Lambert*

MAKE AHEAD The Sautéed Chickpeas with Ham and Kale can be refrigerated overnight. Reheat gently.

Vegetables à la Grecque

 TOTAL: 45 MIN

8 SERVINGS ● ● ●

In France, mixed vegetables such as carrots, onions and mushrooms prepared *à la Grecque* ("in the Greek style") are cooked with vinegar or lemon, olive oil and coriander and other seasonings, then allowed to marinate in the refrigerator and served cool. The vegetables can be served as a first course, perhaps with a slice of pâté, or as a piquant accompaniment to cold roasted meats or poultry.

- ¼ **cup plus 2 tablespoons extra-virgin olive oil**
- ½ **cup dry white wine**
- ½ **cup water**
- ¼ **cup white wine vinegar**
- 1 **teaspoon coriander seeds**
- 3 **bay leaves**
- ½ **teaspoon whole black peppercorns**
- ½ **teaspoon fennel seeds**
- ½ **teaspoon dried thyme**

Salt

- 1 **pound carrots, peeled and cut into 2-by-½-inch sticks**
- 1½ **pounds medium onions, cut into eighths**
- 12 **ounces small white mushrooms, quartered**

Freshly ground black pepper

1. In a large, deep skillet, combine ¼ cup of the olive oil with the white wine, water, white wine vinegar, coriander seeds, bay leaves, black peppercorns, fennel seeds, dried thyme and 1 teaspoon of salt. Bring the mixture to a boil over high heat. Stir in the carrot sticks until well coated with the liquid and seasonings. Cover and simmer over moderate heat, stirring occasionally, until the carrots are barely tender, about 5 minutes. Stir in the onion wedges and mushroom quarters, cover the skillet and simmer, stirring occasionally, until the onions are crisp-tender, about 3 minutes.

2. Transfer the vegetables, seasonings and cooking liquid to a large bowl and let cool to room temperature, stirring occasionally. Stir in the remaining 2 tablespoons of olive oil and season with salt and black pepper. Remove and discard the bay leaves and black peppercorns before serving the vegetables at room temperature or chilled.

—*Jacques Pépin*

MAKE AHEAD The Vegetables à la Grecque can be refrigerated in a covered container for up to 1 week. Serve chilled or bring to room temperature before serving.

● HEALTHY ● MAKE AHEAD ● VEGETARIAN ● STAFF FAVORITE

desserts & brunch

desserts

Poached Pear and Brown Butter Tart

ACTIVE: 1 HR; TOTAL: 2 HR 30 MIN

12 SERVINGS ● ○ ○

CRUST

Vegetable oil spray, such as
    canola, for the pan

1¾ cups all-purpose flour

¼ cup sugar

Pinch of salt

1½ sticks unsalted butter,
    cut into ½ inch pieces
    and chilled

1 large egg yolk mixed with
    4 tablespoons of ice water

PEARS

6 cups water

2 cups semidry white wine,
    such as Riesling

2 cups sugar

1 sage leaf

4 whole cloves

One 3-inch cinnamon stick

1 vanilla bean, split and
    seeds scraped

4 Bosc pears—peeled,
    quartered and cored

FILLING

4 tablespoons unsalted butter

2 large eggs

½ cup sugar

½ vanilla bean, split
    and seeds scraped

½ teaspoon finely grated
    orange zest

Pinch of salt

¼ cup all-purpose flour

1. MAKE THE CRUST: Preheat the oven to 375°. Spray an 11-inch tart pan with a removable bottom with vegetable oil spray. In a food processor, pulse the flour with the sugar and salt once or twice until combined. Add the butter and pulse until it is the size of small peas. Lift the lid and sprinkle with the egg yolk mixture. Pulse 5 or 6 times, until crumbly.

2. Place the dough into the tart pan and press to form an even crust. Use a flat-bottomed glass dipped in flour to tamp it down. Bake in the lower third of the oven for about 25 minutes, until golden brown. Lower the oven temperature to 350°.

3. MEANWHILE, POACH THE PEARS: In a large saucepan, combine the water with the wine, sugar, sage, cloves, cinnamon and vanilla bean and seeds and bring to a boil.

Simmer for 5 minutes, then add the quartered pears. Cover with a large sheet of parchment paper and a lid slightly smaller than the saucepan and cook over moderate heat until the pears are just softened, 25 to 30 minutes. Using a slotted spoon, transfer the poached pears to a paper towel–lined plate and let cool slightly. Cut each wedge in half lengthwise.

4. MAKE THE FILLING: In a small skillet, cook the butter over moderate heat until golden brown and fragrant, about 4 minutes, then pour it into a small cup. In a medium bowl, using an electric mixer, beat the eggs with the sugar, vanilla seeds, orange zest and salt. Add the flour and beat at low speed until smooth. Add the brown butter and beat the filling at low speed until the ingredients are well combined.

5. Pour the filling into the baked crust. Arrange all but 3 of the pear wedges on the custard in a slightly overlapping circle, with the narrow ends pointing toward the center. Trim the remaining 3 pear wedges and arrange them neatly in the center. Place the tart pan on a baking sheet and bake for about 1 hour, until the custard is golden and set. Let the pear tart cool completely before serving. —*John Besh*

PÈRE ROUX'S CAKE (P. 92)
AND POACHED PEAR AND
BROWN BUTTER TART (P. 88)

BRÛLÉED KEY LIME TART

JACQUES PÉPIN'S FAVORITE POUND CAKE

Brûléed Key Lime Tarts

ACTIVE: 25 MIN; TOTAL: 3 HR 30 MIN

4 SERVINGS ● ○ ○

- 10 Oreo cookies
- 2 tablespoons melted butter
- 5 egg yolks

One 14-ounce can sweetened
    condensed milk

- ⅔ cup Key lime juice

Finely grated zest of 1 lime

- 3 tablespoons granulated sugar,
    plus 8 teaspoons for sprinkling
- 3 kaffir lime leaves
    (optional; see Note)

Pinch of salt

1. Preheat the oven to 350°. In a food processor, finely grind the Oreos. Pulse in the butter. Lightly spray four 4½-inch fluted tartlet pans with removable bottoms; press the ground Oreos into the bottoms. Set the pans on a baking sheet and bake for 8 minutes, or until the edges look dry. Let cool.

2. In a bowl, whisk the egg yolks, condensed milk, ⅓ cup of the Key lime juice and the grated lime zest. Pour the filling into the prepared pans and bake at 325° for about 15 minutes, until the edges are just firm. Let cool for 30 minutes, then freeze until very cold, about 2 hours.

3. In a small saucepan, combine the 3 tablespoons of sugar with 3 tablespoons of water, the lime leaves and the salt. Cook until the sugar has dissolved, then let cool. Discard the lime leaves. Stir in the remaining ⅓ cup of lime juice and refrigerate.

4. Sprinkle 2 teaspoons of sugar over each tart and caramelize with a blow torch. Unmold the tarts and place in shallow bowls. Pour in the Key lime sauce and serve.
—*Gray Kunz*

SERVE WITH Sweetened whipped cream.
NOTE Native to Southeast Asia, aromatic fresh kaffir lime leaves are available from Asian markets and importfood.com.

Jacques Pépin's Favorite Pound Cake

ACTIVE: 15 MIN; TOTAL: 2 HR PLUS
COOLING

MAKES ONE 10-INCH LOAF ● ● ○

The French call pound cake *quatre-quarts* ("four-fourths") because it is made with equal parts flour, sugar, eggs and butter. Contributing editor Jacques Pépin's mother, aunt and cousin all have their versions. Pépin likes to fold in candied citrus peels to make a French fruit cake; he also loves plain slices dipped in espresso.

- 2½ sticks unsalted butter,
    softened
- 1¼ cups sugar
- 1 teaspoon pure vanilla extract
- ¼ teaspoon salt
- 6 large eggs
- ¼ cup milk, at room
    temperature
- 2½ cups cake flour

1. Preheat the oven to 325°. Butter a 10-by-5-inch loaf pan. Line the bottom with a strip of parchment paper that extends 2 inches past the short ends of the pan.

2. In a bowl, using an electric mixer, beat the butter with the sugar, vanilla and salt at medium speed until fluffy, 3 minutes. Add the eggs 2 at a time, beating between additions. Beat in the milk. Sift the flour over the batter and whisk it in until smooth. Scrape the batter into the prepared pan and smooth the surface.

3. Bake the cake for 1½ hours, until it is cracked down the center, golden on top and a toothpick inserted into the center comes out clean. Let the cake cool in the pan on a wire rack for 10 minutes, then unmold the cake and let cool completely. —*Jacques Pépin*

MAKE AHEAD The cooled pound cake can be kept at room temperature, covered, for up to 3 days.

Lemon Chess Pie

ACTIVE: 30 MIN; TOTAL: 2 HR PLUS COOLING

MAKES ONE 9-INCH PIE ● ○

Chess pie, a classic Southern dessert, is basically a very simple custard in a pie crust. A common variation, like the one here, uses lemon juice. The origin of the name is not clear, but some speculate that it's based on an old custom of calling custard "cheese." Atlanta baker Angie Mosier's take on the pie has a wonderfully tender, flaky crust and a sweet, puckery filling.

PASTRY

1⅓ cups all-purpose flour,
    plus more for rolling
1½ teaspoons sugar
½ teaspoon salt
4 tablespoons chilled unsalted
    butter, cut into cubes
¼ cup plus ½ tablespoon
    chilled solid vegetable
    shortening
3 tablespoons ice water

FILLING

4 large eggs
1½ cups sugar
1 tablespoon white cornmeal
1 tablespoon all-purpose
    flour
½ teaspoon salt
5 tablespoons unsalted
    butter, melted
½ cup buttermilk
⅓ cup fresh lemon juice
Finely grated zest of 1 lemon
1 teaspoon pure vanilla extract

1. MAKE THE PASTRY: In a food processor, pulse the flour with the sugar and salt until combined. Add the butter and shortening and pulse just until the butter is the size of small peas. Sprinkle the ice water over the mixture and pulse 4 or 5 times, until the pastry just comes together. Turn the pastry out onto a floured work surface and pat it into a disk. Wrap in plastic and refrigerate until chilled, about 30 minutes.

2. Preheat the oven to 350°. On a floured work surface, roll out the pastry to a 14-inch round. Carefully roll the pastry around the rolling pin and unroll it over a 9-inch pie plate; ease the pastry into the plate without stretching or tearing. Trim the overhanging dough to ½ inch and tuck it under itself; crimp the edge decoratively. Freeze the pie shell just until chilled, about 5 minutes.

3. Line the pastry with parchment paper and pie weights or dried beans and bake for about 20 minutes, until nearly set. Remove the parchment paper and weights and bake the pie shell for 5 minutes longer, until set but not colored.

4. MEANWHILE, MAKE THE FILLING: In a bowl, beat the eggs with the sugar. Add all of the remaining ingredients one at a time and in order, whisking until smooth.

5. Pour the filling into the warm pie shell. Bake for about 30 minutes, until the custard is golden and nearly set but still quite jiggly; cover the edge of the pie shell with

foil halfway through baking. Transfer the Lemon Chess Pie to a rack to cool completely before serving. —*Angie Mosier*

MAKE AHEAD The pie can be refrigerated overnight. Serve at room temperature.

Applesauce–Chocolate Chip Bundt Cake

ACTIVE: 15 MIN; TOTAL: 2 HR

12 SERVINGS ● ● ●

2½ cups all-purpose flour, plus
    more for dusting
1½ cups granulated sugar
2 teaspoons baking soda
2 teaspoons cinnamon
1 teaspoon ground cardamom
1 teaspoon salt
½ teaspoon ground cloves
½ teaspoon freshly ground pepper
2 cups unsweetened applesauce
2 large eggs, lightly beaten
½ cup vegetable oil
1 stick unsalted butter, melted
One 12-ounce bag semisweet
    chocolate chips
Confectioners' sugar, for dusting
Crème fraîche, for serving

1. Preheat the oven to 350°. Butter and flour a 12-cup Bundt pan. In a large bowl, whisk the flour with the granulated sugar, baking soda, cinnamon, cardamom, salt, cloves and pepper. Whisk in the applesauce, eggs, oil and melted butter. Fold in the chocolate chips.

2. Scrape the batter into the prepared pan. Bake for 1 hour and 15 minutes, or until a toothpick inserted in the center comes out with a few crumbs attached.

3. Transfer the pan to a rack and let the cake cool for 10 minutes, then invert it onto the rack and let cool completely, about 20 minutes. Sift confectioners' sugar over the cake, slice and serve with crème fraîche. —*Kristin Donnelly*

MAKE AHEAD The Bundt cake can be stored in an airtight container at room temperature for up to 3 days.

Lane Cake

TOTAL: 2 HR PLUS 4 HR STANDING

12 TO 16 SERVINGS ● ○

Lane cake, a Southern specialty, was created by Emma Rylander Lane, an Alabamian who wrote the cookbook *Some Good Things to Eat* around the turn of the 20th century. Typically, it's a large white cake with a filling of egg yolks, sugar, raisins, pecans, fresh coconut and lots of bourbon. The bourbon in the filling is key—it helps cut the sweetness a bit.

CAKE

- 3½ cups all-purpose flour
- 1 tablespoon baking powder
- ¼ teaspoon salt
- 2 sticks unsalted butter, at room temperature
- 2 cups sugar
- 1 teaspoon pure vanilla extract
- 1 cup milk
- 8 large egg whites (reserve the yolks for the filling)

FILLING

- 1½ cups pecans (6 ounces)
- 1½ sticks unsalted butter
- 12 large egg yolks
- 1½ cups sugar
- 1½ cups unsweetened shredded coconut
- 1½ cups golden raisins, coarsely chopped
- ¼ cup bourbon

TECHNIQUE

making candied nuts

Beat 1 egg white with ½ cup of sugar until foamy. Toss with 1 cup of unsalted nuts. With a fork, transfer to a buttered baking sheet and bake at 300° until brown, about 35 minutes; let cool.

BUTTERCREAM

- 2 sticks unsalted butter, at room temperature
- 1 teaspoon pure vanilla extract
- ¼ teaspoon salt
- 1 pound confectioners' sugar, sifted
- ¼ cup half-and-half or milk

1. MAKE THE CAKE: Preheat the oven to 325°. Butter three 9-inch round cake pans. Line the bottoms with parchment paper; butter the paper and flour the pans. In a large bowl, whisk the flour, baking powder and salt. In a standing electric mixer fitted with a paddle attachment, beat the butter and sugar at medium speed until light and fluffy. Beat in the vanilla. At low speed, beat in the dry ingredients and the milk in 3 alternating batches; be sure to scrape the side and bottom of the bowl.

2. In a clean bowl, beat the egg whites until soft peaks form. Beat one-third of the egg whites into the cake batter. Using a rubber spatula, fold in the remaining beaten whites until combined. Divide the cake batter among the prepared pans. Bake for 25 to 30 minutes, until the cakes are lightly golden and springy to the touch. Let the cakes cool in the pans for a few minutes, then invert them onto wire racks to cool completely. Peel off the parchment paper from the bottoms.

3. MEANWHILE, MAKE THE FILLING: Spread the pecans on a baking sheet and toast for 10 minutes, until fragrant. Let cool, then coarsely chop. In a medium saucepan, melt the butter over low heat. Remove the saucepan from the heat and whisk in the egg yolks and sugar until smooth. Return the pan to moderate heat and cook, stirring constantly, until the filling is slightly thickened and an instant-read thermometer reads 180°; be sure not to let it boil. Remove from the heat and stir in the chopped pecans, coconut, raisins and bourbon. Transfer the filling to a bowl and let cool.

4. MAKE THE BUTTERCREAM: In a medium bowl, beat the butter until creamy. Add the vanilla and salt, then gradually beat in the confectioners' sugar, being sure to scrape the side and bottom of the bowl. Add the half-and-half and beat the buttercream until fluffy, about 1 minute.

5. ASSEMBLE THE CAKE: Place a cake layer on a serving plate and top with one-third of the pecan filling, spreading it almost to the edge. Top with a second cake layer and another third of the pecan filling. Top with the last cake layer. Using an offset spatula, spread a thin layer of the buttercream all around the cake, being sure to fill in any gaps between the layers. Refrigerate the cake for 10 minutes, to firm up the buttercream.

6. Spread the remaining buttercream evenly around the side of the cake only, leaving the top with just the thin layer of buttercream. Spread the remaining pecan filling over the top of the cake. Let the cake stand at room temperature for at least 4 hours before cutting. —*Angie Mosier*

Père Roux's Cake

ACTIVE: 1 HR 30 MIN; TOTAL: 3 HR PLUS 2 HR CHILLING

12 SERVINGS ● ○

Père Roux refers to Father Roux, a New Orleans priest and cook who is one of chef John Besh's friends. Besh fashioned this recipe after one that Père Roux bakes for himself every year on his birthday.

CAKE

- 2¾ cups all-purpose flour, plus more for dusting
- 1 tablespoon baking powder
- ½ teaspoon salt
- 1 cup solid vegetable shortening
- 2¼ cups sugar
- 1½ cups skim milk
- 7 large egg whites, at room temperature
- 1 teaspoon pure vanilla extract
- ½ teaspoon pure almond extract

FILLING

2 sticks unsalted butter

1¾ cups lightly packed
light brown sugar

½ teaspoon cinnamon

6 overripe bananas,
coarsely mashed

½ cup plus 2 tablespoons
Myers's dark rum

FROSTING

2 sticks unsalted butter, softened

1½ cups confectioners' sugar

1½ teaspoons pure vanilla extract

¼ teaspoon pure almond extract

¼ pound cream cheese, softened

1. MAKE THE CAKE: Preheat the oven to 350°. Butter two 9-inch round cake pans. Line the bottoms with rounds of wax paper and butter the paper. Dust the pans with flour, tapping out the excess.

2. In the bowl of a standing electric mixer fitted with a paddle, mix the flour, baking powder and salt. Add the shortening and mix at low speed until evenly blended. Add the sugar and mix at medium speed until a mass forms around the paddle. At low speed, gradually add ¾ cup of the milk and beat until smooth, scraping down the side of the bowl from time to time.

3. In a medium bowl, whisk the egg whites with the remaining ¾ cup of milk and the vanilla and almond extracts. With the machine on, gradually beat the egg white mixture into the batter at medium speed until silky, about 5 minutes. Scrape the batter into the prepared pans and bake for 30 to 35 minutes, until golden and springy. Transfer the cakes to a rack and let cool for 15 minutes in the pans, then invert them onto the rack and let cool completely. Peel off the wax paper and slice each cake in half horizontally.

4. MEANWHILE, MAKE THE FILLING: In a large saucepan, cook the butter, brown sugar and cinnamon over moderately high heat until the butter and sugar have melted. Remove from the heat and add the bananas and ½ cup of the rum. Cook over moderate heat, stirring frequently, until the filling is very thick and the butter just begins to separate, about 25 minutes.

5. Transfer the filling to a food processor. Add the remaining 2 tablespoons of rum and puree until smooth. Let the filling cool to room temperature, about 30 minutes.

6. MAKE THE FROSTING: In the bowl of a standing electric mixer fitted with a whisk, beat the butter at medium speed until creamy and fluffy, about 3 minutes. Add the confectioners' sugar and beat at low speed until incorporated. Scrape down the side of the bowl; add the vanilla and almond extracts and beat at medium-high speed until fluffy, about 3 minutes. Beat in the cream cheese until light and fluffy, about 3 minutes.

7. Place a cake layer on a large plate, spoon one-third of the filling on top and spread it to the edge. Top with another cake layer, pressing gently; spread with another third of the filling. Repeat with the remaining cake layers and filling, ending with a cake layer. Spread the frosting over the top and side of the cake and refrigerate for at least 2 hours, or until set. Bring the cake to room temperature before serving.

—John Besh

MAKE AHEAD The cake can be refrigerated overnight. Bring to room temperature before serving.

Cardamom-Spiced Crumb Cake

**ACTIVE: 30 MIN; TOTAL: 1 HR 30 MIN
PLUS COOLING**

15 SERVINGS ●●

CRUMB TOPPING

2 cups pecans

2 sticks unsalted butter, melted

¾ cup light brown sugar

½ cup granulated sugar

½ teaspoon ground cardamom

½ teaspoon salt

2⅔ cups all-purpose flour

CAKE

3 cups all-purpose flour

1¼ cups sugar

1½ teaspoons baking powder

1 teaspoon salt

2 large eggs

1 cup whole milk

1½ sticks unsalted butter, melted

2 teaspoons pure vanilla extract

GLAZE

½ cup confectioners' sugar

2 tablespoons unsalted butter,
melted

2 teaspoons whole milk

½ teaspoon pure vanilla extract

1. Preheat the oven to 350°. Position a rack in the center of the oven. Butter a 9-by-13-inch metal baking pan.

2. MAKE THE CRUMB TOPPING: Spread the pecans on a rimmed baking sheet and toast for 8 minutes, until browned. Let cool, then coarsely chop the nuts.

3. In a medium bowl, stir the melted butter with both sugars, the cardamom and salt. Add the flour and stir until clumpy. Stir in the chopped nuts.

4. MAKE THE CAKE: In a large bowl, whisk the flour with the sugar, baking powder and salt. In a medium bowl, whisk the eggs with the milk, melted butter and vanilla. Add the egg mixture to the dry ingredients and stir until just combined. Scrape the batter into the prepared baking pan, smoothing the surface. Scatter the crumbs in large clumps over the cake; the crumb layer will be quite deep.

5. Bake for about 55 minutes, until the crumbs are golden and firm and a tester inserted in the center of the cake comes out clean. If the crumbs brown before the cake is done, cover the cake loosely with foil. Transfer to a rack to cool.

6. MAKE THE GLAZE: In a bowl, whisk all of the glaze ingredients together. Drizzle the glaze over the cake; let cool slightly. Serve warm or at room temperature.

—Kate Heddings

Walnut Cake with Cinnamon Glaze

ACTIVE: 20 MIN; TOTAL: 2 HR 30 MIN

12 SERVINGS ● ●

New York City chef Tom Valenti's inspiration for this cake was a holiday memory: "When I was a kid, a huge bowl of mixed nuts would always appear on the table around Christmastime."

    1   cup walnut halves
    2   cups all-purpose flour
 1¼   teaspoons cinnamon
    1   teaspoon baking powder
    1   teaspoon baking soda
   ½   teaspoon salt
    2   sticks unsalted butter, softened
    1   cup granulated sugar
    1   teaspoon pure vanilla extract
    3   large eggs, separated
    1   cup crème fraîche (8 ounces)
    1   cup confectioners' sugar
    2   tablespoons half-and-half

1. Preheat the oven to 350°. Butter and flour a 10-cup Bundt pan. Spread the walnut halves in a pie plate and toast for about 8 minutes, until golden brown. Let cool, then coarsely chop.

2. In a medium bowl, whisk the flour with 1 teaspoon of the cinnamon, the baking powder, baking soda and salt. In a large bowl, using a handheld electric mixer, beat the butter until creamy. Beat in the granulated sugar and vanilla until fluffy. Beat in the egg yolks 1 at a time, then beat in the crème fraîche. Beat in the dry ingredients at low speed. Fold in the walnuts.

3. In a clean bowl, using clean beaters, beat the egg whites until firm peaks form. Beat one-third of the whites into the batter, then fold in the remaining whites until no streaks remain. Scrape the batter into the prepared pan and smooth the surface. Bake in the middle of the oven for 50 minutes, until a toothpick inserted in the center comes out clean. Let cool in the pan for 20 minutes, then invert the cake onto a rack and let cool completely.

4. Whisk the confectioners' sugar with the half-and-half and the remaining ¼ teaspoon of cinnamon. Pour the glaze over the cake, allowing it to drip down the side; let cool until set. —*Tom Valenti*

MAKE AHEAD The glazed walnut cake can be stored in an airtight container at room temperature for up to 3 days.

Feta Cheesecake and Wine-Poached Dates

ACTIVE: 40 MIN; TOTAL: 5 HR

12 SERVINGS ● ● ●

  10   ounces feta (preferably French), crumbled (2 cups)
 2¼   cups sugar
 1½   teaspoons all-purpose flour
  22   ounces cream cheese, at room temperature
    5   large eggs
    2   large egg yolks
    2   tablespoons heavy cream
 1½   cups dry red wine
    1   vanilla bean, split lengthwise and seeds scraped
    3   white peppercorns
    2   tablespoons fresh lemon juice
  24   Medjool dates, pitted (8 ounces)
    4   sheets of phyllo dough
    6   tablespoons unsalted butter, melted

1. Preheat the oven to 300°. Spray a 9-by-13-by-2-inch glass baking dish with vegetable oil spray. Line the dish with aluminum foil, making sure to press it into the corners; spray the foil.

2. In a standing electric mixer fitted with a paddle, beat the feta with 1½ cups of the sugar and the flour at medium-low speed until creamy. Add the cream cheese and beat until blended. Add the whole eggs and egg yolks 1 at a time, beating well between additions; scrape down the side of the bowl as necessary. Beat in the heavy cream. Pour the cheesecake mixture into the prepared baking dish.

3. Set the dish in a large roasting pan. Add enough warm water to the pan to reach halfway up the side of the dish. Bake on the bottom rack of the oven for about 1 hour, until firm and set. Transfer the baking dish to a rack and let cool to room temperature, then freeze until very firm but not frozen solid, 3 to 4 hours.

4. Meanwhile, in a large saucepan, combine the red wine with the vanilla bean and seeds, peppercorns, lemon juice and the remaining ¾ cup of sugar and bring to a simmer over moderate heat. Add the dates and simmer until plump, about 10 minutes. Transfer the dates to a bowl and boil the liquid until it has reduced to 1 cup, about 10 minutes. Let the syrup cool completely, then strain it over the dates.

5. Preheat the oven to 350°. Brush 1 sheet of the phyllo dough with melted butter. Cover with a second sheet and brush with butter. Repeat with the remaining 2 phyllo sheets, buttering between them. Cut the layered phyllo into 3-inch squares (you should have 24). Transfer the squares to a large baking sheet. Cover with a sheet of parchment paper and top with a baking sheet to keep the phyllo flat. Bake for about 15 minutes, until golden and crisp. Remove the top baking sheet and let the phyllo squares cool.

6. Invert the chilled cheesecake onto a cutting board and peel off the foil. Using a hot, moist knife, cut the cake into twelve 3-inch squares. Set a cheesecake square on each of 12 phyllo squares and top with the remaining squares. Transfer the cheesecakes to plates. Drizzle some of the red wine syrup around each plate and garnish with the dates. —*Eric Estrella*

MAKE AHEAD The cheesecake can be covered and refrigerated for up to 2 days. The dates can be stored in their syrup in an airtight container in the refrigerator for up to 3 days. The baked phyllo squares can be stored in an airtight container for up to 2 days; crisp them again in the oven.

Lebanese Rice Pudding with Cinnamon and Caraway

TOTAL: 1 HR 25 MIN PLUS OVERNIGHT SOAKING AND CHILLING

8 SERVINGS ●○

This pudding is made with finely milled rice flour, seasoned with cinnamon and caraway and garnished with walnuts, pine nuts and slivered almonds. Known as *meghli,* the sweet is traditionally served in Lebanon at birthdays and holidays.

- 1 tablespoon caraway seeds
- 9 cups water
- 1 cup rice flour (see Note)
- 2 cups granulated sugar
- ½ teaspoon cinnamon
- 1 cup walnut halves
- ½ cup slivered almonds
- ½ cup pine nuts

Confectioners' sugar, for dusting

1. In a spice grinder, grind the caraway seeds to a coarse powder.

2. Pour the water into a large saucepan. Whisk in the rice flour, granulated sugar, ground caraway and cinnamon. Bring to a boil over moderate heat, whisking constantly. Reduce the heat to moderately low and simmer, whisking often, until the pudding is very thick, about 1 hour and 10 minutes. Transfer to a bowl and let cool to room temperature. Cover the pudding and refrigerate overnight.

3. Meanwhile, place the walnuts, almonds and pine nuts in separate small bowls and cover with water. Let them stand at room temperature overnight. Drain well.

4. To serve, spoon the pudding into bowls and sprinkle with the nuts. Dust with confectioners' sugar and serve. —*Rita Nakouzi*

NOTE Rice flour is made from milled white rice and has the fine texture of cornstarch. It is available at major supermarkets and online at kalustyans.com.

MAKE AHEAD The pudding can be refrigerated for up to 3 days.

Pumpkin Cheesecake

ACTIVE: 50 MIN; TOTAL: 3 HR 50 MIN PLUS OVERNIGHT CHILLING

MAKES ONE 9-INCH CAKE ●○

Fresh cream cheese, which has a light, creamy texture, gives this cheesecake its wonderful mousselike airiness.

- 6 ounces broken gingersnaps
- 4 tablespoons unsalted butter, melted

Vegetable oil, for oiling

One 2-pound sugar pumpkin or buttercup or kabocha squash, halved and seeded

- 1½ pounds cream cheese, softened
- 1 teaspoon cinnamon
- ½ teaspoon ground ginger
- ¼ teaspoon ground allspice
- ¼ teaspoon ground cloves
- ½ teaspoon salt
- 1¼ cups granulated maple sugar (see Note)
- 1 cup heavy cream
- 5 large eggs

1. Preheat the oven to 350°. In a food processor, pulse the broken gingersnaps until they're finely ground. Transfer the crumbs to a medium bowl and stir in the melted butter. Pat the crumbs evenly into the bottom of a 9-inch springform pan. Wrap the bottom and side of the pan in a single large sheet of foil. Bake for 8 to 10 minutes, until the crust is firm. Let the crust cool to room temperature.

2. Lightly oil the cut sides of the pumpkin. Place the pumpkin cut side down on a rimmed baking sheet. Bake until tender, about 1 hour. Scoop out the pumpkin flesh and measure out 2 cups. Transfer to a food processor and puree. Let cool.

3. Reduce the oven temperature to 325°. In a large bowl, using a handheld electric mixer, beat the softened cream cheese until smooth. Add the cinnamon, ginger, allspice, cloves, salt and half of the maple sugar and beat until combined. Add the remaining maple sugar and beat until incorporated. Scrape down the side of the bowl and beat in the pumpkin puree, followed by the heavy cream. Add the eggs 1 at a time, beating until blended. Scrape down the side of the bowl again and beat until thoroughly blended, about 1 minute. Pour the pumpkin cheesecake batter into the foil-wrapped springform pan.

4. Set the pan in a baking dish or small roasting pan. Add enough hot water to the dish to reach halfway up the side of the springform pan. Bake the cheesecake for 1 hour, or until the filling is set around the edge and slightly jiggly in the center when the pan is gently shaken. Turn off the oven, close the oven door and leave the cheesecake in for about 1 hour to gradually slow the cooking. Transfer the cheesecake to a wire rack and let cool completely. Cover the cake with plastic wrap and refrigerate overnight.

5. Remove the foil and the springform pan ring. Using a hot knife, cut the cheesecake into wedges, rinsing the blade with hot water between each slice. Transfer to plates and serve. —*Jeremy Silansky*

NOTE Maple sugar is made by boiling down maple sap until it crystallizes. It is available from many maple syrup producers, such as vermontmapleoutlet.com.

MAKE AHEAD The Pumpkin Cheesecake can be refrigerated for up to 3 days.

TECHNIQUE

making fruit sorbets

When a dessert calls for poaching and then draining fruit, save the syrupy cooking liquid to churn into sorbet in an ice cream maker or to freeze into granita (as in the recipe on p. 100).

Rich and Creamy Butterscotch Pudding

TOTAL: 45 MIN PLUS 4 HR COOLING

6 SERVINGS ● ○

- 3½ cups plus 1½ tablespoons heavy cream
- 2 teaspoons Scotch
- 1½ teaspoons dark brown sugar
- 1 teaspoon water
- ½ teaspoon salt
- 5 large egg yolks
- ½ vanilla bean, split lengthwise and seeds scraped
- 1 cup butterscotch chips (6 ounces)

Whipped cream and store-bought caramel sauce, for serving

1. Fill a medium bowl with ice water. Set a fine-mesh sieve in another medium bowl; set the bowl in the ice water bath.

2. In a small skillet, combine 1½ tablespoons of the cream with the Scotch, brown sugar, water and salt and cook over moderate heat just until the sugar is dissolved. Let cool slightly.

3. Put the egg yolks in a medium bowl. In a heavy, medium saucepan, bring the remaining 3½ cups of cream to a simmer with the vanilla bean and seeds. Remove from the heat. Add the butterscotch chips to the hot cream and let stand until melted, 2 to 3 minutes. Whisk until smooth. Gradually add the hot butterscotch mixture to the egg yolks, whisking constantly.

4. Return the mixture to the saucepan and cook over low heat, stirring constantly with a heatproof rubber spatula, until thick, about 15 minutes. Do not let it boil. Strain the pudding into the bowl in the ice bath and stir in the Scotch mixture.

5. Pour the pudding into glasses and refrigerate until thoroughly set, at least 4 hours or overnight. Serve the pudding with whipped cream and caramel sauce.
—*Lisa Sewall*

MAKE AHEAD The pudding can be refrigerated for up to 3 days.

Sticky Toffee Pudding

ACTIVE: 30 MIN; TOTAL: 2 HR 30 MIN

12 SERVINGS ● ○

CAKE

- ½ pound Medjool dates (about 14), pitted and coarsely chopped

Two 4-inch cinnamon sticks

- 2 cups boiling water
- 4 ounces unsalted butter, softened
- 2 cups dark brown sugar
- 1 vanilla bean, split lengthwise and seeds scraped (reserve the pod for another use)
- 2 large eggs
- 3 cups all-purpose flour
- 1 teaspoon baking soda

TOFFEE SAUCE

- 2 cups heavy cream
- 1 pound dark brown sugar (2¼ cups)
- 2 sticks unsalted butter

Sweetened whipped cream, for serving

1. MAKE THE CAKE: Preheat the oven to 350°. Butter an 8-by-12-inch glass baking dish. In a heatproof bowl, cover the dates and cinnamon sticks with the boiling water and let stand for 30 minutes. Drain in a colander and discard the cinnamon.

2. In a large bowl, using an electric mixer, beat the softened butter with the brown sugar and vanilla seeds until the mixture is fluffy. Beat in the eggs 1 at a time, scraping down the side of the bowl after each addition. In a medium bowl, whisk the flour with the baking soda. Add the dry ingredients to the brown sugar mixture and beat at low speed until blended, then stir in the chopped dates. Scrape the batter into the baking dish and bake for 45 minutes, or until the cake is springy and a toothpick inserted in the center comes out clean.

3. MEANWHILE, MAKE THE TOFFEE SAUCE: In a medium saucepan, bring the heavy cream to a boil with the brown sugar. Add the butter and stir over moderate heat until melted; keep warm.

4. Using a fork, poke holes all over the top of the warm date cake. Drizzle 2 cups of the hot toffee sauce over the cake. Return the cake to the oven and bake for 5 minutes longer, until the toffee sauce is bubbling around the edges but not fully absorbed. Let the cake cool until most of the sauce has been absorbed, about 1 hour, poking additional holes from time to time to help it absorb more sauce.

5. Cut the cake into squares and serve on plates with a dollop of whipped cream and the remaining toffee sauce on the side.
—*Michel Nischan*

MAKE AHEAD The cake can be prepared through Step 4 and kept covered overnight at room temperature.

Gianduja Mousse

 **TOTAL: 30 MIN**

4 SERVINGS ● ○

The chocolate-hazelnut spread gianduja is delicious straight off the spoon, but when F&W's Grace Parisi folds in whipped cream and crème fraîche, she creates a truly decadent (and ridiculously easy) mousse. For a supereasy ice cream sandwich, spoon the mousse between chocolate wafers and freeze overnight.

- ½ cup chocolate-hazelnut paste, such as Nutella
- ¼ cup crème fraîche
- 1½ teaspoons brandy or hazelnut liqueur
- ½ cup heavy cream

Chocolate wafer cookies, for serving

In a medium bowl, using an electric mixer, beat the chocolate-hazelnut paste with the crème fraîche and brandy at low speed until smooth. In another bowl, beat the heavy cream until firm peaks form. Using a rubber spatula, fold the whipped cream into the chocolate-hazelnut mixture until no streaks remain. Spoon the mousse into small bowls and refrigerate for 20 minutes. Serve with the chocolate wafer cookies.
—*Grace Parisi*

RICH AND CREAMY
BUTTERSCOTCH PUDDING

New Year's Eve revelers enjoy Palma D'Orazio's Classic Tiramisù.

Kabocha Bread Pudding with Pisco-Soaked Prunes

ACTIVE: 50 MIN; TOTAL: 2 HR 30 MIN

12 SERVINGS ● ○

- 1 cup pitted prunes, coarsely chopped (6 ounces)
- ½ cup pisco or grappa
- 1 pound peeled and cubed kabocha (see Note) or buttercup squash or pumpkin
- One 1-pound loaf of peasant bread, crusts discarded and bread cut into 1-inch cubes (8 cups)
- 1 cup milk
- One 14-ounce can sweetened condensed milk
- Two 12-ounce cans evaporated milk
- ¾ cup dark brown sugar
- 1 teaspoon anise seeds
- 5 whole cloves
- Two 4-inch cinnamon sticks
- 8 allspice berries
- 6 tablespoons unsalted butter, softened
- 6 large egg yolks
- 1 teaspoon pure vanilla extract
- 2 cups granulated sugar
- ¾ cup water
- Crème fraîche and cocoa nibs (see Note), for garnish

1. Preheat the oven to 350°. In a small bowl, cover the prunes with the pisco and let stand for 1 hour, until plump. Meanwhile, bring a medium saucepan of water to a boil. Add the kabocha squash and simmer until tender, about 10 minutes. Drain well. Transfer the squash to a food processor and puree until smooth.

2. Place the bread on a rimmed baking sheet; bake for 15 minutes, until just dry.

3. In a large saucepan, combine the 3 milks with the brown sugar, anise seeds, cloves, cinnamon and allspice and bring just to a simmer, stirring, until the sugar is dissolved, about 2 minutes. Whisk in the pureed squash. Strain the mixture through a fine-mesh sieve set over a large bowl; discard the solids. Whisk the butter, egg yolks and vanilla into the mixture and stir in the toasted bread cubes. Drain the prunes, pressing to extract as much of the soaking liquid as possible, then discard the liquid. Add the prunes to the bowl. Let the bread pudding mixture stand for 20 minutes, pressing to submerge the bread and stirring occasionally, until most of the liquid has been absorbed.

4. Set a 9-by-13-inch baking dish near the stove. In a medium, heavy saucepan, combine the granulated sugar with ½ cup of the water and cook over high heat, stirring until the sugar is dissolved. Using a wet pastry brush, wash down the side of the pan to dissolve any crystals. Cook without stirring until a medium-amber caramel forms, about 8 minutes. Immediately pour half of the caramel into the baking dish, swirling it to coat the bottom. Return the saucepan to the heat and add the remaining ¼ cup of water. Cook until the caramel liquefies, 2 to 3 minutes. Transfer the caramel sauce to a heatproof cup.

5. Pour the bread mixture into the prepared baking dish and smooth the surface. Bake for about 40 minutes, until the pudding is set and lightly browned. Let cool for 20 minutes. Run a knife around the edge of the pudding, set a cutting board on top and invert. Remove the baking dish and cut the bread pudding into squares. Top with a dollop of crème fraîche, a drizzle of the caramel sauce and a sprinkling of cocoa nibs. —*Maricel Presilla*

NOTE Kabocha squash is a sweet-tasting winter squash with pale orange flesh. Cocoa nibs are cocoa beans without their shells. They're available at specialty food stores and online at amazon.com.

MAKE AHEAD The kabocha bread pudding can be covered and refrigerated in the baking dish overnight. Bring the pudding back to room temperature before serving straight from the dish.

Classic Tiramisù

TOTAL: 25 MIN PLUS OVERNIGHT CHILLING

10 SERVINGS ● ○

It's hard to believe that this espresso-flavored Italian dessert (its name means "pick me up") didn't enter the culinary lexicon until the 1960s, when it was invented in the city of Treviso.

- 5 large egg whites
- Salt
- 4 large egg yolks
- ⅓ cup sugar
- Two 8¾-ounce containers mascarpone, at room temperature
- ½ cup strong brewed espresso, cooled
- About 17 ladyfingers (from a 17-ounce package)
- Unsweetened cocoa powder, for dusting
- ½ cup semisweet or bittersweet chocolate curls, made with a vegetable peeler

1. In a medium bowl, using a handheld electric mixer, beat the egg whites with a pinch of salt at high speed until firm peaks form. In another medium bowl, beat the egg yolks with the sugar until pale and thickened. At low speed, beat the mascarpone into the yolk mixture. Fold the beaten whites into the mascarpone mixture.

2. Spread half of the mascarpone mixture in a 9-by-13-inch glass baking dish. Pour the espresso into a shallow bowl. Dip the ladyfingers in the espresso until evenly moistened and arrange in a layer on the mascarpone mixture; you may need to break a few in half to make them fit. Spread the remaining mascarpone mixture on top. Sift cocoa powder over the tiramisù. Cover and refrigerate overnight.

3. Scatter the chocolate curls evenly over the tiramisù and serve. —*Palma D'Orazio*

MAKE AHEAD The tiramisù can be refrigerated for up to 2 days.

Rich Baked Chocolate Puddings

 TOTAL: 40 MIN
8 SERVINGS ●●

Although food blogger Pim Techamuanvivit's deep, dark chocolate pudding is easily made in ramekins, it's also fun to bake and serve in small glass jars. Pim likes the charm of old, mismatched jam jars.

10 ounces bittersweet
    chocolate, coarsely
    chopped
4 large egg yolks
2 large eggs
¼ cup sugar
1 stick plus 6 tablespoons
    (7 ounces) unsalted butter
Sweetened whipped cream
    and chocolate shavings,
    for garnish

1. Preheat the oven to 325°. Arrange eight ½-cup ramekins or 1-cup wide-mouthed jars in a large roasting pan.
2. In a microwave-safe bowl, melt the chocolate at medium power for about 2 minutes, stirring every 30 seconds; let cool.
3. In a large bowl, beat the egg yolks with the whole eggs and sugar until thick and pale, about 4 minutes.
4. In a medium saucepan, melt the butter over moderate heat until sizzling. Remove the saucepan from the heat and whisk in the chocolate until smooth. Add to the egg mixture and beat until thoroughly combined.
5. Spoon the pudding into the ramekins. Carefully fill the roasting pan with enough hot water to reach halfway up the sides of the ramekins. Bake the puddings for about 20 minutes, or until the edges are firm but the centers are still a bit soft. Remove the ramekins from the water bath and let the puddings cool completely. Serve with whipped cream and chocolate shavings. —*Pim Techamuanvivit*

MAKE AHEAD The baked chocolate puddings can be refrigerated for up to 3 days. Serve chilled or at room temperature.

Cartellata Cookies

TOTAL: 1 HR 15 MIN PLUS
OVERNIGHT DRYING
MAKES ABOUT 48 COOKIES ●●

The recipe for these crisp, deep-fried spiral sweets comes from Elena D'Orazio, a cousin of New York City chef Palma D'Orazio. In their native Puglia, *cartellate* are traditionally made around Christmas by bakers and home cooks alike. The cookies are usually drizzled with honey, but for parties, D'Orazio simply sprinkles them with lemon zest and cinnamon sugar.

3 cups all-purpose flour
⅓ cup granulated sugar
½ teaspoon salt
½ cup dry white wine, warmed
¼ cup extra-virgin olive oil
Vegetable oil, for frying
Finely grated zest of 1 lemon
Confectioners' sugar and
    cinnamon, for dusting

1. In a large bowl, whisk the flour with the granulated sugar and salt. Make a well in the center, pour in the wine and olive oil and stir, gradually incorporating the dry ingredients until a dough forms. Transfer to a work surface and knead lightly until smooth. Cut the dough in half and flatten each piece into a disk. Wrap them in plastic and let rest at room temperature for 30 minutes.
2. On a lightly floured work surface, roll out one of the disks to a 12-inch square about ⅛ inch thick. Cut the dough into ½-inch-wide strips. Wrap each strip around itself to form a loose coil; transfer the coils to a cookie sheet. Repeat with the remaining disk of dough. Let the coils dry overnight, turning once.
3. In a medium saucepan, heat 2 inches of oil to 300°. Set a rack over a large baking sheet. Using a wire skimmer, transfer 4 or 5 coils to the hot oil and fry until browned and crisp, about 50 seconds. Transfer the coils to the rack to drain. Repeat with the remaining coils. Sprinkle with the lemon zest. Mix equal amounts of confectioners' sugar and cinnamon and sift over the cookies. Serve warm or at room temperature. —*Elena D'Orazio*

MAKE AHEAD The cookies can be fried earlier in the day. Dust them with lemon zest and cinnamon sugar just before serving.

Blood Orange Granita with Vanilla Ice Cream

TOTAL: 2 HR 45 MIN
8 SERVINGS ●●

When he's grilling outside in winter, Colorado chef Lachlan Mackinnon Patterson likes to make his granita outside too. He'll place a bowl of fresh, bright red blood orange juice in the snow near the grill; as it freezes, he'll occasionally scrape it with a fork to form crystals, and then serve the granita for dessert.

1 cup water
½ cup plus 2 tablespoons sugar
4 cups chilled fresh blood
    orange juice or fresh orange
    juice, strained
1 pint vanilla ice cream,
    for serving

1. In a small saucepan, combine the water and sugar and bring to a simmer, stirring to dissolve the sugar. Remove from the heat and let cool to room temperature.
2. In a 9-by-13-inch glass or ceramic baking dish, stir the sugar syrup into the blood orange juice. Freeze for about 1 hour, or until ice crystals form around the edge. Using a fork, stir the crystals into the center and freeze for about 30 minutes, until a thicker rim of crystals forms around the edge. Stir again and freeze for about 1 hour longer, stirring every 15 minutes or so until all the juice is frozen.
3. Scoop the granita into 8 bowls, top with vanilla ice cream and serve immediately. —*Lachlan Mackinnon Patterson*

MAKE AHEAD The granita can be frozen in an airtight container for up to 2 days; rescrape before serving.

Bacon Baklava

ACTIVE: 50 MIN; TOTAL: 2 HR PLUS
OVERNIGHT SOAKING

MAKES ABOUT 35 PIECES ● ●

Bacon is subtly making its way into desserts. And not so subtly, too: When bacon impresario Dan Philips of the Grateful Palate collaborated on a bacon-themed dinner at the Brown Hotel in Louisville, Kentucky, pastry chef Brian Logsdon created this bacon-studded baklava.

1½ pounds sliced bacon
1 cup whole blanched almonds, toasted and coarsely chopped
¾ cup coarsely chopped dates
1 package phyllo dough
10 tablespoons unsalted butter, melted
1½ cups sugar
1 cup pure maple syrup
½ cup water
2 tablespoons bourbon
Finely grated zest of ½ orange

1. Preheat the oven to 400°. In a skillet, fry the bacon in batches until crisp. Drain well and crumble. In a food processor, finely chop the bacon with the almonds and dates.

2. Butter a 9-by-13-inch metal baking pan. Lay a sheet of phyllo in the pan; trim the edges to fit and brush with butter. Repeat with 4 more phyllo sheets and butter. Spread 1 cup of the filling over the phyllo. Repeat this layering of 5 phyllo sheets and filling twice more. Top with 5 buttered phyllo sheets; butter the top well.

3. With a small, sharp knife, cut the baklava into diamonds and bake for 10 minutes. Turn the oven to 325° and bake for 1 hour longer, or until nicely browned.

4. Meanwhile, combine the sugar, maple syrup, water, bourbon and orange zest in a saucepan and bring to a boil. Simmer for 5 minutes, then let cool to room temperature. Pour the cooled syrup over the hot baklava and let stand at room temperature uncovered overnight.
—*Brian Logsdon*

Salted Fudge Brownies

TOTAL: 45 MIN PLUS 2 HR COOLING

MAKES 16 BROWNIES ● ○ ○

F&W's Kate Krader has been making these fudgy, sweet-salty brownies since she was 10 years old. As a kid she used regular table salt; now she recommends a flaky sea salt like Maldon, because the flavor is less harsh and it melts so nicely into the batter, accentuating the chocolaty sweetness.

1½ sticks unsalted butter
2 ounces unsweetened chocolate, finely chopped
¼ cup plus 2 tablespoons unsweetened cocoa
2 cups sugar
3 large eggs
1½ teaspoons pure vanilla extract
1 cup all-purpose flour
½ teaspoon Maldon sea salt

1. Preheat the oven to 350°. Line a 9-inch square metal cake pan with foil, draping the foil over the edges. Lightly butter the foil.

2. In a large saucepan, melt the butter with the unsweetened chocolate over very low heat, stirring occasionally. Remove from the heat. Whisking them in one at a time until thoroughly incorporated, add the cocoa, sugar, eggs, vanilla and flour. Pour the batter into the prepared pan and smooth the surface. Sprinkle the salt evenly over the batter. Using a butter knife, swirl the salt into the batter.

3. Bake the brownies in the center of the oven for about 35 minutes, until the edges are set but the center is still a bit soft and a toothpick inserted into the center comes out coated with a little of the batter. Let cool at room temperature in the pan for 1 hour, then refrigerate just until they are firm, about 1 hour. Lift the brownies from the pan and peel off the foil. Cut into 16 squares and serve. —*Kate Krader*

MAKE AHEAD The brownies can be refrigerated for up to 3 days and frozen for up to 1 month.

Honey-Lemon Curd with Crème Fraîche

TOTAL: 30 MIN PLUS 3 HR CHILLING

4 SERVINGS ● ○

Honey adds richness to this tart lemon curd and eliminates the need for refined sugar. Dede Sampson, a Bay Area chef who is committed to cooking only with locally grown ingredients, serves the honey-lemon curd with crème fraîche and locally made shortbread cookies.

5 large egg yolks
1 large egg
⅔ cup fresh lemon juice
1 teaspoon finely grated lemon zest, plus more for garnish
¼ cup plus 2 tablespoons honey
4 tablespoons unsalted butter, cut into 8 pieces
Crème fraîche, for serving

1. In a medium heatproof bowl, whisk the egg yolks with the whole egg, the fresh lemon juice, the teaspoon of grated lemon zest and the honey. In a medium saucepan, bring 1 inch of water to a boil. Set the bowl with the lemon mixture over the boiling water, reduce the heat to moderate and cook the mixture, whisking constantly, until the curd has thickened to the consistency of mayonnaise, about 7 minutes. Remove the bowl from the heat and whisk in the butter pieces until smoothly combined. Pass the curd through a fine-mesh strainer into a medium bowl.

2. Ladle the strained curd into 4 cups or ramekins. Press a piece of plastic wrap directly on the surface of the lemon curd to prevent a skin from forming; refrigerate until chilled, at least 3 hours. Top the curd with dollops of crème fraîche and garnish with the remaining lemon zest.
—*Dede Sampson*

SERVE WITH Shortbread cookies.
MAKE AHEAD The lemon curd can be refrigerated for up to 2 days.

Best-Ever Nut Brittle

TOTAL: 50 MIN

MAKES 2 POUNDS ●○

2 cups sugar
½ cup water
1 stick unsalted butter
⅓ cup light corn syrup
½ teaspoon baking soda
12 ounces roasted salted
   peanuts, cashews, pistachios
   and/or pecans
Fleur de sel or crushed Maldon
   sea salt

In a large saucepan, combine the sugar, water, butter and corn syrup and bring to a boil. Cook over moderately high heat, stirring occasionally, until the caramel is light brown and registers 300° on a candy thermometer, 10 minutes. Remove from the heat and carefully stir in the baking soda. The mixture will bubble. Stir in the nuts, then immediately scrape the brittle onto a large rimmed nonstick baking sheet. Using the back of a large spoon (oil it lightly if it sticks), spread the brittle into a thin, even layer. Sprinkle with salt. Let cool completely, about 30 minutes. Break the brittle into large shards and serve.
—Tina Ujlaki

MAKE AHEAD The brittle can be stored in an airtight container at room temperature for up to 1 month.

Coffee-Rum Truffettes

TOTAL: 3 HR 30 MIN

MAKES ABOUT 36 TRUFFETTES ●○○

F&W contributing editor Jacques Pépin flavors truffles with many ingredients, but he is especially fond of the coffee-rum combination in this recipe.

1 pound bittersweet
   chocolate, chopped
3 tablespoons unsalted
   butter, thinly sliced
2 large egg yolks
1½ tablespoons brewed espresso
1 tablespoon dark rum

1. Melt ½ pound of the chocolate in a double boiler over simmering water. Remove from the heat and whisk in the butter. Whisk in the egg yolks, espresso and rum. Refrigerate the chocolate mixture until it is firm enough to roll into balls, about 1 hour.

2. Line a baking sheet with wax paper. Roll rounded teaspoons of the chocolate mixture into balls and place them on the prepared baking sheet. Refrigerate for 1 hour.

3. Melt the remaining ½ pound of chocolate in the double boiler over simmering water. Remove from the heat and let cool, about 10 minutes. Using a skewer, spear each truffette, dip it in the chocolate and return it to the baking sheet. Refrigerate until ready to serve. *—Jacques Pépin*

MAKE AHEAD The truffettes can be frozen for up to 2 months.

Pecan Sandies

TOTAL: 50 MIN PLUS OVERNIGHT CHILLING

MAKES 4 DOZEN COOKIES ●●○

The secret to these light, delicate and crisp cookies is to chill the dough overnight.

2 sticks unsalted butter,
   at room temperature
⅓ cup sugar, plus more
   for sprinkling
½ teaspoon salt
1 teaspoon pure vanilla extract
2 cups all-purpose flour
1 cup pecans, coarsely chopped

1. In a medium bowl, using an electric mixer, beat the butter with the ⅓ cup of sugar and the salt at medium speed until light and fluffy, about 3 minutes. Beat in the vanilla, then beat in the flour at low speed, scraping the side and bottom of the bowl, until the dough just comes together. Add the pecans and beat just until they are incorporated and lightly broken up. Divide the cookie dough in half and form it into two 2-inch-thick logs. Wrap the cookie dough tightly in plastic and refrigerate overnight.

2. Preheat the oven to 350°. Line 3 baking sheets with parchment paper. Working with 1 log at a time and keeping the other one chilled, cut the cookie dough into scant ¼-inch-thick slices and arrange them on the baking sheets. Repeat with the second log of dough.

3. Bake for 25 to 30 minutes, until the cookies are lightly golden around the edge and on the bottom, shifting the baking sheets halfway through. Let the cookies cool on the baking sheets for a few minutes, then transfer them to a wire rack to cool completely. *—Angie Mosier*

MAKE AHEAD The dough can be refrigerated for up to 3 days before baking. The baked cookies can be stored in an airtight container for up to 3 days.

Double-Ginger Sugar Cookies

TOTAL: 1 HR 15 MIN

MAKES 6½ DOZEN COOKIES ●○○

2½ cups all-purpose flour
⅓ cup finely chopped
   crystallized ginger
   (3 ounces)
1½ teaspoons ground ginger
½ teaspoon baking soda
½ teaspoon salt
2 sticks (½ pound) unsalted
   butter, softened
1¼ cups sugar
1 large egg yolk
1 teaspoon pure vanilla extract

1. In a medium bowl, whisk the flour with the crystallized and ground ginger, baking soda and salt. In a standing electric mixer fitted with a paddle, or using a hand mixer in a large bowl, beat the butter with the sugar at medium speed until light and fluffy, about 3 minutes. Beat in the egg yolk and vanilla, scraping the side and bottom of the bowl. Beat in the dry ingredients at medium-low speed. Divide the dough in half. Pat each half into a round, wrap them in plastic and refrigerate the dough for 15 minutes.

2. Preheat the oven to 350°. Position the racks in the upper and lower thirds of the oven. On a lightly floured surface, roll out each piece of cookie dough ⅛ inch thick. Using a 2-inch biscuit cutter, stamp out rounds as close together as possible. Arrange the rounds on large baking sheets about 1 inch apart. Gather the scraps and reroll them, cutting out more cookies.

3. Bake the cookies in batches for about 20 minutes, until golden; shift the pans from top to bottom and front to back halfway through baking. Transfer to wire racks and let the cookies cool on the baking sheets for 5 minutes, then transfer the cookies direcly onto the racks and let them cool completely. —*Grace Parisi*

HAZELNUT-NUTELLA SANDWICH COOKIE VARIATION In a food processor, finely grind ⅔ cup roasted and salted hazelnuts. Replace both gingers with the ground hazelnuts. Sandwich the cooled cookies with Nutella or another chocolate spread.

COCOA NIB–CHOCOLATE CHIP COOKIE VARIATION Finely chop two 3-ounce milk chocolate bars with cocoa nibs. Replace both gingers with the chopped chocolate and nibs, folding them in after beating in the dry ingredients.

COCONUT-RASPBERRY THUMBPRINT VARIATION Replace both gingers with ¾ cup shredded unsweetened coconut. Roll the dough into 1-inch balls and bake for 14 minutes. Make a dent in the cookies, then fill them with jam and bake for about 10 minutes.

MAKE AHEAD The dough can be prepared through Step 1, wrapped in plastic and then foil and refrigerated for up to 1 week or frozen for up to 1 month. Thaw the dough overnight in the refrigerator before dividing it in half and rolling it out. The baked, cooled cookies can be stored in an airtight container for up to 1 week or wrapped in plastic and foil and then frozen for up to 1 month. Thaw in the refrigerator, then bring to room temperature.

DOUBLE-GINGER SUGAR COOKIES AND VARIATIONS

PECAN SANDIES

Superrich Hot Chocolate with Coconut Cream

 TOTAL: 10 MIN
8 SERVINGS •

Lachlan Mackinnon Patterson, the chef at Frasca Food and Wine in Boulder, Colorado, created this drink for his partner's wife, who has a sweet tooth. "We make a lot of desserts with chocolate or coconut, so we just kept going and came up with this," he says.

One 13.5-ounce can unsweetened
    coconut milk
¼ cup sugar
1¾ cups heavy cream
1⅔ cups whole milk
3 cups bittersweet chocolate
    chips (18 ounces)
Marshmallows, for serving (optional)

In a small saucepan, combine the coconut milk and sugar and heat, stirring to dissolve the sugar; keep warm. In a medium saucepan, combine the cream and whole milk and bring to a simmer. Add the chocolate chips and remove from the heat. Let stand, stirring occasionally, until the chocolate is melted; whisk until smooth. Pour the chocolate into 8 mugs and spoon some of the coconut milk on top. Garnish with the marshmallows and serve.
—*Lachlan Mackinnon Patterson*

Cream Puffs with Chocolate Sauce

ACTIVE: 45 MIN; TOTAL: 3 HR
8 SERVINGS •
½ cup milk
½ cup water
9 tablespoons unsalted butter
½ teaspoon salt
1 cup all-purpose flour
3 large eggs
2¼ cups heavy cream
¼ cup confectioners' sugar
1½ teaspoons pure vanilla extract
6 ounces bittersweet chocolate,
    chopped

1. Preheat the oven to 400°. Line 2 large baking sheets with parchment paper.
2. In a large saucepan, bring the milk, water, 1 stick of the butter and the salt to a boil over high heat. Add the flour and remove from the heat. Stir until the dough forms a shiny mass. Using a mixer, beat the dough at low speed for 2 to 3 minutes, just until slightly cooled. Increase the speed to medium and beat in the eggs 1 at a time, beating well between additions; be sure to scrape down the saucepan.
3. Transfer the dough to a pastry bag fitted with a ¾-inch plain tip. Pipe twelve 1½-inch mounds onto each sheet. Using a moistened finger, round the tops of the dough. Bake for about 25 minutes, until the puffs are golden, shifting the pans halfway through.
4. Poke a ¼-inch-deep hole into the side of each puff and return them to the oven. Turn off the oven, leave the door ajar and let the puffs cool and dry out for 2 hours.
5. Meanwhile, in a bowl, using a mixer, beat 1½ cups of the cream with the confectioners' sugar until firm. Beat in the vanilla.
6. Cut off the top third of each puff and scoop out the soft dough in the center. Spoon the cream into the puffs, replace the tops and stack them on a plate. Chill for 10 minutes.
7. In a small saucepan, bring the remaining ¾ cup of cream just to a boil. Remove from the heat. Add the chocolate and the remaining 1 tablespoon of butter and let stand just until the chocolate is melted. Whisk until smooth. Drizzle some of the sauce over the puffs and serve the remaining sauce on the side. —*Elizabeth Katz*

Apricot Pâtes de Fruits

TOTAL: 40 MIN PLUS COOLING AND OVERNIGHT CHILLING
MAKES ABOUT 5 DOZEN PIECES •

In France, *pâtes de fruits* (fruit jellies) are rolled in sanding sugar, which has large crystals that cling without melting. Table sugar also works, as long as the jellies are rolled in it just before serving.

One 15-ounce can apricots in syrup
12 dried apricot halves
    (4 ounces)
1¼ cups apricot preserves
½ cup sugar, plus more for coating
2 envelopes unflavored powdered
    gelatin (4½ teaspoons)
⅓ cup cold water

1. Lightly oil an 8-by-8-inch baking dish. Line the dish with a sheet of wax paper that extends 4 inches beyond the rim.
2. Strain the apricot syrup from the can into a saucepan; reserve the apricots. Add the dried apricots to the saucepan and bring to a boil. Reduce the heat and simmer until the apricots are tender and most of the liquid has evaporated, 7 minutes.
3. Transfer the contents of the saucepan to a food processor. Add the reserved canned apricots, the apricot preserves and the ½ cup of sugar. Process until smooth. Transfer the apricot puree to the saucepan and boil over moderately high heat, stirring often, until it has thickened and any excess liquid has evaporated, about 8 minutes.
4. In a bowl, sprinkle the powdered gelatin over the cold water in an even layer. Let stand until the gelatin softens, then microwave the mixture for 20 seconds to dissolve the gelatin completely. Stir the gelatin into the apricot puree. Scrape the mixture into the prepared baking dish and smooth the surface. Let cool to room temperature, then cover with plastic wrap and refrigerate overnight.
5. Just before serving, unmold the apricot *pâte de fruit* onto a work surface. Peel off and discard the wax paper. Using a sharp knife, cut the *pâte* into 1-inch squares or triangles. Spread about ½ cup of sugar in a shallow bowl. Roll the pieces in the sugar to coat, arrange on a platter and serve.
—*Jacques Pépin*

MAKE AHEAD The *pâte de fruit* can be prepared through Step 4 and refrigerated, covered, for up to 1 week. Dab with paper towels before proceeding.

CREAM PUFFS WITH CHOCOLATE SAUCE

Warm Churros and Hot Chocolate

TOTAL: 1 HR 40 MIN

8 SERVINGS ● ●

2 sticks unsalted butter (½ pound)
Kosher salt
1¼ cups all-purpose flour
4 large eggs
1 large egg white
4½ cups whole milk
7 ounces bittersweet chocolate, finely chopped
⅔ cup unsweetened cocoa powder
1 cup plus 2 tablespoons sugar
1 quart vegetable oil, for frying
2 tablespoons cinnamon

1. In a large saucepan, bring 1¾ cups of water to a boil with the butter and ½ teaspoon of salt. Remove from the heat, add the flour and stir vigorously until incorporated. Return to moderate heat and cook, stirring, until the dough pulls away from the side, 3 minutes. Remove from the heat.

2. Using an electric mixer, beat the dough at low speed for 1 minute, just until slightly cooled. Increase the speed to medium-high and beat in the eggs and egg white 1 at a time. Transfer the dough to a bowl, press a sheet of plastic wrap directly on the surface and refrigerate until cooled to room temperature, about 15 minutes.

3. Meanwhile, in a large saucepan, heat the milk with ½ cup of water until small bubbles appear around the edge. Add the chocolate, cocoa powder, ½ cup plus 2 tablespoons of the sugar and a pinch of salt and whisk over low heat until the chocolate is melted. Keep warm over very low heat.

4. In another large saucepan, heat the oil to 375°. Set a rack on a large baking sheet and cover with paper towels. In a pie plate, combine the remaining ½ cup of sugar with the cinnamon. Scoop the dough into a large pastry bag fitted with a large star tip.

5. Working quickly, squeeze 6-inch lengths of the dough into the hot oil, cutting them off with a knife. Fry no more than 8 churros

at a time; they expand a bit as they cook. Fry over moderately high heat, turning once or twice, until browned, about 8 minutes. Drain on the rack for 2 minutes, then toss with the cinnamon sugar. Serve at once, with hot chocolate. —*Andrew Zimmerman*

Raspberry Pâtes de Fruits

TOTAL: 30 MIN PLUS COOLING AND OVERNIGHT CHILLING

MAKES ABOUT 5 DOZEN PIECES ●

Two 12-ounce bags frozen raspberries, thawed (4 cups)
1¼ cups seedless raspberry jam
1 cup sugar, plus more for coating
3 envelopes unflavored powdered gelatin (2 tablespoons)
¾ cup cold water

1. Lightly oil an 8-by-8-inch baking dish. Line the dish with a piece of wax paper that extends 4 inches beyond the rim.

2. In a food processor, puree the thawed raspberries with the raspberry jam and the 1 cup of sugar. Strain the puree through a mesh sieve set into a medium saucepan. Bring the puree to a boil over moderately high heat, stirring often, until it has reduced to 3 cups, about 10 minutes.

3. In a small bowl, sprinkle the gelatin over the water in an even layer. Let stand until the gelatin softens, then heat in a microwave for 20 seconds, until the gelatin dissolves completely. Stir the melted gelatin into the raspberry puree, then pour the mixture into the prepared dish. Let cool to room temperature, then cover with plastic wrap and refrigerate overnight.

4. Just before serving, unmold the *pâte de fruit* onto a work surface. Peel off and discard the wax paper. Using a sharp knife, cut the *pâte* into 1-inch squares or triangles. Spread about ½ cup of sugar in a shallow bowl. Roll the pieces in the sugar to coat and serve. —*Jacques Pépin*

MAKE AHEAD The *pâte de fruit* can be prepared through Step 3 and refrigerated, covered, for up to 1 week. Dab with paper towels before proceeding.

Dried Fruit Compote in Spiced Syrup

TOTAL: 45 MIN

10 SERVINGS ● ● ●

"Adding a couple of shots of brandy will only make this recipe better," says Tom Valenti, chef of Ouest in New York City. He suggests making a large batch of the poached fruit well in advance. "You'll find lots of uses for it," he says, such as a topping for French toast.

1½ cups dry white wine
¾ cup sugar
1 cinnamon stick
8 whole cloves
1¼ pounds mixed dried apricots and pitted prunes, coarsely chopped (3 cups)
2 cups cold water
1½ tablespoons pure vanilla extract
Vanilla ice cream, gelato or crème fraîche, for serving

In a large saucepan, combine the white wine, sugar, cinnamon stick and cloves and bring the liquid to a boil over high heat. Reduce the heat to low and simmer for 10 minutes. Add the mixed dried fruit, cold water and vanilla extract, increase the heat to moderately high and bring to a boil. Reduce the heat again and simmer over low heat, stirring occasionally, until the fruit is plumped and the poaching liquid has thickened to a slightly syrupy consistency, about 25 minutes. Remove and discard the cinnamon stick and cloves. Spoon the warm fruit compote over ice cream, drizzle it with the spiced syrup and serve immediately. —*Tom Valenti*

MAKE AHEAD The fruit compote can be refrigerated for up to 1 week. Warm gently in a saucepan over moderately low heat before serving.

brunch

Honey Spelt Bread

ACTIVE: 25 MIN; TOTAL: 4 HR

8 SERVINGS ● ● ○

4½ cups whole-wheat spelt flour,
    plus more for dusting
2 teaspoons fine sea salt
2 teaspoons active dry yeast
1¾ cups cool (70°) water
2 tablespoons honey

1. In a standing mixer fitted with a dough hook, combine the flour, salt and yeast. Turn the machine to medium-low, add the water and honey and mix until the flour is moistened, about 2 minutes, scraping down the side of the bowl with a rubber spatula as needed. Increase the speed to medium and knead until a stiff dough forms, about 2 minutes longer.

2. Transfer the dough to a lightly floured work surface and shape into a ball. Set the dough in a well-floured bowl, cover with plastic wrap and let rise in a warm place until doubled in bulk, about 1½ hours.

3. Preheat the oven to 450° and spray a 9-by-5-inch loaf pan with vegetable cooking spray. Invert the dough onto a lightly floured work surface and gently punch it down. Fold the dough into a loaf, tucking in the sides and pinching the seams. Transfer the dough to the loaf pan seam side down. Cover with plastic wrap and let stand until doubled in bulk, about 1 hour.

4. Remove the plastic wrap and lightly dust the dough with flour. Using a razor blade or sharp knife, make a shallow lengthwise gash down the center of the loaf. Bake for about 35 minutes, until the loaf is risen and golden on top and an instant-read thermometer inserted into the center of the loaf reads 180°. Let cool in the pan for 10 minutes, then cool completely on a rack before serving. —*Lionel Vatinet*

MAKE AHEAD The bread can be wrapped in plastic and kept at room temperature for up to 4 days.

Raisin Rye Bread

ACTIVE: 20 MIN; TOTAL: 4 HR

8 SERVINGS ● ● ○

North Carolina baker Lionel Vatinet developed this hearty bread to satisfy customers of Eastern European descent.

2 cups unbleached all-purpose flour,
    plus more for dusting
1½ cups dark rye flour
1¼ teaspoons fine sea salt
1 teaspoon active dry yeast
1½ cups cool (60°) water
1 cup golden raisins

1. In a standing mixer fitted with a dough hook, combine both flours, the salt and the yeast. Turn the machine to medium-low, add the water and mix until the flour is moistened, about 2 minutes, scraping down the side of the bowl with a rubber spatula as needed. Increase the speed to medium and knead until a soft dough forms, about 2 minutes longer. Add the raisins and knead just until evenly distributed.

2. Transfer the dough to a lightly floured work surface and form into a ball. Set the dough in a well-floured bowl, cover with plastic and let rise in a warm place until doubled in bulk, about 1½ hours.

3. Preheat the oven to 450° and spray a 9-inch enameled cast-iron casserole with vegetable cooking spray. Turn the dough out into the casserole. Cover with plastic wrap and let stand until the dough is doubled in bulk, about 1 hour.

4. Remove the plastic. Dust the top of the dough with all-purpose flour. Using a razor blade or sharp knife, make a shallow X in the top of the dough. Bake for about 35 minutes, until the loaf is risen and lightly golden on top and an instant-read thermometer inserted into the center of the loaf reads 200°. Tip the bread out onto a wire rack. Let the bread cool slightly before slicing and serving. —*Lionel Vatinet*

MAKE AHEAD The bread can be wrapped in plastic and kept at room temperature for up to 4 days.

Blueberry Muffins with Crumb Topping

ACTIVE: 20 MIN; TOTAL: 1 HR

MAKES 18 MUFFINS ● ○

These muffins are easy to make: Simply mix the dry and wet ingredients separately, then combine them. Baking powder, which lightens the muffins, is activated by moisture, so get the batter into the oven immediately once it's mixed. For soft edges, use liners; for crisp edges, use a well-greased unlined pan. You can replace the blueberries with other fresh fruit, such as raspberries, peaches (chopped into small pieces) or cranberries. You can also use individually quick-frozen fruit; there's no need to thaw.

CRUMB TOPPING

1 cup all-purpose flour
3 tablespoons light brown sugar
2 tablespoons granulated sugar
1 teaspoon baking powder
Pinch of salt
6 tablespoons unsalted
    butter, melted

MUFFINS

1¾ cups all-purpose flour
2¼ teaspoons baking powder
½ teaspoon salt
1 cup granulated sugar
2 large eggs
½ cup canola oil
¾ cup whole milk
1 teaspoon pure vanilla extract
1½ cups blueberries

1. Preheat the oven to 375°. Line 18 muffin cups with paper or foil liners or spray 2 muffin tins with cooking spray.

2. MAKE THE CRUMB TOPPING: In a medium bowl, combine the flour with the brown sugar, granulated sugar, baking powder and salt. Stir in the melted butter, then pinch the mixture until it forms pea-size clumps.

3. MAKE THE MUFFINS: In a medium bowl, whisk the flour with the baking powder and salt. In a large bowl, combine the sugar,

eggs and canola oil and beat with a hand-held electric mixer at low speed until combined. Beat in the whole milk and vanilla. Add the flour mixture all at once and beat at low speed until the batter is smooth. Stir in the blueberries.

4. Spoon the batter into 18 of the muffin cups, filling them about three-quarters full. Sprinkle the crumb topping on top of each one and bake for about 30 minutes, or until the muffins are golden and a toothpick inserted in the center comes out with a few moist crumbs attached. Let the blueberry muffins cool in the pan for 10 minutes before serving. —*Grace Parisi*

MAKE AHEAD Once cooled, the blueberry muffins can be kept overnight in an airtight container.

Meyer Lemon Marmalade

ACTIVE: 1 HR; TOTAL: 2 HR PLUS 2 DAYS OF STANDING

MAKES FIVE ½-PINT JARS ● ●

F&W's Emily Kaiser devised this fail-safe recipe while living in Oakland, California, with two extravagantly productive Meyer lemon trees.

  12 medium organic Meyer
       lemons (3 pounds)
  3 cups sugar

1. Rinse the lemons and pat dry. Halve the lemons crosswise and juice them, reserving the juice. Using a spoon, scrape the pulp and seeds from the halves. Using a sharp knife, slice the peels ⅛ inch thick.

2. In a large, heavy saucepan, cover the strips of lemon peel with 8 cups of cold water and bring to a boil; boil for 1 minute. Drain the strips and rinse under cold running water. Blanch twice more; the final time, drain the lemon peel strips but do not rinse them.

3. Return the strips to the saucepan. Add the reserved juice and the sugar. Simmer over moderate heat, stirring to dissolve the sugar, then skimming any foam, until the marmalade sets, about 30 minutes.

4. Spoon the marmalade into 5 hot ½-pint canning jars, leaving ¼ inch of space at the top, and close with the lids and rings. To process, boil the jars for 15 minutes in water to cover. Let stand at room temperature for 2 days before serving.
—*Emily Kaiser*

MAKE AHEAD The processed marmalade can be stored in a cool, dark place for up to 1 year. Refrigerate after opening.

Granola with Maple-Glazed Walnuts

ACTIVE: 10 MIN; TOTAL: 1 HR
MAKES 4 POUNDS ● ●

This granola, from F&W's Grace Parisi, is the standard by which the F&W staff measures all others. Says Grace, "Like any true zealot, I love to turn people on to my one big passion."

  4 tablespoons unsalted butter
  ½ cup all-purpose flour
  ½ teaspoon baking soda
  ½ cup light brown sugar
  ½ teaspoon salt
Large pinch of cinnamon
Large pinch of freshly grated nutmeg
  2 pounds thick-cut oats

  ¾ cup plus 2 tablespoons pure
       maple syrup
  2 cups walnut halves (11 ounces)
  3 cups dried cranberries,
       cherries or golden raisins
       (1 pound)

1. Preheat the oven to 375°. Butter a roasting pan. In a mini food processor, pulse the butter, flour, baking soda, brown sugar, salt, cinnamon and nutmeg until crumbly. Transfer to a large bowl. Stir in the oats and ¾ cup of the maple syrup; transfer to the prepared pan. Bake for 50 minutes, stirring occasionally, until crisp. Let cool.

2. Meanwhile, in a small bowl, toss the walnut halves with the remaining 2 tablespoons of maple syrup. Spread the walnuts onto a small rimmed baking sheet and toast in the oven for about 20 minutes, tossing occasionally, until golden and caramelized. Transfer the walnuts to a cutting board and let cool.

3. Chop the maple-glazed walnuts and add them to the granola along with the dried fruit. Transfer to an airtight container.
—*Grace Parisi*

MAKE AHEAD The granola can be kept in an airtight container for up to 2 weeks.

TIPS

great muffins

TECHNIQUE Avoid overbeating the batter; this makes muffins dense and tough. Mix the ingredients until just combined, then bake right away.

SIZE To bake mini muffins, count on making three mini muffins for each standard-size muffin; they will take about half as long to bake.

ESSENTIAL TOOL A medium-size ice cream scoop measures just the right amount of batter for each muffin cup.

Cranberry-Walnut Power Bars

ACTIVE: 20 MIN; TOTAL: 1 HR 15 MIN

MAKES 16 BARS ● ● ○

These gingery, nutrient-packed bars use only natural sweeteners like brown rice syrup and natural cane sugar.

1¼ cups walnut halves (5 ounces)
1½ cups puffed brown rice cereal
1¼ cups rolled oats
 1 cup dried cranberries, chopped
½ cup oat bran
 3 tablespoons finely chopped crystallized ginger
 1 cup brown rice syrup (see Note)
¼ cup natural cane sugar (see Note)
½ teaspoon salt
 1 teaspoon pure vanilla extract

1. Preheat the oven to 350°. Lightly spray an 8-by-11-inch baking dish with cooking spray. Spread the walnuts on a baking sheet and toast until fragrant and golden, about 9 minutes. Let cool, then coarsely chop. Transfer the walnuts to a large bowl. Add the puffed rice, rolled oats, cranberries, oat bran and ginger and toss well.

2. In a small saucepan, combine the brown rice syrup, cane sugar and salt and bring to a boil over moderate heat. Cook, stirring occasionally, until the mixture is slightly thickened, about 4 minutes. Remove from the heat and stir in the vanilla. Pour the syrup into the rice-oat mixture and toss to coat thoroughly. Transfer the warm mixture to the prepared baking dish and pack lightly with a spatula greased with cooking spray. Let cool for at least 45 minutes before cutting into 16 bars.
—*Heidi Swanson*

NOTE Natural sweeteners, such as brown rice syrup and natural cane sugar, are available at specialty and health food shops and from shopnatural.com.

MAKE AHEAD The cranberry-walnut bars can be wrapped individually in plastic or wax paper and kept in an airtight container for up to 4 days.

Frasca's Gorp

 TOTAL: 5 MIN

8 SERVINGS ● ○

"We call this the snack food of champions," says Lachlan Mackinnon Patterson, chef at Frasca Food and Wine in Boulder, Colorado. The chocolate-and-raisin-studded mix gives him energy during long bike rides and long nights in the kitchen.

 2 cups salted roasted almonds (7 ounces)
 2 cups salted dry-roasted peanuts (7 ounces)
1½ cups golden raisins (8 ounces)
1½ cups dark chocolate chips (9 ounces)
½ cup unsweetened coconut flakes

In a large bowl, combine all of the gorp ingredients and serve.
—*Lachlan Mackinnon Patterson*

MAKE AHEAD The gorp can be kept in an airtight container at room temperature for up to 1 week.

Chunky Granola

ACTIVE: 10 MIN; TOTAL: 1 HR

10 SERVINGS ● ● ○ ○

⅔ cup light brown sugar
½ cup canola oil
½ cup honey
 3 cups rolled oats
 1 cup sliced almonds
⅓ cup unsalted roasted sunflower seeds
⅓ cup sesame seeds
⅓ cup flaxseeds

Plain low-fat yogurt, for serving

1. Preheat the oven to 300° and position a rack in the center. Line a large rimmed baking sheet with parchment paper; spray the paper with vegetable oil spray.

2. In a small saucepan, combine the brown sugar, oil and honey. Cook over low heat until just warmed through. In a large bowl, stir the honey mixture into the rest of the ingredients until evenly distributed. Spread the mixture on the prepared baking sheet and bake until golden, about 45 minutes. Transfer the baking sheet to a rack and let the granola cool.

3. Invert the baking sheet onto a work surface and tap out the brittle. Peel off the parchment paper. Break the granola into chunks. Return it to the pan and cool on a wire rack. Serve with the yogurt.
—*Lionel Vatinet*

MAKE AHEAD The granola can be stored in an airtight container for up to 4 days.

Pat's Popovers

ACTIVE: 15 MIN; TOTAL: 1 HR

MAKES 12 POPOVERS

If you've made roast beef, you can use some of the leftover beef fat in this batter. Cook the popovers until they're well browned and crusty or they may collapse.

1½ cups milk
1½ cups all-purpose flour
 4 large eggs
1½ teaspoons kosher salt
 3 tablespoons rendered beef fat (from the Horseradish-and-Herb-Crusted Beef Rib Roast on p. 54) or vegetable oil

1. Preheat the oven to 425°. Put a large 12-cup muffin pan in the oven to heat. In a medium bowl, combine the milk with the flour, eggs, salt and 1 tablespoon of the beef fat. Using a handheld electric mixer, beat until very smooth.

2. Remove the hot muffin pan from the oven and add ½ teaspoon of the beef fat to each cup. Return the muffin pan to the oven and heat until the fat is very hot, about 5 minutes. Carefully and quickly pour the popover batter into the muffin cups and bake for 20 minutes; don't open the oven door. Reduce the heat to 350° and bake for about 20 minutes longer, until the popovers are golden brown and puffed. Serve immediately.
—*Pat Berrigan*

Potato Frittata with Prosciutto and Gruyère

⏱ **TOTAL: 40 MIN**
10 SERVINGS ●

This cheesy frittata is the kind of dish—fast, flexible and easy to reheat—that New York City chef Tom Valenti likes to have around for all sorts of holiday eating. "A frittata is just as good, or maybe better, at midnight," he says.

- 1 dozen large eggs
- 2 tablespoons water

Salt and freshly ground pepper

- 1 packed cup shredded Gruyère
- 4 ounces prosciutto, sliced ¼ inch thick and cut into ¼-inch dice
- ¼ cup extra-virgin olive oil
- 1 pound Yukon Gold potatoes, peeled and cut into ½-inch dice
- 2 scallions, thinly sliced

1. Preheat the oven to 375°. In a bowl, beat the eggs with the water and season with ¾ teaspoon of salt and ½ teaspoon of pepper. Beat in the shredded Gruyère and diced prosciutto.

2. Heat the olive oil in a large nonstick ovenproof skillet. Add the diced potatoes and cook over moderately high heat, stirring occasionally, until they are tender and golden brown, about 7 minutes. Add the scallions and cook, stirring, for 1 minute. Stir the egg mixture and add to the skillet. Stir to distribute the potatoes. Cook until the bottom of the frittata is just set, about 3 minutes; lift the frittata to allow the uncooked eggs to seep underneath.

3. Bake the frittata for about 10 minutes, until nearly set in the center.

4. Preheat the broiler. Broil the frittata about 8 inches from the heat for 1 minute, until the top is just beginning to brown. Cut the frittata into wedges and serve hot or at room temperature. —*Tom Valenti*

MAKE AHEAD The unmolded frittata can be kept at room temperature for 4 hours.

FRASCA'S GORP

POTATO FRITTATA WITH PROSCIUTTO AND GRUYÈRE

Yukon Gold Potato, Leek and Fromage Blanc Frittata

ACTIVE: 30 MIN; TOTAL: 1 HR
6 SERVINGS ●

Bay Area chef Dede Sampson prepared this frittata for the Oliveto staff when she applied for a position at the restaurant in Oakland, California. This recipe gets its extra-creamy texture from *fromage blanc,* an extremely soft cow's-milk cheese with a sour cream–like tang. A devotee of locally grown foods, Sampson buys her cheese from San Francisco's Cowgirl Creamery.

  2 **medium Yukon Gold potatoes (¾ pound)**
  2 **tablespoons unsalted butter**
  2 **leeks, white and tender green parts only, halved lengthwise and thinly sliced**
   Salt and freshly ground black pepper
 10 **large eggs**
 ⅓ **cup whole milk**
  4 **ounces *fromage blanc* (see Note) or crumbled feta cheese (1 cup)**

1. Preheat the oven to 375°. In a medium saucepan, cover the potatoes with water and bring to a boil over high heat. Boil the potatoes until completely tender, about 15 minutes. Drain the potatoes well and let cool slightly. When cool enough to handle, cut into ½-inch dice.

SUPERFAST

breakfast burritos

Burritos are fun and easy for brunch. Roll warm flour tortillas around fluffy scrambled eggs, warm refried beans, salsa, grated cheese, sliced scallions and chopped cilantro and serve.

2. In a 10-inch nonstick ovenproof skillet, melt the butter. Add the sliced leeks and cook over moderate heat, stirring occasionally, until tender, about 4 minutes. Add the diced potatoes and cook, stirring occasionally, for 3 minutes longer. Season with salt and black pepper.

3. In a large bowl, whisk the eggs with the milk and season with salt and black pepper. Pour the beaten eggs over the leeks and potatoes in the skillet and cook for 5 minutes without stirring. Dollop the *fromage blanc* or sprinkle the feta cheese over the leeks and potatoes. Transfer the skillet to the oven and bake until the eggs are just set in the center, about 18 minutes. Carefully slide the frittata onto a large serving plate, cut it into 6 wedges and serve right away. —*Dede Sampson*

NOTE *Fromage blanc,* a tangy, fresh white cow's-milk cheese, has a spreadable texture similar to that of strained yogurt. It is available at some cheese shops and specialty food stores. You can also buy it online from igourmet.com.

Baked Eggs with Chorizo and Potatoes

 TOTAL: 45 MIN
8 SERVINGS ●

Chef David Kinch of Manresa in Los Gatos, California, loves to say that this hearty combination of crumbled chorizo, chunks of crispy potatoes and eggs—all cooked together in a big cast-iron skillet—is his Mexican-Californian twist on rösti, the classic Swiss fried-potato breakfast.

  2 **pounds medium Yukon Gold potatoes**
1½ **pounds fresh chorizo, casings removed (see Note)**
  1 **large onion, finely chopped**
  2 **tablespoons extra-virgin olive oil**
   Salt and freshly ground pepper
  8 **large eggs**
   Toast and hot sauce, for serving

1. Preheat the oven to 375°. Put the potatoes in a large saucepan and cover with cold water. Bring the water to a boil over high heat, then reduce the heat and simmer over moderate heat until completely tender, about 25 minutes; drain the potatoes and let cool. When cool enough to handle, peel the potatoes and cut them into ¾-inch pieces.

2. Meanwhile, heat a 12-inch cast-iron skillet. Add the chorizo, break it into chunks with a wooden spoon and cook over moderate heat, turning, until it is cooked through and lightly browned, about 8 minutes. Add the chopped onion and cook, stirring, until softened, about 5 minutes. Scrape the chorizo mixture into a large bowl and wipe out the skillet.

3. Heat the olive oil in the skillet. Add the diced potatoes, season with salt and pepper and cook over moderate heat, turning occasionally, until the potatoes are golden and crispy, about 6 minutes. Stir in the cooked chorizo mixture. Remove the skillet from the heat.

4. Using the bowl of a ladle, make 8 indentations in the potato-chorizo mixture about 1 inch apart; crack an egg into each one. Place the skillet in the middle of the oven and bake for about 12 minutes, or until the egg whites are just set but the yolks are still runny. Spoon an egg, accompanied by potatoes and chorizo, onto each plate and serve immediately, passing toast and hot sauce at the table.
—*David Kinch*

NOTE Spicy fresh chorizo, which looks a lot like Italian sausage links, gets its distinctive red color and smoky flavor from the smoked Spanish paprika called pimentón de la Vera. It is available at Whole Foods markets and many Latin American food stores. Mexican chorizo is typically dried and should not be substituted.

MAKE AHEAD The potatoes can be boiled a day ahead and refrigerated. Bring them to room temperature before proceeding.

BAKED EGGS WITH CHORIZO AND POTATOES

Chilean winemakers Agustin and
Valeria Huneeus serve a spectacular
Easter dinner at their family villa.

spring

starters & drinks 116

main courses 130

side dishes 174

desserts & brunch 190

starters & drinks

starters

Asian Chicken Noodle Soup

TOTAL: 30 MIN
4 SERVINGS ●

- 4 ounces sugar snap peas or snow peas
- 4 ounces green tea buckwheat noodles (soba; see Note)
- 1 tablespoon plus 1 teaspoon Asian sesame oil
- ¾ pound skinless, boneless chicken cutlets, cut into ¼-inch strips

Salt and freshly ground pepper

- ½ pound shiitake mushrooms, stems discarded and caps thinly sliced
- 6 cups low-sodium chicken broth
- 3 tablespoons low-sodium soy sauce
- 3 tablespoons oyster sauce
- 8 canned water chestnuts, thinly sliced
- 2 scallions, thinly sliced

1. Bring a medium saucepan of salted water to a boil over high heat. Add the sugar snaps and cook until bright green, about 1 minute. With a slotted spoon, transfer the sugar snaps to a large plate

to cool. Add the buckwheat noodles to the saucepan and boil until the noodles are al dente, about 5 minutes. Drain the noodles in a colander; rinse them with cold water and drain again.

2. In a large saucepan, heat 1 tablespoon of the sesame oil. Add the chicken strips, season with salt and ground pepper and cook over moderately high heat, stirring occasionally, until the chicken strips are lightly browned outside and white throughout, about 3 minutes. Transfer the cooked chicken to the large plate.

3. Add the remaining 1 teaspoon of sesame oil and the sliced shiitake to the saucepan and season with salt and pepper. Cover and cook over moderate heat, stirring a few times, until the mushrooms are tender, about 5 minutes. Add the chicken broth, soy sauce and oyster sauce and bring to a boil. Add the cooked noodles, chicken and sugar snaps and the sliced water chestnuts and scallions and bring to a simmer over moderate heat. Season with salt and pepper and serve. —*Nichole Birdsall*

NOTE Green tea buckwheat noodles (soba) are available at health food stores and Japanese markets.

WINE Tart, citrusy Riesling.

Lemony Artichoke and Potato Soup

ACTIVE: 1 HR; TOTAL: 1 HR 45 MIN
6 SERVINGS ● ● ○

- 2 lemons—1 halved, 1 cut into wedges
- 6 medium artichokes
- ¼ cup extra-virgin olive oil, plus more for drizzling
- 1 medium head of garlic, cloves peeled and very thinly sliced (½ cup)
- 1½ pounds Yukon Gold potatoes, peeled and cut into 1-inch cubes
- 6½ cups water

Salt

- 2 tablespoons whole black peppercorns

1. Fill a large bowl with water and squeeze the lemon halves into it. Working with 1 artichoke at a time, trim the base, removing the stem and trimming the tough outer leaves beneath the heart. Cut off the top two-thirds of the leaves, leaving only the heart. With a small spoon, scrape out the hairy choke. Submerge the trimmed artichoke heart in the lemon water to keep it from browning. Repeat this process with the remaining 5 artichokes. Once all the artichokes hearts have been trimmed, slice them ¼ inch thick and return them to the lemon water.

2. In a large, deep saucepan, heat the ¼ cup of olive oil. Add the garlic and cook over low heat until softened but not browned, 5 minutes. Drain the artichokes and add them to the saucepan along with the potatoes, the water and a pinch of salt. Bring to a boil. Put the peppercorns in a tea ball or tie them up in cheesecloth and immerse in the soup. Simmer until the artichokes and potatoes are tender, 30 minutes. Discard the peppercorns.

3. Using a fork or potato masher, partially mash the potatoes to thicken the broth. Season the soup with salt, ladle into bowls and drizzle with olive oil. Serve with the lemon wedges. —*Salvatore Denaro*

MAKE AHEAD The soup can be refrigerated overnight. Reheat gently.

WINE Zippy, fresh Pinot Bianco.

Lemony Asparagus Soup

TOTAL: 35 MIN
6 SERVINGS ● ●

3 pounds asparagus, twelve 3-inch tips reserved, the rest cut into ½-inch pieces

2 tablespoons extra-virgin olive oil

1 small white onion, halved and very thinly sliced

4 cups chicken stock

Two 1-inch wide strips of lemon zest, plus 1 teaspoon finely grated lemon zest for garnish

2 teaspoons fresh lemon juice

Salt and freshly ground white pepper

1. Bring a large saucepan of water to a boil over high heat. Fill a large bowl with ice water. Add all the asparagus to the boiling water and cook until bright green and barely tender, about 3 minutes. Drain and transfer to the ice water to cool, then drain again. Cut the 12 asparagus tips in half lengthwise and set aside.

2. Wipe out the saucepan. Add the olive oil and heat over high heat until shimmering. Add the onion and cook over moderately high heat, stirring, until softened, about 5 minutes. Add the chicken stock and lemon zest strips, bring to a boil and simmer for 5 minutes. Add the asparagus pieces and cook until tender, about 5 minutes. Discard the lemon zest strips.

3. Puree the soup in a blender. Return it to the saucepan, stir in the lemon juice and season with salt and white pepper; reheat if necessary. Ladle into bowls and garnish with the asparagus tips and grated lemon zest; serve hot or chilled.
—*Shelley Lindgren*

WINE Zesty, fresh Albariño.

Asparagus Egg Drop Soup

TOTAL: 25 MIN
4 SERVINGS ● ●

"With its wispy bits of egg and bright green asparagus spears, this dish is like a spring storm," says Sara Kate Gillingham-Ryan, food blogger and author of *The Greyston Bakery Cookbook*.

2 tablespoons extra-virgin olive oil

1 onion, halved and thinly sliced

4 cups vegetable or chicken broth

½ pound asparagus, cut on the diagonal into 1-inch lengths

2 eggs

Kosher salt and freshly ground pepper

½ cup shaved Pecorino Romano

1. In a large saucepan, heat the oil. Add the onion and cook over moderate heat until softened, 8 minutes. Pour in the broth and bring to a simmer. Add the asparagus and cook until just tender, 3 minutes.

2. In a bowl, whisk the eggs and season with salt and pepper. Slowly pour the eggs into the simmering broth, stirring gently and constantly, until cooked, about 30 seconds. Season with salt and pepper. Ladle the soup into bowls and top with the pecorino. —*Sara Kate Gillingham-Ryan*

WINE Peppery, refreshing Grüner Veltliner.

Fallen Polenta and Goat Cheese Soufflé with Mixed Salad

TOTAL: 40 MIN
4 SERVINGS ● ○

½ cup plus 1 tablespoon instant polenta

1 tablespoon freshly grated Parmigiano-Reggiano cheese

2 cups milk

5½ ounces fresh goat cheese (⅔ cup)

4 large eggs, separated

2 tablespoons snipped chives

Kosher salt and freshly ground pepper

2 tablespoons extra-virgin olive oil

1 tablespoon fresh lemon juice

1 bunch arugula (6 ounces), thick stems removed

1 small head of radicchio, leaves torn into bite-size pieces

1. Preheat the oven to 425°. In a small bowl, mix 1 tablespoon of the polenta with the Parmigiano-Reggiano. Generously butter an 8-inch glass or ceramic baking dish and coat it with the polenta-cheese mixture.

2. In a medium saucepan, bring the milk to a simmer. Whisk in the remaining ½ cup of polenta and cook over moderate heat, stirring, until thickened, about 5 minutes. Remove from the heat. Whisk in the goat cheese, egg yolks, chives, 2 teaspoons of kosher salt and ½ teaspoon of pepper.

3. In a large bowl, beat the egg whites until stiff. Beat one-fourth of the whites into the polenta, then fold the polenta into the remaining whites. Pour the mixture into the prepared baking dish and bake on the lowest rack of the oven for about 20 minutes, until the soufflé is golden, risen and only slightly jiggly in the center.

4. In a medium bowl, whisk the olive oil with the lemon juice and season with salt and pepper. Add the arugula and radicchio, toss and transfer to 4 plates. Spoon the soufflé, hot or at room temperature, alongside and serve. —*Grace Parisi*

WINE Minerally, complex Sauvignon Blanc.

Egg White Soufflés with Ratatouille

ACTIVE: 35 MIN; TOTAL: 1 HR

4 SERVINGS ● ●

Ratatouille contains all kinds of vegetables, including zucchini, yellow squash, eggplant, tomatoes and peppers. Sandro Gamba, executive chef at the Four Seasons in Westlake Village, California, sometimes makes his in a skillet, then tops it with fluffy egg whites that puff up in the oven. "People look at it like it's candy," he says. "They see how pretty it is, and they want to eat it."

One 6-ounce zucchini

One 6-ounce yellow squash

 1 red bell pepper

 1 yellow bell pepper

 ½ pound Italian eggplant

 1 medium tomato, peeled
    and seeded

 1 medium onion

 2 tablespoons extra-virgin
    olive oil

 2 garlic cloves, smashed

 1 tablespoon tomato paste

 1 tablespoon ketchup

 ¼ cup chopped basil

Salt and freshly ground
    white pepper

 4 large egg whites

 2 tablespoons freshly grated
    Parmigiano-Reggiano cheese

1. Preheat the oven to 400°. Cut the zucchini, yellow squash, red and yellow bell peppers, eggplant, tomato and onion into 1-inch dice and keep in separate piles. In a large skillet, heat the oil. Add the onion and garlic and cook over moderate heat until softened, 6 minutes. Add the zucchini, yellow squash and bell peppers, cover and cook over moderate heat, stirring occasionally, until softened, 10 minutes. Add the eggplant, tomato, tomato paste and ketchup and cook over low heat, stirring occasionally, until the eggplant is soft, 10 minutes. Stir in the chopped basil and season with salt and white pepper. Spoon the ratatouille into four 8-ounce ramekins and set aside.

2. In a large stainless steel bowl, beat the egg whites with a pinch of salt until firm peaks form. Spoon the beaten egg whites over the ratatouille in each ramekin, gently spreading them in an even layer. Sprinkle the Parmigiano-Reggiano on top of the egg whites and bake the soufflés in the upper third of the oven until the egg whites are golden brown and crisp, about 10 minutes. Serve the soufflés immediately.
—*Sandro Gamba*

WINE Lively, tart Sauvignon Blanc.

Two-Cheese Enchiladas

ACTIVE: 1 HR; TOTAL: 2 HR

6 SERVINGS

Louis Lambert, chef-owner of Lamberts Downtown Barbecue in Austin, dips corn tortillas in hot oil to soften them, then stuffs them with Monterey Jack cheese and *queso blanco* and covers them in a pungent *salsa roja*—a red sauce made with dried chiles and tomatoes.

 ½ cup vegetable oil, plus more
    for the baking dish

 3½ cups Salsa Roja
    (recipe follows)

Twelve 6-inch corn tortillas

 2 cups shredded *queso blanco*
    (½ pound)

 2 cups shredded Monterey Jack
    cheese (½ pound)

 ¾ cup very finely chopped
    onion

 2 cups finely shredded
    green cabbage

 2 medium plum tomatoes, very
    finely chopped

1. Preheat the oven to 350°. Lightly oil a 9-by-13-inch glass or ceramic baking dish. In a medium skillet, heat the ½ cup of vegetable oil over moderate heat. In another medium skillet, warm ½ cup of the Salsa Roja over moderate heat. Using tongs, dip the tortillas in the hot vegetable oil, coating both sides, until they are softened, about 5 seconds. Dip each tortilla in the Salsa Roja to coat and transfer to a plate, stacking the sauce-coated tortillas on top of each other.

2. In a medium bowl, mix the *queso blanco* with the Monterey Jack cheese. Set a sauce-coated tortilla on a work surface and spoon ¼ cup of the cheese and about 1 tablespoon of the finely chopped onion in the center. Loosely roll up the tortilla like a cigar and set it in the prepared baking dish, seam side down. Repeat with the remaining tortillas, onion and all but 1 cup of the cheese. Pour the remaining 3 cups of Salsa Roja over the enchiladas and sprinkle the remaining cheese on top.

3. Bake the enchiladas for 25 minutes, or until the cheese is melted, the enchiladas are heated through and the Salsa Roja is bubbling. Scatter the cabbage and tomatoes over the enchiladas and serve.
—*Louis Lambert*

WINE Fresh, fruity rosé.

SALSA ROJA

TOTAL: 35 MIN

MAKES 5 CUPS ●

The key to a great enchilada is the sauce. Mexican cooks refer to it as "gravy," and each region of Texas has its own distinct version. Salsa Roja is most common in the high desert of western Texas, where, Lambert found, whole dried chiles are a mainstay. In his opinion, this slightly sweet, richly flavored peppery sauce is the very best enchilada gravy.

 8 large ancho chiles, stemmed
    and seeded

 1 small dried red chile, stemmed
    and most seeds discarded

 1 quart chicken stock or
    low-sodium broth

 3 plum tomatoes, chopped

 3 garlic cloves, chopped

 1 small onion, chopped

 1 tablespoon light brown sugar

1 tablespoon vegetable oil
2 teaspoons ground cumin
2 teaspoons kosher salt
1 teaspoon freshly ground
   black pepper
1 tablespoon cider vinegar

In a medium saucepan, combine all of the ingredients except the cider vinegar and bring to a boil over moderately high heat; boil for 2 minutes. Cover, remove from the heat and let stand for 10 minutes. Working in batches, puree the sauce in a blender until smooth. Transfer to a bowl and stir in the cider vinegar. —*L.L.*

MAKE AHEAD The sauce can be refrigerated for up to 1 week.

Fromage Fort

TOTAL: 10 MIN
4 SERVINGS ● ○ ○

Fromage fort (French for "strong cheese") is the ultimate way of using leftover cheese. F&W contributing editor Jacques Pépin's father used to combine Camembert, Brie, Swiss, blue cheese and goat cheese with his mother's leek broth, white wine and garlic. These ingredients marinated in a cold cellar for up to a week and a half (he liked it very strong). Jacques' wife, Gloria, makes a milder version in a food processor that takes only seconds. It freezes well.

½ pound of cheese pieces
1 garlic clove
¼ cup dry white wine
Freshly ground black pepper
Salt
Crackers or sliced bread, for serving

In a food processor, combine the cheese with the garlic, wine and a big grinding of black pepper. Process for about 30 seconds, until creamy but not too soft. Taste and add salt if desired. Pack the mixture into small containers. Serve cold with crackers, or spread on bread and broil for a few minutes until the cheese is browned and fragrant. —*Jacques Pépin*

WINE Lively, tart Sauvignon Blanc.

EGG WHITE SOUFFLÉS WITH RATATOUILLE

FROMAGE FORT

CRISPY TURKEY KATHI ROLLS
WITH MINT-AND-DATE DIPPING SAUCE

Chicken Liver Pâté

TOTAL: 35 MIN PLUS OVERNIGHT CHILLING

6 TO 8 SERVINGS ●

This silky-smooth pâté is inexpensive and simple to make. The chicken livers are briefly simmered in water with aromatics before they're blended with butter in a food processor. If you have the opportunity to choose, shop for pale-colored chicken livers; they tend to have a mellower, richer flavor than deep red ones.

- ½ pound chicken livers, well-trimmed
- ½ small onion, thinly sliced
- 1 small garlic clove, smashed and peeled
- 1 bay leaf
- ¼ teaspoon thyme leaves
Kosher salt
- ½ cup water
- 1½ sticks unsalted butter, at room temperature
- 2 teaspoons Cognac or Scotch whisky
Freshly ground pepper

1. In a medium saucepan, combine the chicken livers, onion, garlic, bay leaf, thyme and ½ teaspoon of salt. Add the water and bring to a simmer. Cover, reduce the heat to low and cook, stirring occasionally, until the livers are barely pink inside, about 3 minutes. Remove from the heat and let stand, covered, for 5 minutes.

2. Discard the bay leaf. Using a slotted spoon, transfer the livers, onion and garlic to a food processor; process until coarsely pureed. With the machine on, add the butter, 2 tablespoons at a time, until incorporated. Add the Cognac, season with salt and pepper and process until completely smooth. Scrape the pâté into 2 or 3 large ramekins. Press a piece of plastic wrap directly onto the surface of the pâté and refrigerate until firm. Serve chilled.
—*Jacques Pépin*

SERVE WITH Toasted baguette slices.

MAKE AHEAD The pâté can be covered with a thin layer of melted butter, then wrapped in plastic and refrigerated for up to 1 week or frozen for up to 2 months.

WINE Lush, fragrant Viognier.

Crispy Turkey Kathi Rolls with Mint-and-Date Dipping Sauce

TOTAL: 1 HR 20 MIN

MAKES 16 ROLLS ● ●

Kathi rolls, a popular street food in India, are made by rolling vegetables or meat in roti, an Indian flat bread. In her fabulous take on the recipe, television cooking show host and cookbook author Padma Lakshmi wraps flour tortillas around a succulent filling of ground turkey, fresh ginger, curry and basil, then pan-fries the rolls until crispy. These decadent hors d'oeuvres can be eaten as finger food.

- 1½ tablespoons canola oil, plus more for frying
- ½ cup finely chopped onion
- 1½ teaspoons minced, peeled fresh ginger
- ½ teaspoon very finely chopped garlic
- ½ teaspoon Madras curry powder
- ½ teaspoon *amchoor* (optional; see Note)
- ¾ pound ground turkey
- 1 tablespoon soy sauce
- 2 tablespoons minced basil
- 1 tablespoon fresh lemon juice
Salt
Sixteen 6-inch flour tortillas, warmed
Mint-and-Date Dipping Sauce (recipe follows), for serving

1. In a large skillet, heat the 1½ tablespoons of canola oil. Add the onion, ginger and garlic and cook over moderate heat, stirring a few times, until the onion is translucent, about 5 minutes. Add the curry powder and *amchoor* and cook, stirring, until the spices become fragrant, about 1 minute. Add the turkey and soy sauce and cook, breaking up the meat, until

no trace of pink remains in the turkey, about 10 minutes. Stir in the basil and lemon juice and season with salt.

2. In a medium saucepan, heat 2 inches of canola oil to 350° over moderately high heat. Lay a tortilla on a work surface and spoon 2 tablespoons of the turkey filling across the lower third of it. Roll the tortilla around the filling, folding in the sides as you roll. Secure the rolls with 2 toothpicks. Repeat to form the remaining rolls.

3. Fry the rolls 3 or 4 at a time, turning once, until browned and crisp, about 4 minutes per batch. Drain on paper towels. Remove the toothpicks and serve the rolls with the Mint-and-Date Dipping Sauce.
—*Padma Lakshmi*

NOTE *Amchoor*, dried mango powder, adds a distinctive tart flavor to foods. It's available at Indian markets and from kalustyans.com.

MAKE AHEAD The fried rolls can be kept at room temperature for up to 2 hours. Reheat in the oven before serving.

WINE Fresh, fruity rosé.

MINT-AND-DATE DIPPING SAUCE

TOTAL: 20 MIN

MAKES ABOUT 1 CUP

● ● ● ●

- 2 cups mint leaves
- 3 pitted Medjool dates, finely chopped
- 1 serrano chile, seeded and chopped
- 3 tablespoons fresh lemon juice
- 2 tablespoons water
Salt

In a blender, combine the mint leaves, dates, serrano chile, lemon juice and water and puree until smooth. Transfer the dipping sauce to a bowl and season with salt. Serve at room temperature. —*P.L.*

MAKE AHEAD The dipping sauce can be prepared and kept at room temperature up to 4 hours before serving.

Sweet and Savory Pork Empanadas

TOTAL: 2 HR 30 MIN

MAKES 18 EMPANADAS ●

DOUGH

4 large egg yolks

1 large egg

3½ cups all-purpose flour, plus more for dusting

2 teaspoons salt

6 tablespoons cold unsalted butter, cut into tablespoons

½ cup dry white wine

¼ cup plus 1 tablespoon milk

FILLING

3 tablespoons unsalted butter

3 tablespoons extra-virgin olive oil

1 large white onion, minced

1 tablespoon sugar

1¼ pounds pork tenderloin, finely chopped

Salt and freshly ground pepper

½ cup amber beer

2 tablespoons soy sauce

1½ teaspoons paprika

1 teaspoon Chinese chile-garlic paste or *sambal oelek*

1 teaspoon ground cumin

½ jalapeño, seeded and minced

3 hard-cooked eggs, coarsely chopped

6 kalamata olives, thinly sliced

1 tablespoon golden raisins

INGREDIENT

empanada pastry

A shortcut for making empanadas is to buy rounds of Goya pastry *discos,* which are available in the frozen-food section of the supermarket. They can be filled as in the recipe above.

1. MAKE THE DOUGH: In a small bowl, beat 3 of the egg yolks with the whole egg. In a large bowl, whisk the 3½ cups of flour with the salt. With a pastry cutter or 2 knives, cut in the butter until it's evenly distributed in tiny flecks. Add the wine, ¼ cup of the milk and the beaten eggs and stir until a soft dough forms. Pat the dough into 2 disks, wrap in plastic and refrigerate for 30 minutes, until firm.

2. In a small bowl, whisk the 1 remaining egg yolk with the remaining 1 tablespoon of milk; cover the bowl and keep the egg wash chilled.

3. MAKE THE FILLING: In a medium skillet, melt 1 tablespoon of the butter in 1 tablespoon of the oil. Add the onion and cook over moderate heat, stirring occasionally, until softened and starting to brown, about 10 minutes. Stir in the sugar and cook, stirring occasionally, until the onion is browned, about 8 minutes longer.

4. Meanwhile, in a large skillet, melt the remaining 2 tablespoons of butter in the remaining 2 tablespoons of olive oil. Add the chopped pork, season with salt and pepper and cook over high heat until the pork is golden brown on the bottom, about 4 minutes. Stir and cook until no pink remains, about 3 minutes longer. Stir in the browned onions, beer, soy sauce, paprika, chile paste, cumin and jalapeño and cook for 1 minute. Transfer the filling to a large bowl. Stir in the hard-cooked eggs, olives and raisins and season with salt and pepper.

5. Preheat the oven to 350°. Turn 1 disk of dough out onto a floured work surface and sprinkle with flour. Roll out the dough ⅛ inch thick. Cut the dough into a 15-by-12-inch rectangle; discard the scraps. Cut the dough into nine 4-by-5-inch rectangles. Spoon about 3 tablespoons of filling onto one side of each rectangle. Moisten the edges with water and close the empanadas, pressing the edges to seal. Transfer the empanadas to a large rimmed baking sheet. Repeat with the second disk of dough and the remaining filling.

6. Brush the empanadas with the egg wash. Bake for about 20 minutes, rotating the baking sheets halfway through, until the empanadas are golden brown, then serve. —*Valeria Huneeus*

MAKE AHEAD The baked empanadas can be refrigerated overnight. Reheat them before serving.

WINE Rustic, peppery Malbec.

Scallop Fritters

TOTAL: 1 HR

6 SERVINGS

Vegetable oil, for frying

½ cup all-purpose flour

½ cup yellow cornmeal

2 teaspoons baking powder

Kosher salt and freshly ground pepper

2 large eggs, lightly beaten

¼ cup bottled clam broth

¼ cup pilsner beer

½ pound sea scallops, coarsely chopped

3 scallions, white and green parts, thinly sliced

¼ cup finely chopped red onion

1 small jalapeño with seeds, minced

Tartar sauce and lemon wedges, for serving

1. In a large saucepan, heat 2 inches of oil to 350°. Meanwhile, in a medium bowl, whisk the all-purpose flour with the cornmeal, baking powder, 1¼ teaspoons of salt and a pinch of pepper. Add the eggs, clam broth and beer and whisk until the batter is smooth. Fold in the scallops, scallions, onion and jalapeño.

2. Working in batches, drop heaping teaspoons of the batter into the oil and fry, turning occasionally, until golden brown all over, about 7 minutes. Using a slotted spoon, transfer the fritters to paper towels. Serve with tartar sauce and lemon wedges. —*Jimmy Bradley*

WINE Fresh, lively Soave.

L.A. designer Thomas Schoos pours O-Hurricanes (P. 128).

BLOOD ORANGE–SCALLOP CEVICHE

Blood Orange–Scallop Ceviche

ACTIVE: 45 MIN; TOTAL: 2 HR

8 SERVINGS ●

E. Michael Reidt, chef at the Penthouse restaurant at the Huntley Hotel in Santa Monica, California, garnishes this zesty ceviche with popcorn, a nod to Peruvian and Ecuadoran cuisine. "Whenever you go to a bar in Peru, you're given a big bowl of ceviche and a bowl of popcorn with your beer," Reidt says. "This puts them both together on one plate."

1¼ pounds sea scallops, quartered
½ cup fresh lime juice
½ cup fresh lemon juice
¼ cup pineapple juice
¼ cup fresh orange juice
2 tablespoons unsweetened coconut milk
1 tablespoon soy sauce
1 teaspoon Sriracha hot sauce
Salt and freshly ground black pepper
2 tablespoons extra-virgin olive oil
2 tablespoons rice vinegar
1 teaspoon sugar
1 red bell pepper, julienned
1 medium cucumber—peeled, seeded and julienned
1 medium carrot, julienned
One 1½-inch piece of fresh ginger, peeled and julienned
1 blood orange
1 cup lightly salted popcorn

1. Bring a medium saucepan of salted water to a boil over high heat. Add the sea scallops and cook for 1 minute. Drain the scallops and spread them out on a large plate. Cover with plastic wrap and refrigerate the scallops until well chilled.

2. In a large nonreactive bowl, whisk together the lime, lemon, pineapple and orange juices. Whisk in the coconut milk, soy sauce and Sriracha hot sauce and season with salt and black pepper. Stir in the chilled scallops, cover and marinate in the refrigerator for 1 hour.

3. In a medium bowl, whisk the olive oil with the rice vinegar and sugar and season with salt and black pepper. Add the julienned bell pepper, cucumber, carrot and fresh ginger and toss until the vegetables are well combined with the dressing.

4. Using a very sharp paring knife, peel the blood orange, carefully removing all of the bitter white pith. Cut in between the membranes, releasing the orange sections into a small bowl.

5. Divide the julienned vegetable mixture among 8 serving bowls. Using a slotted spoon, top the vegetables with the marinated scallops and pour a little of the marinade over each portion. Garnish with the orange sections and sprinkle with popcorn. Serve right away.
—*E. Michael Reidt*

WINE Lively, tart Sauvignon Blanc.

●HEALTHY ●MAKE AHEAD ·VEGETARIAN ●STAFF FAVORITE

KING CRAB AND AVOCADO SHOOTERS

CUCUMBER-GRAPEFRUIT CRAB SALAD

King Crab and Avocado Shooters

TOTAL: 30 MIN
8 SERVINGS ●

Zapallar, the small Chilean beach town in which Veramonte winery proprietors Agustin and Valeria Huneeus's family villa is located, has a wonderful fish market where Valeria buys excellent fresh crab. She loves tossing it with sweet and soft avocados, a little coconut milk and fresh ginger, then serving it in a glass, shooter-style, with a thick slice of avocado on top.

- 2 small Hass avocados—
  1 cut into ½-inch dice,
  1 cut into 8 wedges
- 2 tablespoons heavy cream
- 1 tablespoon fresh lemon juice
- 1 tablespoon finely chopped
  cilantro

Salt and freshly ground
  black pepper
- ½ pound king crab in the shell or
  6 ounces lump crabmeat
- 3 tablespoons unsweetened
  coconut milk
- ¼ teaspoon finely grated, peeled
  fresh ginger

1. In a shallow bowl, coarsely mash the diced avocado with a fork. Add the heavy cream and lemon juice and mash the mixture just until combined. Stir in the chopped cilantro and season generously with salt and pepper.

2. With kitchen scissors, cut the crab leg shells and pull out the crabmeat. Cut the crabmeat crosswise into 1-inch pieces and shred the crab. In a small bowl, combine the coconut milk and ginger. Fold in the shredded crabmeat and season with salt and black pepper.

3. Spoon the crab and avocado into 8 small glasses. Top each shooter with an avocado wedge and serve. —*Valeria Huneeus*

MAKE AHEAD The shelled crabmeat can be refrigerated overnight.

WINE Ripe, luxurious Chardonnay.

Cucumber-Grapefruit Crab Salad

TOTAL: 25 MIN
4 SERVINGS ●

Sandro Gamba, executive chef at the Four Seasons in Westlake Village, California, uses yogurt in many of his sauces and salad dressings. Here he mixes it with succulent Dungeness crab.

- ¼ cup plain nonfat yogurt
- 2 tablespoons fresh lime juice
- ½ teaspoon finely grated lime zest
- 2 tablespoons extra-virgin olive oil

Tabasco sauce
Salt and freshly ground white pepper

- ½ pound Dungeness crabmeat
- 1 teaspoon Champagne vinegar
- 1 seedless cucumber, peeled and sliced into thin half-moons
- 1 medium pink grapefruit, peeled and cut into segments
- ½ cup shelled edamame, steamed

1. In a large bowl, whisk the nonfat yogurt with the lime juice, lime zest, olive oil and a few dashes of Tabasco sauce. Season with salt and white pepper. Place the crabmeat in a bowl and fold in 3 tablespoons of the yogurt dressing.

2. Stir the Champagne vinegar into the remaining yogurt dressing. Fold in the cucumber slices, grapefruit segments and steamed edamame. Spoon the salad onto plates, top with the crab and serve.
—*Sandro Gamba*

Red Pepper and Walnut Dip

TOTAL: 25 MIN
MAKES 2 CUPS ●● ○

Muhammara, a smooth Middle Eastern bell pepper and walnut dip with a spicy kick, is traditionally served alongside fresh pita bread or roasted meats. Chris Hanna, president of Hanna Winery in Sonoma County, California, likes to serve the dip with crunchy raw fennel wedges.

- 3 medium red bell peppers
- ¾ cup walnuts (3 ounces)
- ¼ cup crushed whole-wheat crackers
- 1 tablespoon pomegranate molasses (see Note)
- 1 tablespoon fresh lemon juice
- ½ teaspoon ground cumin
- ½ teaspoon Aleppo pepper or ¼ teaspoon crushed red pepper
- 1 tablespoon extra-virgin olive oil, plus more for drizzling

Salt and freshly ground black pepper

- 1 tablespoon chopped parsley

Fennel bulbs, cored and cut in wedges

1. Light a grill. Grill the red bell peppers over moderately high heat, turning with tongs, until their skins are blackened all over. Transfer the charred red peppers to a bowl and let them cool completely. Use a paper towel to wipe the charred skins from the cooled red peppers. Core the peeled red peppers, wipe away any remaining seeds, and coarsely chop the peeled red pepper flesh.

2. In a food processor, combine the peppers, walnuts, crushed crackers, pomegranate molasses, lemon juice, cumin and Aleppo pepper and process until fairly smooth. With the machine on, add the 1 tablespoon of olive oil and process until creamy. Season with salt and pepper and transfer to a bowl. Drizzle the Red Pepper and Walnut Dip with olive oil, garnish with the chopped parsley and serve with the fennel wedges.
—*Chris Hanna*

NOTE Sweet-tart pomegranate molasses, made by reducing pomegranate juice to a dark, sticky syrup, gives dishes an exotic, tangy flavor. It is available at specialty food shops and Middle Eastern markets.

MAKE AHEAD The Red Pepper and Walnut Dip can be refrigerated in a covered container for up to 2 days. Bring to room temperature before serving with the fennel.

drinks

Virgin Strawberry Bellinis

TOTAL: 30 MIN
MAKES 5 DRINKS ○

The latest nonalcoholic mocktails at top restaurants and bars are as inventive and delicious as cocktails. David Slape, the bartender at Manhattan's PDT, makes this Virgin Bellini with strawberry puree and a sparkling cider from Normandy.

- 14 ounces hulled fresh strawberries
- 6 ounces water
- ½ cup granulated sugar
- 1½ ounces fresh lemon juice
- 15 ounces sparkling apple cider, chilled

In a medium saucepan over moderately high heat, combine the hulled strawberries, water and granulated sugar. Bring the mixture to a boil, stirring once or twice until the sugar has dissolved. Remove the saucepan from the heat and let the strawberries cool in their syrup. Stir the fresh lemon juice into the strawberry mixture. Transfer the cooled strawberries and their syrup to a food processor and blend until smooth; strain the puree through a fine sieve and discard the solids. Pour 1 ounce of strawberry puree into each of 5 Champagne flutes and top each drink with 3 ounces of sparkling apple cider.
—*David Slape*

SUPERFAST

a quick, easy crab dip

Blend together ½ cup each of cream cheese and mayonnaise and season with chopped chives, salt, pepper and hot sauce. Fold in 1 pound of lump crabmeat. Serve with crackers.

cheese plate

The perfect cheese plate should include a mix of fresh, aged, soft and hard cheeses, arranged in the order in which they should be tasted: from the lightest and freshest to the ripest and most intense. Here, cheese expert **Laura Werlin** lists quintessential American cheeses by style, including examples of each, starting with fresh cheeses and ending with washed-rind varieties.

fresh cheeses

These are ready to eat as soon as they're made—no aging required. They tend to have the mild, minerally flavors of their primary ingredients: milk and salt.

BASKET-MOLDED CHÈVRE Pure Luck Grade A Goat Dairy, Dripping Springs, TX (1) For this silky chèvre, the cheesemakers ladle curds made from the farm's goat milk into basket molds to drain (purelucktexas.com).

semisoft cheeses

Mild semisoft cheeses are most often aged from a few days to a few months. They melt beautifully under the slightest heat.

CRESCENZA Bellwether Farms, Petaluma, CA (2) This handmade cheese has the perfect texture for a semisoft cheese: creamy yet firm (bellwetherfarms.com).

soft-ripened cheeses

With white "bloomy" rinds and creamy interiors, these cheeses soften as they age.

GREEN HILL Sweet Grass Dairy, Thomasville, GA (3) This cheese gets its grassy flavors from the pasture that feeds the cows at Green Hill Dairy (sweetgrassdairy.com).

surface-ripened cheeses

Surface-ripened cheeses can be firm or molten, but they all have similarly wrinkly rinds and intensely flavored interiors. They are innoculated with special kinds of mold that ensure their exteriors ripen first.

BIJOU Vermont Butter & Cheese Company, Websterville, VT (4) This unctuous two-ounce goat's-milk round was introduced in 2006. Unwrap it and store it in the fridge, and it firms up to become a fantastic grating cheese; keep it covered and it just gets creamier (vtbutter andcheeseco.com).

semihard cheeses

A broad category that ranges from cheddar to Gouda, semihard cheeses can be aged for as little as a few months and up to a few years, or even longer.

FLAGSHIP RESERVE Beecher's Handmade Cheese, Seattle, WA (5) A cheddarlike cow's-milk cheese, Beecher's Flagship Reserve develops its nutty, sharp flavors while it ages in cloth wrapping for at least a year (beechershandmade cheese.com).

hard cheeses

Hard cheeses like Parmigiano-Reggiano are defined by their firm, granular texture and salty-sharp taste.

SARVECCHIO PARMESAN Sartori Foods, Plymouth, WI (6) SarVecchio is the closest thing to an American Parmigiano. It has a nutty, salty caramel taste (sartorifoods.com).

blue cheeses

Blue cheeses get their color from rich veins of mold and range in texture from creamy to hard.

ROGUE RIVER BLUE Rogue Creamery, Central Point, OR (7) This salty-sweet raw cow's-milk cheese is aged in grape leaves soaked in pear brandy (roguecreamery.com).

washed-rind cheeses

These cheeses get their characteristic orange-pink rinds from being "washed" (rubbed, really) with a solution of salt water and beneficial bacteria. Often described as stinky (in a good way), washed-rind cheeses can smell stronger than they taste.

GRAYSON Meadow Creek Dairy, Galax, VA (8) Prepared from the milk of Jersey cows, this soft, square-shaped cheese has earned a cult following for its beefy brown-butter flavors (meadowcreekdairy.com).

Pomelo-Mint Mojito

TOTAL: 5 MIN
MAKES 1 DRINK ●

This refreshing take on the classic mojito is made with sections of pomelo, an Asian citrus fruit that resembles a thick-skinned grapefruit. If pomelo is hard to find, grapefruit works wonderfully here.

- 4 peeled sections of pomelo or grapefruit, chopped
- 6 mint leaves
- 2 tablespoons orange juice concentrate or orange sorbet
- 1½ ounces white rum

Ice

Club soda

- 1 lime wedge

In a cocktail shaker, muddle the chopped pomelo sections with the mint leaves and orange juice concentrate. Add the white rum and ice and shake well. Pour the mixture into a highball glass. Top with club soda and garnish with the lime wedge. Serve the drink at once.

—*Jean-Georges Vongerichten*

Grilled-Lime Caipirinha

TOTAL: 10 MIN
MAKES 1 DRINK ●

E. Michael Reidt, chef at the Penthouse restaurant in the Huntley Hotel in Santa Monica, California, had used grilled limes

INGREDIENT

cachaça

A clear, fermented sugarcane alcohol made in Brazil, cachaça (pronounced kah-SHAH-sah) is the key ingredient in a caipirinha cocktail. Look for an artisanal cachaça, which will have more refined flavors than an industrially produced variety.

---

only to garnish fish before he realized they would also be amazing in a caipirinha. "They add a slight smokiness to the drink," he says. "We've also muddled in a few slices of jalapeño, and that was awesome."

- 1 lime
- 2 tablespoons superfine sugar, plus more for dusting

Ice cubes

- 3 ounces cachaça
- ½ ounce lemon-lime soda (optional)

1. Light a grill or preheat a grill pan over high heat. Trim the ends off the lime and slice the lime crosswise into ¼-inch-thick rounds. Dust both sides of the lime wheels with superfine sugar and grill the lime slices over high heat, turning them once, until the sugar is lightly caramelized, about 20 seconds per side.

2. In a rocks glass, muddle the grilled lime wheels with the 2 tablespoons of superfine sugar. Fill the glass with ice cubes, pour in the cachaça and top with the lemon-lime soda, if using. Stir the drink thoroughly and serve immediately.

—*E. Michael Reidt*

Ginger Margarita

TOTAL: 5 MIN
MAKES 1 DRINK ●

F&W contributing editor Jean-Georges Vongerichten's genius as a chef is unquestioned; less known are his gifts as a mixologist. In fact, he created most of the cocktails served at Lagoon restaurant, in the St. Regis Resort in Bora Bora, like this piquant Ginger Margarita.

Kosher salt

- 1 quarter-size slice of fresh ginger

One ¼-inch slice of Thai chile

- 1 teaspoon sugar
- 1 teaspoon fresh lemon juice
- 1½ ounces añejo tequila
- ½ ounce Cointreau

Ice

- 1 lime wedge

Fill a shallow dish with kosher salt. Moisten the rim of a margarita glass and press it into the salt. In a cocktail shaker, muddle the ginger slice, chile slice, sugar and fresh lemon juice. Add the tequila, Cointreau and ice and shake. Fill the salt-rimmed glass with ice and strain the cocktail over the ice. Squeeze the juice from the lime wedge into the cocktail and fasten the wedge to the glass; serve immediately.

—*Jean-Georges Vongerichten*

O-Hurricane Cocktail

TOTAL: 5 MIN
MAKES 1 DRINK ●

This classic New Orleans party drink is traditionally made with rum and sweet-tart passion fruit syrup and served in large, curvy glasses that are shaped like hurricane lamps. James Matusky, formerly the bar manager at O-Bar in West Hollywood, California, offers his interpretation: a sweet blend of grenadine and pineapple and orange juices amped up with berry schnapps and two kinds of rum.

Ice

- 3 ounces white rum
- ½ ounce DeKuyper Pucker Berry Fusion schnapps
- 1 ounce grenadine
- 1½ ounces lemon-lime soda
- ½ ounce pineapple juice
- ½ ounce orange juice
- ½ ounce Rose's lime juice
- ½ ounce Bacardi 151 rum
- 1 orange wedge
- 1 lime wedge

Fill a cocktail shaker with ice. Add the white rum, Berry Fusion schnapps, grenadine, lemon-lime soda, pineapple and orange juices and Rose's lime juice; shake well. Fill a hurricane glass or large wineglass with ice and strain the mixture over the ice. Top with the Bacardi 151 rum. Garnish the cocktail with the orange and lime wedges and serve immediately.

—*James Matusky*

O-HURRICANE COCKTAILS

main courses

Stir-Fried Tofu with Bok Choy

ACTIVE: 20 MIN; TOTAL: 50 MIN

4 SERVINGS ●

This nutritious dish, adapted from a recipe in Harumi Kurihara's *Harumi's Japanese Cooking*, is seasoned with a sprinkling of flavor-packed chicken bouillon.

- ¾ **pound firm tofu, drained**
- 2 **tablespoons sesame seeds**
- 1 **tablespoon Asian sesame oil**
- 1 **tablespoon vegetable oil**
- 1 **head of bok choy (about ¾ pound), leaves and stalks sliced crosswise 1 inch thick**
- 4 **cups bean sprouts (9 ounces)**
- 1 **teaspoon crushed or grated chicken bouillon cube**

Salt and freshly ground black pepper

1. Wrap the tofu in paper towels and drain in a strainer set over a bowl for 30 minutes. In a skillet, toast the sesame seeds over moderate heat until fragrant, 1 minute. Transfer the seeds to a plate and let cool, then grind to a coarse powder.

2. In a large skillet, heat the sesame oil. Add the drained tofu, breaking it up into chunks with a spoon, and stir-fry over moderately high heat until lightly browned, about 3 minutes. Transfer to a plate.

3. In the same skillet, heat the vegetable oil. Add the bok choy and stir-fry over moderately high heat until the stalks are just tender, 5 minutes. Add the bean sprouts and stir-fry until heated through. Stir in the browned tofu and season with the bouillon, salt and black pepper. Transfer to a bowl and garnish with the toasted sesame seeds. —*Harumi Kurihara*

WINE Light, fresh Pinot Grigio.

Lemony Shrimp Salad

 TOTAL: 30 MIN

4 SERVINGS ●

Richard Reddington, chef and owner of Redd in Yountville, California, tosses butter lettuce and shrimp in a lemony vinaigrette, then tops the dish with a second salad of romaine, tomato, avocado and bacon in a Caesar dressing. Here, the F&W kitchen combines the best elements of both salads to create one amazing dish.

- ½ **lemon, plus 2 tablespoons fresh lemon juice**
- ½ **teaspoon black peppercorns**

Salt

- 1 **pound shelled and deveined medium shrimp**
- 2 **tablespoons extra-virgin olive oil**
- 2 **tablespoons grapeseed or vegetable oil**

Pinch of sugar

Freshly ground black pepper

- 2 **hearts of romaine, cut into 1-inch-wide ribbons**
- 1 **cup grape tomatoes, halved**
- 1 **Hass avocado, diced**
- 2 **tablespoons snipped chives**

1. Fill a medium saucepan with water. Squeeze the lemon half into the water, then add the squeezed lemon rind along with the peppercorns and a generous pinch of salt; bring to a boil. Add the shrimp and simmer until they are curled and just pink, about 3 minutes. Using a slotted spoon, transfer the cooked shrimp to a paper towel–lined plate. Place the shrimp in the freezer until they are just chilled, about 5 minutes.

2. Meanwhile, in a large bowl, whisk the lemon juice with the olive oil, grapeseed oil, sugar and a generous pinch each of salt and ground black pepper. Add the romaine ribbons, halved grape tomatoes, diced avocado and chilled shrimp and toss the salad well. Transfer to plates, garnish with the snipped chives and serve immediately. —*Richard Reddington*

WINE Lively, tart Sauvignon Blanc.

Poached Salmon Salad with Lettuce and Asparagus

TOTAL: 45 MIN
4 SERVINGS ●

The simple poaching-in-a-bag technique used to cook this salmon eliminates the need for extra oil or butter. "The fish becomes buttery and just flakes away," says chef Erik Oberholtzer of Tender Greens in Los Angeles. "It's the juiciest salmon you'll ever have."

Salt
24 large asparagus stalks, peeled
¼ cup fresh lemon juice, preferably Meyer lemon, plus four 3-by-1-inch strips of zest
¼ cup extra-virgin olive oil
1 medium shallot, minced
1 tablespoon very finely chopped fresh tarragon
1 teaspoon Dijon mustard
Freshly ground black pepper
Four 6-ounce center-cut skinless salmon fillets
½ pound Boston lettuce or miner's lettuce, torn into bite-size pieces

1. Bring a large, deep skillet of salted water to a boil over high heat. Add the asparagus stalks and cook until they are tender, about 4 minutes. Using tongs, transfer the cooked asparagus to a platter; reserve the water in the skillet.
2. In a small bowl, whisk the lemon juice with the olive oil, shallot, tarragon and Dijon mustard. Season the vinaigrette with salt and black pepper.
3. Season the salmon fillets with salt and black pepper. Make four long cuts in each strip of lemon zest to make a fan. Place a lemon zest fan on each salmon fillet; place each fillet in a small resealable freezer-safe plastic bag and seal, pressing out the air. Bring the water in the skillet to a simmer. Add the salmon in the bags and poach at a gentle simmer until just cooked through, about 10 minutes.

4. Meanwhile, in a large bowl, toss the lettuce with half of the vinaigrette. Spread the lettuce on plates, top with the asparagus and drizzle with more of the vinaigrette. Remove the salmon from the bags and arrange over the asparagus; discard the zest. Drizzle the salmon with the remaining vinaigrette and serve right away.
—*Matt Lyman and Erik Oberholtzer*
WINE Fruity, low-oak Chardonnay.

Chinese Chicken Salad

TOTAL: 45 MIN
4 SERVINGS ●

Even though it's cooked without extra fat, the chicken in this crunchy, colorful main-course salad stays flavorful and moist because it's poached with the skin on (the skin is removed before serving).

1 whole bone-in chicken breast with skin (1¼ pounds)
4 scallions, 1 thinly sliced
One 1-inch piece of peeled fresh ginger, thinly sliced, plus 1½ teaspoons finely grated ginger
Salt
3 tablespoons vegetable oil, plus more for frying
8 wonton wrappers, cut into ⅓-inch strips
3 tablespoons unseasoned rice vinegar
1 tablespoon Asian sesame oil
2 teaspoons soy sauce
Freshly ground pepper
¾ pound baby bok choy, stems halved, leaves left whole
2 cups mizuna (1 ounce)
1 cup mung bean sprouts (3 ounces)
1 medium carrot, julienned
1 tablespoon chopped cilantro
¼ cup chopped roasted, salted peanuts

1. In a medium saucepan, cover the chicken breast with water and bring to a simmer over moderately high heat. Reduce the heat to low and skim the surface. Add the

3 whole scallions, the sliced ginger and a pinch of salt. Simmer until the chicken breast is cooked through, about 25 minutes. Transfer the chicken to a plate and let cool to room temperature. Discard the skin and bones and shred the meat.
2. Meanwhile, in a medium saucepan, heat ½ inch of vegetable oil over moderately high heat until shimmering. Add a small handful of the wonton strips and fry over moderate heat until they are crisp and golden brown, about 10 seconds. Use a slotted spoon or spider to transfer the fried strips to a paper towel–lined plate; repeat with the remaining wonton strips.
3. In small bowl, whisk the rice vinegar with the sesame oil, soy sauce, grated ginger and 3 tablespoons of vegetable oil. Season the dressing with salt and pepper.
4. In a large bowl, toss together the sliced scallion, the bok choy stems and leaves, mizuna, bean sprouts, julienned carrot, chopped cilantro and peanuts. Add the chicken, wonton strips and dressing; toss the salad and serve at once.
—*Matt Lyman and Erik Oberholtzer*
MAKE AHEAD The poached chicken breast can be refrigerated overnight. The fried wonton strips can be stored overnight at room temperature.
WINE Zippy, fresh Pinot Bianco.

Flatiron Steak Salad with Thai Dressing

TOTAL: 40 MIN
4 SERVINGS ●

"This is the dish that I make to show wine geeks what beer can do with food," says Sang Yoon, chef and owner of Father's Office, a bar and restaurant in Santa Monica, California. "I really love the acidity of the lime juice and fish sauce in Thai food. Those high-pitched flavors are impossible with wine, but a silky-smooth Belgian beer allows them to come through. I serve this salad to my sommelier friends and say, 'Put your Riesling away.'"

2 tablespoons vegetable oil, plus more for brushing

2½ tablespoons fresh lime juice

2 tablespoons Asian fish sauce

2 tablespoons soy sauce

1 garlic clove, quartered

½ serrano chile, seeded and coarsely chopped

One ½-inch piece of peeled fresh ginger, coarsely chopped (about ½ tablespoon)

1 teaspoon sugar

Salt and freshly ground pepper

1 pound flatiron steak or top blade steak, about 1 inch thick

2 heads of baby romaine, leaves separated (and torn if large)

¾ pound cherry tomatoes, halved

1 medium cucumber—peeled, halved, seeded and sliced ¼ inch thick

½ large red onion, thinly sliced

2 scallions, thinly sliced

½ cup basil leaves

½ cup cilantro leaves

1. Light a grill. In a blender, puree the 2 tablespoons of oil with the lime juice, fish sauce, soy sauce, garlic, chile, ginger and sugar. Season with salt and pepper.

2. Brush the steak with vegetable oil and season with salt and pepper. Grill over high heat until the meat is charred outside and medium-rare within, about 5 minutes per side. Transfer to a work surface and let it rest for 5 minutes.

3. Meanwhile, in a bowl, toss the romaine with the cherry tomatoes, cucumber, onion, scallions, basil and cilantro leaves. Pour two-thirds of the dressing over the salad and toss. Divide among 4 plates. Slice the steak ⅓ inch thick across the grain and serve alongside the salad. Pass the remaining dressing at the table.
—*Sang Yoon*

MAKE AHEAD The citrus-and-soy dressing can be refrigerated overnight.

BEER Smooth, fruity Belgian ale.

Spicy Vietnamese Chicken Sandwiches

ACTIVE: 30 MIN; TOTAL: 1 HR 30 MIN

6 SERVINGS ●

The Vietnamese accents here come from Sriracha (Southeast Asian chile sauce) and sweet-salty pickled onions.

¾ pound skinless, boneless chicken breast, sliced ¼ inch thick

2 tablespoons soy sauce

1 tablespoon mayonnaise, plus more for spreading

1 large shallot, thinly sliced

2 carrots, halved crosswise and thinly sliced lengthwise

½ cup pickled cocktail onions, halved, plus ¼ cup of the pickling liquid from the jar

One 10-ounce baguette, split lengthwise and toasted

Sriracha or other hot sauce, for spreading

1 Kirby cucumber, very thinly sliced lengthwise

Cilantro sprigs

1. In a bowl, toss the chicken with the soy sauce, 1 tablespoon of mayonnaise and the sliced shallot. Cover and let marinate in the refrigerator for 1 hour.

2. Meanwhile, in another bowl, mix the sliced carrots with the pickled onions and their liquid and let stand at room temperature for 1 hour.

3. Heat a grill pan. Grill the chicken and shallot slices over high heat until charred and the chicken is just cooked through, about 2 minutes per side.

4. Spread mayonnaise on the cut sides of the baguette, then spread with Sriracha. On the bottom half of the baguette, layer the carrots, pickled onions and sliced cucumber, then top with the grilled chicken and shallot slices. Lay cilantro sprigs over the chicken and close the sandwich. Cut crosswise into 6 pieces and serve.
—*Marcia Kiesel*

WINE Tart, citrusy Riesling.

Deviled Ham Salad on Marbled Rye Bread

TOTAL: 25 MIN

4 SERVINGS ●

½ pound smoked ham, coarsely chopped

½ cup mayonnaise

3 tablespoons chopped flat-leaf parsley

1 jalapeño, seeded and minced

1 tablespoon Dijon mustard

½ teaspoon sweet paprika

Hot sauce and salt, for seasoning

8 slices of bakery-style marbled rye bread, crusts removed, or 32 slices of cocktail rye

1½ cups alfalfa sprouts

1. Pulse the ham in a food processor until finely chopped. Transfer the ham to a medium bowl. Stir in the mayonnaise, parsley, jalapeño, mustard and paprika; season the deviled ham salad with hot sauce and salt.

2. Lay half of the bread slices on a work surface and spread them with the deviled ham. Top with the alfalfa sprouts and close the sandwiches. If making larger sandwiches, quarter them before serving.
—*Marcia Kiesel*

MAKE AHEAD The deviled ham salad can be refrigerated overnight.

WINE Fresh, fruity rosé.

SUPERFAST

making salad sandwiches

Any main-course salad makes a great filling for a crisp toasted baguette. Drizzle in some extra dressing and add plenty of crunchy ingredients like grated carrot and sliced cucumber.

● HEALTHY ●MAKE AHEAD ○ VEGETARIAN ● STAFF FAVORITE

SOFT PORK TACOS WITH SPICY BLACK BEANS

BARBECUED SALMON SANDWICH

Soft Pork Tacos with Spicy Black Beans

ACTIVE: 50 MIN; TOTAL: 4 HR PLUS OVERNIGHT SOAKING

4 SERVINGS ● ●

BEANS

1½ cups dried black beans
   (10½ ounces), soaked
   overnight in cold water
   and drained
 1 tablespoon vegetable oil
 1 medium onion, very finely
   chopped
 4 medium garlic cloves,
   very finely chopped
 1 large jalapeño, seeded
   and very finely chopped
 1 medium tomato,
   coarsely chopped
 1 teaspoon dried oregano
Salt and freshly ground
   black pepper

PORK

 ¾ cup low-sodium chicken broth
 1 head of garlic, cloves
   peeled and thinly sliced
 1 medium onion, finely chopped
 1 habanero chile, seeded
   and minced
 1 large serrano chile, seeded
   and minced
 1 bay leaf
 ½ teaspoon ground cumin
Salt and freshly ground pepper
One 1-pound pork loin roast,
   trimmed of excess fat
Warm corn tortillas and salsa,
   for serving

1. PREPARE THE BEANS: In a large sauce-pan, cover the beans with 2 inches of water and bring to a boil. Simmer over low heat for 1 hour, stirring occasionally.
2. In a medium skillet, heat the oil. Add the onion, garlic and jalapeño and cook over moderate heat until softened, about 7 min-utes. Add to the beans, along with the tomato, oregano and water to cover. Season with salt and pepper and simmer until the beans are tender, about 2 hours longer, replenishing the water if necessary.
3. MEANWHILE, COOK THE PORK: Preheat the oven to 300°. In a small enameled cast-iron casserole, combine the broth, garlic, onion, habanero and serrano chiles, bay leaf, cumin and ½ teaspoon each of salt and pepper; bring to a simmer. Season the pork with salt and pepper and add it to the cas-serole. Cover with foil and bake for about 1 hour, turning the pork once, until tender. Transfer the pork to a plate and cover with plastic wrap until cool enough to handle.
4. Remove the bay leaf. Shred the pork and stir into the broth. Season with salt. Fill the tortillas with pork and serve with the black beans and salsa. —*Nichole Birdsall*
WINE Rustic, peppery Malbec.

134

Dry-Rubbed Salmon Tacos with Tomatillo-Avocado Slaw

TOTAL: 40 MIN
4 SERVINGS ● ●

For maximum flavor in minimal time, Jeff Smith, the owner of Hourglass winery in Napa Valley, opts for spice rubs over marinades. After trying out spice blends for heartier fish, he discovered that ground coffee lends earthiness to the rub.

- 1 teaspoon ground cumin
- 1 teaspoon chile powder
- 1 teaspoon brown sugar
- ¼ teaspoon finely ground coffee

Salt and freshly ground pepper

Two 8-ounce skinless center-cut salmon fillets

Extra-virgin olive oil, for brushing

- 2 tomatillos, husked and quartered
- 2 tablespoons chopped cilantro
- 1 small jalapeño, seeded and quartered
- 1 garlic clove, peeled
- 6 tablespoons sour cream
- 1 ripe Hass avocado—halved, peeled and pitted
- 4 cups finely shredded red and green cabbages (12 ounces)
- 8 corn tortillas

Hot sauce and lime wedges, for serving

1. In a small bowl, stir the cumin with the chile powder, brown sugar and coffee. Season generously with salt and pepper. Brush the salmon fillets with olive oil and dredge them in the spice mixture.
2. Meanwhile, in a food processor or blender, puree the tomatillos with the cilantro, jalapeño and garlic until smooth. Add the sour cream and process until smooth, then add the avocado and pulse until creamy. Transfer the dressing to a large bowl and season with salt and pepper. Add the cabbage and toss to coat.
3. Preheat the oven to 300°. Preheat a grill pan. Lightly brush each tortilla with olive oil. Stack the tortillas and wrap them in foil. Bake for 10 minutes. Meanwhile, brush the grill pan with olive oil and grill the salmon fillets over high heat, turning once, until nearly cooked through, 8 to 9 minutes. Transfer the salmon to a plate and flake with a fork.
4. Fill the tortillas with the salmon. Top with the cabbage slaw and serve right away with the hot sauce and lime wedges.
—*Jeff Smith*

WINE Intense, fruity Zinfandel.

Barbecued Salmon Sandwiches

TOTAL: 30 MIN
4 SERVINGS ● ●

This barbecue sauce, made with ketchup, cider vinegar, Worcestershire and a canned chipotle pepper in adobo, comes together quickly in a blender. The chipotle gives the sauce an appealing smokiness.

- 1 tablespoon vegetable oil
- ¼ cup finely chopped onion
- 1 garlic clove, minced
- ½ cup ketchup
- 1 chipotle in adobo, finely chopped
- 1 teaspoon Worcestershire sauce
- ½ teaspoon dry mustard
- 2 tablespoons cider vinegar
- 3 tablespoons mayonnaise

Kosher salt and freshly ground pepper

- 1½ cups coleslaw mix
- 1½ tablespoons finely chopped cilantro
- 1 scallion, thinly sliced

Four 5-ounce salmon fillets with skin

- 4 hot dog buns, preferably brioche-style or split-top

1. Light a grill. In a medium skillet, heat the oil. Add the onion and garlic and cook over moderate heat until tender, about 4 minutes. Reduce the heat to low and stir in the ketchup, chipotle, Worcestershire, dry mustard and 1 tablespoon of the vinegar and cook for 1 minute, until warm. Transfer to a blender and puree until smooth. Scrape the barbecue sauce into a bowl.
2. In a medium bowl, whisk the mayonnaise with the remaining 1 tablespoon of cider vinegar and season with salt and pepper. Add the coleslaw mix, cilantro and scallion and toss well.
3. Season the salmon with salt and pepper and grill skin side up over moderately high heat for 3 minutes. Turn and brush with the barbecue sauce. Grill until the skin is crisp and the fish is just cooked through, 4 minutes longer. Toast the buns on the grill.
4. Transfer the salmon to the buns and top with the slaw. Serve, passing the remaining barbecue sauce at the table.
—*Melissa Rubel*

WINE Fruity, light-bodied Beaujolais.

Swordfish Spiedini

TOTAL: 25 MIN
6 SERVINGS ●

For these *spiedini* (Italian grilled skewers), Food Network host Giada De Laurentiis cuts swordfish into chunks and cooks them on skewers so the fish is done extra fast. Alternatively, "I like to skewer the swordfish on rosemary sticks," De Laurentiis says. "They infuse the fish with such a nice flavor."

- 2 tablespoons extra-virgin olive oil
- 1 teaspoon herbes de Provence

Salt and freshly ground pepper

- 1½ pounds skinless swordfish steak, cut into 1-inch cubes
- 6 slices of pancetta or bacon

1. Light a grill. In a medium bowl, mix the oil with the herbes de Provence and ½ teaspoon each of salt and pepper. Add the swordfish cubes and toss to coat. Thread one-sixth of the swordfish cubes and 1 slice of pancetta onto each of 6 skewers (or soaked rosemary sprigs), wrapping the pancetta around the fish as you go.
2. Grill over high heat, turning occasionally, until cooked through and lightly charred, 8 to 9 minutes. Transfer to plates; serve.
—*Giada De Laurentiis*

WINE Fresh, lively Soave.

the perfect pizza

After my grandfather moved from Sicily to Brooklyn, he opened
several restaurants, including a small pizzeria. I remember him
twirling pizza dough in his famously showy fashion. I've worked hard
to develop a pie that would meet his standards, and after dozens of attempts
with myriad cheese, tomato and flour varieties, I've finally done it.
Mine is a Neapolitan-style pie with a chewy-yet-crisp crust, a well-seasoned
raw tomato sauce and fresh buffalo mozzarella cheese. —*Grace Parisi*

Perfect Pizza Margherita

ACTIVE: 45 MIN; TOTAL: 2 HR PLUS OVERNIGHT RESTING

MAKES FOUR 13-INCH PIZZAS ● ●

Letting the dough rest in the refrigerator overnight results in
a chewy crust with a slight tang. Letting it sit for up to three
days adds even more texture and complexity.

DOUGH

- 1 envelope active dry yeast
- 2 cups warm water (90° to 105°)
- ½ teaspoon sugar
- 4 cups all-purpose flour, plus more for kneading
- 2½ teaspoons kosher salt
- Extra-virgin olive oil

TOPPINGS

- One 14-ounce can peeled whole San Marzano tomatoes, drained
- ½ teaspoon dried oregano, crumbled
- ¼ cup plus 1 tablespoon extra-virgin olive oil
- Coarse sea salt and freshly ground pepper
- 2 pounds buffalo mozzarella, thinly sliced
- 32 large basil leaves, torn into pieces

1. MAKE THE DOUGH: In a large bowl, mix the yeast with
½ cup of the warm water and the sugar and let stand until
foamy, about 5 minutes. Add the remaining 1½ cups of warm
water, the 4 cups of flour and the kosher salt and stir until a
soft dough forms. Turn the dough out onto a well-floured work
surface and knead, adding flour as necessary. Transfer the
dough to a lightly oiled bowl and brush all over with olive oil.
Cover the bowl with plastic wrap and refrigerate overnight or
for up to 3 days.

2. Transfer the dough to a lightly floured work surface, then
punch down and divide it into 4 pieces. Form each piece into
a ball. Rub each ball with oil and transfer to a baking sheet.
Cover the balls loosely with plastic wrap and let rise in a draft-
free place for 1 hour.

3. PREPARE THE TOPPINGS: Meanwhile, set a pizza stone in
the oven and preheat the oven to 500°, allowing at least
45 minutes for the stone to heat. Pass the tomatoes through
a food mill set over a medium bowl or pulse them in a food
processor until coarsely chopped. Stir in the oregano and
1 tablespoon of the olive oil and season generously with salt
and pepper.

4. On a lightly floured surface, stretch one ball of dough into a
13-inch round; transfer to a floured pizza peel, adding flour
where the dough sticks. Spread ¼ cup of the tomato sauce over
the dough to within 1 inch of the edge. Spread one-fourth of
the cheese over the pizza and drizzle with 1 tablespoon of oil.
Season with sea salt and pepper and slide the pizza onto the
stone. Bake until the bottom is charred and the cheese is melted,
about 8 minutes. Scatter one-fourth of the basil on top and let
stand for 3 minutes before serving. Repeat with the remaining
dough and toppings. —*G.P.*

---

kitchen-tested pizza essentials

BUFALUS BUFFALO MOZZARELLA
We sampled a dozen mozzarellas;
this won out for its tangy, salty flavor
(available at Whole Foods).

LA VALLE SAN MARZANO TOMATOES
These triumphed in our taste
test for their fresh, extra-ripe flavor
(lavallefoodsusa.com).

TYPHOON PIZZA SLICER
This mezzaluna-style cutter (like the
one at left) is easier to control than
wheel cutters ($18; typhoonus.com).

Grilled Seafood Kebabs and Orecchiette with Arugula

 **TOTAL: 45 MIN**
4 SERVINGS

8 jumbo scallops, about 2 ounces each, halved

16 large shrimp, shelled and deveined (about 1 pound)

16 cherry tomatoes

2 tablespoons extra-virgin olive oil, plus more for brushing

Salt and freshly ground pepper

2 cups orecchiette (6 ounces)

2 tablespoons unsalted butter

1 shallot, minced

2 garlic cloves, minced

½ cup chicken stock or low-sodium broth

4 ounces baby arugula (4 cups packed)

1 tablespoon fresh lemon juice

½ cup freshly grated Parmigiano-Reggiano cheese

1. Bring a large pot of salted water to a boil. Preheat a grill pan or light a grill. Using 8 pairs of wooden skewers, double-skewer the scallops, shrimp and cherry tomatoes. Brush the kebabs with olive oil and season with salt and pepper.

2. Boil the pasta until al dente. Drain, reserving ½ cup of the cooking water.

3. Grill the kebabs over high heat until they are browned and cooked through, turning once, about 7 minutes.

4. Meanwhile, in a large skillet, melt the butter in the 2 tablespoons of oil. Add the shallot and garlic and cook over high heat, stirring, until softened, about 2 minutes. Add the stock and boil until reduced by half, about 3 minutes. Add the pasta, arugula, lemon juice and cheese and season with salt and pepper. Toss until the arugula is slightly wilted, adding a few tablespoons of the reserved pasta water if necessary. Serve immediately with the kebabs.
—*Jeff Smith*

WINE Light, fresh Pinot Grigio.

Swordfish Steaks with Smoky Tomato Ketchup

ACTIVE: 45 MIN; TOTAL: 1 HR 15 MIN
4 SERVINGS ●
SWORDFISH

Four 7-ounce swordfish steaks, cut ¾ inch thick

Salt and freshly ground pepper

2 garlic cloves, minced

2 tablespoons fresh lemon juice

2 tablespoons extra-virgin olive oil
KETCHUP

1 tablespoon vegetable oil

1 garlic clove, minced

½ small red onion, very finely chopped

½ teaspoon finely grated lemon zest

3 tablespoons light brown sugar

2 tablespoons fresh lemon juice

2 tablespoons red wine vinegar

2 teaspoons drained capers

½ teaspoon ground allspice

½ teaspoon ground ginger

½ teaspoon dry mustard

4 medium tomatoes (1¼ pounds)

Salt and freshly ground pepper

1. PREPARE THE SWORDFISH: Arrange the swordfish in a shallow dish and season with salt and pepper. Rub the garlic onto both sides of the steaks, then drizzle the lemon juice and olive oil over the fish. Cover and refrigerate for up to 1 hour.

2. MAKE THE KETCHUP: In a saucepan, heat the oil. Add the garlic, onion and lemon zest and cook over moderately high heat until lightly browned, 4 minutes. Stir in the brown sugar, lemon juice, vinegar, capers, allspice, ginger and mustard and boil for 3 minutes. Remove from the heat.

3. Light a charcoal grill. Oil the grate and grill the tomatoes over high heat, turning frequently, until lightly charred. Core and finely chop the tomatoes, then stir them into the ketchup. Simmer over low heat, stirring occasionally, until thickened, about 10 minutes. Season with salt and pepper.

4. Grill the swordfish over high heat for 5 minutes, shifting them after 2 minutes to create a crosshatch pattern, if desired. Flip and grill for 3 minutes longer. Transfer to plates and serve with the grilled-tomato ketchup. —*Steven Raichlen*
WINE Fresh, fruity rosé.

Swordfish in Creamy Tomato Sauce

ACTIVE: 30 MIN; TOTAL: 1 HR
4 SERVINGS

2 tablespoons unsalted butter

4 garlic cloves, crushed

1 poblano or Anaheim pepper, cut into ¼-inch dice

Salt and freshly ground pepper

One 16-ounce can whole tomatoes, drained and finely chopped

½ cup water

2 tablespoons heavy cream

Four 6-ounce swordfish steaks, about 1 inch thick

1 teaspoon red wine vinegar

Pinch of dried oregano

Turkish Ridged Flat Bread (p. 184), for serving

1. Preheat the oven to 325°. In a large oven-proof skillet, flameproof clay pot or enameled cast-iron baking dish, melt the butter. Add the garlic and poblano, season with salt and pepper and cook over moderate heat until the poblano starts to soften, about 5 minutes. Stir in the chopped tomatoes, water and cream and bring to a simmer.

2. Season the swordfish steaks with salt and pepper and nestle them in the tomato mixture. Cover with foil and bake in the oven for about 20 minutes, turning the steaks once, until just cooked through.

3. Using a slotted spatula, transfer the swordfish to plates. Stir the vinegar and oregano into the sauce; season with salt and pepper. Pour the sauce over the fish and serve with Turkish Ridged Flat Bread. —*Paula Wolfert*

WINE Fresh, fruity rosé.

Grilled Mahimahi with Tomatoes Two Ways

ACTIVE: 30 MIN; TOTAL: 2 HR 45 MIN

4 SERVINGS ●

- 4 large plum tomatoes, halved lengthwise
- 1 pound yellow cherry tomatoes, halved

Extra-virgin olive oil, for drizzling

Salt and freshly ground black pepper

- 1 garlic clove, thinly sliced
- 2 teaspoons red wine vinegar

Four 6-ounce skinless mahimahi fillets

- 8 small basil leaves, for garnish

1. Preheat the oven to 225°. Arrange the plum tomatoes and half of the cherry tomatoes cut side up on a rimmed baking sheet. Drizzle the tomatoes with olive oil and season with salt and pepper. Scatter the garlic slices on top. Turn the plum tomatoes cut side down. Bake the tomatoes for about 2½ hours, or until they are shriveled but still moist. Transfer the tomatoes to a bowl. Pull off and discard the plum tomato skins.

2. Meanwhile, puree the remaining cherry tomatoes in a food processor. Working over a medium bowl, pass the puree through a fine-mesh strainer, pressing on the solids. Stir the red wine vinegar into the tomato jus and season with salt.

3. Light a grill or heat a grill pan. Lightly rub the mahimahi fillets with olive oil and season with salt and black pepper. Grill the fillets over high heat, turning once, until they are lightly charred and cooked through, about 8 minutes.

4. Pour the tomato jus onto 4 plates and set the mahimahi fillets on top; spoon the roasted tomatoes alongside. Garnish with the basil leaves and serve.

—*Jean-Georges Vongerichten*

MAKE AHEAD The roasted tomatoes and tomato jus can be refrigerated overnight. Rewarm before serving.

WINE Tart, citrusy Riesling.

GRILLED SEAFOOD KEBABS AND ORECCHIETTE WITH ARUGULA

SWORDFISH IN CREAMY TOMATO SAUCE

Mahimahi Coconut Curry Stew with Carrots and Fennel

ACTIVE: 40 MIN; TOTAL: 1 HR 10 MIN
8 SERVINGS ●

Television cooking show host and cookbook author Padma Lakshmi always makes extra portions of this excellent coconut-curried mahimahi stew so she can reheat it the next day and eat it over noodles.

Eight 6-ounce skinless
    mahimahi fillets
½ cup fresh lemon juice
Salt
½ cup vegetable oil
8 garlic cloves, peeled
3 large shallots, thinly sliced (1 cup)
8 small dried red chiles
12 fresh curry leaves (see Note)
2 tablespoons very finely chopped
    fresh ginger
8 kaffir lime leaves (see Note)
1 large fennel bulb—halved, cored
    and cut into 1-inch pieces (4 cups)
4 cups carrots, cut into
    1-inch pieces
1 teaspoon Madras curry powder
Two 15-ounce cans unsweetened
    coconut milk
1 cup cilantro leaves, for garnish

1. Put the mahimahi fillets in a large, shallow dish. Pour the lemon juice over the fish and season lightly with salt. Cover and refrigerate for 30 minutes.
2. In a very large enameled cast-iron casserole, heat the oil. Add the garlic cloves and cook over moderately high heat until sizzling, about 2 minutes. Add the shallots and cook over moderate heat, stirring, until softened, about 3 minutes. Add the chiles and curry leaves and cook for 2 minutes. Add the ginger and lime leaves and cook for 2 minutes. Add the fennel, carrots and curry powder and season lightly with salt. Cover and cook, stirring occasionally, until the vegetables begin to soften, about 5 minutes. Add the coconut milk and bring to a boil. Cover and cook over low heat, stirring a few times, until the carrots are tender, about 10 minutes longer.
3. Add the mahimahi and any accumulated juices to the casserole, nestling the fish into the stew. Cover and simmer over low heat, shifting the fish a few times, until it is just cooked, about 15 minutes. Transfer the fillets to a large, deep platter. Pour the sauce over and around the fish. Garnish with the cilantro and serve.
—Padma Lakshmi

NOTE Fresh curry leaves are small, shiny, bright green and fragrant. Kaffir lime is a citrus fruit with dark green leaves that are very floral and citrusy-smelling.
MAKE AHEAD The coconut-curry broth can be kept at room temperature for up to 4 hours.
WINE Rich Alsace Gewürztraminer.

Mirin-Glazed Halibut

ACTIVE: 20 MIN; TOTAL: 45 MIN
4 SERVINGS ●

Japanese cooking expert Hiroko Shimbo worked with the importer New York Mutual Trading to bring products like artisanal *akasake* mirin (a rich-flavored sweet cooking wine made from sake) to America. She uses the mirin here to make a teriyaki-like sauce that has sweetness and depth but isn't at all cloying.

2 cups *akasake* mirin or
    sweet oloroso sherry
1 cup dry sake
1 cup *marudaizu shoyu* (see Note)
    or other soy sauce
¼ cup light brown sugar
5 to 6 small, dried hot red chiles
Four 6-ounce skinless halibut fillets
2 tablespoons vegetable oil

1. Preheat the oven to 375°. In a medium saucepan, bring the mirin and sake to a simmer. Add the *marudaizu shoyu* and light brown sugar and simmer over low heat for 10 minutes, stirring occasionally. Add the dried red chiles and let cool to room temperature.
2. Pick out the chiles and transfer 1 cup of the sauce to an 8-inch square baking dish. Refrigerate the remaining sauce for another use. Add the halibut to the sauce in the baking dish; marinate at room temperature for 20 minutes, turning several times.
3. Remove the fish from the marinade and blot dry; reserve the marinade. Heat the oil in a large nonstick ovenproof skillet. Add the halibut and cook over moderately high heat for 2 minutes. Turn the fillets. Transfer the skillet to the oven and cook for about 5 minutes, until the fish flakes with a fork.
4. Meanwhile, pour the reserved marinade into a small saucepan and boil over moderately high heat until slightly reduced, 5 minutes. Transfer the halibut to plates and drizzle with the sauce. *—Hiroko Shimbo*
NOTE *Marudaizu shoyu*, made from whole soy beans, has a deeper flavor than commercial soy sauces made with defatted soy meal. It's available at Asian markets.
WINE Light, crisp white Burgundy.

Prosciutto-Wrapped Halibut with Asparagus Sauce

TOTAL: 45 MIN
4 SERVINGS ●

5 tablespoons unsalted butter
4 scallions, thinly sliced
1 pound asparagus, spears
    sliced ½ inch thick, tips
    reserved separately
1 cup water
1 cup packed baby spinach leaves
Salt and freshly ground pepper
8 thin slices of prosciutto
4 skinless halibut fillets
    (about 5 ounces each)
8 small sage leaves, halved
    lengthwise
1 tablespoon extra-virgin olive oil

1. Preheat the oven to 450°. In a skillet, melt 4 tablespoons of the butter. Add the scallions and cook over low heat until softened, about 3 minutes. Add the asparagus spears and the water and cook until the spears are tender and the water is reduced to ¼ cup, about 5 minutes. Add the spinach and cook just until wilted, about 2 minutes. Puree the mixture in a blender until smooth; season with salt and pepper. Transfer the sauce to a small saucepan and keep warm.

2. Arrange the prosciutto slices in pairs, overlapping them slightly. Place a halibut fillet in the center of the prosciutto and top each fillet with 2 sage leaves. Season with salt and pepper and wrap the prosciutto around the fish.

3. In a large ovenproof skillet, melt the remaining 1 tablespoon of butter in the olive oil. Add the halibut and cook over high heat until browned on the bottom, about 3 minutes. Carefully flip the fish and add the asparagus tips to the skillet. Transfer to the oven and roast the prosciutto-wrapped halibut for 5 minutes.

4. Spoon the asparagus sauce onto plates. Arrange the halibut and asparagus tips alongside and serve immediately.
—*Richard Reddington*
WINE Complex, aromatic Chenin Blanc.

Halibut with Tartar-Style Dressing

TOTAL: 20 MIN
4 SERVINGS ●

This fun twist on tartar sauce omits the usual mayo, instead mixing capers, cornichons and olive oil for a chunky dressing.

- ½ small shallot, finely chopped
- 1½ tablespoons fresh lemon juice
- 4 cornichons, diced
- 3 tablespoons chopped flat-leaf parsley
- 1 tablespoon capers, rinsed and coarsely chopped
- ¼ teaspoon sweet paprika
- 3 tablespoons extra-virgin olive oil, plus more for brushing
- Four 6-ounce skinless halibut fillets (1 inch thick)
- Kosher salt and freshly ground black pepper

1. Light a grill. In a small bowl, stir together the chopped shallot and lemon juice. Let stand for 5 minutes. Stir in the cornichons, parsley, capers, paprika and the 3 tablespoons of olive oil.

2. Brush the grate with oil. Season the halibut with salt and pepper and grill over moderately high heat, turning, until opaque, 6 minutes. Transfer the fish to plates, spoon the dressing on top and serve.
—*Melissa Rubel*
MAKE AHEAD The tartar dressing can be made up to 3 hours in advance and kept covered at room temperature.
WINE Creamy, supple Pinot Blanc.

Striped Bass with Spiced Vegetables and Cilantro Dressing

ACTIVE: 45 MIN; TOTAL: 1 HR 30 MIN
4 SERVINGS

- Seeds from 2 cardamom pods
- 1 teaspoon cumin seeds
- 1 teaspoon coriander seeds
- ½ teaspoon caraway seeds
- ½ teaspoon black peppercorns
- 4 tablespoons unsalted butter, melted
- 2 medium garlic cloves, very finely chopped
- One 1-inch piece of peeled fresh ginger, minced
- 12 fingerling potatoes, quartered
- ½ head cauliflower (10 ounces), separated into 1-inch florets
- Salt and freshly ground black pepper
- ½ pound green beans, cut into 1-inch pieces
- 10 cherry tomatoes, halved
- Four 6-ounce striped bass fillets with skin (about ¾ inch thick)
- Extra-virgin olive oil, for drizzling
- Cilantro Dressing (recipe follows)

1. Preheat the oven to 400°. In a small skillet, toast the cardamom, cumin, coriander and caraway seeds and black peppercorns over moderate heat until the spices are

fragrant, 2 minutes. Let cool. Transfer the spices to a mortar and grind to a powder. Transfer to a bowl and stir in the butter, chopped garlic and minced ginger.

2. Put the potatoes on one side of a large rimmed baking sheet and the cauliflower on the other. Toss each vegetable with one-third of the spiced butter, spread the vegetables in the pan in an even layer and season with salt and pepper. Roast in the upper third of the oven for 25 minutes, or until the vegetables are tender and lightly browned. Transfer to a bowl.

3. Light a grill. Put the beans on one side of the baking sheet, the tomatoes on the other and toss each with half of the remaining spiced butter. Roast in the oven until tender, 5 minutes for the tomatoes and 10 for the green beans. Mix the tomatoes and beans with the other roasted vegetables; cover and keep warm.

4. Drizzle the striped bass with olive oil and season with salt and black pepper. Grill the fillets skin side down over high heat until the skin is crisp, 4 minutes. Turn the fillets over and grill until they are just cooked through, 5 minutes longer. Transfer the striped bass to plates, pile the roasted vegetables alongside and serve, drizzled with the Cilantro Dressing.
—*Sang Yoon*
WINE Fresh, minerally Vermentino.

CILANTRO DRESSING

TOTAL: 10 MIN
MAKES ABOUT ½ CUP ● ●

- 1 cup packed cilantro leaves
- ½ cup packed mint leaves
- ½ small onion, very finely chopped
- ¼ cup vegetable oil
- 2 tablespoons rice vinegar
- Salt and freshly ground pepper

In a blender, combine the cilantro, mint, onion, oil and vinegar and puree until smooth. Season the dressing with salt and pepper. —*S.Y.*

Wild Striped Bass with Scallions and Herb Salad

TOTAL: 45 MIN
4 SERVINGS ●

12 scallions
1 tablespoon extra-virgin olive oil
¼ teaspoon crushed red pepper
Four 6-ounce skinless wild
   striped bass fillets
Kosher salt and freshly ground pepper
1½ teaspoons finely grated
   lemon zest
1 tablespoon unsalted butter,
   cut into 4 pieces
¼ cup fresh orange juice
2 tablespoons walnut oil
1½ teaspoons fresh lemon juice
½ cup dill, coarsely chopped
½ cup flat-leaf parsley leaves,
   very coarsely chopped
⅓ cup mint leaves, finely chopped
⅓ cup fresh tarragon leaves,
   finely chopped
⅓ cup snipped chives

1. Preheat the oven to 500°. Discard the top 2 inches of the scallions. Halve them crosswise and thinly slice lengthwise.
2. In a medium skillet, heat the oil. Add the scallions and red pepper and cook over moderate heat until the scallions are tender and beginning to brown, 4 minutes.
3. Season the bass with salt and pepper and transfer the fillets to a 9-by-13-inch baking dish. Top with the scallions and sprinkle with the lemon zest. Dot each fillet with a piece of the butter. Pour the orange juice over or around the fish. Cover tightly with foil and bake for about 16 minutes, until the fish is just opaque.
4. Just before serving, in a medium bowl, whisk the walnut oil with the lemon juice and season with salt and pepper. Add the herbs and toss to coat. Transfer the fish to plates and spoon the juices on top. Serve the herb salad alongside.
—*Sara Kate Gillingham-Ryan*
WINE Lively, tart Sauvignon Blanc.

Sea Bass with Popcorn Ponzu

TOTAL: 1 HR
4 SERVINGS ●

1 teaspoon vegetable oil
2 tablespoons popping corn
1 quart water
2 tablespoons bonito flakes or
   1 teaspoon Asian fish sauce
2 Thai green chiles, halved
2 rosemary sprigs
1 thyme sprig
1 teaspoon allspice berries, crushed
2 tablespoons soy sauce
1 tablespoon fresh yuzu juice
8 large shiitake, stems discarded
   and caps cut into 1-inch pieces
2 medium shallots, thinly sliced
2 tablespoons julienned ginger
Four 6-ounce skinless sea bass fillets
Salt and freshly ground pepper
Extra-virgin olive oil, for drizzling

1. In a medium saucepan, heat the vegetable oil. Add the corn, cover and shake over high heat until the kernels have popped. Add the the water, bonito flakes, chiles, rosemary, thyme and allspice and bring to a boil. Remove the saucepan from the heat, cover and let stand for 15 minutes. Strain the broth into a bowl and add the soy sauce and yuzu juice.
2. Light a grill. For each papillote, layer two 14-inch sheets of heavy-duty aluminum foil on a work surface. Fold up the sides of the foil to hold the broth. Divide the shiitake, shallots and ginger among the foil sheets. Season the fish with salt and pepper and set the fillets on the vegetables. Pour about 1 cup of popcorn broth over each fillet. Seal the packets, crimping tightly.
3. Grill the packets over high heat until the broth bubbles vigorously, about 10 minutes. Carefully open each packet. Transfer the fish to shallow bowls and drizzle with olive oil. Spoon the vegetables and broth over the fish and serve.
—*Jean-Georges Vongerichten*
WINE Peppery, refreshing Grüner Veltliner.

Crispy Tuna with Tuna-Caper Sauce

TOTAL: 30 MIN
4 SERVINGS ●

Be sure to buy sushi-grade tuna fillets for this incredibly simple recipe.

One 3-ounce can imported tuna
   in olive oil, drained
¼ cup chicken stock or
   low-sodium broth
¼ cup mayonnaise
1½ teaspoons drained capers
1 anchovy fillet
2 small cornichons
½ teaspoon Dijon mustard
½ teaspoon white wine vinegar
Salt and freshly ground black pepper
½ cup plain dry bread crumbs
1 teaspoon chopped thyme
1 teaspoon chopped
   flat-leaf parsley
¼ cup extra-virgin olive oil
Four 7-ounce tuna steaks,
   cut 1 inch thick

1. In a blender, puree the canned tuna with the chicken stock, mayonnaise, capers, anchovy, cornichons, mustard and white wine vinegar. Season the sauce with salt and black pepper.
2. In a small bowl, toss the bread crumbs, thyme, parsley and 1 tablespoon of the oil; season with salt and black pepper. Rub the tuna steaks with 1 tablespoon of olive oil and sprinkle the fish with the seasoned bread crumbs.
3. In a large nonstick skillet, heat the remaining 2 tablespoons of olive oil. Add the seasoned tuna steaks and cook them over high heat, turning once, until the steaks are golden outside but very rare within, about 5 minutes. Transfer the tuna steaks to a cutting board and cut them into ½-inch-thick slices.
4. Spoon the tuna-caper sauce onto plates and top with the seared tuna slices. Serve immediately. —*Lidia Bastianich*
WINE Fresh, minerally Vermentino.

WILD STRIPED BASS
WITH SCALLIONS AND
HERB SALAD

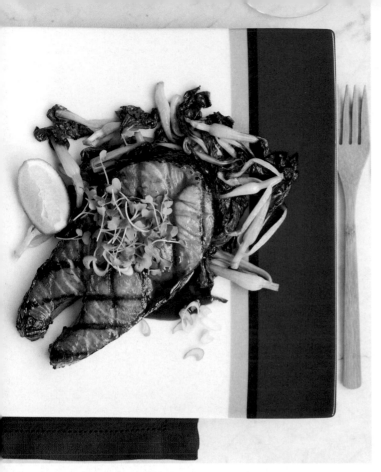

SALMON STEAK WITH SOY-MAPLE GLAZE

SCALLOPS WITH CAULIFLOWER, CAPERS AND RAISINS

Mustard-and-Coriander-Crusted Salmon

 **TOTAL: 25 MIN**
4 SERVINGS ●

This roasted salmon fillet is coated with a delicious, fragrant mix of Dijon mustard and spices.

- 1 tablespoon coriander seeds
- 1 teaspoon mustard seeds

Pinch of crushed red pepper

1¼ pounds skinless salmon fillet in one piece

Salt and freshly ground black pepper

- 1 tablespoon plus ½ teaspoon Dijon mustard
- 1 tablespoon plus 1 teaspoon extra-virgin olive oil
- 1 tablespoon fresh lemon juice
- 1 bunch watercress (6 ounces), thick stems discarded
- 1 cup tightly packed flat-leaf parsley leaves

1. Preheat the oven to 425°. In a coffee grinder, coarsely grind the coriander seeds with the mustard seeds and crushed red pepper. Season the salmon fillet with salt and black pepper and spread 1 tablespoon of the mustard evenly over the fillet. Press the ground spices into the mustard.

2. In a large nonstick ovenproof skillet, heat 1 teaspoon of the oil. Add the salmon, coated side down, and cook over high heat until lightly browned, 2 to 3 minutes. Turn the fish and transfer the skillet to the oven for 6 minutes, or until cooked through. Transfer the fish to a cutting board.

3. Meanwhile, in a medium bowl, whisk the lemon juice with the remaining 1 tablespoon of oil and ½ teaspoon of mustard. Add the watercress and parsley, season with salt and pepper and toss to coat. Cut the salmon fillet into 4 pieces and serve with the salad. —*Grace Parisi*

WINE Full-bodied, rich Pinot Gris.

Salmon Steaks with Soy-Maple Glaze

TOTAL: 35 MIN PLUS 2 HR MARINATING

4 SERVINGS ●

"Every year I come up with one preparation that's embarrassingly simple but incredibly versatile," says cookbook author and grilling maven Steven Raichlen. This year's go-to recipe is a glaze made from maple syrup, soy sauce and Asian sesame oil, which adds a trifecta of sweet, salty and nutty flavors to all sorts of grilled meats and fish.

- ¼ cup soy sauce
- 3 tablespoons pure maple syrup
- 3 tablespoons Asian sesame oil

Four 8-ounce wild salmon steaks, cut 1 inch thick

One 2-inch piece of fresh ginger— peeled, thinly sliced and smashed

- 2 garlic cloves, smashed
- 2 scallions, thinly sliced

1. In a large, shallow dish, whisk the soy sauce with the maple syrup and sesame oil. Add the salmon steaks and turn to coat. Press the ginger and garlic onto both sides of the steaks. Cover and refrigerate for 2 hours, turning the salmon a few times.

2. Light a charcoal grill. Remove the salmon from the marinade. Pour the marinade into a small saucepan and boil over high heat until syrupy, about 3 minutes. Strain the glaze into a small bowl.

3. Oil the grate and grill the salmon over moderately high heat for 6 minutes, rotating the steaks slightly after 2 minutes to make crosshatches, if desired. Turn the steaks and grill for 6 minutes longer. Transfer to plates and spoon the glaze on top. Sprinkle with the scallions and serve. —*Steven Raichlen*

WINE Ripe, juicy Pinot Noir.

Pan-Roasted Salmon with Tomato Vinaigrette

TOTAL: 30 MIN
4 SERVINGS ● ●

Ted Allen, the culinary expert on the Bravo TV show *Queer Eye for the Straight Guy*, used this recipe to teach a 22-year-old fast-food junkie how to cook a healthy meal. The simple sauce on the salmon is a bright, tangy combination of sautéed tomatoes, shallots, capers and vinegar. Allen likes the recipe so much he put it in his cookbook, *The Food You Want to Eat.*

1 pint grape tomatoes, halved
1 medium shallot, thinly sliced
1 tablespoon drained capers
2 tablespoons red wine vinegar
Salt
3 tablespoons extra-virgin olive oil
4 center-cut salmon fillets with skin (about 7 ounces each)
Freshly ground pepper
½ teaspoon ground cumin
2 tablespoons canola oil
1 tablespoon minced parsley
1 tablespoon chopped basil

1. Preheat the oven to 425°. In a bowl, toss the tomatoes with the shallot, capers, vinegar and ½ teaspoon of salt.

2. In a medium ovenproof skillet, heat 1 tablespoon of the olive oil. Season the salmon with salt and pepper and add it to the skillet, skin side up. Cook over moderately high heat until well-browned on the bottom, about 3 minutes. Carefully flip the fillets. Transfer the skillet to the oven and roast until the salmon is cooked through, about 7 minutes. Transfer the fish to plates and pour off any fat in the skillet.

3. Place the skillet over moderate heat and add the tomato mixture along with the cumin, canola oil and the remaining 2 tablespoons of olive oil. Cook, scraping up any bits stuck to the skillet, until the tomatoes just soften, about 2 minutes. Pour the sauce over the salmon, sprinkle with the parsley and basil and serve right away. —*Ted Allen*

WINE Fresh, fruity rosé.

Seared Scallops with Cauliflower, Capers and Raisins

TOTAL: 30 MIN
4 SERVINGS ●

½ small head of cauliflower, cut into small florets (4 cups)
1 tablespoon extra-virgin olive oil
12 jumbo scallops (1½ pounds), side muscles removed
Salt and freshly ground pepper
2 tablespoons unsalted butter
¼ cup chopped roasted almonds, preferably marcona
2 tablespoons drained small capers
2 tablespoons golden raisins
2 tablespoons balsamic vinegar
1 tablespoon chopped flat-leaf parsley

1. Bring a medium saucepan of salted water to a boil. Add the cauliflower and boil over high heat until just tender, 3 to 4 minutes. Drain well.

2. In a large skillet, heat the oil until shimmering. Season the scallops with salt and pepper, add to the skillet in a single layer and cook over high heat until golden and crusty, about 2 minutes. Flip, then add the butter, cauliflower, almonds, capers and raisins; cook undisturbed until the scallops are white throughout and the cauliflower is browned in spots, about 1 minute. Stir in the vinegar, transfer to plates and garnish with parsley. —*Richard Reddington*

WINE Lush, fragrant Viognier.

Grilled Scallops with Parsley Salad

TOTAL: 25 MIN
4 SERVINGS ●

1 tablespoon fresh lemon juice
½ small shallot, minced
2½ tablespoons extra-virgin olive oil
Kosher salt and freshly ground pepper
1 pink grapefruit
1 large fennel bulb—halved, cored and thinly sliced
1 cup flat-leaf parsley leaves
16 sea scallops (about 1 pound), side muscles removed

1. Light a grill. In a small bowl, pour the lemon juice over the minced shallot and let stand for 5 minutes. Whisk in 2 tablespoons of the olive oil and season the dressing with salt and pepper.

2. Using a sharp knife, peel the grapefruit, making sure to remove all of the bitter white pith. Working over a medium bowl, cut in between the membranes to release the sections into the bowl. Toss the fennel and parsley with the grapefruit.

3. Brush the scallops with the remaining ½ tablespoon of olive oil and season with salt and pepper. Grill over moderately high heat, turning once, until just cooked through, about 5 minutes.

4. Toss the salad with dressing and season with salt and pepper. Transfer to plates, top with scallops and serve. —*Melissa Rubel*

WINE Lively, tart Sauvignon Blanc.

Curried Mussels in White Ale

ACTIVE: 25 MIN; TOTAL: 45 MIN
4 SERVINGS

2 tablespoons vegetable oil
1 tablespoon Thai red curry paste
6 medium garlic cloves, finely chopped
1 tablespoon finely grated fresh ginger
1 large fresh lemongrass stalk, bottom two-thirds of the inner bulb only, smashed and chopped
⅔ cup mirin (sweet rice wine)
One 15-ounce can unsweetened coconut milk
¼ cup soy sauce
3 tablespoons Asian fish sauce
½ cup basil leaves, plus ¼ cup chopped basil
Two 12-ounce bottles Belgian-style white ale
2 pounds mussels, scrubbed and debearded
¼ cup chopped cilantro

1. In a saucepan, heat the oil. Add the curry paste, garlic, ginger and lemongrass; cook over moderate heat for 2 minutes, stirring. Add the mirin, coconut milk, soy sauce, fish sauce and basil leaves; simmer over low heat for 15 minutes. Strain the sauce.
2. In a saucepan, bring the ale to a boil. Add the mussels, cover and cook over high heat, about 5 minutes. Using a slotted spoon, transfer the mussels to 4 bowls; discard any that don't open. Add the curry sauce to the ale and boil for 1 minute. Pour over the mussels, sprinkle with the chopped basil and cilantro and serve. —*Sang Yoon*
WINE Spicy American Gewürztraminer.

Shrimp Boil Hobo Packs

TOTAL: 30 MIN
4 SERVINGS ●

24 shelled and deveined large shrimp (about 1¼ pounds)
16 mussels (about 10 ounces), scrubbed
6 ounces kielbasa, sliced ½ inch thick
1 large ear of corn, shucked and cut into 8 rounds
4 thyme sprigs
1½ tablespoons unsalted butter, cut into 4 pieces
Old Bay seasoning
¼ cup dry white wine
¼ cup water

1. Light a grill. Lay four 24-by-18-inch sheets of heavy-duty foil on a work surface. Fold each sheet in half crosswise. On the lower half of each sheet, arrange the seafood, kielbasa, corn, thyme and butter; season with Old Bay. Fold the top half of each sheet over the bottom half and seal tightly on 2 sides. Into each packet, pour 1 tablespoon each of wine and water; seal tightly.
2. Grill the packets over moderately high heat, turning once, until puffed, about 10 minutes. Pour the contents of the packets into bowls and serve. —*Melissa Rubel*
WINE Ripe, luxurious Chardonnay.

Bacon-Wrapped Shrimp with Passion Fruit Mustard

ACTIVE: 30 MIN; TOTAL: 50 MIN
2 SERVINGS

1 cup passion fruit juice
1 Thai red chile, halved lengthwise
½ teaspoon cumin seeds
3 tablespoons honey
1 Thai green chile, coarsely chopped
1 tablespoon water
1 tablespoon dry mustard
1 tablespoon Dijon mustard
Salt
8 large shrimp, shelled and deveined with tails left on
8 thin slices of lean bacon
1 Hass avocado, quartered and thinly sliced
Extra-virgin olive oil, for drizzling
1 passion fruit, halved and seeds scooped out (optional)
Cilantro leaves, for garnish

1. In a small saucepan, boil the passion fruit juice with the red chile until reduced to ¼ cup, about 20 minutes.
2. Meanwhile, in another saucepan, toast the cumin seeds over moderate heat until fragrant. Add the honey and green chile and bring to a simmer. Remove from the heat and let stand for 15 minutes. Strain the honey and stir in 1 teaspoon of the water.
3. In a bowl, blend the dry mustard with the remaining 2 teaspoons of water; let stand for 5 minutes. Stir in the Dijon mustard. Strain the reduced passion fruit juice into the mustard and season with salt.
4. Light a grill. Wrap each shrimp in bacon. Grill over moderately high heat, turning, until the bacon is lightly charred and the shrimp are cooked through, about 4 minutes.
5. Fan the avocado slices on each plate and top with the shrimp. Spoon the mustard around the shrimp, then spoon the honey around the mustard. Drizzle with oil; garnish with passion fruit seeds and cilantro. —*Jean-Georges Vongerichten*
WINE Ripe, luxurious Chardonnay.

INGREDIENT

wild shrimp

More than 85 percent of the shrimp sold in the U.S. is imported. But we're thrilled about these varieties of wild American shrimp (wildamericanshrimp.com):

BROWN SHRIMP An iodine-rich diet makes these hearty Atlantic- and Gulf-coast shrimp perfect for gumbo.

PINK SHRIMP Our favorite variety is briny and sweet; delicious sautéed simply or steamed for shrimp cocktail.

WHITE SHRIMP Sweet and firm with crablike flavor, these bayou-dwellers are best for soups, ceviche and salads.

Sichuan Peppercorn Shrimp

TOTAL: 40 MIN
4 SERVINGS ●

1½ teaspoons Sichuan peppercorns
(see Note)

1 pound large shrimp—shelled,
deveined and butterflied

Salt

¼ cup vegetable oil

3 scallions—2 coarsely chopped,
1 thinly sliced

3 garlic cloves, minced

3 jalapeños, seeded and
thinly sliced

1 dried pasilla or small ancho chile,
seeded and very thinly sliced

1 tablespoon fresh lime juice

Chile-sesame oil, for drizzling

1. In a small skillet, toast the peppercorns over moderate heat until fragrant, about 30 seconds; let cool. Transfer the peppercorns to a mortar or spice grinder and grind to a powder. Put the shrimp in a bowl, toss with 1 teaspoon of the ground peppercorns and season with salt.

2. In a medium skillet, heat 1 tablespoon of the vegetable oil. Add the shrimp and stir-fry over moderate heat until almost cooked through, 4 minutes. Transfer to a plate.

3. Heat the remaining 3 tablespoons of vegetable oil in the skillet. Add the chopped scallions, garlic, jalapeños and chile and cook over moderate heat, stirring, until the scallions and garlic are softened, 5 minutes. Add the remaining ½ teaspoon of ground peppercorns and cook, stirring, for 1 minute. Add the shrimp and lime juice and stir until the shrimp are just cooked through, 1 minute. Season with salt and transfer to a bowl. Garnish with the sliced scallion, drizzle with chile oil and serve.
—*Sang Yoon*

NOTE Fragrant, mouth-numbing Sichuan peppercorns from China are increasingly available at Asian markets and on websites like thespicehouse.com.

WINE Peppery, refreshing Grüner Veltliner.

SHRIMP BOIL HOBO PACK

BACON-WRAPPED SHRIMP WITH PASSION FRUIT MUSTARD

Crispy Pan-Fried Shrimp and Chorizo Fideo Cakes

ACTIVE: 1 HR; TOTAL: 4 HR

6 SERVINGS

- ½ pound *fideos* (fine pasta nests) or angel-hair pasta, broken into 1-inch lengths
- 2 cups chicken stock
- 1 cup dry white wine

Large pinch of saffron threads

- ½ pound medium shrimp—shelled, deveined and cut into ½-inch pieces, shells reserved
- 7 tablespoons extra-virgin olive oil
- 4 ounces chorizo, finely diced
- 2 tablespoons sliced garlic, plus 1 garlic clove minced

Large pinch of crushed red pepper

Salt

- 4 large egg whites
- ½ cup mayonnaise
- 4 teaspoons fresh lemon juice

1. Preheat the oven to 350°. Spread the *fideos* on a rimmed baking sheet; bake for 8 minutes, or until lightly browned.

2. In a saucepan, combine the stock, wine, saffron and shrimp shells; bring to a boil. Remove from the heat, cover and let stand for 1 hour. Discard the shrimp shells.

3. In a large saucepan, heat 1 tablespoon of the oil. Add the chorizo and sliced garlic and cook over moderate heat until the garlic is golden. Add the crushed red pepper, *fideos* and the shrimp stock and bring to a boil, stirring. Cook over moderate heat, stirring constantly, until the *fideos* are al dente and the sauce is creamy, 5 minutes. Stir in the shrimp and season with salt. Remove from the heat and let cool to room temperature. Stir in the egg whites and refrigerate for 1 hour.

4. Shape the mixture into twelve 3½-inch cakes about ½ inch thick. Set them on a baking sheet and refrigerate for 1 hour.

5. In a bowl, blend the mayonnaise, minced garlic and lemon juice. Whisk in 2 tablespoons of the oil and season with salt.

6. In a large cast-iron skillet, heat 1 tablespoon of the oil. Add 3 cakes and cook over moderately high heat until browned on the bottom, about 4 minutes. Turn the cakes, reduce the heat to moderate and cook until heated through, about 3 minutes longer. Transfer to a plate and keep warm. Repeat with the remaining oil and cakes. Top the *fideo* cakes with the garlic mayonnaise and serve warm. —*Ilan Hall*

WINE Fresh, fruity rosé.

Chipotle Chilaquiles

 TOTAL: 40 MIN

4 SERVINGS

Chilaquiles is a basic Mexican dish created to make good use of leftovers like tortillas, chiles, shredded chicken and cheese.

One 28-ounce can whole tomatoes, drained and ½ cup liquid reserved

- 2 chipotles in adobo
- 1½ tablespoons vegetable oil
- 1 large white onion, thinly sliced
- 3 garlic cloves, very finely chopped
- 1½ cups chicken stock or low-sodium broth

Salt

- 8 ounces tortilla chips
- 1½ cups shredded chicken
- ¼ cup freshly grated Parmesan cheese or *queso añejo* (see Note)
- ⅓ cup sour cream
- ¼ cup finely chopped cilantro leaves

1. In a blender, combine the tomatoes with their reserved ½ cup of liquid and the chipotles; blend until almost smooth.

2. In a very large, deep skillet, heat the oil. Add two-thirds of the onion and cook over moderately high heat until browned around the edges, about 6 minutes. Add the garlic and cook for 1 minute. Pour in the tomato puree and simmer, stirring, until slightly thickened, about 5 minutes. Stir in the stock and boil the sauce over

moderately high heat until slightly thickened, about 2 minutes. Season with salt and remove from the heat.

3. Gently stir the tortilla chips into the sauce, making sure they are well coated. Top with the remaining onion, the shredded chicken and the Parmesan cheese. Dollop the sour cream over the *chilaquiles,* sprinkle with the cilantro and serve immediately. —*Rick Bayless*

NOTE *Queso añejo* is an aged Spanish white cheese that's slightly salty.

MAKE AHEAD The recipe can be prepared through Step 2 and refrigerated overnight. Reheat the chipotle-tomato sauce before proceeding.

WINE Intense, fruity Zinfandel.

Chile-Chicken Sauté

 TOTAL: 30 MIN

4 SERVINGS

A cross between a fajita and chili, this saucy stir-fry can be served in warm tortillas or over rice. It can even be baked between layers of tortilla chips, cheddar cheese and sour cream to make *chilaquiles,* a Mexican-style lasagna (see the recipe at left).

- 3 tablespoons extra-virgin olive oil
- 1½ pounds skinless, boneless chicken thighs, cut into ½-inch strips, or skinless, boneless breasts, cut into 1½-inch chunks

Salt and freshly ground pepper

- 1 small onion, thinly sliced
- 1 red bell pepper, cut into ½-inch strips
- 2 large garlic cloves, very finely chopped
- 1 tablespoon pure chile powder
- 1 teaspoon ground cumin
- ½ cup canned tomato sauce
- 2 ears of corn, kernels cut off the cob (1¼ cups)
- ½ cup water

Warmed corn tortillas, sour cream and chopped cilantro, for serving

1. In a very large skillet, heat 2 tablespoons of the oil. Season the chicken with salt and pepper and add it to the skillet in a single layer. Cook over high heat, turning once, until browned but not cooked through, 4 to 5 minutes. Using a slotted spoon, transfer to a plate. Pour off the fat in the skillet.

2. Add the remaining 1 tablespoon of oil to the skillet. Add the onion and bell pepper and cook over high heat, stirring occasionally, until crisp-tender, about 3 minutes. Add the garlic, chile powder and cumin and cook, stirring, until fragrant, 1 minute.

3. Return the chicken and any accumulated juices to the skillet and cook for 1 minute. Add the tomato sauce, corn and water and cook over moderate heat, scraping up any bits stuck to the skillet, until the chicken is cooked through and the sauce is reduced, about 5 minutes. Transfer to a bowl and serve with corn tortillas, sour cream and cilantro. —*Grace Parisi*
WINE Intense, fruity Zinfandel.

Sautéed Chicken with Olives, Capers and Roasted Lemons

TOTAL: 40 MIN
4 SERVINGS ●

¼ cup plus 2 tablespoons extra-virgin olive oil, plus more for drizzling

2 lemons, sliced ¼ inch thick

Salt and freshly ground black pepper

Two 5-ounce bags baby spinach

2 tablespoons plain dry bread crumbs

Four 6-ounce skinless, boneless chicken breast halves

¼ cup all-purpose flour

½ cup pitted green Sicilian or Spanish olives, sliced

2 tablespoons drained capers

1 cup chicken stock or low-sodium broth

3 tablespoons unsalted butter, cut into small dice

2 tablespoons chopped parsley

1. Preheat the oven to 375°. Line a baking sheet with parchment paper. Drizzle some olive oil on the parchment paper, then arrange the lemon slices on the parchment in a single layer. Drizzle the lemons lightly with a little more olive oil and season with salt and black pepper. Roast the lemons for about 20 minutes, until they begin to brown around the edges.

2. Meanwhile, heat a large, deep skillet. Add the baby spinach and cook over high heat, tossing frequently, until the leaves are all wilted, about 2 minutes. Transfer the spinach to a strainer and press out the liquid. Wipe out the skillet and heat 2 tablespoons of the olive oil in it. Add the bread crumbs and cook over moderate heat, stirring, until toasted, 2 minutes. Add the spinach, season with salt and pepper and cook for 1 minute.

3. In a medium, deep skillet, heat the remaining ¼ cup of oil. Season the chicken with salt and pepper and dust with the flour, shaking off the excess. Cook the chicken over high heat, turning once, until golden, about 6 minutes. Add the olives, capers and stock and bring to a boil. Cook over high heat until the stock is reduced by about two-thirds, about 5 minutes. Add the roasted lemons, butter and parsley, season with salt and pepper and simmer just until the chicken is cooked through, about 1 minute longer.

4. Transfer the chicken to plates, spoon the sauce on top and serve the spinach on the side. —*Lidia Bastianich*
WINE Fresh, fruity rosé.

Stir-Fried Chicken in Lettuce Leaves

TOTAL: 40 MIN
4 SERVINGS ●

For this quick, flavorful dish, the chicken is marinated for just 10 minutes before stir-frying, then served with shredded carrot, sliced scallions and fresh mint, plus green-leaf lettuce leaves for wrapping.

1 pound skinless, boneless chicken thighs, cut into ½-inch dice

3 large garlic cloves, very finely chopped

1½ tablespoons very finely chopped fresh ginger

½ teaspoon crushed red pepper

3 tablespoons vegetable oil

Salt and freshly ground black pepper

1 tablespoon soy sauce

1½ teaspoons dry sherry

1½ teaspoons Chinese black bean sauce

1½ teaspoons sugar

¾ teaspoon cornstarch dissolved in 2 tablespoons water

1 head of green-leaf lettuce, leaves separated

1 large carrot, coarsely shredded on a box grater

4 scallions, thinly sliced

¼ cup shredded mint

1. In a medium bowl, toss the diced chicken thighs with the garlic, ginger, crushed red pepper and 1 tablespoon of the oil and season with salt and black pepper. Let the chicken stand for 10 minutes.

2. Meanwhile, in a small cup, combine the soy sauce with the dry sherry, black bean sauce and sugar. Stir in the dissolved cornstarch.

3. Heat a large skillet or wok until very hot to the touch. Add the remaining 2 tablespoons of vegetable oil and heat until smoking, swirling the skillet to coat with the hot oil. Add the marinated chicken and stir-fry over high heat until browned all over, about 10 minutes. Stir the sauce and add it to the chicken, stirring to coat; cook just until the sauce is thickened and glossy, about 1 minute.

4. Arrange the lettuce leaves, shredded carrot, sliced scallions and shredded mint in separate serving bowls and serve with the chicken. —*Richard Reddington*
WINE Earthy, medium-bodied Tempranillo.

Stir-Fried Chicken with Bok Choy

TOTAL: 30 MIN
4 SERVINGS ●

¾ cup chicken stock or low-sodium broth
2 tablespoons Chinese black bean sauce
1 tablespoon dry sherry
1 tablespoon sugar
1 teaspoon Chinese chile-garlic sauce
2 teaspoons cornstarch
¼ cup vegetable oil
1½ pounds skinless, boneless chicken thighs, cut into ½-inch strips, or skinless, boneless breasts, cut into 1½-inch chunks
Salt and freshly ground pepper
2 tablespoons minced fresh ginger
1 pound bok choy, cut into ¾-inch pieces
1 cup snow peas
Steamed white rice, for serving

1. In a small bowl, whisk the chicken stock with the black bean sauce, sherry, sugar, chile-garlic sauce and cornstarch.
2. Heat a large wok or skillet until very hot. Add 2 tablespoons of the oil and heat until just smoking. Season the chicken with salt and pepper and add it to the wok in a single layer. Cook over high heat, turning once, until it is browned but not cooked through, 4 to 5 minutes. Transfer to a plate and pour off the fat in the wok.
3. Add the remaining 2 tablespoons of oil to the wok. Add the ginger and stir-fry until fragrant, about 30 seconds. Add the bok choy and snow peas and stir-fry until bright green and crisp-tender, 2 to 3 minutes. Return the chicken and its juices to the wok. Stir the sauce, then add it to the wok and simmer, stirring, until thickened, about 5 minutes. Transfer to a bowl and serve with rice. —*Grace Parisi*
WINE Light, fresh Pinot Grigio.

Spicy Red Curry Chicken

TOTAL: 30 MIN
4 SERVINGS

⅔ cup unsweetened coconut milk
2 to 3 teaspoons Thai red curry paste
1 tablespoon Asian fish sauce
3 tablespoons vegetable oil
1½ pounds skinless, boneless chicken thighs, cut into ½-inch strips, or skinless, boneless breasts, cut into 1½-inch chunks
Salt and freshly ground pepper
½ pound shiitake mushrooms, stemmed, caps quartered
1 tablespoon very finely chopped fresh ginger
2 large garlic cloves, very finely chopped
½ cup water
1 cup frozen baby peas
Toasted peanuts and cilantro leaves, for garnish
Steamed rice and lime wedges, for serving

1. In a small bowl, whisk the coconut milk with the curry paste and fish sauce.
2. Heat a large wok or skillet until very hot. Add 2 tablespoons of the oil and heat until just smoking. Season the chicken with salt and pepper and add it to the wok in a single layer. Cook over high heat, turning once, until browned but not cooked through, 4 to 5 minutes. Transfer to a plate and pour off the fat in the wok.
3. Add the remaining 1 tablespoon of oil to the wok. Add the shiitake and stir-fry over high heat until lightly browned, about 5 minutes. Add the ginger and garlic and stir-fry for 1 minute. Return the chicken and its juices to the wok. Add the curry mixture and water and bring to a boil. Add the peas and simmer until the liquid is slightly reduced and the peas are warm, 2 to 3 minutes. Transfer the curry to a serving bowl and garnish with peanuts and cilantro. Serve with rice and lime wedges. —*Grace Parisi*
WINE Vivid, lightly sweet Riesling.

Chicken with Coconut-Caramel Sauce and Citrus Salad

TOTAL: 1 HR 20 MIN
4 SERVINGS ●

¼ cup plus 2 teaspoons sugar
1½ teaspoons ground coriander
1½ teaspoons ground cumin
½ teaspoon turmeric
½ teaspoon freshly ground black pepper
Cayenne pepper
4 skin-on boneless chicken breast halves
2 tablespoons water
½ cup unsweetened coconut milk
2 tablespoons Asian fish sauce
1 Thai green chile, minced
Salt
1 grapefruit—peeled with a knife, sectioned and diced
1 lime—peeled with a knife, sectioned and diced
1 cup diced fresh pineapple
Extra-virgin olive oil, for drizzling
2 tablespoons thinly sliced cilantro
Fleur de sel, for garnish

1. Mix 2 teaspoons of the sugar with the coriander, cumin, turmeric, black pepper and ½ teaspoon of cayenne. Rub over the chicken, cover and refrigerate for 1 hour.
2. In a saucepan, mix the remaining ¼ cup of sugar with the water and bring to a boil. Simmer until an amber caramel forms, about 10 minutes. Off the heat, stir in the coconut milk until the caramel dissolves. Add the fish sauce and chile, then let stand for 5 minutes. Strain and season with salt.
3. In a bowl, gently toss the three fruits with a pinch each of salt and cayenne.
4. Light a grill. Rub the chicken with oil and season with salt. Grill over moderate heat, turning once, until the skin is charred and the meat is white throughout, 12 minutes. Serve with the citrus salad and sauce, drizzled with oil, sprinkled with cilantro and fleur de sel. —*Jean-Georges Vongerichten*
WINE Fruity, luscious Shiraz.

Berber-Spiced Chicken Breasts

ACTIVE: 20 MIN; TOTAL: 1 HR PLUS
1 HR MARINATING

4 SERVINGS ● ●

Grill expert Steven Raichlen is ambivalent about chicken breasts: "You could describe them two ways," he says. "They're the canvases upon which a grill master paints his colors. Or, to put a less charitable spin on it, they're the meat that grill masters love to hate because they're so intrinsically bland." Here, he rubs chicken breasts with a blend of North African spices that, when grilled, forms a crispy crust full of what Raichlen calls "gutsy, in-your-face flavors."

- 3 garlic cloves, quartered
- 1 small onion, coarsely chopped

One 1-inch piece of fresh ginger, peeled and chopped

- 3 tablespoons sweet paprika
- 2 teaspoons kosher salt
- 1 teaspoon ground coriander
- 1 teaspoon freshly ground pepper
- 1 teaspoon finely grated lemon zest
- ½ teaspoon ground cinnamon
- ¼ teaspoon ground cardamom
- 3 tablespoons fresh lemon juice
- 3 tablespoons extra-virgin olive oil
- 4 chicken breast halves on the bone with skin (2 pounds)

Lemon wedges, for serving

1. In a food processor, combine all of the ingredients except the chicken and lemon wedges and process to a paste. Spread the paste all over the chicken and refrigerate for at least 1 hour or up to 4 hours.
2. Light a charcoal grill. When the coals are hot, move them to one side of the grill. Oil the grate and place the chicken on it, skin side up, opposite the coals. Cover and grill the chicken until browned and just cooked through, about 30 minutes. Flip and grill over high heat until the skin is crisp and lightly charred, about 2 minutes longer. Let the breasts rest for 5 minutes, then serve with lemon wedges. —*Steven Raichlen*
WINE Juicy, spicy Grenache.

Grilled Garlic Chicken with Salsa Verde

ACTIVE: 1 HR 15 MIN; TOTAL: 2 HR PLUS
OVERNIGHT MARINATING

4 SERVINGS ●

CHICKEN

One 3½-pound chicken, backbone removed
- 4 garlic cloves, smashed and finely chopped
- 1 tablespoon chopped rosemary

Finely grated zest of 1 lemon
- 2 teaspoons crushed red pepper
- 1 teaspoon kosher salt
- ½ teaspoon freshly ground black pepper
- 3 tablespoons extra-virgin olive oil, plus more for brushing

SALSA VERDE
- 1 medium shallot, minced
- 1 tablespoon white wine vinegar
- 2 cups flat-leaf parsley leaves
- ½ cup mint leaves
- 2 garlic cloves, chopped
- 2 anchovy fillets, chopped
- 1 tablespoon small capers, drained
- ½ cup extra-virgin olive oil

Salt

Sage Polenta (p. 182), for serving

1. MARINATE THE CHICKEN: Set the chicken skin side up on a large rimmed baking sheet. Flatten the bird, fold the wing tips under the wingettes, point the drumsticks out and arrange the thighs next to the breasts. In a bowl, mix the garlic, rosemary, lemon zest, crushed red pepper, salt and black pepper with the 3 tablespoons of olive oil. Turn the chicken over and rub one-fourth of the marinade on the meat. Turn the chicken skin side up and rub the remaining marinade over the skin. Cover with plastic wrap and refrigerate overnight or for up to 24 hours.
2. MAKE THE SALSA VERDE: In a small bowl, combine the minced shallot and vinegar and let stand for 10 minutes. In a food processor, combine the parsley, mint,

garlic, anchovies and capers and process until finely chopped. Add the shallot and vinegar mixture. With the machine on, slowly pour in the olive oil until incorporated. Season with salt.
3. Light a charcoal fire. When the coals are hot, push them to one side of the grill. Brush the side of the grill opposite the coals with oil. Set the chicken on the oiled side of the grill, skin side down. Cover and grill for about 25 minutes, or until lightly charred on the bottom. Turn the chicken, cover and grill for about 20 minutes longer, or until cooked through. Transfer the chicken to a carving board and let rest for 10 minutes before carving.
4. Spoon the Sage Polenta onto warm plates. Arrange the chicken pieces alongside and serve with the salsa verde.
—*Shelley Lindgren*
MAKE AHEAD The salsa verde can be refrigerated overnight. Let return to room temperature before serving.
WINE Fresh, fruity rosé.

Brazilian Beer– Marinated Chicken

TOTAL: 30 MIN PLUS 4 HR
MARINATING

4 SERVINGS

Steven Raichlen flavors this chicken dish with Xingu (a Brazilian black lager that has a distinctive colalike flavor), plus mustard and onion—evoking the classic combination of beer and bratwursts. "The marinade brings a lot of flavor to a meat that really needs it," he says.

- 4 garlic cloves, smashed

Four ¼-inch slices of peeled fresh ginger, smashed
- 1 medium onion, thinly sliced
- 1 tablespoon sweet paprika
- 1 teaspoon kosher salt
- 1 teaspoon freshly ground black pepper
- ½ teaspoon caraway seeds
- ½ green bell pepper, finely chopped

¼ cup Dijon mustard

2 cups dark lager or stout, preferably Xingu Black Beer (see Note)

¼ cup vegetable oil

Four 6-ounce boneless, skinless chicken breast halves

2 tablespoons unsalted butter, melted

¼ cup chopped cilantro

Lime wedges, for serving

1. In a shallow dish, mix the garlic, ginger, onion, paprika, salt, black pepper, caraway seeds, green pepper, mustard, beer and oil. Add the chicken, cover and refrigerate for 4 hours, turning a few times.

2. Light a grill. Remove the chicken from the marinade and grill over high heat until nicely browned and just cooked through, about 5 minutes per side. Transfer the chicken to a platter and brush with the melted butter. Scatter the cilantro over the top and serve with lime wedges. —*Steven Raichlen*

NOTE Xingu Black Beer is an anise-scented, bittersweet black lager from Brazil. It's available in most states.

WINE Rustic, peppery Malbec.

Chicken in Tarragon-Mustard Cream Sauce

 **TOTAL: 30 MIN**
4 SERVINGS ●

F&W's Grace Parisi steals the flavors from a classic French pan sauce (mustard, tarragon, white wine and cream) for this quick, flavorful chicken sauté.

3 tablespoons extra-virgin olive oil

1½ pounds skinless, boneless chicken thighs, cut into ½-inch strips, or skinless, boneless breasts, cut into 1½-inch chunks

Salt and freshly ground pepper

½ pound white mushrooms, thinly sliced

1 large shallot, minced

¾ cup dry white wine

1¼ cups chicken stock or low-sodium broth

½ cup heavy cream

2 tablespoons grainy mustard

2 tablespoons chopped tarragon

Buttered noodles, for serving

1. In a very large skillet, heat 2 tablespoons of the olive oil. Season the chicken with salt and pepper and add it to the skillet in a single layer. Cook over high heat, turning once, until browned but not cooked through, 4 to 5 minutes. Using a slotted spoon, transfer the chicken to a plate. Pour off any fat in the skillet.

2. Add the remaining 1 tablespoon of oil to the skillet. Add the mushrooms and cook over high heat, stirring occasionally, until browned, 4 to 5 minutes. Add the shallot and cook, stirring, for 2 minutes. Add the wine and cook until reduced to 2 tablespoons, about 4 minutes. Add the stock, cream and mustard and bring to a boil. Cook until the sauce has reduced by half, about 6 minutes.

3. Return the chicken and any accumulated juices to the skillet and simmer over moderate heat until the chicken is cooked through, 2 to 3 minutes; season with salt and pepper. Stir in the tarragon. Serve with buttered noodles. —*Grace Parisi*

WINE Light, crisp white Burgundy.

Chicken with Carrots and Olives

 TOTAL: 40 MIN
4 SERVINGS ●

Middle Eastern cooks often stew chicken slowly in clay pots. This intensely flavorful recipe borrows ingredients common in Tunisian stews—ground cumin, cinnamon, lemon, garlic and olives—for a fast and fragrant sauté.

¼ cup extra-virgin olive oil

1½ pounds skinless, boneless chicken thighs, cut into ½-inch strips, or skinless, boneless breasts, cut into 1½-inch chunks

Salt and freshly ground pepper

½ lemon, seeded and very thinly sliced

3 large carrots, very thinly sliced, preferably on a mandoline

3 large garlic cloves, very thinly sliced

1 tablespoon water

1 teaspoon ground cumin

1 teaspoon sweet paprika

Pinch of cinnamon

1 cup chicken stock or low-sodium broth

¾ cup mixed, herb-marinated pitted olives (3 ounces)

Chopped roasted almonds and couscous, for serving

1. In a very large skillet, heat 2 tablespoons of the olive oil. Season the chicken with salt and pepper and add it to the skillet in a single layer. Cook the chicken over high heat, turning once, until it is browned but not cooked through, 4 to 5 minutes. Using a slotted spoon, transfer the chicken to a plate, leaving as much of the oil in the skillet as possible.

2. Add the lemon to the skillet in a single layer. Cook, turning once, until browned on both sides, about 2 minutes. Add the remaining 2 tablespoons of oil, the carrots and garlic and cook over moderate heat, stirring occasionally, until the carrots are slightly softened, about 2 minutes. Add the water and cook until the carrots are crisp-tender and the liquid has evaporated, about 2 minutes. Stir in the cumin, paprika and cinnamon and cook for 1 minute.

3. Return the chicken and any accumulated juices to the skillet and cook, stirring, for 1 minute. Add the chicken stock and olives, season with salt and pepper and simmer over moderate heat until the chicken is cooked through, about 5 minutes. Transfer the chicken to a serving bowl and sprinkle with the almonds. Serve with couscous. —*Grace Parisi*

WINE Fruity, light-bodied Beaujolais.

Chicken Saltimbocca

TOTAL: 40 MIN
4 SERVINGS

Four 6-ounce skinless,
   boneless chicken breast
   halves, butterflied and
   lightly pounded
Salt and freshly ground pepper
8   large sage leaves
4   thin slices of prosciutto di Parma
All-purpose flour, for dusting
2   tablespoons extra-virgin olive oil
4   tablespoons unsalted butter,
   cut into tablespoons
¼   cup plus 2 tablespoons dry
   white wine
1   cup chicken stock or
   low-sodium broth

1. Season the chicken with salt and pepper. Place 2 sage leaves on each breast. Top with a slice of prosciutto, trimming it to fit. Press the prosciutto to help it adhere to the chicken. Dust the chicken with flour, shaking off the excess.

2. Heat a large skillet. Add the olive oil and 2 tablespoons of the butter. Add 2 of the chicken breasts, prosciutto side up, and cook over high heat until nearly cooked through, about 3 minutes. Turn the chicken and cook just until the prosciutto begins to shrink, about 1 minute. Transfer the chicken to a plate; repeat with the remaining chicken. Pour off any fat from the skillet and wipe it clean with paper towels.

3. Add the remaining 2 tablespoons of butter to the skillet. Add the wine and cook over high heat until reduced by half, 2 minutes. Add the stock and bring to a boil. Cook until reduced by half, 3 minutes.

4. Return the chicken to the skillet, prosciutto side up, and simmer over moderate heat until the chicken is cooked through, about 2 minutes; season with salt and pepper. Transfer the chicken to plates, pour the sauce on top and serve.
—*Lidia Bastianich*

WINE Cherry-inflected, earthy Sangiovese.

Cornish Hens with Challah Stuffing

ACTIVE: 40 MIN; TOTAL: 2 HR
4 SERVINGS ●
¼   cup plus 1 tablespoon
   vegetable oil
½   teaspoon sweet paprika
½   teaspoon garlic powder
Kosher salt and freshly ground pepper
4   Cornish hens (about
   1½ pounds each)
3   medium white mushrooms
   (3 ounces), sliced ¼ inch thick
1   medium onion, finely chopped
1   celery rib, cut into ¼-inch dice
1   cup water
Six ½-inch-thick slices of challah
   bread, crust removed
2   tablespoons chopped parsley

1. Preheat the oven to 350°. In a bowl, mix the ¼ cup of oil with the paprika, garlic powder and 2 teaspoons of salt; season with pepper. Place the hens in a large roasting pan and loosen the breast skin. Brush the seasoned oil over the hens and between the breast meat and the skin. Let stand at room temperature for 30 minutes.

2. In a medium skillet, heat the remaining 1 tablespoon of oil. Add the mushrooms and cook over moderately high heat until golden brown, about 3 minutes. Add the onion and celery and cook over moderate heat until tender, about 5 minutes. Season with salt and pepper and transfer to a bowl.

3. In another bowl, pour the water over the challah and let stand for 1 minute. Squeeze most of the water from the challah, then chop it into ½-inch pieces. Add the challah to the mushroom mixture. Stir in the parsley and season with salt and pepper.

4. Spoon ½ cup of the challah stuffing into the cavity of each hen. Spoon the remaining stuffing between the skin and breast. Using butcher string, tie the legs of each hen together. Roast, breast side up, for 1 hour, or until the skin is golden brown and an instant-read thermometer inserted into the stuffing registers 165°. Transfer the hens to plates and let rest for 5 minutes. Drizzle with the pan juices and serve. —*Joan Nathan*

WINE Ripe, juicy Pinot Noir.

Zesty Braised Chicken with Lemon and Capers

ACTIVE: 25 MIN; TOTAL: 1 HR 30 MIN
4 SERVINGS ●
8   bone-in chicken thighs with skin
   (6 ounces each)
Salt and freshly ground black pepper
All-purpose flour, for dusting
2   tablespoons unsalted butter
2   tablespoons extra-virgin olive oil
4   large garlic cloves, peeled
1½   cups Sauvignon Blanc
1½   cups chicken stock, preferably
   homemade
Four 1-inch strips of lemon zest
4   thyme sprigs
1   tablespoon capers, drained
1   bay leaf

1. Preheat the oven to 350°. Season the chicken with salt and pepper and dust with flour. In a large ovenproof skillet, melt the butter in the oil. Add the chicken skin side down and cook over high heat, turning once, until browned, 12 to 14 minutes. Transfer to a large plate and pour off all but 1 tablespoon of the fat.

2. Add the garlic to the skillet and cook over low heat until softened, about 5 minutes. Add the wine and boil over high heat until reduced by half, about 5 minutes. Add the chicken stock, lemon zest, thyme sprigs, capers and bay leaf and bring to a boil. Return the chicken to the pan, skin side up. Transfer the skillet to the oven and braise for about 45 minutes, until the meat is tender.

3. Return the skillet to the stove and boil until the sauce is slightly reduced, about 5 minutes. Discard the thyme, bay leaf and lemon zest, if desired, before serving.
—*Grace Parisi*

WINE Lively, tart Sauvignon Blanc.

ZESTY BRAISED CHICKEN
WITH LEMON AND CAPERS

Smoked Chicken Pizza with Red Pepper Pesto

ACTIVE: 1 HR 15 MIN;
TOTAL: 2 HR 30 MIN
8 SERVINGS ●

Chef E. Michael Reidt's favorite new toy at the Huntley Hotel in Santa Monica, California—a superhot wood-burning oven—helped him solve a perpetual problem in his kitchen: what to do with leftover chicken? Now he smokes the meat and tosses it with a roasted-red-pepper pesto and goat cheese to make a topping for his wickedly addictive flat bread pizzas.

RED PEPPER PESTO

1 head of garlic, top third sliced off and discarded
2 tablespoons extra-virgin olive oil, plus more for drizzling
1 red bell pepper
½ cup basil leaves
1 tablespoon oregano leaves
Salt and freshly ground black pepper

PIZZA

1 pound pizza dough
All-purpose flour, for dusting
½ pound smoked chicken breast, shredded (2 cups)
1 small red bell pepper, thinly sliced
6 ounces Manchego cheese, coarsely shredded (2 cups)
4 ounces soft goat cheese, crumbled (1 cup)
Arugula, for garnish

1. MAKE THE RED PEPPER PESTO: Preheat the oven to 350°. Place the head of garlic cut side up on a double sheet of foil and drizzle with olive oil. Wrap the foil around the garlic and bake until the cloves are very soft, about 1 hour. Let cool. Squeeze the garlic onto a plate.

2. Roast the red pepper directly over a gas flame or under the broiler, turning frequently, until charred all over. Transfer the pepper to a plate to cool. Discard the charred skin, seeds and core, and coarsely chop the pepper. In a food processor, puree the pepper with the roasted garlic, basil, oregano and the 2 tablespoons of oil. Season with salt and pepper.

3. MAKE THE PIZZA: Set a pizza stone on the bottom of the oven and preheat the oven to 500° for at least 45 minutes. On a lightly floured work surface, cut the pizza dough into quarters and roll each piece into a ball. Flatten each ball, dust with flour and roll out to a 5-inch round. Cover the rounds with plastic wrap and let them rest at room temperature for 20 minutes.

4. Flour a pizza peel. Place a dough round on the peel and roll it out to an ⅛-inch thickness. Spread 2 tablespoons of the red pepper pesto over the dough to within ½ inch of the edge. Scatter ½ cup of the chicken and one-fourth of the red pepper strips over the pizza, then top with ½ cup of the Manchego and ¼ cup of the goat cheese. Carefully slide the pizza onto the hot stone and bake until browned on the bottom and bubbling on top, about 6 minutes. Transfer to a

TASTE TEST

great sauces & rubs

1 **Doc Jack's Original Formula Grillin' Soss** is spiked with apple cider vinegar ($5 for 16.5 oz; docjacks.com).

2 **Carolina Pig Pucker Sauce** has an excellent mustardy punch ($4 for 10 oz; extremebarbecuethebook.com).

3 **Tramonto's Dry Rub,** by Chicago chef Rick Tramonto, has zesty orange-peel flavor ($7 for 2 oz; cenitare.com).

4 **Jule's Gourmet Jerk Marinade,** by Arizona chef Bradford Thompson, is superfiery ($6 for 4 oz; julesgourmetjerk.com).

5 **Plantation Roast Coffee Rub**'s subtle coffee flavor is a great match with pork ($7 for 5.25 oz; fireandflavor.com).

6 **Trim Tabb's Pig Powder** has a superb sweet-salty-spicy balance ($7 for 12 oz; woodchicksbbq.com).

cutting board, scatter some arugula on top and cut into pieces. Repeat with the remaining dough, pesto and toppings.
—E. Michael Reidt

MAKE AHEAD The red pepper pesto can be refrigerated overnight.

WINE Full-bodied, rich Pinot Gris.

Smoky Barbecued Chicken

ACTIVE: 1 HR 15 MIN; TOTAL: 5 HR PLUS
OVERNIGHT MARINATING
6 TO 8 SERVINGS ●

This chicken is incredibly delicious thanks to an overnight marinade, a spice-and-sugar rub, a sweet-sour mop (brushing sauce) and four hours on the grill. To make the chicken extra moist, stand it upright inside the grill on top of a half-filled can of beer.

CHICKEN
1 cup balsamic vinegar
¼ cup Dijon mustard
¼ cup honey
4 garlic cloves, minced
3 small shallots, minced
½ teaspoon kosher salt
½ teaspoon freshly ground pepper
¾ cup olive oil
Two 3½-pound chickens

RUB
1 tablespoon plus ½ teaspoon granulated sugar
1 tablespoon plus ½ teaspoon light brown sugar
1 tablespoon plus ½ teaspoon garlic salt
1 tablespoon plus ½ teaspoon smoked sweet paprika
1 teaspoon dehydrated onion flakes
1 teaspoon pure chile powder
1 teaspoon freshly ground black pepper
½ teaspoon celery seeds
½ teaspoon dried basil
½ teaspoon dried tarragon
½ teaspoon dried oregano
¼ teaspoon cayenne pepper

MOP
½ cup dry white wine
½ cup apple juice
Kansas City–Style Barbecue Sauce (recipe follows), for serving

1. MARINATE THE CHICKEN: In a bowl, combine the vinegar, mustard, honey, garlic, shallots, salt and pepper. Slowly whisk in the olive oil. Put the chickens in a 2-gallon resealable plastic bag and pour in the marinade. Seal and turn to thoroughly coat the chickens. Refrigerate overnight, turning a few times.

2. Light 50 charcoal briquettes using a chimney. Run the wand of a thermometer through a cork and use the cork to plug one of the air vents in the grill lid. Leave the remaining lid vents open and adjust the lower vents as needed (if the fire gets too hot, close the vents; too cold, open them).

3. MAKE THE RUB AND THE MOP: Combine all of the rub ingredients in a bowl. Combine the wine and apple juice in a spray bottle or small bowl.

4. Drain the chickens. Set them on a large rimmed baking sheet and sprinkle all over with the rub, inside and out.

5. When the coals are hot, push them to one side of the grill and set a drip pan half-filled with water on the other side. Using tongs, transfer 4 of the hot coals to the chimney to light an additional 25 briquettes. Set the chickens breast side up on the grill grate over the drip pan, with their cavities facing the coals. Cover the grill and cook for 2 hours, spraying the chickens with the mop every hour. Check the thermometer to maintain a temperature of 250° to 275°. Add more coals, 25 at a time, every hour or so as needed.

6. After 2 hours, turn the chickens 90°, still breast side up, so that their sides are facing the coals. Be careful when turning to keep the juices inside the cavities. Spray with the mop. Cover and cook for 1 hour, then turn the chickens so that their opposite sides are facing the coals. Spray again,

then cover and cook for 1 to 1½ hours longer, until a thermometer inserted in the inner thigh reads 170°.

7. Transfer the chickens to a rimmed baking sheet. Pour the cavity juices into a serving bowl. Let the chickens rest for 10 minutes. Cut off the whole legs and transfer them to a platter. Slice the breast meat off the bone and transfer to the platter. Add any accumulated juices to the serving bowl. Serve the chicken with the juices and barbecue sauce. —Paul Kirk

WINE Intense, fruity Zinfandel.

KANSAS CITY–STYLE BARBECUE SAUCE

TOTAL: 40 MIN
MAKES ABOUT 1 QUART ● ●

Pit master Paul Kirk, a Kansas City native, jokes that this sauce reflects the style of his hometown "because I said so." But it also has the characteristic tomato base of Kansas City's classic sauces, unlike the vinegar-based sauces of the Carolinas.

3 cups ketchup
⅔ cup dark brown sugar
½ cup water
½ cup white wine vinegar
½ cup tomato paste
2 tablespoons yellow mustard
2 tablespoons pure chile powder
1 tablespoon freshly ground black pepper
1 teaspoon salt
1 teaspoon granulated onion powder
1 teaspoon granulated garlic powder
½ teaspoon ground ginger

In a medium saucepan, combine all of the ingredients and bring to a boil over moderate heat. Reduce the heat to low and simmer the sauce for 30 minutes, stirring often to prevent scorching. —P.K.

MAKE AHEAD The barbecue sauce can be refrigerated for up to 1 month. Rewarm gently before serving.

Mini Turkey Meat Loaves with Red Pepper Sauce

ACTIVE: 45 MIN; TOTAL: 1 HR 30 MIN

4 SERVINGS ●●

- 5 tablespoons extra-virgin olive oil
- 1 medium carrot, very finely chopped
- 1 medium celery rib, very finely chopped
- 1 medium garlic clove, very finely chopped
- 1 large onion, finely chopped

Kosher salt and freshly ground white pepper

- 1½ pounds ground lean turkey, white meat only
- 2 large egg whites
- ½ cup *panko*
- ½ cup low-fat cottage cheese
- 3 red bell peppers, sliced
- 1 thyme sprig
- ½ cup water
- 1 tablespoon half-and-half
- 1 yellow bell pepper, sliced

Cooked wild rice, for serving

1. Preheat the oven to 400°. Lightly oil two 6-by-3½-inch metal loaf pans. In a skillet, heat 2 tablespoons of the olive oil. Add the chopped carrot, celery, garlic and two-thirds of the chopped onion; season with salt and white pepper and cook over moderate heat, stirring, until the vegetables are softened, about 10 minutes. Let cool.

2. Add the ground turkey and cooked vegetables to a large bowl. Add the egg whites, *panko*, cottage cheese, 2 teaspoons of salt and ½ teaspoon of white pepper. Knead until blended and divide the meatloaf mixture between the pans. Place the pans on a baking sheet and bake in the upper third of the oven for 35 minutes, or until an instant-read thermometer registers 160°. Remove the meat loaves from the oven and preheat the broiler.

3. Meanwhile, in a skillet, heat 2 table-spoons of the olive oil. Add two-thirds of the sliced red peppers, the remaining chopped onion and the thyme sprig. Cover and cook over moderate heat until the vegetables are softened, 10 minutes. Add the water, cover and simmer until the peppers are very tender, 7 minutes. Discard the thyme sprig. Carefully transfer the contents of the skillet to a blender, add the half-and-half and puree. Season with salt and white pepper.

4. In a skillet, heat the remaining 1 table-spoon of olive oil. Add the remaining sliced red and yellow peppers and cook over moderate heat until softened, 10 minutes. Season with salt and white pepper.

5. Broil the meat loaves 4 inches from the heat until browned, 2 minutes. Turn the loaves out onto a plate and cut into ½-inch slices. Spoon some of the pepper sauce onto plates. Top with the meat loaf and peppers, then serve with wild rice and the remaining sauce. —*Sandro Gamba*

MAKE AHEAD The red pepper sauce can be refrigerated overnight. Reheat gently before serving.

WINE Juicy, fresh Dolcetto.

Asian Baby Back Ribs with Panko-Crusted Mushrooms

ACTIVE: 20 MIN; TOTAL: 1 HR 15 MIN

4 SERVINGS

Hourglass winery owner Jeff Smith gives these roasted baby back ribs an Asian nudge by basting them with a sweet soy sauce–based marinade, which makes them more wine-friendly than ribs with traditional barbecue sauce. "Barbecue sauce has a strong flavor that dominates most American-style ribs," he says, "but here, the delicate flavors in the marinade allow you to still taste the pork."

Two 1½-pound racks of pork baby back ribs, papery membrane removed from the underside of each rack

- 4 medium garlic cloves, very finely chopped
- 4 scallions, minced
- 2 tablespoons soy sauce
- 2 tablespoons extra-virgin olive oil
- 2 tablespoons light brown sugar
- 1 tablespoon rice vinegar

Salt and freshly ground black pepper

Panko-Crusted Mushrooms (recipe follows), for serving

1. Preheat the oven to 400°. Set the baby back ribs on a large rimmed baking sheet, skinned side up. In a small bowl, stir together the chopped garlic with the minced scallions, soy sauce, olive oil, brown sugar and rice vinegar. Season the ribs lightly with salt and generously with black pepper. Brush some of the sauce on the skinned side of the ribs and turn them over; brush the remaining sauce over the tops of the ribs.

2. Roast the ribs in the upper third of the oven for about 45 minutes, until browned and tender. Let them rest for 10 minutes, then slice into individual ribs and serve with the Panko-Crusted Mushrooms. —*Jeff Smith*

MAKE AHEAD The baby back ribs can be brushed with sauce, covered and refrigerated overnight.

WINE Firm, complex Cabernet Sauvignon.

PANKO-CRUSTED MUSHROOMS

TOTAL: 20 MIN

4 SERVINGS ●

- 2 cups vegetable oil, for frying
- 2 large eggs
- 2 cups *panko* (Japanese bread crumbs)
- 12 large white mushrooms, stems discarded

Salt

In a medium skillet, heat the vegetable oil until shimmering. In a small bowl, lightly beat the eggs with a fork. Spread the *panko* in a shallow bowl. Dip each mushroom into the beaten egg and let the excess drip off, then coat thoroughly with *panko*. Carefully add 4 of the *panko*-coated mushrooms to the hot oil and fry over moderately high heat until golden brown, about 2 minutes per side. Transfer the fried mushrooms to a wire rack set over a baking sheet to drain. Repeat with the remaining mushrooms, working in batches of 4. Season with salt and serve the mushrooms immediately. —*J.S.*

Missouri Baby Back Ribs with Apple Slaw

ACTIVE: 45 MIN; TOTAL: 4 HR 30 MIN

10 SERVINGS ● ●

These luscious, extra-porky ribs are based on a recipe that Michel Nischan's mother, a talented Southern cook, used to make. "Mom would stand in front of the grill, flipping the ribs and basting them with ham stock every few minutes until they got incredibly tender. It took forever, but it was so worth it," recalls Nischan, chef and owner of Dressing Room in Westport, Connecticut. This version uses a broiler and a warm oven instead of a grill.

- 8 pounds baby back ribs, membranes removed, cut into 4-rib sections
- Finely grated zest of 2 lemons
- ¼ cup finely chopped flat-leaf parsley
- 2 tablespoons very finely chopped chives
- 1 tablespoon very finely chopped tarragon
- 1 tablespoon very finely chopped thyme leaves
- 1½ cups Ham Hock Stock (recipe follows)
- Salt and freshly ground black pepper
- 3 tablespoons grapeseed oil or canola oil
- 2 tablespoons cider vinegar
- 1 pound napa cabbage, finely shredded (4 cups)
- 2 large Granny Smith apples, julienned

1. Preheat the broiler. Peel the membrane from the underside of the baby back ribs and place them skinned side up on 2 rimmed baking sheets. Broil the ribs 6 inches from the heat, turning once, until they are browned on both sides, 8 to 10 minutes per sheet.

2. Preheat the oven to 350°. In a small bowl, mix the grated lemon zest with 2 tablespoons of the chopped parsley and the chopped chives, tarragon and thyme. Brush the ribs with some of the Ham Hock Stock and sprinkle with half of the herb and lemon zest mixture. Season the ribs with salt and black pepper and bake for about 1 hour, without turning, until the meat is very tender; baste the ribs with the stock and sprinkle with the herb mixture several times while baking. Transfer the ribs to a cutting board and cut into individual ribs.

3. Meanwhile, in a large bowl, whisk the grapeseed oil with the cider vinegar and season with salt and black pepper. Add the shredded cabbage, julienned apples and the remaining 2 tablespoons of chopped parsley; toss to coat the cabbage and apples with dressing. Serve the slaw with the ribs. —*Michel Nischan*

MAKE AHEAD The baked ribs can be refrigerated overnight. Reheat before serving.

WINE Rustic, peppery Malbec.

HAM HOCK STOCK

ACTIVE: 10 MIN; TOTAL: 2 HR 30 MIN

MAKES 3½ QUARTS ●

- 4 smoked ham hocks
- 1 carrot, roughly chopped
- 1 onion, quartered
- 2 bay leaves
- 1 teaspoon black peppercorns
- 4 quarts water

Combine the smoked ham hocks, chopped carrot and onion, bay leaves, black peppercorns and water in a large soup pot and bring to a boil over high heat. Cover the pot partially and simmer until the ham hock stock is flavorful and the meat is falling off the bones, about 2 hours. Strain the stock and skim off any fat from the surface. —*M.N.*

MAKE AHEAD The stock can be refrigerated in an airtight container for up to 3 days or frozen for up to 1 month.

Pork and Bacon Kebabs

ACTIVE: 30 MIN; TOTAL: 1 HR 30 MIN

4 SERVINGS

This double dose of pork was inspired by a dish Steven Raichlen encountered on a recent trip to Serbia, where he researched native barbecue traditions for his upcoming book, *Planet Barbecue*. "The grilling there was amazing, as sophisticated as any grill culture in the world," he says.

- 3 medium garlic cloves, very finely chopped
- 2 teaspoons sweet paprika
- 1 teaspoon kosher salt
- 1 teaspoon caraway seeds
- 1 teaspoon dry mustard
- ½ teaspoon freshly ground black pepper
- 2 tablespoons vegetable oil
- 1½ pounds pork tenderloin, cut into 1½-inch cubes
- 1 large sweet onion, cut into 2-inch dice
- ½ pound lean slab bacon, cut into 1-inch dice

1. In a large bowl, mix the chopped garlic with the paprika, salt, caraway seeds, dry mustard, black pepper and vegetable oil. Add the pork and toss well to coat. Cover the bowl and let marinate in the refrigerator for 1 to 2 hours.

2. Light a charcoal grill. Thread the pork, onion and bacon onto 8 skewers. Grill the skewers over high heat, turning a few times, until they are browned and the pork is just cooked through, 15 minutes. Transfer the skewers to a platter and serve. —*Steven Raichlen*

WINE Intense, fruity Zinfandel.

DOUBLE-PORK, DOUBLE-CHEESE BURGER

ROAST PORK SHOULDER WITH FENNEL AND POTATOES

Double-Pork, Double-Cheese Burgers

 **TOTAL: 35 MIN**
4 SERVINGS ●

In these impressive burgers, smoky bacon enriches ground pork. Just before the burgers are done cooking, they're topped with two kinds of cheese: Camembert (for creaminess) and Gorgonzola (for more creaminess, as well as pungency).

½ cup finely chopped bacon
1½ pounds ground pork
1 large garlic clove, very finely chopped
2 teaspoons finely chopped thyme leaves
1 teaspoon kosher salt
½ teaspoon freshly ground black pepper
Four ½-inch-thick red onion slices
Olive oil, for drizzling
4 hamburger buns or ciabatta rolls
2 tablespoons unsalted butter, melted
6 ounces Camembert, cut into eight ⅓-inch-thick slices
2 ounces Gorgonzola cheese, cut into four ⅓-inch-thick slices
Arugula and 4 tomato slices

1. In a skillet, cook the bacon over moderate heat, stirring, until cooked through, about 3 minutes. Transfer to a paper towel–lined plate to drain; let cool. In a large bowl, mix the bacon with the pork, garlic, thyme, salt and pepper. Shape into four 1-inch-thick patties.

2. Light a grill. Drizzle the onion slices with olive oil and grill over moderately high heat until lightly charred, about 2 minutes per side. Transfer to a platter. Brush the cut sides of the buns with the melted butter and grill, cut side down, until toasted, about 1 minute. Turn and grill for 30 seconds longer. Transfer to the platter.

3. Grill the burgers until they are charred outside and cooked through, about 5 minutes per side. Arrange 2 Camembert slices and 1 Gorgonzola slice on each burger and cook until the cheese is melted, about 1 minute longer.

4. On the bottom halves of the buns, layer the arugula, tomato, burgers and grilled onion. Close the burgers and serve.
—*Sang Yoon*
WINE Intense, fruity Zinfandel.

Stir-Fried Pork Belly with Kimchi

 TOTAL: 15 MIN
2 SERVINGS

Chef Isamu Soumi, formerly of Ten in New York City, adds kimchi, the pungent Korean condiment, to a pork stir-fry. Fresh pork belly, available at Japanese markets, has the ideal fat-to-lean-meat ratio to temper the kimchi's intensity.

1 tablespoon vegetable oil
¾ pound thinly sliced
   fresh pork belly, cut into
   2-inch strips
¾ pound kimchi
1½ tablespoons soy sauce
¼ teaspoon Asian sesame oil
1 scallion, top 2 inches trimmed,
   very thinly sliced

1. In a large skillet, heat the vegetable oil until shimmering. Add the thinly sliced pork belly to the skillet in a single layer and cook over high heat, turning the slices once, until crisp, 6 minutes. Transfer the fried pork slices to a paper towel–lined plate to drain and pour off all but 2 tablespoons of the fat from the skillet.

2. Add the kimchi to the skillet and stir-fry over high heat for 2 minutes. Return the drained pork to the skillet and toss to combine with the kimchi. Stir in the soy sauce and transfer to a large serving bowl. Drizzle the stir-fry with the sesame oil and garnish with the sliced scallion. Serve immediately. —*Isamu Soumi*

SERVE WITH Steamed rice.
WINE Complex, aromatic Nebbiolo.

Roast Pork Shoulder with Fennel and Potatoes

ACTIVE: 20 MIN; TOTAL: 4 HR 30 MIN
6 SERVINGS ●

Porchetta can be found at weekly markets in the country towns around Foligno, Italy: whole roasted young pigs seasoned with *fiore di finocchio* (wild fennel pollen) and sold either sliced and stuffed into panini (small round buns) for a snack or by the kilo to take home for lunch. For this recipe, a pork shoulder is slow-roasted with similar seasonings (pork belly is equally delicious roasted for 1 hour at 400°).

¼ cup fennel pollen or ground
   fennel seeds (see Note)
1½ tablespoons kosher salt
1½ tablespoons freshly
   ground black pepper

One 6- to 7-pound bone-in pork
   shoulder, skin removed
   and thick layer of fat scored
1 tablespoon extra-virgin
   olive oil
3 pounds medium Yukon Gold
   potatoes, peeled and quartered
1 cup dry white wine

1. Preheat the oven to 325°. In a small bowl, mix the fennel pollen, salt and black pepper. Coat the pork shoulder all over with the spice mixture and set it in a large roasting pan, fat side up. Pour the olive oil around the pork. Roll the quartered potatoes in the oil to coat and arrange them cut side down. Roast until the pork is tender and the potatoes are browned on the bottom, about 3 hours.

2. Transfer the roasted potatoes to an ovenproof bowl. Pour the white wine into the pan around the pork, return the pan to the oven and continue to roast for 1 hour longer, or until an instant-read thermometer inserted into the thickest part of the pork shoulder registers 185°.

3. Transfer the pork to a board and let rest for 20 minutes. Meanwhile, reheat the potatoes in the oven. Carve the pork into thick slices and serve on a platter with the potatoes. —*Salvatore Denaro*

NOTE Wild fennel pollen is available in the U.S. from specialty purveyors such as chefshop.com and zingermans.com.
WINE Rustic, peppery Malbec.

Rack of Lamb with Coconut-Mint Sauce and Glazed Peas

 TOTAL: 45 MIN
4 SERVINGS

The vibrant, Thai-influenced coconut-mint sauce that Napa vineyard owner Jeff Smith serves with this roasted rack of lamb is a delicious example of his homespun Mediterranean-Asian cuisine. Substituting brown sugar for white when glazing vegetables "adds a deeper kind of sweet note to them," Smith says.

Two 1½-pound racks of lamb
   (16 chops), frenched (see Note)
Salt and freshly ground
   black pepper
Extra-virgin olive oil
½ cup unsweetened
   coconut milk
¼ cup mint leaves
Three ¼-inch slices of fresh ginger
2 garlic cloves
2 tablespoons fresh lime juice
1 jalapeño, seeded
1 tablespoon cilantro,
   roughly chopped
1 tablespoon unsalted butter
1 shallot, minced
10 ounces frozen baby
   peas, thawed
1 tablespoon brown sugar

1. Preheat the oven to 400°. Set the lamb in a medium roasting pan. Season with salt and pepper and drizzle with oil. Roast until an instant-read thermometer inserted into the center registers 125° for medium-rare, about 35 minutes. Transfer to a cutting board and let rest for about 5 minutes.

2. Meanwhile, in a blender or food processor, puree the coconut milk, mint, ginger, garlic, lime juice, jalapeño and cilantro until smooth. Season with salt and pepper.

3. In a medium skillet, melt the butter. Add the minced shallot and cook over moderate heat, stirring, until softened, about 3 minutes. Add the peas and brown sugar, season with salt and pepper and cook until the peas are lightly coated with the glaze, 2 to 3 minutes longer. Carve the lamb into chops and serve with the coconut-mint sauce and peas. —*Jeff Smith*

NOTE Have your butcher french the racks of lamb, or do it yourself by scraping the fat and gristle from the bones with a boning or paring knife.
MAKE AHEAD The coconut-mint sauce can be refrigerated for up to 2 days.
WINE Firm, complex Cabernet Sauvignon.

Rack of Lamb with Arugula Pesto

 ACTIVE: 20 MIN; TOTAL: 45 MIN
4 SERVINGS

"This combination was a huge hit while I was chef at Michael's in Santa Monica," says Sang Yoon (chef and owner of Father's Office, also in Santa Monica, California) of his grilled lamb paired with a simple, pleasantly tangy arugula-and-Parmesan pesto. The mustard seeds in the spice coating add alluring crunch to the lamb.

- **2 teaspoons mustard seeds**
- **1½ teaspoons cumin seeds**
- **Two 1½-pound racks of lamb, chine bone removed and bones frenched**
- **Salt and freshly ground pepper**
- **5 cups arugula leaves (3 ounces)**
- **2 garlic cloves, quartered**
- **2 tablespoons fresh lemon juice**
- **½ cup extra-virgin olive oil**
- **¼ cup freshly grated Parmesan cheese**

1. Light a grill. In a small skillet, toast the mustard and cumin seeds over moderately high heat until fragrant, about 1 minute. Let cool, then transfer the seeds to a mortar or spice grinder and grind to a powder. Rub the spices all over the lamb and season with salt and pepper.

2. Grill the lamb over moderately high heat, turning and rotating the racks occasionally, until lightly charred outside and medium-rare within, about 30 minutes total. Transfer the lamb to a carving board and let rest for 10 minutes.

3. Meanwhile, in a food processor, puree the arugula with the garlic, lemon juice and olive oil. Add the cheese and season the pesto with salt and pepper.

4. Carve the lamb racks into individual chops and transfer to plates. Serve the arugula pesto alongside. —*Sang Yoon*

MAKE AHEAD The pesto can be refrigerated for 2 days. Serve at room temperature.

WINE Round, deep-flavored Syrah.

Grilled Lamb Shwarma

TOTAL: 1 HR 30 MIN PLUS OVERNIGHT MARINATING

8 SERVINGS ●

Shwarma, thin slices of roasted meat and condiments that are often wrapped in a pita, is a popular street food throughout the Middle East. Rather than roasting meat on a spit in the traditional style, Sonoma vintner Chris Hanna simply grills a butterflied leg of lamb to achieve similar results. The lamb should sit overnight in a spicy, garlicky marinade before grilling, though three days would be even better.

- **½ cup plus 2 tablespoons extra-virgin olive oil**
- **6 garlic cloves, minced**
- **Juice of 2 lemons**
- **1 tablespoon ground cumin**
- **1 tablespoon ground cardamom**
- **1 teaspoon Aleppo pepper or ½ teaspoon crushed red pepper**
- **Freshly ground black pepper**
- **Kosher salt**
- **One 6- to 7-pound butterflied leg of lamb**
- **2 orange bell peppers, cut into ¼-inch strips**
- **1 yellow bell pepper, cut into ¼-inch strips**
- **3 medium red onions, thinly sliced**
- **Yogurt-Tahini Sauce and Syrian Pita Bread (recipes follow), for serving**

1. In a bowl, mix ½ cup of the oil with the garlic, lemon juice, cumin, cardamom, Aleppo pepper, 1 teaspoon of black pepper and 1½ tablespoons of salt. Set the lamb on a rimmed baking sheet and coat it with the marinade. Cover and refrigerate overnight or, preferably, for 2 or 3 days.

2. Light a grill. In a large skillet, heat 1 tablespoon of the oil. Add the bell peppers, cover and cook over moderately low heat, stirring occasionally, until tender, about 10 minutes. Season with salt and ground black pepper and transfer to a serving bowl. Heat the remaining 1 tablespoon of olive oil in the skillet and add the onions. Cook over moderate heat, stirring occasionally, until lightly browned, about 10 minutes. Season the onions with salt and ground black pepper and transfer them to another serving bowl.

3. Grill the leg of lamb over moderately high heat, turning and shifting often, until an instant-read thermometer inserted into the thickest part of the meat registers 130° for medium-rare, about 25 minutes. Transfer the lamb to a carving board and let rest for 10 minutes. Thinly slice the lamb across the grain and serve with the peppers, onions, Yogurt-Tahini Sauce and Syrian Pita Bread. —*Chris Hanna*

WINE Bright, tart Barbera.

YOGURT-TAHINI SAUCE

 TOTAL: 10 MIN
MAKES ABOUT 2 CUPS ● ●

Blending this lightly spiced tahini sauce with whole-milk yogurt makes it extra-creamy. It's delicious and cooling with the pepper-dusted lamb *shwarma.*

- **¼ cup tahini paste, at room temperature**
- **Juice of ½ lemon**
- **1 tablespoon extra-virgin olive oil**
- **2 cups plain whole-milk yogurt**
- **1 teaspoon ground cumin**
- **½ teaspoon Aleppo pepper or freshly ground black pepper**
- **Salt**
- **1 tablespoon finely chopped parsley, for garnish**

In a food processor, blend the tahini paste, lemon juice and olive oil until smooth. Add the yogurt and blend the mixture thoroughly. Scrape the tahini sauce into a bowl; stir in the cumin and Aleppo pepper. Season with salt and garnish with the parsley. —*C.H.*

MAKE AHEAD The Yogurt-Tahini Sauce can be refrigerated for up to 3 days. Serve at room temperature.

SYRIAN PITA BREAD

ACTIVE: 45 MIN; TOTAL: 2 HR 30 MIN

MAKES SIXTEEN 6-INCH PITAS ● ● ●

Hanna learned to make these airy pitas from her Syrian grandmother, and she still insists on baking them from scratch when serving *shwarma.* "It isn't that hard to make your own, and the flavor and texture are far superior to the flaccid, sweet kind you find in most grocery stores," she says.

- ¾ **cup warm water**
- 1½ **envelopes (3⅜ teaspoons) active dry yeast**
- 6 **cups bread flour**
- 1½ **teaspoons salt**
- 1½ **cups warm milk**

Extra-virgin olive oil, for the bowl

1. Set a pizza stone on the bottom rack of the oven and preheat the oven to 500°. In a bowl, combine the water and yeast and let stand until foamy, about 10 minutes.

2. In a food processor, pulse the flour with the salt. With the machine on, pour in the yeast mixture and then the warm milk and process until the dough forms a ball. Turn the dough out onto a lightly floured work surface and knead it a few times. Form the dough into a ball. Lightly oil a bowl. Transfer the dough to the bowl and turn to coat; cover with plastic wrap and let rise in a warm place until doubled in bulk, about 1 hour.

3. Lightly dust a work surface with flour. Punch down the dough and cut it in half. Cut each half into 8 pieces and roll them into balls, then flatten into 6-inch rounds. Arrange the rounds on the work surface or on floured baking sheets; cover with plastic wrap. Let rise until puffy, 25 minutes.

4. Using a lightly floured pizza peel, slide 4 of the rounds onto the hot pizza stone at a time and bake for about 5 minutes, until the pitas puff up. Serve hot or wrap in foil to keep warm. —*C.H.*

MAKE AHEAD The flattened, unbaked pita rounds can be frozen for up to 1 month. Let thaw completely, then let rest at room temperature for 20 minutes before baking.

RACK OF LAMB WITH ARUGULA PESTO

GRILLED LAMB SHWARMA

Rosemary Lamb Chops

TOTAL: 40 MIN
4 SERVINGS

¼ cup extra-virgin olive oil
4 scallions, thinly sliced
1 cup frozen baby peas
1 cup frozen baby lima beans
1 small zucchini, cut into
    ½-inch dice
¼ teaspoon crushed red pepper
Salt and freshly ground
    black pepper
6 romaine leaves, cut crosswise
    into ¼-inch ribbons
¼ cup shredded mint leaves
12 baby lamb rib chops (about
    2½ pounds), bones
    frenched (see Note)
1 tablespoon minced rosemary

1. In a medium saucepan, heat 3 tablespoons of the olive oil. Add the sliced scallions and cook over moderate heat, stirring frequently, until softened, about 4 minutes. Add the baby peas, baby lima beans, diced zucchini and crushed red pepper and season with salt and black pepper. Cover and cook over very low heat until the vegetables are barely softened, about 15 minutes. Add the lettuce ribbons and 2 tablespoons of the shredded mint leaves, cover and cook until the lettuce is very tender, about 10 minutes.

2. Meanwhile, preheat a grill pan. Rub the lamb chops with the remaining 1 tablespoon of olive oil and season with salt and black pepper. Rub the rosemary onto the chops. Grill the chops over high heat for 6 minutes, turning them once or twice, for medium-rare meat.

3. Spoon the vegetables onto plates and top with the lamb. Garnish with the remaining 2 tablespoons of mint and serve.
—*Lidia Bastianich*

NOTE Have your butcher french the lamb chops, removing the meat from the ends of the bones.

WINE Bright, tart Barbera.

Tandoori Leg of Lamb

ACTIVE: 40 MIN; TOTAL: 2 HR 45 MIN
PLUS 6 HR MARINATING
6 TO 8 SERVINGS

½ cup plus 2 tablespoons
    fresh lemon juice
Kosher salt
One 6-pound bone-in leg of lamb
2 cups plain whole-milk yogurt
½ cup vegetable oil
2 garlic cloves, minced
2 tablespoons minced fresh ginger
2 tablespoons dry mustard
2 teaspoons ground cumin
1 teaspoon ground nutmeg
1 teaspoon ground cardamom
1 teaspoon freshly ground
    black pepper
1 teaspoon ground cinnamon
1 teaspoon turmeric
1 teaspoon cayenne pepper
2 medium sweet onions,
    thinly sliced
½ cup chopped cilantro
4 tablespoons unsalted
    butter, melted
Lemon wedges, for serving

1. In a large roasting pan, mix ½ cup of the lemon juice with 2 teaspoons of salt. Place the lamb in the pan and coat well with the lemon juice. Let the lamb stand in the juice for 30 minutes, then drain.

2. In a large bowl, stir together the yogurt, oil, garlic, ginger, dry mustard, cumin, nutmeg, cardamom, black pepper, cinnamon, turmeric and cayenne. Add 2 teaspoons of salt and the remaining 2 tablespoons of lemon juice. With a small knife, make 1-inch-deep slits all over the lamb. Coat the lamb thoroughly with the marinade, pushing it into the slits. Refrigerate for at least 6 hours or overnight.

3. Light a charcoal grill. Remove the lamb from the marinade, leaving on a thick layer of the marinade seasonings. Move the hot coals to one side of the grill and place a drip pan opposite the coals. Set the lamb over the drip pan, cover the grill and cook until the lamb is glazed and an instant-read thermometer registers 140° for medium, about 2 hours.

4. Line a platter with the onion slices and sprinkle with the cilantro. Place the lamb on top, brush it with the melted butter and let rest for 15 minutes. Carve into slices and serve with the lemon wedges.
—*Steven Raichlen*

WINE Juicy, spicy Grenache.

Herb-Crusted Leg of Lamb

ACTIVE: 20 MIN; TOTAL: 2 HR 40 MIN
8 SERVINGS ●

6 tablespoons fresh bread crumbs
6 tablespoons unsalted butter,
    softened
6 garlic cloves, minced
6 tablespoons chopped
    flat-leaf parsley
3 tablespoons thyme leaves
3 tablespoons chopped rosemary
2 tablespoons fresh lemon juice
One 7- to 8-pound bone-in leg of lamb
    at room temperature, fat trimmed
Salt and freshly ground pepper
¼ cup Dijon mustard

1. Preheat the oven to 325°. In a bowl, mix the bread crumbs with the butter, garlic, parsley, thyme, rosemary and lemon juice. Season the lamb all over with salt and pepper. Rub some of the herb mixture on the underside of the lamb and set in a roasting pan, fat side up. Spread the mustard over the top of the lamb, then pat the remaining herb mixture over the top of the lamb.

2. Bake for about 2 hours, until browned on top and an instant-read thermometer inserted in the thickest part of the meat registers 150° for medium meat.

3. Transfer the lamb to a carving board and let rest for 15 minutes. Carve into slices and serve. —*Valeria Huneeus*

MAKE AHEAD The unroasted, herb-rubbed lamb can be refrigerated overnight.

WINE Rich, ripe Cabernet Sauvignon.

Tex-Mex Porterhouse Steaks

ACTIVE: 45 MIN; TOTAL: 1 HR 45 MIN

4 SERVINGS

1½ tablespoons kosher salt

1½ tablespoons pure ancho or
    mulato chile powder

1½ teaspoons coarsely cracked
    black pepper

  1 teaspoon garlic powder

  1 teaspoon crumbled dried oregano

  ½ teaspoon cayenne pepper

  ½ teaspoon ground cumin

Two 2½-pound porterhouse steaks,
    cut 2 inches thick

  4 tablespoons unsalted butter

  ¼ cup lager beer

  ¼ cup strong brewed coffee

  ¼ cup Worcestershire sauce

1. Soak 1 cup of hardwood chips in water for 1 hour and drain.

2. Light a charcoal grill. In a bowl, mix the salt with the chile powder, black pepper, garlic powder, oregano, cayenne pepper and cumin. Sprinkle all over the steaks. In a small saucepan, melt the butter over moderate heat. Stir in the beer, coffee and Worcestershire sauce and simmer for 5 minutes.

3. Move two-thirds of the hot coals to one side of the grill to create a high-heat zone and leave the remaining third in the center to create a moderate-heat zone. Oil the grate, sprinkle the wood chips over the high-heat zone and grill the steaks over high heat for 3 minutes. Slide the steaks to the moderate-heat zone and grill for 10 minutes, rotating them after 2 minutes to make crosshatches, if desired. Turn them over and grill over high heat for 3 minutes. Brush the steaks with the coffee mop and move them to moderate heat. Grill the steaks for 10 minutes longer, or until an instant-read thermometer registers 125° for medium-rare, mopping twice more. Transfer the steaks to a carving board and let rest for 10 minutes, then carve into thick slices. —*Steven Raichlen*

WINE Fruity, luscious Shiraz.

Barbecued Brisket and Burnt Ends

ACTIVE: 3 HR; TOTAL: 11 HR

10 TO 12 SERVINGS ●

MOP

  2 cups beef broth or
    low-sodium consommé

  ½ cup cider vinegar

  ½ cup Worcestershire sauce

  4 garlic cloves, smashed

  ¼ cup grated onion

  1 bay leaf

  1 teaspoon kosher salt

  1 teaspoon freshly ground pepper

SLATHER

  ¼ cup Dijon mustard

  2 tablespoons pickle juice
    (from a jar of dill pickles)

  1 tablespoon dark brown sugar

  ½ tablespoon Worcestershire sauce

  ¾ teaspoon hot sauce

RUB

  2 tablespoons granulated sugar

  2 tablespoons light brown sugar

  2 tablespoons smoked
    sweet paprika

  2 tablespoons garlic salt

1½ teaspoons onion salt

1½ teaspoons pure chile powder

1½ teaspoons freshly ground
    black pepper

  1 teaspoon celery seeds

  ½ teaspoon ground cumin

  ¼ teaspoon cayenne pepper

  ¼ teaspoon dried thyme

  ⅛ teaspoon dried oregano

One 9-pound whole packer beef
    brisket, fat trimmed to ¼ inch

Kansas City–Style Barbecue Sauce
    (p. 157), for serving

1. Light 50 charcoal briquettes using a chimney. Run the wand of a thermometer through a cork and use the cork to plug one of the air vents in the grill lid. Leave the remaining lid vents open and adjust the lower vents as needed (if the fire gets too hot, close the vents; too cold, open them).

2. MAKE THE MOP: Combine all the ingredients in a saucepan and bring to a boil. Reduce the heat; simmer for 10 minutes. Strain, cool and transfer to a spray bottle.

3. MAKE THE SLATHER AND RUB: Mix the slather ingredients in a bowl. In another bowl, stir together the rub ingredients.

4. Coat the brisket with the slather, then sprinkle with the rub.

5. When the coals are hot, push them to one side of the grill and set a drip pan half-filled with water on the other side. Using tongs, transfer 4 of the hot coals to the chimney to light another 25 briquettes. Set the brisket on the grill over the drip pan, fat side up, with the widest end facing the coals. Cover and cook for about 5 hours, maintaining a steady temperature inside the grill of 250° to 275° (add more lit coals, 25 at a time, every hour or so, as needed). Spray with the mop every hour.

6. After 5 hours, carefully flip the brisket and rotate it 180° so the opposite end is facing the coals. Cover, then cook for 2 hours, spraying every hour with the mop and adding more hot coals as necessary.

7. Flip the brisket and rotate it 90°. Spray with the mop, cover and cook for 1½ hours. Flip the brisket a final time and rotate it 180°. Spray with the mop, cover and cook for about 1 hour longer, or until an instant-read thermometer inserted into the thickest part registers 185°.

8. To make the burnt ends, transfer the brisket to a board and cut off the point, slicing through the layer of fat that separates it from the brisket. Return the point to the grill. Spray it with the mop, cover and cook for 1 hour, or until the meat is almost black on the outside. Transfer the point to the board and let rest for 15 minutes. Slice into cubes and serve, or save for making Grandma Kirk's Baked Beans (p. 185). Thinly slice the brisket against the grain. Serve with Kansas City–Style Barbecue Sauce on the side. —*Paul Kirk*

WINE Intense, fruity Zinfandel.

Grilled Steaks with Ancho Mole Sauce

ACTIVE: 50 MIN; TOTAL: 2 HR

6 SERVINGS

- 1 tablespoon sesame seeds
- 1 cup Salsa Roja (p. 118)
- ½ cup chicken stock or low-sodium broth
- ⅓ cup chopped Mexican chocolate (2 ounces; see Note)
- 2 tablespoons raisins

Pinch of ground cinnamon

Pinch of freshly grated nutmeg

Salt and freshly ground pepper

Six 10-ounce boneless strip steaks, about 1 inch thick

- 2 tablespoons unsalted butter

1. In a medium saucepan, toast the sesame seeds over moderate heat until golden. Add the Salsa Roja, stock, chocolate, raisins, cinnamon and nutmeg. Cook over moderate heat, stirring, until the chocolate has melted, about 4 minutes. Transfer the sauce to a blender and puree until smooth. Season with salt and pepper and return to the saucepan.

2. Brush each steak with 1 tablespoon of the mole sauce and let the steaks stand at room temperature for 1 hour.

3. Light a grill. Season the steaks on both sides with salt and pepper. Grill them over high heat for 3 to 4 minutes per side for rare to medium-rare meat. Transfer to a platter and let rest for 5 minutes.

4. Meanwhile, bring the remaining mole sauce to a simmer. Whisk in the butter, 1 tablespoon at a time. Serve the steaks with the mole sauce on the side.

—*Louis Lambert*

NOTE Mexican chocolate, a sweet chocolate flavored with cinnamon, is sold at Latin markets and specialty food stores.

MAKE AHEAD The mole sauce can be covered and refrigerated for up to 3 days. Reheat the sauce gently and add the butter just before serving.

WINE Rustic, peppery Malbec.

Grilled Hanger Steak with Bacon Chimichurri

TOTAL: 45 MIN PLUS 4 HR MARINATING

8 SERVINGS ●

STEAK

- 8 garlic cloves, smashed
- 4 thyme sprigs, coarsely chopped
- 2 rosemary sprigs, coarsely chopped
- 1 cup dry red wine
- 1 medium red onion, minced
- 2 tablespoons extra-virgin olive oil

Eight 6-ounce hanger steaks, trimmed

Salt and freshly ground pepper

CHIMICHURRI

- 4 garlic cloves, quartered, with germ removed
- ½ cup packed flat-leaf parsley leaves
- ¼ cup packed oregano leaves
- ¼ cup rice vinegar

Juice of 1 lemon

- 1 cup extra-virgin olive oil

Salt and freshly ground pepper

- ½ pound sliced bacon

1. MARINATE THE STEAK: In a large, shallow dish, combine the smashed garlic, chopped thyme and rosemary, red wine, minced red onion and olive oil. Stir well, then add the steaks and turn to coat them thoroughly in the marinade. Cover and refrigerate the steaks in the marinade for at least 4 hours or overnight.

2. MAKE THE CHIMICHURRI: In a food processor, pulse the quartered garlic, parsley and oregano leaves, rice vinegar, fresh lemon juice and olive oil until the herbs are pureed. Scrape the chimichurri into a medium bowl and season it with salt and ground pepper. In a large skillet, cook the bacon in 2 batches over moderate heat until crisp, about 8 minutes. Drain on paper towels and let cool, then finely chop. Pour all but 2 tablespoons of the bacon fat from the skillet. Reserve the bacon.

3. Light a grill. Remove the steaks from the marinade and scrape off the marinade

seasonings. Season the steaks with salt and ground pepper; grill over high heat until charred, about 10 minutes for medium-rare meat. Transfer to a cutting board and let rest for 5 minutes.

4. Meanwhile, heat the bacon fat in the skillet. Carefully pour in the chimichurri and bring to a simmer over high heat. Remove from the heat and stir in the chopped bacon. Pour the sauce into a serving bowl. Carve the steaks crosswise into thick slices and serve immediately with the bacon chimichurri.

—*E. Michael Reidt*

WINE Rich, ripe Cabernet Sauvignon.

Four-Pepper Steak au Poivre

TOTAL: 30 MIN

4 SERVINGS

- 1½ teaspoons black peppercorns
- 1½ teaspoons white peppercorns
- 1½ teaspoons dried green peppercorns
- 1½ teaspoons Sichuan peppercorns
- 1½ teaspoons kosher salt
- 2 tablespoons soy sauce
- 1 tablespoon wasabi powder
- 1 tablespoon Asian sesame oil
- 1½ pounds tri-tip steak in 1 piece

1. Light a charcoal grill. In a mortar or spice grinder, coarsely grind the black, white, green and Sichuan peppercorns; transfer the ground pepper to a small bowl and stir in the salt. In another small bowl, whisk the soy sauce with the wasabi and sesame oil to make a paste. Spread the wasabi paste all over the steak, then sprinkle the steak with the ground pepper, gently pressing the seasonings into the meat.

2. Grill the steak over moderately high heat, turning once, 10 minutes per side for medium-rare. Transfer the steak to a carving board and let it rest for 5 minutes before carving. Thinly slice the steak against the grain and serve.

—*Steven Raichlen*

WINE Rustic, peppery Malbec.

GRILLED HANGER STEAK
WITH BACON CHIMICHURRI

BEEF STEW IN RED WINE SAUCE

TUSCAN-STYLE VEAL CHOP

Tuscan-Style Veal Chops

 **TOTAL: 30 MIN**
4 SERVINGS ●

"Grill masters all over the world have noticed that when you grill a piece of meat and then anoint it with some kind of fat, the fat mixes with the meat juices and creates an instant sauce," says grilling expert Steven Raichlen. "At Peter Luger Steakhouse, in Brooklyn, steaks get finished with a pat of butter; other places use beef tallow." In Tuscany, olive oil is the fat of choice for finishing steaks and herbed veal chops like these.

> 2 **tablespoons extra-virgin olive oil, plus more for drizzling**
> 2 **garlic cloves, minced**
> 1 **tablespoon rosemary leaves**
> ¼ **cup sage leaves**
> Four 12-ounce veal rib chops, cut 1 inch thick

Salt and freshly ground pepper

Light a charcoal grill. On a platter, mix the 2 tablespoons of olive oil with the garlic, rosemary and sage. Season the veal chops with salt and black pepper and drizzle generously with olive oil. Grill the chops over moderately high heat, turning once, about 6 minutes per side for medium. Transfer the chops to the platter and turn to coat with the olive oil and herbs. Generously drizzle the veal with olive oil and let stand for 3 minutes, turning the chops a few times. Spoon the juices and oil over the chops and serve. —*Steven Raichlen*
WINE Cherry-inflected, earthy Sangiovese.

T-Bone Fiorentina with Sautéed Spinach

ACTIVE: 40 MIN; TOTAL: 1 HR 20 MIN
4 SERVINGS

Mario Batali, who hosts *Ciao America* and *Molto Mario* on Food Network, loves to drizzle giant, juicy T-bone steaks with a peppery olive oil just before serving. For this recipe, he grills the steak very briefly to give it a charred, smoky flavor, then finishes it in the oven.

1 tablespoon chopped rosemary
1 tablespoon chopped sage
1 tablespoon chopped thyme
Kosher salt and freshly ground pepper
One 3¾-pound T-bone steak,
    about 3 inches thick
6 tablespoons extra-virgin olive oil
6 garlic cloves, thinly sliced
4 pounds fresh spinach—stemmed,
    washed and dried
3 tablespoons fresh lemon juice

1. Preheat the oven to 350° and preheat a grill pan. In a small bowl, combine the chopped rosemary, sage and thyme with 2 tablespoons each of kosher salt and ground pepper. Rub the T-bone steak with 2 tablespoons of the olive oil, then rub the meat with the herb, salt and pepper mixture. Grill the seasoned steak over moderately high heat, turning it over halfway through, until the steak is lightly charred all over, about 10 minutes. Transfer the meat to a small roasting pan and roast for about 40 minutes, or until an instant-read thermometer inserted into the thickest part of the steak registers 120°. Transfer to a cutting board and let rest for 10 minutes before slicing.

2. Meanwhile, in a large, deep skillet, heat the remaining ¼ cup of olive oil over high heat until smoking. Add the sliced garlic and cook over high heat until the garlic is lightly browned, about 20 seconds. Add the spinach leaves in large handfuls and cook, tossing constantly, until the spinach is wilted, about 5 minutes. Season the spinach with kosher salt and ground pepper and stir in the fresh lemon juice. Serve the spinach with the sliced steak.
—*Mario Batali*

NOTE Since T-bone steak is such a thick cut, consider taking it out of the refrigerator and letting it sit, wrapped, at room temperature for about 30 minutes before grilling it. This will help ensure that the meat cooks more evenly.

WINE Cherry-inflected, earthy Sangiovese.

Beef Stew in Red Wine Sauce
ACTIVE: 1 HR; TOTAL: 2 HR 40 MIN
4 SERVINGS

For many Americans, the quintessential French stew is *boeuf bourguignon*—beef cooked in Burgundy red wine. This stew featured regularly at contributing editor Jacques Pépin's mother's restaurant, where it was made from tougher, cheaper cuts of beef that required long braising to get tender and to stay moist.

For his beef stew, Pépin likes to use a piece of the shoulder called the flatiron steak. This long, narrow cut is extremely lean, tender and moist, which makes it ideal for stew. Because he uses only a robust red wine rather than also adding stock, demiglace or water, the stew ends up rich and winey. Pépin recommends making this dish in a cast-iron pot that is attractive enough to bring to the table.

1 tablespoon unsalted butter
2 tablespoons extra-virgin
    olive oil
2 pounds beef from the flatiron
    part of the shoulder, skin
    removed from the top, meat
    cut into 8 pieces (see Note)
Salt and freshly ground
    black pepper
1 cup finely chopped onion
1 tablespoon very finely
    chopped garlic
1 tablespoon flour
1 bottle dry red wine
2 bay leaves
1 thyme sprig
One 5-ounce piece of pancetta
2¼ cups water
15 cipollini or pearl onions,
    peeled
15 cremini mushrooms,
    wiped clean
15 baby carrots, peeled
Dash of sugar
Chopped flat-leaf parsley,
    for serving

1. Preheat the oven to 350°. In a large oven-to-table cast-iron pot over moderate heat, melt the butter in 1 tablespoon of the olive oil. Arrange the pieces of beef in a single layer in the pot and season them with salt and ground pepper. Cook the beef over high heat for about 8 minutes, turning to brown the pieces on all sides. Stir in the finely chopped onion and garlic. Cook over moderate heat for another 5 minutes, stirring occasionally. Add the flour, stirring well so it doesn't form lumps, then stir in the red wine. Add the bay leaves, thyme sprig, salt and ground pepper and bring to a boil. Stir well and cover the pot.

2. Carefully transfer the pot to the oven and braise for about 1½ hours; the meat should be soft and tender and the liquid reduced to a rich sauce.

3. Meanwhile, in a medium saucepan, cover the pancetta with 2 cups of the water and bring to a boil over high heat. Simmer over moderate heat for about 30 minutes; drain. Cut the pancetta into ½-inch slices, then cut the slices into 1-inch-wide lardons.

4. Combine the cipollini onions, cremini mushrooms, baby carrots and pancetta lardons in a skillet with the remaining 1 tablespoon of olive oil and ¼ cup of water and a good dash each of sugar, salt and ground pepper. Bring to a boil and simmer, covered, over moderate heat for about 15 minutes; there should be very little water left. Uncover and cook over high heat, sautéing the vegetables until well browned all over, about 4 minutes.

5. Stir some of the vegetables and lardons into the stew and sprinkle the rest on top. Discard the bay leaves and thyme sprig. Garnish with the parsley and serve at once.
—*Jacques Pépin*

NOTE If you prefer, lean beef chuck can be substituted for the flatiron.

MAKE AHEAD This recipe can be prepared through Step 2 up to a day ahead. Rewarm gently before proceeding.

WINE Intense, spicy Syrah.

Farfalle with Yogurt and Zucchini

TOTAL: 25 MIN
4 TO 6 SERVINGS ● ●

One of the best (and simplest) pasta dishes from this year's crop of cookbooks comes from Johanne Killeen and George Germon, the chefs and owners of Al Forno in Providence, Rhode Island, and the authors of *On Top of Spaghetti*. This recipe calls for quickly boiling shredded zucchini in the same pot as the pasta, and then tossing everything together in a sauce made with yogurt instead of cream. Yogurt may seem strange in a pasta sauce, but the result is brilliant.

- 1 **pound farfalle**
- 4 **medium zucchini (about 1½ pounds), coarsely shredded**
- 4 **tablespoons unsalted butter**
- 1 **cup plain whole-milk Greek yogurt**
- 1 **cup freshly grated Parmigiano-Reggiano cheese, plus more for serving**

Freshly grated nutmeg
Kosher salt and freshly ground black pepper

1. In a large pot of boiling salted water, cook the farfalle until al dente; about 1 minute before the farfalle is done, add the shredded zucchini to the pot. Drain the farfalle and zucchini, reserving ¼ cup of the pasta cooking water.

2. Meanwhile, in a large, deep skillet, melt the butter. Remove from the heat. Stir in the Greek yogurt and the 1 cup of grated Parmigiano-Reggiano and season the yogurt sauce with freshly grated nutmeg, salt and black pepper.

3. Add the farfalle, zucchini and reserved pasta water to the skillet and cook over low heat, tossing, until the sauce coats the pasta; transfer to warmed bowls and serve with the extra cheese.
—*George Germon and Johanne Killeen*
WINE Peppery, refreshing Grüner Veltliner.

Broken Pappardelle with Shrimp and Zucchini

TOTAL: 30 MIN
4 SERVINGS ●

This recipe starts with large, flat sheets of pappardelle noodles, which are broken into bite-size, charmingly irregular pieces that fit perfectly onto a fork. You can leave in the jalapeño seeds for more heat or discard them for a milder flavor.

- ½ **pound pappardelle, broken into 2-inch lengths**
- 3 **tablespoons extra-virgin olive oil**
- 1 **pound small zucchini, thinly sliced (3½ cups)**

Salt and freshly ground black pepper

- 1 **medium garlic clove, very thinly sliced**
- 1 **large jalapeño, seeded (optional) and thinly sliced**
- 1 **pound shelled and deveined medium shrimp, halved lengthwise**
- ½ **pound thin asparagus, cut into ½-inch lengths**
- ½ **cup heavy cream**
- 3 **tablespoons snipped chives**

1. Bring a large pot of salted water to a boil over high heat. Add the broken pappardelle and cook until just al dente. Drain the pappardelle, reserving ½ cup of the pasta cooking water.

2. Meanwhile, in a very large skillet, heat the olive oil over high heat. Add the sliced zucchini, season with salt and black pepper and cook over high heat, stirring occasionally, until the zucchini slices are browned in spots, about 3 minutes. Add the sliced garlic and jalapeño and cook, stirring, for 1 minute. Season the halved shrimp with salt and black pepper and add them to the skillet along with the asparagus pieces. Cook, stirring occasionally, until the shrimp are curled but not cooked through, about 3 minutes.

3. Add the cooked pappardelle, heavy cream and ¼ cup of the reserved pasta cooking water to the skillet and simmer over moderately low heat, tossing, until the shrimp are cooked through and the sauce is slightly thickened, about 2 minutes; add more of the pasta cooking water if the sauce seems dry. Stir in the snipped chives, transfer the pappardelle to shallow bowls and serve immediately.
—*Grace Parisi*
WINE Fresh, minerally Vermentino.

Penne with Salmon Puttanesca

TOTAL: 30 MIN
4 SERVINGS

A traditional puttanesca gets complex, savory flavor from a mix of olives, capers, tomatoes and anchovies (which essentially melt into the sauce). This version omits the anchovies in favor of salmon, which stays firm and makes for a heartier dish.

- ¾ **pound penne rigate or other ridged tubular pasta**
- ¼ **cup extra-virgin olive oil**
- 1 **pound skinless center-cut salmon fillet in 1 piece**

Salt and freshly ground pepper

- 2 **garlic cloves, thinly sliced**
- ½ **teaspoon crushed red pepper**
- 1 **pint grape tomatoes**
- ¼ **cup pitted kalamata olives, coarsely chopped**
- 1 **tablespoon drained capers, rinsed and coarsely chopped**
- ¼ **cup finely shredded basil leaves**

1. Bring a large pot of salted water to a boil. Add the pasta and cook until barely al dente. Drain, reserving 1¼ cups of the pasta cooking water.

2. Meanwhile, in a very large skillet, heat 2 tablespoons of the oil. Season the salmon with salt and pepper, add it to the skillet and cook over high heat until browned on both sides but not cooked through, about 6 minutes. Transfer the salmon to a plate and pour off the oil in the skillet.

FARFALLE WITH YOGURT AND ZUCCHINI

PENNE WITH SALMON PUTTANESCA

3. Add the remaining 2 tablespoons of olive oil to the skillet along with the sliced garlic and crushed red pepper. Cook over moderate heat until the garlic is lightly browned in spots, about 30 seconds. Add the grape tomatoes and cook until just softened, 2 to 3 minutes. Add 1 cup of the reserved pasta cooking water and bring to a boil, gently crushing the tomatoes with a wooden spoon. Add the cooked pasta and chopped olives and capers and cook over moderate heat, stirring, until the liquid is slightly absorbed by the pasta, about 2 minutes. Add the salmon to the skillet and break it up into chunks. Cook, tossing, until the salmon is nearly cooked through and the pasta is al dente, about 2 minutes; add more of the pasta cooking water if the sauce seems dry. Stir in the shredded basil, transfer the pasta to bowls and serve.
—*Grace Parisi*
WINE Fresh, fruity rosé.

Orecchiette with Grilled Squid, Arugula and Chickpeas

TOTAL: 30 MIN
4 SERVINGS ●

The orecchiette in this lemony, bright-flavored pasta dish holds the delicious chickpeas like little cups.

¾ **pound orecchiette**
½ **pound cleaned squid**
¼ **cup plus 1 tablespoon extra-virgin olive oil**
Kosher salt and freshly ground black pepper
2 **garlic cloves, thinly sliced**
Pinch of crushed red pepper
2 **tablespoons fresh lemon juice**
4 **packed cups baby arugula**
¾ **cup canned chickpeas, rinsed**

1. Light a grill. In a large pot of boiling salted water, cook the pasta until al dente. Drain, reserving 6 tablespoons of the cooking water. Return the pasta to the pot.

2. Meanwhile, in a bowl, toss the squid with 1 tablespoon of the oil; season with salt and black pepper and grill over moderately high heat, turning once, until lightly charred and white throughout, 4 minutes. Transfer the squid to a work surface. Slice the bodies crosswise into ¼-inch-thick rings and quarter the tentacles.

3. In a small skillet, heat the remaining ¼ cup of olive oil. Add the garlic and cook over moderate heat until golden, about 3 minutes. Add the crushed red pepper and cook for 30 seconds. Remove from the heat and stir in the lemon juice.

4. Stir the lemon-garlic sauce into the pasta. Stir in the arugula, chickpeas, squid and the reserved pasta cooking water. Cook over low heat, tossing, until the arugula is wilted, about 1 minute. Season with salt and pepper, transfer to bowls and serve.
—*Melissa Rubel*
WINE Fresh, minerally Vermentino.

Bucatini with Pancetta, Pecorino and Pepper

TOTAL: 30 MIN
4 TO 6 SERVINGS ●

"I love knowing that I have leftovers in the refrigerator," says Shelley Lindgren, wine director and co-owner of A16 and SPQR in San Francisco. She'll often make pasta during the day—like this rich, pancetta-studded bucatini that's tossed with plenty of freshly ground black pepper and grated Pecorino Romano cheese—and then reheat a big bowl of it when she comes home from work late at night.

- 1 **pound bucatini, perciatelli or thick spaghetti**
- 2 **tablespoons extra-virgin olive oil**
- 5 **ounces pancetta, sliced ½ inch thick and cut into 1-inch-long pieces (1 cup)**
- 1¼ **cups freshly grated Pecorino Romano cheese, plus more for serving**
- 1 **teaspoon freshly ground black pepper**

Salt

1. In a large pot of boiling salted water, cook the pasta until al dente. Drain, reserving 1 cup of the cooking water.

2. Meanwhile, heat the oil in a large, deep skillet. Add the pancetta pieces and cook over moderately high heat, stirring, until the meat is lightly browned and most of the fat is rendered, 4 to 5 minutes.

3. Add the bucatini to the skillet and toss over moderate heat to coat with the fat and pancetta. Add ¾ cup of the reserved cooking water, the 1¼ cups of Pecorino Romano cheese and the pepper and season with salt. Toss the pasta until the sauce becomes very thick and creamy, 2 to 3 minutes; add more of the cooking water if necessary. Serve immediately, passing additional cheese at the table.
—*Shelley Lindgren*
WINE Intense, fruity Zinfandel.

Linguine with Spicy Sausage and Scallion Sauce

TOTAL: 35 MIN
4 SERVINGS ●

This fun take on pesto uses scallions and parsley in place of basil to create a bright, flavorful sauce that coats the linguine beautifully. The hot Italian sausage adds a nice, meaty kick.

- ¾ **pound linguine**
- 4 **scallions, cut into ½-inch lengths**
- ½ **cup flat-leaf parsley**
- 2 **tablespoons pine nuts**
- ¼ **cup plus 1 tablespoon extra-virgin olive oil**
- ½ **cup freshly grated Parmigiano-Reggiano cheese, plus more for serving**
- **Salt and freshly ground black pepper**
- ¾ **pound hot Italian sausage (about 4 links), casings removed**

1. Bring a large pot of generously salted water to a boil over high heat. Add the linguine and cook until just al dente. Drain the pasta, reserving 1 cup of the pasta cooking water.

2. Meanwhile, in a mini food processor, combine the scallions, parsley, pine nuts and ¼ cup of the olive oil and process until pureed. Add the ½ cup of Parmigiano-Reggiano cheese, season with salt and black pepper and process the scallion pesto just until blended.

3. In a large skillet, heat the remaining 1 tablespoon of olive oil. Add the sausage and cook over high heat, breaking up the meat with a wooden spoon, until it is lightly browned and no trace of pink remains, about 5 minutes. Use a slotted spoon to transfer the sausage to a paper towel–lined sieve to drain, and pour off any fat in the skillet.

4. Return the sausage to the skillet. Add the scallion pesto, pasta and ¾ cup of the reserved pasta cooking water and simmer over moderate heat, tossing, until a thick, creamy sauce forms, about 2 minutes; add more of the reserved pasta cooking water if the sauce seems dry. Transfer the linguine to shallow bowls and serve immediately, passing extra Parmigiano-Reggiano on the side. —*Grace Parisi*
WINE Bright, tart Barbera.

Creamy Risotto with Edamame

TOTAL: 30 MIN
4 SERVINGS

Vineyard owner Jeff Smith loves cooking with his children and often lets them pick the ingredients. "Kids come up with cool flavor combinations that an adult would never think of," he says. "I learn a lot that way." This risotto was created when Smith's daughter, Isabelle, tossed some Laughing Cow cheese into a pot of risotto. "It adds a lot of richness without making the dish taste too sharp," Smith says. The cup of beer is his own addition, a last-minute fix on a night he found himself without white wine in the house. "I ended up preferring it to wine in this dish," he says.

- ½ **cup frozen shelled edamame**
- 1 **tablespoon unsalted butter**
- 2 **tablespoons extra-virgin olive oil**
- 2 **medium shallots, very finely chopped (¼ cup)**
- 3 **medium garlic cloves, very finely chopped**
- 1 **cup arborio rice**
- 3 **cups low-sodium chicken broth, warmed**
- 1 **cup lager beer, such as Budweiser**
- **Salt and freshly ground black pepper**
- **Three ¾-ounce wedges Laughing Cow cheese**

1. Bring a small saucepan of salted water to a boil over high heat. Add the shelled edamame and cook until they are tender, about 5 minutes; drain well.

2. In a large saucepan, melt the butter in the olive oil. Add the chopped shallots and garlic and cook over moderate heat, stirring, until the shallots are softened, about 3 minutes. Add the arborio rice and cook, stirring, until the grains are slightly translucent, about 2 minutes.

3. Mix the chicken broth with the beer and season generously with salt and black pepper. Add 1 cup of the beer broth to the rice and cook over moderately high heat, stirring constantly, until nearly absorbed. Continue adding the broth, about 1 cup at a time, stirring until it is absorbed by the rice before adding more liquid. The rice is done when it's al dente and suspended in a thick, creamy sauce, about 17 minutes total. Add the edamame and cheese and stir until the cheese is melted. Season with salt and pepper and serve right away. —*Jeff Smith*

WINE Dry, fruity sparkling wine.

Almond Skordalia

ACTIVE: 10 MIN; TOTAL: 30 MIN

MAKES ABOUT 2 CUPS ● ● ●

Ana Sortun, chef and owner of Oleana in Cambridge, Massachusetts, serves a number of variations on skordalia, a Greek garlic sauce that makes a terrific accompaniment to plain grilled red meat. Here, Sortun does a traditional version with fluffy baking potatoes and plenty of olive oil. It's important to use a blender, not a food processor, to achieve the desired silky consistency. If the skordalia seems too thick, simply stir in a little water.

- **2** baking potatoes (1 pound)
- **1** cup extra-virgin olive oil
- **¾** cup blanched almonds, coarsely chopped
- **½** cup water
- **1½** tablespoons coarsely chopped garlic
- **1** tablespoon fresh lemon juice
- **Salt**

1. In a medium saucepan, cover the potatoes with cold water and bring to a boil over moderately high heat. Boil the potatoes until they are tender when pierced with a knife, about 20 minutes. Drain and peel the cooked potatoes, then pass them through a ricer into a medium bowl while they're still hot.

2. In a blender, combine the olive oil, blanched almonds, water, chopped garlic and fresh lemon juice and puree until very smooth. Stir the almond mixture into the riced potatoes until smooth. Season the skordalia with salt and serve warm or at room temperature. —*Ana Sortun*

SERVE WITH Grilled beef or lamb.

MAKE AHEAD The skordalia can be kept at room temperature for up to 3 hours.

WINE Earthy, medium-bodied Tempranillo.

Tahini Remoulade

TOTAL: 20 MIN

MAKES 2½ CUPS ● ●

Sortun likes to serve this tangy Middle Eastern twist on the classic French sauce with oily fish like bluefish. But the intense flavor of the tahini stands up equally well to charred lamb.

- **1¼** cups plain Greek yogurt
- **1** cup tahini, well-stirred, at room temperature
- **¼** cup fresh lemon juice
- **¼** cup minced cornichons
- **¼** cup drained and rinsed small capers
- **2** tablespoons finely chopped fresh dill
- **2** peperoncini—stemmed, seeded and minced
- **2** medium garlic cloves, very finely chopped
- **Salt and freshly ground black pepper**

In a medium bowl, stir all of the ingredients together and season with salt and black pepper. Serve immediately.
—*Ana Sortun*

SERVE WITH Bluefish or grilled lamb.

Spicy Zhoug

TOTAL: 20 MIN

MAKES 1¼ CUPS ● ● ●

Falafel stands throughout the Middle East often have some version of this hot chile sauce, called *zhoug,* for giving a spicy kick to pita sandwiches. Sortun adds pumpkin seeds to her take on this fiery sauce to thicken it and deepen the flavor. In addition to spicing up falafel, *zhoug* is also great with grilled chicken and fish.

- **Two 3-ounce Hungarian wax peppers, seeded and coarsely chopped**
- **1** cup cilantro leaves and stems
- **½** cup flat-leaf parsley leaves
- **2** garlic cloves
- **½** teaspoon ground coriander
- **½** teaspoon ground cumin
- **¼** cup extra-virgin olive oil
- **1½** teaspoons sherry vinegar
- **¼** cup toasted shelled pumpkin seeds
- **Salt and freshly ground black pepper**

In a blender, combine all of the ingredients and blend until smooth. Season the *zhoug* with salt and black pepper and serve.
—*Ana Sortun*

SERVE WITH Grilled chicken or fish.

MAKE AHEAD The *zhoug* can be covered and refrigerated for up to 2 days. Bring to room temperature before serving.

making remoulade

The tahini version at left riffs on this sauce: ¾ cup mayo, ½ cup each parsley and chives, 1 tablespoon each lemon juice, mustard, capers and gherkins.

● HEALTHY ● MAKE AHEAD ● VEGETARIAN ● STAFF FAVORITE

side dishes

Arugula Salad with Ricotta Salata

 **TOTAL: 20 MIN**
4 SERVINGS ●

Chef, cookbook author and television personality Lidia Bastianich likes to use young dandelion greens for this crunchy, nutty salad. Although tender dandelion greens aren't always easy to find, widely available arugula is a perfect stand-in.

- ¼ cup plus 2 tablespoons extra-virgin olive oil
- 2 tablespoons red wine vinegar
- 1 teaspoon honey
- ½ cup salted roasted almonds, coarsely chopped
- 3 bunches of arugula, thick stems discarded
- ½ pound *ricotta salata* cheese, shaved with a peeler

Salt and freshly ground pepper

In a blender, combine the olive oil, red wine vinegar, honey and 2 tablespoons of the chopped almonds. Blend and transfer to a large salad bowl. Add the remaining almonds, the arugula and the cheese and season with salt and pepper. Toss the salad well, transfer to 4 salad plates and serve right away. —*Lidia Bastianich*

Endive, Radish and Lemon Salad

 TOTAL: 25 MIN
6 SERVINGS ● ●

This lemony, minty salad dresses up grilled poultry or lamb particularly well. For added flavor, toss in some thinly sliced preserved lemons (available at specialty food shops) with the fresh lemon.

- 2 lemons
- 4 Belgian endives—halved, cored and leaves thinly sliced crosswise or left whole
- 6 radishes, very thinly sliced
- 12 mint leaves, torn into small pieces
- ¼ cup extra-virgin olive oil

Salt and freshly ground black pepper

1. Using a sharp knife, peel the lemons, removing all of the bitter white pith. Working over a strainer, cut in between the membranes to release the lemon sections; drain the juice from the sections and reserve for another use.

2. In a large bowl, toss the endives with the lemon sections, radishes, mint and olive oil. Season with salt and black pepper and serve. —*Andy Nusser*

Ten-Vegetable Salad with Lemon Vinaigrette

 TOTAL: 40 MIN
4 SERVINGS ● ● ●

- 3 tablespoons fresh lemon juice, preferably Meyer lemon
- ¼ cup extra-virgin olive oil
- 1 tablespoon chopped chervil or parsley
- 1 teaspoon honey

Salt and freshly ground pepper

- 6 jumbo asparagus stalks, peeled
- 6 baby carrots, peeled and quartered lengthwise
- 2 ounces sugar snap peas (½ cup), trimmed
- 3 ounces assorted baby lettuce leaves or mesclun (4 packed cups)
- 4 radishes, julienned
- 2 white mushrooms, stemmed and thinly sliced
- 1 fennel bulb—halved, cored and thinly sliced
- 1 Kirby cucumber, julienned
- 1 ripe Hass avocado, cut into 2-by-¼-inch slices
- 1 cup pea sprouts or broccoli sprouts
- ¼ cup raw cashew halves

1. In a small bowl, whisk the lemon juice with the olive oil, chervil and honey and season with salt and pepper.

2. Bring a medium saucepan of salted water to a boil. Add the asparagus and carrots and cook until the asparagus is bright green and the carrots are barely tender, about 2 minutes. Using a slotted spoon, transfer the asparagus and carrots to a platter. Add the sugar snap peas to the saucepan and cook until they turn bright green, about 30 seconds; transfer to the platter. Cut the sugar snap peas into julienne strips. Halve the asparagus stalks lengthwise, then halve the asparagus pieces crosswise.

3. In a large bowl, toss the lettuce, asparagus, carrots, sugar snap peas, radishes, mushrooms, fennel, cucumber, avocado, sprouts and cashews. Add the vinaigrette and toss well. Serve right away.
—*Matt Lyman and Erik Oberholtzer*
MAKE AHEAD The blanched vegetables and vinaigrette can be refrigerated overnight.

Chopped Salad with Apple Vinaigrette

TOTAL: 40 MIN
10 SERVINGS ● ● ●
½ cup apple juice
1 cinnamon stick
Three 1-inch strips of lemon zest
2 tablespoons cider vinegar
1 medium shallot, minced
Salt and freshly ground pepper
¼ cup grapeseed or vegetable oil
1 small celery root (½ pound), peeled and finely diced
1 medium seedless cucumber, peeled and diced
2 large carrots, finely diced
2 cups red seedless grapes, halved
4 ounces feta cheese, cut into small dice (1 cup)
5 ounces mesclun or other mixed greens (5 cups)
2 romaine lettuce hearts, coarsely chopped

1. In a small saucepan, bring the apple juice to a boil with the cinnamon stick and the lemon zest. Simmer over moderate heat until the liquid is reduced to 2 tablespoons, about 5 minutes. Discard the cinnamon stick and lemon zest and pour the liquid into a small bowl; let cool slightly. Add the cider vinegar and shallot and season with salt and pepper. Whisk in the grapeseed oil until emulsified.

2. In a large bowl, toss the celery root, cucumber, carrots, grapes, feta cheese, mesclun and romaine. Whisk the apple vinaigrette again and add to the salad, season with salt and pepper and toss to coat. Serve the salad right away.
—*Michel Nischan*
MAKE AHEAD The apple vinaigrette can be refrigerated overnight. The vegetables and lettuce can be tossed together and refrigerated for up to 4 hours before tossing with the vinaigrette.

Gazpacho Salad
ACTIVE: 35 MIN; TOTAL: 1 HR
6 SERVINGS ● ●
Chef Andy Nusser of Casa Mono in New York City teases apart the elements of a traditional Spanish gazpacho—tomatoes, vinegar, bread and olive oil—to recombine them in a summery salad with real zing. He candies cherry tomatoes in a cinnamon-and-chile-spiked syrup. "I like how they explode like water balloons and taste like Red Hots," he says. Sea beans, crisp marine sprigs resembling slender green beans, add a salty crunch.
CANDIED TOMATOES
1 pint cherry tomatoes
1 cup water
1 cup sugar
1 tablespoon kosher salt
1 tablespoon crushed red pepper
One 2½-inch cinnamon stick
SALAD
One 3½-inch piece of baguette, cut into ½-inch dice (about 1½ cups)

2 tablespoons plus 2 teaspoons extra-virgin olive oil
Salt and freshly ground black pepper
¼ pound sea beans, thick ends trimmed (see Note)
1 cucumber—peeled, seeded and thinly sliced
2 scallions, top 2 inches trimmed, thinly sliced
1 tablespoon sherry vinegar

1. CANDY THE TOMATOES: Bring a saucepan of water to a boil. Fill a bowl with ice water. Cut a slit in the base of each tomato. Add the tomatoes to the boiling water and blanch them until the skins start to split, about 15 seconds. Drain the tomatoes, then transfer them to the ice water to cool. Drain and peel the tomatoes, then transfer them to a small bowl.

2. In the same saucepan, combine the 1 cup of water, sugar, salt, crushed red pepper and cinnamon stick; simmer over moderate heat, stirring a few times, until the sugar dissolves. Strain the syrup over the tomatoes and let stand until cool, 45 minutes. Drain, discarding the syrup.

3. MEANWHILE, PREPARE THE SALAD: Preheat the oven to 350°. On a baking sheet, toss the bread with 2 teaspoons of the olive oil and season with salt and pepper. Bake until golden, about 8 minutes.

4. Bring a medium saucepan of water to a boil. Add the sea beans and blanch for 30 seconds. Drain in a colander and cool under running water, then pat dry.

5. In a bowl, toss the candied cherry tomatoes, seasoned croutons, blanched sea beans, sliced cucumber and scallions, sherry vinegar and the remaining 2 tablespoons of olive oil. Season with salt and black pepper and serve immediately.
—*Andy Nusser*
NOTE Sea beans, also known as samphire, grow on the coastlines of Europe and the northeastern U.S. Fresh sea beans are available from melissas.com.

Cannellini and Green Bean Salad

**ACTIVE: 25 MIN; TOTAL: 2 HR 25 MIN
PLUS OVERNIGHT SOAKING**

8 SERVINGS ● ●

This simple and bright-tasting salad, with lots of salty kalamata olives and cilantro, is an appealing way to showcase fresh beans. The salad can be made with dried cannellini beans or, in a pinch, canned white beans.

1½ cups dried cannellini beans
    (3 ounces), soaked overnight
    in cold water and drained
1 bay leaf
1 thyme sprig
½ small onion
¾ pound green beans
¼ cup plus 2 tablespoons
    extra-virgin olive oil
¼ cup fresh lemon juice
¼ cup chopped cilantro
½ cup pitted kalamata olives
    (2½ ounces), chopped
Salt and freshly ground
    black pepper
Lime wedges, for serving

1. In a medium saucepan, cover the soaked and drained cannellini beans with 2 inches of water. Add the bay leaf, thyme sprig and onion half and bring to a simmer. Simmer over moderately low heat, stirring occasionally and adding more water to cover as necessary, until the beans are tender, about 2 hours. Drain and let cool completely. Discard the bay leaf, thyme sprig and onion half.
2. Meanwhile, in a medium saucepan of boiling salted water, cook the green beans until they are crisp-tender, about 3 minutes. Drain the green beans well and spread them out on a large rimmed baking sheet and let cool. Pat the beans dry with paper towels. Cut the green beans on the diagonal into 1-inch lengths.
3. In a large bowl, combine the olive oil, fresh lemon juice, chopped cilantro and kalamata olives and season with salt and black pepper. Fold in the cooked, cooled cannellini and green beans and season with salt and black pepper. Serve the Cannelli and Green Bean Salad with the lime wedges. —*Valeria Huneeus*

MAKE AHEAD The cooked and cooled cannellini and green beans can be refrigerated, separately, overnight. Bring the beans back to room temperature before tossing them with the dressing.

Chilean Tomato and Onion Salad

 TOTAL: 30 MIN

8 SERVINGS ● ●

This juicy, crunchy and slightly spicy salad combines tomatoes (which are ubiquitous in Chile) with sweet onions, cilantro and jalapeños. It's terrific alongside rich meat like a leg of lamb.

1 large sweet onion, very
    thinly sliced
2 tablespoons red wine vinegar
Salt and freshly ground
    black pepper
¼ cup extra-virgin olive oil
3 tablespoons coarsely
    chopped cilantro
½ jalapeño, seeded and
    very finely chopped
8 medium tomatoes (about
    6 ounces each), cored and
    cut into 8 wedges each

1. In a medium bowl, toss the sliced sweet onion with the red wine vinegar and season with salt and black pepper. Let the onion slices marinate at room temperature for 15 minutes, tossing a few times.
2. In a small bowl, combine the olive oil, chopped cilantro and jalapeño and season with salt and black pepper. Arrange the tomatoes on a platter and season with salt and pepper. Scatter the marinated onion slices over the tomatoes, drizzle with the dressing and serve the salad.
—*Valeria Huneeus*

Wax Bean and Cherry Tomato Salad with Goat Cheese

TOTAL: 1 HR

4 SERVINGS ●

Some lovely fresh French goat cheese in the kitchen at his Bora Bora restaurant, Lagoon, inspired star chef Jean-Georges Vongerichten to create this Provençal-style combination.

2 cups packed basil leaves
¾ pound yellow wax beans
¼ cup vegetable oil
Salt
6 ounces fresh goat cheese,
    plus 2 tablespoons crumbled
2 tablespoons buttermilk
1 tablespoon fresh lime juice
3 tablespoons extra-virgin olive oil
½ pound cherry tomatoes, halved
1 shallot, thinly sliced
1 Thai green chile, minced
1 tablespoon red wine vinegar

1. In a large saucepan of boiling salted water, blanch the basil for 20 seconds. Plunge the basil leaves into a bowl of ice water; drain and squeeze dry.
2. Cook the beans in the boiling water until just tender, 4 minutes. Transfer the beans to the ice water; drain and pat dry. Cut the beans on the bias into 1-inch lengths.
3. In a blender, puree the basil with the vegetable oil. Strain and season with salt.
4. In a food processor, puree the 6 ounces of goat cheese with the buttermilk, lime juice and 1 tablespoon of the olive oil. Season with salt.
5. In a large bowl, toss together the cherry tomatoes, shallot, chile, red wine vinegar and remaining 2 tablespoons of olive oil. Season with salt. Let stand for 15 minutes, tossing a few times.
6. Toss the wax beans with the goat cheese dressing. Mound the beans on plates and top with the cherry tomato salad. Drizzle with the basil oil, sprinkle with the crumbled goat cheese and serve.
—*Jean-Georges Vongerichten*

CANNELLINI AND GREEN BEAN SALAD

Grilling vegetables intensifies their sweetness.

WARM LENTIL AND HAM SALAD

Grilled-Pepper Salad with Currants, Capers and Feta

TOTAL: 50 MIN

4 SERVINGS ● ● ●

This simple grilled-pepper salad gets a burst of Mediterranean flavors from the addition of sweet dried currants, tart capers and salty feta cheese.

    1 large red bell pepper
    1 large yellow bell pepper
    1 large orange bell pepper
    1 large green bell pepper
    ¼ cup plus 2 tablespoons
       extra-virgin olive oil
    2 garlic cloves, minced
    2 tablespoons pine nuts
    2 tablespoons dried currants
    1 tablespoon drained small capers
    2 tablespoons sherry vinegar
    ¼ cup chopped parsley
    ½ cup crumbled feta cheese
Salt and freshly ground pepper

1. Light a charcoal grill. Grill all the bell peppers over high heat, turning, until the pepper skins are charred all over. Transfer the grilled peppers to a large plate and let stand until they are cool enough to handle. Peel the peppers and discard the charred skins, seeds and stems. Quarter the grilled peppers lengthwise and arrange them on a large serving platter.

2. In a small skillet, heat 2 tablespoons of the olive oil. Add the minced garlic and pine nuts and cook over moderate heat until golden, about 4 minutes. Stir in the dried currants and drained capers. Remove the skillet from the heat and stir in the remaining ¼ cup of olive oil. Let this mixture cool to room temperature, then whisk in the sherry vinegar and stir in the chopped parsley and crumbled feta; season with salt and pepper. Pour the dressing over the grilled peppers and serve.

—Steven Raichlen

Grilled Romaine Salad with Roasted Garlic Dressing

ACTIVE: 20 MIN; TOTAL: 1 HR 30 MIN

8 SERVINGS ● ●

Sturdy hearts of romaine become marvelously smoky on the grill. They create a unique spin on Caesar salad that's a delicious accompaniment to grilled steak.

    1 head of garlic, top third sliced
       off and discarded
    1 cup extra-virgin olive oil, plus
       more for drizzling
    ¼ cup buttermilk
    3 tablespoons fresh lemon juice
Salt and freshly ground pepper
    4 romaine hearts, halved lengthwise
    3 ounces Manchego cheese,
       shaved (1 cup)

1. Preheat the oven to 350°. Place the garlic cut side up on a double sheet of foil and drizzle with oil. Wrap the garlic in the foil and bake until very soft, 1 hour. Let cool.

2. Light a grill. Squeeze the roasted garlic cloves out of their peels into a blender. Add the buttermilk and lemon juice and blend to a puree. With the machine on, slowly pour in the 1 cup of olive oil until blended. Season the roasted garlic dressing with salt and pepper.

3. Drizzle the cut side of the romaine hearts with olive oil and sprinkle with salt and pepper. Grill the romaine over high heat, cut side down, until charred in spots, about 20 seconds. Turn the romaine over and grill for 20 seconds longer. Transfer the grilled hearts to a serving platter, cut side up. Drizzle the roasted garlic dressing over the romaine, sprinkle with the shaved Manchego and serve right away.
—*E. Michael Reidl*

MAKE AHEAD The roasted garlic dressing can be refrigerated overnight.

Grilled Eggplant Salad

 TOTAL: 20 MIN
8 SERVINGS ● ●

Smoky grilled eggplant gives this simple, refreshing salad an unexpected depth.

1½   pounds small eggplants, sliced 1 inch thick
¼   cup plus 2 tablespoons extra-virgin olive oil
Salt and freshly ground black pepper
1   tablespoon balsamic vinegar
1   tablespoon fresh lemon juice
1   pint cherry tomatoes, halved
4   ounces baby arugula (4 packed cups)
4   ounces feta cheese, crumbled (1 cup)
1   tablespoon chopped fresh mint

1. Light a grill. Brush the eggplant slices with 3 tablespoons of the olive oil and season with salt and black pepper. Grill the slices over moderately high heat until softened and lightly charred in spots, about 10 minutes. Let cool slightly, then cut each slice into bite-size pieces.

2. In a large bowl, whisk the balsamic vinegar and lemon juice with the remaining 3 tablespoons of olive oil and season with salt and pepper. Add the eggplant, cherry tomatoes, arugula, feta cheese and mint; toss gently and serve. —*Chris Hanna*

Warm Lentil and Ham Salad

 TOTAL: 40 MIN
4 TO 6 SERVINGS ●

2   tablespoons unsalted butter
1   medium onion, finely chopped
3   light-green celery ribs, finely diced
2   carrots, cut into ½-inch dice
1   cup brown lentils, picked over
2   cups chicken stock or low-sodium broth
3   cups water
Salt and freshly ground pepper
¾   pound thickly sliced smoked ham, cut into ½-inch dice
1   tablespoon Dijon mustard
2   tablespoons sherry vinegar
1   garlic clove, minced
2   tablespoons grapeseed or vegetable oil
2   tablespoons extra-virgin olive oil
2   tablespoons minced flat-leaf parsley
¼   cup snipped chives

1. In a large saucepan, melt the butter. Add the onion, celery and carrots and cook over moderately high heat, stirring, until softened, about 5 minutes. Add the lentils, stock and water and bring to a boil. Simmer over moderate heat until the lentils are tender, about 25 minutes. Season with salt and pepper. Add the ham and cook until heated through, about 2 minutes. Drain and return the lentils and ham to the saucepan.

2. Meanwhile, in a small bowl, whisk the mustard with the vinegar and garlic. Whisk in the grapeseed and olive oils and season with salt and pepper. Stir the dressing into the lentils and fold in the parsley and chives. Serve warm or at room temperature.
—*Richard Reddington*

Spinach and Ricotta Pappardelle

 TOTAL: 30 MIN
4 SERVINGS ●

Lidia Bastianich, one of the matriarchs of Italian cooking in America, stuffs home-made ravioli with ricotta, leeks, scallions and spinach, then serves them in a butter-sage sauce. In this deconstructed version of her dish, pappardelle are simply tossed with all the ingredients in the filling except the labor-intensive leeks.

12   ounces pappardelle
2   tablespoons extra-virgin olive oil
4   scallions, thinly sliced
1   tablespoon chopped sage
Two 5-ounce bags baby spinach
2   tablespoons unsalted butter, cut into cubes
1   cup fresh ricotta cheese
¼   cup freshly grated Parmigiano-Reggiano cheese, plus more for serving
Salt and freshly ground black pepper

1. Bring a large pot of salted water to a boil over high heat. Add the pappardelle and cook until al dente. Drain the pappardelle thoroughly, reserving 1 cup of the pasta cooking water.

2. Meanwhile, in a large, deep skillet, heat the olive oil over high heat. Add the sliced scallions and chopped sage and cook over high heat until lightly browned, 2 to 3 minutes. Add the baby spinach in large handfuls and cook, stirring, until the leaves are all wilted. Add the drained pappardelle, butter and ricotta cheese and toss until well combined. Add ¾ cup of the reserved pasta cooking water and the grated Parmigiano cheese and season generously with salt and black pepper. Cook over moderately low heat, tossing, until the sauce is thick and creamy, adding more of the pasta water as needed. Transfer the pappardelle to shallow bowls and serve right away, with grated Parmigiano.
—*Lidia Bastianich*

Orecchiette with Sautéed Greens and Scallion Sauce

TOTAL: 30 MIN
4 SERVINGS ● ●

At Redd, his restaurant in Yountville, California, chef Richard Reddington fills homemade ravioli with fresh ricotta, mascarpone, arugula, spinach and Swiss chard, then serves them in a green garlic–and–white wine sauce. These flavors are also great together in this simpler version, which features store-bought orecchiette tossed with arugula and Swiss chard (both are more flavorful than spinach) and a sauce made with scallions instead of the harder-to-find green garlic.

- ¾ pound orecchiette
- 4 tablespoons unsalted butter
- 1 bunch of scallions, thinly sliced
- 3 garlic cloves, thinly sliced
- ¾ cup dry white wine
- ½ cup water
- Salt and freshly ground black pepper
- 2 tablespoons extra-virgin olive oil
- One 5-ounce bag baby arugula
- 6 large Swiss chard leaves, stems and central ribs discarded, leaves coarsely chopped
- ¼ cup mascarpone cheese

1. Bring a large pot of salted water to a boil over high heat. Add the orecchiette and cook until al dente. Drain the pasta, reserving ¼ cup of the cooking water.

2. Meanwhile, in a medium saucepan, melt the butter. Add the sliced scallions and garlic and cook over low heat, stirring a few times, until softened, about 5 minutes. Add the white wine and simmer over moderate heat until the wine has reduced by half, about 5 minutes. Add the ½ cup of water and transfer the mixture to a blender. Puree until smooth. Season the scallion sauce with salt and pepper.

3. Wipe out the pasta pot and heat the olive oil in it over high heat. Add the arugula and Swiss chard leaves; cook the greens over high heat, stirring frequently, until wilted, about 5 minutes. Add the drained pasta, scallion sauce and the reserved pasta cooking water and simmer, tossing and stirring, until the sauce is thick, about 3 minutes. Stir in the mascarpone cheese, season the pasta with salt and black pepper and serve immediately.
—*Richard Reddington*

Fusilli with Creamy Leek Sauce

TOTAL: 30 MIN
6 SERVINGS ●

- ¼ cup extra-virgin olive oil
- 6 medium leeks, white parts only, halved lengthwise and thinly sliced crosswise
- ½ cup chicken stock or low-sodium broth
- 1 tablespoon fresh lemon juice
- 1 teaspoon finely grated lemon zest
- 1 tablespoon flat-leaf parsley leaves
- Salt and freshly ground black pepper
- 1 pound fusilli
- ½ cup freshly grated Parmigiano-Reggiano cheese, plus more for serving

1. Bring a large pot of water to a boil over high heat. In a large, deep skillet, heat the olive oil. Add the sliced leeks and cook over moderate heat, stirring occasionally, until they are softened and just beginning to brown, about 10 minutes. Add the chicken stock, fresh lemon juice, grated lemon zest and parsley leaves and bring to a boil. Transfer the mixture to a blender and puree until smooth. Season the leek sauce with salt and black pepper.

2. Meanwhile, add salt to the pot of boiling water. Add the fusilli and cook until it's almost al dente. Drain the pasta, reserving ½ cup of the cooking water. Return the pasta to the pot.

3. Add the leek sauce and the reserved cooking water to the pot of drained fusilli and cook over moderate heat, stirring occasionally, until the pasta is al dente and coated with a thick sauce, about 3 minutes. Sprinkle in the ½ cup of grated Parmigiano-Reggiano cheese and season with salt and black pepper. Toss well and serve the fusilli immediately, passing additional grated Parmigiano-Reggiano at the table.
—*Shelley Lindgren*

MAKE AHEAD The creamy leek sauce can be refrigerated overnight.

Creamy Pear, Mascarpone and Pecorino Farfalle

TOTAL: 30 MIN
4 SERVINGS ●

- 12 ounces farfalle
- 3 tablespoons unsalted butter
- 2 large Bartlett pears—peeled, cored and thinly sliced
- Salt and freshly ground pepper
- ½ cup mascarpone cheese
- ½ cup freshly grated Pecorino Romano cheese, plus more for serving
- 2 tablespoons finely chopped flat-leaf parsley

1. Bring a large pot of salted water to a boil over high heat. Add the farfalle pasta and cook until al dente. Drain the farfalle thoroughly, reserving ¾ cup of the pasta cooking water.

2. Meanwhile, in a large, deep skillet, melt the butter. Add the sliced pears and cook over moderately high heat, stirring occasionally, until softened but not browned, about 5 minutes. Season the pears with salt and pepper.

3. Add the drained farfalle, mascarpone, ½ cup of grated pecorino and ½ cup of the pasta cooking water to the skillet and cook over moderately low heat, stirring, until the sauce is thick and creamy, about 2 minutes; add more pasta cooking water as needed. Season the pasta with salt and pepper and stir in the chopped parsley. Transfer the pasta to bowls and serve.
—*Lidia Bastianich*

Fettuccine with Escarole and Brie

TOTAL: 30 MIN
4 SERVINGS

F&W's Grace Parisi makes brilliant use of Brie here. After removing the rind from the cheese, she combines it with some of the pasta cooking water to make a rich, silky sauce for the fettuccine.

- ¾ **pound fettuccine**
- 2 **tablespoons extra-virgin olive oil**
- 2 **ounces thinly sliced pancetta or bacon, coarsely chopped**
- 1 **large garlic clove, minced**
- 1 **shallot, minced**
- 1 **pound escarole, cut into 1-inch ribbons**

Salt and freshly ground black pepper

- ½ **pound Brie (preferably a wedge), rind removed**

1. In a large pot of generously salted boiling water, cook the pasta until just al dente. Drain the pasta, reserving 1¼ cups of the cooking water.

2. Meanwhile, in a very large skillet, heat the olive oil. Add the pancetta and cook

TIP

pasta pointers

There are a few simple secrets to making perfect pasta:

SALT THE WATER just before adding the pasta (to be sure you don't forget).

SAVE SOME OF THE STARCHY COOKING WATER (before draining) to help thicken, season and round out the flavors in the finished dish.

USE THE RIGHT QUANTITIES For every ½ pound of pasta, boil at least 3 quarts of water and add 2 tablespoons of kosher salt.

over high heat, stirring, until lightly browned, about 2 minutes. Add the garlic and shallot and cook until fragrant, about 1 minute. Add the sliced escarole, season with salt and pepper and cook, stirring, just until wilted.

3. Add the pasta to the skillet along with 1 cup of the reserved pasta cooking water. Tear the Brie into 1-inch pieces and add to the skillet. Cook the pasta over moderate heat, tossing, until the Brie is melted and the sauce is thick and creamy, about 4 minutes; add more of the pasta cooking water if the sauce is dry. Season the pasta with salt and pepper. Transfer the fettuccine to bowls and serve immediately.
—*Grace Parisi*

Gnocchi Parisienne

ACTIVE: 20 MIN; TOTAL: 1 HR
4 SERVINGS ● ●

These very tasty gnocchi are made with *pâte à choux*—the same dough used for profiteroles, cream puffs and éclairs—that is poached and then baked. You don't need a light hand to make these, as you do for other forms of gnocchi; in fact, the dough comes together quickly in a saucepan and requires vigorous stirring.

- 1 **cup water**
- 1 **teaspoon salt**
- ¼ **teaspoon freshly grated nutmeg**
- 3 **tablespoons unsalted butter, cut into tablespoons**
- 1 **cup all-purpose flour**
- 3 **large eggs**
- ¼ **cup plus 2 tablespoons freshly grated Parmigiano-Reggiano, Gruyère or Asiago cheese**

1. In a small saucepan, combine the water, salt and nutmeg with 2 tablespoons of the butter and bring to a boil over high heat. As soon as the water boils, add the flour all at once and beat the dough with a wooden spoon until it is thick and comes away from the side of the pan. Cook, stirring to dry out the dough, about 30 seconds. Transfer the

dough to a medium bowl and let cool slightly, about 5 minutes.

2. Beat 1 egg into the dough until incorporated. Beat in ¼ cup of the cheese and another egg until blended, then beat in the last egg until the dough is very smooth.

3. Preheat the oven to 350°. Bring a large pot of salted water to a boil. Set a bowl of ice water near the stove. With a large spatula, transfer the dough to a resealable plastic bag, pressing it into one corner. Cut off the tip of the bag; the opening should be about ½ inch long (see Note).

4. Reduce the heat to maintain a gentle simmer. Carefully hold the bag over the water and press out the dough, using a small, sharp knife to cut it into 1½-inch lengths before dropping it into the pot. Simmer the gnocchi for 3 minutes. With a slotted spoon, transfer the gnocchi to the ice water bath to stop the cooking. Transfer the gnocchi to paper towels and pat dry.

5. Grease a 9-by-12-inch baking dish with the remaining 1 tablespoon of butter. Arrange the gnocchi in the dish and sprinkle with the remaining 2 tablespoons of cheese. Bake until puffed, about 25 minutes. Preheat the broiler. Broil the gnocchi 6 inches from the heat for 1 to 2 minutes, or until browned. Serve right away.
—*Jacques Pépin*

NOTE The gnocchi dough can also be shaped with 2 teaspoons.

MAKE AHEAD The gnocchi can be prepared through Step 4 and refrigerated overnight before baking and broiling.

Sage Polenta

TOTAL: 50 MIN
4 SERVINGS ● ◐

Sage-infused melted butter adds a luxurious, rich herb flavor to creamy polenta.

- 1 **quart water**

Salt

- 1 **cup coarse yellow polenta (not instant)**
- 3 **tablespoons unsalted butter**

4 sage leaves

¼ cup freshly grated Parmigiano-
Reggiano cheese

Freshly ground black pepper

1. In a large saucepan, bring the water to a boil. Add salt to the water, then slowly whisk in the polenta. Cover the saucepan and cook over moderate heat, whisking often, until the polenta is very thick and creamy, about 45 minutes.

2. Meanwhile, in a small saucepan, cook the butter over moderate heat until starting to brown, about 3 minutes. Add the sage leaves to the saucepan and fry until crisp, about 1 minute. Discard the sage leaves and set the butter aside.

3. Stir the sage butter and grated Parmigiano cheese into the polenta. Season with salt and black pepper and serve hot.
—*Shelley Lindgren*

MAKE AHEAD The cooked polenta can stand, covered, for 1 hour. Reheat, whisking vigorously, and stir in the sage butter and cheese before serving.

Ginger Rice

TOTAL: 25 MIN
4 SERVINGS

This ginger-scented basmati rice is versatile enough to pair with many Asian- and Indian-inflected dishes.

1 tablespoon unsalted butter

2 tablespoons very finely
chopped peeled fresh ginger

1 cup basmati rice, rinsed

1½ cups chicken stock or
low-sodium broth

½ teaspoon salt

In a medium saucepan, melt the butter. Add the chopped ginger, basmati rice, chicken stock and salt and bring to a boil. Cover and cook over low heat for 12 minutes, or until the basmati rice is tender and the water has fully evaporated. Fluff the Ginger Rice, transfer to a large bowl and serve immediately.
—*Jean-Georges Vongerichten*

FETTUCCINE WITH ESCAROLE AND BRIE

GNOCCHI PARISIENNE

Bacon Fried Rice

TOTAL: 45 MIN
4 SERVINGS

Australian chef, cooking show host and cookbook author Kylie Kwong says, "The secret to good fried rice is cooking the eggs first. You scramble the eggs and take them out of the wok. Then you stir-fry onion, bacon, ginger and all of the aromatics, put in the rice and soy, then lastly the eggs, so you have fluffy eggs throughout the dish."

- 3 tablespoons peanut oil
- 4 eggs, lightly beaten

Kosher salt and freshly ground
   black pepper

- 4 thick-cut slices of bacon, sliced crosswise into ½-inch pieces
- 4 medium garlic cloves, very finely chopped
- 1½ tablespoons very finely chopped fresh ginger
- 1 medium onion, finely chopped
- 2 tablespoons dry sherry
- 1 teaspoon sugar
- 6 cups cooked white rice, chilled or at room temperature
- 2½ tablespoons oyster sauce
- 2½ tablespoons soy sauce
- 1 teaspoon Asian sesame oil
- 5 scallions, thinly sliced

1. In a large wok, heat 2 tablespoons of the peanut oil until very hot. Season the eggs with salt and pepper and pour into the wok. Scramble the eggs over high heat until just cooked through, about 1 minute. Transfer to a paper towel–lined plate.
2. Add the bacon to the wok and cook, stirring occasionally, until crisp, about 4 minutes. Using a slotted spoon, transfer the bacon to the plate with the eggs. Drain off the bacon grease and wipe out the wok.
3. Heat the remaining 1 tablespoon of peanut oil in the wok. Add the garlic and ginger and cook over high heat for 1 minute. Add the onion and cook until golden, about 3 minutes. Stir in the sherry and sugar and cook until the sherry is reduced by half,

about 30 seconds. Add the rice, oyster sauce, soy sauce, sesame oil, reserved eggs and bacon and all but 2 tablespoons of the scallions. Season with salt and stir-fry until the rice is hot, 2 minutes. Transfer to a serving bowl, sprinkle with the remaining scallions and serve. —*Kylie Kwong*

Turkish Ridged Flat Bread

ACTIVE: 30 MIN; TOTAL: 4 HR 30 MIN
PLUS OVERNIGHT RESTING
MAKES 4 LOAVES ● ●

This bread's long rise creates an assertive, yeasty flavor. The crisp, chewy texture is a satisfying complement to meaty fish like tuna or swordfish.

SPONGE

- ½ cup warm water
- ¼ teaspoon active dry yeast
- 1 cup all-purpose flour

DOUGH

- 1¼ cups warm water
- 1 teaspoon active dry yeast
- ½ teaspoon sugar
- 2 tablespoons extra-virgin olive oil
- 3 cups bread flour
- ½ cup whole wheat flour
- 1 tablespoon plus 1 teaspoon salt

Cornmeal, for dusting
Nigella or sesame seeds, for sprinkling

1. MAKE THE SPONGE: In a medium bowl, mix the water with the yeast and let stand until foamy, about 10 minutes. Stir in the flour. Cover the bowl loosely with plastic wrap and let stand overnight.
2. MAKE THE DOUGH: In a large bowl, mix ¼ cup of the water with the yeast and sugar and let stand until foamy. Add the sponge, the remaining 1 cup of water and the olive oil. Stir in the flours and salt until a dough forms. Turn the dough out onto a lightly floured work surface and knead until smooth. Place the dough in a large, oiled bowl, cover with plastic wrap and let stand until doubled in bulk, about 3 hours.
3. Place a baking stone on the bottom of the oven and preheat the oven to 450°.

Punch down the dough and divide it into 4 pieces. Flatten each piece into a round. Cover the rounds with plastic and let rise until puffy, about 30 minutes.
4. Sprinkle a pizza peel with cornmeal. On a floured work surface, with wet hands, flatten each round into an 8-by-10-inch oval. Make 6 or 7 deep grooves with your fingertips down the length of each oval. Sprinkle the ovals with the nigella seeds. Slide the ovals onto the peel, then onto the hot stone in the oven. Bake until crisp on the bottom, about 10 minutes. Serve warm.
—*Paula Wolfert*

Crispy, Creamy Potato Puffs

TOTAL: 1 HR 40 MIN
MAKES ABOUT 60 PUFFS ● ●

These enticing Chilean potato puffs, known as *papas duquesas,* are a cross between mashed potatoes and french fries.

- 2¼ pounds baking potatoes, peeled and cut into 2-inch chunks

Salt

- 1 large egg, beaten
- 1 tablespoon unsalted butter
- 2 tablespoons nonfat dry milk
- 2 tablespoons freshly grated Parmigiano-Reggiano cheese
- ½ cup all-purpose flour

Pinch of freshly grated nutmeg
Vegetable oil, for frying

1. Put the potatoes in a large saucepan and cover with water. Add a large pinch of salt and bring to a boil. Simmer over moderate heat until tender, about 20 minutes. Drain the potatoes and return them to the saucepan. Cook for 1 minute over high heat, shaking the pan frequently to dry out the potatoes.
2. Pass the potatoes through a ricer into a large bowl. Stir in the egg, butter, dry milk, cheese, flour and nutmeg; season with salt. Using floured hands, roll the potato mixture into 1-inch balls; you should have about 60.

3. Preheat the oven to 350°. In a large nonstick skillet, heat ½ inch of vegetable oil until shimmering. Working in batches of about 12, fry the potato balls over moderately high heat until they are browned on 3 sides, 2 to 3 minutes per side. Drain on paper towels, season lightly with salt and transfer the fried potato puffs to a large rimmed baking sheet. Repeat with the remaining balls.

4. When all of the puffs are fried, reheat them in the oven for about 10 minutes. Serve at once. —*Valeria Huneeus*

MAKE AHEAD The recipe can be prepared through Step 2 and refrigerated overnight. Bring the potato balls to room temperature before frying them.

Grandma Kirk's Baked Beans

ACTIVE: 25 MIN; TOTAL: 5 HR PLUS OVERNIGHT SOAKING

8 TO 10 SERVINGS ●

Paul Kirk, author of *Paul Kirk's Championship Barbecue,* learned this recipe for soft red-brown beans in a brothy liquid from his 89-year-old mother. The Burnt Ends in this recipe are optional but add a nice smoky flavor to the beans along with the bacon.

 2 **pounds dried navy beans, soaked overnight in cold water and drained**

 1 onion, coarsely chopped
 1 garlic clove, minced
 ¾ cup light molasses or sorghum syrup
 ¾ cup light brown sugar
 1 tablespoon soy sauce
 1½ teaspoons salt
 1 teaspoon Worcestershire sauce
 ¼ teaspoon dry mustard
 ½ pound slab bacon in 1 piece
 Burnt Ends (optional; see Barbecued Brisket, p. 165)

1. Put the beans in a large enameled cast-iron casserole and add enough water to cover by ½ inch. Bring to a simmer and cook until the skins on the beans curl up when you blow on them, about 30 minutes.
2. Preheat the oven to 300°. Stir the onion, garlic, molasses, brown sugar, soy sauce, salt, Worcestershire and mustard into the beans, then nestle in the bacon. Cover and bake for 3 hours, until the beans are tender, stirring occasionally and adding water as needed to cover the beans by ½ inch.
3. Stir in the Burnt Ends (if using), then bake the beans uncovered about 1½ hours longer, until richly browned on top. Remove the bacon piece, chop into cubes and return to the beans before serving. —*Paul Kirk*
MAKE AHEAD The baked beans can be refrigerated for up to 3 days.

Grilled Fava Bean Pods with Chile and Lemon

 TOTAL: 15 MIN
 6 SERVINGS ● ● ●

"Trust me," says San Francisco chef Nate Appleman about this unorthodox recipe. He quickly grills whole fava beans, tosses them with crushed red pepper or Chinese chile sauce and serves them hot. They can be eaten whole—the tender pods develop a delightful charred flavor on the grill—but it's also easy to eat them in the traditional way by popping the beans out of their pods and outer skins.

 1 **pound very fresh fava beans in the pods, rinsed**
 2 **tablespoons extra-virgin olive oil**
 1 **scallion, thinly sliced crosswise**
 ½ **teaspoon crushed red pepper or Chinese chile sauce**
Kosher salt
Lemon wedges, for serving

Light a grill. In a large bowl, toss the fava bean pods with the olive oil. Grill the favas over high heat for about 5 minutes, turning occasionally, until the pods are softened and charred in spots. Return the beans to the bowl and toss with the sliced scallion, crushed red pepper and salt. Transfer to a platter and serve with lemon wedges. —*Nate Appleman*

● HEALTHY ● MAKE AHEAD ● VEGETARIAN ● STAFF FAVORITE

PEPPERY SALAD AND GINGER DRESSING

perfect salad dressings

These three basic salad dressing recipes should be indispensable parts of any cook's repertoire; by adding just an ingredient or two, they can be transformed into dozens of fantastic variations. —Grace Parisi

Dijon Vinaigrette

TOTAL: 5 MIN, MAKES ½ CUP ● ●

2 tablespoons sherry vinegar • ½ tablespoon minced shallot • ½ tablespoon Dijon mustard • ⅓ cup extra-virgin olive oil • salt and freshly ground pepper

In a small bowl, whisk the sherry vinegar with the shallot and Dijon mustard. In a thin, steady stream, whisk in the olive oil until emulsified. Season with salt and pepper. —G.P.

HERB VINAIGRETTE Add ¼ teaspoon chopped thyme and ½ teaspoon chopped tarragon.

LEMON VINAIGRETTE Substitute 1½ tablespoons lemon juice for the vinegar and add ¼ teaspoon grated lemon zest.

Buttermilk Dressing

TOTAL: 5 MIN, MAKES ⅔ CUP ● ● ● ●

1 small garlic clove, smashed • salt • 3 tablespoons sour cream • 3 tablespoons mayonnaise • 1 tablespoon white wine vinegar • ¼ cup buttermilk • freshly ground pepper

Sprinkle the garlic with a pinch of salt and mash to a paste. In a bowl, whisk together the mashed garlic, sour cream, mayonnaise and vinegar. Whisk in the buttermilk and season the dressing with pepper. —G.P.

BLUE CHEESE DRESSING Add 2 ounces crumbled blue cheese.

TZATZIKI DRESSING Add 2 ounces crumbled feta cheese and 1 tablespoon chopped dill.

Ginger Dressing

TOTAL: 10 MIN, MAKES ⅔ CUP ● ●

1 tablespoon minced fresh ginger • 1 tablespoon minced shallot • 2 tablespoons rice vinegar • 2 tablespoons mayonnaise • 1 tablespoon low-sodium soy sauce • ⅓ cup vegetable oil • salt and freshly ground pepper

In a blender, puree the ginger, shallot, vinegar, mayonnaise and soy sauce. With the machine on, add the vegetable oil and blend until smooth. Season with salt and pepper. —G.P.

MISO DRESSING Add 2 tablespoons white miso paste.

SESAME DRESSING Add 1 tablespoon toasted sesame seeds and ½ teaspoon Asian sesame oil.

matching salad and dressing

1 Leafy Salad + Dijon Vinaigrette
Improvise with lettuces like Boston and romaine; vegetables such as cucumbers and green beans; fruit such as apples and grapes; toasted nuts.

2 Crunchy Salad + Buttermilk Dressing
Improvise with bitter greens such as endive; sturdy greens such as baby spinach; vegetables such as cherry tomatoes; shaved cheeses; toasted croutons.

3 Peppery Salad + Ginger Dressing
Improvise with sturdy greens such as watercress; vegetables such as avocados and radishes; fruit such as Asian pears; poached shrimp and seared tuna.

Brussels Sprouts with Cranberries

TOTAL: 30 MIN
10 SERVINGS ● ●

Because brussels sprouts are slightly bitter, chef Michel Nischan of Dressing Room in Westport, Connecticut, likes to pair them with something sweet; here he adds sweet-tart dried cranberries that have been plumped in an off-dry Riesling. "I don't like to overdress vegetables," he explains. "It takes just one counterpoint to bring the sprouts to a place where people say, 'This is really good.'"

- 1 cup dried cranberries
- 2 cups off-dry Riesling
- 3 tablespoons grapeseed or vegetable oil
- 2 large shallots, finely chopped
- 2½ pounds brussels sprouts, trimmed and halved lengthwise
- 1¼ cups water
- Salt and freshly ground pepper
- 3 tablespoons unsalted butter

1. In a microwave-safe bowl, heat the dried cranberries in the Riesling at high power for 2 minutes. Let stand until the cranberries are slightly plumped, about 10 minutes. Drain the soaked cranberries and discard the liquid.
2. In a large skillet, heat the grapeseed oil. Add the chopped shallots and cook over low heat until softened, about 2 minutes. Add the brussels sprouts and cook over moderately high heat until bright green, about 2 minutes. Add the water and drained cranberries; season with salt and pepper. Cover and cook over moderate heat until the brussels sprouts are tender, about 12 minutes. Uncover and continue cooking until the liquid has evaporated, about 2 minutes. Add the butter and toss to coat. Serve right away.
—*Michel Nischan*

MAKE AHEAD The brussels sprouts can be prepared up to 4 hours ahead. Reheat gently in a skillet.

Sweet-and-Spicy Ketchup

TOTAL: 40 MIN
MAKES 1¼ CUPS ● ● ● ●

Chef Paul Virant of Vie restaurant in Western Springs, Illinois, keeps this simple house-made ketchup on hand for staff meals when burgers or Chicago dogs are on offer for his cooks. For the base, Virant uses tomatoes his staff has canned during the summer, but store-bought tomato sauce also works.

- 1 tablespoon extra-virgin olive oil
- 1 small onion, finely chopped
- 2 garlic cloves, minced
- ¼ cup light brown sugar
- ½ teaspoon smoked paprika or pimentón de la Vera
- ¼ teaspoon ground allspice
- ¼ teaspoon ground cloves
- ⅓ cup distilled white vinegar
- 1 tablespoon tomato paste
- Two 8-ounce cans tomato sauce
- Salt and freshly ground black pepper

1. In a saucepan, heat the oil. Add the onion and garlic and cook over moderately low heat, stirring occasionally, until softened, about 7 minutes. Add the brown sugar, paprika, allspice and cloves and cook, stirring occasionally, until the sugar melts. Add the vinegar and tomato paste and cook over moderate heat until thick, about 3 minutes. Stir in the tomato sauce and simmer over moderate heat, stirring occasionally, until very thick, 15 to 20 minutes.
2. Transfer the ketchup to a blender or food processor and puree until smooth. Season with salt and pepper.
—*Paul Virant*

MAKE AHEAD The ketchup can be refrigerated for up to 2 weeks.

Golden Yellow Mustard

TOTAL: 15 MIN PLUS OVERNIGHT RESTING
MAKES 1¼ CUPS ● ● ●

Like most homemade mustards, this one tastes best after resting overnight, which gives the flavors time to mellow. The classic sauce has a refreshing piquancy that makes it work perfectly as either a condiment or a marinade. Slather it on a burger or steak, or spread it on chicken breasts a few hours before grilling.

- ⅓ cup yellow mustard seeds
- 1 tablespoon sugar
- 1½ teaspoons salt
- 2 teaspoons turmeric
- ¼ cup Champagne vinegar
- 2 tablespoons extra-virgin olive oil
- 1 teaspoon Worcestershire sauce
- Dash of Tabasco
- ⅓ cup water plus 3 tablespoons

1. In a small skillet, toast the mustard seeds over moderate heat until they begin to pop, 1 minute. Immediately transfer them to a bowl and cover with a lid to stop the popping. Let the seeds cool completely.
2. Transfer the cooled mustard seeds to a spice grinder. Add the sugar and salt and grind to a powder.
3. Return the powder to the skillet. Add the turmeric, vinegar, oil, Worcestershire sauce, Tabasco and 3 tablespoons of the water. Cook the paste over moderate heat, stirring constantly, until it's sizzling, about 5 minutes. Stir in the remaining ⅓ cup of water and transfer to a bowl. Refrigerate the mustard overnight before serving.
—*Paul Virant*

MAKE AHEAD The mustard can be refrigerated for up to 2 weeks.

Lemon-Dijon Mayonnaise

TOTAL: 10 MIN
MAKES 1¼ CUPS ● ●

"When it's made fresh," says Paul Virant, "plain mayonnaise is a great little sauce"— a savory complement to grilled chicken, pork or even asparagus. For added punch, Virant suggests adding a quarter cup of finely grated fresh horseradish and up to a half tablespoon of Sriracha chile-garlic sauce to the food processor before adding the vegetable oil.

1 large egg
1 large egg yolk
1 teaspoon Dijon mustard
Finely grated zest and juice
     of 1 lemon
1 cup grapeseed, canola or other
     neutral vegetable oil
Salt and freshly ground black pepper

In a food processor, combine the egg, egg yolk, mustard, lemon zest and lemon juice and process until very smooth. With the machine running, add the oil in a very thin stream until it is fully incorporated and the mayonnaise is thick and creamy. Season with salt and pepper. —*Paul Virant*
MAKE AHEAD The mayonnaise can be refrigerated for up to 2 days.

Superfast Salt-and-Sugar Pickles

TOTAL: 30 MIN
6 TO 8 SERVINGS ● ●

In Japan, salt pickles are a staple. David Chang of New York City's Momofuku restaurants serves his right after seasoning, while they're still vibrant and crunchy.

1 teaspoon fine sea salt
1 teaspoon sugar
3 very large radishes, halved
     and sliced into thin wedges
     (1½ cups)
2 thin daikon radishes, sliced
     crosswise ⅛ inch thick
     (1½ cups)
2 Kirby cucumbers, sliced
     crosswise ¼ inch thick
     (1½ cups)
2 pounds seedless watermelon—
     rind removed, flesh sliced ⅓ inch
     thick and cut into 2-inch wedges

In a small bowl, combine the salt and sugar. Arrange the radishes, daikon, cucumbers and watermelon in separate bowls; sprinkle ½ teaspoon of the salt mixture over each and toss. Let the pickles stand for 5 to 10 minutes. Serve immediately. —*David Chang*

Sweet-and-Sour Pickles

TOTAL: 40 MIN PLUS OVERNIGHT SOAKING
MAKES 5 PINTS ● ● ○ ○

2 pounds seedless watermelon,
     sliced ¾ inch thick
12 pearl onions
3 ears of corn, shucked,
     kernels cut from the cobs
1 serrano chile, seeded and minced
½ pound yellow wax beans
1 large Asian pear—peeled, cored
     and cut into ¼-inch-thick wedges
2 cups honeydew melon, cut
     into 1-inch cubes
4 cups water
2 cups sugar
¼ cup kosher salt
2 cups rice vinegar
1 large star anise pod

1. Trim the watermelon slices, removing the green rind and leaving ½ inch of the red flesh on ½ inch of the white rind. Cut these pieces into ¾-inch dice and transfer them to a 1-pint jar.
2. Bring a saucepan of water to a boil. Add the onions and cook for 2 minutes. Drain the onions, peel them and add them to another 1-pint jar with the corn and the chile. Trim the beans to fit upright in another 1-pint jar. Pack the pear and the honeydew into separate 1-pint jars.
3. In a saucepan, combine the water, sugar, salt, vinegar and star anise and bring to a boil. Simmer for 10 minutes, then discard the star anise. Return the liquid to a boil and carefully pour it into the jars, filling them to the top. Close the jars and refrigerate overnight or for up to 2 weeks. —*David Chang*

Quick Kimchi Cucumbers

TOTAL: 45 MIN
MAKES 1 POUND ●

Koreans eat kimchi—a garlicky, chile-laden pickle—at almost every meal. Traditionally, kimchi needs days, even weeks, to ferment, but this kimchi is ready in 45 minutes. Great on hot dogs, it's best served right away, when the cucumbers are still juicy.

1 pound Kirby cucumbers,
     halved lengthwise and cut
     into ½-inch spears
1½ teaspoons salt
2½ tablespoons sugar
1½ tablespoons Korean red chile
     flakes or 2 teaspoons crushed
     red pepper
1½ tablespoons thinly sliced strips
     of peeled fresh ginger
4 garlic cloves, thinly sliced
1 tablespoon Asian fish sauce
1 tablespoon soy sauce
½ teaspoon dried shrimp
     (optional), minced
1 small carrot and 1 scallion, thinly
     sliced into 2-inch matchsticks
¼ small onion, thinly sliced

1. In a colander, toss the cucumbers with ¼ teaspoon of the salt and ½ tablespoon of the sugar and let stand for 10 minutes.
2. In a bowl, mix the remaining 1¼ teaspoons of salt and 2 tablespoons of sugar with the chile flakes, ginger, garlic, fish sauce, soy sauce and dried shrimp. Toss in the carrot, scallion, onion and cucumbers. Arrange the cucumbers in a shallow dish, spooning the shredded vegetables and liquid on top. Let stand for 15 minutes, turning once or twice, then serve. —*David Chang*

SUPERFAST

dressing up mayonnaise

To make a fast condiment for seafood, asparagus or grilled chicken, fold together ½ cup of jarred mayonnaise, 1 teaspoon of grated lemon zest and ½ teaspoon of Dijon mustard.

desserts & brunch

desserts

Double-Chocolate Layer Cake

**ACTIVE: 40 MIN; TOTAL: 1 HR 30 MIN
PLUS 1 HR CHILLING**

MAKES ONE 8-INCH CAKE ● ○ ○

"This is the most fabulous chocolate cake," says Ina Garten, host of Food Network's *Barefoot Contessa.* "It's so easy and so moist and light. There's buttermilk and a cup of coffee in the batter! The frosting is just buttercream and a little coffee."

CAKE

1¾ cups all-purpose flour,
      plus more for dusting
2   cups sugar
¾   cup unsweetened
      cocoa powder
2   teaspoons baking soda
1   teaspoon baking powder
1   teaspoon kosher salt
1   cup buttermilk
½   cup vegetable oil
2   large eggs
1   teaspoon pure vanilla extract
1   cup freshly brewed hot coffee

FROSTING

6   ounces semisweet chocolate,
      coarsely chopped

2   sticks (½ pound) unsalted butter,
      at room temperature
1   large egg yolk
1   teaspoon pure vanilla extract
1   cup plus 1 tablespoon
      confectioners' sugar, sifted
1   tablespoon instant coffee
      granules

1. MAKE THE CAKE: Preheat the oven to 350°. Butter two 8-inch round cake pans and line them with parchment paper; butter the paper. Dust the pans with flour, tapping out any excess.

2. In the bowl of an electric mixer fitted with a paddle, mix the 1¾ cups of flour with the sugar, cocoa powder, baking soda, baking powder and salt at low speed. In a medium bowl, whisk the buttermilk with the oil, eggs and vanilla. Slowly beat the buttermilk mixture into the dry ingredients until just incorporated, then slowly beat in the hot coffee until fully incorporated.

3. Pour the batter into the prepared pans. Bake for 35 minutes, or until a toothpick inserted in the center of each cake comes out clean. Let the cakes cool in the pans for 30 minutes, then invert the cakes onto a rack to cool completely. Peel off the parchment paper.

4. MAKE THE FROSTING: In a microwave-safe bowl, heat the chocolate at high power in 30-second intervals, stirring, until most of the chocolate is melted. Stir until completely melted, then set aside to cool to room temperature.

5. In the bowl of an electric mixer fitted with a paddle, beat the room-temperature butter at medium speed until pale and fluffy. Add the egg yolk and vanilla extract and beat for 1 minute, scraping down the side of the bowl. At low speed, gradually beat in the confectioners' sugar, about 1 minute. In a small bowl, dissolve the instant coffee granules in 2 teaspoons of hot water. Slowly beat the coffee mixture and the cooled chocolate into the butter mixture until just combined.

6. Set a cake layer on a plate with the flat side facing up. Evenly spread one-third of the frosting over the cake to the edge. Top with the second cake layer, rounded side up. Spread the remaining frosting over the top and side of the cake. Refrigerate for at least 1 hour before slicing.
—*Ina Garten*

MAKE AHEAD The frosted cake can be refrigerated, covered, for 2 days. Let stand for 1 hour before serving.

Mascarpone-Swirled Brownies with Nutty Caramel Corn

ACTIVE: 30 MIN; TOTAL: 1 HR 30 MIN

9 SERVINGS ● ●

- ⅔ cup all-purpose flour
- ½ teaspoon baking powder
- ¼ teaspoon salt
- 4 ounces semisweet chocolate, chopped
- 2 ounces unsweetened chocolate, chopped
- 1 stick unsalted butter, softened
- 1¼ cups sugar
- 1 tablespoon plus ½ teaspoon pure vanilla extract
- 3 large eggs
- 8 ounces mascarpone cheese
- 1 large egg yolk

Nutty Caramel Corn (recipe follows) and vanilla ice cream, for serving

1. Preheat the oven to 325°. Butter and flour a 9-inch-square baking pan. In a small bowl, whisk together the flour, baking powder and salt. In a medium saucepan, melt the semisweet and unsweetened chocolate with the butter over low heat. Remove from the heat and whisk in 1 cup of the sugar and 1 tablespoon of the vanilla. Whisk in the whole eggs 1 at a time. Whisk the dry ingredients into the chocolate mixture until the brownie batter is smooth.

2. In a bowl, whisk the mascarpone with the egg yolk and the remaining ¼ cup of sugar and ½ teaspoon of vanilla. Pour half of the brownie batter into the baking pan. Dollop half of the mascarpone mixture on top and cover with the remaining batter. Dollop on the remaining mascarpone mixture and swirl the batter a few times with a knife to create a marbled effect.

3. Bake the brownies for about 55 minutes, until a toothpick inserted in the center comes out with a few crumbs attached. Let cool before cutting. Serve with the caramel corn and ice cream. —*Kate Jennings*

MAKE AHEAD The brownies can be refrigerated for 3 days.

NUTTY CARAMEL CORN

ACTIVE: 20 MIN; TOTAL: 2 HR

MAKES 18 CUPS ● ●

- 12 cups unsalted popped popcorn
- 1 cup salted cocktail peanuts
- 1 cup light brown sugar
- 1 stick unsalted butter
- ¼ cup light corn syrup
- ½ teaspoon salt
- ½ teaspoon baking soda
- ⅛ teaspoon cream of tartar

1. Preheat the oven to 225°. Line a baking sheet with parchment paper. Put the popcorn and peanuts in a large bowl.

2. In a medium saucepan, combine the brown sugar, butter, corn syrup and salt and bring to a boil. Add the baking soda and cream of tartar and boil over moderate heat, stirring occasionally, until the syrup is deep amber, about 4 minutes. Pour the hot syrup over the peanuts and popcorn and stir with a wooden spoon until evenly coated. Spread the mixture on the baking sheet and bake until slightly dry, about 1 hour. The caramel corn will harden as it cools; let it cool completely.

3. Invert the caramel corn onto a cutting board. Peel off the paper and break into chunks before serving. —*K.J.*

MAKE AHEAD The caramel corn can be stored in an airtight container for 4 days.

Chocolate-Oatmeal Carmelitas

ACTIVE: 30 MIN; TOTAL: 1 HR PLUS OVERNIGHT RESTING

MAKES 24 BARS ● ●

- 3 cups plus 3 tablespoons all-purpose flour
- 1½ teaspoons baking soda
- ½ teaspoon salt
- 4 sticks (1 pound) unsalted butter, softened
- 3 cups quick-cooking rolled oats
- 2¼ cups light brown sugar
- 1½ cups dulce de leche (see Note)
- 1½ cups semisweet chocolate chips
- ¾ cup chopped pecans

1. Preheat the oven to 350°. Butter a 9-by-13-inch metal baking pan. In a large bowl, whisk 3 cups of the flour with the baking soda and salt. Add the butter, quick-cooking oats and light brown sugar and mix until combined. In a small bowl, mix the dulce de leche with the remaining 3 tablespoons of flour.

2. Pat half of the oat mixture into the baking pan. Bake for 15 minutes. Scatter half of the chocolate chips and pecans over the crust. Dollop half of the dulce de leche mixture on top. Crumble the remaining oat mixture evenly into the pan. Cover with the remaining chocolate chips, pecans and dulce de leche. Bake for about 35 minutes, or until the edges are set. Let stand uncovered at room temperature overnight. Cut the *carmelitas* into bars and serve. —*Louis Lambert*

NOTE Dulce de leche, the Latin caramel sauce, is available at most supermarkets and specialty food shops.

MAKE AHEAD Once cooled, the *carmelitas* can be kept in an airtight container at room temperature for up to 3 days or frozen for up to 1 month.

Dulce de Leche Napoleons

ACTIVE: 1 HR 20 MIN;

TOTAL: 2 HR 20 MIN

8 SERVINGS ●

- 1 cup milk
- 2 large eggs
- 2 large egg yolks
- ¼ cup granulated sugar
- 2 tablespoons all-purpose flour
- 2 tablespoons cornstarch
- 1 teaspoon pure vanilla extract
- 1 cup heavy cream
- ¼ cup confectioners' sugar, plus more for dusting
- 12 sheets of phyllo dough
- 1½ sticks unsalted butter, melted
- 1¼ cups dulce de leche, warmed
- 8 large strawberries, thinly sliced lengthwise, for garnish

1. In a medium saucepan, heat the milk until hot to the touch. Meanwhile, in a medium heatproof bowl, whisk the whole eggs with the egg yolks and granulated sugar. Whisk in the flour, cornstarch and vanilla until smooth. Slowly whisk in the hot milk. Pour the mixture into the saucepan and cook over moderate heat, whisking constantly, until bubbles appear around the edge and the custard is hot and thick, about 4 minutes. Pass the custard through a fine strainer into a bowl and refrigerate until chilled, stirring occasionally, about 20 minutes.

2. In a large stainless steel bowl, using an electric mixer, beat the heavy cream until stiff. Beat in the ¼ cup of confectioners' sugar until combined. Fold the custard into the whipped cream. Cover with plastic wrap and refrigerate.

3. Preheat the oven to 350°. Line 2 large rimmed baking sheets with parchment paper. Lay 1 sheet of phyllo dough on a work surface and brush with melted butter. Top with another phyllo sheet and brush with butter. Repeat twice more so you have 4 layers. Cut out nine 4-inch squares. Cut each square in half diagonally so you have 18 triangles. Transfer the triangles to the lined baking sheets and cover with another sheet of parchment paper. Top with another baking sheet and bake for about 20 minutes, until the triangles are nicely browned. Repeat with the remaining phyllo sheets and butter in 2 batches, making another 36 triangles.

4. Place a phyllo triangle on each plate. Spread with ½ tablespoon of dulce de leche and 1 tablespoon of the custard cream; top with another phyllo triangle. Repeat 4 more times, finishing with a sixth phyllo triangle. Top each napoleon with a sliced strawberry. Dust with confectioners' sugar and serve. —*Valeria Huneeus*

MAKE AHEAD The phyllo triangles can be stored overnight in an airtight container at room temperature. The custard cream can be refrigerated for up to 2 days.

Chocolate Tartlets with Candied Grapefruit Peel

ACTIVE: 45 MIN; TOTAL: 1 HR 15 MIN
MAKES 10 TARTLETS ● ●
TART SHELLS

- 1 cup all-purpose flour
- 6 tablespoons unsalted butter, cut into pieces
- 3 tablespoons confectioners' sugar
Salt
- 1 large egg yolk
- 1 tablespoon milk

FILLING

- 5 ounces bittersweet or semisweet chocolate, chopped
- ⅔ stick (5 tablespoons plus 1 teaspoon) unsalted butter, cut into pieces
- 2 tablespoons granulated sugar
- 1 large egg
- 1 large egg yolk

Confectioners' sugar, for sprinkling
Candied Grapefruit Peel (recipe follows), for garnish

1. **MAKE THE TART SHELLS:** Preheat the oven to 350°. In the bowl of a food processor, combine the flour, butter, confectioners' sugar and a dash of salt. Process for 15 seconds, until well mixed. In a bowl, mix the egg yolk with the milk. Add to the processor and process for another 15 seconds, until the dough forms a ball. Roll out immediately or chill for about 1 hour before rolling.

2. Arrange ten 3-inch fluted tartlet molds side by side on a work surface. Roll the dough between 2 sheets of plastic wrap to a thickness of ¼ inch. Remove the top sheet of plastic and invert the dough over the molds. Press the dough through the plastic into the molds. Peel away the plastic wrap and trim the excess dough overhanging the tartlet pans. Refrigerate the tartlet shells for about 2 hours.

3. Bake the tartlet shells for about 20 minutes, until they are golden. Transfer to a cooling rack. Leave the oven on.

4. **MEANWHILE, MAKE THE FILLING:** In a 4-cup glass measuring cup, combine the chocolate, butter and granulated sugar. Microwave for 1 minute, stir, leave for a few minutes, then microwave for 1 minute longer, until melted. In a small bowl, beat together the whole egg and yolk, then whisk into the chocolate.

5. Divide the filling among the tartlet shells. Bake for 5 minutes. Let cool just to room temperature before serving, so that the filling is slightly soft. Slide the tartlets out of the molds, sprinkle with confectioners' sugar and garnish with the Candied Grapefruit Peel. —*Jacques Pépin*

CANDIED GRAPEFRUIT PEEL

ACTIVE: 30 MIN; TOTAL: 1 HR
MAKES ABOUT 40 STRIPS ● ●

- 10 strips of ruby red grapefruit zest (use a vegetable peeler to remove only the surface and not the white pith), cut into ¼-inch-wide julienne
- 2⅔ cups water
- ⅔ cup sugar

1. In a saucepan, cover the grapefruit zest strips with 2 cups of the water, bring to a boil and cook for 10 seconds over high heat. Drain them in a strainer, then rinse under cold water.

2. Return the zest strips to the saucepan with ⅓ cup of the sugar and the remaining ⅔ cup of water. Bring to a boil and cook, uncovered, until the mixture starts to thicken, about 8 minutes. At this point, the syrup should be a bit gooey and the zest strips should be almost transparent.

3. Spread the remaining ⅓ cup of sugar on a tray. Use a slotted spoon or fork to transfer the zest to the tray and toss, separating the pieces so that each strip is coated with sugar. Transfer the strips to a plate; let stand for at least 30 minutes, until dry. Store in the refrigerator in a jar with a tight-fitting lid (the zest will keep for months). —*J.P.*

Syrian Walnut-Semolina Cake with Figs and Chocolate

ACTIVE: 30 MIN; TOTAL: 2 HR

8 SERVINGS ●○

This crumbly cake is Sonoma vintner Chris Hanna's riff on a baklava-like Syrian pastry made with semolina, honey and walnuts. The sweet dried figs, common in Middle Eastern cooking, are a natural addition, but the less traditional chocolate chips really make this version stand out. Hanna tops the cake with homemade cardamom ice cream, but good vanilla ice cream is delicious, too.

All-purpose flour, for dusting

1½ cups walnut halves (6 ounces)

1 cup semolina flour

1½ teaspoons baking powder

½ teaspoon salt

1½ sticks (12 tablespoons) unsalted butter, softened

½ cup honey

¼ cup sugar

3 large eggs, at room temperature

½ teaspoon pure vanilla extract

⅓ cup dried black Mission figs, finely chopped

⅓ cup semisweet or bittersweet chocolate chips

Vanilla ice cream, for serving

1. Preheat the oven to 350°. Butter a 9-inch round cake pan. Line the bottom of the pan with wax paper and butter the paper. Flour the pan, tapping out the excess.

2. Spread the walnut halves in a pie plate and toast them in the oven for 9 minutes, until fragrant. Let them cool completely.

3. In a food processor, combine the walnuts and semolina flour and pulse to a finely ground meal; do not overprocess. Add the baking powder and salt and process until just incorporated.

4. In a large bowl, using a handheld electric mixer, beat the butter with the honey and sugar at medium speed until fluffy, about 3 minutes. Add the eggs 1 at a time, beating well between each addition. Beat in the vanilla. At low speed, beat in the semolina and walnut mixture. Add the chopped figs and chocolate chips and beat at low speed just until evenly distributed, or fold them in with a spoon.

5. Scrape the cake batter into the prepared pan and bake the cake on the middle rack of the oven for 1 hour and 5 minutes, or until a toothpick inserted into the center comes out clean. Let the cake cool in the pan for 10 minutes, then carefully run a thin-bladed knife or offset spatula around the side of the pan to loosen the cake and turn it out onto a wire rack; let cool completely. Gently peel off the wax paper and invert the cake onto a large serving plate. Cut the walnut-semolina cake into wedges and serve with the vanilla ice cream.
—*Chris Hanna*

MAKE AHEAD The cake can be stored at room temperature for up to 3 days.

Malt-Ball Cake

ACTIVE: 1 HR; TOTAL: 3 HR

12 TO 14 SERVINGS ●○○

The staff at Baked, in Brooklyn, New York, created this tall, fluffy cake to gratify their love of malted-milk balls. Although the bakery prefers to use a brewer's malt like the one from nearby Sixpoint Craft Ales, this recipe calls for the more readily available malted-milk powder, which has a mellow, nutty flavor.

CAKE

2¼ cups cake flour

¾ cup all-purpose flour

1 cup malted-milk powder

1 tablespoon baking powder

¼ teaspoon baking soda

¾ teaspoon salt

¼ teaspoon freshly grated nutmeg

1 stick unsalted butter, at room temperature

½ cup solid vegetable shortening, at room temperature

2 cups sugar

1 tablespoon pure vanilla extract

2 cups ice water

4 large egg whites, at room temperature

FROSTING AND GARNISH

10 ounces bittersweet chocolate, finely chopped

10 ounces milk chocolate, finely chopped

1¾ cups heavy cream

3 tablespoons light corn syrup

4 sticks (1 pound) unsalted butter, cut into 1-inch chunks, softened

Malted-milk balls, for garnish

1. MAKE THE CAKE: Preheat the oven to 325°. Butter and flour three 8-inch round cake pans and line the bottoms with parchment paper. In a large bowl, combine the cake flour and all-purpose flour with the malt powder, baking powder, baking soda, salt and grated nutmeg; whisk the ingredients until well combined.

INGREDIENT

best honey

Chef **Felix Vaquero** of New York City's Blue Ribbon restaurants is especially close to one of his suppliers: His extra-thick, intense-tasting Mexican honeys come from his father's farm ($12; deandeluca.com).

2. In the bowl of a standing electric mixer fitted with the paddle, beat the butter with the shortening until creamy. Add the sugar and vanilla and beat at medium speed until fluffy, about 3 minutes. Beat in the dry ingredients in 3 batches at low speed, alternating with the ice water, occasionally scraping down the side of the bowl.

3. In a clean bowl, beat the egg whites at medium-high speed until soft peaks form. Fold the egg whites into the batter. Divide the batter between the pans, spreading it evenly, and bake the cakes for 40 to 45 minutes, until a toothpick inserted into the center comes out clean. Let the cakes cool in the pans for 20 minutes, then invert them onto a rack and let cool completely. Peel off the parchment.

4. MEANWHILE, MAKE THE FROSTING: Place the chocolate in a large bowl. In a small saucepan, bring the cream to a boil, then remove from the heat. Add the corn syrup, then pour the mixture over the chocolate. Let stand for 2 to 3 minutes, until the chocolate has melted; whisk until smooth. Let cool to room temperature.

5. Transfer the mixture to the bowl of a standing electric mixer fitted with a wire whisk. Gradually beat in the butter at medium speed, a few chunks at a time, and beat until thoroughly incorporated between additions. The frosting should be smooth and silky. Refrigerate the frosting just until it is thick enough to hold its shape, 10 to 15 minutes.

6. Place 1 cake layer on a platter and spread 1¼ cups of the frosting over the top in an even layer. Repeat to form 2 more layers. Spread a thin layer of frosting over the side of the cake and refrigerate briefly until the frosting is firm. Frost the side again with the remaining frosting. Garnish with the malted-milk balls, chill briefly to firm the frosting and serve. —*Matt Lewis*

MAKE AHEAD The cake can be refrigerated in an airtight container for up to 4 days. Serve at room temperature.

Yellow Layer Cake with Vanilla Frosting

ACTIVE: 30 MIN; TOTAL: 2 HR ● ● ●
MAKES ONE 9-INCH CAKE ● ● ●
F&W's Grace Parisi says this cake recipe is her ideal: moist, spongy layers and sweet, buttery frosting.

CAKE

- 3 cups sifted all-purpose flour, plus more for dusting
- 1 tablespoon baking powder
- ¾ teaspoon salt
- 1 cup milk, at room temperature
- 2 teaspoons pure vanilla extract
- 1½ sticks unsalted butter, softened
- 2 cups granulated sugar
- 4 large eggs, at room temperature

FROSTING

- ½ pound unsalted butter, softened
- 1 large egg yolk (optional)
- 1 pound confectioners' sugar
- ¼ cup plus 2 tablespoons heavy cream
- 1 teaspoon pure vanilla extract

Pinch of salt

1. MAKE THE CAKE: Preheat the oven to 350°. Butter two 9-by-2-inch round cake pans and line with parchment paper; butter and dust with flour. In a bowl, mix the 3 cups of flour, baking powder and salt. In a cup, mix the milk with the vanilla.

2. In a standing mixer fitted with the paddle, beat the butter at medium speed until light and creamy. Add the granulated sugar and beat until fluffy, 4 minutes. Beat in the eggs 1 at a time, scraping down the bowl. Beat in the dry ingredients in 3 batches, alternating with the milk mixture and scraping down the bowl.

3. Scrape the batter into the pans. Bake in the lower third of the oven for about 35 minutes, until the tops of the layers feel springy to the touch. Let cool for 15 minutes, then run a knife around the edges and invert onto a rack. Peel off the parchment paper, turn the cakes upright and let them cool completely.

4. MAKE THE FROSTING: In a standing mixer fitted with the whisk, beat the butter and egg yolk at medium-high speed until creamy. Beat in the confectioners' sugar at low speed. Beat in the cream, vanilla and salt, then beat at medium-high speed until fluffy, 3 minutes longer.

5. Spread 1 cup of frosting over a cake layer and top with the second layer, then frost the top and side. Let the cake stand for 1 hour before serving. —*Grace Parisi*

Easy Vanilla Bean Panna Cotta

ACTIVE: 15 MIN; TOTAL: 3 HR 15 MIN
8 SERVINGS ●
Panna cotta is typically served unmolded, but this version is so creamy that it's served in ramekins.

- 1 quart heavy cream
- ½ cup sugar
- ½ vanilla bean, split lengthwise, seeds scraped
- 2¼ teaspoons unflavored powdered gelatin
- 3 tablespoons water

Mixed berries, for serving

1. In a medium saucepan, combine the cream, sugar and vanilla bean and seeds. Bring the mixture just to a simmer over moderate heat. Remove from the heat, cover and let steep for 15 minutes.

2. Meanwhile, in a small bowl, sprinkle the gelatin over the water and let stand until evenly moistened, about 5 minutes.

3. Uncover the cream mixture and bring just to a simmer over moderately high heat. Remove from the heat, add the gelatin and stir until dissolved. Remove the vanilla bean and save for another use. Pour the panna cotta mixture into eight 4-ounce ramekins and let cool to room temperature. Cover with plastic wrap and refrigerate until the panna cotta is set but still jiggly, at least 3 hours. Serve the panna cotta in the ramekins, with berries. —*E. Michael Reidt*

MAKE AHEAD The panna cottas can be refrigerated for up to 3 days.

LEMON CAKE WITH
CRACKLY CARAMEL GLAZE
AND LIME-YOGURT MOUSSE

Vanilla Tapioca Pudding

TOTAL: 25 MIN PLUS 2 HR COOLING

6 SERVINGS ● ○

Louis Lambert, chef and owner of Lamberts Downtown Barbecue in Austin, believes that the best way to finish off a spicy meal is with a cool and creamy custard. He combined his grandmother's tapioca recipe and his own recipe for crème brûlée to make this sumptuous pudding.

- 2 large eggs
- 1 cup sugar
- ¼ cup plus 3 tablespoons quick-cooking tapioca
- 1 vanilla bean, split lengthwise and seeds scraped
- 1 quart half-and-half
- 1½ teaspoons pure vanilla extract

1. In a medium, heavy saucepan, whisk the eggs with the sugar, tapioca and vanilla bean and seeds until the mixture is pale yellow. Add the half-and-half and bring to a simmer over moderately high heat, whisking constantly. Simmer, whisking, until the mixture is very thick, about 10 minutes. Discard the vanilla bean, then whisk in the vanilla extract.

2. Pour the pudding into a heatproof dish and let cool for 2 hours before serving. Alternatively, cover the pudding and refrigerate overnight, then serve chilled. —*Louis Lambert*

Lemon Cake with Crackly Caramel Glaze and Lime-Yogurt Mousse

ACTIVE: 45 MIN; TOTAL: 2 HR

10 SERVINGS ●

CAKE

- 6 large eggs, separated
- ½ teaspoon cream of tartar
- 1½ cups sugar
- 2¼ cups cake flour
- 1 tablespoon baking powder
- ½ teaspoon salt
- ¾ cup water
- ½ cup pure olive oil
- 2 teaspoons pure vanilla extract
- Finely grated zest of 2 lemons

LIMONCELLO SYRUP

- ¼ cup water
- ¼ cup sugar
- 2 tablespoons limoncello liqueur or ½ teaspoon pure lemon extract

CARAMEL TOPPING

- 1 cup sugar
- ¼ teaspoon cream of tartar
- 2 tablespoons water

Lime-Yogurt Mousse (recipe follows), for serving

1. MAKE THE CAKE: Preheat the oven to 375°. Butter and flour a 12-cup Bundt pan. In a large bowl, using an electric mixer, beat the egg whites with the cream of tartar until soft peaks form. Gradually beat in ½ cup of the sugar.

2. In a medium bowl, whisk the cake flour with the baking powder and salt. In a large bowl, using an electric mixer, beat the 6 egg yolks with the water, olive oil, vanilla extract, lemon zest and the remaining 1 cup of sugar. Add the dry ingredients and beat until the batter is smooth. Using a spatula, fold in the beaten egg whites until no streaks remain.

3. Spoon the batter into the prepared Bundt pan. Bake the cake for 35 to 40 minutes, until springy to the touch. Let cool for 20 minutes, then invert the cake onto a rack to cool completely. Lower the oven temperature to 350°.

4. MAKE THE LIMONCELLO SYRUP: In a small saucepan, simmer the water and sugar over moderate heat just until the sugar dissolves, about 5 minutes. Let cool, then stir in the limoncello. Brush the syrup all over the cake, allowing it to soak in.

5. MAKE THE CARAMEL TOPPING: Line a large baking sheet with parchment paper. In a heavy saucepan, stir the sugar with the cream of tartar and water until sandy. Wash down the side of the pan with a moistened pastry brush to remove any sugar crystals. Bring the mixture to a boil over moderately high heat and cook without stirring until an amber caramel forms, about 5 minutes. Remove from the heat. Carefully swirl the pan to cool the caramel slightly, then pour it onto the baking sheet in a rough round. Using an offset spatula, spread the caramel into a 13-inch round and let stand until slightly cooled but still pliable, about 5 minutes.

6. Invert the caramel round over the cake and peel off the parchment paper. Gently press the caramel onto the cake before it hardens to help it conform. If the caramel hardens as you work, place the caramel-coated cake in the oven for 2 to 3 minutes, just to soften the caramel. When the caramel has hardened, serve the cake with the Lime-Yogurt Mousse. —*Lynn Moulton*

MAKE AHEAD The caramel-coated cake is best served the day it's assembled.

LIME-YOGURT MOUSSE

ACTIVE: 20 MIN; TOTAL: 1 HR 20 MIN

10 SERVINGS ●

- 1½ teaspoons unflavored gelatin
- 2 tablespoons cold water
- 6 tablespoons fresh lime juice
- ½ cup sugar
- 1 cup plain whole-milk Greek yogurt
- 1 cup heavy cream

1. In a small bowl, sprinkle the gelatin over the water and let stand until softened, about 5 minutes. In a small saucepan, combine the lime juice with 6 tablespoons of the sugar and simmer over moderate heat just until the sugar is dissolved, about 3 minutes. Remove the saucepan from the heat and stir in the softened gelatin until melted. Transfer the lime gelatin to a medium bowl and let cool slightly. Whisk in the Greek yogurt.

2. In another bowl, beat the heavy cream with the remaining 2 tablespoons of sugar until softly whipped. Fold the whipped cream into the lime-yogurt mixture and refrigerate until the mousse is chilled and set, at least 1 hour. —*L.M.*

Lemon-Ricotta Puddings

ACTIVE: 20 MIN; TOTAL: 1 HR 30 MIN

4 SERVINGS ● ◐

Besides being so much creamier and silkier than the store-bought version, homemade ricotta cheese is also surprisingly easy to prepare. San Francisco chef and cookbook author Daniel Patterson likes to use it in this very versatile lemon-accented pudding, which can be served as a starter with a cherry tomato and basil salad or at the end of a meal with honey or strawberries. Any leftover fresh ricotta cheese is excellent spread on toast.

RICOTTA

- ½ gallon whole milk
- 1 cup heavy cream
- 3 tablespoons plus 1 teaspoon white vinegar, plus more if needed

PUDDING

- ¾ cup heavy cream
- Finely grated zest of 1 lemon
- Salt and freshly ground pepper
- 2 large eggs, lightly beaten

1. MAKE THE RICOTTA: Line a strainer with a double layer of cheesecloth and set over a large bowl. In a large saucepan, heat the milk and cream over moderately high heat to 180°. Remove from the heat and slowly add the vinegar until you see the milk separate; add more vinegar as needed. Cover the saucepan and let stand for 2 minutes.

INGREDIENT

meyer lemons

Meyer lemons are slightly rounder than standard lemons, with smoother, often orange-tinted skin. They are fragrant, sweet and only mildly acidic, making them a great choice in recipes like the shortcakes on this page, where they complement the sweet berries.

2. Pour the contents of the saucepan into the strainer; shake vigorously to remove the water (a.k.a. whey). You should have about 2 cups of ricotta; let cool.

3. MAKE THE PUDDING: Preheat the oven to 325°. Butter the sides and bottoms of four 1-cup ramekins. In a large bowl, combine 1¾ cups of the ricotta with the heavy cream and grated lemon zest and whisk well, breaking up any large ricotta curds; season with salt and pepper. Whisk in the lightly beaten eggs.

4. Pour the pudding mixture into the prepared ramekins and set them in a larger baking dish. Place the dish in the oven and add enough hot water to reach halfway up the sides of the ramekins. Bake the puddings for about 55 minutes, or just until set. Let the puddings cool to room temperature or refrigerate until chilled. Serve the puddings in the ramekins.

—*Daniel Patterson*

MAKE AHEAD The puddings can be refrigerated overnight.

Lemon Pudding Cakes

ACTIVE: 20 MIN; TOTAL: 1 HR 15 MIN

6 SERVINGS ● ◐ ○ ○

These pillowy little cakes are adapted from *The Greyston Bakery Cookbook.* "When you overwhelm dry ingredients with wet ones, an amazing texture separation happens," author Sara Kate Gillingham-Ryan says. "These cakes are rich without being too heavy."

- ¾ cup sugar
- ⅓ cup all-purpose flour
- 3 large eggs, separated
- 2 tablespoons unsalted butter, at room temperature
- 1 cup skim milk
- 5 tablespoons fresh lemon juice
- 1 teaspoon finely grated lemon zest
- ¼ teaspoon salt
- Fresh raspberries or blackberries, for serving

1. Preheat the oven to 350°. Spray six 6-ounce ramekins with vegetable oil spray. In a medium bowl, whisk the sugar with the flour. In another bowl, whisk the egg yolks with the butter until well blended. Whisk in the skim milk, fresh lemon juice and grated lemon zest. Pour the lemon mixture into the sugar mixture and whisk until smoothly combined.

2. In a medium bowl, beat the egg whites with the salt until firm peaks form. Gently fold the egg whites into the lemon mixture.

3. Pour the batter into the prepared ramekins and transfer them to a small roasting pan. Place the pan in the oven and pour in enough hot water to reach halfway up the sides of the ramekins. Bake the pudding cakes for 35 minutes, or until they are puffy and golden on top. Using tongs, carefully transfer the ramekins to a rack to cool for 20 minutes. Serve the cakes in the ramekins or run a knife around the edge of each cake and unmold them onto plates. Serve the cakes warm or at room temperature with the fresh berries.

—*Sara Kate Gillingham-Ryan*

MAKE AHEAD The Lemon Pudding Cakes can be refrigerated for 2 days.

Strawberry Shortcakes with Meyer Lemon Cream

ACTIVE: 40 MIN; TOTAL: 1 HR 30 MIN

6 SERVINGS ○

Pastry chef Michelle Polzine of Range in San Francisco makes these strawberry shortcakes with sweet, intensely flavored Seascape strawberries and fragrant Meyer lemon cream. But the growing seasons for Seascapes and Meyer lemons overlap for only a few weeks. Happily, Polzine's recipe is also terrific with standard lemons and any variety of strawberry, as long as the berries are juicy and sweet.

BISCUITS

- 1½ cups all-purpose flour, plus more for dusting
- ¾ cup cake flour

LEMON PUDDING CAKE

STRAWBERRY SHORTCAKE WITH MEYER LEMON CREAM

3 tablespoons granulated sugar

2 teaspoons baking powder

½ teaspoon salt

6 tablespoons cold unsalted butter, cubed, plus 1½ tablespoons melted butter

1 cup heavy cream

1½ tablespoons turbinado sugar

LEMON CREAM

Finely grated zest of 1 lemon

¼ cup fresh lemon juice, preferably from Meyer lemons

2½ tablespoons sugar

1 large egg

1 large egg yolk

Pinch of salt

3 tablespoons unsalted butter

1 cup heavy cream

STRAWBERRIES

2 pints strawberries, hulled and quartered

2 tablespoons sugar

1. MAKE THE BISCUITS: Preheat the oven to 375°. In a bowl, whisk the flours, granulated sugar, baking powder and salt. Using a pastry blender or 2 knives, cut in the cold butter until it is the size of peas. Stir in the cream until a shaggy dough forms.

2. Turn the dough out onto a lightly floured surface and knead 2 or 3 times, just until it comes together. Roll into a 7-inch round about ¾ inch thick. Using a 2¾-inch or 3-inch biscuit cutter, cut 5 biscuits. Gently gather the scraps and reroll them; cut out 1 more round for a total of 6 biscuits.

3. Transfer the biscuits to a baking sheet and brush with the melted butter. Sprinkle the turbinado sugar on top and bake for 25 to 30 minutes, until the biscuits are golden. Let cool.

4. MEANWHILE, MAKE THE LEMON CREAM: Set a strainer over a bowl. In a saucepan, combine half the lemon zest with the lemon juice, sugar, egg, egg yolk,

salt and 1 tablespoon of the butter. Cook over moderate heat, whisking constantly, until thickened, about 5 minutes. Immediately strain into the bowl. Whisk in the remaining lemon zest and 2 tablespoons of butter. Press plastic wrap directly onto the curd and chill for about 15 minutes.

5. In a medium bowl, softly whip the cream. Fold the lemon curd into the whipped cream and refrigerate for at least 15 minutes.

6. PREPARE THE STRAWBERRIES: In a medium bowl, toss the strawberries with the sugar and let stand for 15 minutes.

7. Split the biscuits in half and arrange the bottom halves on plates. Mound the lemon cream on the biscuits, top with the strawberries and their juices, replace the tops and serve. —*Michelle Polzine*

MAKE AHEAD The biscuits can be stored overnight. Recrisp in a warm oven and let cool before serving. The lemon curd can be refrigerated for up to 2 days.

ALMOND AND CREAM SPICED BUN

CRÊPES WITH STRAWBERRIES AND MUSCAT-YOGURT SAUCE

Almond and Cream Spiced Buns

ACTIVE: 30 MIN; TOTAL: 3 HR

8 SERVINGS ●

- ¾ cup milk
- 1 envelope active dry yeast
- 3 cups all-purpose flour, plus more for dusting
- 5 tablespoons granulated sugar
- 3½ tablespoons unsalted butter, softened
- 1½ teaspoons ground cardamom
- ¾ teaspoon salt
- 2 large eggs
- 6 ounces almond paste (1 cup plus 1 tablespoon), broken up
- 1 cup heavy cream

Confectioners' sugar, for dusting

1. In a small saucepan, warm the milk over moderate heat, about 2 minutes. Stir in the yeast until dissolved. In the bowl of a standing mixer fitted with the dough hook, mix the 3 cups of flour with the granulated sugar. With the mixer at medium speed, pour in the warm milk and beat until incorporated. Add the butter, cardamom, salt and 1 of the eggs. Mix until a smooth dough forms, about 8 minutes.

2. Cover a large baking sheet with parchment paper and sprinkle with flour. Roll the dough into 8 balls. Place the dough on the prepared baking sheet and wrap the sheet with plastic wrap. Set aside in a warm place until the balls have doubled in size, about 2 hours.

3. Preheat the oven to 375°. Bake the buns for about 10 minutes, rotating the pan halfway through, until golden brown. Meanwhile, in a small bowl, whisk the remaining egg with 2 tablespoons of water. Immediately brush the hot buns with the egg wash, then transfer them to a rack to cool, about 30 minutes.

4. In a bowl, using an electric mixer, beat the almond paste with 3½ tablespoons of water until creamy. In another bowl, beat the heavy cream until stiff.

5. Using a small paring knife, cut a deep 1¾-inch round plug out of the top of each bun, making sure not to cut through the bottom; reserve the plugs. Fill the buns with the almond paste and top with some whipped cream. Replace the plugs. Dust with confectioners' sugar and serve.
—*Carina Ahlin*

Crêpes with Strawberries and Muscat-Yogurt Sauce

TOTAL: 1 HR

4 SERVINGS ●●

These crêpes are topped by an orangey sauce sweetened with dessert wine.

- ½ cup all-purpose flour
- ½ teaspoon salt
- ¾ cup skim milk
- 1 large egg

Vegetable oil

- 1 cup plain low-fat yogurt
- 2 tablespoons honey
- 1 tablespoon Muscat dessert wine
- ¼ teaspoon grated orange zest
- 24 strawberries, sliced

Confectioners' sugar, for dusting

1. In a small bowl, whisk the flour with the salt. Add the milk, egg and 1 tablespoon of oil and whisk until smooth. Cover and let rest for 20 minutes. In another small bowl, whisk the yogurt, honey, Muscat and zest.
2. Preheat the oven to 350°. Heat an 8-inch nonstick skillet. Rub the pan with an oiled paper towel. Add about 3 tablespoons of the crêpe batter, swirling the pan to coat evenly; pour off any excess. Cook the crêpe over moderate heat until the bottom is brown in spots and the edge is crisp, about 2 minutes. Flip the crêpe and cook for 1 minute longer. Transfer to a baking sheet; repeat to make 7 more crêpes.
3. Fold the crêpes into quarters and bake until hot, 4 minutes. Place 2 crêpes on each plate. Top with the yogurt sauce and garnish with the strawberries. Dust with confectioners' sugar and serve immediately.
—*Nichole Birdsall*

brunch

Poached Eggs with Chicken Hash

TOTAL: 30 MIN
4 SERVINGS ●

Napa Valley chef Richard Reddington prepares this hash with a chicken jus made from chicken bones, vegetables, white wine and chicken stock, serving slices of bacon alongside. That appealing combination is simplified here into a hash spiked with bits of chopped, meaty bacon.

Salt

- 1 large baking potato (¾ pound), peeled and cut into ½-inch dice
- 1 tablespoon extra-virgin olive oil
- ¾ pound skinless, boneless chicken thighs, cut into ½-inch dice

Freshly ground pepper

- 2 slices of meaty bacon (2 ounces), cut into ¼-inch dice
- 1 small onion, very finely chopped
- 2 light green celery ribs, finely chopped
- 4 large eggs

Hot sauce, for serving

1. Bring a small saucepan of water to a boil. Add a pinch of salt and the diced potato and boil over high heat until just tender, about 5 minutes; drain.
2. In a large skillet, heat the olive oil until shimmering. Season the chicken with salt and pepper and add it to the skillet along with the diced bacon. Cook over high heat, stirring occasionally, until the chicken is browned all over, about 5 minutes. Add the onion and celery and cook until they are softened, about 3 minutes. Add the cooked diced potato, season with salt and pepper and cook over moderately high heat, pressing gently on the chicken hash with a spatula and turning it once, until browned, about 10 minutes; keep warm.

3. Meanwhile, bring a skillet of water to a boil. Crack an egg into a small bowl and carefully slide it into the simmering water. Repeat with the remaining 3 eggs. Simmer over moderately low heat until the whites are set and the yolks are still runny, about 4 minutes.
4. Transfer the chicken hash to plates. Using a slotted spoon, gently transfer a poached egg to each plate and serve, passing hot sauce on the side.
—*Richard Reddington*

Spicy Indian-Style Scrambled Eggs

TOTAL: 25 MIN
2 SERVINGS ●●●

- 4 large eggs
- ¼ teaspoon ground cumin

Pinch of turmeric

Kosher salt

- 1 tablespoon vegetable oil
- 1 small red onion, cut into ¼-inch dice
- 1 small hot red or green chile, seeded and very finely chopped
- 1 garlic clove, minced
- 1½ teaspoons very finely chopped fresh ginger
- 1 tomato—halved, seeded and cut into ¼-inch dice

Pinch of sugar

- 2 teaspoons chopped cilantro

Roti or toast, for serving

In a medium bowl, whisk the eggs with the cumin, turmeric and ½ teaspoon of salt. In a medium nonstick skillet, heat the vegetable oil. Add the onion, chile, garlic and ginger and cook over high heat until the onion just begins to brown, about 3 minutes. Add the tomato, season with salt and the sugar and cook for 1 minute. Reduce the heat to moderately low and pour in the eggs. Cook, stirring constantly, until the eggs are just set, about 1 minute. Fold in the cilantro and serve with roti or toast.
—*Sarah Woodward*

Asparagus with Poached Eggs and Citrus-Ginger Vinaigrette

TOTAL: 30 MIN
4 SERVINGS ● ●

Pino Maffeo, executive chef and owner of Boston Public in Boston, makes this dish with green and white asparagus topped by a sweet-spicy vinaigrette flavored with *kalamansi* (an Asian citrus that's similar to a mandarin orange) and *sudachi* (a small green citrus used in Japan that's similar to lemon and lime). Here, the F&W kitchen pares the dish down by omitting the white asparagus and replacing the exotic citrus with fresh orange and lime juices.

- 1 tablespoon fresh orange juice
- 1 tablespoon fresh lime juice
- 1 tablespoon pickled ginger juice (see Note)
- 1 teaspoon soy sauce
- 2 teaspoons wasabi powder mixed with 2 teaspoons water
- 1 small shallot, minced
- 1 tablespoon extra-virgin olive oil
- Salt
- 1 cup *panko* (Japanese bread crumbs)
- 1 pound medium asparagus, trimmed
- 2 large egg yolks, lightly beaten
- 4 large eggs, at room temperature
- Canola oil, for frying
- Radish sprouts, for garnish

1. In a small bowl, whisk the fresh orange and lime juices with the pickled ginger juice, soy sauce, wasabi-water mixture and minced shallot until combined. Drizzle in the olive oil, whisking until emulsified. Season the citrus-ginger vinaigrette with salt. Put the *panko* in a large resealable plastic bag and crush the bread crumbs finely with a rolling pin.

2. Bring a wide, deep skillet of salted water to a boil. Add the asparagus and cook until crisp-tender, 3 to 4 minutes. Using tongs, transfer half of the asparagus to a large plate and the remaining asparagus to a bowl. Add the egg yolks to the bowl and toss to coat the asparagus. Transfer the coated asparagus to the bag and shake to coat with the *panko*.

3. Return the asparagus water to a simmer. Carefully crack each whole egg into a small bowl and slip each one into the water. Poach over moderate heat for 4 minutes. Using a slotted spoon, carefully transfer the poached eggs to another plate.

4. Heat ¼ inch of oil in a medium skillet. Add the breaded asparagus and fry over high heat until they are golden and crisp, about 4 minutes. Transfer the fried asparagus to a paper towel–lined plate to drain.

5. Spoon the citrus-ginger vinaigrette onto 4 plates and add the blanched and fried asparagus. Top with the poached eggs, garnish with radish sprouts and serve right away. —*Pino Maffeo*

NOTE Pickled ginger juice is the liquid found in a jar of pickled ginger. It's available at most supermarkets.

Smoked Salmon Panini

TOTAL: 15 MIN
4 SERVINGS

- 8 slices of brioche
- Dijon mustard, for spreading
- 8 thin slices of Gruyère cheese
- ½ pound thinly sliced smoked salmon
- Finely grated zest of 1 lemon
- Salt and freshly ground black pepper

Heat a panini press. Spread 4 of the brioche slices with Dijon mustard and top each one with 1 slice of Gruyère; divide all of the smoked salmon and the grated lemon zest among the 4 slices of brioche. Season lightly with salt and black pepper and cover with the remaining slices of Gruyère. Close the sandwiches and grill in the panini press for 2 to 3 minutes, until the bread is toasted and the cheese is melted. Cut the panini in half and serve. —*Richard Reddington*

SMOKED SALMON PANINI

BACON, CHEESE AND EGG SANDWICHES WITH HOLLANDAISE

Bacon, Cheese and Egg Sandwiches with Hollandaise

TOTAL: 1 HR

4 SERVINGS ●

- 2 tablespoons extra-virgin olive oil
- 1 medium onion, finely chopped

Four ¼-inch-thick slices of Canadian bacon (3 ounces), cut into ¼-inch dice

- ½ cup sliced pitted kalamata olives
- 2 pickled jalapeños, seeded and diced
- 1 tomato, diced
- 6 large eggs, lightly beaten
- 1 cup shredded Gruyère cheese (3½ ounces)

Salt and freshly ground pepper

- 4 split English muffins, toasted

Classic Hollandaise Sauce (recipe follows)

- 1 tablespoon snipped chives

1. In a large nonstick skillet, heat the olive oil. Add the onion and cook over high heat until softened, about 4 minutes. Add the bacon and cook, stirring, until very lightly browned, about 2 minutes. Add the olives, jalapeños and tomato and cook, stirring, for 1 minute. Add the eggs and scramble, scraping down the side with a rubber spatula, until just set, about 2 minutes. Add the Gruyère and stir just until melted. Season lightly with salt and pepper.

2. Arrange the toasted English muffins on plates. Spoon the scrambled eggs on the muffins and top with the Classic Hollandaise Sauce. Garnish with the chives and serve right away. —*Greg Lindgren*

CLASSIC HOLLANDAISE SAUCE

TOTAL: 10 MIN

MAKES ABOUT 1 CUP ●

- 2 large egg yolks
- 1 tablespoon cold water

Pinch of salt

- 1 stick unsalted butter, melted
- 1 tablespoon fresh lemon juice

Dash of hot sauce

Dash of Worcestershire sauce

In a medium heatproof bowl set over (but not in) a large saucepan filled with 2 inches of gently simmering water, whisk the egg yolks with the cold water and salt until the mixture is just warm to the touch. Slowly drizzle half of the melted butter into the egg mixture in a thin stream, whisking constantly until the butter is thoroughly incorporated. Continue whisking in the melted butter until the sauce is thick and smoothly emulsified. Whisk in the fresh lemon juice, hot sauce and Worcestershire sauce and serve warm. —*G.L.*

MAKE AHEAD The hollandaise sauce can be kept warm over the hot water bath off the heat for 30 minutes. Whisk occasionally and reheat gently over hot water.

● HEALTHY ● MAKE AHEAD ○ VEGETARIAN ● STAFF FAVORITE

Chef Laurent Tourondel celebrates the Fourth of July by preparing a globally accented American meal.

summer

starters & drinks 206
main courses 220
side dishes 258
desserts & brunch 270

starters & drinks

starters

Creamy Sun-Dried Tomato Soup with Cheese Panini

 **TOTAL: 35 MIN**
4 SERVINGS

This recipe riffs on the classic American combination of cream of tomato soup alongside grilled cheese sandwiches. In addition to fresh tomato, F&W's Grace Parisi adds plump, oil-packed sun-dried tomatoes, which contribute loads of flavor and give the soup a thick, luscious texture.

- 1 tablespoon unsalted butter
- 1 tablespoon extra-virgin olive oil
- 1 small onion, chopped
- 1 garlic clove, sliced
- ½ cup oil-packed sun-dried tomatoes, drained and coarsely chopped
- 1 tomato, diced
- 3 cups chicken stock or low-sodium broth
- 2 thyme sprigs
- Salt and freshly ground pepper
- ¼ cup heavy cream
- 4 ciabatta rolls, split
- ½ pound Italian Fontina cheese, sliced

1. In a large saucepan, melt the butter in the olive oil. Add the onion and garlic and cook over moderately high heat, stirring until softened, about 4 minutes. Add the sun-dried tomatoes, diced tomato, stock and thyme. Season with salt and pepper; bring to a boil. Cover and simmer over low heat until the vegetables are very soft, about 20 minutes. Discard the thyme.

2. Preheat a panini press. Transfer the soup to a blender, add the cream and puree until smooth. Return the soup to the saucepan and season with salt and pepper. Keep the sun-dried tomato soup warm over moderate heat.

3. Fill the ciabatta rolls with the sliced cheese and press them until the bread is crispy and the cheese is melted. Serve the tomato soup with the cheese panini on the side. —*Grace Parisi*

WINE Cherry-inflected, earthy Sangiovese.

Pappa al Pomodoro

ACTIVE: 30 MIN; TOTAL: 1 HR
6 SERVINGS ●●

For this classic Tuscan tomato-bread soup, Joe Sponzo (rock star Sting's private chef) says, "You want a dense, crusty bread, then let it get stale for two days."

- 5 pounds tomatoes
- ½ cup extra-virgin olive oil, plus more for drizzling
- 1 large onion, halved lengthwise and thinly sliced
- 4 garlic cloves, thinly sliced
- Pinch of crushed red pepper
- Salt
- ½ pound stale, crustless 1-inch Italian bread cubes (4 cups)
- 1 cup basil leaves, torn
- Ricotta cheese, for serving

1. Bring a large pot of water to a boil. Fill a large bowl with ice water. Cut a slit in the base of each tomato. Add the tomatoes to the boiling water and blanch just until the skins start to split, about 10 seconds. Transfer the blanched tomatoes to the ice water to cool.

2. Peel and halve the tomatoes crosswise. Working over a mesh strainer set over a large bowl, pry out the seeds and press the tomato juice and pulp through the strainer. Discard the seeds and reserve the juice. Coarsely chop the tomatoes.

3. Wipe out the pot and heat the ½ cup of olive oil. Add the onion and cook over moderate heat, stirring, until softened, about 6 minutes. Add the garlic and cook for

1 minute. Add the tomatoes and crushed red pepper and season with salt. Cover partially and simmer over moderately high heat until the tomatoes have cooked down, about 30 minutes.

4. Add the bread and the reserved tomato juice to the soup and cook, mashing the bread until fully incorporated, and season with salt. Stir in the basil leaves. Spoon the soup into shallow bowls, drizzle lightly with olive oil, top with a dollop of ricotta and serve right away. —*Joe Sponzo*

MAKE AHEAD The soup can be prepared through Step 3 and refrigerated overnight. Reheat before proceeding.

WINE Cherry-inflected, earthy Sangiovese.

E.J.'s Vegetable Noodle Soup

ACTIVE: 25 MIN; TOTAL: 50 MIN
4 SERVINGS ●

- 2 tablespoons vegetable oil
- 2 small onions, cut into ¼-inch dice
- 3 celery ribs, cut into ¼-inch dice
- 4 carrots, thinly sliced
- 1 garlic clove, minced
- ¾ teaspoon chopped thyme
- 6 cups low-sodium chicken broth
- 1 cup water
- 1 bay leaf
- Kosher salt and freshly ground pepper
- ⅔ cup alphabet pasta
- ½ cup frozen peas, thawed
- 2 tablespoons snipped chives

1. Heat the vegetable oil in a large saucepan. Add the onions, celery and carrots and cook over moderate heat, stirring, for 8 minutes. Add the garlic and thyme and cook for 1 minute. Add the chicken broth, water and bay leaf; simmer until the vegetables are tender, about 20 minutes. Season with salt and pepper.

2. Stir in the pasta and simmer until tender, 5 minutes. Remove from the heat and stir in the peas and chives. Cover and let stand for 5 minutes. Discard the bay leaf. Ladle the soup into bowls and serve.
—*Emeril Lagasse*

Vegetable Soup with Fennel, Herbs and Parmesan Broth

ACTIVE: 30 MIN; TOTAL: 1 HR
4 SERVINGS ● ● ○

Cookbook author Viana La Place simmers Parmigiano-Reggiano rinds in the broth to give this soup a rich, cheesy flavor.

- 2 tablespoons extra-virgin olive oil
- 4 garlic cloves, minced
- 3 carrots, halved lengthwise and thinly sliced crosswise
- 2 celery ribs, halved lengthwise and thinly sliced crosswise
- 2 leeks, white parts only, halved lengthwise and thinly sliced crosswise
- 1 fennel bulb—halved, cored and thinly sliced
- 1 medium tomato, diced (½ inch)
- 2 bay leaves, preferably fresh
- 6 cups water
- One 3-inch square Parmigiano-Reggiano rind
- 1 tablespoon chopped parsley
- 1 tablespoon chopped basil
- Salt and freshly ground pepper
- ¼ cup freshly grated Parmigiano-Reggiano cheese

1. Heat the olive oil in a large soup pot. Add the garlic and cook over moderate heat, stirring, until fragrant, about 2 minutes. Add the carrots, celery, leeks and fennel and cook, stirring, until the vegetables begin to soften, about 5 minutes. Add the tomato and bay leaves and cook until the vegetables are tender, about 5 minutes. Add the water and the cheese rind and bring to a simmer. Cover partially and cook over moderately low heat until very tender, about 30 minutes.

2. Discard the cheese rind and bay leaves. Stir in the parsley and basil and season the soup with salt and pepper. Ladle into bowls, sprinkle with the grated cheese and serve. —*Viana La Place*

WINE Fresh, minerally Vermentino.

Sunchoke and Cauliflower Soup

ACTIVE: 40 MIN; TOTAL: 1 HR 10 MIN
4 SERVINGS ●

- 2 tablespoons unsalted butter, plus 2 teaspoons softened butter
- 1 small celery rib, minced
- ½ small onion, minced
- 2 cups chicken stock or broth
- ¾ cup whole milk
- 1 pound cauliflower, cut into 1-inch florets
- 6 ounces sunchokes, peeled and cut into 1-inch pieces
- 1 thyme sprig
- 1 small garlic clove, minced
- Salt
- Four ¼-inch-thick baguette slices
- 1 tablespoon freshly grated Parmigiano-Reggiano cheese
- Freshly ground pepper
- ½ cup sunflower sprouts

1. In a large saucepan, melt the 2 tablespoons of butter. Add the celery and onion and cook over low heat until softened, about 6 minutes. Add the stock and milk and bring to a simmer over high heat. Add the cauliflower, sunchokes and thyme and bring to a boil. Simmer over low heat until the sunchokes are very tender, about 30 minutes; discard the thyme sprig. Meanwhile, preheat the oven to 350°.

2. In a small bowl, mix the 2 teaspoons of softened butter with the garlic and season with salt. Spread the garlic butter on the baguette slices and place on a baking sheet. Sprinkle with the cheese and bake for about 8 minutes, until crisp.

3. Working in batches, puree the soup in a blender until smooth. Return it to the saucepan; season with salt and pepper. Ladle into bowls and top with the sunflower sprouts. Serve with the cheese toasts.
—*Ian Schnoebelen*

MAKE AHEAD The soup can be refrigerated overnight. Reheat gently.

WINE Ripe, luxurious Chardonnay.

Summertime Ribollita

 TOTAL: 40 MIN
4 SERVINGS ● ● ○

In her variation on a classic *ribollita*—the thick, hearty Italian soup typically made with winter vegetables, beans, bread and cheese—F&W's Grace Parisi uses summer vegetables like tomatoes, squash and green beans. Instead of putting the bread in the soup, she serves it alongside, and before serving, she drizzles the vegetable soup with a quick, smoky and delicious paprika-fennel oil.

¼ cup plus 2 tablespoons
   extra-virgin olive oil
1 pound yellow squash, halved
   lengthwise and sliced
   ½ inch thick
1 medium onion, thinly sliced
2 large garlic cloves, thinly sliced
1½ teaspoons tomato paste
½ cup water
1½ pounds tomatoes, cored and
   coarsely chopped
½ pound green beans or yellow
   wax beans, cut into
   1-inch pieces
Salt and freshly ground pepper
½ pound Swiss chard, stems
   discarded, leaves coarsely
   chopped
¼ teaspoon pimentón de la Vera
   (smoked Spanish paprika)

TECHNIQUE

giving soup a flavor boost

To garnish soups with a sizzling spice oil (as for the *ribollita* above), heat 2 tablespoons of oil with ½ teaspoon of spices until sizzling. Use seasonings that complement your recipe.

¼ teaspoon fennel seeds, coarsely
   chopped
Toasted Italian bread, for serving

1. In a medium enameled cast-iron casserole or Dutch oven, heat ¼ cup of the olive oil. Add the yellow squash, onion and garlic and cook over moderately high heat, stirring frequently, until the vegetables are lightly browned, about 5 minutes. Add the tomato paste, water, chopped tomatoes and green beans and season with salt and pepper. Cover and cook over moderately low heat, stirring occasionally, until the vegetables are softened, approximately 12 minutes. Add the Swiss chard, cover and cook for 5 minutes, until the chard is completely wilted.
2. In a small skillet, heat the remaining 2 tablespoons of olive oil with the paprika and fennel seeds over moderate heat until sizzling, about 2 minutes. Ladle the *ribollita* into shallow bowls, drizzle with the paprika-fennel oil and serve at once with the toasted Italian bread. —*Grace Parisi*
MAKE AHEAD The vegetable soup can be made through Step 1 up to 1 day ahead and refrigerated overnight. Reheat the soup and make the paprika-fennel oil just before serving.
WINE Fruity, soft Chenin Blanc.

Watermelon Gazpacho

ACTIVE: 40 MIN; TOTAL: 1 HR 40 MIN
12 SERVINGS ● ● ○

This cool, sweet-tangy twist on the Spanish staple was inspired by an abundance of watermelons.

6½ pounds tomatoes, cored
2 pounds seedless watermelon,
   rind removed—2 cups coarsely
   chopped, 2 cups cut into
   ½-inch dice
2 pounds cucumbers, peeled
   and seeded—2 cups coarsely
   chopped, 2 cups cut into
   ½-inch dice
¼ cup sherry vinegar

3 tablespoons extra-virgin olive oil
Salt and freshly ground
   black pepper
6 scallions, thinly sliced
2 jalapeños, seeded and very
   finely chopped
½ cup chopped cilantro
¼ cup fresh lime juice
½ cup very finely chopped chives,
   for garnish

1. Bring a large pot of water to a boil. Add the tomatoes and blanch just until the skins are loosened, about 30 seconds. Use a slotted spoon to transfer the blanched tomatoes to a large rimmed baking sheet and let cool.
2. Peel the tomatoes and halve them crosswise. Working over a coarse sieve set over a large bowl, squeeze the tomato halves to release the seeds and juice. Press on the seeds; you should have about 2 cups of tomato juice in the bowl. Coarsely chop enough of the tomatoes to make 4 cups. Cut the remaining tomatoes into ½-inch dice. Discard the seeds.
3. In a food processor, puree the coarsely chopped tomatoes with the reserved tomato juice as well as the 2 cups each of chopped watermelon and cucumber until very smooth. Transfer the soup to a large bowl. Stir in the diced tomato, watermelon and cucumber, the vinegar and 1 tablespoon of the olive oil and season with salt and pepper. Refrigerate until the soup is chilled, at least 1 hour.
4. In a small bowl, toss the sliced scallions with the chopped jalapeños, cilantro and lime juice, and season with salt and black pepper. Ladle the Watermelon Gazpacho into bowls, drizzle each serving with some of the remaining 2 tablespoons of olive oil and sprinkle the chopped chives on top. Serve the gazpacho immediately, passing the scallion relish at the table.
—*Gabriel Frasca and Amanda Lydon*
MAKE AHEAD The Watermelon Gazpacho can be refrigerated overnight.

WATERMELON GAZPACHO

CORN AND BACON SOUP WITH JALAPEÑO CREMA

POTATO PANCAKES WITH SMOKED SALMON AND CAVIAR

Corn and Bacon Soup with Jalapeño Crema

ACTIVE: 45 MIN; TOTAL: 1 HR 30 MIN
6 SERVINGS ●

Star chef Wolfgang Puck uses both creamy grated corn and sautéed kernels to make this satisfying soup, which he serves with a chile-spiked cream.

- 10 medium ears of corn, shucked
- 3 tablespoons extra-virgin olive oil
- 2 ounces lean bacon, finely diced (½ cup)
- 1 celery rib, finely diced
- ½ cup very finely chopped onion
- ½ cup finely diced yellow bell pepper
- 3 cups whole milk
- 1½ cups heavy cream
- Kosher salt
- Pinch of cayenne pepper
- ¼ cup sour cream
- 1 jalapeño, seeded and very finely chopped
- 2 tablespoons chopped cilantro, plus cilantro leaves for garnish
- ½ teaspoon fresh lemon juice
- Freshly ground white pepper

1. Set a box grater in a wide, shallow bowl and coarsely grate 6 ears of corn; you should have 2 cups of grated corn. Cut the kernels from the remaining 4 ears; you should have 2 cups of kernels.

2. In a large saucepan, heat 1 tablespoon of the olive oil. Add the bacon, celery, onion and yellow pepper, cover and cook over low heat, stirring a few times, until softened, about 10 minutes. Add the grated corn, the milk and 1 cup of the heavy cream and bring to a boil. Reduce the heat to moderately low and simmer, stirring often, until the soup is thickened, about 20 minutes. Season with salt and the cayenne pepper and keep warm.

3. Meanwhile, in a large skillet, heat the remaining 2 tablespoons of olive oil until shimmering. Add the corn kernels to the skillet and cook over moderately high heat, stirring a few times, until they are lightly browned, about 7 minutes. Season with salt. Stir the cooked corn kernels into the soup and keep warm.

4. In a blender, whip the remaining ½ cup of cream to soft peaks, about 20 seconds. Add the sour cream, jalapeño, chopped cilantro and lemon juice and blend until thick. Season with salt and white pepper.

5. Ladle the soup into bowls, top with spoonfuls of the jalapeño *crema* and garnish with cilantro leaves; serve at once.
—*Wolfgang Puck*

MAKE AHEAD The corn soup can be refrigerated overnight and reheated gently. The jalapeño *crema* can be refrigerated for up to 4 hours.

WINE Ripe, luxurious Chardonnay.

Summer Melon Soup with Crab

TOTAL: 20 MIN
4 SERVINGS ● ●

- 1 medium shallot, very finely chopped
- 2 tablespoons snipped chives
- 3½ tablespoons fresh lemon juice
- 2 tablespoons extra-virgin olive oil
- 1 pound jumbo lump crabmeat

Salt and freshly ground white pepper
- 2 tablespoons water
- 2 tablespoons sugar
- 4 cups cubed cantaloupe or muskmelon

1. In a medium bowl, toss the shallot and chives with 2 tablespoons of the lemon juice. Whisk in the olive oil and fold in the crabmeat. Season the crab salad with salt and white pepper.

2. In a small saucepan, boil the water with the sugar. Transfer the syrup to a blender and let cool. Add the melon and the remaining lemon juice to the cooled syrup, season lightly with salt and puree the melon soup until very smooth.

3. Mound the crab in the center of 4 shallow bowls. Pour the soup around the crab and serve right away. —*David Myers*
MAKE AHEAD The melon soup can be refrigerated overnight.

Smoked Bluefish Pâté

TOTAL: 15 MIN
12 SERVINGS ● ●

- 8 ounces cream cheese, softened
- 1 tablespoon Worcestershire sauce
- 1 tablespoon fresh lemon juice
- 1 tablespoon chopped parsley
- ½ medium red onion, minced

4 to 6 dashes of hot sauce
- ¼ cup minced chives
- ½ pound skinless, boneless smoked bluefish, flaked

Toasts or crackers, for serving

In a bowl, blend the cream cheese with the Worcestershire sauce, lemon juice, parsley, onion, hot sauce and half of the chives. Fold the smoked bluefish into the cream cheese mixture. Sprinkle the bluefish pâté with the remaining chives and serve with the toasts or crackers.
—*Gabriel Frasca and Amanda Lydon*
MAKE AHEAD The pâté can be refrigerated for up to 3 days.

Goat Cheese–Garlic Toasts

TOTAL: 25 MIN
6 SERVINGS ●

Six ½-inch-thick diagonal baguette slices
Extra-virgin olive oil, for brushing
- ½ cup fresh goat cheese, softened (3½ ounces)
- 1 tablespoon chopped parsley
- 1 tablespoon minced chives
- 1 teaspoon chopped thyme

Salt and freshly ground pepper
- 1 garlic clove, halved

1. Preheat the oven to 350° or light a grill. Brush the bread with olive oil and bake for 7 minutes, until crisp. Alternatively, grill the bread over moderately high heat for about 30 seconds per side, until browned.

2. Meanwhile, in a bowl, blend the goat cheese with the parsley, chives and thyme; season with salt and pepper.

3. Rub the toasts with the garlic. Spread the goat cheese on top and serve warm or at room temperature. —*Wolfgang Puck*

Potato Pancakes with Smoked Salmon, Caviar and Dill Cream

TOTAL: 35 MIN
6 SERVINGS ●

Best known for putting smoked salmon, caviar and dill-flecked crème fraîche on his designer pizzas, Wolfgang Puck also loves this trio on his crispy potato pancakes. All three are wonderfully decadent together; still, you can leave out the smoked salmon or the caviar if you like.

- ½ cup crème fraîche or sour cream
- 1 teaspoon chopped dill
- 1 teaspoon fresh lemon juice

Kosher salt and freshly ground black pepper
- 1 tablespoon snipped chives
- 2 medium baking potatoes (1 pound), peeled
- 1 small onion
- 1 large egg, lightly beaten
- 2 tablespoons all-purpose flour
- ½ teaspoon baking powder
- ½ cup vegetable oil
- ½ pound thinly sliced smoked salmon
- 2 ounces caviar

1. In a small bowl, fold together the crème fraîche, dill and lemon juice. Season the cream with salt and black pepper and sprinkle with the chives. Refrigerate until ready to serve.

2. In a food processor or on a box grater, coarsely shred the potatoes and the onion. Transfer to a large, clean kitchen towel and squeeze dry.

3. In a medium bowl, mix the shredded potatoes and onion with the egg, flour, baking powder, 1 teaspoon of salt and ¼ teaspoon of black pepper.

4. In a large nonstick skillet or on a griddle, heat the vegetable oil until shimmering. Drop 2 tablespoons of the potato mixture into the skillet and flatten with the back of a spoon to make a 3-inch round. Make about 5 more pancakes and cook over moderately high heat until the pancakes are golden on the bottom, about 4 minutes. Flip the pancakes and cook until golden on the second side, about 2 minutes longer. Transfer to paper towels to drain. Repeat with the remaining potato mixture; you should have 12 pancakes.

5. Arrange the potato pancakes on a platter. Serve them at once, topped with the dill cream, smoked salmon and caviar.
—*Wolfgang Puck*
WINE Dry, light Champagne.

Grilled Shrimp Summer Rolls

TOTAL: 45 MIN
4 SERVINGS ●

- 2 ounces dried cellophane noodles
- 16 large shrimp (¾ pound), shelled and deveined

Salt and freshly ground pepper

- ½ cup low-sodium soy sauce
- ½ cup rice vinegar
- 2 tablespoons honey
- 2 garlic cloves, minced
- 1 tablespoon minced fresh ginger
- 1 teaspoon sesame seeds (optional)
- 1 teaspoon minced scallion (optional)
- 2 teaspoons Asian sesame oil

Eight 8½-inch rice paper wrappers

- 4 romaine lettuce leaves, torn
- 32 small mint leaves
- 32 small cilantro leaves
- 1 carrot, peeled and julienned

1. In a medium bowl, cover the cellophane noodles with hot water and let stand until soft, 30 minutes. Drain and cover with a damp paper towel until ready to use.

2. Light a grill. Season the shrimp with salt and pepper and grill over moderately high heat until they're just cooked through, about 2 minutes per side. Let cool, then cut each shrimp in half lengthwise.

3. Meanwhile, in a medium bowl, whisk the soy sauce with the rice vinegar, honey, garlic, ginger, sesame seeds and scallion, if using, and sesame oil.

TECHNIQUE

cutting corn off the cob

To cut kernels from an ear of corn without scattering them across the kitchen, snap the ear in half. Hold each half upright in a wide bowl and slice along the cob to release the kernels.

4. Soak 1 wrapper in hot water until pliable. Lay the wrapper on a cutting board and blot dry. Arrange 2 pieces of romaine on the bottom third of the wrapper. Top with some of the cellophane noodles, shrimp, mint, cilantro and carrot. Roll up the wrapper, tucking in the ends as you roll. Cover with a damp paper towel. Repeat with the remaining wrappers and fillings. Cut each roll in half and serve with the dipping sauce.
—*Emeril Lagasse*

WINE Tart, citrusy Riesling.

Corn and Shiitake Fritters

TOTAL: 40 MIN
4 SERVINGS ●●○

Sweet corn kernels take two different forms in these crispy cakes. Half the corn is pureed into the batter; the other half is sautéed with shiitake mushrooms and onion to give the fritters crunch.

- 3 ears of corn, shucked
- 1 large egg
- ¼ cup milk
- ½ cup plus 1 tablespoon vegetable oil
- 3 large shiitake mushrooms (2 ounces), stems discarded and caps cut into ½-inch dice
- ¼ cup diced sweet onion
- ¾ cup all-purpose flour
- 1 teaspoon baking powder
- 1½ teaspoons kosher salt
- ½ teaspoon freshly ground pepper

1. Cut the corn kernels from the cobs and transfer half of them to a blender. Using the dull side of a knife, scrape the pulp from the cobs into the blender. Add the egg and milk; puree until smooth.

2. In a very large nonstick skillet, heat 1 tablespoon of the oil. Add the shiitake and onion and cook over high heat, stirring occasionally, until lightly browned, about 5 minutes. Add the remaining corn and cook, stirring, for 1 minute. Scrape the mixture onto a plate and freeze just until no longer hot, about 5 minutes.

3. In a bowl, whisk the flour with the baking powder, salt and pepper. Stir in the puree, then fold in the shiitake mixture.

4. Wipe out the skillet and add the remaining ½ cup of oil. When it is hot, add 8 level ¼-cup mounds of batter to the skillet and spread them to a ½-inch thickness. Fry over moderately high heat, turning once, until the fritters are golden and crusty, about 4 minutes. Drain on paper towels and serve warm. —*Grace Parisi*

WINE Fruity, soft Chenin Blanc.

Two-Corn Crêpes

TOTAL: 1 HR 10 MIN
4 SERVINGS ○

These double-corn crêpes are made with masa harina (a corn-based flour) and filled with corn-flecked mashed potatoes, then broiled until crisp on top.

CRÊPES

- 2 large eggs
- 1¼ cups milk
- ¼ cup all-purpose flour
- ⅓ cup instant masa harina (see Note)
- ½ teaspoon sugar
- ½ teaspoon salt

Vegetable oil

FILLING

- 1 medium Yukon Gold potato (8 ounces), peeled and diced

Salt

- ½ cup heavy cream, plus more for brushing
- 1 tablespoon unsalted butter
- 2 tablespoons minced onion
- 1 jalapeño, seeded and minced
- 2 cups fresh corn kernels
- 2 tablespoons minced scallions

Freshly ground pepper

Freshly grated Parmigiano-Reggiano cheese, for serving

1. MAKE THE CRÊPES: In a bowl, whisk the eggs. Whisk in the milk, flour, masa harina, sugar and salt until blended. Let the batter stand for 30 minutes.

2. MEANWHILE, MAKE THE FILLING: In a saucepan, cover the potato with water, add a pinch of salt and bring to a boil. Simmer over moderately high heat until the potato is tender, about 8 minutes. Drain in a colander and return to the saucepan. Shake the pan over high heat to dry the potato, about 20 seconds; transfer the potato to a microwave-safe bowl and mash until it is slightly chunky. Stir in the ½ cup of heavy cream.

3. In a medium skillet, melt the butter. Add the onion and jalapeño and cook over moderate heat until softened, about 5 minutes. Add the corn, cover and cook, stirring a few times, until the corn is tender, about 6 minutes. Stir in the scallions. Stir the corn mixture into the mashed potatoes and season with salt and pepper.

4. Heat an 8-inch nonstick skillet and rub it with vegetable oil. When the pan is hot, add 2 tablespoons of the crêpe batter, swirl to coat the bottom and cook over moderately high heat until lightly browned on the bottom, about 1½ minutes. Carefully turn the crêpe over and continue cooking until brown in spots, about 1 minute longer. Transfer the finished crêpe to a baking sheet and repeat with the remaining batter to make 7 more crêpes.

5. Preheat the broiler. Reheat the potato-corn filling in a microwave oven for 45 seconds. Spoon 2 tablespoons of the filling onto one side of each crêpe and fold the crêpes in half. Transfer the filled crêpes to a baking sheet and brush the tops with cream. Broil until browned on top, about 10 seconds. Place the corn crêpes on plates, sprinkle with the cheese and serve at once. —*Alex Roberts*

SERVE WITH Arugula salad.

NOTE Masa harina is made from corn treated with limewater. It can be found in the Latin section of most supermarkets. Do not substitute other types of cornmeal in this recipe.

WINE Full-bodied, rich Pinot Gris.

GRILLED SHRIMP SUMMER ROLLS

CORN AND SHIITAKE FRITTERS

Greek Salad with Feta Mousse

ACTIVE: 30 MIN; TOTAL: 1 HR

4 SERVINGS

Gavin Kaysen, a 2007 F&W Best New Chef, makes his Greek salad with most of the usual ingredients, like tomatoes and olives—but he gives the salad an inspired twist by turning the traditional feta cheese into a creamy, light feta mousse.

- 6   ounces Greek feta cheese, crumbled (1½ cups)
- ½   cup heavy cream
- ¾   teaspoon unflavored gelatin softened in 1½ tablespoons water

  Freshly ground white pepper
- 2½ pounds mixed heirloom tomatoes, cut into thick slices, quartered or halved

  Fleur de sel and coarsely ground black pepper
- ¼   cup extra-virgin olive oil
- 16 pitted kalamata olives, halved
- ¼   cup thinly sliced red onion
- 1   tablespoon finely chopped fresh oregano

1. In a small skillet, combine the feta and cream and simmer, stirring, over moderate heat until the feta is slightly melted, about 1 minute. Stir in the softened gelatin until dissolved; transfer the feta mixture to a blender. Puree until fairly smooth. Season with white pepper. Scrape the mousse into a shallow bowl and refrigerate until set, about 30 minutes.

2. Bring the feta mousse back to room temperature, about 20 minutes. Whisk the mousse until loosened. Spread the feta mousse in the center of each plate. Top with the tomatoes, lightly seasoning each layer with fleur de sel and black pepper. Drizzle the salads with the olive oil, garnish with the olives, red onion and oregano and serve at once. —*Gavin Kaysen*

MAKE AHEAD The feta mousse can be refrigerated for up to 2 days.

Summer Squash and Tomato Tart

ACTIVE: 30 MIN; TOTAL: 1 HR 15 MIN

4 SERVINGS ● ○

For this elegant tart, a crispy puff pastry base is topped with a simple mix of soft, pesto-spiked goat cheese, sautéed vegetables and slices of fresh tomato, all sprinkled with chopped green olives.

- 2   tablespoons extra-virgin olive oil
- 1   pound small yellow squash, sliced ¼ inch thick
- 1   large onion, halved and thinly sliced

  Salt and freshly ground white pepper
- 2   tablespoons prepared pesto
- 5   ounces fresh goat cheese, softened

  All-purpose flour, for dusting
- 14 ounces puff pastry, chilled
- 1   plum tomato, very thinly sliced
- 1   large egg beaten with 2 tablespoons water
- 10 small pitted green olives, coarsely chopped

1. Preheat the oven to 425° and line a baking sheet with parchment paper. In a large skillet, heat the olive oil. Add the squash and onion and season with salt and white pepper. Cover and cook over moderately high heat, stirring occasionally, until the squash and onion are lightly browned, about 5 minutes. Remove the skillet from the heat and let stand, covered, for 5 minutes. Transfer the vegetables to a strainer and press lightly.

2. Meanwhile, in a small bowl, blend the pesto with the goat cheese. On a lightly floured surface, roll out the puff pastry to a 13-inch square; trim the square to 12 inches. Prick the pastry all over with a fork and invert it onto the parchment-lined baking sheet.

3. Spread the goat cheese all over the pastry, leaving a 1-inch border all around. Top with the squash mixture. Arrange the tomato slices on the tart and sprinkle with salt and white pepper. Fold up the sides, pressing the corners together. Trim any excess pastry at the corners. Brush the pastry with the egg wash and bake in the lower third of the oven for approximately 45 minutes, until the edges are golden and the bottom is completely cooked through. Sprinkle with the olives, cut into squares and serve the tart right away. —*Bruce Sherman*

MAKE AHEAD The Summer Squash and Tomato Tart can be assembled and refrigerated for 2 hours before baking.

WINE Lively, tart Sauvignon Blanc.

Eggplant Caponatina

TOTAL: 40 MIN PLUS STANDING AND COOLING

6 SERVINGS ● ● ○

Little mustard-yellow terra-cotta bowls filled with *caponatina* (a finely chopped version of the traditional Sicilian sweet-and-sour eggplant dish caponata) often appear on the tables at Il Bacco Felice in Foligno, Italy, soon after guests have been seated. Chef-owner Salvatore Denaro insists on making his *caponatina* with exquisite salted capers from Malfa on the Sicilian island of Salina.

INGREDIENT

puff pastry: a quick snack

Puff pastry scraps are great for making into snacks to serve alongside soup or cocktails. Cut pieces into squares or strips and brush lightly with beaten egg. Sprinkle with a pinch of sesame seeds, black pepper, coarse salt or grated Parmigiano-Reggiano cheese. Bake for about 10 minutes, until golden and puffed.

½ cup salt-packed capers (see Note)

2 medium eggplants (1¾ pounds)

Vegetable oil, for frying

3 tablespoons extra-virgin olive oil

2 medium onions, thinly sliced

3 bay leaves

3 tender inner celery ribs,
    thinly sliced crosswise

20 cherry tomatoes, halved

½ cup coarsely chopped pitted
    green olives

¼ cup pine nuts

2 teaspoons sugar

¼ cup red wine vinegar

Salt and freshly ground black pepper

1. In a small bowl, cover the capers with warm water and let stand for 1 hour. Drain well. Meanwhile, partially peel the eggplant in vertical stripes and cut into 1-inch dice.

2. In a large skillet, heat 1 inch of vegetable oil to 350°. Add one-fourth of the eggplant at a time and fry over moderately high heat until golden brown, about 2 minutes. Drain on paper towels.

3. Discard the vegetable oil and wipe out the pan. In the same saucepan, heat the olive oil. Add the onions and bay leaves and cook over moderately low heat until the onions are soft but not browned, about 10 minutes. Add the capers, celery, tomatoes, olives and pine nuts and simmer over low heat, stirring a few times, until the vegetables are heated through, about 5 minutes. Discard the bay leaves.

4. In a small saucepan, dissolve the sugar in the vinegar over moderate heat. Stir the vinegar mixture and reserved eggplant into the vegetables. Transfer to a serving bowl. Season with salt and pepper; let cool to room temperature. —*Salvatore Denaro*

NOTE One source for salt-packed capers is Market Hall Foods (888-952-4005 or markethallfoods.com).

MAKE AHEAD The *caponatina* can be refrigerated for up to 2 days. Bring to room temperature before serving.

WINE Juicy, spicy Grenache.

Grilled Vegetable Bruschetta

TOTAL: 1 HR

10 SERVINGS ●

What could be more summery than grilled peppers and squash heaped on toasted country bread that's slathered with fresh basil pesto? This versatile recipe works as a first course or even a whole meal.

PESTO

6 cups lightly packed basil leaves

6 garlic cloves

¾ cup extra-virgin olive oil

1 cup freshly grated
    Parmigiano-Reggiano

Salt and freshly ground pepper

BRUSCHETTA

2 each of red bell pepper, yellow
    bell pepper, yellow squash and
    zucchini, all halved lengthwise

1 sweet onion, sliced ¼ inch thick

¾ cup extra-virgin olive oil,
    plus more for brushing

Salt and freshly ground pepper

5 large ripe tomatoes, diced

1 small red onion, thinly sliced

¼ cup fresh lemon juice

¼ cup chopped parsley

3 tablespoons sherry vinegar

2 tablespoons minced garlic

1 tablespoon thyme

Ten 1-inch slices of country bread

4 ounces *ricotta salata*,
    thinly sliced, for garnish

1. MAKE THE PESTO: Light a grill. In a food processor, mince the basil and garlic, then add the oil and process to a paste. Transfer to a bowl and fold in the grated cheese. Season the pesto with salt and pepper.

2. PREPARE THE BRUSCHETTA: Brush the bell peppers, squash, zucchini and sweet onion with oil; season with salt and pepper. Grill the vegetables over moderately high heat, turning once, until charred and just tender. Discard the charred skin from the peppers. Cut the grilled vegetables into 1-inch squares and transfer to a large bowl. Add the tomatoes and red onion.

3. In a small bowl, whisk the ¾ cup of olive oil with the lemon juice, parsley, sherry vinegar, garlic and thyme. Season with salt and pepper, pour it over the vegetables and toss.

4. Brush the bread on both sides with oil. Grill over moderately high heat, turning once, until toasted, 2 minutes. Spread each toast with a rounded tablespoon of the pesto, then top with the grilled vegetables and the *ricotta salata* and serve. —*Laurent Tourondel*

MAKE AHEAD The pesto can be refrigerated overnight.

WINE Fresh, lively Soave.

drinks

Cucumber-Basil Martini

 TOTAL: 10 MIN

MAKES 1 DRINK ●

For this cocktail, chef Laurent Tourondel muddles basil and cucumber the same way he'd mash the ingredients for a mojito.

1 tablespoon sugar

1 tablespoon hot water

1 teaspoon finely grated
    fresh ginger

One 3-inch piece of cucumber—
    peeled, seeded and diced, plus
    1 round for garnish

3 basil leaves, 2 torn

2 ounces gin

1 tablespoon fresh lime juice

Ice

1. In a small bowl, dissolve the sugar in the hot water. Press the grated ginger through a fine strainer set over the bowl, releasing the juice.

2. In a cocktail shaker, muddle the diced cucumber with the 2 torn basil leaves. Add the ginger syrup, gin, lime juice and a handful of ice. Shake well, then strain into a martini glass. Garnish the martini with the cucumber slice and the whole basil leaf and serve. —*Laurent Tourondel*

the best new pisco cocktails

Peru and Chile have famously fought over the right to call pisco—
the fiery, grappa-like spirit—their own. Now the debate is being played out
in North America, as both countries are sending more (and better)
pisco to the U.S. each year. Many bartenders still use oak-aged Chilean pisco,
but the grapey, unoaked flavors of Peruvian pisco are more appealing.
It's made in two styles: *puro,* distilled from a single grape variety,
and *acholado,* a blend of two or more varieties. I use both for refreshing
summer cocktails like the three drinks below. —*Nick Fauchald*

the pisco	*the cocktail*
Acholado This blended style is best for the pisco sour, said to have been invented in California, then sent to Peru. **TOP PICK** La Diablada ($38), a blend of Italia, Quebranta and Moscatel grapes, has sweet, spicy fruit notes and a long finish.	**Key Lime Pisco Sour** TOTAL: 15 MIN, MAKES 1 DRINK In the U.S., pisco sours are usually made with lemon juice, but fresh (not bottled) Key lime juice tastes even better. **1 medium egg white • 1½ ounces pisco, preferably *acholado* • ¾ ounce fresh Key lime juice • ¾ ounce simple syrup • Angostura bitters • ice** In a cocktail shaker, combine the egg white, pisco, Key lime juice, simple syrup and 1 dash of Angostura bitters and shake vigorously for 10 seconds. Fill the cocktail shaker with ice and shake vigorously for 20 seconds. Strain into a chilled cocktail glass and top with 3 drops of Angostura. —*N.F.*
Italia With their floral scent and delicate fruit flavors, piscos made from the Italia grape are great in light citrus cocktails. **TOP PICK** Barsol Italia ($20) shows elegant balance, with layers of tropical fruit flavors.	**Pisco Cup** TOTAL: 5 MIN, MAKES 1 DRINK This cocktail is bright and fruity enough for a summertime aperitif; the floral aromas of the Italia pisco shine through. Making it with a tawny or late-vintage port instead of ruby port will result in a more complex, year-round drink. **ice • 1 ounce pisco, preferably Italia • 2 ounces ruby port • 2 dashes of orange bitters • 1 orange twist** Fill a cocktail shaker with ice. Add the pisco, port and bitters and stir briskly for 20 seconds. Strain into a chilled cocktail glass; garnish with the orange twist. —*N.F.*
Quebranta The Quebranta grape makes a robust pisco—a good substitute for brandy—often with earthy and chocolaty notes. **TOP PICK** The big, bold **Ocucaje Pure** ($15) is full of aromatic lemongrass and anise flavors.	**Pisco Smash** TOTAL: 10 MIN, MAKES 1 DRINK High-quality pisco, even if made from hearty Quebranta, retains a fresh, grapey flavor, which is amplified in this refreshing cocktail by the addition of muddled red grapes and Riesling. **8 seedless red grapes • 1½ ounces pisco, preferably Quebranta • 2 ounces Riesling • ½ ounce simple syrup • ¾ ounce fresh lemon juice • ice** In a cocktail shaker, gently muddle the grapes until they burst. Add the remaining ingredients and enough ice to fill a rocks glass and shake well for 20 seconds. Pour the contents of the shaker into the rocks glass. —*N.F.*

Sweet-Tart Tarragon Lemonade

ACTIVE: 30 MIN; TOTAL: 1 HR

12 SERVINGS ● ● ○ ○

Gabriel Frasca and Amanda Lydon offer infused lemonades on the lunch menu at their Nantucket restaurant Straight Wharf. Frasca prefers to make his lemonade at "face-puckering levels"—holding back on the sugar. But this version has a gentle sweetness, like a tarragon-zapped lemon drop. Give it a try with other summer herbs, too, like fresh mint or basil.

- 10   cups water
- 2¼ cups sugar
- 17   tarragon sprigs
- 6   cups fresh lemon juice, strained (from about 40 lemons), plus 12 thin lemon slices for garnish

Salt

Ice

1. In a medium saucepan, combine 4 cups of the water with the sugar and bring to a boil over high heat, stirring to dissolve the sugar. Simmer over moderately high heat, stirring occasionally, until the syrup is reduced to 3¼ cups, about 25 minutes. Remove the sugar syrup from the heat and add 5 of the tarragon sprigs. Let stand, stirring often, until the infused sugar syrup is cooled to room temperature, about 30 minutes. Discard the tarragon sprigs.

2. In a large glass pitcher, combine the remaining 6 cups of water with the tarragon syrup and lemon juice. Stir in a pinch of salt. Serve the lemonade over ice, garnished with the lemon slices and the remaining 12 tarragon sprigs.
—*Gabriel Frasca and Amanda Lydon*

MAKE AHEAD The lemonade can be refrigerated overnight.

Thai-Basil Sangria

 **ACTIVE: 20 MIN; TOTAL: 40 MIN**

12 SERVINGS ● ○

The Spanish drink sangria draws its name from the blood-red (*sangre*) color of its traditional red wine base. This stripped-down version gets its golden hue—and zingy flavors—from white wine, fresh-squeezed orange juice and a kick of brandy.

- ¼   cup sugar
- ¼   cup water
- 8   Thai basil sprigs

Zest of 1 lemon, peeled in 3-inch strips

Zest of 1 orange, peeled in 3-inch strips

- 2   bottles chilled Pinot Grigio
- ¾   cup brandy
- ½   cup fresh orange juice, strained

Ice

Chilled club soda

12 thin orange slices, for garnish

1. In a small saucepan, combine the sugar and water and bring to a boil, stirring until the sugar is dissolved. Remove the saucepan from the heat. Add the basil sprigs and lemon and orange zests. Let the syrup stand, stirring often, until cooled to room temperature, about 20 minutes. Remove and discard the basil sprigs and lemon and orange zest strips.

2. In a large pitcher, combine the basil syrup with the Pinot Grigio, brandy and fresh orange juice. Pour the sangria into ice-filled glasses, top each glass with club soda and garnish each drink with one of the orange slices.
—*Gabriel Frasca and Amanda Lydon*

Prosecco-Saba Cocktail

 **TOTAL: 5 MIN**

MAKES 1 DRINK ○

This tart Italian cocktail can be mixed before serving or served as a layered drink for guests to stir themselves.

- 1   teaspoon *saba* (see Note)

About 4 ounces Prosecco, chilled

Pour the *saba* into a flute. Carefully add the Prosecco without disturbing the *saba*. Stir in the *saba* just before drinking.
—*Efisio Farris*

NOTE *Saba,* the Italian condiment made from reduced grape must, is available in specialty food stores and by mail-order at igourmet.com and gourmetsardinia.com.

COCKTAIL UPDATE

best summer spirits

TEA LIQUEUR Distilled in the same Bay Area facility as Hangar One vodka, the orangey **Qi White Tea Liqueur** is excellent with club soda ($39; qispirits.com).

TEQUILA Bottled right after being double-distilled, **Dos Lunas Silver** tequila has loads of herbal, smoky agave flavor as well as a nice smoothness ($50; doslunas.com).

RUM The newly imported **Rhum Blanc J.M,** made from sugarcane in Martinique, has strong white pepper notes to give daiquiris an unexpected zip ($37; rhumclement.net).

main courses

Lemongrass Salad with Chinese Sausage and Mango

 TOTAL: 45 MIN
6 SERVINGS

¾ pound Chinese sausage

3 stalks of fresh lemongrass, first 2 layers peeled off and bottom 6 inches very thinly sliced

1 garlic clove, thinly sliced

1 shallot, thinly sliced

1 red Thai chile, thinly sliced

1 green Thai chile, thinly sliced

¼ cup fresh lime juice

3 tablespoons soy sauce

2 tablespoons finely julienned fresh ginger

2 tablespoons *gula Jawa* (see Note) or dark brown sugar

1 teaspoon canola oil

½ teaspoon Asian sesame oil

1 large, slightly underripe mango, peeled and cut into 2-by-¼-inch matchsticks (2 cups)

1 bunch of watercress, coarsely chopped

¼ cup chopped cilantro

1. Steam the sausage over boiling water until plump, about 15 minutes. Let cool slightly and pat dry, then slice thinly.

2. Meanwhile, in a medium bowl, toss the sliced lemongrass with the garlic, shallot, chiles, lime juice, soy sauce, ginger, *gula Jawa,* canola oil and sesame oil, tossing until the *gula* is dissolved.

3. Add the Chinese sausage, mango, watercress and cilantro to the dressing in the bowl and toss well. Serve the salad warm or at room temperature. —*Zak Pelaccio*

NOTE *Gula Jawa* is a type of palm sugar. It can be ordered from indomart.us.

WINE Light, fresh Pinot Grigio.

Seared Chicken Liver Salad

 TOTAL: 45 MIN
6 SERVINGS ●

1 lemon, halved

5 baby artichokes (about ¾ pound)

6 tablespoons extra-virgin olive oil

1 large red onion, halved and thinly sliced

1 pound chicken livers, halved

Salt and freshly ground pepper

3 rosemary sprigs

½ cup red wine vinegar

2 tablespoons fresh lemon juice

2 heads of baby Bibb lettuce, torn

1. Fill a bowl with water and squeeze the lemon into it. Working with 1 artichoke at a time, snap off the outer leaves. Trim the stem and cut off the top two-thirds of the leaves. Thinly slice the artichoke lengthwise and add to the water. Repeat with the remaining baby artichokes.

2. In a large skillet, heat 2 tablespoons of the oil until shimmering. Add the onion and cook over moderate heat, stirring occasionally, until lightly browned, 15 minutes. Transfer to a plate and wipe out the skillet.

3. Heat 2 tablespoons of the oil in the skillet until shimmering. Season the livers with salt and pepper; add them to the pan in a single layer along with the rosemary. Cook over moderate heat until lightly browned on the bottom, about 1 minute. Return the onion to the pan and cook, turning the livers until they're just pink in the center, about 1 minute. Add the vinegar, lemon juice and the remaining 2 tablespoons of oil to the skillet and cook over high heat until reduced by half, about 1 minute. Discard the rosemary sprigs.

4. Drain the artichokes and pat thoroughly dry. Arrange the lettuce and artichokes on a platter. Spoon the chicken livers and pan sauce on top and serve at once.
—*Scott Conant*

WINE Juicy, fresh Dolcetto.

Fennel Slaw with Bresaola and Walnut Pesto

TOTAL: 25 MIN
4 SERVINGS ●

F&W's Nick Fauchald uses *bresaola* (salty, air-dried beef) to add savoriness to this crunchy fennel slaw.

- ¾ cup walnut halves
- 12 basil leaves
- 1 small garlic clove
- ¼ cup extra-virgin olive oil
- 3 tablespoons mayonnaise
- 1 tablespoon fresh lemon juice
- Kosher salt and freshly ground pepper
- 1 large fennel bulb—halved, cored and thinly sliced
- 1 pound napa cabbage, cored and shredded
- 6 ounces thinly sliced *bresaola,* cut into thin ribbons

1. In a food processor, pulse ½ cup of the walnuts with the basil and garlic until finely chopped. Add the oil, mayonnaise and lemon juice and process until smooth. Season with salt and pepper.

2. Coarsely chop the remaining ¼ cup of walnuts. In a large bowl, toss the fennel with the cabbage, *bresaola,* chopped walnuts and pesto. Transfer to plates and serve. —*Nick Fauchald*

WINE Earthy, medium-bodied Tempranillo.

Grilled Squid with Miner's Lettuce Salad and Green Sauce

ACTIVE: 1 HR; TOTAL: 3 HR
4 SMALL SERVINGS

The green sauce accompanying this salad is loaded with flavor from anchovies and capers and an abundance of fresh herbs. It's terrific on everything from seafood to pork to chicken.

SQUID
- Finely grated zest and juice of 1 lemon
- 1 garlic clove, very finely chopped
- 1 teaspoon pimentón de la Vera (smoked Spanish paprika)
- ¼ cup extra-virgin olive oil
- ¼ cup chopped flat-leaf parsley
- 1 pound cleaned small squid bodies
- Salt

GREEN SAUCE
- 4 anchovy fillets, chopped
- 2 tablespoons drained capers
- 1 medium shallot, chopped
- 1 large garlic clove, chopped
- 1½ cups flat-leaf parsley
- ½ cup mint leaves
- ½ cup minced chives
- Finely grated zest and juice of 1 lemon
- ½ cup extra-virgin olive oil
- Salt and freshly ground pepper

SALAD
- 2 tablespoons fresh lemon juice
- 1 medium shallot, thinly sliced
- ¼ cup extra-virgin olive oil
- Salt and freshly ground pepper
- ¼ pound miner's lettuce (see Note) or baby arugula
- ½ cup cooked chickpeas
- ¼ cup torn mint leaves
- ¼ cup flat-leaf parsley

1. **PREPARE THE SQUID:** In a medium bowl, combine the lemon zest and juice with the garlic, pimentón, olive oil and parsley. Add the squid and toss to coat. Cover and refrigerate for 2 hours.

2. **MAKE THE GREEN SAUCE:** In a food processor, combine the anchovies with the capers, shallot, garlic, parsley, mint, chives and lemon zest and juice and process until minced. With the machine on, slowly pour in the olive oil. Season the green sauce with salt and pepper.

3. **MAKE THE SALAD:** In a large bowl, mix the lemon juice and shallot and let stand for 10 minutes. Whisk in the oil and season with salt and pepper. Add the miner's lettuce, chickpeas, mint and parsley; toss.

4. Meanwhile, light a grill. Remove the squid from the marinade and season with salt. Grill the squid over high heat until it is lightly charred and just cooked, about 2 minutes per side.

5. Mound the salad on 2 plates. Spoon the green sauce onto the plates, top with the grilled squid and serve right away. —*Matthew Dillon*

NOTE Miner's lettuce is a delicious and delicate salad green that's also commonly known as winter purslane. Look for it at farmers' markets.

MAKE AHEAD The green sauce can be refrigerated for up to 3 days. Bring to room temperature before serving.

WINE Lively, tart Sauvignon Blanc.

Smoked Trout Salad with Apple and Manchego

TOTAL: 30 MIN
4 SERVINGS

Pairing smoked trout with green apples creates a sweet tart smoky combination. A little mayonnaise in the dressing gives the salad a lovely creaminess.

- 3 tablespoons mayonnaise
- 3 tablespoons cider vinegar
- 1 tablespoon extra-virgin olive oil
- Kosher salt and freshly ground pepper
- 1 head of frisée, torn into bite-size pieces (3 cups)
- ½ pound skinless smoked trout fillets, flaked and pin bones removed
- 3 ounces Manchego cheese, coarsely shredded (about 1 cup)
- 1 Granny Smith apple, cored and cut into ⅛-inch-thick matchsticks
- ½ cup flat-leaf parsley, coarsely chopped
- ¼ cup thinly sliced red onion

1. In a small bowl, whisk the mayonnaise with the cider vinegar and olive oil and season with salt and pepper.

2. In a large bowl, combine the frisée with the flaked trout, shredded Manchego, apple, parsley and red onion. Add the dressing and toss to coat. Transfer the salad to plates and serve.
—*Nick Fauchald*

WINE Fresh, minerally Vermentino.

● HEALTHY ● MAKE AHEAD ● VEGETARIAN ● STAFF FAVORITE

Asian Shrimp and Cabbage Salad

ACTIVE: 30 MIN; TOTAL: 50 MIN

6 SERVINGS ● ●

An appealing combination of shrimp, carrots, cucumbers, peanuts and cilantro in a spicy Asian dressing makes this slaw fresh-tasting and even slightly addictive.

- 1 pound medium shrimp, shelled and deveined
- 3 tablespoons extra-virgin olive oil
- 1½ tablespoons Asian fish sauce

Finely grated zest and juice of 1 lime, plus lime wedges for serving

- 1 tablespoon light brown sugar
- 1 teaspoon Thai red curry paste
- 1 small shallot, very finely chopped
- ½ small green cabbage, cored and finely shredded (6 packed cups)
- 2 carrots, julienned
- 2 Kirby cucumbers, very thinly sliced
- 1 cup unsalted roasted peanuts, coarsely chopped
- 1 cup cilantro leaves

1. Bring a large pot of salted water to a boil and fill a bowl with ice water. Add the shrimp to the boiling water and cook until pink and curled, about 1 minute. Drain the shrimp and transfer them to the ice water to cool. Drain and pat dry.

2. In a large bowl, whisk the olive oil with the fish sauce, lime zest, lime juice, brown sugar, red curry paste and chopped shallot. Add the cabbage, carrots, cucumbers and cooked shrimp and toss until evenly coated. Let the salad stand at room temperature for about 20 minutes, until the cabbage is very slightly wilted. Toss the salad, top with the peanuts and cilantro and serve with the lime wedges.
—*Melissa Clark*

MAKE AHEAD The spicy dressing can be refrigerated overnight.

WINE Tart, citrusy Riesling.

Cajun-Spiced Shrimp and Corn Salad

TOTAL: 1 HR 15 MIN

10 SERVINGS ● ●

PICKLED RED ONION

- ½ cup red wine vinegar
- ½ tablespoon kosher salt
- ½ tablespoon sugar
- ½ tablespoon freshly ground pepper
- 1 red onion, halved and thinly sliced

SALAD

- 1 teaspoon Old Bay seasoning
- 1 teaspoon Cajun spice blend
- 1 teaspoon hot pimentón de la Vera (smoked Spanish paprika)
- 1 teaspoon chopped rosemary
- ¼ teaspoon cayenne pepper
- 2 tablespoons extra-virgin olive oil
- 20 large shrimp, shelled and deveined
- 7 ears of corn, shucked
- 2 tablespoons unsalted butter

Salt and freshly ground pepper

- 4 Kirby cucumbers, diced
- 2 Medjool dates, pitted and diced
- ¼ cup chopped cilantro
- ¼ cup fresh lime juice

Pea shoots, for garnish (optional)

1. **PICKLE THE ONION:** In a small saucepan, bring the vinegar to a boil with the salt, sugar and pepper. Cook over high heat until the salt and sugar dissolve, about 2 minutes. Remove from the heat, stir in the onion slices, and let the onion pickle at room temperature for 1 hour.

2. **MEANWHILE, MAKE THE SALAD:** Light a grill. In a large bowl, mix the Old Bay, Cajun spice, smoked paprika, rosemary, cayenne and 1 tablespoon of the olive oil. Add the shrimp and toss well. Grill the shrimp over high heat, turning once, until the shrimp are lightly charred and white throughout, about 2 minutes.

3. Rub the corn with the butter and season with salt and black pepper. Grill over moderately high heat, turning occasionally, until the kernels are charred and tender, about 10 minutes. Let the ears cool slightly.

4. Using a serrated knife, cut the kernels from the ears over a large bowl. Toss the corn with the cucumbers, dates, cilantro, lime juice and the remaining 1 tablespoon of olive oil. Drain the pickled onion strips and add them to the salad. Season with salt and black pepper and toss well. Transfer to a platter, top with the shrimp, garnish with the pea shoots and serve.
—*Laurent Tourondel*

MAKE AHEAD The pickled onion can be refrigerated for up to 3 days. The dressed salad can be refrigerated for up to 2 hours; serve lightly chilled.

WINE Spicy American Gewürztraminer.

Tuna Salad with Fennel, Cucumber and Tarragon

TOTAL: 25 MIN

4 SERVINGS ●

The key to any delicious uncooked recipe is great ingredients. Here, a good-quality oil-packed tuna is essential. You can wrap the salad in lettuce or stuff it into pitas.

- 1 small shallot, finely chopped
- ¼ cup white wine vinegar
- 3 tablespoons extra-virgin olive oil
- 1½ teaspoons sugar
- 1 tablespoon chopped tarragon
- 1 small fennel bulb, cored and cut into ¼-inch dice
- ½ English cucumber—peeled, seeded and diced

Two 6-ounce cans olive oil–packed tuna, drained

Kosher salt and freshly ground pepper

Lettuce leaves or pita bread, for serving

1. In a bowl, whisk the shallot, vinegar, oil, sugar and tarragon. Add the fennel and cucumber and toss. Let the salad stand for 5 minutes.

2. Add the tuna to the salad and season with salt and pepper. Spoon the salad into lettuce leaves or pita bread and serve.
—*Nick Fauchald*

WINE Peppery, refreshing Grüner Veltliner.

TUNA, OLIVE AND BREAD SALAD WITH FARINATA

PIADINA WITH RICOTTA, PROSCIUTTO AND ARUGULA

Tuna, Olive and Bread Salad

TOTAL: 30 MIN
8 SERVINGS ●

Eight ¾-inch-thick slices of dense
    Italian bread from a long loaf
1 garlic clove
2 tablespoons water
2 tablespoons red wine vinegar
1 pound tomatoes, diced
1 seedless cucumber, peeled and
    cut into ½-inch pieces
1 scallion, thinly sliced
1 cup pitted kalamata olives
½ cup torn basil leaves
1 tablespoon chopped oregano
1 tablespoon drained capers
4 anchovy fillets, chopped
Two 6-ounce cans or jars Italian
    tuna in oil, drained and flaked
⅓ cup extra-virgin olive oil
Salt and freshly ground pepper
Farinata (recipe follows), for serving

1. Preheat the broiler. Toast the bread for about 1 minute, turning once, until golden. Let cool, then rub the toasts with the garlic. In a bowl, combine the water and vinegar; sprinkle on the bread and let stand for 1 minute, until moistened slightly.
2. Break the bread into chunks; transfer to a bowl. Add the tomatoes, cucumber, scallion, olives, basil, oregano, capers, anchovies, tuna and oil to the bowl. Season the salad with salt and pepper and toss. Serve with the *farinata.* —*Michela Larson*
WINE Fresh, minerally Vermentino.

FARINATA

ACTIVE: 20 MIN; TOTAL: 3 HR
8 SERVINGS ● ● ●

Farinata is a thin chickpea cake from Liguria, on Italy's northwest coast. Typically cooked in a wood-burning oven, it makes a perfect snack and is often eaten like a piece of pizza.

4 cups warm water
3 cups chickpea flour (15 ounces)
1 tablespoon kosher salt
1 teaspoon finely chopped
    rosemary leaves
½ cup plus 2 tablespoons
    extra-virgin olive oil
Freshly ground pepper

1. Pour the water into a bowl. Slowly whisk in the chickpea flour until smooth. Let stand at room temperature for 2 hours.
2. Preheat the oven to 500°. Skim any foam off the batter. Stir in the salt, rosemary and ¼ cup plus 2 tablespoons of the oil.
3. Heat two 10-inch cast-iron skillets in the oven for 10 minutes. Add 2 tablespoons of oil to each skillet, swirling to coat. Divide the batter between the skillets; it should be less than ½ inch thick. Bake for 25 to 30 minutes, until crisp around the edges. Slide the *farinata* onto a board; cut into wedges. Sprinkle with pepper and serve. —*M.L.*

Bagna Cauda Salad Sandwiches

TOTAL: 30 MIN
4 SERVINGS

Traditionally, bagna cauda is a warm Italian anchovy-and-garlic vegetable dip; here, it's used as a hearty dressing for fantastic, substantial sandwiches.

- 4 large eggs
- 12 cherry tomatoes, halved
- 10 cups mixed greens, such as romaine hearts, endive and watercress, coarsely chopped
- 1 Hass avocado, cut into 1-inch dice

Eight ¾-inch-thick slices of Tuscan or peasant bread, cut from a large oval loaf

- ½ cup extra-virgin olive oil, plus more for brushing
- 10 anchovy fillets, coarsely chopped
- 3 large garlic cloves, thinly sliced
- ¼ cup fresh lemon juice

Salt and freshly ground pepper

1. Put the eggs in a small saucepan, cover with cold water and bring to a boil. Remove the pan from the heat, cover and let stand for 12 minutes. Drain and rinse under cold water, shaking the pan to crack the shells. Peel and chop the eggs; transfer to a bowl. Add the tomatoes, greens and avocado.

2. Meanwhile, light a grill or heat a grill pan. Brush the bread lightly on both sides with oil and grill until toasted.

3. In a medium skillet, cook the anchovies and garlic in the ½ cup of olive oil over moderate heat, stirring, until the garlic is lightly browned and the anchovies are nearly dissolved, about 2 minutes. Remove from the heat and add the lemon juice; gently swirl the pan to blend. Immediately pour the hot dressing into the salad and toss to coat. Season with salt and pepper. Mound the salad on half of the toasts and close the sandwiches. Cut the sandwiches in half and serve right away.
—*Grace Parisi*

WINE Fruity, low-oak Chardonnay.

Italian Tuna Melts

TOTAL: 30 MIN
4 SERVINGS

- 3 tablespoons extra-virgin olive oil, plus more for brushing
- 1 tablespoon red wine vinegar
- 1 teaspoon Dijon mustard

Two 6-ounce cans Italian tuna in olive oil, drained and flaked

- 9 ounces marinated artichokes, coarsely chopped (1½ cups)
- 3½ ounces pitted green olives, coarsely chopped (½ cup)
- ½ cup thinly sliced red onion
- 1½ tablespoons shredded basil

Salt and freshly ground pepper

- 4 long ciabatta rolls or 1 long ciabatta loaf, split lengthwise
- 1 garlic clove
- ½ pound Robiola cheese or Brie, rind removed and cheese sliced

1. Preheat the broiler. In a medium bowl, whisk the 3 tablespoons of oil with the vinegar and mustard until combined. Add the tuna, artichokes, olives, red onion and basil and toss gently. Season lightly with salt and pepper.

2. Using a pastry brush, brush the cut sides of the ciabatta lightly with olive oil and broil cut side up on a baking sheet for 2 minutes, until golden and lightly toasted; shift the baking sheet for even browning. Rub the garlic clove over the toasted ciabatta and mound the tuna salad on top. Cover with the sliced cheese and broil until just melted, about 1 minute. Serve at once.
—*Grace Parisi*

WINE Fresh, fruity rosé.

Piadina with Ricotta, Prosciutto and Arugula

ACTIVE: 45 MIN; TOTAL: 1 HR 20 MIN
6 SERVINGS ●

Chef Paul Bartolotta describes *piadina* (an Italian flat bread) as Italy's defense against fast food: Even though it's fast to make, it's real food with a cultural past.

- 3½ cups all-purpose flour
- ½ teaspoon baking soda

Kosher salt

- 4 ounces lard or vegetable shortening (½ cup), at room temperature
- ¾ cup water
- 1 tablespoon extra-virgin olive oil, plus more for brushing
- 1½ cups fresh ricotta cheese

Freshly ground pepper

- 4 ounces baby arugula (4 cups)
- 1 teaspoon fresh lemon juice
- ¼ pound thinly sliced prosciutto, mortadella or salami

1. In a standing electric mixer fitted with the dough hook, combine the flour, baking soda and 2 teaspoons of salt. Add the lard and mix at medium-low speed until evenly combined. Slowly add the water, mixing until the dough forms a mass around the hook. Increase the speed to medium and knead the dough until smooth, 5 minutes. Divide the dough into 6 pieces and roll each piece into a ball. Wrap the balls individually in plastic and let rest at room temperature for 30 minutes.

2. Preheat the oven to 225°. Heat a cast-iron griddle until very hot. On an unfloured work surface, roll out each ball to a 10-inch round about ⅛ inch thick. Brush both sides of each round very lightly with oil and grill over moderate heat, turning once, until golden and cooked through, 3 to 4 minutes. Wrap in foil and keep the breads warm in the oven while you cook the rest.

3. In a small bowl, season the ricotta lightly with salt and pepper. In a medium bowl, toss the arugula with the 1 tablespoon of oil and the lemon juice and season with salt and pepper. Arrange 3 breads on a work surface and spread with the ricotta. Top with the prosciutto, followed by the arugula salad. Cover with the remaining breads, cut into quarters and serve warm.
—*Paul Bartolotta*

WINE Dry, earthy sparkling wine.

SOFT-SHELL CRAB SANDWICH WITH PANCETTA

KNUCKLE SANDWICH

Soft-Shell Crab Sandwiches with Pancetta and Remoulade

TOTAL: 45 MIN
4 SERVINGS ●

These hefty soft-shell crab sandwiches are made by layering salty slices of pancetta, slabs of tomato and a remoulade based on store-bought mayonnaise.

- ½ cup mayonnaise
- 3 cornichons, finely chopped
- 1 tablespoon minced red onion
- 2 teaspoons chopped tarragon
- 1 teaspoon capers, chopped
- 1 teaspoon Dijon mustard

Salt and freshly ground pepper

- 4 slices of pancetta (2 ounces)
- 2 tablespoons unsalted butter
- 2 tablespoons extra-virgin olive oil
- 4 jumbo soft-shell crabs

All-purpose flour, for dusting

- 4 large brioche buns, split and toasted

One 5-ounce bunch of arugula, trimmed

- 1 large tomato, thinly sliced

1. In a small bowl, whisk the mayonnaise, cornichons, red onion, tarragon, capers and mustard. Season with salt and pepper.

2. In a large skillet, arrange the pancetta slices in a single layer. Place a flat pot lid, slightly smaller than the skillet, directly on the pancetta to weight it down. Cook over moderate heat, turning once, until the pancetta is crisp, about 6 minutes. Transfer the pancetta to paper towels and wipe out the skillet.

3. In the skillet, melt the butter in the oil. Season the crabs with salt and pepper and dust them generously with flour. Add the crabs to the skillet and cook over high heat, turning once, until crisp, about 7 minutes.

4. Spread the remoulade on the cut sides of the buns. Arrange the pancetta on the buns and top with arugula, tomato and crabs. Close the sandwiches, cut them in half and serve. —*Bruce Sherman*

WINE Fresh, fruity rosé.

Knuckle Sandwich

ACTIVE: 1 HR; TOTAL: 2 HR

4 SERVINGS

A fun take on a New England lobster roll, this sandwich comes from 2007 F&W Best New Chef Steve Corry. He flavors delicious meaty lobster salad with basil, chives and lemon zest, then layers it between crispy, tart slices of fried green tomatoes instead of bread. The whimsical name only adds to the appeal.

1 **ear of corn, shucked**

One 2-pound lobster

1 **small garlic clove, mashed**

Salt

⅓ **cup mayonnaise**

2 **tablespoons finely chopped basil**

2 **tablespoons snipped chives**

2 **tablespoons very finely chopped red onion**

1 **teaspoon finely grated lemon zest**

Freshly ground pepper

1 **cup all-purpose flour**

1 **teaspoon sweet smoked paprika**

2 **large eggs**

¼ **cup milk**

8 **large ½-inch-thick slices of green tomato or extra-large tomatillos**

1 **cup vegetable oil**

1. Bring a large pot of salted water to a boil and fill a large bowl with ice water. Add the corn to the pot and boil for 2 minutes, until glossy. Let cool, then cut the kernels from the cob.

2. Return the water to a boil and add the lobster. Cook over high heat for 13 minutes, just until the lobster turns red. Immediately plunge the lobster into the ice water to cool. Twist off the tail and claws. Crack the shells and remove the meat. Cut four ½-inch-thick slices from the tail and another 4 from a claw and reserve for garnish. Coarsely chop the remaining lobster.

3. In a medium bowl, using the back of a spoon, mash the garlic to a paste with a pinch of salt. Add the mayonnaise, chopped basil, snipped chives, finely chopped red onion, lemon zest and a generous pinch of pepper. Fold in the chopped lobster and the corn and refrigerate the lobster salad until chilled, about 1 hour.

4. In a shallow bowl, mix the flour with the smoked paprika and a generous pinch of salt. In another shallow bowl, beat the eggs with the milk and season with salt and pepper. Dredge the green tomato slices in the flour mixture, tapping off the excess. Dip the slices in the egg mixture and then in the flour again.

5. In a large skillet, heat the oil until shimmering. Add the tomato slices and fry over high heat, turning once, until golden and crisp, about 4 minutes. Drain on paper towels and sprinkle lightly with salt.

6. Transfer 4 tomato slices to plates. Top with the lobster salad and another fried tomato; press lightly to compact the sandwiches. Garnish the sandwiches with the reserved lobster pieces and serve at once. —*Steve Corry*

MAKE AHEAD The lobster salad can be refrigerated overnight.

WINE Full-bodied, rich Pinot Gris.

Chicken Quesadillas with Blue Cheese and Caramelized Onions

ACTIVE: 30 MIN; TOTAL: 1 HR 15 MIN

6 SERVINGS ●●

8 **skinless chicken thighs on the bone (about 4 pounds)**

3 **tablespoons extra-virgin olive oil**

1 **tablespoon chopped rosemary**

2 **garlic cloves, minced**

Kosher salt

3 **tablespoons unsalted butter**

2 **large onions, thinly sliced**

2 **tablespoons chopped thyme**

1½ **tablespoons sherry vinegar**

Pinch of sugar

Freshly ground pepper

Twelve 6-inch flour tortillas

4 **ounces blue cheese, crumbled (1 cup)**

1. In a bowl, toss the chicken with 2 table-spoons of the oil, the rosemary, garlic and a generous pinch of salt. Cover and let stand at room temperature for 30 minutes or refrigerate for 4 hours or overnight.

2. Meanwhile, in a large, deep skillet, melt the butter in the remaining 1 tablespoon of olive oil. Add the sliced onions, thyme, vinegar, sugar and a generous pinch of pepper. Cook over moderately low heat, stirring occasionally, until the onions are softened, about 30 minutes; add a few tablespoons of water from time to time to keep the onions moist.

3. Light a grill and preheat the oven to 500°. Season the chicken with salt and pepper and grill over moderately high heat, turning, until lightly charred and cooked through, about 15 minutes. Let the chicken cool, then pull the meat from the bones and tear into shreds.

4. Arrange 6 tortillas on 2 large baking sheets. Spoon the onions onto the tortillas and top with the chicken and cheese. Cover with the remaining tortillas, pressing to flatten slightly. Bake for about 6 minutes, until the quesadillas are golden and toasted. Transfer the quesadillas to plates and serve right away. —*Melissa Clark*

MAKE AHEAD The unbaked quesadillas can be tightly wrapped in plastic and refrigerated overnight.

WINE Intense, fruity Zinfandel.

INGREDIENT

tortillas

For last-minute meals, keep tortillas and cheese on hand for quesadillas. You can dress up the basic cheese quesadilla with drained beans, sliced scallions, corn, pickled jalapeños or shredded leftover chicken. Serve with salsa and sour cream.

Grilled Chicken Sandwiches with Mozzarella, Tomato and Basil

ACTIVE: 15 MIN; TOTAL: 50 MIN

6 SERVINGS

These warm sandwiches are best made with chewy Italian bread. You can add pesto, tapenade or garlicky aioli to make them even more delicious.

- ¼ cup plus 2 tablespoons extra-virgin olive oil
- Finely grated zest of 1 lemon
- 1½ tablespoons fresh lemon juice
- 1 tablespoon thyme leaves
- 2 garlic cloves, very finely chopped
- Kosher salt and freshly ground pepper
- 2 tomatoes, thinly sliced
- Twelve ½-inch-thick chicken breast cutlets (2½ pounds)
- 6 ciabatta rolls, split
- Six ⅓-inch-thick slices of fresh mozzarella
- 6 large basil leaves (optional)

1. In a large bowl, whisk ¼ cup of the olive oil with the lemon zest, lemon juice, thyme, garlic and a generous pinch each of salt and pepper. Spoon 1½ tablespoons of the mixture into a medium bowl, add the tomatoes and turn to coat. Add the chicken to the large bowl and turn to coat. Let the tomatoes and chicken stand at room temperature for 30 minutes.

2. Light a grill. Brush the cut sides of the rolls with the remaining 2 tablespoons of olive oil and grill over high heat until golden. Add the chicken to the grill, season with salt and pepper and grill over high heat, turning once, until cooked through and lightly charred, about 6 minutes. Place the chicken on the rolls and top with the mozzarella, tomato and basil. Spoon any tomato juices on the top half of the bun, close the sandwiches and serve.
—*Melissa Clark*

WINE Zippy, fresh Pinot Bianco.

Indian Pulled-Chicken Sandwiches

 TOTAL: 20 MIN

4 SERVINGS ● ●

- ¾ cup plain whole-milk yogurt
- ¾ cup mango chutney
- 2 tablespoons fresh lime juice
- 2 teaspoons mild curry powder
- 1 small rotisserie chicken, meat shredded, skin and bones discarded (4 cups)
- 2 scallions, thinly sliced
- ½ cup cilantro leaves, coarsely chopped
- Kosher salt and freshly ground pepper
- 1 cup baby arugula leaves
- 4 brioche rolls or other rolls, split

In a food processor, pulse the yogurt, mango chutney, fresh lime juice and curry powder until the mixture is blended but not completely smooth. Scrape the yogurt mixture into a medium bowl, add the shredded chicken meat, sliced scallions and chopped cilantro and toss. Season the pulled chicken salad with salt and pepper. Lay the arugula on the rolls, spoon the chicken salad on top and serve.
—*Nick Fauchald*

MAKE AHEAD The pulled chicken salad can be refrigerated overnight.

WINE Spicy American Gewürztraminer.

Easy Chicken Fajitas

 TOTAL: 45 MIN

4 SERVINGS ●

Eight-year-old Dani Shaub, 2007 F&W Kid Cook Contest runner-up, loves making these juicy fajitas—a recipe she based on the ingredients list from a packet of fajita seasoning. Why? Because it involves lots of slicing (one of her favorite cooking tasks) and "everyone gets to participate and pick their own toppings," she says.

- 1 teaspoon pure chile powder
- 1 teaspoon kosher salt
- ½ teaspoon ground cumin
- ½ teaspoon onion powder
- ¼ teaspoon garlic powder
- 1 tablespoon cornstarch
- ¼ cup water
- 3 tablespoons extra-virgin olive oil
- 1 whole skinless, boneless chicken breast (about 1 pound), cut into ½-inch strips
- 1 green bell pepper—cored, seeded and cut into thin strips
- 1 medium onion, thinly sliced
- 2 tablespoons fresh lime juice, plus lime wedges for serving
- 8 flour tortillas, warmed in the microwave
- Shredded lettuce, shredded cheddar cheese, salsa and sour cream, for serving

1. In a large resealable plastic bag, combine the chile powder with the salt, cumin, onion powder, garlic powder, cornstarch, water and 2 tablespoons of the olive oil. Add the chicken breast strips, bell pepper strips and sliced onion. Seal the bag and knead gently to coat the chicken strips evenly with the spice mixture. Refrigerate the chicken strips and marinade in the plastic bag for 15 minutes.

2. Heat the remaining 1 tablespoon of olive oil in a large nonstick skillet over high heat until the oil is shimmering. Carefully empty the contents of the bag into the hot skillet and cook over high heat, stirring occasionally, until the pepper strips and onion slices are crisp-tender and the chicken strips are cooked through, about 6 minutes. Remove the chicken and vegetables from the heat and stir in the 2 tablespoons of fresh lime juice.

3. Transfer the cooked chicken and vegetables to a large serving bowl and serve with the warmed flour tortillas, shredded lettuce, shredded cheddar cheese, salsa, sour cream and lime wedges.
—*Dani Shaub*

WINE Rustic, peppery Malbec.

Sweet-and-Sour Eggplant with Ricotta Salata

ACTIVE: 25 MIN; TOTAL: 1 HR 15 MIN

6 SERVINGS ● ● ○

- 2 tablespoons water
- 2 tablespoons sugar
- 2 tablespoons red wine vinegar

One 28-ounce can peeled Italian tomatoes, crushed

- 2 garlic cloves, thinly sliced
- ½ cup extra-virgin olive oil

Salt and freshly ground white pepper

- 2 large eggplants (about 1¼ pounds each), sliced crosswise ¾ inch thick
- ½ cup shredded ricotta salata
- 2 tablespoons chopped mint

1. In a saucepan, combine the water and sugar and stir over high heat until the sugar dissolves. Cook the syrup without stirring until a light amber caramel forms, about 2 minutes. Off the heat, add the vinegar. Cook the caramel over very low heat just until it softens, about 1 minute. Add the tomatoes, garlic and ¼ cup of the oil and season with salt and white pepper. Simmer the sauce over moderately low heat until thickened, about 30 minutes.

2. Preheat the oven to 400°. Brush a large rimmed baking sheet with 2 tablespoons of the oil. Arrange the eggplant on the sheet and brush with the remaining 2 tablespoons of oil; season with salt and white pepper. Roast the eggplant for 10 minutes, then flip and roast for 10 minutes longer, until tender and lightly golden.

3. Arrange the eggplant slices in an 8-by-11-inch baking dish in slightly overlapping rows. Spoon two-thirds of the tomato sauce on top and bake for 20 minutes, until bubbling and browned around the edges. Sprinkle the shredded cheese and chopped mint on top of the eggplant and serve warm or at room temperature, passing the remaining sauce on the side.

—*Frank Castronovo and Frank Falcinelli*

WINE Light, fresh Pinot Grigio.

Baked Eggplant Marinara with Basil

ACTIVE: 40 MIN; TOTAL: 1 HR 40 MIN

4 SERVINGS ● ○

Salt

- 2 medium eggplants (1¾ pounds), sliced crosswise ⅓ inch thick

Vegetable oil, for frying

- ¼ cup fine, dry bread crumbs
- 2 cups thick marinara sauce
- 3 large hard-cooked eggs, sliced ¼ inch thick
- ¼ pound fresh mozzarella, sliced ⅛ inch thick
- 1 cup loosely packed basil leaves

Freshly ground black pepper

- 1 tablespoon extra-virgin olive oil

1. Salt the eggplant and lay in a colander. Cover with a plate and weight with a can. Let stand for 30 minutes. Pat dry.

2. Preheat the oven to 400°. In a large skillet, heat ⅛ inch of oil. Fry the eggplant in batches over moderately high heat until browned and tender, about 2 minutes per side. Drain the eggplant on paper towels. Add more oil to the skillet as needed.

3. Sprinkle 2 tablespoons of the bread crumbs in the bottom of a 10-inch round baking dish. Arrange half of the eggplant on top, overlapping them slightly. Spread the marinara sauce over the eggplant and arrange the hard-cooked egg slices on top. Cover with the mozzarella. Scatter the basil over and season with pepper. Arrange the remaining eggplant on top. Cover the eggplant with foil and bake until the eggplant is heated through and the mozzarella is just melted, about 20 minutes.

4. Preheat the broiler. Uncover the eggplant and sprinkle with the remaining bread crumbs and the olive oil; broil until browned, about 2 minutes. Let rest for a minimum of 10 minutes and up to 30. Cut into wedges and serve warm or at room temperature.

—*Salvatore Denaro*

WINE Fresh, fruity rosé.

Baked Sole with Pecorino and Butter

 TOTAL: 30 MIN

4 SERVINGS ●

- 4 tablespoons unsalted butter, thinly sliced, plus more for coating

Four 6- to 8-ounce sole or flounder fillets

- 2 tablespoons extra-virgin olive oil

Freshly ground pepper

- 1 tablespoon chopped flat-leaf parsley
- 1 teaspoon finely chopped thyme leaves
- ⅓ cup freshly grated pecorino cheese, preferably Pecorino Sardo (about 1 ounce)
- ½ ounce *bottarga* (optional; see Note)

1. Preheat the oven to 350°. Generously butter a shallow baking dish that is large enough to accommodate all of the fish fillets in a single layer. Arrange the fish fillets in the baking dish, top with the butter slices and drizzle with the olive oil. Season the fish fillets with black pepper and scatter the chopped parsley and thyme evenly on top of the fish. Bake the sole fillets for about 10 minutes, or until the fish is just cooked through.

2. Preheat the broiler. Sprinkle the fish fillets with the grated pecorino cheese, then broil for about 2 minutes, or until the cheese is golden brown. Let the fish fillets stand for 5 minutes, then transfer them to plates, grate the *bottarga* on top, if using, and serve immediately.

—*Efisio Farris*

NOTE Salty and flavorful, *bottarga* is an Italian delicacy made by salting, pressing and drying tuna or mullet roe; it can be grated or sliced paper-thin. *Bottarga* is available at specialty food stores and can be ordered online from amazon.com or gourmetsardinia.com.

WINE Fresh, minerally Vermentino.

Seared Scallops with Basil, Anchovy and Sweet Corn Pudding

ACTIVE: 50 MIN; TOTAL: 1 HR 20 MIN

4 SERVINGS

The quality of the seafood is key in this lemony, piquant dish. April Bloomfield, a 2007 F&W Best New Chef, recommends seeking out day-boat scallops that haven't been treated with any preservatives.

CORN PUDDING

1⅔ cups corn kernels
     (from 4 ears of corn)
⅔ cup whole milk
⅔ cup heavy cream
1 tablespoon unsalted butter
1½ tablespoons all-purpose flour
Salt
2 large eggs, separated

SCALLOPS

3½ tablespoons extra-virgin olive oil
16 sea scallops (about 1 pound)
Salt
4 anchovy fillets, minced
1 tablespoon plus 1 teaspoon
     fresh lemon juice
2 tablespoons water
⅓ cup chopped basil
2 cups pea shoots (1 ounce)

1. MAKE THE CORN PUDDING: Preheat the oven to 400°. Butter four 1-cup ramekins. In a medium saucepan, combine the corn, milk and heavy cream and simmer over moderately high heat for 2 minutes. Puree half of the mixture in a blender. Return the puree to the saucepan.

2. In another medium saucepan, melt the butter. Add the flour and cook over moderately high heat, stirring, for 1 minute. Gradually whisk in the corn mixture and bring to a boil, then simmer, whisking, for 1 minute; season with salt. Remove from the heat and whisk in the egg yolks. Let cool until warm, about 20 minutes.

3. In a large stainless steel bowl, using a handheld mixer, beat the egg whites with a pinch of salt to firm peaks. Fold one-third of the whites into the corn mixture, then fold in the remaining whites. Spoon the mixture into the ramekins. Set the ramekins in a small baking dish and add enough water to the dish to reach one-third of the way up the sides of the ramekins. Bake for about 30 minutes, until the puddings are just slightly jiggly in the center.

4. MEANWHILE, PREPARE THE SCALLOPS: In a large skillet, heat 3 tablespoons of the oil until smoking. Season the scallops with salt, add them to the skillet and cook over high heat until browned on the bottom, about 3 minutes. Turn and cook 1 minute longer. Transfer the scallops to a plate.

5. Add the anchovies to the skillet and cook over moderately high heat, stirring, until they dissolve, about 2 minutes. Add 1 tablespoon of the lemon juice and the water to the skillet and simmer until thickened, scraping up the browned bits on the bottom of the pan, about 1 minute. Remove from the heat. Stir in the basil and any accumulated juices from the scallops. Season with salt. Return the scallops to the skillet and keep warm.

6. In a bowl, toss the pea shoots with the remaining ½ tablespoon of olive oil and 1 teaspoon of the lemon juice; season with salt. Arrange the seared scallops on 4 plates and pour the basil-anchovy sauce on top. Mound the pea shoot salad alongside and serve with the corn puddings.

—April Bloomfield

WINE Ripe, luxurious Chardonnay.

Halibut with Avocado Mash and Green Papaya Slaw

 TOTAL: 45 MIN

4 SERVINGS ●

In this healthy recipe, chef David Myers of Sona in Los Angeles pairs simple poached halibut fillets with a crunchy, Southeast Asian–inspired green papaya slaw and creamy mashed avocado.

8 cups water
4 medium shallots, thinly sliced
6 garlic cloves, halved
12 thyme sprigs
2 tablespoons whole black
     peppercorns
2 tablespoons kosher salt
¼ cup extra-virgin olive oil
1 lemon, halved
2 tablespoons sugar
3 tablespoons rice vinegar
Crushed red pepper
1 pound green papaya—peeled
     seeded and julienned (2 cups)
Sea salt and freshly ground
     black pepper
1 tablespoon fresh lime juice
1 large Hass avocado, mashed
Four 6-ounce skinless halibut fillets

1. In a large saucepan, combine the water, shallots, garlic, thyme sprigs, whole peppercorns, kosher salt and olive oil. Squeeze the lemon halves over the saucepan and add the squeezed halves to the pan. Bring to a boil over high heat, then simmer over moderate heat for 30 minutes.

2. Meanwhile, in a medium microwave-safe bowl, combine the sugar and rice vinegar and microwave at high power for 1 minute; stir to dissolve the sugar. Add a pinch of crushed red pepper and the green papaya. Season with sea salt and black pepper and toss to coat.

3. In a small bowl, mash the lime juice into the avocado and season with sea salt and crushed red pepper.

4. Place the halibut in a deep, medium skillet, leaving some space between the fillets. Strain enough of the aromatic poaching liquid over the fish to just cover it. Simmer the halibut gently over very low heat just until the fish flakes easily with a fork, about 10 minutes.

5. Spoon the avocado mixture onto each of 4 plates and top with the fish. Using a slotted spoon, mound the papaya slaw on the halibut and serve right away.

—David Myers

WINE Zesty, fresh Vinho Verde.

●HEALTHY ●MAKE AHEAD ○VEGETARIAN ●STAFF FAVORITE

COD WITH HAM POWDER AND GARLIC WAFERS

TUNA WITH PROVENÇAL VEGETABLES

Cod with Ham Powder and Garlic Wafers

ACTIVE: 40 MIN; TOTAL: 2 HR 15 MIN
4 SERVINGS ●

The traditional Basque dish that inspired this recipe, called *merluza en salsa verde,* consists of hake (a flaky white fish similar to cod) pan-cooked and topped with a thick sauce of parsley mashed with garlic. Chefs Juan Mari Arzak and Elena Arzak of Restaurante Arzak in San Sebastián, Spain, recast the classic by lightly poaching cod or hake fillets in an ethereal clam broth and transforming the sauce's components into airy distillations: the parsley into crunchy sprigs, the garlic into crisp wafers.

Twenty 2-inch, 3-pronged
    parsley stems
¼ cup extra-virgin olive oil,
    plus more for drizzling
3 medium garlic cloves,
    very finely minced
½ cup water
1 dozen littleneck clams,
    scrubbed
Four 6-ounce cod or
    hake fillets with skin
Salt and freshly ground
    black pepper
Ham Powder and Garlic Wafers
    (recipes follow), for garnish

1. Bring a saucepan of salted water to a boil over high heat. Fill a small bowl with ice water. Blanch the parsley stems in the boiling water until they turn bright green, about 30 seconds. Using a slotted spoon, transfer the stems to the ice water, then drain and pat them dry with a paper towel. In a small bowl, drizzle the parsley stems with a little olive oil to keep them moist.

2. In a large, deep skillet, heat the ¼ cup of olive oil. Add the minced garlic and cook over moderately high heat until the garlic is fragrant, about 2 minutes. Add the water and bring to a boil. Add the clams, cover and cook over high heat, shaking the skillet a few times, until the clams open, about 5 minutes. Discard any that don't open. Using a slotted spoon, transfer the clams to a plate, leaving their juices in the skillet.

3. Season the cod fillets with salt and pepper. Add the fillets to the clam juices in the skillet. Cook over moderate heat, turning the fillets once, until the flesh is white throughout, about 8 minutes.

4. Transfer the cod fillets to plates along with some of the broth, then sprinkle the fish with some of the Ham Powder. Arrange the clams in their shells and the parsley stems around the fish. Lean the Garlic Wafers against the fillets and serve.
—*Elena Arzak and Juan Mari Arzak*

MAKE AHEAD The parsley stems can be blanched up to 2 hours ahead; cover and refrigerate.

WINE Dry, earthy sparkling wine.

HAM POWDER

ACTIVE: 10 MIN; TOTAL: 1 HR 10 MIN
MAKES ABOUT ¼ CUP ● ●

You can also try this ingenious recipe sprinkled over scrambled eggs or a pan-seared chicken breast. Just be sure to use serrano ham, which is lean enough to grind into a powder when dried.

  1 **ounce thinly sliced serrano ham, torn into 3-inch pieces**
Kosher salt

1. Preheat the oven to 200°. Arrange the ham pieces in a single layer on a large baking sheet or cookie sheet and bake until dried and crisp, about 1 hour. Let the ham pieces cool completely.

2. In a mini food processor or spice grinder, grind the ham to a fine powder. Season with a pinch of salt. —*E.A. and J.M.A.*

MAKE AHEAD The Ham Powder can be stored for up to a week at room temperature in an airtight container.

GARLIC WAFERS

ACTIVE: 15 MIN; TOTAL: 1 HR 40 MIN
MAKES TWO 6-INCH WAFERS ● ● ○

In this recipe, softened garlic cloves are pureed, then dehydrated in a very low-heat oven to create crispy wafers. Serve the wafers as a garnish with any dish that calls for sautéed garlic.

 16 **garlic cloves, peeled**
Salt
Freshly grated nutmeg

1. Preheat the oven to 200°. Fill a medium saucepan with water and bring to a boil over high heat. Add the garlic cloves and simmer over moderately low heat until they become very tender, about 25 minutes. Drain the cloves and pat them dry. In a small bowl, use a fork to mash the garlic to a smooth paste. Season with salt and freshly grated nutmeg.

2. Line a large baking sheet with parchment paper or a nonstick liner. Using a metal spatula, spread the garlic paste on the paper in two 6-by-4-inch sheets. Bake until the wafers are crisp, about 1 hour. Let cool. Slowly and carefully peel the garlic wafers off the parchment paper and slice each into quarters to make 8 pieces. —*E.A. and J.M.A.*

MAKE AHEAD The Garlic Wafers can be stored overnight in an airtight container. Serve at room temperature or recrisp for a few minutes in a 325° oven.

Tuna with Provençal Vegetables

 TOTAL: 40 MIN
     4 SERVINGS ●

Chef Bruce Sherman of North Pond in Chicago poaches tuna in an exquisite homemade tomato oil, then serves it alongside an array of vegetables and homemade herbed pasta. In this simplified version of his recipe, tuna steaks are seared in a garlicky oil, then served with a flavorful vegetable sauté.

  ½ **cup extra-virgin olive oil**
  1 **pound zucchini, halved lengthwise and thinly sliced**
  1 **red bell pepper, cut into thin strips**
  ½ **small red onion, very thinly sliced**
  4 **thyme sprigs**
  4 **garlic cloves—2 thinly sliced, 2 halved**
Salt and freshly ground pepper
  1 **tomato, coarsely chopped**
  1 **small fennel bulb—halved, cored and sliced paper-thin**
  ¼ **cup pitted kalamata olives, coarsely chopped**
  1 **tablespoon drained capers**
Four 5-ounce tuna steaks, cut 1 inch thick

1. In a large, deep skillet, heat ¼ cup of the olive oil. Add the sliced zucchini, bell pepper strips, sliced onion, thyme sprigs and sliced garlic and season with salt and pepper. Cook the vegetables over high heat, stirring occasionally, until the zucchini, pepper, and onions are crisp-tender, about 7 minutes. Add the chopped tomato, sliced fennel, chopped olives and capers, season with salt and pepper and cook, stirring, until the vegetables are completely tender, 2 to 3 minutes longer. Discard the thyme sprigs.

2. In a medium skillet, heat the remaining ¼ cup of olive oil with the halved garlic cloves over moderately high heat. Season the tuna steaks with salt and pepper and add them to the skillet; cook over moderate heat for 3 minutes, turning the steaks halfway through. Cover the skillet and cook the fish over very low heat for 2 minutes longer; the tuna should still be slightly rare in the center.

3. Spoon the vegetables onto plates. Top with the tuna steaks and the browned garlic halves and serve immediately. —*Bruce Sherman*

MAKE AHEAD The Provençal vegetables can be refrigerated overnight. Rewarm before serving.

WINE Fresh, fruity rosé.

INGREDIENT

sustainable seafood

Leading chefs around the country are making a point of serving sustainable fish. According to California's Monterey Bay Aquarium, the **best choices** include tilapia, Alaskan wild-caught salmon and pole-caught tuna. Among the varieties to **avoid:** Chilean sea bass, red snapper and imported shrimp. For up-to-date regional information about making sustainable seafood choices, check out the Monterey Bay Aquarium website: mbayaq.org/cr/seafoodwatch.asp.

Grilled Trout with Smoky Tomatillo Sauce and Cucumber Salad
TOTAL: 50 MIN
4 SERVINGS ●

Chef Alex Roberts of Restaurant Alma in Minneapolis is known for using locally grown ingredients. Here, he uses chiles and tomatillos to make the base for this smoky sauce, which he pairs with grilled local trout and a tart cucumber salad.

- 1 medium cucumber—peeled, seeded and sliced into thin half-moons
- Salt
- 2 dried *guajillo* chiles
- 1 dried chipotle chile
- 2 cups boiling water
- 5 medium tomatillos, husked and rinsed (6 ounces)
- 2 tablespoons vegetable oil, plus more for brushing
- 3 medium garlic cloves, very finely chopped
- 1 small onion, diced
- 1 tablespoon finely chopped cilantro
- 2 tablespoons very finely chopped mint leaves
- Freshly ground pepper
- ¼ cup sour cream
- 1 jalapeño, seeded and very finely chopped
- 1 tablespoon chopped flat-leaf parsley
- Four 6- to 8-ounce trout fillets, with skin

1. In a colander, toss the cucumber slices with ½ teaspoon of salt and let stand until wilted, about 25 minutes. Pat dry.

2. Meanwhile, soak the *guajillo* and chipotle chiles in the boiling water until softened, 20 minutes. Discard the stems and seeds and coarsely chop the chiles.

3. Light a grill. Grill the tomatillos over high heat until they are charred all over, about 5 minutes. Discard the charred skins and coarsely chop the tomatillos.

4. In a small skillet, heat the 2 tablespoons of vegetable oil. Add two-thirds of the chopped garlic and the onion and cook them over moderate heat until softened, about 7 minutes. Transfer to a blender, then add the chopped chiles and tomatillos and the cilantro and mint. Puree the sauce and season with salt and pepper.

5. In a medium bowl, toss the wilted cucumbers with the sour cream, jalapeño, parsley and the remaining chopped garlic. Season with salt and pepper.

6. Brush the trout fillets with vegetable oil and season with salt and pepper. Oil the grate and grill the fish over high heat, skin side down, until the skin is crisp, about 3 minutes. Turn the fish fillets over and grill until they are just cooked through, about 2 minutes longer. Transfer the grilled trout to plates and serve with the chile-tomatillo sauce and cucumber salad. —*Alex Roberts*

MAKE AHEAD The sauce can be refrigerated overnight; serve at room temperature.
WINE Fresh, fruity rosé.

INGREDIENT
tamarind

Tropical tamarind pods contain a sweet-tart pulp that is pressed into blocks and sold in Indian and Latin markets. Mashed with water and strained, the fruit turns into a tangy liquid that can be used to brighten dishes like the fish curry at right.

Fish Curry with Tamarind
TOTAL: 1 HR 30 MIN
6 SERVINGS ●

Tangy tamarind, creamy coconut milk and a homemade spice paste give this grouper and vegetable curry many layers of deep flavor. If you're feeling particularly adventurous, ask your fishmonger to give you a fish head or two to add to the pot.

- 8 cups water
- Salt
- 6 skinless grouper fillets (6 to 7 ounces each)
- 4 ounces pressed tamarind, cut into large chunks
- 4 dried small red chiles, soaked in hot water for 10 minutes and drained
- 4 garlic cloves, thickly sliced
- 2 tablespoons mild curry powder
- 1 tablespoon coriander seeds
- 1 tablespoon cumin seeds
- ½ tablespoon *belacan* (see Note), crushed
- ¼ cup plus 2 tablespoons vegetable oil
- ½ teaspoon mustard seeds
- 1 large onion, very thinly sliced
- 12 fresh curry leaves
- 1 stalk of fresh lemongrass, bottom 6 inches only, smashed
- One 14.5-ounce can unsweetened coconut milk (1⅓ cups)
- ½ pound okra, stem ends trimmed
- 1 Japanese eggplant, cut into 1-inch pieces
- 2 medium tomatoes, each cut into 6 wedges
- 2 to 3 Thai chiles, halved and seeded
- 1 teaspoon sugar

1. In a large, deep skillet, bring the water to a simmer with 1 tablespoon of salt over high heat and stir to dissolve the salt. Add the grouper fillets to the salted water and poach over low heat for 6 minutes, until the fish is partially cooked. Using a slotted spoon, transfer the grouper fillets to a large platter. Carefully pour 4 cups of the fish poaching liquid into a medium bowl and discard the rest.

2. Pour 2 cups of the reserved poaching liquid into another bowl. Add the tamarind and use a potato masher to break it up as

much as possible. Strain the tamarind juice into a small bowl, pressing on the solids; discard the solids.

3. In a small skillet, combine the soaked red chiles, sliced garlic, curry powder, whole coriander seeds, whole cumin seeds and *belacan* and toast over moderate heat, stirring constantly, until fragrant, 1 to 2 minutes. Transfer the seasonings to a spice grinder and let cool. Grind the seasonings to a dry paste.

4. Wipe out the deep skillet and add the vegetable oil. Add the mustard seeds and cook over moderately low heat until they begin to pop, about 30 seconds. Add the spice paste and cook, stirring, until the color deepens slightly, about 3 minutes. Add the sliced onion, curry leaves and smashed lemongrass and cook, stirring occasionally, until the onion is softened, about 8 minutes.

5. Add the tamarind juice to the skillet and bring to a boil. Add the coconut milk, okra, eggplant, tomatoes, Thai chiles, sugar and the remaining 2 cups of fish poaching liquid and bring to a simmer over high heat. Season with salt and cook the curry sauce over low heat until the vegetables are tender and the liquid is thickened slightly, about 40 minutes.

6. Cut the grouper fillets into 2-inch pieces and nestle them in the curry sauce. Simmer the curry over moderately high heat until the grouper is just cooked through, about 5 minutes longer.

—*Zak Pelaccio*

SERVE WITH Steamed rice.

NOTE *Belacan,* a pungent seasoning made by grinding small shrimp into a paste that is fermented, dried and pressed into cakes, is available from indomart.us. It is often toasted, as it is here.

MAKE AHEAD The recipe can be prepared through Step 5 and refrigerated overnight. Return the curry to a simmer before adding the pieces of grouper.

WINE Ripe, luxurious Chardonnay.

GRILLED TROUT WITH SMOKY TOMATILLO SAUCE AND CUCUMBERS

FISH CURRY WITH TAMARIND

Marinated Fish with Salmoriglio Sauce

ACTIVE: 30 MIN; TOTAL: 1 HR

4 SERVINGS ●

FISH

White vinegar

2 pounds fish fillets, such as wild salmon, arctic char, ruby trout or halibut, with or without skin

Salt

2 tablespoons fresh lemon juice

⅓ cup fine, dry bread crumbs

2 tablespoons extra-virgin olive oil

SALMORIGLIO SAUCE

2 tablespoons thyme leaves

1½ tablespoons fresh lemon juice

1 tablespoon Dijon mustard

Salt

2 tablespoons unsalted butter, softened

3 tablespoons extra-virgin olive oil

1. PREPARE THE FISH: Pour a little of the vinegar over the fish fillets, then rinse them under cold running water. Pat dry and arrange on an ovenproof glass or ceramic platter. Rub a little salt over the skinless sides of the fillets and sprinkle with the lemon juice. Spread half of the bread crumbs over the fish and drizzle with 1 tablespoon of the olive oil; turn the fillets over and repeat with the remaining bread crumbs and oil. Cover and let marinate at room temperature for 30 minutes.

2. MEANWHILE, MAKE THE SALMORIGLIO SAUCE: In a mini food processor, combine the thyme, lemon juice, mustard and salt. Pulse for 1 minute. Add the butter and process until completely smooth. With the machine on, add the oil in a thin, constant stream until fully incorporated. Season the sauce with salt and pour into a sauceboat.

3. Preheat the oven to 400° or light a grill. Bake the fish on the platter until just cooked through, about 12 to 15 minutes. Alternatively, grill the fish, skin side down for skin-on fillets, for about 5 minutes; turn and grill just until they flake, about 4 minutes longer. Transfer the fish to a serving platter. Pour the sauce over the fillets and serve right away. —*Marcella Hazan*

WINE Rich, complex white Burgundy.

Nantucket Clambake

ACTIVE: 2 HR; TOTAL: 4 HR

12 SERVINGS

A classic New England clambake is a terrific weekend activity. It does require some planning, however. Here are a few key points:

Most public beaches prohibit fires. Ask the local fire, parks and health departments if permits are required. Keep a fire extinguisher and bucket of seawater close by.

Avoid flooding your pit. Check the tide tables to plan the clambake for low tide. To ensure the water table is low enough, dig a small, two-foot-deep test hole. If the hole is still dry after an hour, dig your pit.

Be sure to get the right-sized rocks: too small and they'll lose their heat too quickly; too large, and they won't heat through.

Don't use just any seaweed. The pockets of water and air in rockweed produce the necessary steam and flavor.

Hold all the ingredients in coolers while you build the pit and fire.

EQUIPMENT

Fire extinguisher

1 large bucket

1 or 2 full-size shovels

120 rocks, about the size of grapefruits

50 hardwood logs, each about 2 feet long and 8 inches in diameter

Screwdriver

Twelve 9-by-13-by-1½-inch disposable aluminum baking pans

Heavy-duty oven mitts

25 pounds rockweed

Three 10-by-8-foot canvas tarps, soaked in water

INGREDIENTS

3 pounds new potatoes

Twelve 1-pound lobsters

12 pounds littleneck clams, scrubbed and rinsed

2 pounds dried chorizo sausage

1 dozen ears of unhusked corn

6 sticks (1½ pounds) unsalted butter, melted

1. In a large, deep pot, cover the potatoes with cold, salted water and bring to a boil. Simmer for 5 minutes. Drain well.

2. On a flat beach, dig a 6-by-4-foot pit 2 feet deep. Line the pit with 90 rocks. Dig a 2-foot-wide pit nearby, also 2 feet deep.

3. Using 8 logs, build a bonfire in the large pit. Over the next hour and 45 minutes, add 6 logs to the fire every 15 minutes, building the fire outward so that it covers the base of the pit. After the first 45 minutes, as the logs turn to coals, add 20 rocks to the fire. When the logs have completely turned to coals, after about 2 hours, shovel the 20 rocks to the sides. Leaving a 1-inch-thick layer of coals atop and between the rocks, shovel the rest of the coals into the smaller pit and extinguish with water.

4. Meanwhile, use a screwdriver to perforate the baking pans, punching holes in the bottoms about every inch.

5. Arrange the potatoes and lobsters together in 6 of the pans. Arrange the clams, chorizo and corn in the 6 remaining pans.

6. Wearing mitts, line the pit with a ½-inch-thick layer of rockweed. Arrange the pans on the rockweed in a single layer. Top the pans with a 1-inch-thick layer of rockweed. Fold the tarps in half lengthwise to measure 5 by 8 feet. Stack them on top of the rockweed. Weight down the edges of the top tarp with the remaining 10 rocks to trap the steam. Bake for about 1 hour, checking after 45 minutes. The lobsters and potatoes should be done; the clams, corn and chorizo will need another 15 minutes. When cooked, the lobsters will be bright red, the clams open and the corn and potatoes fork-tender. Serve with melted butter.

—*Gabriel Frasca and Amanda Lydon*

WINE Zesty, fresh Albariño.

Grilled Shrimp with Orange Aioli

ACTIVE: 30 MIN; TOTAL: 1 HR 30 MIN

6 SERVINGS

Three simple ingredients in this creamy aioli—orange, honey and garlic—evoke the flavors of Provence.

SHRIMP

- 2 pounds large shrimp, shelled and deveined
- ¼ cup extra-virgin olive oil
- 1 tablespoon fresh orange juice
- 2 garlic cloves, very finely chopped

Freshly ground black pepper

AIOLI

- 1½ cups mayonnaise
- 3 tablespoons fresh orange juice
- 2 teaspoons finely grated orange zest
- 2 teaspoons honey
- 1 garlic clove, very finely chopped

Kosher salt

1. MARINATE THE SHRIMP: In a medium bowl, toss the shelled shrimp with the olive oil, fresh orange juice, chopped garlic and a generous pinch of black pepper. Cover and refrigerate the shrimp and its marinade for 1 hour or overnight.

2. MAKE THE AIOLI: Meanwhile, in a medium bowl, whisk the mayonnaise with the fresh orange juice, grated orange zest, honey and chopped garlic; season the aioli with salt.

3. Light a grill or preheat a ridged grill pan. Thread the shrimp onto 6 pairs of bamboo skewers and season the shrimp with salt. Grill the skewers over high heat, turning occasionally, until the shrimp are lightly charred and cooked through, 5 to 6 minutes. Transfer the shrimp skewers to plates and serve with the orange aioli.
—*Melissa Clark*

MAKE AHEAD The aioli can be refrigerated for up to 2 days.

WINE Complex, aromatic Chenin Blanc.

Rock Shrimp Poke with Ginger Soy Sauce and Hijiki

ACTIVE: 30 MIN; TOTAL: 50 MIN

2 SERVINGS ●

Sean O'Brien, a 2007 F&W Best New Chef, got hooked on a traditional Hawaiian dish called *poke* (which consists of raw fish chopped into bite-size pieces and seasoned) after honeymooning on the islands. O'Brien boils his shrimp, however, then adds Japanese and Hawaiian ingredients, including hijiki, edamame and roasted macadamia nuts.

- 1 pound shelled rock shrimp
- 3 tablespoons soy sauce
- 1 tablespoon rice vinegar
- 1 tablespoon fresh lemon juice
- 1 tablespoon finely grated fresh ginger
- 1 garlic clove, minced
- 1 small shallot, minced
- 1 teaspoon Asian sesame oil
- 1 teaspoon sugar
- ½ teaspoon *sambal oelek* chile paste or Sriracha
- 2 tablespoons dried hijiki seaweed
- 1 teaspoon mixed black and white sesame seeds
- 1½ cups tatsoi leaves or mâche
- ½ cup minced peeled cucumber
- 5 shiso leaves (perilla), chopped
- ¼ cup frozen shelled edamame, thawed
- 1 tablespoon minced chives

Salt

- 8 salted roasted macadamia nuts, chopped

1. In a medium saucepan of boiling, salted water, cook the shrimp until curled and cooked through, about 3 minutes. Drain and let cool, then cover and refrigerate.

2. In a small saucepan, combine the soy sauce, vinegar, lemon juice, ginger, garlic, shallot, sesame oil, sugar and *sambal oelek* and simmer over low heat for 3 minutes. Pass the dressing through a fine strainer into a small bowl, pressing on the solids.

3. Put the dried hijiki in a bowl and cover with hot water. Let stand until rehydrated, about 10 minutes. Drain well.

4. In a small skillet, toast the sesame seeds over moderately high heat until the white seeds are golden, about 30 seconds. Transfer to a plate to cool.

5. Pat the shrimp dry, then toss them with 2 tablespoons of the ginger-soy dressing. Let stand for 5 minutes.

6. In a large bowl, toss the tatsoi with the hijiki, sesame seeds, cucumber, shiso, edamame and chives. Add the shrimp and dressing and toss well. Season the *poke* with salt and toss again. Spoon the *poke* onto plates, top with the macadamia nuts and serve immediately. —*Sean O'Brien*

WINE Fresh, lively Verdicchio.

Cornish Hens with Porcini-Rice Stuffing

ACTIVE: 40 MIN; TOTAL: 2 HR 30 MIN

4 SERVINGS

Cornish hens, roasted and stuffed with buttery porcini-flecked arborio rice, make for a terrific dinner-party meal.

- ½ cup dried porcini (½ ounce)
- ½ cup boiling water
- 3 cups chicken stock or low-sodium broth
- 1 cup arborio rice
- 4 tablespoons unsalted butter, 1 tablespoon softened
- 1 small onion, minced
- 1 celery rib, minced, plus 1 tablespoon minced celery leaves
- ¼ cup freshly grated Parmigiano-Reggiano cheese

Salt and freshly ground pepper

Two 1¼-pound Cornish game hens

- ¼ cup dry red wine, such as Barbera

1. Preheat the oven to 350°. In a heatproof bowl, cover the dried porcini with the boiling water and let stand until the mushrooms are softened, about 15 minutes.

2. Meanwhile, in a medium saucepan, bring the chicken stock to a boil. Add the rice and

simmer over moderate heat until al dente, about 10 minutes. Drain the rice; reserve the cooking broth in a covered container in the refrigerator.

3. In the same pan, melt 3 tablespoons of the butter. Add the onion, celery and celery leaves and cook over moderate heat, stirring occasionally, until softened, about 7 minutes. Drain the porcini, reserving the soaking liquid. Coarsely chop the porcini, add to the saucepan and cook for 3 minutes. Remove from the heat. Pour in ¼ cup of the mushroom-soaking liquid; reserve the rest. Stir the rice into the saucepan along with the cheese; season with salt and pepper.

4. Put the Cornish hens in a medium flame-proof roasting pan. Stuff the cavities with the porcini-rice mixture; you will have about 1 cup of stuffing left over. Wrap the remaining rice in a foil packet. Spread the 1 tablespoon of softened butter over both hens' breasts and legs and season the hens inside and out with salt and pepper.

5. Roast the hens in the upper third of the oven until they are nicely browned and an instant-read thermometer inserted in the thickest part of a thigh registers 165°, about 1 hour and 20 minutes. Transfer the hens to a platter and let rest in a warm place for 10 minutes. Increase the oven temperature to 400°. Bake the foil packet of stuffing until hot, about 10 minutes.

6. Meanwhile, set the roasting pan over moderately high heat. Add the wine and scrape up the browned bits from the bottom of the pan with a spoon. Add in the reserved rice-cooking broth. Pour in the reserved mushroom-soaking liquid, stopping before you reach the grit at the bottom. Simmer over moderate heat until reduced to 1 cup, 10 minutes. Season the gravy with salt and pepper and pour into a warm gravy boat.

7. Using a sharp, heavy knife, cut the hens in half and arrange on a platter, stuffing side down. Pass the gravy at the table along with the extra rice stuffing. —*Marcia Kiesel* **WINE** Complex, elegant Pinot Noir.

GRILLED SHRIMP WITH ORANGE AIOLI

ROCK SHRIMP POKE WITH GINGER SOY SAUCE AND HIJIKI

marinades for chicken

×××××× **step 1:** *pick your favorite flavors* ××××××

Vietnamese

4 SERVINGS ●

Hot, sour, salty and sweet are the dominant flavors in this vibrant Vietnamese-inspired marinade from F&W's Melissa Rubel.

SERVE WITH Shredded carrot, onion, mint, cilantro and lettuce leaves for wrapping.

- 5 tablespoons fresh lime juice
- ¼ cup vegetable oil
- 4 garlic cloves, crushed
- 1 jalapeño, halved lengthwise and thinly sliced
- 1 shallot, thinly sliced
- 2 tablespoons Asian fish sauce
- 2 teaspoons sugar

Salt and freshly ground pepper

Peruvian

4 SERVINGS ● ●

This recipe is based on Peruvian rotisserie chicken. Melissa Rubel says it's deliciously lemony and garlicky. Vinegar and hot paprika make the marinade even brighter-tasting.

SERVE WITH Avocado and red onion salad.

- ½ cup vegetable oil
- ¼ cup fresh lemon juice
- ¼ cup white wine vinegar
- 8 large garlic cloves, coarsely chopped
- 1 teaspoon turmeric
- 1 tablespoon hot paprika
- ½ teaspoon ground cumin

Salt and freshly ground pepper

Greek

4 SERVINGS ●

Melissa Rubel suggests marinating the chicken for 30 minutes for a mild taste or up to 4 hours for a more intense flavor.

SERVE WITH Cucumber and herb salad.

- ½ cup chopped dill
- ¼ cup extra-virgin olive oil
- 1 small onion, thinly sliced
- 3 garlic cloves, crushed

Six 1-inch strips of lemon zest

Juice of 1 lemon

- 2 tablespoons ouzo
- 1 teaspoon fennel seeds, crushed

Salt and freshly ground pepper

×××××× **step 2:** *make the marinade* ××××××

1. In a bowl, whisk all the ingredients. Place the chicken in a resealable bag and add the marinade. Seal the bag and toss to coat. Refrigerate for at least 30 minutes, up to 4 hours.

2. Light a grill or preheat a grill pan and brush liberally with vegetable oil. Scrape any marinade off the chicken, season generously with salt and pepper and grill.

×××××× **step 3:** *grill over moderate heat* ××××××

4 SKINLESS, BONELESS BREASTS *6 ounces each*	15 MIN, covered: turn once
4 SKIN-ON, BONE-IN BREASTS *12 ounces each*	30 MIN TOTAL, covered: 5 MIN skin side down, then 25 MIN on the other side
8 SKINLESS, BONELESS THIGHS *5 ounces each*	20 MIN TOTAL, covered: 10 MIN skinned side down, then 10 MIN on the other side
8 SKIN-ON, BONE-IN THIGHS *6 ounces each*	30 MIN TOTAL, covered: 10 MIN skin side down, then 20 MIN on the other side
8 LEGS *4 ounces each*	30 MIN, covered: turn twice

Rosemary-Grilled Chicken with Mushroom Sauce

ACTIVE: 35 MIN; TOTAL: 1 HR

4 SERVINGS ●

Cookbook author Viana La Place gets wild mushrooms from a forager who also supplies San Francisco restaurants. She combines the mushrooms with tomatoes to make a chunky sauce for chicken that is also delicious spread on grilled bread.

- 4 skinless, boneless chicken breast halves (1¼ pounds)
- 5 tablespoons extra-virgin olive oil
- 1 tablespoon chopped rosemary

Freshly ground black pepper

- 1 pound shiitake mushrooms, stems discarded and caps thinly sliced
- ½ pound cremini mushrooms, stems discarded and caps thinly sliced
- 1 small onion, very finely chopped
- 2 medium garlic cloves, very finely chopped
- 1 teaspoon chopped thyme leaves
- 3 medium tomatoes—halved, seeded and cut into ½-inch dice

Salt

1. Light a grill or preheat a ridged grill pan over moderately high heat. In a medium baking dish, brush the chicken breasts with 1 tablespoon of the olive oil and rub with the chopped rosemary. Season with black pepper and let stand for 30 minutes.

2. Meanwhile, heat the remaining ¼ cup of olive oil in a large skillet. Add the shiitake and cremini mushrooms and cook over moderately high heat, stirring occasionally, until browned, about 6 minutes. Add the chopped onion, chopped garlic and chopped thyme leaves and cook, stirring occasionally, until the onion is translucent, about 4 minutes. Add the diced tomatoes with their liquid and season the vegetables with salt and black pepper. Cover the skillet partially and cook over low heat, stirring occasionally, until the mushrooms are tender, about 15 minutes.

3. Season the chicken breasts with salt and grill over moderately high heat, turning the chicken breasts once, until they are cooked through, about 8 minutes.

4. Meanwhile, rewarm the mushroom sauce over low heat. Season the sauce with salt and pepper and spoon some sauce onto each of 4 dinner plates. Slice the grilled chicken breasts on the diagonal into ½-inch-thick strips. Arrange the chicken slices over the mushroom sauce and serve. —*Viana La Place*

MAKE AHEAD The mushroom sauce can be refrigerated for up to 2 days. Rewarm the sauce before serving.

WINE Ripe, juicy Pinot Noir.

Chicken alla Diavola

ACTIVE: 30 MIN; TOTAL: 3 HR PLUS
2 DAYS INFUSING

4 SERVINGS

Less fiery than the classic version, this variation on *pollo alla diavola* ("devil's-style chicken") is nonetheless intensely seasoned. It's marinated in white wine vinegar infused with dried Sicilian oregano, then rubbed with an exotic herb mixture, or *condimento,* that includes Turkish bay laurel and myrtle leaves. Feel free to experiment with a variety of herbs for the *condimento. Pollo alla diavola* is traditionally grilled over wood embers, but the chicken can also be grilled over a charcoal or gas fire, or broiled in an oven.

- ½ cup white wine vinegar
- 1 tablespoon dried oregano
- ½ cup extra-virgin olive oil

Two 3- to 3¼-pound chickens

- 2 teaspoons dried sage
- 1 teaspoon kosher salt
- 1 teaspoon piment d'Espelette or Aleppo pepper, or ½ teaspoon crushed red pepper
- 1 teaspoon dried rosemary
- ½ teaspoon freshly ground black pepper

1. In a small jar, combine the white wine vinegar with the dried oregano. Cover and let infuse at room temperature for 2 days. Strain the oregano-infused vinegar into a small bowl and stir in the olive oil.

2. Using kitchen shears, remove the wing tips and the backbones from the chickens. Set the chickens on a large rimmed baking sheet, skin side up, and press down firmly on the breastbones to flatten the chickens so that the legs face the breasts. Score each breast, drumstick, thigh and wing halfway to the bone in two places per part. Drizzle all but 2 tablespoons of the oregano vinegar–olive oil mixture over both sides of the chickens and rub the mixture into the meat. Cover and refrigerate the chicken for 1 hour.

3. In a small bowl, combine the dried sage with the kosher salt, piment d'Espelette, dried rosemary and ground black pepper. Rub this seasoning mixture all over the chickens. Let the seasoned chickens stand at room temperature for 30 minutes.

4. Preheat the oven to 425°. Roast the chickens in the baking pan in the upper third of the oven, skin side up, basting both chickens with the remaining oregano vinegar–olive oil mixture halfway through, until the chickens are just cooked and an instant-read thermometer inserted into the thickest part of the thigh registers 165°, about 45 minutes.

5. Preheat the broiler. Pour the pan juices into a small saucepan. Transfer the pan to the broiler and broil the chickens about 4 inches from the heat, rotating the pan for even browning, until the chicken skins are browned and crisp, about 3 minutes. Using a sharp, heavy knife, cut each chicken in half lengthwise. Reheat the pan juices and serve with the chicken. —*Salvatore Denaro*

MAKE AHEAD The oregano-infused vinegar can be refrigerated in a tightly covered container for up to 2 weeks.

WINE Cherry-inflected, earthy Sangiovese.

Caribbean Jerk Chicken

TOTAL: 1 HR PLUS OVERNIGHT MARINATING

10 SERVINGS

The spirit of Jamaica's jerk sauce comes through in this superspicy, fragrant grilled chicken. To punch up the flavor even more, let the marinade sit for an additional 24 hours before coating the meat. To lower the heat, swap out Scotch bonnet chiles (among the world's hottest) for jalapeños.

- 8 scallions, chopped
- 4 large garlic cloves, chopped
- 3 Scotch bonnet chiles, chopped
- 1 small onion, chopped
- ¼ cup dark brown sugar
- 2 tablespoons chopped thyme
- 2 tablespoons ground allspice
- 1¼ teaspoons freshly grated nutmeg
- 1 teaspoon cinnamon
- ½ cup white vinegar
- ¼ cup soy sauce
- ¼ cup fresh lime juice
- ¼ cup fresh orange juice
- ¼ cup vegetable oil

Three 4-pound chickens,
    each cut into 8 pieces
Salt and freshly ground pepper
Green Tomato Salsa (recipe follows),
    for serving

1. In a food processor, combine all of the ingredients up through the oil; process to a paste. Put the chicken in a bowl, pour the marinade over and coat the chicken. Cover and refrigerate overnight.

2. Light a grill. Remove the chicken pieces from the marinade, leaving on a coating of spice paste. Season the chicken pieces with salt and pepper. Grill the chicken over moderately high heat, turning often, until the skin is nicely charred and the chicken is cooked through, about 30 minutes. Transfer to a platter and serve.
—*Laurent Tourondel*

MAKE AHEAD The jerk marinade can be refrigerated overnight.

WINE Intense, fruity Zinfandel.

GREEN TOMATO SALSA

 TOTAL: 20 MIN
    MAKES 4 CUPS ●●○

This salsa makes inventive use of unripened tomatoes, which can be very sour. Mixed with fresh lime juice and sweet grilled Vidalia onion, they make for a surprisingly bright accompaniment to spicy jerk chicken.

- 1 medium Vidalia onion,
    sliced ½ inch thick
- 2 tablespoons extra-virgin olive oil,
    plus more for brushing

Salt and freshly ground pepper
- 1 pound green, unripe tomatoes
- 2 tablespoons chopped cilantro
- 1 large red tomato, cored
    and coarsely chopped
- 1 tablespoon fresh lime juice

1. Light a grill. Brush the onion with oil; season with salt and pepper. Grill the onion and the green tomatoes over high heat, turning once, until charred; about 6 minutes for the onion, and 8 minutes for the tomato.

2. Chop the onion into 1-inch pieces and transfer to a bowl. Core, peel and coarsely chop the green tomatoes and add to the bowl. Stir in the cilantro, red tomato, lime juice and the 2 tablespoons of oil. Season the salsa with salt and pepper and serve.
—*L.T.*

Crispy Twice-Fried Chicken

 TOTAL: 40 MIN
    4 SERVINGS

In Kuala Lumpur, Malaysia, there are as many permutations of fried chicken as there are purveyors. This version is one of the simplest, as it doesn't require long brining or dredging the chicken in flour and battering it. Instead, using easy-to-find ingredients, the recipe calls for mixing up a spice paste quickly in a food processor, then massaging it into the chicken. The spice-rubbed chicken is fried once until nearly cooked through, then fried again to ensure crispy skin.

SPICE PASTE
- 4 small shallots, quartered
- 2 teaspoons pure chile powder
- 1 teaspoon *belacan* (see Note)
- 1 teaspoon ground coriander
- 1 teaspoon ground cumin
- 1 teaspoon ground fennel seeds
- 1 teaspoon ground turmeric
- 1 teaspoon freshly ground
    black pepper
- 1 teaspoon salt
- 1 teaspoon sugar
- ¼ teaspoon ground cloves
- ¼ teaspoon ground cinnamon

CHICKEN
- 3 cups vegetable oil, for frying

One 4-pound chicken cut into
    12 pieces (each breast half
    cut into thirds)

1. **MAKE THE SPICE PASTE:** In a mini food processor, combine all of the ingredients and process to a dry paste.

2. **PREPARE THE CHICKEN:** In a large, deep skillet, heat the vegetable oil to 365°. Rub the spice paste all over the chicken pieces, massaging it in. When the oil is ready, carefully add the chicken and fry over moderately high heat until partially cooked, about 8 minutes for the breast and 15 minutes for the thighs, drumsticks and wings. Using a slotted spoon, transfer the chicken to a rack to cool for 10 minutes.

3. Reheat the vegetable oil to 365°. Add the chicken pieces and fry them again until they are browned and cooked through, about 3 minutes for breast pieces, 5 to 6 minutes for the wings and dark meat. Drain the fried chicken on paper towels and serve. —*Zak Pelaccio*

NOTE *Belacan* is a pungent seasoning made by grinding small shrimp into a paste that is fermented, dried and pressed into cakes. It is available from indomart.us.

MAKE AHEAD The chicken can be rubbed with the spice paste and refrigerated for 2 hours before frying.

WINE Complex, elegant Pinot Noir.

10
easy ways to master the grill

Steven Raichlen, host of TV's *Barbecue University,*
has written dozens of books on grilling.
Here, he distills a library of advice into 10 simple tips.

1 *grill over wood*
Forget about the gas-versus-charcoal debate: Wood is the only fuel that adds real flavor to food. If possible, use whole hardwood logs in a wood-burning grill. The next best option is to burn hardwood chunks in a regular grill. (Light them in a chimney starter as you would charcoal.) As a last resort, toss some wood chips onto the coals of your charcoal grill—you use hardwood charcoal, right?—or in the smoker box of your gas grill just before you begin grilling.

2 *keep your cool*
You don't need to bring steaks to room temperature before grilling: There's no appreciable difference in cooking time. Steak houses keep meat refrigerated until they're ready to cook it—for reasons of convenience and food safety—and so should you.

3 *line it up*
Align the food on your grill in a neat row with soldierly precision. This helps you keep track of which foods went on the fire first, so you can turn them and take them off in order. Plus, it looks more professional—and looking professional is half the battle.

4 *flip just once*
You can't get killer grill marks (the signature of master grillmanship) or accurately gauge cooking time if you're compulsively turning over your steak every 10 seconds. To lay on a handsome set of crosshatches, rotate the steak 90 degrees after a couple of minutes of grilling.

5 *season before grilling*
You might have heard that salt "bleeds" the juices out of raw meat: It doesn't. Instead, it helps steaks form a savory crust as they cook. Just before putting the steaks on the grill, sprinkle on a generous amount of coarse salt and freshly ground black pepper.

6 *keep the grate hot, clean and oiled*
This is the grill master's mantra. Following it will prevent food from sticking and give it excellent grill marks. Before grilling, scrub the hot grate with a wire brush, then rub it with a tightly folded paper towel dipped in oil. Scrub the grate again when you're finished cooking.

7 *grill your veggies*
The dry heat of a grill intensifies a vegetable's natural sweetness. Grill tender, watery vegetables, such as bell peppers and onions, directly over the coals. Grill dense or starchy vegetables, such as sliced potatoes and eggplant, using indirect heat, as far away from the coals as possible.

8 *grip, don't stab*
Use a pair of tongs—not a barbecue fork or, worse, a knife—to turn meat or move it around on the grill. Forks and knives poke holes in the meat that can allow precious juices to drain out. If you must cut and peek to check doneness, make a small slit with a knife.

9 *know when it's done*
For steaks, chops and chicken, poke the meat with your finger: If it feels soft and squishy, it's rare; yielding, medium-rare; only slightly yielding, medium; firm and springy, well-done. For large cuts of meat, use an instant-read meat thermometer (even barbecue experts use them). Just don't let it touch any bones, or you'll get a false reading.

10 *let it rest*
When you grill a piece of meat, its muscle fibers contract and drive the juices to the center of the cut. Meat served right off the grill will taste tough and dry, but a post-grill rest allows the muscle fibers to reabsorb the juices, resulting in a tender and succulent cut. Larger pieces of meat, like leg of lamb and pork shoulder, need to rest longer than steaks and chops—for about 15 minutes.

GRILLED PORK CHOPS WITH SWISS CHARD

SLOW-ROASTED PORK WITH EGGPLANT AND FENNEL

Grilled Pork Chops with Anchovies and Swiss Chard

 **TOTAL: 45 MIN**
6 SERVINGS

Marinating these pork chops in garlic-and-anchovy-infused olive oil at room temperature for 30 minutes yields juicier meat after grilling and gives the chops another layer of flavor.

    10 oil-packed anchovies, drained
     5 medium garlic cloves, very
        finely chopped
     5 tablespoons extra-virgin
        olive oil
Six 8- to 10-ounce pork rib chops,
        about 1 inch thick
     ¼ teaspoon crushed red pepper
     3 pounds Swiss chard, stems
        and inner ribs discarded,
        leaves coarsely chopped
Kosher salt and freshly ground
        black pepper

1. In a small bowl, mash the anchovies with three-fourths of the garlic and stir in 3 tablespoons of the oil. Arrange the chops on a baking sheet and rub with the anchovy mixture. Let stand for 30 minutes.

2. Light a grill. In a large, deep skillet, cook the remaining garlic in the remaining 2 tablespoons of oil over moderately high heat until fragrant, 20 seconds. Add the crushed red pepper and cook for 20 seconds. Add the chard in handfuls, allowing it to wilt slightly before adding more. Cook the chard until tender, about 10 minutes. Season the chard with salt and black pepper and keep warm.

3. Season the pork with salt and pepper and grill over high heat, turning twice, until the chops are charred in spots and cooked through, 8 to 10 minutes. Transfer to a platter and serve with the Swiss chard.
—*Melissa Clark*

WINE Fruity, light-bodied Beaujolais.

Slow-Roasted Pork Belly with Eggplant and Pickled Fennel

ACTIVE: 1 HR; TOTAL: 5 HR
2 SERVINGS

Paul Virant, chef and owner of Vie restaurant in Western Springs, Illinois, swears by a very slow, four-hour method of roasting pork belly to render a lot of the fat and make the meat superbly succulent and tender. Seasoning the pork liberally with a mix of salt, black pepper, smoked paprika and herbes de Provence before cooking results in an amazing crust.

One 1-pound square piece of fresh
        pork belly, skin removed and
        top thick layer of fat scored
Salt and freshly ground
        black pepper
     2 teaspoons sweet pimentón
        de la Vera (smoked Spanish
        paprika)
     1 tablespoon herbes de Provence

½ teaspoon each of black peppercorns, yellow mustard seeds, fennel seeds and coriander seeds

2 cups water

1 cup Champagne vinegar or white wine vinegar

½ cup sugar

2 tablespoons kosher salt

2 medium fennel bulbs (about 1½ pounds)—cored, trimmed and thinly sliced on a mandoline

1 pound eggplant, cut into ½-inch dice

3 tablespoons plus 2 teaspoons extra-virgin olive oil

1 medium shallot, thinly sliced

1 small red chile, thinly sliced

1 tablespoon mixed small mint and flat-leaf parsley leaves, plus 2 tablespoons each of chopped mint and parsley

1. Preheat the oven to 400°. Place the pork belly fat side up in a shallow baking dish. Season the pork all over with salt, pepper, the smoked paprika and the herbes de Provence. Roast for 1 hour. Reduce the oven temperature to 200° and bake for 3 hours longer, rotating the dish a few times, until the pork is very tender and richly browned. Remove the pork from the oven and let stand for 15 minutes.

2. Meanwhile, in a large saucepan, toast the peppercorns, mustard seeds, fennel seeds and coriander seeds over moderately high heat until fragrant, about 30 seconds. Transfer the seeds to a spice grinder and let cool completely. Grind the seeds very coarsely.

3. Return the ground spices to the saucepan. Add the water, vinegar, sugar and salt and bring to a boil, stirring to dissolve the sugar. Spread the fennel slices in a large, shallow, heatproof dish in an even layer. Pour the pickling liquid over the fennel and let cool to room temperature. Cover and refrigerate for at least 2 hours.

4. In a colander, toss the eggplant with ½ teaspoon of salt. Set a small plate on the eggplant and let stand for 1 hour to release the bitter juices. Pat the eggplant dry.

5. In a large skillet, heat 3 tablespoons of the olive oil. Add the eggplant and cook over moderately high heat, stirring occasionally, until browned and tender, about 4 minutes. Add the shallot and chile and cook, stirring, until softened, about 2 minutes. Season with salt and pepper and stir in the mint and parsley leaves. In a small bowl, toss the chopped mint and parsley with the remaining 2 teaspoons of olive oil and season with salt.

6. Spoon the eggplant onto plates. Using a serrated knife, cut the pork belly into ¼-inch-thick slices; set the slices next to the eggplant. Using a slotted spoon, transfer the pickled fennel to the plates. Garnish with the chopped herbs and serve.

—*Paul Virant*

MAKE AHEAD The pickled fennel can be refrigerated in its liquid for up to 1 week.

WINE Intense, spicy Syrah.

Roast Pork Loin with Saba

ACTIVE: 30 MIN; TOTAL: 1 HR 30 MIN PLUS OVERNIGHT MARINATING

4 SERVINGS

Saba (reduced grape must) adds a tangy-sweet richness to this glazed roast pork.

½ cup plus 2 tablespoons extra-virgin olive oil

8 thyme sprigs

4 rosemary sprigs

2 garlic cloves, minced

1 bay leaf

½ cup plus 2 tablespoons *saba* (see Note) or *vincotto*

One 2-pound pork loin

Salt and freshly ground pepper

1 cup dry red wine

1 cup vegetable stock or low-sodium broth

1 teaspoon cornstarch dissolved in 1 tablespoon water

1. In a large bowl, combine ½ cup of the olive oil with the thyme sprigs, rosemary sprigs, minced garlic, bay leaf and 2 tablespoons of the *saba*. Add the pork loin and turn to coat with the marinade. Cover and refrigerate overnight, turning the pork in the marinade a few times.

2. Preheat the oven to 350°. In a large ovenproof skillet, heat the remaining 2 tablespoons of olive oil. Remove the pork loin from the marinade; reserve the marinade. Season the pork all over with salt and pepper, add the meat to the skillet and cook over moderate heat until it is browned all over, about 2 minutes per side. Transfer the pork to a plate.

3. Add the red wine to the skillet and bring to a boil over high heat, scraping up any browned bits from the bottom of the skillet. Add the vegetable stock and the reserved marinade and bring to a boil. Add the pork, fat side up, and roast in the oven for about 50 minutes, or until an instant-read thermometer inserted in the center of the loin registers 140°.

4. Transfer the pork to a rimmed baking sheet and let rest for 10 minutes. Strain the liquid from the skillet into a medium saucepan and bring to a simmer over moderate heat. Add ¼ cup of the *saba* and stir in the cornstarch slurry. Simmer the sauce, stirring, until thickened, about 3 minutes. Season with salt and pepper.

5. Preheat the broiler. Brush the top of the roast with 2 tablespoons of the *saba* and broil for about 1 minute, or until glazed. Turn the roast, brush with the remaining 2 tablespoons of *saba* and broil for 1 minute. Let the pork rest for 10 minutes. Carve the roast and serve with the sauce.

—*Efisio Farris*

NOTE *Saba*, the molasses-thick Italian condiment made from reduced grape must (unfermented juice), is available at specialty food stores and by mail-order from igourmet.com and gourmetsardinia.com.

WINE Intense, spicy Syrah.

Crispy Pork Milanese

TOTAL: 30 MIN
6 SERVINGS ●

The mix of *panko* (Japanese bread crumbs) and Parmesan cheese in this crust gets delightfully crunchy when pan-fried.

- 6 pork cutlets (1½ pounds), pounded ¼ inch thick

Kosher salt and freshly ground pepper

- 1 cup *panko* (Japanese bread crumbs)
- ½ cup freshly grated Parmigiano-Reggiano cheese (2 ounces)
- ¼ teaspoon dried oregano, crumbled
- ⅛ teaspoon freshly grated nutmeg
- ½ cup all-purpose flour
- 2 large eggs, beaten

Olive oil, for frying

Lemon wedges, for serving

1. Season the cutlets with salt and pepper. In a shallow bowl, mix the *panko* with the cheese, oregano and nutmeg. Put the flour and eggs in 2 bowls. Line a baking sheet with paper towels. Dredge the cutlets in the flour, tapping off the excess, then dip them in the eggs, allowing excess to drip back into the bowl. Coat the cutlets with the *panko* mixture, pressing to help them adhere.

2. In each of 2 large skillets, heat ¼ inch of olive oil until shimmering. Add the cutlets to the skillets and fry over high heat, turning once, until crisp, golden brown and cooked through, about 4 minutes total. Drain the pork on paper towels and serve at once with lemon wedges. —*Melissa Clark*

SERVE WITH Tomato salad.
WINE Juicy, fresh Dolcetto.

Milk-Braised Pork Tenderloin with Spinach and Strawberry Salad

ACTIVE: 40 MIN; TOTAL: 1 HR 20 MIN
4 SERVINGS

Four 6-ounce pieces of trimmed pork tenderloin

Salt and freshly ground white pepper

- 1½ tablespoons tarragon mustard or Dijon mustard
- 3 tablespoons extra-virgin olive oil
- 2 cups whole milk
- 4 garlic cloves, halved
- 1 sage sprig
- 2 large sage leaves, minced, plus 12 small sage leaves for garnish
- 1 tablespoon tawny port or oloroso sherry
- 2 cups baby spinach leaves
- 4 large strawberries, cut into matchsticks

1. Season the pork with salt and white pepper, then slather it with the mustard. In a medium nonstick skillet, heat 2 tablespoons of the olive oil. Add the pork and cook over moderately high heat, turning twice, until browned, about 9 minutes. Transfer the pork to a plate.

2. Pour off the oil in the skillet. Add the milk, garlic and sage sprig. Simmer over moderately low heat until the garlic is almost tender, about 20 minutes.

3. Add the pork to the skillet along with any accumulated juices and simmer, turning the pieces every 5 minutes, until an instant-read thermometer inserted at the thickest part of a piece of pork registers 140°, about 20 minutes. Transfer the pork to a plate. Cover with foil and keep warm. Discard the sage sprig.

4. In a blender, puree the milk with the garlic until smooth. Return the sauce to the skillet, stir in the minced sage and season with salt and white pepper.

5. In a medium bowl, combine the remaining 1 tablespoon of oil with the port and season with salt and white pepper. Slice the pork 1 inch thick and arrange on plates. Spoon the garlic-sage milk sauce on top. Garnish with the small sage leaves. Toss the spinach and strawberries in the dressing and serve the salad alongside the pork. —*Elena Arzak and Juan Mari Arzak*

WINE Earthy, medium-bodied Tempranillo.

Smoky Strip Steaks with Chimichurri Sauce

ACTIVE: 30 MIN; TOTAL: 1 HR
10 SERVINGS

- ½ cup vegetable oil
- ½ cup extra-virgin olive oil
- 2 tablespoons white wine vinegar
- ½ cup chopped parsley
- ½ cup chopped cilantro
- 4 piquillo or roasted red bell peppers (from a jar), chopped
- 4 garlic cloves, minced
- 2 tablespoons minced onion
- 1 tablespoon fresh lime juice
- 2 teaspoons crushed red pepper

Salt and freshly ground pepper

Ten 10-ounce strip steaks, cut ¾ inch thick

- 2 tablespoons unsalted butter, melted

Smoked sea salt (like Halen Môn) and smoked black pepper (like Cattleman's; see Note)

1. Light a grill. In a bowl, whisk the oils with the vinegar. Stir in the parsley, cilantro, piquillos, garlic, onion, lime juice and crushed red pepper. Season with salt and pepper and let stand for 20 minutes.

2. Brush the steaks on both sides with the melted butter and season them with the smoked salt and pepper. Grill the steaks over moderately high heat, turning once, until nicely charred and medium-rare, about 8 minutes. Transfer to a platter and let rest for 10 minutes.

3. Slice the steaks 1 inch thick and arrange on the platter; spoon some of the chimichurri sauce on top. Serve, passing more smoked salt and pepper and the remaining chimichurri on the side. —*Laurent Tourondel*

NOTE Smoked black pepper is available at adrianascaravan.com.

MAKE AHEAD The chimichurri sauce can be refrigerated overnight. Bring to room temperature before serving.

WINE Rustic, peppery Malbec.

Grilled Steaks with Sweet-Spicy Hoisin Sauce

TOTAL: 50 MIN

6 SERVINGS

This sweet-and-savory Asian-inspired sauce, flavored with hoisin, ginger and soy, is delicious with the grilled beef.

- ¼ cup vegetable oil, plus more for rubbing
- 4 medium shallots, very thinly sliced
- 4 garlic cloves, minced
- 1 tablespoon finely grated ginger
- ½ teaspoon crushed red pepper
- ⅓ cup chopped cilantro
- ⅓ cup hoisin sauce
- 3 tablespoons soy sauce
- ½ cup chicken stock
- 3 tablespoons honey
- 3 tablespoons unsalted butter

Six ½-pound strip steaks

- 2 large sweet onions, sliced crosswise ½ inch thick

Salt and freshly ground black pepper

1. Light a grill. In a medium saucepan, heat the ¼ cup of vegetable oil. Add the shallots, garlic, ginger, crushed red pepper and cilantro and cook over moderate heat, stirring occasionally, until softened, about 7 minutes. Add the hoisin, soy sauce and chicken stock, raise the heat to moderately high and boil until thickened, about 5 minutes. Stir in the honey. Remove from the heat and stir in the butter until blended; keep the sauce warm.
2. Generously rub the steaks and onions with oil and season with salt and pepper. Grill the steaks over high heat for 4 minutes per side, or until nicely browned and medium-rare. Transfer the steaks to a carving board and let rest for 5 minutes. Grill the onions for 4 minutes per side, or until charred. Transfer the onions to a platter.
3. Thickly slice the steaks and arrange on the platter. Serve with the steak sauce. —*Wolfgang Puck*

WINE Intense, fruity Zinfandel.

Vitello Tonnato

ACTIVE: 30 MIN; TOTAL: 2 HR PLUS 4 HR CHILLING

6 SERVINGS ●

In chef Scott Conant's version of the classic *vitello tonnato,* succulent chilled veal is smothered in a tangy, creamy sauce of canned tuna, egg yolks, anchovies, fresh lemon juice and capers.

- ¾ cup plus 2 tablespoons extra-virgin olive oil

One 2½-pound veal top-loin roast, tied

Salt and freshly ground pepper

- 3 large eggs, at room temperature
- 4 anchovy fillets
- 1 tablespoon drained capers
- 2 tablespoons white wine vinegar
- 2 tablespoons fresh lemon juice

One 6-ounce can Italian tuna in oil, drained and flaked

- 1 tablespoon water
- 2 tablespoons chopped parsley

1. Preheat the oven to 325°. In a medium skillet, heat 2 tablespoons of the oil. Season the veal with salt and pepper and cook over high heat, turning, until golden brown, 8 minutes. Roast for 1 hour and 20 minutes, until an instant-read thermometer inserted in the center of the meat registers 135°. Let the roast cool, then wrap in plastic and refrigerate until chilled, at least 4 hours.
2. Meanwhile, in a saucepan of boiling water, cook the eggs for 4 minutes. Drain and cool slightly in cold water. Cut off the tops and scoop the soft yolks into a blender. Blend in the anchovies, capers, vinegar and lemon juice until smooth. With the machine on, add the remaining ¾ cup of oil in a very thin stream, blending until creamy. Blend in the tuna until smooth, then add the water to thin the sauce slightly; season with salt and pepper. Refrigerate until chilled.
3. Thinly slice the roast. Arrange the slices on plates and spoon the sauce on top. Garnish with the parsley and serve. —*Scott Conant*

WINE Fresh, lively Soave.

Ham-and-Cheese-Stuffed Veal Chops

TOTAL: 35 MIN

4 SERVINGS

- 4 veal rib chops (about ¾ pound each)

Salt and freshly ground pepper

- 4 slices of ham (2 ounces)
- 4 slices of truffled pecorino cheese (2 ounces)
- ¼ cup extra-virgin olive oil
- 5 tablespoons unsalted butter— 2 tablespoons at room temperature, 3 tablespoons diced and chilled
- ½ cup Madeira
- ½ cup chicken stock or low-sodium broth

1. Preheat the oven to 425°. Using a paring knife, cut a 3-inch-deep horizontal pocket in the center of each chop. Season the chops and pockets with salt and pepper. Tuck 1 slice each of ham and cheese into each pocket and seal with toothpicks.
2. In each of 2 large skillets, heat 2 tablespoons of the oil. Add 2 chops to each skillet and cook over moderately high heat for about 1 minute. Add 1 tablespoon of the room-temperature butter to each skillet and cook, turning once, until browned, about 8 minutes. Transfer the chops to a large rimmed baking sheet and roast in the oven until the veal is pink and an instant-read thermometer inserted at the thickest point registers 130°, about 8 to 10 minutes. Discard the toothpicks.
3. Meanwhile, add ¼ cup of the Madeira to each skillet and swirl to deglaze. Scrape the juices from 1 skillet into the other. Add the stock and simmer over moderate heat until reduced to ½ cup. Remove from the heat and gradually whisk in the cold butter. Season the sauce with salt and pepper.
4. Add any juices from the baking sheet to the sauce. Pour the sauce over the chops and serve at once. —*Marcia Kiesel*

WINE Bright, tart Barbera.

the perfect burger

All-Time-Favorite Hamburger

TOTAL: 20 MIN
4 SERVINGS

The ideal hamburger combines the fattiness of chuck with the rich, beefy flavor of sirloin. F&W's Grace Parisi uses equal parts of both cuts in her mix, a foundation you can transform into all sorts of variations. When she has the time, she grinds her own meat after salting it overnight: It's an extra step that makes the burger truly superb.

- ¾ pound ground chuck, about 80 percent lean
- ¾ pound ground sirloin, about 90 percent lean

Vegetable oil

Salt and freshly ground pepper

- 4 kaiser rolls or hamburger buns, split and toasted

Grilled Chile Relish (recipe opposite), for serving

Light a grill. In a bowl, mix the ground meats and gently form into four 4-inch patties about 1½ inches thick. Make a ½-inch-deep indentation in the center of each patty, then rub lightly with the oil and season generously with salt and pepper. Grill the burgers over high heat, turning once, about 6 minutes for medium-rare; transfer to the buns, top with the relish and serve right away. —*Grace Parisi*

HOME-GROUND HAMBURGER MEAT Trim the fat around ¾ pound each of chuck roast and sirloin steak until it's ¼ inch thick. Cut the meat into 2-by-1-inch strips, transfer to a nonreactive bowl and toss with 1½ teaspoons of kosher salt. Cover and refrigerate overnight. Using a meat grinder fitted with a medium disk, grind the meat.

GRILLED CHILE RELISH

TOTAL: 20 MIN
MAKES 3 CUPS ● ● ○

- 4 poblano chiles
- 4 Anaheim chiles
- 1 large sweet onion, sliced ½ inch thick

Vegetable oil

- ¼ cup light brown sugar
- ¼ cup each of whole-grain mustard and Dijon mustard
- 2 tablespoons cider vinegar

Salt and freshly ground pepper

Light a grill. Rub the chiles and onion with oil and grill until charred, 8 minutes. Peel and seed the chiles and cut into thin strips; chop the onion. Transfer the vegetables to a saucepan. Add the remaining ingredients and bring to a simmer over moderate heat, then serve. —*G.P.*

---

three more great burgers

1 Chorizo-Olive Burgers with Fried Egg

In a food processor, mince 2 ounces of cured chorizo. Add it to the ground meat along with ¼ cup of chopped green olives. Grill the burgers. Top with roasted red peppers and a fried egg and serve right away.

2 Double-Decker Burgers with Goat Cheese

Form the ground meat into 8 patties and grill them for 2 minutes per side. Top 4 of the patties with a disk of goat cheese, some of the Grilled Chile Relish (above) and another burger and transfer to a bun.

3 Pimiento Cheese–Stuffed Burgers

In a processor, blend 4 ounces of shredded sharp cheddar, ½ teaspoon of dry mustard, ¼ teaspoon of pepper, 1 tablespoon of mayonnaise and 2 tablespoons of chopped pimientos. Stuff the burgers before grilling.

SHELLFISH PAELLA WITH FREGOLA

Lamb Chops and Ragù with Malloreddus

ACTIVE: 35 MIN; TOTAL: 1 HR

4 TO 6 SERVINGS ●

- 3 tablespoons extra-virgin olive oil
- ¼ pound ground lamb

Salt and freshly ground pepper

- 2 medium shallots, minced
- ½ small onion, finely chopped
- 2 thyme sprigs, plus 1 teaspoon chopped thyme
- 1 rosemary sprig, plus 1 teaspoon chopped rosemary
- 1 bay leaf
- 1 cup dry red wine
- ½ cup chicken stock or low-sodium broth
- 2 cups prepared tomato sauce
- 2 tablespoons chopped basil
- 8 lamb rib chops, about ½ inch thick
- 1 pound *malloreddus* pasta (see Note), *gnochetti* or *cavatelli*
- ½ cup freshly grated pecorino cheese (1½ ounces), preferably Pecorino Sardo

1. In a medium saucepan, heat 2 tablespoons of the oil. Add the lamb, season with salt and pepper and cook over moderately high heat, stirring to break up the meat, until browned, about 4 minutes. Add the shallots, onion, thyme and rosemary sprigs and bay leaf and cook over moderate heat, stirring occasionally, until softened, about 4 minutes. Add the wine and boil over high heat until reduced by three-quarters, about 4 minutes. Add the stock and tomato sauce and simmer over low heat, stirring occasionally, until thickened, about 20 minutes. Stir in the basil and season with salt and pepper. Discard the herb sprigs and bay leaf and keep warm.
2. In a large skillet, heat the remaining oil until shimmering. Season the lamb with salt and pepper and pat the chopped thyme and rosemary onto the meat. Add the chops to the skillet and cook over moderately high heat until browned outside and medium-rare within, about 3 minutes per side.
3. Meanwhile, in a large pot of boiling, salted water, cook the *malloreddus* until al dente. Drain and return to the pot. Add the lamb ragù and stir well. Stir in the cheese. Transfer the pasta to plates, top with the lamb chops and serve. —*Efisio Farris*

NOTE *Malloreddus*, a small and curved ridged pasta often flavored with saffron, is available at specialty food stores.

MAKE AHEAD The lamb ragù can be covered and refrigerated for up to 3 days.

WINE Juicy, spicy Grenache.

Shellfish Paella with Fregola

TOTAL: 1 HR

4 SERVINGS ●

Fregola, a toasted pearl-size Sardinian pasta that is quite similar to couscous, replaces rice in this Sardinian seafood-only version of paella.

- 1 quart fish stock or bottled clam juice
- ¼ teaspoon saffron threads
- 1 pound fresh fava beans, shelled (1 cup)
- ¼ cup extra-virgin olive oil
- 1 medium onion, finely chopped
- 2 cups *fregola* (11 ounces; see Note)
- 16 littleneck clams, scrubbed and rinsed
- 16 mussels, scrubbed and debearded
- 1 cup dry sherry
- 1 red bell pepper, thinly sliced
- 1 green bell pepper, thinly sliced
- 3 plum tomatoes—halved, seeded and coarsely chopped
- ½ cup drained sun-dried tomatoes, coarsely chopped
- 5 thyme sprigs
- 2 bay leaves
- 1 rosemary sprig
- 4 ounces medium shrimp, shelled and deveined
- 4 ounces squid, bodies cut crosswise into 1-inch rings, tentacles left whole

One 4-ounce piece of monkfish, cut into 2-inch pieces

- 3 tablespoons chopped dill

Salt and freshly ground pepper

1. In a medium saucepan, bring the fish stock to a simmer. Transfer 1 cup of the hot cooking liquid to a measuring cup and crumble in the saffron. Add the fava beans to the remaining stock and cook over moderate heat until bright green, about 1 minute. Using a slotted spoon, transfer the favas to a plate. Squeeze the beans out of their tough outer skins. Cover the remaining stock and keep warm over low heat.
2. In a large, deep skillet, heat the olive oil. Add the chopped onion and cook over moderate heat, stirring occasionally, until softened, about 7 minutes. Add the *fregola,* raise the heat to moderately high and cook, stirring frequently, until well coated with the oil, about 2 minutes. Add the clams, mussels and 1 cup of the hot stock and stir constantly until the shellfish start to open, about 4 minutes; discard any clams or mussels that don't open.
3. Add the sherry and simmer until reduced by half, about 3 minutes. Stir in the fava beans, bell peppers, plum tomatoes, sun-dried tomatoes, thyme, bay leaves and rosemary. Add the remaining 2 cups of hot fish stock and the saffron-infused stock to the *fregola.* Lower the heat to moderate and cook, stirring frequently, until the *fregola* is just tender, about 10 minutes.
4. Add the shrimp, squid and monkfish and cook over moderate heat, stirring a few times, until the seafood is just cooked through, about 5 minutes. Discard the bay leaves and thyme and rosemary sprigs. Stir in the dill and season with salt and pepper. Serve immediately. —*Efisio Farris*

NOTE *Fregola* is available at specialty food shops and some supermarkets.

WINE Fresh, minerally Vermentino.

Saffron Risotto with Mussels and Bottarga

TOTAL: 1 HR

4 SERVINGS

Carnaroli superfino rice from Sardinia is known for its ability to soak up flavor and to become creamier than the more widely available arborio rice. In this recipe, the rice is simmered in fish stock, creating a delicious complement to the white wine–steamed mussels.

- 6 cups fish stock or bottled clam juice

Small pinch of saffron threads

- ¼ cup extra-virgin olive oil
- 2 garlic cloves, smashed
- 3 pounds mussels, scrubbed and debearded
- 1 cup dry white wine
- 2 tablespoons chopped parsley
- 1 medium shallot, very finely chopped
- 2 cups *carnaroli superfino* or arborio rice (12 ounces)
- 2 tablespoons unsalted butter

Salt

- 1 ounce *bottarga,* thinly sliced (optional; see Note)

1. In a small saucepan, bring ½ cup of the fish stock to a simmer. Transfer the fish stock to a measuring cup and crumble in the saffron threads.

2. In a large skillet, heat 2 tablespoons of the olive oil. Add the smashed garlic and cook over moderate heat until fragrant, about 2 minutes. Add the mussels, cover and cook until the mussels start to open, about 4 minutes. Add ½ cup of the white wine and simmer over moderate heat until reduced by half, about 4 minutes. Add the saffron-infused fish stock and the chopped parsley and simmer for 3 minutes; discard any mussels that don't open. Transfer 16 of the mussels to a large bowl. Take the remaining mussels out of their shells and transfer them to another bowl along with their cooking liquid.

3. In a large saucepan, bring the remaining 5½ cups of fish stock to a simmer over low heat. In another large saucepan, heat the remaining 2 tablespoons of olive oil. Add the chopped shallot and cook over moderate heat, stirring, until softened, about 4 minutes. Add the rice and cook, stirring, until thoroughly coated with oil, about 3 minutes. Add the remaining ½ cup of white wine to the rice and simmer until the wine is reduced by half.

4. Add enough hot fish stock to the saucepan to just cover the rice and cook over moderate heat, stirring, until the stock has been absorbed by the rice. Repeat with the remaining fish stock, adding just enough each time to cover the rice and stirring until it has been absorbed before adding more. The rice is done when it's just tender and bound with a creamy sauce, about 20 minutes total. Stir in the butter and the shelled mussels and their cooking liquid. Season with salt. Divide the rice among 4 bowls and top each with a few of the mussels in their shells and the *bottarga.* Serve right away.

—Efisio Farris

NOTE *Bottarga* is a salty, flavorful Italian delicacy made by salting, pressing and drying the roe of tuna or mullet; it can be grated or sliced paper-thin. It is available at specialty food stores and online at amazon.com or gourmetsardinia.com.

WINE Fresh, fruity rosé.

Shrimp Fried Rice

TOTAL: 45 MIN

4 SERVINGS ●

Rice is a staple at every Malaysian meal, so there are always plenty of leftovers—which are, in fact, what you want when you're making this Malaysian fried rice. This dish is seasoned with *belacan* (shrimp paste), oyster sauce, soy sauce and white pepper, but it's the pickled mustard greens, which are available at Chinese markets, that provide a memorable tang.

- 3 tablespoons vegetable oil
- 2 large eggs, lightly beaten
- 2 red Thai chiles, seeded and minced
- 2 medium shallots, thinly sliced
- 2 garlic cloves, thinly sliced
- 1 teaspoon *belacan* (see Note) or 2 tablespoons Asian fish sauce
- ½ pound medium shrimp—shelled, deveined and coarsely chopped
- 3½ cups cold cooked white rice

Water, for sprinkling

- 1 teaspoon oyster sauce
- 1 teaspoon soy sauce
- ¼ to ½ teaspoon freshly ground white pepper
- ½ teaspoon sugar
- 2 scallions, thinly sliced
- ¼ cup chopped cilantro
- ⅓ cup chopped pickled mustard greens

1. Heat 1 tablespoon of the vegetable oil in a wok. Add the eggs and scramble lightly with a wooden spoon over high heat. Transfer the eggs to a plate.

2. Add the remaining 2 tablespoons of vegetable oil to the wok. When the oil is hot, add the chiles, shallots, garlic and *belacan* and stir-fry over high heat until aromatic, about 2 minutes. Add the shrimp and stir-fry for 1 minute. Add the rice, reduce the heat to moderate and cook, stirring, until heated through, 3 to 4 minutes; sprinkle the rice with water as necessary to keep it moist. Stir the oyster sauce, soy sauce, white pepper and sugar into the rice. Stir in the scrambled eggs. Transfer the rice to a platter or bowl, garnish with the scallions, cilantro and pickled mustard greens and serve.

—Zak Pelaccio

NOTE *Belacan* is a pungent seasoning made by grinding small shrimp into a paste that is fermented, dried and pressed into cakes. It is often toasted, as it is here, before being used. It is available from indomart.us.

WINE Tart, citrusy Riesling.

Bucatini with Sausage and Peas

ACTIVE: 20 MIN; TOTAL: 1 HR

6 SERVINGS ●

Bucatini is a tubular pasta (like thick spaghetti with a hole in the middle). It's great with chunky sauces, such as this tomato-based sauce enhanced with peas and wild boar sausage.

- 2 tablespoons extra-virgin olive oil
- ½ pound hot Italian sausage, casings removed
- 2 garlic cloves, minced
- 1 small shallot, minced
- 2½ cups prepared tomato sauce
- ¼ cup heavy cream
- ½ cup frozen baby peas
- Salt
- 1 pound bucatini or *perciatelli*
- ½ cup freshly grated Parmigiano-Reggiano cheese
- 2 tablespoons shredded basil

1. In a large saucepan, heat the olive oil. Add the sausage and cook over moderately high heat, breaking up the meat into small pieces with a wooden spoon, until lightly browned, about 8 minutes. Add the minced garlic and shallot and cook, stirring, until softened, about 2 minutes. Add the tomato sauce and bring to a simmer.

2. Partially cover and cook the sauce over low heat for 30 minutes. Stir in the cream and peas and simmer over low heat for 10 minutes longer. Season with salt.

3. Meanwhile, cook the pasta in boiling salted water until al dente. Drain and return the pasta to the pot. Add the tomato sauce and ¼ cup of the grated Parmigiano-Reggiano cheese and toss over low heat until the pasta absorbs some of the sauce. Transfer the pasta to bowls, top with the remaining ¼ cup of grated cheese and the shredded basil and serve. —*Joe Sponzo*

MAKE AHEAD The sauce can be refrigerated for up to 3 days.

WINE Cherry-inflected, earthy Sangiovese.

Malay Gnocchi with Shredded Pork Sauce

ACTIVE: 1 HR; TOTAL: 4 HR 30 MIN

6 SERVINGS

This dish is based on a Malay specialty called abacus seeds, which resembles gnocchi but uses a dough made with purple yam and sticky rice flour. Zak Pelaccio of Fatty Crab in New York City bases his version on roasted taro and sauces the gnocchi with a hearty East-West ragù.

GNOCCHI

- 1 pound small taro roots (about 5), scrubbed
- 2 cups all-purpose flour, plus more for dusting
- 1 extra-large egg
- 3 tablespoons unsalted butter, melted
- 3 tablespoons extra-virgin olive oil
- 1 tablespoon kosher salt

SHREDDED PORK SAUCE

- 2 tablespoons unsalted butter
- 2 tablespoons extra-virgin olive oil
- ¾ pound roasted pork, pulled into large shreds
- 1 shallot, minced
- 2 large garlic cloves, minced
- 2 green Thai chiles, thinly sliced
- ½ tablespoon tomato paste
- 1½ pounds tomatoes—peeled, seeded and coarsely chopped
- Salt and freshly ground pepper
- 1 cup chicken stock or broth
- 1 long red chile, seeded and cut into long, thin strips
- 2 scallions, thinly sliced
- 2 tablespoons coarsely chopped mint
- 2 tablespoons coarsely chopped basil

1. **MAKE THE GNOCCHI:** Preheat the oven to 350°. Wrap the taro roots individually in foil and bake for 1 hour, or until they are tender when pierced. Unwrap and let cool.

2. Slice one end off of each taro root and use a small spoon to scoop out the flesh. Press the taro through a ricer into a medium bowl. Add the 2 cups of flour and the egg, butter, oil and salt. Using your hands, knead the mixture together to form a dough. Transfer the dough to a floured work surface and knead until smooth.

3. Cut the taro dough into 3 pieces. On a lightly floured work surface, roll each piece of dough into a 1-inch-thick rope. Using a sharp knife, cut the ropes into ½-inch pieces, dipping the knife in flour as necessary to prevent sticking. Transfer the taro gnocchi to a floured baking sheet and freeze until firm, about 3 hours.

4. **MAKE THE SHREDDED PORK SAUCE:** In a large, deep skillet, melt the butter in the oil. Add the roasted pork, shallot and garlic and cook over high heat, stirring occasionally, until the shallot and garlic are lightly browned, about 5 minutes. Add the sliced Thai chiles and the tomato paste and cook, stirring, for 1 minute. Stir in the chopped tomatoes and season with salt and pepper. Add the chicken stock, red chile strips, scallions, mint and basil and cook, scraping up any browned bits stuck to the bottom of the skillet. Remove from the heat, cover and keep warm.

5. In a large saucepan of boiling salted water, cook the taro gnocchi until they rise to the surface, then simmer them until tender, about 5 minutes longer. Drain the gnocchi in a colander.

6. Add the taro gnocchi to the shredded pork sauce in the skillet. Cook over moderate heat, tossing gently, just until the gnocchi are thoroughly coated and the sauce is heated through, about 3 minutes. Season with salt and black pepper and serve right away in deep bowls. —*Zak Pelaccio*

MAKE AHEAD The taro gnocchi dough can be frozen for 2 weeks. The pork sauce can be refrigerated overnight.

WINE Cherry-inflected, earthy Sangiovese.

PAPPARDELLE WITH MILK-ROASTED BABY GOAT RAGÙ

Pappardelle with Milk-Roasted Baby Goat Ragù

ACTIVE: 1 HR; TOTAL: 3 HR 30 MIN
PLUS OVERNIGHT CHILLING
4 SERVINGS ● ●

This is a signature dish at Komi in Washington, DC. Johnny Monis, a 2007 F&W Best New Chef, slowly roasts the baby goat in milk until it's meltingly tender, then simmers it in tomato sauce before spooning it over fresh, eggy pappardelle noodles. The key to the dish is giving all of the elements enough time to come together: "We *never* serve our ragù the same day we make it," Monis says. "When the ragù is allowed to cool overnight, the flavor and texture completely change."

- ¼ cup extra-virgin olive oil
- 1½ pounds baby goat shoulder on the bone (see Note)
- Salt and freshly ground black pepper
- 1 cup whole milk
- 2 thyme sprigs
- 1 bay leaf
- ½ small cinnamon stick
- 2 tablespoons tomato paste
- 2 cups canned peeled Italian tomatoes, crushed
- 1¼ cups chicken stock or low-sodium broth
- Homemade Pappardelle (recipe follows)
- Freshly grated Pecorino Romano cheese, for serving

1. Preheat the oven to 300°. In a medium enameled cast-iron casserole, heat 3 tablespoons of the olive oil over moderately high heat. Season the goat meat with salt and black pepper and add it to the casserole. Cook over moderately high heat, turning once, until lightly browned on both sides, about 15 minutes. Spoon off the excess fat in the casserole.

2. Carefully pour in the milk, then add the thyme sprigs, bay leaf and cinnamon stick to the casserole; bring the liquid to a boil over high heat. Cover the casserole with foil and then with a lid and transfer the casserole to the oven. Braise for about 1 hour 40 minutes, turning the goat meat occasionally and spooning the cooking liquid over the meat from time to time. The goat is done when it's tender enough to pull off the bone.

3. Remove the goat meat from the casserole and let cool on a large plate. Pour the pan juices into a heatproof glass measuring cup. There should be about ½ cup of liquid. Discard the thyme sprigs, bay leaf and cinnamon stick. Pull the goat meat from the bones and cut it into ½-inch pieces. Reserve the large bones.

4. Add the remaining 1 tablespoon of olive oil to the casserole along with the tomato paste and cook, stirring, over moderate heat until sizzling, about 2 minutes. Stir in the reserved pan juices. Add the crushed tomatoes and chicken stock and bring to a boil. Season with salt and black pepper. Return the meat and bones to the casserole and simmer over very low heat until the sauce is thick and reduced to about 3½ cups, about 1 hour; discard the bones. Let cool, then cover and refrigerate the goat ragù overnight.

5. The next day, rewarm the goat ragù in the casserole. Bring a large pot of salted water to a boil. Add the pappardelle and cook until al dente, about 3 minutes. Drain well and add the pasta to the ragù; toss well. Serve the pasta and ragù in warmed, shallow bowls, passing the grated Pecorino Romano cheese on the side.
—*Johnny Monis*

NOTE You can find goat shoulder meat (preferably from a baby goat) at halal meat markets, or you can order it in advance from your butcher.

MAKE AHEAD The baby goat ragù can be refrigerated for up to 5 days or frozen for up to 1 month. Reheat the ragù gently before proceeding.

WINE Complex, aromatic Nebbiolo.

HOMEMADE PAPPARDELLE

ACTIVE: 30 MIN; TOTAL: 1 HR
MAKES 1 POUND ● ●

- 1¾ cups plus 2 tablespoons all-purpose flour, plus more for rolling
- ⅓ cup fine semolina
- 3 large eggs, at room temperature
- 3 large egg yolks, at room temperature

1. In a food processor, combine the flour and semolina and pulse several times to combine. In a measuring cup, use a fork to briefly beat the whole eggs and egg yolks together until just combined. With the food processor running, pour in the lightly beaten eggs and process until the flour is moistened; the dough may still be a bit crumbly. Turn the dough out onto a floured work surface and knead until it becomes silky smooth, about 3 minutes. Wrap the pappardelle dough in plastic and let stand at room temperature to rest for 30 minutes.

2. Divide the pasta dough into 3 pieces. Work with 1 piece of dough at a time, keeping the other pieces wrapped in plastic. Flatten the remaining piece of dough, dust it with flour and roll it through a hand-cranked pasta machine, beginning at the widest setting and stopping at (or just before) the thinnest; dust the dough lightly with flour between settings. Cut the strip into 4 pieces, 10 to 12 inches each, and dust with flour. Roll up each piece loosely and slice ¾ inch thick. Uncoil the pappardelle and toss them with flour to keep them from sticking. Transfer the finished pappardelle to a flour-dusted baking sheet. Repeat with the remaining 2 pieces of pasta dough. Toss the pappardelle occasionally to dry them out evenly and keep them from clumping. —*J.M.*

MAKE AHEAD The pappardelle can be prepared earlier in the day and kept uncovered at room temperature.

Loh Shi Fun

TOTAL: 1 HR 15 MIN

8 SERVINGS ●

Ground pork and Chinese sausage flavor this slightly sweet and supersavory hot pot of chewy rice noodles with shiitake mushrooms, pea shoots and pickled mustard greens. A just-cooked poached egg tops it all off, adding richness to the sauce, which Fatty Crab chef-owner Zak Pelaccio compares to an Italian Bolognese.

3 tablespoons vegetable oil
½ pound shiitake mushrooms, stems discarded and caps quartered
¼ cup plus 1 tablespoon Shaoxing wine (see Note) or dry sherry
¾ pound ground pork
¼ cup plus 2 tablespoons *kecap manis* (see Note)
Salt
1 teaspoon Asian sesame oil
1 pound dried pearl noodles or frozen rice cakes
6 ounces Chinese sausage, thinly sliced
6 ounces snow pea shoots or 1 bunch watercress, thick stems discarded
¾ cup chicken stock
¼ cup black vinegar
1 tablespoon soy sauce
1 tablespoon Asian fish sauce
8 large eggs
½ cup cilantro leaves
¼ cup chopped pickled mustard greens (see Note)

1. In a large, deep skillet, heat 2 tablespoons of the vegetable oil over high heat until the oil is smoking. Add the shiitake mushroom caps and stir-fry over high heat until golden and crisp in spots, about 7 minutes. Remove from the heat and carefully pour in ¼ cup of the Shaoxing wine. Return the skillet to the heat and cook, stirring, until the wine has completely evaporated, about 3 minutes. Transfer the shiitake mushroom caps to a bowl.

2. In the same skillet, heat the remaining 1 tablespoon of vegetable oil over high heat until almost smoking. Add the ground pork in clumps and cook over high heat, turning once, until the pork clumps are browned on both sides, about 6 minutes; break up the clumps. Spoon off the fat in the skillet. Add ¼ cup of the *kecap manis*, season the pork lightly with salt and cook over low heat, stirring, until the pork is nicely glazed, about 5 minutes. Stir in the sesame oil and add the reserved stir-fried shiitake mushroom caps.

3. In a medium casserole of boiling salted water, cook the pearl noodles or rice cakes until al dente, 4 to 8 minutes; drain the noodles or rice cakes thoroughly.

4. Add the noodles to the skillet along with the Chinese sausage and snow pea shoots. Add the remaining 1 tablespoon of Shaoxing wine and 2 tablespoons of *kecap manis* along with the chicken stock, black vinegar, soy sauce and fish sauce. Cover and simmer for 5 minutes, stirring occasionally.

5. Meanwhile, bring another large, deep skillet of water to a simmer. Crack the eggs into individual ramekins. Slip the eggs into the barely simmering water and cook until the whites are set but the yolks are still runny, about 4 minutes. Using a slotted spoon, transfer the poached eggs to a large plate; carefully blot the eggs dry.

6. Ladle the *loh shi fun* into deep bowls and set the poached eggs on top. Sprinkle with the cilantro and pickled mustard greens and serve right away.
—*Zak Pelaccio*

NOTE Shaoxing wine is an aged Chinese rice wine often used in cooking. It can be found in Chinese markets, as can pickled mustard greens. Dry sherry can be substituted for the rice wine. *Kecap manis* is a thick, slightly sweet Indonesian seasoning, sometimes called sweet soy sauce, that's flavored with garlic and/or star anise. It can be ordered from indomart.us.
WINE Dry, earthy sparkling wine.

Chicken Noodle Stir-Fry

TOTAL: 35 MIN

4 SERVINGS ●

Emeril Lagasse's son, E.J. (Emeril John), helped create this superquick dish.

1 pound skinless, boneless chicken breast halves, cut into 2-by-½-inch strips
2 tablespoons oyster sauce
6 ounces dried chow mein noodles
2 tablespoons vegetable oil
2 carrots, cut into ½-inch dice
1 medium onion, diced
½ red bell pepper, diced
4 canned whole baby corns, sliced crosswise ½ inch thick
2 scallions, thinly sliced
½ cup frozen shelled edamame, thawed
2 medium garlic cloves, very finely chopped
1½ teaspoons minced fresh ginger
¼ cup plus 2 tablespoons low-sodium soy sauce
2 teaspoons cornstarch mixed with 1 tablespoon water

1. In a bowl, toss the chicken strips with the oyster sauce and let stand at room temperature for 20 minutes.

2. Meanwhile, bring a large pot of salted water to a boil over high heat. Add the noodles and cook until al dente. Drain the noodles and rinse them under cold running water. Drain well and reserve.

3. In a large skillet, heat the oil over high heat until shimmering. Add the carrots, onion and bell pepper and stir-fry over high heat for 1 minute. Add the marinated chicken strips and stir-fry for 2 minutes. Add the sliced baby corn, sliced scallions, edamame, chopped garlic and minced ginger and stir-fry until the chicken is white throughout, 2 minutes. Reduce the heat to moderate. Add the noodles, soy sauce and cornstarch slurry and toss well. Transfer to bowls and serve. —*Emeril Lagasse*
WINE Fruity, low-oak Chardonnay.

Spaghettini with Eggplant and Fried Capers

TOTAL: 30 MIN
4 SERVINGS ●

When capers hit hot oil, they puff up into crispy little blossoms that can add intense flavor and crunch to pasta. Keep in mind that the longer you soak the capers before cooking them, the less salty they will be.

- ¼ cup salted capers
- 12 ounces spaghettini
- ¾ cup extra-virgin olive oil
- 1 large eggplant, peeled and cut into 1-inch dice

Salt and freshly ground pepper

- 3 medium garlic cloves, 2 very thinly sliced

Large pinch of crushed red pepper

- 1 cup ⅓-inch diced crustless Italian bread
- ¼ cup freshly grated young pecorino cheese, preferably Sardinian, plus more for serving

1. In a large cup, soak the salted capers in plenty of cold water for 15 minutes. Drain the capers and squeeze dry.

2. Meanwhile, bring a large pot of salted water to a boil over high heat. Add the spaghettini and cook until just al dente. Drain the pasta well, reserving ¾ cup of the cooking water.

3. In a large, deep nonstick skillet, heat ¼ cup of the oil until shimmering. Add the eggplant, season lightly with salt and pepper and cook over high heat, stirring occasionally, until tender, about 6 minutes. Add the sliced garlic and crushed red pepper and cook until the garlic is softened, about 2 minutes longer.

4. Meanwhile, in a small skillet, heat the remaining ½ cup of oil until shimmering. Add the capers and fry over high heat, shaking the pan slightly, until the capers are golden and puffed, 2 minutes. Using a slotted spoon, transfer the capers to a paper towel–lined plate. Add the whole garlic clove and the diced bread to the oil

and fry, stirring, until the bread is golden, about 2 minutes. Using a slotted spoon, transfer the croutons to the plate with the capers. Discard the garlic clove.

5. Add the pasta to the eggplant. Add the pecorino and the reserved cooking water and simmer, tossing, just until the water is nearly absorbed, about 2 minutes. Serve the pasta in shallow bowls, sprinkled with the fried capers and croutons. Pass freshly grated pecorino at the table.
—*Grace Parisi*

WINE Juicy, spicy Grenache.

Orecchiette with Pistachio Pesto

TOTAL: 30 MIN
6 SERVINGS ● ● ●

- 1 pound orecchiette
- 7 ounces unsalted roasted shelled pistachios (1½ cups)
- ½ cup extra-virgin olive oil
- 2 tablespoons chopped mint
- 1 garlic clove, minced
- ½ cup finely shredded pecorino cheese, plus more for serving
- 2 scallions, cut into 2-inch lengths and julienned

Salt

1. In a large pot of boiling salted water, cook the pasta until al dente.

2. Meanwhile, in a food processor, pulse the pistachios until coarsely chopped. Add the oil, mint and garlic and pulse just to combine. Transfer to a pasta bowl, stir in the cheese and scallions; season with salt.

3. Drain the pasta, reserving ½ cup of the cooking water. Return the pasta to the pot. Add the cooking water and the pesto and cook over low heat, tossing, until coated, 1 minute. Transfer the pasta to the bowl and serve, passing extra cheese on the side.
—*Frank Castronovo and Frank Falcinelli*

MAKE AHEAD The pistachio pesto can be refrigerated for up to 2 days. Bring to room temperature before proceeding.

WINE Fresh, minerally Vermentino.

Cold Peanut Noodles with Tofu and Red Peppers

TOTAL: 30 MIN
4 SERVINGS ● ●

A vast improvement on the usual sesame noodles made famous by Chinese take-out menus, this silky version includes chunks of tofu and sweet, crunchy slices of red bell pepper.

- ½ pound firm tofu, cut into ½-inch dice
- ¼ cup plus 2 tablespoons soy sauce
- ¾ pound Chinese chow mein noodles or thin linguine
- ½ cup creamy peanut butter
- ½ cup chicken stock or low-sodium broth
- 1 tablespoon rice vinegar
- ¾ teaspoon Chinese chile-garlic sauce
- 1 tablespoon chopped fresh ginger
- 1 garlic clove
- ¾ teaspoon Asian sesame oil
- 2 large red bell peppers, thinly sliced
- 3 large scallions, cut into 2-inch lengths and julienned

Cilantro sprigs, for garnish

1. In a large bowl, toss the tofu with 2 tablespoons of the soy sauce and let stand for 10 minutes.

2. Bring a large saucepan of water to a boil. Add the chow mein noodles and cook until they are al dente. Drain and rinse the noodles under cold water. Shake out any excess water and add the noodles to the tofu and soy sauce.

3. Meanwhile, in a blender, combine the remaining ¼ cup of soy sauce with the peanut butter, chicken stock, rice vinegar, chile-garlic sauce, ginger, garlic and sesame oil and puree until a smooth sauce forms. Pour the peanut sauce over the noodles, add the sliced red bell peppers and scallions and toss. Garnish with the cilantro and serve. —*Grace Parisi*

WINE Fresh, lively Gavi.

SUMMER
side dishes

Fennel Salad with Tarragon and Creamy Tapenade

 TOTAL: 20 MIN
4 SERVINGS ● ● ●

¼ cup extra-virgin olive oil

2 tablespoons fresh lemon juice

Salt and freshly ground pepper

2 fennel bulbs (2 pounds)—halved, cored and shaved on a mandoline, fronds coarsely chopped

1½ teaspoons chopped tarragon

1 tablespoon black olive tapenade

⅓ cup nonfat *fromage blanc* or nonfat Greek yogurt

¼ teaspoon fennel pollen or finely ground fennel seeds

1. In a large bowl, whisk the olive oil with the lemon juice and season generously with salt and pepper. Add the shaved fennel and chopped tarragon and toss well.

2. In a small bowl, stir the black olive tapenade into the *fromage blanc.* Spread a thin layer of tapenade cream in the center of each plate. Mound the fennel salad on top and garnish each salad with some of the chopped fennel fronds and fennel pollen. Serve the fennel salad right away.
—*David Myers*

Watermelon and Arugula Salad with Walnuts

ACTIVE: 20 MIN; TOTAL: 50 MIN
4 SERVINGS ● ●

This salad is a fabulous blend of juicy (watermelon) and crunchy (red onions and walnuts). For anyone who thinks raspberry vinegar went out with the '90s, the fruity vinaigrette will be a revelation.

3 pounds watermelon, cut into 1-inch cubes

1 small red onion, thinly sliced

1½ cups arugula

⅓ cup fresh orange juice

2 tablespoons fresh lime juice

2 tablespoons raspberry vinegar

Salt and freshly ground pepper

½ cup shredded *ricotta salata*

1 cup coarsely chopped walnuts

2 tablespoons extra-virgin olive oil

1. In a large bowl, toss the watermelon with the red onion. Cover and refrigerate until chilled, about 30 minutes.

2. Add the arugula to the watermelon. In a small bowl, combine the orange and lime juices and vinegar. Pour the dressing over the salad and season with salt and pepper. Top with the cheese and nuts; drizzle with the olive oil and serve. —*Efisio Farris*

Raw Corn and Radish Salad with Spicy Lime Dressing

 TOTAL: 25 MIN
4 SERVINGS ● ●

2 tablespoons fresh lime juice

1 small jalapeño, seeded and coarsely chopped

1½ teaspoons honey

¼ teaspoon cumin

¼ cup vegetable oil

Kosher salt and freshly ground black pepper

4 cups fresh corn kernels (from 4 ears)

6 medium radishes, halved and thinly sliced crosswise

½ cup coarsely chopped flat-leaf parsley

¼ small red onion, very thinly sliced

1. In a blender, puree the lime juice, jalapeño, honey and cumin. With the machine on, add the vegetable oil. Season with salt and black pepper.

2. In a large bowl, toss the corn with the radishes, parsley, red onion and dressing. Season the salad with salt and black pepper, transfer to plates and serve.
—*Nick Fauchald*

Mixed Grilled Vegetables with Fontina Fonduta

TOTAL: 45 MIN
6 SERVINGS ●

Chef and cookbook author Scott Conant says that *fonduta* (melted cheese sauce) is traditional throughout the Piedmont region. It is often laced with white truffles when they're in season, making it superbly rich and luxurious.

- 2 zucchini (½ pound each), cut into ½-inch rounds
- 2 yellow squash (½ pound each), cut into ½-inch rounds
- 3 large portobello mushrooms, stemmed, brown gills scraped out
- 3 plum tomatoes, halved
- 1 medium red onion, sliced ½ inch thick
- ½ cup extra-virgin olive oil
- Salt and freshly ground pepper
- 1 tablespoon thyme leaves
- ½ cup milk
- ¼ cup heavy cream
- ¾ pound Italian fontina cheese, cut into ½-inch dice (3 cups)
- 2 tablespoons freshly grated Parmigiano-Reggiano cheese
- 2 tablespoons snipped chives

1. Light a grill. Brush the zucchini, yellow squash, portobellos, tomatoes and onion with the olive oil and season with salt and black pepper. Sprinkle with the thyme leaves and grill over high heat, turning occasionally, until the vegetables are lightly charred, about 8 minutes. Transfer to a platter and keep warm.

2. Meanwhile, in a saucepan, bring the milk and cream to a boil. Add the fontina and cook over low heat, stirring, until creamy, 2 minutes. Stir in the Parmigiano-Reggiano. Strain the *fonduta* through a fine sieve and pour it into a pitcher. Season with salt and pepper. Sprinkle the vegetables with the chives and serve the *fonduta* on the side.
—*Scott Conant*

Grilled Vegetable Salad

TOTAL: 1 HR
6 SERVINGS ● ●

- 1 red bell pepper, halved and cored
- 1 yellow bell pepper, halved and cored
- 1 small fennel bulb, sliced lengthwise ⅓ inch thick
- 1 Asian eggplant, sliced lengthwise ½ inch thick
- 1 ear of corn, shucked
- 1 small onion, sliced ⅓ inch thick and separated into rings
- 1 medium zucchini or yellow squash, sliced lengthwise ½ inch thick
- 1 jalapeño
- 2 tablespoons extra-virgin olive oil, plus more for brushing
- Salt and freshly ground pepper
- 1½ cups cherry tomatoes, halved
- ⅓ cup fresh lime juice
- ¼ cup chopped cilantro
- ¾ teaspoon ground cumin

1. Light a grill. Brush the bell peppers, fennel, eggplant, corn, onion, zucchini and jalapeño with olive oil and season with salt and pepper. Grill the vegetables over moderately high heat for about 15 minutes, turning often, until their skins are lightly charred and the vegetables tender.

2. Peel the jalapeño, cut it in half and discard the stem and seeds. Coarsely chop the jalapeño and put it in a blender. Peel the bell peppers; coarsely chop them and transfer to a large bowl. Using a large knife, cut the corn kernels from the cob and add them to the bowl. Coarsely chop the remaining vegetables; add them to the bowl along with the cherry tomatoes.

3. Add the 2 tablespoons of olive oil and the lime juice, cilantro and cumin to the blender and puree until smooth. Pour the dressing over the vegetables, toss well and season with salt and pepper.
—*Wolfgang Puck*

SERVE WITH Goat Cheese–Garlic Toasts (p. 211) or grilled bread.

Salad of Bitter Greens with Balsamic-Glazed Prosciutto

TOTAL: 45 MIN
6 SERVINGS ●

Crisp, balsamic-glazed prosciutto is tossed into a salad of bitter greens and chopped egg in this brilliant combination.

- 5 tablespoons balsamic vinegar
- 3 tablespoons red wine vinegar
- 1½ teaspoons Dijon mustard
- ¼ cup extra-virgin olive oil
- Salt and freshly ground pepper
- 1 small head of frisée, leaves torn
- 3 ounces baby arugula (3 cups)
- 1 small head of radicchio, leaves torn (3 cups)
- 3 ounces dandelion greens, stems discarded and leaves torn (3 cups)
- 2 hard-cooked eggs, chopped
- 5 tablespoons unsalted butter
- 6 ounces thinly sliced prosciutto, cut into ½-inch-wide ribbons

1. In a large bowl, whisk 1 tablespoon each of the balsamic and red wine vinegars with the Dijon mustard. Whisk in 2 tablespoons of the olive oil and season with salt and pepper. Add the frisée, arugula, radicchio, dandelion greens and the chopped eggs, but don't toss the salad.

2. In a large skillet, melt 2 tablespoons of the butter in the remaining 2 tablespoons of olive oil. Cook over moderately high heat until the butter begins to brown, about 1 minute. Add the sliced prosciutto and cook, stirring occasionally, until crisp, 2 to 3 minutes. Add the remaining ¼ cup of balsamic vinegar and 2 tablespoons of red wine vinegar and cook until the liquid is slightly reduced, about 2 minutes. Remove from the heat. Swirl in the remaining 3 tablespoons of butter until melted.

3. Toss the greens and chopped eggs, season with salt and pepper and transfer to salad plates. Spoon the hot dressing over the salads and serve immediately.
—*Paul Bartolotta*

WARM SUMMER VEGETABLE SALAD
WITH BROWN BUTTER DRESSING

Warm Summer Vegetable Salad with Brown Butter Dressing

TOTAL: 45 MIN
4 SERVINGS ● ● ●

For this exquisitely simple recipe, wedges of crunchy radish are tossed in a warm dressing made with brown butter and Spanish Moscatel vinegar, which is golden and slightly bittersweet.

2 small leeks or 16 baby leeks, white and tender green parts only, halved and washed

½ pound green beans

2 ounces baby arugula (4 cups)

2½ tablespoons unsalted butter

¼ cup Moscatel, white balsamic or late-harvest wine vinegar

¼ cup thinly sliced red onion

16 small radishes, quartered

Salt and freshly ground pepper

¼ cup small or torn mint leaves

1. Bring a medium saucepan of salted water to a boil over high heat. Add the leeks, cover and simmer over low heat until tender, about 10 minutes (3 minutes for baby leeks). Using a slotted spoon, transfer the cooked leeks to a paper towel–lined plate to drain. Cut the leeks lengthwise into long, thin strands.

2. Add the green beans to the saucepan. Cook until just tender, 4 minutes. Drain well and pat dry with paper towels.

3. Put the baby arugula in a large salad bowl. In a large skillet, heat the butter and cook over moderately high heat until richly browned, about 2 minutes. Add the leeks, green beans, vinegar, sliced red onion and quartered radishes and toss until the vegetables are warmed. Spoon the vegetables and brown butter dressing over the baby arugula and toss the salad well; season with salt and ground pepper. Arrange the salad on 4 small salad plates, garnish each plate with 1 tablespoon of the torn mint leaves and serve immediately.
—*Gabriel Rucker*

Tomato, Cucumber and Onion Salad

TOTAL: 20 MIN
4 SERVINGS ● ●

Lightly salting the tomato wedges and letting them stand briefly concentrates their flavor significantly. Be sure to use a sweet onion to maintain the balance in this refreshing salad.

2 medium tomatoes, preferably an heirloom variety

Salt

½ teaspoon red wine vinegar

1 small sweet onion, such as Vidalia, coarsely chopped

1 cucumber—peeled, halved lengthwise, seeded and cut into ½-inch dice

¼ cup extra-virgin olive oil

Basil leaves, torn if large

1. Halve the tomatoes lengthwise and gently peel them using a swivel-bladed vegetable peeler in a back-and-forth motion. Cut the peeled tomato halves into bite-size, irregular wedges, discarding any runny seeds. In a small bowl, toss the peeled tomato wedges with a pinch of salt and the red wine vinegar. Let the tomato wedges and red wine vinegar stand at room temperature for at least 10 minutes and up to 30 minutes.

2. Meanwhile, in a mini food processor, pulse the sweet onion until it is very finely chopped; be careful not to overprocess the onion into a puree.

3. Shortly before serving, use a slotted spoon to transfer the marinated tomato wedges to a medium bowl, leaving the tomato juices behind. Add the diced cucumber and finely chopped onion and toss well, then season with salt. Add the olive oil and toss the salad well to coat the vegetables with oil, then add the basil leaves and toss once more, until well combined. Serve the Tomato, Cucumber and Onion Salad immediately.
—*Marcella Hazan*

Tomato and Bread Salad with Watercress Salsa Verde

TOTAL: 25 MIN
4 SERVINGS

A bright-tasting salsa verde, made with watercress, capers, garlic and anchovy, lends flavor to a luscious salad of juicy tomatoes, chewy bread cubes and salty pecorino cheese. The salsa verde is good on almost anything, from fish to meat.

2 cups watercress leaves, thick stems discarded

2 tablespoons capers, drained

1 garlic clove

1 oil-packed anchovy fillet

½ cup extra-virgin olive oil

¼ cup red wine vinegar

Kosher salt and freshly ground pepper

8 cups diced ciabatta bread (1¼-inch dice)

1 pound tomatoes, cut into 1-inch dice

1½ ounces shaved pecorino cheese (¾ cup)

1. In a food processor, pulse the watercress, capers, garlic and anchovy until finely chopped. Add the oil and vinegar and process until the dressing is smooth. Season with salt and pepper.

2. In a large bowl, toss the ciabatta, tomatoes, shaved pecorino and dressing; season with salt and pepper and serve.
—*Nick Fauchald*

TECHNIQUE

making brown butter

Brown butter can be a quick sauce for fish, ravioli or vegetables. It's made (as in the warm salad at left) by melting butter until the solids turn a toasty brown and take on a rich, nutty flavor.

Bread Salad with Tomatoes and Olives

TOTAL: 35 MIN
6 SERVINGS ● ● ○

Salvatore Denaro, chef-owner of Il Bacco Felice in Foligno, Italy, makes a *panzanella* that's quite different from the typical summer bread salad served at other Umbrian trattorias. His zesty version includes southern Italian green olives, dried oregano and whole-grain barley rolls from Puglia called *friselle*. Any good grainy, country-style loaf works nicely in this recipe; just make sure it's *pane raffermo,* what the Italians call bread that is "firmed up" and quite stale.

- 1 cup water
- 3 tablespoons red wine vinegar
- 1 piece of stale, rustic whole-grain bread, cut into 1-inch cubes (6 ounces)
- 1/3 cup extra-virgin olive oil
- 1 pint cherry tomatoes, halved
- 1 cup thinly sliced celery
- 1 cup coarsely chopped green olives
- 1 medium sweet onion, thinly sliced
- 1/2 cup coarsely chopped basil
- 1/2 cup coarsely chopped mint
- 1 tablespoon dried oregano

Salt and freshly ground pepper

1. In a large bowl, mix the water with 2 tablespoons of the red wine vinegar. Add the stale bread cubes to the vinegar and water and swirl briefly, then drain the bread in a colander, gently squeezing out any excess moisture.

2. In a small bowl, mix the olive oil with the remaining 1 tablespoon of red wine vinegar. In a large bowl, stir together the halved cherry tomatoes, sliced celery, chopped green olives, sliced sweet onion and chopped basil, mint and oregano. Gently fold in the soaked bread cubes. Add the dressing and toss well. Season with salt and ground pepper and serve.
—*Salvatore Denaro*

Rice Salad with Merguez and Preserved Lemon Dressing

TOTAL: 40 MIN
6 SERVINGS ●

- 1 cup jasmine rice
- 1½ cups water

Salt

- ½ cup extra-virgin olive oil
- 2½ tablespoons fresh lemon juice
- ¼ preserved lemon, rind only, minced (see Note)
- 2 garlic cloves, minced
- 1 tablespoon *harissa*
- ¾ teaspoon ground cumin
- ½ fennel bulb, cored and finely diced
- 1/3 cup pitted Picholine olives, chopped (2 ounces)
- 1 pound merguez sausage, cut into ¾-inch-thick slices
- 1 pint grape tomatoes, halved
- 1 cup coarsely chopped parsley

1. In a medium saucepan, combine the rice with the water and ½ teaspoon of salt. Bring to a boil, cover and cook over low heat until tender, about 18 minutes. Fluff with a fork and transfer to a medium bowl.

2. Meanwhile, in a small bowl, whisk all but 1 teaspoon of the oil with the lemon juice, preserved lemon, garlic, *harissa* and cumin. Toss the dressing with the rice. Add the fennel and olives and season lightly with salt.

3. In a large skillet, heat the remaining 1 teaspoon of olive oil. Add the merguez sausage and cook over moderately high heat, stirring once or twice, until browned and cooked through, about 8 minutes. Using a slotted spoon, transfer the sausage to the salad. Stir in the tomatoes and parsley and serve. —*Melissa Clark*

NOTE Preserved lemons are a common Moroccan ingredient made from lemons that have been cured in lemon juice and salt for several days, until very soft. Look for them at specialty food shops.

MAKE AHEAD The rice salad can be prepared several hours ahead and served at room temperature.

Lemony Rice-Parsley Salad

TOTAL: 25 MIN
4 SERVINGS ● ● ○

"Parsley grows like wildfire in my garden," cookbook author Viana La Place says. "It's wonderful to rediscover an herb that is so flavorful and so good for you, too. It has a mineral richness you just can't beat."

- 1 cup arborio rice
- ¼ cup extra-virgin olive oil
- 1 tablespoon fresh lemon juice
- 1 cup tightly packed flat-leaf parsley leaves, coarsely chopped
- ½ small sweet Italian frying pepper, cut into ¼-inch dice
- 1/3 cup oil-cured pitted black olives, coarsely chopped
- 1 tablespoon capers, rinsed and drained
- 1½ teaspoons grated lemon zest

Salt and freshly ground black pepper

Lemon wedges, for serving

1. Bring a large saucepan of salted water to a boil. Add the rice and simmer over moderate heat until just tender, about 14 minutes. Drain thoroughly.

2. In a large bowl, toss the rice with the olive oil and lemon juice. Stir in the parsley, frying pepper, olives, capers and lemon zest and season with salt and pepper. Serve warm or at room temperature with lemon wedges. —*Viana La Place*

Fresh Corn Risotto

TOTAL: 45 MIN
6 SERVINGS

- 6 cups chicken stock or low-sodium broth
- 1 bay leaf
- 3 tablespoons extra-virgin olive oil
- 1 medium onion, minced
- 1½ cups arborio rice (12 ounces)
- ½ cup dry white wine
- 1 cup white corn kernels (from 2 ears)

RICE SALAD WITH MERGUEZ

LEMONY RICE-PARSLEY SALAD

1 cup freshly grated Parmigiano-Reggiano cheese

2 tablespoons unsalted butter, cubed

Salt and freshly ground pepper

1. In a medium saucepan, bring the chicken stock to a boil with the bay leaf. Keep the stock warm over very low heat.

2. In a large saucepan, heat the olive oil. Add the onion and cook over moderately high heat, stirring, until softened, about 2 minutes. Add the rice and cook, stirring, until opaque, about 3 minutes. Add the white wine and cook, stirring, until completely absorbed, about 1 minute. Add 1 cup of the warm stock and cook over moderate heat, stirring, until nearly absorbed. Continue adding the stock 1 cup at a time and stirring until it is absorbed between additions. After about half of the stock has been added, stir in the corn, then add the remaining stock. The rice is done when it's al dente and creamy, about 25 minutes total. Stir in the cheese and butter; season with salt and pepper. Discard the bay leaf and serve.
—*Melissa Clark*

Beet and Cheddar Risotto

 TOTAL: 30 MIN

4 SERVINGS ● ●

1 medium beet, peeled and quartered

2 cups loosely packed beet greens, stems trimmed

2 cups water

2 cups vegetable broth

2 tablespoons extra-virgin olive oil

1 medium onion, minced

1 cup arborio rice

8 ounces shredded sharp cheddar cheese (2 cups)

Salt and freshly ground pepper

Freshly grated Parmigiano-Reggiano cheese, for serving

1. Place the quartered beet in a food processor and pulse until it is finely chopped. Add the beet greens and pulse until finely chopped.

2. In a medium saucepan, bring the water and vegetable broth to a simmer. Heat the olive oil in a large saucepan. Add the minced onion and cook over moderately high heat, stirring, until softened, 3 minutes. Add the rice and cook, stirring, for 2 minutes. Stir in the chopped beets and beet greens and cook for 1 minute. Add the hot vegetable broth and water to the large saucepan, 1 cup at a time, and cook over moderate heat, stirring until the liquid is nearly absorbed between additions, 20 minutes. Add the shredded cheddar cheese; season with salt and ground pepper. Cook, stirring, until the risotto is creamy and thick, 3 minutes longer. Serve in deep bowls, passing the Parmigiano-Reggiano on the side.
—*Alexander Donowitz*

Potato Salad with Bacon and Barbecue Sauce

ACTIVE: 45 MIN; TOTAL: 1 HR 30 MIN

10 SERVINGS ●

The mayonnaise dressing for this potato salad gets pungency from mustard oil (store-bought spicy mustard works fine, too) and a hit of smoky-sweet flavor from bacon and bottled barbecue sauce.

- 4 pounds small red potatoes
- ½ pound lean bacon, preferably applewood-smoked, thinly sliced
- 1¼ cups mayonnaise
- 2 tablespoons barbecue sauce
- 2 tablespoons mustard oil or spicy mustard
- 2 tablespoons sherry vinegar
- 2 celery ribs, diced
- 1 small red onion, minced
- ¼ cup chopped parsley
- 1 tablespoon chopped tarragon
- Salt and freshly ground pepper
- ¼ cup onion sprouts, for garnish (optional)

1. In a large pot, cover the potatoes with cold salted water and bring to a boil over moderately high heat. Cook until the potatoes are tender, about 35 minutes. Drain the potatoes and, when they are cool enough to handle, slice them in half.

2. Meanwhile, in a medium skillet, cook the bacon slices over moderate heat until crisp, about 6 minutes. Drain the strips on paper towels until cool enough to handle, then coarsely crumble.

INGREDIENT

sprouts

Crunchy little sprouts make a flavorful garnish for salads, pastas and other dishes. Look for onion, radish and pea shoot sprouts in specialty food markets, or order seeds to grow on your own from sproutpeople.com.

3. In a large bowl, mix the mayonnaise with the barbecue sauce, mustard oil and sherry vinegar. Fold the potatoes into the dressing while they are still warm. Let the potato salad stand, stirring a few times, until the potatoes have cooled and absorbed most of the dressing, about 20 minutes.

4. Add the celery, red onion, parsley and tarragon to the potatoes and season with salt and pepper. Let stand for an additional 20 minutes, stirring a few times. Garnish with the bacon and sprouts, then serve.
—*Laurent Tourondel*

MAKE AHEAD The ungarnished salad can be refrigerated overnight. Serve lightly chilled or at room temperature.

Asian-Style Spicy Coleslaw

 TOTAL: 40 MIN

10 SERVINGS ●

Chef Laurent Tourondel traveled throughout Southeast Asia before founding his BLT restaurant empire; the fish sauce and peanut dressing in this coleslaw come straight out of Vietnam.

- ¼ cup plus 2 tablespoons smooth peanut butter
- 3 tablespoons fresh lime juice
- 3 tablespoons Asian fish sauce
- 3 tablespoons water
- 3 tablespoons sugar
- 3 medium garlic cloves, very finely chopped
- 1 tablespoon Sriracha chile sauce
- 2 pounds napa cabbage, thinly sliced (12 cups)
- ¾ pound red cabbage, thinly sliced (3 cups)
- 3 medium carrots, julienned
- 2 red bell peppers, very thinly sliced
- 3 tablespoons chopped cilantro
- 15 mint leaves
- Salt and freshly ground pepper

1. In a medium bowl, whisk the peanut butter with the lime juice, fish sauce, water, sugar, garlic and Sriracha.

2. In a large bowl, toss the sliced napa and red cabbages with the carrots, peppers, cilantro and mint. Toss the coleslaw with the peanut dressing and season with salt and black pepper. Serve right away.
—*Laurent Tourondel*

Bread-and-Butter Pickles

TOTAL: 1 HR PLUS OVERNIGHT SALTING

MAKES 3 QUARTS ● ● ○ ○

Chef Linton Hopkins of Atlanta's Restaurant Eugene has endless uses for these sweet and tangy pickles, which he even deep-fries to make pickle chips. Brining before pickling helps keep them crunchy.

- 1 cup kosher salt
- 1½ gallons water
- 5½ pounds Kirby cucumbers, sliced crosswise on a mandoline ⅛ inch thick
- 5 cups cider vinegar
- 5 cups sugar
- 1¼ pounds onions, thinly sliced
- 2 tablespoons yellow mustard seeds
- 1 tablespoon celery seeds
- 1 tablespoon turmeric
- 1 tablespoon coarsely cracked black pepper

1. In a very large bowl or pot, dissolve the salt in the water. Add the cucumbers, cover and soak overnight in the refrigerator.

2. In a large, heavy pot, combine the vinegar and sugar; cook until the sugar dissolves. Stir in the remaining ingredients. Drain the cucumbers and add them to the pot. Stir gently and bring to a boil, then turn off the heat. Ladle the hot cucumbers and their liquid into 6 hot 1-pint glass canning jars, leaving ½ inch of space at the top. Close with the lids and rings.

3. To process, boil the jars for 10 minutes (see Canning 101, p. 266). Cool the pickles to room temperature and serve immediately, or store them in a cool, dark place for up to 1 year. Refrigerate after opening.
—*Linton Hopkins*

ASIAN-STYLE SPICY COLESLAW

Chowchow

ACTIVE: 1 HR 15 MIN;

TOTAL: 2 HR 45 MIN PLUS OVERNIGHT
SALTING

MAKES 6 QUARTS ● ● ○

Chowchow, a slightly tangy Southern vegetable relish, is terrific with everything from hot dogs to corn bread. It's a perfect way to preserve summer produce like bell peppers and green tomatoes.

- 4 pounds green bell peppers, cut into ¼-inch dice
- 4 pounds red bell peppers, cut into ¼-inch dice
- 3 pounds green tomatoes, cut into ¼-inch dice
- 4 pounds sweet onions, cut into ¼-inch dice
- One 3¼-pound head of green cabbage, cored and finely chopped
- ½ cup kosher salt
- 6 cups sugar
- 4 cups cider vinegar
- 2 cups water
- 2 tablespoons yellow mustard seeds
- 1 tablespoon dry mustard
- 1 tablespoon crushed red pepper
- 1 tablespoon celery seeds
- 2 teaspoons ground ginger
- 1½ teaspoons turmeric

1. In a very large bowl, toss the bell peppers, tomatoes, onions and cabbage with the salt; cover and refrigerate overnight.

2. Drain the vegetables, discarding the liquid. In a large, heavy pot, bring the sugar, vinegar and water to a boil. Add the mustard seeds, dry mustard, crushed red pepper, celery seeds, ginger and turmeric and stir well. Add the drained vegetables and bring to a boil. Simmer over moderate heat, stirring occasionally, until the relish is thick and saucy, about 1 hour. Pack the chowchow into 6 hot 1-quart canning jars, leaving ½ inch of space at the top, and close with the lids and rings.

3. To process, simmer the jars at 180° for 30 minutes (see Canning 101, below left); monitor the water temperature with a thermometer. Store the jars in a cool, dark place for at least 2 weeks before serving, to allow the flavors to meld; store unopened for up to 1 year. Refrigerate after opening.
—Linton Hopkins

Savory Baked Carrot and Broccoli Rabe Terrine

ACTIVE: 1 HR; TOTAL: 2 HR 30 MIN

6 SERVINGS ● ● ○

"It's impressive and somewhat different," says superchef Wolfgang Puck of this terrine, one of his home-entertaining staples. He prepares a mixture of sautéed carrots, mushrooms, cheddar cheese and eggs, then layers it with sautéed broccoli rabe before baking.

- 6 tablespoons unsalted butter, plus more for coating
- 2 pounds carrots, sliced crosswise ¼ inch thick
- ½ cup water
- Salt and freshly ground pepper
- 6 ounces broccoli rabe—thick stems discarded, the rest chopped
- 5 large eggs
- 4 ounces shiitake mushrooms, stemmed, caps thinly sliced
- 4 ounces sharp white cheddar cheese, shredded (1½ cups)

1. Preheat the oven to 400°. In a large, deep skillet, melt 4 tablespoons of the butter. Add the carrots and water. Cover and cook over moderately low heat, stirring occasionally, until the carrots are tender, about 30 minutes. Uncover, raise the heat to high and boil off any excess water. Season with salt and pepper.

2. Meanwhile, in a large skillet, melt 1 tablespoon of the butter. Add the chopped

TECHNIQUE

canning 101

Home canning—as for the chowchow above—requires just a few basic pieces of equipment and knowledge of some simple techniques:

1. GET THE PROPER JARS In addition to ladles and big pots, you will need special jars (which work with lids and rings) that create a vacuum seal. Ball and Kerr are good brands. Canning tongs made for gripping jars are also helpful.

2. KEEP THE EQUIPMENT HOT Bring a large pot of water to 180° and simmer the canning jars, lids and rings and other utensils (ladles, tongs and spoons) for at least 10 minutes. Immediately before using, carefully remove everything from the pot, shaking off as much of the hot water as possible. If necessary, you can hold the jars in a 200° oven until you're ready to fill them.

3. PROCESS THE JARS Set a metal rack in a large pot. Fill the pot with water and heat to the temperature recommended in the recipe. Using canning tongs, carefully set the filled jars on the rack; make sure the jars are covered by at least 1 inch of water. Cover the pot and process according to the recipe. Again using canning tongs, carefully lift the jars from the pot and set them on a work surface until the lids seal (they will look concave) and the jars cool to room temperature. Refrigerate any jars that do not seal.

broccoli rabe, cover and cook over moderately high heat until just tender, about 2 minutes. Season with salt and pepper and transfer to a bowl. Lightly beat 1 of the eggs and stir into the broccoli rabe.

3. Wipe out the skillet and melt the remaining 1 tablespoon of butter. Add the shiitake, season with salt and pepper and cook over moderately high heat, stirring, until tender, about 5 minutes.

4. Line an 8½-by-4½-inch metal loaf pan with foil. Butter the foil. In a large bowl, using a pastry cutter or 2 sharp knives, coarsely chop the carrots. Lightly beat the remaining 4 eggs and add them to the carrots with the shiitake, cheddar, 1½ teaspoons of salt and ½ teaspoon of pepper. Spread half of the carrot mixture in the prepared loaf pan in an even layer. Top with the broccoli rabe mixture. Cover with the remaining carrot mixture, smoothing the surface.

5. Set the loaf pan in a large baking dish. Add enough hot water to the dish to reach halfway up the side of the loaf pan. Bake for about 1 hour and 15 minutes, or until the terrine is firm throughout. Let cool for 10 to 15 minutes.

6. Unmold the carrot terrine onto a platter. Cut into 1-inch-thick slices and serve.
—*Wolfgang Puck*

MAKE AHEAD The baked carrot terrine can be refrigerated overnight in the pan. Bring to room temperature, cover with foil and reheat in a hot water bath in a 350° oven until heated through, about 30 minutes.

Swiss Chard Soufflé

ACTIVE: 45 MIN; TOTAL: 2 HR

4 SERVINGS ●

½ ounce dried porcini mushrooms
    (½ cup)
6 tablespoons unsalted butter
½ cup all-purpose flour
3 cups whole milk
Salt and freshly ground
    black pepper
Pinch of freshly grated nutmeg

½ cup freshly grated young
    pecorino cheese, such as Pecorino
    Toscano Fresco (1½ ounces)
3 large egg yolks
1½ pounds Swiss chard, stems
    and inner ribs discarded
4 large egg whites

1. In a small bowl, cover the porcini mushrooms with hot water and let stand until they are softened, about 20 minutes. Lift the porcini from the water, squeeze dry and coarsely chop.

2. Meanwhile, preheat the oven to 350°. In a medium saucepan, melt 3 tablespoons of the butter over moderate heat. Stir in the flour until blended. Gradually whisk in the milk until smooth. Bring the béchamel to a boil over moderately high heat, whisking constantly until slightly thickened. Reduce the heat to low and simmer, whisking often, until no floury taste remains and the béchamel is very thick, about 20 minutes. Season with salt, pepper and nutmeg. Transfer the béchamel to a large bowl and, while it is still hot, whisk in the pecorino and egg yolks.

3. In a large skillet, cook the Swiss chard over moderately high heat in batches, a handful at a time, until the leaves are wilted, about 2 minutes per batch. Transfer the chard to a colander to cool, then squeeze dry. Coarsely chop the chard.

4. In the same large skillet, melt the remaining 3 tablespoons of butter. Add the Swiss chard and cook over moderate heat, stirring, until it's heated through and coated with butter, about 4 minutes. Season with salt and pepper. Stir the chopped chard into the béchamel along with the porcini mushrooms, 1 teaspoon of salt and ¼ teaspoon of pepper.

5. Butter an 8-cup ceramic soufflé dish. In a large stainless steel bowl, beat the egg whites with a pinch of salt until firm peaks form. Fold one-third of the beaten whites into the chard mixture, then fold in the remaining whites. Scrape the batter into

the prepared dish and run your thumb around the inside of the rim to help the soufflé rise evenly. Bake until the soufflé rises and is golden brown on top and slightly soft in the center, about 1 hour and 5 minutes. Serve right away.
—*Alex Roberts*

MAKE AHEAD The soufflé batter can be prepared through Step 4 and refrigerated overnight. Bring the batter to room temperature before proceeding.

Broccoli with Garlicky Tapenade

TOTAL: 30 MIN

6 SERVINGS ● ●

1 cup pitted kalamata olives
    (5 ounces)
3 tablespoons extra-virgin
    olive oil
2 tablespoons shredded
    basil leaves
1½ tablespoons drained capers
1 tablespoon fresh lemon juice
5 oil-packed anchovies
3 garlic cloves, smashed
Freshly ground pepper
1 pound broccoli, cut into 1-inch
    florets with about 2 inches of
    stem attached

1. In a food processor, combine the olives, olive oil, shredded basil, capers, lemon juice, anchovies and smashed garlic and pulse until finely chopped. Scrape down the bowl, season the tapenade with pepper and puree until fairly smooth. Transfer the tapenade to a serving bowl.

2. In a large, deep saucepan, bring 1 inch of water to a boil. Fill a steamer basket with the broccoli florets, add it to the saucepan, cover and steam over high heat until the broccoli is crisp-tender, about 5 minutes. Transfer the broccoli florets to a platter and serve with the tapenade.
—*Melissa Clark*

MAKE AHEAD The tapenade can be refrigerated for up to 3 days.

● HEALTHY ● MAKE AHEAD ● VEGETARIAN ● STAFF FAVORITE

GREEN BEANS WITH SOFFRITTO AND COUNTRY HAM

Four Cheese–Stuffed Portobellos

ACTIVE: 35 MIN; TOTAL: 1 HR

10 SERVINGS ● ●

These mushrooms—stuffed with cheese, brightened with lemon zest and topped with toasted bread crumbs—are a perfect side dish or appetizer. *Panko* (Japanese bread crumbs) are lovely here, but if you can't find them at an Asian market or specialty store, substitute any bread crumbs that will provide some satisfying crunch.

10   portobello mushroom caps, black gills removed

3   tablespoons extra-virgin olive oil, plus more for brushing

Salt and freshly ground pepper

3   ounces each of Gruyère, Muenster, mozzarella and Manchego, shredded

Finely grated zest of 2 lemons

1   tablespoon chopped basil

4   medium garlic cloves, very finely chopped

1   cup *panko*

3   tablespoons chopped parsley

1. Preheat the oven to 375°. Brush the mushroom caps on both sides with olive oil and season with salt and pepper. Place on a large rimmed baking sheet, gill side down, and bake until tender, about 20 minutes, then turn gill side up.

2. In a large bowl, combine the cheeses with the zest, basil, three-fourths of the garlic and 1 tablespoon of the olive oil. Season the stuffing with salt and pepper and mound onto the mushroom caps. Bake until the cheese melts, about 5 minutes.

3. Preheat the broiler. In a bowl, mix the *panko* and parsley with the remaining garlic and 2 tablespoons of oil. Sprinkle the *panko* mixture over the mushrooms and broil 4 inches from the heat until browned, about 2 minutes. Serve right away.
—*Laurent Tourondel*

MAKE AHEAD The stuffed mushrooms can be refrigerated overnight before baking.

Green Beans with Soffritto and Country Ham

ACTIVE: 25 MIN; TOTAL: 1 HR

4 SERVINGS ●

Chef Alex Roberts of Restaurant Alma in Minneapolis learned the secret to making a great *soffritto*—an aromatic vegetable mixture used as a base for many Italian soups and sauces—while traveling through Tuscany. "The trick is to cook the *soffritto* really slow—otherwise, the vegetables scorch," he says.

1¼   pounds green beans

¼   cup extra-virgin olive oil

2   medium carrots, finely diced

2   medium celery ribs, finely diced

1   small onion, finely diced

Pinch of crushed red pepper

Pinch of dried oregano

Salt and freshly ground black pepper

1   garlic clove, minced

3   ounces thinly sliced country ham or prosciutto, cut into ¼-inch-thick matchsticks (½ cup)

½   teaspoon finely chopped rosemary leaves

1   tablespoon red wine vinegar

1. Bring a large saucepan of salted water to a boil over high heat. Add the green beans and cook until crisp-tender, about 4 minutes. Drain the green beans well and cut them into 1-inch lengths.

2. In a medium skillet, heat 3 tablespoons of the olive oil. Add the diced carrots, celery, and onion, the crushed red pepper and dried oregano and cook over low heat, stirring occasionally, until the carrots, celery, and onion are just tender, about 25 minutes. Season the *soffritto* with salt and black pepper.

3. In a large skillet, heat the remaining 1 tablespoon of oil. Add the garlic and cook over moderate heat until fragrant, about 1½ minutes. Add the country ham and chopped rosemary and cook over moderately high heat until the ham is sizzling, about 1 minute. Stir in the vinegar. Add the beans and *soffritto* and toss until heated through. Season with salt and pepper and serve. —*Alex Roberts*

MAKE AHEAD The *soffritto* can be made up to 2 days ahead and refrigerated.

Broccoli with Cheddar Cheese "Dunk"

TOTAL: 30 MIN

6 SERVINGS ●

1   pound broccoli, cut into 1-inch florets with about 2 inches of stem attached

3   tablespoons unsalted butter

3   tablespoons all-purpose flour

1¼   cups milk

¼   cup heavy cream

¼   teaspoon dry mustard mixed with ½ tablespoon water

6   ounces sharp or mild white cheddar cheese, shredded (1½ cups)

Kosher salt

1. In a large, deep saucepan, bring 1 inch of water to a boil. Fill a steamer basket with the broccoli florets, add it to the saucepan, cover and steam over high heat until the broccoli is crisp-tender, about 5 minutes. Transfer the broccoli florets to a serving platter.

2. Meanwhile, in a saucepan, melt the butter. Add the flour and whisk over moderately high heat for 2 minutes. Add the milk and heavy cream and cook, whisking, until the sauce is thickened, about 2 minutes. Add the mustard powder mixture and shredded cheddar cheese and cook over moderately low heat, stirring, until the cheddar cheese is completely melted. Season the cheddar cheese sauce with salt, transfer to a serving bowl and serve with the steamed broccoli florets.
—*Melissa Clark*

MAKE AHEAD The broccoli florets can be made up to 1 hour ahead and served at room temperature.

desserts & brunch

desserts

Sour Cherry Turnovers

ACTIVE: 45 MIN; TOTAL: 2 HR 30 MIN
MAKES 12 TURNOVERS ● ○

Small, juicy, ruby-red sour cherries are excellent for baking because, unlike their sweet counterparts, they retain their shape as they cook. Here, they are roasted with lemon and sugar, then baked into delectable puff pastry turnovers.

- 2 cups pitted sour cherries (10 ounces), fresh or thawed frozen (see Note)
- 1 tablespoon cornstarch
- ¼ cup plus 2 tablespoons granulated sugar
- 2 tablespoons fresh lemon juice
- 1½ teaspoons finely grated lemon zest
- ½ teaspoon pure vanilla extract
- Salt
- 4 tablespoons unsalted butter, softened
- ¾ cup confectioners' sugar
- 1 large egg
- 2 tablespoons all-purpose flour, plus more for rolling
- 1¼ pounds all-butter puff pastry

- 1 egg yolk mixed with 1 tablespoon water
- Pearl sugar or granulated sugar, for sprinkling
- Vanilla ice cream, for serving

1. Preheat the oven to 350°. In an 8-inch glass or ceramic baking dish, mix the cherries with the cornstarch, granulated sugar, lemon juice, ½ teaspoon of the lemon zest, ¼ teaspoon of the vanilla and a pinch of salt. Bake for about 35 minutes, until the juices are thickened and bubbling. Drain the cherries, reserving the juices for another use. Chill the cherries.

2. In a medium bowl, whisk the butter with the confectioners' sugar until smooth. Whisk in the egg, then whisk in the 2 tablespoons of flour, the remaining 1 teaspoon of lemon zest and ¼ teaspoon of vanilla; whisk in a pinch of salt. Chill until firm.

3. Line a large baking sheet with parchment paper. On a lightly floured work surface, roll out the puff pastry to a 15-by-20-inch rectangle about ⅛ inch thick. Cut into twelve 5-inch squares, transfer to a plate and refrigerate for 10 minutes.

4. Arrange 3 pastry squares at a time on a work surface, keeping the rest chilled. Brush 2 adjoining edges of each square with the egg wash. Dollop a tablespoon of the lemon filling in the center of each square and top with 7 cherries. Fold the pastry over the filling to form a triangle, pressing out the air as you go. Press the edges firmly and crimp with a fork. Transfer the turnovers to the parchment-lined baking sheet. Repeat with the remaining pastry squares, lemon filling and sour cherries. Refrigerate the turnovers for about 15 minutes, or until firm.

5. Heat the oven to 400°. Using a sharp knife, trim the edges of the turnovers slightly. Brush the top of each turnover with egg wash and sprinkle with pearl sugar. Cut 2 or 3 small slashes in the tops to allow steam to escape. Bake for about 40 minutes, until the pastry is deep golden brown and the filling is bubbling out of the vents. Let the turnovers cool slightly, then serve with vanilla ice cream.

—Marc Meyer

NOTE Excellent frozen sour cherries are available online from Friske Orchards at friske.com. Jarred, pitted sour cherries can also be substituted.

MAKE AHEAD The turnovers can be kept at room temperature overnight. Rewarm before serving.

Almond-Plum Cake with Crème Fraîche

ACTIVE: 15 MIN; TOTAL: 1 HR 20 MIN
PLUS COOLING
8 SERVINGS ● ○ ●

For this incredibly moist almond cake, Minneapolis chef Alex Roberts demands the very best just-picked plums, which sink into the batter as they cook. "You can also use all kinds of seasonal fruit, like cherries or apricots," he says.

- 1 cup cake flour
- 1 teaspoon baking powder
- ¼ teaspoon salt
- 1¼ cups granulated sugar
- 1 cup almond paste (9 ounces)
- 6 tablespoons unsalted butter, at room temperature
- 6 eggs, at room temperature
- 1 teaspoon pure vanilla extract
- 1 vanilla bean—split lengthwise, seeds scraped, pod reserved for another use
- 3 large plums (12 ounces)—halved, pitted and cut into ½-inch wedges

Crème fraîche and slivered almonds, for serving

1. Preheat the oven to 350°. Butter and flour a 9-inch springform pan. In a small bowl, mix the cake flour with the baking powder and salt.

2. In the bowl of a standing mixer fitted with a paddle, beat the sugar with the almond paste until crumbly. Add the butter and beat at high speed until light in color and fluffy, about 2 minutes. Add the eggs, one at a time, beating until fully incorporated between additions. Beat in the vanilla extract and vanilla seeds. Gently fold in the flour mixture until fully incorporated.

3. Scrape the batter into the prepared pan. Arrange the plums over the top of the batter. Bake for 1 hour and 5 minutes, or until the cake is deeply golden and a toothpick inserted in the center comes out clean.

4. Transfer the cake to a rack and let cool for 15 minutes. Run a knife around the edge of the cake and remove the outside ring of the pan. Let the cake cool for at least 30 minutes longer. Serve the plum cake warm or at room temperature topped with crème fraîche and slivered almonds.
—Alex Roberts

Peach-Apricot Cobbler with Almond Ice Milk

ACTIVE: 45 MIN; TOTAL: 2 HR
10 SERVINGS ● ○

Peaches, apricots and almonds all come from the same plant family, so pairing them is only natural—literally. To boost the almond flavor, Laurent Tourondel, chef-owner of New York City's BLT restaurants, folds toasted slivered almonds into the fluffy cobbler topping and serves the dessert with Almond Ice Milk.

FILLING

- 8 ripe but firm peaches (2¾ pounds)—halved, pitted and cut into ½-inch wedges
- 5 ripe but firm apricots (12 ounces)—halved, pitted and cut into ½-inch wedges
- ¼ cup granulated sugar
- 2 tablespoons peach schnapps
- 1 tablespoon freshly squeezed lemon juice

TOPPING

- ½ cup slivered almonds
- 1½ cups all-purpose flour
- ½ cup granulated sugar, plus more for sprinkling
- 1 tablespoon baking powder
- ½ teaspoon salt
- 5 tablespoons cold unsalted butter, cut into ½-inch pieces
- ½ cup whole milk
- 1 large egg

Almond Ice Milk (recipe follows), for serving

1. MAKE THE FILLING: Preheat the oven to 375°. In a large bowl, toss the peach and apricot wedges with the sugar, peach schnapps and fresh lemon juice. Transfer the fruit filling mixture to a 9-by-13-inch baking dish.

2. MAKE THE TOPPING: Spread the slivered almonds evenly in a pie plate and toast them in the oven until they are lightly browned and fragrant, about 5 minutes. Let cool in the pie plate.

3. Meanwhile, in a bowl, whisk the flour with the ½ cup of sugar, the baking powder and the salt. Use a pastry cutter or 2 butter knives to cut the butter into the flour until the pieces are pea-size, then stir in the cooled toasted almonds.

4. In a medium bowl, whisk the milk with the egg to combine and pour the liquid over the flour mixture. Mix with a spoon just until a sticky dough forms. Spoon 10 evenly spaced mounds of the dough over the fruit. Sprinkle each mound of dough with a pinch of sugar. Bake the cobbler until the filling is bubbly and the topping is puffed and golden brown, about 45 minutes. Let stand for 20 minutes, then serve with the Almond Ice Milk.
—Laurent Tourondel

ALMOND ICE MILK

ACTIVE: 20 MIN; TOTAL: 1 HR 15 MIN
MAKES 5 CUPS ● ● ○

- 1 quart whole milk
- ⅔ cup honey
- ⅓ cup ground blanched almonds
- ½ teaspoon pure almond extract

In a medium saucepan, bring the milk and honey to a simmer over moderate heat, stirring to dissolve the honey, 4 minutes. Remove the saucepan from the heat and stir in the ground blanched almonds and the almond extract until completely combined. Fill a large bowl with water and ice. Place a medium bowl in this ice bath. Strain the almond milk through a fine-mesh sieve into the medium bowl and let cool completely, stirring occasionally. Transfer the chilled almond milk to an ice cream maker and freeze it according to the manufacturer's instructions. —L.T.

Zucchini Cupcakes with Cream Cheese Frosting

ACTIVE: 30 MIN; TOTAL: 1 HR

MAKES 18 CUPCAKES ● ◦

CUPCAKES

    2 cups walnuts (8 ounces), coarsely chopped
    ½ cup golden raisins
    ¼ cup brandy
    1 cup all-purpose flour
    1 cup whole wheat flour
    1 teaspoon baking soda
    1 teaspoon baking powder
    1 teaspoon cinnamon
    1 teaspoon kosher salt
    ½ teaspoon freshly ground pepper
    ½ cup vegetable oil
    ½ cup dark brown sugar
    ½ cup pure maple syrup
    1 teaspoon pure vanilla extract
    2 large eggs, beaten
    1¼ pounds zucchini, shredded (4 cups)
    2 tablespoons minced candied ginger

FROSTING

    8 ounces cream cheese, softened
    2 tablespoons unsalted butter, softened
    ½ cup confectioners' sugar
    1 teaspoon pure vanilla extract
    ½ teaspoon cinnamon
    ½ teaspoon finely grated orange zest

1. MAKE THE CUPCAKES: Preheat the oven to 350°. Line 18 muffin cups with paper liners. Spread the chopped walnuts on a large rimmed baking sheet and bake them until toasted, about 7 minutes. Let cool.

2. In a microwave-safe bowl, cover the raisins with the brandy and microwave until hot, 30 seconds. Let cool, then drain.

3. In a medium bowl, whisk the all-purpose and wheat flours with the baking soda, baking powder, cinnamon, salt and pepper. In a large bowl, whisk together the oil, brown sugar, maple syrup, vanilla and eggs.

4. Squeeze the zucchini dry. Stir the walnuts, raisins, zucchini and ginger into the wet ingredients. Add the dry ingredients in small batches until thoroughly blended. Spoon the batter into the muffin cups and bake until the muffins spring back when lightly pressed, about 25 minutes. Transfer to a rack and let cool to room temperature.

5. MAKE THE FROSTING: In a bowl, beat the cream cheese with the butter until smooth. Add the confectioners' sugar, vanilla, cinnamon and orange zest; beat until thoroughly mixed. Spread the frosting on the cupcakes and serve.
—Gabriel Frasca and Amanda Lydon

Chilled Peaches with Arborio Rice Pudding and Cinnamon Churros

TOTAL: 1 HR 45 MIN PLUS 4 HR CHILLING

6 SERVINGS ◦ ●

    6 peaches (about 3½ pounds)
    3¼ cups sugar
    Finely grated zest of 1 lime
    Finely grated zest of 1 lemon
    2 tablespoons fresh lemon juice
    4½ cups milk
    ¼ vanilla bean, seeds scraped
    ½ cup arborio rice (3½ ounces)
    Salt
    5½ tablespoons unsalted butter
    ⅔ cup all-purpose flour
    2 large eggs
    Vegetable oil, for deep-frying
    1½ teaspoons ground cinnamon

1. Bring a large saucepan of water to a boil and fill a bowl with ice water. Score a shallow X in the bottom of each peach. Submerge the peaches in the boiling water for 1 minute. Using a slotted spoon, transfer the peaches to the ice water to cool. Peel, cut into eighths and transfer them to a heatproof bowl.

2. Rinse out the saucepan. Add 2 cups of the sugar, the lime and lemon zests, the lemon juice and 2 cups of water and bring to a boil, stirring until the sugar is dissolved.

Pour the hot syrup over the peaches, then top them with a small plate to keep them submerged in the syrup. Refrigerate until chilled, at least 4 hours.

3. Meanwhile, rinse out the saucepan and add 4 cups of the milk, the vanilla bean and seeds and ¼ cup of the sugar. Bring to a boil, stirring until the sugar is dissolved. Stir in the rice and a pinch of salt and cook over moderately low heat, stirring constantly, until the rice is tender and the liquid is very thick and nearly absorbed, about 35 minutes. Remove from the heat; discard the vanilla bean.

4. In a medium saucepan, combine ⅔ cup of water with the butter and ¼ teaspoon of salt; bring to a boil. Off the heat, stir in the flour with a wooden spoon. Return the saucepan to moderate heat and cook, stirring, for 1 minute. Using an electric mixer at medium speed and working off the heat, beat in the eggs 1 at a time, beating well between additions. Transfer the dough to a pastry bag fitted with a ½-inch star tip.

5. Fill a large saucepan with 3 inches of oil and heat to 375°. Line a rack with paper towels. In a bowl, combine the remaining 1 cup of sugar with the cinnamon and a generous pinch of salt. Carefully squeeze the batter into the hot oil in 3-inch lengths, using a knife or kitchen scissors to cut the churros as they gently fall into the oil; fry no more than 8 at a time. Fry the churros over high heat, turning once, until golden brown, about 3 minutes per batch. Using a slotted spoon, transfer the churros to the rack to drain for 30 seconds, then immediately toss them in the cinnamon sugar to coat. Continue frying the churros, coating them as they are done.

6. Using a slotted spoon, transfer the peaches to large glasses; top with 2 tablespoons of the syrup. Stir the remaining ½ cup of milk into the rice pudding and rewarm until hot, about 1 minute. Spoon the pudding over the peaches and serve with the churros. *—Gabriel Bremer*

DEEP-DISH STRAWBERRY-RHUBARB PIE

perfect fruit pies

Deep-Dish Strawberry-Rhubarb Pie

ACTIVE: 40 MIN; TOTAL: 2 HR 40 MIN PLUS COOLING

MAKES ONE 9½-INCH DEEP-DISH PIE ●

The dough for these pies can be made with just butter, but swapping in some lard yields an even flakier crust.

- 1½ pounds strawberries, hulled and quartered (5 cups)
- 1½ pounds rhubarb, sliced ½ inch thick (5 cups)
- 1 cup sugar, plus more for sprinkling
- ¼ cup cornstarch

Pinch of salt

Flaky Pie Dough (recipe follows)

1. Preheat the oven to 375° and position a rack in the lower third. In a bowl, toss the strawberries and rhubarb with the 1 cup of sugar, the cornstarch and the salt.

2. Roll out the larger piece of dough to a 13-inch round about ⅛ inch thick and transfer to a 9½-by-1¾-inch glass pie plate. Brush the overhang with water and spoon in the filling.

3. Roll out the smaller piece of dough to a 12-inch round and lay it over the filling; press the edges together. Trim the overhang to ½ inch, fold it under itself and crimp. Lightly brush the top with water and sprinkle with sugar. Cut a few slits for steam to escape.

4. Bake the pie until the filling is bubbling and the crust is golden brown, about 2 hours. Cover the edge of the pie with foil if it begins to darken. Let cool for 5 hours at room temperature before serving. —*Grace Parisi*

FLAKY PIE DOUGH

ACTIVE: 10 MIN; TOTAL: 40 MIN

MAKES ENOUGH DOUGH FOR ONE 9½-INCH DEEP-DISH, DOUBLE-CRUST PIE ●

- 2½ cups all-purpose flour
- ½ teaspoon salt
- 1½ sticks cold unsalted butter, cut into ½-inch dice
- ¼ cup lard (2 ounces), frozen and cut into ½-inch cubes
- ½ cup ice water

1. In a food processor, pulse the flour and salt. Add the butter and lard and pulse 5 or 6 times, until the crumbs are the size of peas. Drizzle on the ice water; pulse just until moistened.

2. Press the dough into a ball. Divide the dough into 2 pieces, one slightly smaller than the other. Flatten into disks, wrap in plastic and refrigerate until firm, at least 30 minutes. —*G.P.*

---

three more deep-dish fruit pies

1 Peach-Raspberry Pie
Use 3¾ pounds of fresh ripe peaches, peeled and sliced (about 10 cups), 3 cups of raspberries, ¾ cup of granulated sugar, ¼ cup of cornstarch and a pinch of salt. Bake at 375° for 2 to 2¼ hours.

2 Blueberry Pie
Use 2½ pounds of blueberries, ¾ cup of granulated sugar, ⅓ cup plus 1 tablespoon cornstarch, 2 tablespoons of lemon juice, ½ teaspoon of finely grated lemon zest and a pinch of salt. Bake at 375° for 2 to 2¼ hours.

3 Sour Cherry Pie
Use 7½ cups (2 pounds) of pitted sour cherries, 1½ cups of granulated sugar, ¼ cup of cornstarch, 1 tablespoon of freshly squeezed lemon juice and a pinch of salt. Bake at 375° for 2 to 2¼ hours.

Blueberry-Lemon Parfaits

TOTAL: 45 MIN PLUS 2 HR CHILLING

10 SERVINGS ● ● ○

BLUEBERRY COMPOTE

    1 pint blueberries
    ⅓ cup sugar
    2 teaspoons water

LEMON CREAM

    6 large eggs
    1 cup granulated sugar

Finely grated zest of 2 lemons

    1¼ cups fresh lemon juice
    6 tablespoons unsalted butter,
       cut into pieces
    2 cups heavy cream
    ¼ cup confectioners' sugar

1. MAKE THE COMPOTE: In a medium saucepan, combine the blueberries, sugar and water and cook over moderate heat, stirring occasionally, until the sugar dissolves and the berries start to release their juices, about 3 minutes. Transfer the compote to a bowl and refrigerate until cool.

2. MAKE THE LEMON CREAM: Set a strainer over a heatproof bowl. In a heavy saucepan, whisk the eggs with the granulated sugar, lemon zest and juice. Cook over moderate heat, whisking constantly, until warm, about 5 minutes. Whisk in the butter, then continue to cook until just thickened, 5 minutes longer. Immediately strain the lemon curd into the bowl. Place a piece of plastic wrap on top of the curd to prevent a skin from forming. Refrigerate until chilled.

3. In a large bowl, whip the heavy cream until it begins to thicken. Add the confectioners' sugar and whip until the cream forms stiff peaks. Fold the whipped cream into the chilled lemon curd.

4. Divide the blueberry compote between 10 parfait or other tall glasses. Top with the lemon cream. Cover the parfaits and refrigerate until chilled, at least 1 hour. —*Laurent Tourondel*

MAKE AHEAD The blueberry compote and the lemon cream can each be refrigerated separately overnight.

Creamy Rose Panna Cotta

TOTAL: 30 MIN PLUS 5 HR CHILLING

4 SERVINGS ●

    ½ cup whole milk
    ½ cup heavy cream
    ½ vanilla bean, seeds scraped
    1 teaspoon unflavored gelatin
    1 tablespoon water
    3 tablespoons sugar
    ¼ cup plain whole-milk yogurt
    ¼ cup crème fraîche
    ¼ cup rose syrup, plus more for
       drizzling (see Note)

Vegetable oil, for brushing

Organic, unsprayed rose petals,
    for garnish

1. In a small saucepan, combine the milk, cream and vanilla bean and seeds and bring to a boil. Cover and remove from the heat. Let stand for 5 minutes. Discard the vanilla bean.

2. Meanwhile, in a small bowl, sprinkle the gelatin over the water and let stand until softened, about 5 minutes.

3. Whisk the gelatin into the hot milk, then whisk in the sugar, yogurt, crème fraîche and the ¼ cup of rose syrup.

4. Brush four ½-cup ramekins very lightly with vegetable oil. Pour the panna cotta mixture into the ramekins and refrigerate until firm, at least 5 hours.

5. Run a small knife around each panna cotta, then dip the ramekin bottoms in hot water and pat dry. Invert the ramekins onto small plates. Holding both the ramekin and the plate, give each plate a firm tap on a counter to release the panna cotta. Remove the ramekin. Drizzle the panna cotta with rose syrup, top with rose petals and serve. —*Erin Eastland*

NOTE Chef Erin Eastland's favorite organic Italian rose syrup (Sciroppo di Rose) is produced by Azienda Agricola Magliano. It is available at divinepasta.com.

MAKE AHEAD The finished panna cotta can be refrigerated in the ramekins for up to 2 days.

Crème Caramel

ACTIVE: 30 MIN; TOTAL: 2 HR PLUS OVERNIGHT CHILLING

8 SERVINGS ● ○

CARAMEL

    ½ cup plus 1 tablespoon sugar
    3 tablespoons light corn syrup
    3 tablespoons water

CUSTARD

    1 quart whole milk
    1¼ cups plus 3 tablespoons sugar
    5 large eggs
    3 large egg yolks
    2¼ teaspoons pure vanilla extract

1. MAKE THE CARAMEL: Arrange eight 1-cup ramekins in a large roasting pan. In a small saucepan, bring the sugar, corn syrup and water to a simmer over moderate heat, stirring lightly to dissolve the sugar. Simmer until a rich, amber caramel forms, about 25 minutes. Wash down any sugar crystals from the side of the pan with a wet pastry brush. Pour an equal amount of hot caramel into each ramekin; if the caramel gets too hard, gently reheat it.

2. MAKE THE CUSTARD: Preheat the oven to 300°. In a large saucepan, bring the milk and sugar just to a simmer over moderate heat, stirring to dissolve the sugar, about 5 minutes. Let cool until warm. In a large bowl, thoroughly whisk the eggs with the yolks. Slowly whisk in the warm milk mixture and then the vanilla.

3. Strain the custard and pour it into the prepared ramekins. Add enough hot water to the roasting pan to reach halfway up the sides of the ramekins. Cover the pan with 2 layers of plastic wrap. Bake the custards for about 1 hour, or until they are set but still slightly jiggly in the center.

4. Remove the hot custards from the water bath and let them cool on a rack to room temperature, then cover and refrigerate the custards overnight.

5. To serve, pour 2 inches of very hot water into a small bowl. Dip a ramekin in the hot water for about 10 seconds, then run a

BLUEBERRY-LEMON PARFAITS

CREAMY ROSE PANNA COTTA

thin knife around the edge of the ramekin to loosen the custard. Invert the Crème Caramel onto a plate. Repeat with the remaining ramekins and serve.

—*Thomas Keller*

MAKE AHEAD The custards can be refrigerated in their ramekins, covered, for up to 3 days before serving.

Ricotta with Berries and Bitter Honey

 TOTAL: 20 MIN
4 TO 6 SERVINGS ●

"Toast and ricotta is a common part of the morning meal in Sardinia," says Efisio Farris, chef and owner of Arcodoro in Houston and Arcodoro & Pomodoro in Dallas. "But when you drizzle those ingredients with bitter honey and add berries in a syrup, you have a great dessert." The recipe is extremely easy; the only step that requires any effort at all is making the syrup.

2 **cups fresh ricotta, preferably from sheep's milk**
¼ **cup plus 1 tablespoon Sardinian bitter honey (see Note)**
Finely grated zest and juice of 1 orange
Finely grated zest and juice of 1 lemon
1 **tablespoon sugar**
1 **cup raspberries**
8 **large strawberries, stemmed and quartered**
1 to 2 sheets of *pane carasau* (see Note)
1 **tablespoon chopped mint**

1. Preheat the oven to 400°. In a bowl, blend the ricotta with 2 tablespoons of the honey and the orange and lemon zests.
2. In a small saucepan, combine the orange and lemon juices with the sugar and 1 tablespoon of the honey and bring to a boil. Simmer over moderately high heat

until the syrup is reduced to ½ cup, about 5 minutes. Add the raspberries and strawberries and remove the saucepan from the heat. Let the mixture stand, stirring a few times, until the berries are barely softened, about 4 minutes.
3. Put the *pane carasau* directly onto the oven rack and bake for about 4 minutes, or until hot. Drizzle the *pane carasau* with the remaining 2 tablespoons of honey and break into large pieces. Divide the ricotta mixture among shallow bowls. Spoon the berry mixture on top and sprinkle with the chopped mint. Serve the ricotta and berries with the *pane carasau*.

—*Efisio Farris*

NOTE Sardinian bitter honey, which has a nicely acrid aftertaste, and *pane carasau*, or *carta da musica* (a traditional round Sardinian flatbread), are both available at Italian specialty food stores and from gourmetsardinia.com.

APPLE PIE GRANITA

Apple Pie Granita

TOTAL: 15 MIN PLUS 4 HR FREEZING
8 SERVINGS ● ● ○ ○

3 cups natural-style apple juice
½ cup sugar
1½ tablespoons fresh lemon juice
½ teaspoon ground cinnamon
Pinch of freshly grated nutmeg
Pinch of ground allspice

In a saucepan, combine all of the ingredients and cook over moderate heat, stirring, until the sugar has dissolved, 3 minutes. Pour into an 8-inch square glass baking dish. Freeze until icy around the edges, about 1 hour. Using a fork, scrape the icy shards into the center. Continue to freeze, stirring occasionally, until slushy throughout, about 3 hours longer. Scoop the granita into bowls or glasses and serve right away.
—*Emeril Lagasse*

Espresso-Chocolate Semifreddo

TOTAL: 45 MIN PLUS 6 HR FREEZING
8 SERVINGS ●

1½ cups sugar
1¼ cups strongly brewed espresso
½ cup whole milk
1 vanilla bean, split, seeds scraped
1 teaspoon unflavored gelatin dissolved in 2 teaspoons water
2 ounces bittersweet chocolate, chopped
4 large eggs
¼ cup light corn syrup
1½ cups heavy cream
18 dry ladyfingers or *savoiardi* cookies
1 tablespoon unsweetened cocoa, for sprinkling
Raspberries, for serving

1. In a small saucepan, combine 1 cup of the sugar with ¾ cup of water and ¼ cup of the espresso. Bring to a simmer over moderate heat and stir to dissolve the sugar. Let the espresso syrup cool.

2. In a small saucepan, boil the remaining 1 cup of espresso over high heat until reduced to ¼ cup, about 8 minutes. Pour into a medium heatproof bowl.

3. In the same saucepan, warm the milk with the vanilla bean and seeds over moderate heat until bubbles form around the edge, about 2 minutes. Remove from the heat and stir in the gelatin mixture until melted. Discard the vanilla bean. Add the hot milk to the reduced espresso and whisk in the chocolate until melted. Rinse and dry the saucepan.

4. In the bowl of a standing mixer, beat the eggs at high speed until light yellow and foamy. In the small saucepan, bring the corn syrup, the remaining ½ cup of sugar and 2 tablespoons of water to a simmer. Cook over moderately high heat until the syrup registers 235° on a candy thermometer, about 5 minutes. With the mixer at medium-high speed, gradually beat the hot syrup into the eggs. Continue beating until the mixture is very pale and has tripled in volume, about 4 minutes. Fold in the espresso-chocolate mixture.

5. In a bowl, whip the heavy cream until stiff peaks form. Fold into the mousse mixture until no streaks remain.

6. Spoon about one-fourth of the espresso mousse into a 9-inch springform pan. Dip 6 ladyfingers into the espresso syrup until just soaked through. Arrange the ladyfingers over the mousse in rows. Repeat the process twice more with the mousse and the remaining ladyfingers, then top with the remaining mousse. Cover with plastic wrap and freeze for at least 6 hours.

7. Before serving, warm a thin, sharp knife under hot water. Run the knife around the edge of the semifreddo and remove the ring. Sift the cocoa over the top of the semifreddo. Cut the semifreddo into wedges and serve, garnished with raspberries.
—*Wolfgang Puck*

SERVE WITH A dollop of unsweetened whipped cream.

Blanco y Negro

TOTAL: 1 HR PLUS 5 HR 30 MIN FREEZING
6 TALL SERVINGS ● ○ ○

3 cups whole milk
1 cup heavy cream
¾ cup plus 2 tablespoons sugar
Zest strips from 1 lemon, removed with a vegetable peeler
1 cinnamon stick, broken
4 large egg whites, at room temperature
2 tablespoons fresh lemon juice
1 cup strong-brewed espresso, chilled
Whipped cream and ground cinnamon, for serving

1. In a medium saucepan, combine the milk and cream with ¾ cup of sugar. Add the lemon zest and cinnamon stick and bring to a simmer. Cover and let the mixture stand off the heat for 30 minutes.

2. Strain the milk mixture into a bowl. Set the bowl in an ice water bath and stir occasionally until chilled. Pour the milk mixture into a 9-by-13-inch glass dish.

3. In a large bowl, using an electric mixer, beat the egg whites with the remaining 2 tablespoons of sugar and the lemon juice at high speed until soft peaks form. Dollop the beaten whites all over the milk mixture and freeze until solid, about 5 hours.

4. Cut the ice milk into 2-inch squares. Using a sturdy spatula, transfer half of the squares to a food processor. Process until completely smooth, scraping down the sides of the bowl. Scrape the smooth ice milk into a bowl and freeze. Repeat with the remaining ice milk. Freeze until firm but not solid, about 30 minutes.

5. Scoop the ice milk into tall glasses and pour in the chilled espresso. Top with whipped cream and cinnamon. Serve with straws and long spoons. —*Jen Demarest*

MAKE AHEAD The ice milk can be prepared through Step 4 and frozen in an airtight container for up to 3 days.

Gooey Walnut Brownies

ACTIVE: 15 MIN; TOTAL: 1 HR PLUS COOLING

MAKES 16 BROWNIES ● ○

Andrew Zavala, age 11, a 2007 F&W Kid Cook Contest runner-up, discovered the recipe for these gooey brownies in a kids' cookbook by Pamela Gwyther called *Let's Cook!* A self-professed kitchen scientist, he likes to revisit the recipe often, substituting ingredients and noting the results. "My favorite version uses two ounces each of dark, milk and white chocolate," he says.

- 6 ounces bittersweet chocolate, chopped
- 1½ sticks (6 ounces) unsalted butter, softened
- 1¼ cups sugar
- ½ teaspoon kosher salt
- 3 large eggs, beaten
- 2 teaspoons pure vanilla extract
- 1 cup all-purpose flour
- ½ cup coarsely chopped walnuts

1. Preheat the oven to 350°. Butter an 8-inch square baking pan and line it with parchment paper so the paper extends over two opposite sides.

2. In a large saucepan, melt the chocolate and butter over low heat; stir constantly.

TOOL

sharp scooper

Calphalon's new 3-Way Ice Cream Scoop, with a trio of curved points, makes short work of hard ice cream ($10; calphalon.com).

Remove the saucepan from the heat and stir in the sugar and salt. Let cool slightly, then gradually stir in the beaten eggs. Stir in the vanilla extract. Add the flour and stir until blended. Fold in the chopped walnuts and pour into the prepared baking pan.

3. Bake the brownies in the center of the oven for 40 minutes, until they are glossy and cracked in spots and a toothpick inserted just off center comes out with a few crumbs attached. Let cool completely in the pan, at least 4 hours. Run a knife around the edge of the pan and lift out the brownies using the overhanging parchment paper. Cut into squares and serve.
—*Andrew Zavala*

MAKE AHEAD The brownies can be stored in an airtight container for up to 4 days or frozen for 1 month. Cut the brownies while frozen and let thaw at room temperature. If desired, rewarm the brownies in a 300° oven for 15 minutes.

Spotted Porcupine Cookies

ACTIVE: 20 MIN; TOTAL: 1 HR

MAKES ABOUT 24 COOKIES ● ○

Catherine Ralston, an 11-year-old 2007 F&W Kid Cook Contest grand-prize winner, likes animals, polka dots and cookies. Her porcupine cookies have pretzel-stick "quills," with M&M's doubling as polka dots. She says, "I thought pretzels would be good in cookies because salty can go well with sweet." Her other culinary creations include Leaning Tower of Pizza Burgers and Ohana Pineapple Steak.

- 1 cup unsalted butter, softened
- 1 cup (packed) light brown sugar
- ½ cup granulated sugar
- 2 large eggs, at room temperature
- 2 teaspoons pure vanilla extract
- 2½ cups all-purpose flour
- 1 teaspoon baking soda
- 1 teaspoon salt
- ½ cup each of white and semisweet chocolate chips

About 100 thin pretzel sticks, broken in half

- 2 ounces M&M's Minis

1. Preheat the oven to 375° and position 2 racks in the upper and lower thirds of the oven. In a large bowl, using a wooden spoon, beat the butter until creamy. Add the brown and granulated sugars and beat until smooth. Add the eggs and vanilla and beat until smooth. In a small bowl, whisk the flour with the baking soda and salt. Add the dry ingredients to the large bowl and stir until combined. Stir in the white and semisweet chocolate chips.

2. Using a 1½-inch ice cream scoop, scoop 3-tablespoon mounds of the cookie batter onto 3 ungreased baking sheets about 2 inches apart. Using your hands, roll the dough mounds into balls. Insert the pretzel sticks into the dough balls and fill the empty spaces with M&M's Minis. Bake 2 sheets of the cookies until they are lightly browned but still soft in the middle, about 15 minutes, shifting the baking sheets from top to bottom and front to back halfway through. Let the cookies cool on the pans for 10 minutes, then transfer to wire racks to cool completely. Repeat with the remaining baking sheet, rotating it halfway through baking. Serve warm or cooled.
—*Catherine Ralston*

MAKE AHEAD The cookies can be stored in an airtight container for up to 2 days.

Brandied Peaches

TOTAL: 1 HR PLUS COOLING

MAKES 4 QUARTS ● ● ○

One of chef Linton Hopkins's customers at Restaurant Eugene in Atlanta loves these brandied peaches so much that she bought him enough fruit to preserve for a party of 450 people. Since the peaches are not processed in a water bath to maintain freshness, it's best to store the jars in the refrigerator. If you like, bring them to room temperature before serving as a dessert sauce.

6 pounds small to medium
 ripe peaches
3 cups water
2 pounds sugar (4 cups)
4 cups brandy

1. Bring a large pot of water to a boil. Add the peaches and boil just until the skins loosen, 30 seconds; transfer to a large rimmed baking sheet and let cool. Peel the peaches, then halve and pit them.
2. In a large saucepan, combine the 3 cups of water and sugar and bring to a boil over high heat, stirring to dissolve the sugar. Boil the syrup until slightly reduced to 4 cups, about 5 minutes. Add the peaches to the syrup and bring to a boil.
3. Using a slotted spoon, transfer the peaches to 4 hot 1-quart canning jars. Add the brandy to the syrup and bring to a boil. Ladle the hot brandy syrup over the peaches and close the jars tightly with the lids and rings. Let cool to room temperature, then refrigerate for at least 1 week before serving. Store unopened jars in the refrigerator for up to 3 months.
—*Linton Hopkins*

SERVE WITH Ice cream or pound cake.

brunch

Strawberry Preserves
ACTIVE: 45 MIN; TOTAL: 1 HR PLUS COOLING

MAKES 3 PINTS ● ○
The secret to this sweet strawberry preserve is simple: Use ripe berries, and cook them at the proper temperature so that you don't have to add any fruit pectin as a thickener.

Juice of 2 lemons, strained
4½ cups sugar
2 pounds small to medium
 strawberries, hulled

1. In a large, deep skillet, pour the lemon juice around the sugar. Cook over moderate heat undisturbed until most of the sugar is melted, about 10 minutes. Gently stir the sugar until completely melted. Using a moistened pastry brush, wash down any sugar crystals from the side of the skillet.
2. Add the strawberries and boil over moderately high heat, mashing them gently until the preserves reach 220° (or 8° above boiling point, depending on the altitude), about 10 minutes. Continue to boil until thick, 4 minutes longer.
3. Spoon the preserves into 3 hot 1-pint canning jars, leaving ¼ inch of space at the top, and close with the lids and rings.
4. To process, boil the jars for 15 minutes (see Canning 101 on p. 266). Let the jars cool to room temperature and serve the preserves after 2 days, or store the jars in a cool, dark place for up to 1 year. Refrigerate for up to 2 months after opening.
—*Linton Hopkins*

Chanterelle Omelets with Fines Herbes Sauce
TOTAL: 1 HR 15 MIN

4 SERVINGS ●
Why does famed chef Thomas Keller make a one-egg omelet? Because the result is so much more delicate and alluring than the usual supersize omelets prepared with multiple eggs, especially with this creamy chanterelle filling.

2½ cups flat-leaf parsley leaves
2 cups chives, snipped into
 ½-inch lengths
1 cup chervil leaves
½ cup tarragon leaves
¾ cup water
Salt
2 tablespoons plus 1 teaspoon
 unsalted butter
1 small shallot, minced
¼ pound chanterelles, trimmed
 and coarsely chopped
1 tablespoon crème fraîche
½ teaspoon vegetable oil
4 large eggs, at room
 temperature

1. Preheat the oven to 250°. Bring a large saucepan of salted water to a boil over high heat. Prepare a bowl of ice water. Add the parsley, chives, chervil and tarragon to the boiling water and cook for 4 minutes. Using a slotted spoon, transfer the herbs to the ice water to cool completely. Transfer the herbs to a kitchen towel and wring dry, then transfer to a blender and add the ¾ cup of water. Blend at high speed until pureed. Season the herb sauce with salt.
2. In a medium skillet, melt 1 tablespoon of the butter. Add the minced shallot and cook over moderate heat until softened, about 2 minutes. Add the chanterelles, season with salt and cook, stirring, until tender, 8 minutes. Remove from the heat, stir in the crème fraîche and keep warm.
3. In a 6- or 8-inch nonstick, ovenproof skillet, melt 1 teaspoon of the butter in the oil over moderate heat. In a small bowl, beat 1 egg with a pinch of salt until the egg foams. Add the egg to the skillet and cook over low heat until it starts to set, about 10 seconds. Transfer the skillet to the oven and cook until the egg is just set, about 1 minute. Slide the egg onto a plate and spread a rounded tablespoon of chanterelles down the center. Fold both sides of the omelet over the mushrooms and roll the omelet over. Spoon a little herb sauce alongside. Repeat to make 3 more omelets.
—*Thomas Keller*

TECHNIQUE

making a berry sauce

Overripe berries make a luscious sauce for ice cream or pancakes: Simmer 2 cups berries with 3 to 4 tablespoons sugar, depending on their sweetness; stir gently until a syrup forms.

BLT, FRIED EGG AND CHEESE SANDWICH

OVER-THE-TOP MUSHROOM QUICHE

BLT, Fried Egg and Cheese Sandwich

TOTAL: 20 MIN
MAKES 1 SANDWICH

In this scrumptious recipe, chef Thomas Keller combines three of the world's most popular sandwiches—bacon, lettuce and tomato; fried egg; and grilled cheese.

- 4 thick slices of bacon
- 2 slices of Monterey Jack cheese
- 2 thick slices of rustic white bread, toasted and hot
- 1 tablespoon mayonnaise
- 4 tomato slices
- 2 leaves of butter lettuce
- 1 teaspoon unsalted butter
- 1 large egg

1. In a small skillet, cook the bacon slices over moderate heat, turning them halfway through, until they are crisp, about 8 minutes. Transfer the cooked bacon to a paper towel–lined plate to drain.

2. Set the Monterey Jack cheese slices on 1 piece of hot toast. Spread the mayonnaise on the other slice of toast, then top with the bacon, tomato slices and butter lettuce leaves.

3. In a small nonstick skillet, melt the butter. Add the egg and fry over moderate heat, gently flipping the egg after 2 minutes, until it is crisp around the edge, about 4 minutes; the yolk should still be runny. Slide the egg onto the lettuce; close the sandwich and serve immediately.
—Thomas Keller

Over-the-Top Mushroom Quiche

ACTIVE: 1 HR 30 MIN; TOTAL: 6 HR
12 SERVINGS ● ● ●

"I love quiche, but it has to be several inches high and made right," says chef Thomas Keller. This high-rising version, which is adapted from a recipe in his *Bouchon* cookbook, just might be the perfect one, and it's well worth the time it takes to prepare. Layering the sautéed mushrooms and cheese ensures that they're nicely distributed throughout the silky egg custard.

- 1 tablespoon vegetable oil
- 1 pound oyster mushrooms, stems trimmed and large caps halved or quartered
- 1 pound white mushrooms, thinly sliced

Salt and freshly ground white pepper
- 1 tablespoon unsalted butter
- 2 small shallots, very finely chopped
- 1 tablespoon thyme leaves, finely chopped
- ¾ cup shredded Comté or Emmental cheese (2½ ounces)

Buttery Pastry Shell (recipe follows)
- 2 cups milk
- 2 cups heavy cream
- 6 large eggs, lightly beaten

Freshly grated nutmeg

1. Preheat the oven to 325°. In a very large skillet, heat the vegetable oil. Add the halved oyster and sliced white mushrooms and season with salt and white pepper; cook the mushrooms over high heat, stirring frequently, until the mushrooms begin to soften, about 5 minutes. Reduce the heat to moderate. Add the butter, chopped shallots and chopped thyme leaves and cook, stirring often, until the mushrooms are tender, about 12 minutes longer. Season the mushrooms with salt and white pepper and let cool.

2. Scatter ¼ cup of the shredded Comté or Emmental cheese and half of the cooked mushrooms evenly over the bottom of the Buttery Pastry Shell. In a blender, combine 1 cup each of the milk and heavy cream with 3 of the eggs and season with 1½ teaspoons of salt, ⅛ teaspoon of white pepper and a pinch of grated nutmeg; mix at high speed until frothy, about 1 minute. Pour the custard into the pastry shell. Top

with another ¼ cup of the shredded Comté or Emmental cheese and the remaining cooked mushrooms. Make a second batch of custard with the remaining cup each of milk and heavy cream and 3 eggs, plus the same amount of salt, white pepper and grated nutmeg as before and pour into the shell. Scatter the remaining ¼ cup of shredded Comté or Emmental cheese on top of the custard.

3. Bake the mushroom quiche for about 1½ hours, or until the quiche is richly browned on top and the custard is barely set in the center. Let the quiche cool in the pan until very warm.

4. Using a serrated knife, cut the pastry shell flush with the top of the pan. Carefully lift the springform pan ring off the quiche. Cut the mushroom quiche into wedges, transfer to plates and serve warm.
—*Thomas Keller*

MAKE AHEAD The unmolded mushroom quiche can be cooled completely, then refrigerated overnight. To serve, cut the chilled quiche into wedges, arrange the pieces on a baking sheet and bake in a 350° oven until they are warmed through, about 10 minutes.

BUTTERY PASTRY SHELL
ACTIVE: 30 MIN; TOTAL: 3 HR
MAKES ONE 9-INCH SHELL ● ○
Making a butter pastry crust using a standing mixer might seem slightly unorthodox, but the result is an amazingly flaky shell that's equally good for both savory and sweet tarts.
- 2 cups all-purpose flour, sifted, plus more for dusting
- 1 teaspoon kosher salt
- 2 sticks chilled unsalted butter, cut into ¼-inch dice
- ¼ cup ice water

Canola oil, for brushing

1. In the bowl of a standing mixer fitted with the paddle, mix 1 cup of the sifted flour with the salt. At low speed, add the

diced butter pieces, a handful at a time. When all of the butter has been added, increase the speed to medium and mix until the butter is completely incorporated. Reduce the speed to low and add the remaining 1 cup of sifted flour just until blended. Mix in the water just until thoroughly incorporated. Scrape the pastry into a ball and flatten it into an 8-inch disk. Wrap the dough in plastic and refrigerate until chilled, at least 1 hour or overnight.

2. Set the ring of a 9-inch springform pan on a rimmed baking sheet lined with parchment paper, leaving the hinge open. Brush the inside of the ring with oil.

3. Dust the pastry evenly on both sides with flour. On a lightly floured work surface, roll out the pastry to a 16-inch round about ³⁄₁₆ inch thick. Carefully roll the pastry around the rolling pin and transfer to the prepared ring, pressing it into the corners. Trim the overhanging pastry to 1 inch and press it firmly against the outside of the ring. Use the trimmings to fill any cracks and wrap the remaining trimmings in plastic and reserve in the refrigerator. Refrigerate the shell for 20 minutes.

4. Preheat the oven to 375°. Line the pastry shell with a 14-inch round of parchment paper; fill the shell with pie weights, dried beans or rice. Bake the pastry shell for about 40 minutes, or until the edge of the dough is lightly browned. Remove the parchment and pie weights and continue baking the pastry shell for about 15 minutes longer, or until it is richly browned on the bottom. Transfer the baking sheet to a rack and let the pastry cool completely. Fill any cracks with the reserved pastry dough to make sure that the crust will not leak when filled. —*T.K.*

MAKE AHEAD The uncooked pastry disk can be wrapped well in plastic and frozen for up to 1 month. The baked and cooled pastry shell can be wrapped well in plastic and kept at room temperature overnight before it is filled and baked.

Alexis Swanson Traina of Swanson Vineyards in Napa Valley serves Thomas Keller's Lemon-Brined Fried Chicken (P. 313).

autumn

starters & drinks 286

main courses 302

side dishes 340

desserts & brunch 358

AUTUMN

starters & drinks

starters

Creamy Anchoïade
with Crudités

TOTAL: 15 MIN
4 TO 6 SERVINGS ● ●

Anchoïade, a Provençal puree of anchovies, garlic and olive oil, is often served as a dip. Use any combination of crudités— from thin shavings of spicy black radish to florets of *broccoli romanesco,* a relative of broccoli and cauliflower.

One 3-ounce jar anchovies packed
  in olive oil, drained and chopped
3 large garlic cloves, chopped
½ cup extra-virgin olive oil
Assorted vegetables for dipping, such
  as thinly sliced black radishes,
  fennel wedges, treviso leaves and
  florets of *broccoli romanesco*

In a mini processor or blender, puree the anchovies with the garlic. With the machine on, pour in the oil until blended. Transfer to a bowl; serve with the vegetables.
—*Marcia Kiesel*

MAKE AHEAD The *anchoïade* can be refrigerated, covered, for up to 4 hours. Process again before serving.
WINE Fresh, fruity rosé.

Texas Smoked Salmon Tartare

TOTAL: 30 MIN
12 SERVINGS ● ● ●

These spicy, tangy little hors d'oeuvres are Dallas chef Dean Fearing's take on the classic combination of smoked salmon, red onion and capers—he throws in roasted garlic, lime juice and jalapeño and replaces the standard cream cheese with sour cream. Fearing makes the dish especially Southwestern by serving the tartare on tortilla chips. "Everything is good on a chip," he points out.

2 oil-packed anchovy fillets, drained
  and coarsely chopped
2 teaspoons roasted garlic paste
  (see Note)
1 teaspoon ground cumin
1 tablespoon extra-virgin olive oil
½ cup sour cream
2 teaspoons fresh lime juice
One ½-pound piece of skinless
  smoked salmon, cut into
  ¼-inch dice
1 small jalapeño, seeded
  and minced
¼ cup finely chopped red onion
1 tablespoon capers, drained and
  coarsely chopped
1 tablespoon finely chopped
  cilantro, plus 4 dozen cilantro
  leaves for garnish
Salt and freshly ground pepper
4 dozen sturdy corn tortilla chips

1. In a medium bowl, using the back of a fork, mash the chopped anchovies with the roasted garlic paste, cumin and olive oil. Stir in the sour cream and lime juice. Fold in the smoked salmon, jalapeño, red onion, capers and chopped cilantro and season with salt and pepper.
2. Arrange the tortilla chips on a large serving platter. Spoon a heaping teaspoon of the smoked salmon tartare onto each tortilla chip, top the tartare with a cilantro leaf and serve at once. —*Dean Fearing*
NOTE To make your own roasted garlic paste, place 3 unpeeled garlic cloves on a piece of foil and drizzle with 1 teaspoon of olive oil. Close the foil to form a packet and roast in a preheated 350° oven for about 45 minutes. Let the garlic cool slightly, then mash it.
MAKE AHEAD The smoked salmon tartare can be refrigerated, covered, for up to 1 day. Bring to room temperature before spooning onto chips and serving.
WINE Dry, earthy sparkling wine.

Smoked Sablefish and Potato Salad with Capers and Onions

ACTIVE: 25 MIN; TOTAL: 55 MIN

4 SERVINGS ●

This salad gets its lovely piquancy from salty capers and crunchy red onions. Sablefish, a buttery fish also known as black cod, is firmer and slightly smokier than smoked salmon, but the latter can be substituted for it.

¼ cup salt-packed capers, rinsed

1½ pounds medium Yukon
   Gold potatoes

Salt

¼ cup extra-virgin olive oil

1 tablespoon fresh lemon juice

Freshly ground pepper

½ small red onion, very
   thinly sliced

¾ pound smoked sablefish or
   salmon, thinly sliced

2 tablespoons parsley leaves,
   for garnish

Lemon wedges, for serving

1. In a small bowl, cover the rinsed capers with warm water. Let stand at room temperature for 30 minutes. Drain.

2. Meanwhile, in a large saucepan, cover the Yukon Gold potatoes with cold salted water and bring to a boil over high heat. Lower the heat and simmer until tender, about 30 minutes; drain. While the potatoes are still warm, peel and slice them ¼ inch thick. Transfer the sliced potatoes to a large salad bowl.

3. In a small bowl, combine the olive oil, fresh lemon juice and soaked, drained capers and season with salt and pepper. Pour two-thirds of the dressing over the potatoes and toss.

4. Arrange the sliced potatoes, sliced red onion and smoked sablefish on a large platter. Drizzle with the remaining dressing, garnish with the parsley leaves and serve with the lemon wedges.
—*Marcia Kiesel*

WINE Minerally, complex Sauvignon Blanc.

Classic Deviled Eggs

 TOTAL: 30 MIN
8 SERVINGS ● ○

1 dozen large eggs

½ cup mayonnaise

1½ teaspoons Dijon mustard

1½ teaspoons yellow mustard

3 dashes of Worcestershire sauce

Salt

Sweet paprika or pure ancho chile
   powder, for garnish

1. In a medium saucepan, cover the eggs with cold water and bring to a rolling boil. Cover, remove from the heat and let stand for 12 minutes.

2. Immediately drain the eggs and gently shake the pan to lightly crack the shells. Fill the pan with cold water and shake lightly to loosen the eggshells. Let stand until the eggs are cool.

3. Drain and peel the eggs; pat dry. Cut the eggs in half lengthwise. Carefully transfer the yolks to a mini food processor. Add the mayonnaise, Dijon and yellow mustards and Worcestershire sauce and pulse until the yolk mixture is smooth and creamy; season with salt.

4. Using a pastry bag fitted with a star tip or a teaspoon, fill the egg whites with the yolk mixture. Arrange on a platter, garnish with paprika and serve chilled or at room temperature. —*Terry Sweetland*

WINE Fresh, fruity rosé.

Spicy Onion-Garlic Soup with Poached Eggs

ACTIVE: 25 MIN; TOTAL: 1 HR

4 SERVINGS ● ●

Before this soup became a staple on the menu at Two in San Francisco, chef and owner David Gingrass created the recipe in his home kitchen with the most basic pantry ingredients: onions, garlic, day-old bread and a hit of spicy cayenne. To turn it into a soothing one-dish meal, he cracks eggs into the soup and poaches them gently until they are soft and runny.

3 tablespoons extra-virgin olive oil

3 large garlic cloves, minced

1 medium sweet onion,
   cut into ½-inch dice

½ teaspoon sweet paprika

6 cups chicken stock or
   low-sodium broth

¼ teaspoon cayenne pepper
   or to taste

Salt

4 ounces sourdough bread,
   crusts removed, bread cut into
   ¾-inch cubes (2 cups)

4 large eggs

2 tablespoons chopped parsley

1. Preheat the oven to 350°. In a medium saucepan, heat 1 tablespoon of the olive oil. Add two-thirds of the minced garlic and cook over high heat until fragrant, about 30 seconds. Reduce the heat to moderate and cook, stirring, until golden brown, about 1 minute. Add the onion and paprika and cook, stirring, until the onion is translucent, about 5 minutes. Add the chicken stock and bring to a boil over high heat. Reduce the heat to moderate and simmer the soup until reduced to 2½ cups, about 30 minutes. Add the cayenne pepper and season with salt.

2. Meanwhile, spread the bread cubes on a large rimmed baking sheet and toss with the remaining 2 tablespoons of olive oil and minced garlic. Season the cubes with salt and bake for about 12 minutes, or until golden brown and crisp.

3. Crack the eggs into 4 small bowls. Bring the soup to a simmer over moderately low heat. Slide the eggs into the soup and simmer until the whites are firm and the yolks are runny, about 4 minutes.

4. Ladle a poached egg and some soup into soup bowls and sprinkle with the chopped parsley. Serve immediately, passing the croutons. —*David Gingrass*

MAKE AHEAD The soup can be prepared through Step 1 and refrigerated overnight.

WINE Fruity, low-oak Chardonnay.

Creamy Chicken Soup with Baby Peas and Carrots

TOTAL: 45 MIN

4 SERVINGS ●

Rotisserie chicken is a great shortcut; if you've got a few minutes to spare, save the bones and simmer them in store-bought chicken broth for an enriched chicken flavor.

- 2 tablespoons unsalted butter
- 2 large carrots, very thinly sliced
- 1 leek, white and tender green parts, halved lengthwise and thinly sliced
- 1 rotisserie chicken, dark meat and white meat pulled and coarsely shredded separately (3 cups total)
- ½ teaspoon mild curry powder
- 4 cups chicken stock or low-sodium broth

Salt and freshly ground white pepper

- 3 ounces crustless peasant or country white bread, cut into 1-inch cubes (2¼ cups)
- ½ cup half-and-half
- 1 cup frozen baby peas
- 1 tablespoon finely chopped flat-leaf parsley

1. In a medium saucepan, melt the butter. Add the carrots and leek and cook over moderate heat, stirring, until slightly softened, about 4 minutes. Add the dark meat and curry powder and cook, stirring, for 1 minute. Add 3 cups of the stock and season with salt and white pepper. Simmer over moderate heat until the vegetables are tender, about 5 minutes.

2. Meanwhile, in a blender, puree the bread with the remaining 1 cup of stock and the half-and-half.

3. Stir the puree into the soup along with the peas and simmer over low heat until thickened, about 8 minutes. Add the white meat and cook just until heated through, 2 to 3 minutes. Stir in the parsley and serve right away. —*Grace Parisi*

WINE Ripe, luxurious Chardonnay.

Gingered Butternut Squash Soup with Spicy Pecan Cream

ACTIVE: 40 MIN; TOTAL: 2 HR 15 MIN

12 SERVINGS ●

- 2 large butternut squash (5½ pounds), halved lengthwise and seeded
- 1 tablespoon extra-virgin olive oil
- ¾ cup pecans (2 ounces)
- 2 tablespoons unsalted butter
- 1 large onion, cut into ½-inch dice
- 1 small fennel bulb—halved, cored and cut into ½-inch dice

One 1½-inch piece of fresh ginger, peeled and finely chopped

- 6 cups chicken stock

One 14-ounce can unsweetened coconut milk

- ¾ cup chilled heavy cream
- 1 teaspoon hazelnut oil
- ⅛ teaspoon cayenne pepper

Kosher salt

- 1½ tablespoons fresh lemon juice

1. Preheat the oven to 350°. Rub the cut sides of the squash with the olive oil and set them cut side down on a large rimmed baking sheet. Bake the squash for about 1 hour, or until very tender. Remove from the oven and let stand until cool enough to handle. Spoon the squash flesh into a large bowl; discard the skins.

2. In a pie plate, toast the pecans for about 8 minutes, or until lightly browned and fragrant; let the nuts cool.

3. In a large pot, melt the butter. Add the onion, fennel and ginger and cook over moderate heat until softened, about 8 minutes. Add the squash and chicken stock, cover and simmer for 20 minutes, stirring occasionally. Uncover the pot and continue cooking until the squash starts to fall apart, about 10 minutes. Remove from the heat and stir in the coconut milk.

4. Meanwhile, in a food processor, pulse the pecans until they are finely chopped. In a medium bowl, beat the cream until soft peaks form. Fold in the chopped pecans, the hazelnut oil and the cayenne pepper and season with salt.

5. Working in batches, puree the soup in a blender until smooth. Stir in the lemon juice and season with salt. Ladle the soup into bowls, top with a dollop of the pecan cream and serve. —*Dean Fearing*

WINE Lush, fragrant Viognier.

Pumpkin and Yellow Split Pea Soup

ACTIVE: 25 MIN; TOTAL: 4 HR

12 SERVINGS ● ● ○

- 4 tablespoons unsalted butter
- 1 medium red onion, cut into ¼-inch dice
- 4 garlic cloves, minced
- 1 serrano chile, seeded and minced
- 1½ teaspoons ground cumin
- ½ teaspoon cayenne pepper
- 2 cups yellow split peas, soaked in water for 1 hour and drained
- 8½ cups water

One 15-ounce can unsweetened pumpkin puree

- ¾ pound fresh sugar pumpkin or butternut squash, peeled and cut into ¼-inch dice
- 1½ tablespoons fresh lemon juice

Kosher salt and freshly ground pepper

1. In a large pot, melt the butter. Add the red onion, garlic and chile and cook over moderately high heat until the onion is softened, 4 minutes. Add the cumin and cayenne and cook until fragrant, about 1 minute. Add the split peas and the water, then whisk in the pumpkin puree; bring to a simmer. Cover and cook over moderately low heat, stirring occasionally, until the split peas are tender, about 2 hours.

2. Stir the diced pumpkin into the soup and simmer over moderately low heat until the pumpkin pieces are completely tender, about 30 minutes. Remove from the heat. Stir in the lemon juice, season with salt and pepper and serve. —*Melissa Rubel*

WINE Full-bodied, rich Pinot Gris.

Mushroom Barley Soup with Mini Meatballs

TOTAL: 40 MIN

4 SERVINGS ●●

- 4 cups beef stock or low-sodium broth
- 1 cup water
- ½ cup pearl barley
- 1 large thyme sprig

Salt and freshly ground pepper

- 2 tablespoons extra-virgin olive oil
- 1 pound mixed wild and cultivated mushrooms, stemmed and thinly sliced (or ¾ pound presliced mushrooms)
- 1 large shallot, finely chopped
- ½ pound ground sirloin
- 1 large egg
- 2 tablespoons dry bread crumbs
- 2 tablespoons freshly grated Parmigiano-Reggiano cheese
- 2 tablespoons chopped parsley

Sour cream, for serving (optional)

1. In a large saucepan, combine the stock, water, barley and thyme. Season with salt and pepper and bring to a boil. Cover and cook over low heat until the barley is nearly tender, about 18 minutes.

2. Meanwhile, in a large nonstick skillet, heat the oil. Add the mushrooms and shallot, season with salt and pepper and cook over high heat until tender and browned, about 8 minutes.

3. In a medium bowl, combine the sirloin, egg, bread crumbs, cheese, ½ teaspoon of salt and ¼ teaspoon of pepper. Knead until blended, then roll into sixteen 1-inch balls.

4. Add the meatballs and mushrooms to the soup and simmer over moderate heat until the meatballs are cooked through and the barley is tender, about 8 minutes. Discard the thyme. Stir in the parsley and serve with sour cream. —*Grace Parisi*

MAKE AHEAD The soup can be refrigerated for up to 2 days. Reheat gently, adding a little beef stock to thin the soup.

WINE Ripe, juicy Pinot Noir.

Pork and Pink Bean Soup with Corn Muffin Croutons

TOTAL: 40 MIN

4 SERVINGS ●●

This thick and savory soup, reminiscent of cowboy campfire cooking, is a delicious cross between baked beans and tomato soup. The crunchy, sweet corn muffin croutons make it even more rustic.

- 6 ounces thickly sliced bacon, cut into 1-inch strips
- ½ medium sweet onion, very finely chopped
- 2 garlic cloves, finely chopped
- 2 tablespoons tomato paste
- 1 tablespoon pure maple syrup

Two 15-ounce cans pink beans with their liquid

- 3 cups chicken stock or low-sodium broth

Salt

Cayenne pepper

- 1 jumbo corn muffin (about 5 ounces), cut into ¾-inch cubes

Chopped scallions, for garnish

1. Preheat the oven to 400°. In a medium saucepan, cook the bacon over moderately high heat until browned and crisp, about 7 minutes. Transfer the bacon to a plate and pour off all but 2 tablespoons of the fat from the saucepan.

2. Add the onion and garlic to the fat in the saucepan and cook, stirring, until they are softened, about 5 minutes. Add the tomato paste and maple syrup and cook over moderate heat, stirring, until thick, about 3 minutes. Add the pink beans and their liquid and cook until slightly thickened, 2 to 3 minutes. Add the chicken stock and bacon and season lightly with salt and cayenne pepper. Simmer the soup over moderate heat until thickened slightly, about 15 minutes.

3. Meanwhile, spread the corn muffin cubes on a small baking sheet and bake for 7 to 8 minutes, until they are golden and crisp. Let the croutons cool slightly.

4. Ladle the soup into deep bowls, garnish with the corn muffin croutons and chopped scallions and serve. —*Grace Parisi*

MAKE AHEAD The soup can be refrigerated for up to 2 days. Reheat gently, adding a little chicken stock to thin the soup.

WINE Rustic, peppery Malbec.

Mussel and Spinach Bisque

TOTAL: 1 HR

10 SERVINGS ●

- 6 ounces baby spinach (6 cups)
- 1 cup dry white wine
- 1 cup water
- 3 bay leaves
- 4 pounds mussels, scrubbed
- 1½ tablespoons unsalted butter
- 2 medium shallots, minced
- 3 tablespoons all-purpose flour

One 8-ounce bottle clam juice

- 2 teaspoons tomato paste

Pinch of saffron threads, crumbled

- 2½ cups milk
- 1½ cups heavy cream

Salt and freshly ground white pepper

1. In a saucepan of boiling water, cook the spinach until just wilted, 30 seconds. Drain and spread on a baking sheet to cool, then gently squeeze out the excess water.

2. In a large pot, bring the wine and water to a boil with the bay leaves. Add the mussels, cover and cook over high heat, shaking the pot a few times, until the mussels open, about 5 minutes. Transfer the mussels to a large rimmed baking sheet to cool. Discard any mussels that do not open. Carefully pour the mussel cooking liquid into a glass measuring cup, stopping just before you reach the grit at the bottom; discard the bay leaves. Remove the mussels from their shells.

3. In a large saucepan, melt the butter. Add the shallots and cook over moderate heat until softened, about 5 minutes. Stir in the flour. Gradually whisk in the reserved mussel cooking liquid and the clam juice.

Bring to a boil, whisking. Whisk in the tomato paste and saffron; simmer gently, whisking occasionally, until no floury taste remains, about 10 minutes. Stir in the milk and cream and simmer for 5 minutes. Stir in the spinach and mussels, season with salt and pepper and serve. —*Marcia Kiesel*

WINE Lush, fragrant Viognier.

Miso Soup with Shrimp and Tofu

⏱ TOTAL: 20 MIN

4 SERVINGS ●

No soup is quicker to prepare than miso; just whisk miso paste into water. With added shrimp, tofu and greens, it can double as a complete and light meal. Feel free to use leftover chicken or roast pork (or whatever else is at hand) in place of the shrimp.

- 5 cups water
- ¼ cup white or red miso

Salt

- 1 cup frozen shelled edamame
- 4 ounces baby spinach (4 cups)
- ¾ pound shelled and deveined medium shrimp, cut into ½-inch pieces
- 7 ounces firm tofu, cut into ½-inch cubes
- 1 scallion, thinly sliced

Steamed short-grain rice and toasted sesame seeds, for serving

In a small bowl, whisk 1 cup of the water into the miso. In a medium saucepan, bring the remaining 4 cups of water to a boil with a pinch of salt. Add the edamame, cover and cook until tender, about 5 minutes. Add the spinach in bunches and stir to wilt. Add the shrimp and tofu. Stir the miso mixture and add it to the soup. Simmer just until the shrimp are cooked through, about 1 minute. Season the soup with salt and stir in the sliced scallion. Ladle the soup into deep bowls and serve with steamed rice and toasted sesame seeds. —*Grace Parisi*

WINE Light, fresh Pinot Grigio.

MISO SOUP WITH SHRIMP AND TOFU

PORK AND PINK BEAN SOUP WITH CORN MUFFIN CROUTONS

LATTICE-CRUSTED MINESTRONE POT PIE
(P. 293) AND BREADSTICK TWISTS (P. 300)

Lattice-Crusted Minestrone Pot Pies

ACTIVE: 2 HR 15 MIN; TOTAL: 5 HR

8 SERVINGS ●

This hearty dish is based on *ribollita*, the thick Tuscan soup made with leftover minestrone and chunks of bread. Here, a buttery, cheesy pastry lattice is baked on top of the soup. Instead of weaving the strips of dough to make the lattice, you can arrange them in a crisscross pattern; easier still, roll the dough into rounds, cut a few steam vents in the pastry and drape it over the bowls before baking.

SOUP

- 2 tablespoons extra-virgin olive oil
- 3 medium leeks, white and light green parts only, halved lengthwise and thickly sliced
- 3 celery ribs, halved lengthwise and sliced crosswise ¼ inch thick
- 2 carrots, halved lengthwise and sliced crosswise ¼ inch thick
- 4 garlic cloves, minced

One 2-pound butternut squash—peeled, seeded and cut into 1-inch chunks

- 1 bunch of Tuscan kale, leaves only, coarsely chopped

One 24-ounce can diced tomatoes

One 19-ounce can cannellini beans

- 5½ cups low-sodium chicken broth
- 2 teaspoons chopped rosemary
- 1 bay leaf
- 1 Parmigiano-Reggiano rind (optional)

Kosher salt and freshly ground pepper

PASTRY

- 3¾ cups all-purpose flour
- 1 tablespoon coarsely chopped rosemary
- 1½ teaspoons salt
- 1½ teaspoons sugar
- 3 sticks (12 ounces) cold unsalted butter, cut into small cubes
- ½ cup freshly grated Parmigiano-Reggiano cheese

½ to ¾ cup ice water

Egg wash made with 1 egg yolk mixed with 1 tablespoon heavy cream

1. MAKE THE SOUP: Heat the olive oil in a large saucepan. Add the leeks, celery, carrots and garlic and cook over moderate heat until the vegetables are golden and tender, about 12 minutes. Stir in the squash, kale, tomatoes, beans, chicken broth and rosemary and bring to a boil. Add the bay leaf and cheese rind and season with salt and pepper. Cover and simmer the soup gently until the squash is tender, about 25 minutes. Let cool completely. Remove the cheese rind and the bay leaf.

2. MEANWHILE, MAKE THE PASTRY: In a food processor, pulse the flour with the rosemary, salt and sugar. Add the butter and cheese and process until the mixture resembles coarse meal. With the machine on, gradually add the ice water and process just until the dough comes together. Divide the pastry into 8 pieces, flatten into disks and wrap in plastic. Refrigerate for at least 1 hour.

3. On a floured work surface, roll out 1 piece of pastry to a round 1 inch larger than your bowl. Using a pizza cutter, cut the pastry into ½-inch strips. Weave the strips into a lattice; refrigerate on a plate until firm. Repeat with the remaining pastry disks.

4. Preheat the oven to 400°. Ladle the soup into 8 heatproof 2-cup bowls and set them on a large baking sheet. Brush the outer rims of the bowls with the egg wash and top with a pastry lattice. When the pastry softens slightly, fold the overhang over the rims and press to help the pastry adhere. Lightly brush the lattice tops with egg wash. Bake the pot pies for 15 minutes. Reduce the oven temperature to 350° and bake for about 50 minutes longer, until the pastry is golden brown and the soup is bubbling. Serve hot. —*Susan Spungen*

MAKE AHEAD The unbaked minestrone pot pies can be refrigerated for up to 1 day.

WINE Bright, tart Barbera.

Smoked Mozzarella Spread

⏱ TOTAL: 10 MIN

10 SERVINGS ● ● ●

F&W's Marcia Kiesel likes to whiz smoked mozzarella in the food processor with sun-dried tomato pesto and olive oil.

- 1 pound smoked mozzarella, coarsely chopped
- ¼ cup plus 1 tablespoon extra-virgin olive oil
- 3 tablespoons sun-dried tomato pesto
- 1 tablespoon chopped parsley

Salt and freshly ground black pepper

Flatbread crackers, for serving

In a food processor, combine the mozzarella, olive oil and pesto and process to a coarse paste. Scrape into a bowl. Stir in the chopped parsley and season with salt and pepper. Serve with flatbread crackers. —*Marcia Kiesel*

WINE Fruity, low-oak Chardonnay.

TOOLS

dream knives

MISONO The extra-thin blades, perfect for fine dicing, are crafted in Japan's traditional sword-making town of Seki.

MAC The flexible blades on these Japanese knives make effortless work of cutting tough meats and hard vegetables.

WÜSTHOF These German-made knives are among the sturdiest; the Grand Prix II line has ergonomic handles and is made of an alloy designed to hold a sharp edge longer than most.

Winter Squash and Gouda Croquettes

ACTIVE: 45 MIN;

TOTAL: 2 HR 45 MIN

8 SERVINGS ●●

Los Angeles chef Octavio Becerra found the inspiration for this dish at a cheese festival in Petaluma, California, where he tasted an aged Gouda made by Valerie Thomas of Winchester Cheese Company in Riverside County (winchestercheese.com). "Her Gouda has been on my mind for months. Any time I can work it into my food, I do." Here he uses the salty, minerally cheese to season crunchy pastry rounds sweetened with soft-baked winter squash.

　1　tablespoon extra-virgin olive oil

One 2-pound winter squash, such as butternut, split lengthwise

　1　pound small sweet potatoes, split lengthwise

　6　large egg yolks

　1　large egg, beaten

　1　cup finely shredded aged Gouda

　1　teaspoon thyme

Salt and freshly ground pepper

　3　tablespoons water

1½　cups all-purpose flour

1½　cups plain dried bread crumbs

Vegetable oil, for frying

Bitter Orange Compote (recipe follows), for serving

1. Preheat the oven to 400°. Drizzle the olive oil on a large rimmed baking sheet. Arrange the squash and sweet potatoes on the baking sheet cut side down. Roast for about 45 minutes, until tender and lightly browned on the bottom. Let cool.

2. Scoop the squash and potato flesh into a large bowl and mash well. Stir in 2 of the egg yolks, the whole egg, the cheese and the thyme and season with 1 teaspoon of salt and ¼ teaspoon of pepper. Refrigerate until chilled, about 1 hour.

3. In a shallow bowl, beat the remaining 4 egg yolks with the water. Spread the flour and bread crumbs in 2 shallow bowls;

season the bread crumbs with salt and pepper. Line a baking sheet with wax paper or plastic wrap. Working in batches of 4, scoop rounded tablespoons of the croquette mixture into the flour. Roll into balls, dip in the egg wash, coat with the bread crumbs and place on the baking sheet. Repeat to form the remaining croquettes. Let the croquettes stand at room temperature for at least 10 minutes and as long as half an hour to firm up slightly before frying.

4. In a large, deep skillet, heat 1 inch of the vegetable oil to 350°. Line another baking sheet with paper towels and a rack. Add the croquettes to the hot oil in batches, taking care not to crowd the pan, and fry over high heat, turning once, until golden brown. Transfer the croquettes to the rack to drain. Serve hot with the Bitter Orange Compote. —*Octavio Becerra*

WINE Dry, light Champagne.

BITTER ORANGE COMPOTE

ACTIVE: 20 MIN; TOTAL: 1 HR

MAKES 1¼ CUPS ●●○

　4　large oranges

　2　tablespoons unsalted butter

　1　small sweet onion, thinly sliced

　2　tablespoons honey

1. Peel the zest from 1 of the oranges and slice it into very thin strips. Using a serrated knife, peel all the oranges, removing all of the bitter white pith. Working over a bowl, cut in between the membranes to release the sections into the bowl. Squeeze the membranes to extract as much juice as possible; you should have about 1 cup.

2. In a medium saucepan, melt the butter. Add the onion and cook over moderately high heat, stirring, until softened and lightly browned, about 8 minutes. Add the honey and cook until lightly caramelized, 3 minutes. Add the orange zest, sections and juice and bring to a boil. Reduce the heat to low and simmer until the liquid is reduced to a syrup and the sections have nearly broken down, about 30 minutes. —*O.B.*

Stuffed Fried Sardines

 TOTAL: 40 MIN

4 SERVINGS

　2　tablespoons chopped raisins

1½　tablespoons fresh lemon juice

　1　large scallion, minced

　1　tablespoon chopped parsley

　1　tablespoon fine dry bread crumbs

　¼　cup finely chopped serrano ham

　½　teaspoon ground fennel or fennel pollen

Salt and freshly ground pepper

16　sardines—butterflied, spines removed and (optional) heads and tails removed

All-purpose flour, for dredging

　2　large eggs

　1　tablespoon water

Extra-virgin olive oil, for frying

1. In a small bowl, mix the raisins with the lemon juice, scallion, parsley, bread crumbs, chopped ham and ground fennel. Season with salt and pepper. Open a sardine and place a rounded teaspoon of the filling on one side of the fish. Close the sardine, pressing the halves together firmly. Repeat with the remaining sardines and filling.

2. Spread some flour in a shallow bowl. Place the eggs in another shallow bowl and beat the water into the eggs. Dredge the sardines in the flour, then dip them into the egg mixture to thoroughly coat, letting the excess egg drip off. Dredge the sardines again in the flour and shake off any excess.

3. In a large skillet, heat ¼ inch of olive oil until shimmering. Add half of the breaded sardines and fry over moderately high heat until the fish are golden brown and crisp, about 2 minutes per side. Drain the sardines briefly on paper towels and transfer to plates. Fry and drain the second batch of sardines. —*Janet Mendel*

SERVE WITH Lemon wedges and a lightly dressed mesclun salad.

WINE Zesty, fresh Albariño.

STUFFED FRIED SARDINES

Roquefort Gougères

ACTIVE: 35 MIN; TOTAL: 1 HR 40 MIN
MAKES ABOUT 4½ DOZEN ● ○

Savory cheese puffs native to Burgundy, gougères are traditionally made with that region's mild, nutty Comté cheese. These ethereal, crispy rounds substitute Roquefort, a robust blue cheese that mellows out when baked in pastry, providing a deliciously pungent, mildly salty bite.

- 1 cup water
- 3 tablespoons unsalted butter
- ½ teaspoon salt
- 1 cup all-purpose flour
- 4 large eggs
- 2 ounces Roquefort cheese, crumbled (½ cup)

1. Preheat the oven to 425°. Line 2 large rimmed baking sheets with parchment paper. In a small saucepan, combine the water, butter and salt and bring to a boil. Remove from the heat, add the flour all at once and beat vigorously with a wooden spoon until the flour is thoroughly incorporated. Return the pan to moderate heat and cook, stirring constantly, until the dough pulls away from the side of the pan, forming a ball, about 2 minutes. Remove the pan from the heat and let stand at room temperature, stirring a few times, until the dough cools slightly, about 3 minutes.

2. Add the eggs 1 at a time, stirring briskly between additions to thoroughly incorporate each egg. Stir in the cheese.
3. Transfer the dough to a pastry bag fitted with a ½-inch round tip. Pipe 1-inch mounds of dough about 1 inch apart.
4. Bake until golden brown, about 25 minutes. Turn the oven off and prop the door ajar to dry out the gougères completely, about 20 minutes. Serve warm or at room temperature. —*Marcia Kiesel*
MAKE AHEAD The gougères can be frozen for up to 1 month. Reheat in a 350° oven.
WINE Fresh, fruity rosé.

Potato Chips with Chèvre, Pepper Jelly and Bacon

 TOTAL: 25 MIN
12 SERVINGS ●

F&W's Grace Parisi loves using extra-crispy, thick-cut potato chips as the base for quick hors d'oeuvres. Here, she tops the chips with creamy goat cheese, sweet-spicy pepper jelly and smoky bacon.

- 6 ounces sliced bacon
- 36 thick-cut potato chips
- 5 ounces fresh goat cheese, softened
- 3 tablespoons sweet red pepper jelly
- 1 tablespoon snipped chives

In a large skillet, cook the sliced bacon over high heat until crisp. Drain, cool and crumble the bacon. Arrange the potato chips on a serving platter. Spread or pipe 1 teaspoon of the goat cheese onto each potato chip. Top with a small dollop of the pepper jelly, sprinkle with the bacon and chives and serve. —*Grace Parisi*
WINE Lively, tart Sauvignon Blanc.

Green Salad with Tangy Mustard Vinaigrette

TOTAL: 20 MIN
12 SERVINGS ● ○

The combination of grapes, Roquefort cheese and walnuts in this salad makes for a refreshing starter or side.

- 3 tablespoons red wine vinegar
- 2 tablespoons whole-grain mustard
- 1 medium shallot, very finely chopped
- 1 tablespoon very finely chopped parsley
- ½ cup extra-virgin olive oil
- Salt and freshly ground pepper
- 12 ounces mixed baby greens (12 packed cups)
- 1 cup each of halved grapes, chopped and toasted walnuts and crumbled Roquefort cheese

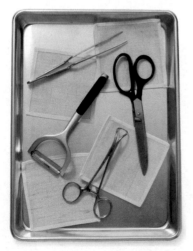

TOOLS

chefs' favorite gadgets

SURGICAL TWEEZERS Sean Brock of McCrady's in Charleston, South Carolina, gives these to his cooks for aligning tiny garnishes (Miltex; $45, Caligor, 212-369-6000).

SEWING SCISSORS Grant Achatz of Chicago's Alinea uses extra-sharp scissors to clean shellfish (Wiss; from $26, amazon.com).

PEELERS "At home, I use them to make carrot noodles for my daughter," says Seis Kamimura of Boka Kitchen + Bar in Seattle ($3; Pearl River, 800-878-2446).

SURGICAL TONGS Vikram Garg of Washington, DC's IndeBleu likes the fine-pointed tips (Misdom-Frank; from $20, Caligor, 212-369-6000).

1. In a medium jar, combine the red wine vinegar, whole-grain mustard and chopped shallot and parsley; cover and shake until smooth. Add the olive oil, season with salt and pepper and shake the vinaigrette until thoroughly blended.

2. In a large bowl, toss the greens, grapes, walnuts and cheese. Shake the vinaigrette again, pour it over the greens and toss. Serve right away. —*Grace Parisi*

WINE Lively, tart Sauvignon Blanc.

Roasted Beet Salad with Lemon Crème Fraîche

ACTIVE: 30 MIN; TOTAL: 1 HR 15 MIN
PLUS OVERNIGHT PICKLING
8 SERVINGS ● ●

This spectacular salad combines earthy-sweet beets, vinegary pickled red onions and a lemony crème fraîche dressing.

- 1 large red onion, sliced crosswise ½ inch thick and separated into rings
- 1½ cups balsamic vinegar
- 1 tablespoon yellow mustard seeds
- 1 tablespoon acacia honey
- 5 bay leaves
- 2 pounds baby beets (without tops)
- 2 tablespoons extra-virgin olive oil
- ¼ cup water
- Salt and freshly ground pepper
- 1 cup dry red wine, such as Syrah
- 1 tablespoon sugar
- ½ cup crème fraîche
- 1 tablespoon fresh lemon juice
- ½ teaspoon finely grated lemon zest
- 1 bunch of watercress, thick stems discarded

1. Place the onion rings in a large heat-proof jar or bowl. In a medium saucepan, combine the balsamic vinegar with the mustard seeds, honey and bay leaves. Bring to a boil, reduce the heat to low and simmer for 15 minutes. Pour the hot liquid over the onion rings; press to submerge them. Cover and refrigerate overnight.

2. Preheat the oven to 375°. In a medium roasting pan, toss the beets with the olive oil and water. Cover tightly with foil and braise until tender, about 45 minutes. Let the beets cool in their braising liquid. Peel the beets, return them to the liquid and season with salt and pepper.

3. Meanwhile, in a small saucepan, boil the red wine with the sugar over high heat until reduced to a syrup, about 10 minutes. Let the wine syrup cool.

4. In a bowl, whisk the crème fraîche with the fresh lemon juice and zest and season with salt. Spread the lemon crème fraîche on a serving platter. Use a slotted spoon to mound the braised beets on the crème fraîche and drizzle with their cooking liquid. Garnish the beets with the pickled onion rings and watercress, drizzle some of the red wine syrup over everything and serve immediately. —*Octavio Becerra*

MAKE AHEAD The roasted beets can be refrigerated in their braising liquid for up to 3 days. The onions can be refrigerated in their pickling brine for up to 3 days.

WINE Fresh, fruity rosé.

Chicory and Endive Salad with Spiced Pistachios

TOTAL: 35 MIN
6 SERVINGS ● ●

- 1 tablespoon hazelnut oil
- 2 tablespoons sherry vinegar
- One 10-ounce head of radicchio, quartered
- ¼ cup shelled unsalted pistachios
- Salt
- Sugar
- Ground cumin
- Cayenne pepper
- Freshly ground black pepper
- ¼ cup extra-virgin olive oil
- 1 large shallot, finely chopped
- ¼ cup balsamic vinegar
- One 6-ounce head of chicory, cut into bite-size pieces (6 cups)

- 1 red Belgian endive, thinly sliced crosswise
- 1 yellow Belgian endive, thinly sliced crosswise
- 1 tablespoon chopped tarragon

1. Preheat the oven to 375°. In a shallow dish, mix the hazelnut oil with the sherry vinegar. Add the radicchio and let marinate for 10 minutes, turning often.

2. Scatter the pistachios on a rimmed baking sheet and sprinkle with a pinch each of salt, sugar, cumin and cayenne. Bake until toasted, about 5 minutes.

3. Light a grill. Season the radicchio with salt and black pepper and grill over high heat until lightly charred on 2 sides, about 2 minutes per side. Transfer to a work surface and let cool slightly. Cut the radicchio into bite-size pieces.

4. In a large skillet, heat the olive oil. Add the shallot and cook over moderate heat until softened, about 4 minutes. Add the balsamic vinegar and bring to a boil over moderate heat. Add the chicory and cook, stirring occasionally, until just tender, about 5 minutes. Add the radicchio, red and yellow endives and tarragon and toss well. Season with salt and black pepper. Mound on plates, garnish with the pistachios and serve. —*Jan Birnbaum*

MAKE AHEAD The spiced pistachios can be stored in an airtight container overnight.

WINE Fresh, lively Soave.

TECHNIQUE

making crème fraîche

For 1½ cups of crème fraîche, combine ½ cup of buttermilk, sour cream or plain yogurt and 1 cup of heavy cream in a glass container. Let sit in a warm place for 6 hours, then stir and refrigerate.

TUSCAN SANGRIA

the new sangria

Sangria has a bad reputation (bargain-basement wine, cheap spirits, soggy fruit), but America's best mixologists are making versions of the drink to be proud of.

Tuscan Sangria

DUGGAN MCDONNELL,
CANTINA, SAN FRANCISCO

MAKES 10 DRINKS ● ● ●

Tuscan red wine and three Italian spirits give this robust sangria authentic regional flavor.

one 750-milliliter bottle Tuscan red wine, such as Sangiovese • 3 cups fresh orange juice • ¾ cup Tuaca (a vanilla-and-citrus-flavored liqueur) • ⅓ cup Punt e Mes (a bittersweet Italian vermouth) • ½ cup fresh lime juice • ½ cup limoncello • ¼ cup sugar • ice • orange slices and cinnamon sticks, for garnish

In a pitcher, combine the red wine, orange juice, Tuaca, Punt e Mes, lime juice, limoncello and sugar. Stir well to dissolve the sugar. To serve, fill wineglasses halfway with ice. Add the sangria and garnish with an orange slice and a cinnamon stick.

Vino Francesca

GARY SULLIVAN, ROCCA KITCHEN & BAR, BOSTON

MAKES 6 DRINKS ● ●

Sullivan created this food-friendly sangria around Rocca's house rosé. "I wanted to maintain the wine's fresh fruit flavors," he says.

⅓ cup honey • ⅓ cup boiling water • 15 sage leaves, plus more for garnish • one 750-milliliter bottle rosé • ice • lemon twists, for garnish

In a small heatproof bowl, stir the honey into the boiling water until dissolved. Add the 15 sage leaves and muddle them with a wooden spoon. Let the syrup cool slightly, then strain it into a pitcher, pressing hard on the sage leaves. Pour in the rosé and stir well. Serve the sangria in wineglasses over ice, garnishing each glass with a lemon twist and sage leaf.

Sangria Flora

LYNNETTE MARRERO, FREEMANS, NYC

MAKES 8 DRINKS ● ●

This delicate sangria is made with St-Germain, an aromatic elderflower liqueur that's delicious with a tropical-fruit-inflected Sauvignon Blanc.

one 750-milliliter bottle Sauvignon Blanc • 1½ cups St-Germain elderflower liqueur (or elderflower cordial) • ¼ cup Cointreau • 6 strawberries, sliced ¼ inch thick • 6 raspberries • 2 peaches, sliced ¼ inch thick • 1 orange, thinly sliced crosswise • 1 pound green and red grapes • ice

Combine all of the ingredients except the ice in a pitcher and let stand at room temperature for 3 hours, or cover and refrigerate overnight. Serve in wineglasses over ice.

Brewsky Sangria

ROGER KUGLER, SUBA, NYC

MAKES 8 DRINKS ● ●

Kugler's tangy beer-based sangria was inspired by a British customer's request for a shandy, a refreshing blend of lager beer and lemonade or soda often served in pubs.

2 Bartlett pears, peeled and chopped • 1 cup plus 2 tablespoons fresh lemon juice • four 12-ounce bottles lager, chilled • 1 cup triple sec • ice • 2 Bosc pears, sliced, for garnish

In a food processor, combine the Bartlett pears with 2 tablespoons of the lemon juice and process to a puree. Slowly pour the beer into a pitcher. Stir in the remaining 1 cup of lemon juice, the triple sec and the pear puree. Fill pint glasses halfway with ice. Add the sangria and garnish with the Bosc pear slices.

Indian Popcorn

TOTAL: 20 MIN

12 SERVINGS ● ● ○ ○

Inspired by the Indian snacks called *chaat,* this crispy, spicy, salty combination of popcorn and bits of fried serrano chiles and shallots is perfect with cocktails.

- ⅓ cup vegetable oil
- 4 medium shallots, very thinly sliced
- 2 serrano chiles, very thinly sliced
- 1½ teaspoons mild curry powder
- 1 teaspoon nigella seeds (also sold as black onion seeds)
- ¾ cup popcorn kernels

Kosher salt

1. In a large pot, heat the vegetable oil. Add the sliced shallots and serrano chiles and fry over moderately high heat, stirring occasionally, until golden, about 4 minutes. With a slotted spoon, transfer the fried shallots and chiles to a paper towel–lined plate to drain.

2. In the same pot, cook the curry powder and nigella seeds over moderate heat until fragrant, about 1 minute. Stir in the popcorn kernels and cover. Cook, shaking the pan every 30 seconds, until the kernels have stopped popping, about 8 minutes. Season the popcorn with salt and transfer to a bowl. Sprinkle with the shallots and chiles and serve. —*Melissa Rubel*

SUPERFAST

jazzing up olives

Warm 2 tablespoons of extra-virgin olive oil with 3 lemon zest strips, 2 smashed garlic cloves and a pinch of crushed red pepper until fragrant. Add 2 cups of olives, toss and serve.

Breadstick Twists

ACTIVE: 45 MIN; TOTAL: 1 HR 10 MIN

MAKES ABOUT 18 TWISTS ● ○

This versatile hors d'oeuvre is made with a simple baking-powder dough that can be rolled out immediately, without resting. The twists can be formed in any length, and flavored with all kinds of spices and seasonings, from curry to fennel.

- 2 cups all-purpose flour
- ½ teaspoon baking powder
- 1½ teaspoons kosher salt, plus more for sprinkling
- 3 tablespoons cold unsalted butter, cut into ½-inch pieces
- ½ cup plus 1 tablespoon ice water

Extra-virgin olive oil, for brushing

1. Preheat the oven to 375°. In a food processor, pulse the flour with the baking powder and the 1½ teaspoons of salt. Add the butter and pulse until the mixture resembles small peas. With the machine on, add the ice water and process just until the dough comes together.

2. Transfer the dough to a lightly floured work surface and gently pat it into a 1-inch-thick rectangle. Roll out the dough to a 10-by-12-inch rectangle about ¼ inch thick. Cut the rectangle crosswise to form strips of dough ¼ inch thick.

3. Gently roll each strip into a 14-inch-long stick. Brush 1 stick with water and twist it with another stick, pressing at the top and the bottom. Arrange the twists on a baking sheet. Repeat, rolling and twisting the remaining strips of dough.

4. Brush the breadsticks with olive oil and sprinkle with kosher salt. Bake the twists for about 25 minutes, until golden. Let cool before serving. —*Susan Spungen*

VARIATIONS To make flavored breadstick twists, add 2 tablespoons of fennel seeds, 2 teaspoons of smoked sweet paprika or 2 teaspoons of curry powder to the flour.

MAKE AHEAD The Breadstick Twists can be stored in an airtight container at room temperature for up to 2 days.

Cashews with Crispy Sage and Garlic

TOTAL: 15 MIN

MAKES 2 CUPS ● ● ○

- 2 tablespoons extra-virgin olive oil
- 2 garlic cloves, thinly sliced
- 12 sage leaves plus 1 tablespoon chopped sage
- 2 cups raw cashews

Salt

In a skillet, heat the oil. Add the garlic and fry over medium heat until lightly golden, about 2 minutes. Add all the sage and cook until crisp, 1 minute; drain on paper towels. Add the cashews and cook, stirring, until golden, 5 minutes; drain on paper towels. Toss with the garlic, sage and salt. Let cool, then serve. —*Susan Spungen*

Asian Bar Mix

ACTIVE: 15 MIN; TOTAL: 1 HR 15 MIN

MAKES 3 CUPS ● ○

- 2 tablespoons unsalted butter, melted
- 2 teaspoons soy sauce
- 1 teaspoon sugar
- ½ teaspoon Chinese five-spice powder
- ½ teaspoon kosher salt
- ¼ teaspoon cayenne pepper
- 1 cup sesame sticks
- 1 cup wasabi peas
- ½ cup raw almonds
- ½ cup unsalted roasted peanuts
- 1 sheet of nori, cut into small rectangles

Preheat the oven to 250°. In a large bowl, mix together the butter, soy sauce, sugar, five-spice powder, salt and cayenne. Add the sesame sticks, wasabi peas, almonds, peanuts and nori; toss well. Spread on a baking sheet and roast for 1 hour, stirring once, until the nuts are toasted and the coating is dry. Let cool before serving. —*Susan Spungen*

ASIAN BAR MIX, TOASTED PUMPKIN SEEDS, CASHEWS WITH SAGE

INDIAN POPCORN

Toasted Pumpkin Seeds

 TOTAL: 5 MIN
MAKES 1 CUP ● ○

¼ cup extra-virgin olive oil
1 cup raw pumpkin seeds
¾ teaspoon kosher salt

In a medium skillet, heat the oil over moderately high heat. When the oil is hot, add the pumpkin seeds and cook until puffed and browned, about 3 minutes; if they start popping, cover the skillet. Transfer to paper towels to drain. Sprinkle with salt, let cool and serve. —*Susan Spungen*

drinks

Mango–Rose Water Cocktail

TOTAL: 5 MIN
MAKES 1 DRINK ○

Fragrant rose water is a popular flavoring in Indian drinks, and it's often blended with mango in a yogurt shake called a *lassi*. Here, those Indian flavors come together in a sophisticated cocktail.

Ice
3 ounces mango nectar
1½ ounces vodka
1 tablespoon fresh lime juice
½ teaspoon rose water

Fill a cocktail shaker with ice. Pour in the mango nectar, vodka, fresh lime juice and rose water and shake well until chilled. Strain the cocktail into a tall glass and serve immediately. —*Melissa Rubel*

Blood Orange Margaritas

TOTAL: 40 MIN
MAKES 12 DRINKS ○

1 quart fresh blood orange juice or fresh orange juice (about 12 blood oranges or 8 large navel oranges)
1½ cups fresh lime juice (about 12 limes)

1½ cups Cointreau or other triple sec
3½ cups silver tequila
Kosher salt
1 blood orange or orange wedge, plus 12 thin blood orange or orange slices for garnish
Ice
12 small sage sprigs or leaves

1. In a large pitcher, combine the blood orange juice with the fresh lime juice, Cointreau and silver tequila and mix well. Refrigerate the mixture until chilled, at least 30 minutes or overnight.

2. Spread a small mound of salt on a small plate. Moisten the outer rims of 12 martini glasses with the orange wedge, then dip the rims into the salt to lightly coat.

3. Add ice to the pitcher and stir well, then strain the blood orange margaritas into the salt-rimmed glasses. Garnish each margarita with a blood orange slice and a sage sprig and serve. —*Chris Beverly*

●HEALTHY ●MAKE AHEAD ○VEGETARIAN ●STAFF FAVORITE

main courses

Spice-Crusted Tuna with Thai Snow Pea Salad

 TOTAL: 35 MIN
4 SERVINGS ● ●

Four 6-ounce tuna steaks,
　　about 1 inch thick

　2　tablespoons vegetable oil,
　　plus more for brushing

Salt

　2　teaspoons cracked coriander seeds

　2　teaspoons cracked peppercorns

　¼　cup fresh lime juice

　2　fresh lemongrass stalks,
　　bottom two-thirds of tender
　　inner bulbs only, thinly sliced

　2　tablespoons Asian fish sauce

　1　tablespoon minced cilantro

　1　fresh long red chile, such as
　　de arbol or cayenne—halved,
　　seeded and thinly sliced

　½　pound snow peas

1. Light a grill. Brush the tuna steaks with vegetable oil and season with salt. Mix the coriander seeds with the cracked peppercorns and press them onto both sides of the tuna steaks.

2. In a bowl, combine the 2 tablespoons of vegetable oil with the lime juice, lemongrass, fish sauce, cilantro and chile.

3. In a medium saucepan, steam the snow peas over ½ inch of boiling water, covered, until bright green and crisp-tender, about 2 minutes. Drain, refresh under cold water and pat dry. Transfer to a bowl.

4. Grill the tuna steaks over a hot fire, turning once, until lightly charred outside and rare in the center, about 2 minutes per side. Transfer to a cutting board.

5. Cut the tuna into thick slices and arrange on plates. Toss the snow peas with 2 tablespoons of the dressing and spoon alongside the tuna. Pass extra dressing at the table. —*Andrew Murray*

WINE Lush, fragrant Viognier.

Crunchy Vietnamese Chicken Salad

 TOTAL: 45 MIN
4 SERVINGS ● ●

　2　tablespoons sugar

　2　tablespoons plus 1 teaspoon
　　Asian fish sauce

　1½　tablespoons fresh lime juice,
　　plus lime wedges for serving

　1½　tablespoons distilled
　　white vinegar

　1　tablespoon water

　1　serrano chile with seeds, minced

　1　small garlic clove, minced

　1　cup vegetable oil, for frying

　2　large shallots, thinly sliced

Salt

　4　cups finely shredded green
　　cabbage (from ½ small head)

　2　carrots, finely shredded

　½　small red onion, thinly sliced

　¼　cup coarsely chopped cilantro

　¼　cup coarsely chopped mint

　3　cups shredded rotisserie chicken
　　(from ½ chicken)

　2　tablespoons extra-virgin olive oil

　3　tablespoons coarsely chopped
　　unsalted roasted peanuts

1. Stir together the sugar, fish sauce, lime juice, vinegar, water, chile and garlic until the sugar dissolves. Let stand 5 minutes.

2. Meanwhile, in a small saucepan, heat the oil until shimmering. Add the shallots and cook over high heat, stirring, until golden, 3 to 4 minutes. Drain on paper towels. Sprinkle with salt and let cool.

3. In a large bowl, toss the cabbage, carrots, onion, cilantro, mint and chicken. Add the olive oil and dressing; toss. Sprinkle with the peanuts and shallots; serve with lime wedges. —*Eric Banh and Sophie Banh*

WINE Lively, tart Sauvignon Blanc.

SPICE-CRUSTED TUNA
WITH THAI SNOW PEA SALAD

Grilled Pork and Onion Tacos

TOTAL: 30 MIN
4 SERVINGS

Grilling pork quickly not only keeps it moist, but adds a charred, smoky flavor that is lovely in these tacos. Remember to grill the cutlets only until they're just cooked through; leave them on the heat any longer, and they can dry out.

Eight ¼-inch-thick pork loin cutlets
   (about 2 pounds)
1 large sweet onion, such as
   Vidalia, cut crosswise into
   ½-inch-thick rounds
2 tablespoons extra-virgin olive oil
Kosher salt and freshly ground pepper
2 teaspoons chile powder
Eight 6-inch flour or corn tortillas,
   warmed, for serving
1 Hass avocado, halved and
   sliced lengthwise, for serving
½ cup cilantro leaves, for serving
Sour cream and lime wedges,
   for serving

1. Light a grill or preheat a grill pan. Arrange the cutlets and onion on a large baking sheet. Brush all over with the oil and season with salt and pepper. Season the cutlets with the chile powder.
2. Grill the onions over moderately high heat, turning once, until charred and tender, about 8 minutes. Transfer to a cutting board and cover with foil to keep warm.

TECHNIQUE

crisping fish

For supercrisp fish skin, follow the technique for **Neil Perry**'s salmon on the opposite page: Preheat a nonstick pan over moderately high heat, rub skin-on fillets with oil and cook skin side down, undisturbed, until the skin is very crisp. Turn to finish cooking.

Grill the cutlets, turning once, until just cooked through, about 2 minutes. Transfer the pork to the cutting board.
3. Coarsely chop the onions and cut the pork into ½-inch strips; transfer to a platter. Serve with the tortillas, avocado, cilantro, sour cream and lime wedges.
—*Melissa Rubel*
WINE Intense, fruity Zinfandel.

Grilled Beef Rolls

TOTAL: 1 HR
MAKES 12 ROLLS ●

Grape leaves make an excellent replacement for the more traditional, hard-to-find *la lot* leaves in these crunchy Vietnamese grilled beef rolls.

¼ cup plus 1 tablespoon vegetable
   oil, plus more for brushing
1 tablespoon Asian fish sauce
1 fresh lemongrass stalk, tender
   inner white bulb only, minced
½ teaspoon five-spice powder
1½ teaspoons honey
4 medium garlic cloves—
   1 very finely chopped,
   3 very thinly sliced
Kosher salt
½ pound flank steak, thinly sliced
   across the grain into ¼-inch-thick
   slices, then halved crosswise
12 large grape leaves from a jar
½ small jicama, peeled and cut
   into 2-by-¼-inch matchsticks
24 small basil leaves
2 scallions, minced
2 tablespoons chopped
   unsalted roasted peanuts

1. Light a grill. In a medium bowl, mix 1 tablespoon of the oil with the fish sauce, lemongrass, five-spice powder, honey, chopped garlic and ½ teaspoon of salt. Add the flank steak and toss to coat.
2. Using scissors, snip off the stems from the grape leaves and spread a few of the leaves out on a work surface. Place 2 slices of the garlic in the center of each leaf. Top

with 2 slices of steak, 2 pieces of jicama and 2 basil leaves. Roll up the leaves into tight cylinders, tucking in the sides as you roll. Repeat with the remaining grape leaves, garlic, steak, jicama and basil. Thread the rolls onto 4 pairs of skewers, so that each pair holds 3 rolls. Lightly brush the skewered rolls with oil.
3. In a small skillet, heat the remaining ¼ cup of oil until just beginning to smoke. Remove from the heat and add the scallions and ½ teaspoon of salt. Immediately pour the hot scallion oil into a ramekin.
4. Grill the rolls over moderately high heat, turning once, until lightly charred outside and firm, about 8 minutes. Transfer the rolls to a platter and drizzle the scallion oil on top. Sprinkle with the peanuts and serve.
—*Eric Banh and Sophie Banh*
WINE Ripe, juicy Pinot Noir.

Steamed Fish with Mushrooms and Noodles

TOTAL: 45 MIN
4 SERVINGS ●

1½ ounces cellophane noodles
1 tablespoon white miso
1 tablespoon oyster sauce
1 tablespoon soy sauce
1½ teaspoons sugar
½ cup chicken stock or
   low-sodium broth
6 ounces large white mushrooms,
   thinly sliced
1½ pounds tilapia or snapper fillets
1 scallion, julienned
3 cilantro sprigs
3 tablespoons canola oil

1. In a small bowl, cover the cellophane noodles with hot water and let stand until softened, about 5 minutes. Drain and cut into 4-inch lengths.
2. In another small bowl, whisk the miso, oyster sauce, soy sauce, sugar and stock.
3. Scatter the mushrooms in a deep-dish pie plate and set the fish on top. Mound the noodles over the fish and drizzle the sauce

on top. Set the pie plate in a steamer basket or a deep skillet large enough to hold it. Add 1 inch of water to the steamer or skillet and bring to a boil. Cover and steam until the fish is cooked through, about 15 minutes. Transfer the plate to a trivet and sprinkle with the scallion and cilantro.

4. Heat the canola oil in a small saucepan until very hot. Drizzle the hot oil over the noodles and fish and serve right away.
—*Eric Banh and Sophie Banh*

WINE Vivid, lightly sweet Riesling.

Pan-Glazed Salmon with Oyster Sauce and Basil

TOTAL: 30 MIN
4 SERVINGS ●

1½ pounds skinless salmon fillet, cut into 1½ inch cubes
2 tablespoons oyster sauce
Salt and freshly ground pepper
1 tablespoon vegetable oil
1 fresh long red chile, thinly sliced on the bias
4 scallions, cut into 1-inch lengths
1 tablespoon dry white wine
2 tablespoons water
3 tablespoons chopped basil
Steamed rice and lime or lemon wedges, for serving

1. In a large bowl, toss the salmon cubes with the oyster sauce and season them lightly with salt and pepper.

2. In a large nonstick skillet, heat the vegetable oil. Add the seasoned salmon cubes and cook over moderately high heat, turning once, until browned but barely cooked through, about 6 minutes. Reduce the heat to moderate; add the chile and scallions. Cook until the scallions soften, about 2 minutes. Stir in the wine and water and simmer until the salmon is just cooked through, 1 minute. Stir in the basil. Transfer the salmon to plates and serve with steamed rice and lime wedges.
—*Marcia Kiesel*

WINE Zesty, fresh Albariño.

Salmon with Tomato-Braised Chickpeas and Herbed Yogurt

TOTAL: 35 MIN
4 SERVINGS ●

The key to this dish is making sure that the salmon skin is completely crisp.

1 cup plain whole-milk Greek yogurt
2 tablespoons coarsely chopped cilantro
2 tablespoons coarsely chopped mint
1 tablespoon fresh lemon juice
Kosher salt and freshly ground black pepper
¼ cup extra-virgin olive oil
8 sage leaves
2 garlic cloves, thinly sliced
Two 15-ounce cans chickpeas, drained and rinsed
One 14-ounce can whole tomatoes, coarsely chopped and juices reserved
Four 6-ounce skin-on salmon fillets

1. In a small bowl, mix the yogurt with the cilantro, mint and lemon juice and season with salt and pepper. Cover the herbed yogurt and refrigerate.

2. In a large skillet, heat 3 tablespoons of the olive oil. Add the sage leaves and sliced garlic and cook over moderate heat until the garlic just begins to turn lightly golden, about 2 minutes. Add the chickpeas and the chopped tomatoes and their juices and season with salt and pepper. Simmer the chickpeas and tomatoes over moderately low heat until the sauce thickens, about 12 minutes.

3. Meanwhile, heat a large nonstick skillet until very hot. Rub the salmon with the remaining 1 tablespoon of olive oil and season with salt and pepper. Add the salmon to the skillet, skin side down, and cook over moderately high heat until the skin is very crisp, about 4 minutes. Turn the fillets and cook until light pink throughout, about 3 minutes longer.

4. Spoon the tomato-braised chickpeas onto plates and top with the salmon, skin side up. Garnish with a dollop of the herbed yogurt and serve immediately, passing the remaining yogurt at the table.
—*Neil Perry*

WINE Ripe, juicy Pinot Noir.

Galician Fish Stew

ACTIVE: 25 MIN; TOTAL: 1 HR 5 MIN
4 SERVINGS ●

This traditional fisherman's stew is punched up by *ajada*, a spicy Galician sauce made with olive oil, garlic and paprika.

Four 6-ounce skinless halibut fillets
Kosher salt
2 pounds Yukon Gold potatoes, peeled and sliced ½ inch thick
1 cup fish stock or clam broth
½ cup dry white wine
2 bay leaves
1 medium onion, quartered
3 cups coarsely chopped Swiss chard leaves (6 ounces)
¼ cup extra-virgin olive oil
4 garlic cloves, thinly sliced
1 tablespoon sweet Spanish paprika
Crushed red pepper

1. Season the halibut with salt and refrigerate for 30 minutes. In a large saucepan, combine the potatoes, stock, wine, bay leaves, onion, chard and 1 tablespoon of salt. Bring to a boil, cover and simmer over low heat for 15 minutes.

2. In a small saucepan, heat the oil. Add the garlic and cook over low heat until golden, 4 minutes. Stir in the paprika and crushed red pepper; remove from the heat.

3. Lay the halibut on top of the potatoes and simmer, turning once, until the fish is just cooked through, about 8 minutes.

4. Transfer the halibut and potato stew to shallow bowls. Ladle 1½ cups of the broth into the garlic oil and bring to a boil. Stir well, pour over the fish and serve.
—*Janet Mendel*

WINE Zesty, fresh Albariño.

SPICY SHRIMP IN CHILE SAUCE

Halibut with Lemon Oil and Sautéed Escarole

 TOTAL: 40 MIN
4 SERVINGS ●

A drizzle of lemon oil over the halibut and a touch of anchovy paste in the escarole give this healthy dish unexpected richness.

¼ cup extra-virgin olive oil
2 garlic cloves—1 crushed, 1 minced
Finely grated zest of 1 lemon
½ teaspoon anchovy paste
Pinch of crushed red pepper
2 heads of escarole (1¾ pounds total), dark green outer leaves discarded and the rest coarsely chopped
Salt and freshly ground black pepper
Four 6-ounce skinless halibut fillets

1. Preheat the oven to 400°. In a small bowl, combine 2 tablespoons of the olive oil with the crushed garlic clove and the lemon zest. Let stand at room temperature for 10 minutes, then discard the garlic.
2. Meanwhile, in a large skillet, heat 1 tablespoon of the olive oil. Add the minced garlic, anchovy paste and crushed red pepper and cook over moderate heat, stirring, until fragrant, about 30 seconds. Add the escarole and cook over moderately high heat, stirring, until barely wilted, about 3 minutes. Season with salt and black pepper.
3. In a large ovenproof skillet, heat the remaining 1 tablespoon of olive oil until shimmering. Season the halibut fillets with salt and black pepper and add them to the skillet. Cook over high heat until beginning to brown on the bottom, about 3 minutes. Transfer the skillet to the oven and roast the halibut for about 5 minutes, or until just white throughout.
4. Briefly warm the escarole over moderately high heat until hot but still crisp-tender, about 1 minute, then spoon it onto plates. Transfer the halibut to the plates browned side up. Drizzle with the lemon-garlic oil and serve. —*David Gingrass*
WINE Ripe, luxurious Chardonnay.

Lemony Herb-Grilled Jumbo Shrimp

ACTIVE: 25 MIN; TOTAL: 1 HR 25 MIN
4 SERVINGS ●

Australian chef Neil Perry likes to use this marinade—a zesty combination of garlic, ginger, lemon zest, crushed red pepper and fresh herbs—to marinate all kinds of seafood, but shrimp is a favorite. When the weather is pleasant, he grills the shrimp outdoors; when it's cooler out, he broils the shrimp in his oven.

16 jumbo shrimp (1½ pounds)
3 garlic cloves
One ¾-inch piece of fresh ginger, peeled and finely grated
1 tablespoon chopped oregano
1 tablespoon chopped sage
1 tablespoon chopped cilantro
1 teaspoon crushed red pepper
1 lemon, zest finely grated and lemon cut in half
Kosher salt
½ cup extra-virgin olive oil, plus more for drizzling
Freshly ground pepper

1. Using kitchen scissors, cut down the back of each shrimp through the shell and halfway through the meat. Remove the dark veins and transfer the shrimp in their shells to a large bowl.
2. In a mortar or food processor, crush the garlic, ginger, oregano, sage, cilantro, crushed red pepper and lemon zest with 1 teaspoon of kosher salt until a coarse paste forms. Stir in the ½ cup of olive oil. Pour the mixture over the shrimp and toss to coat thoroughly. Let stand at room temperature for 1 hour.
3. Light a grill. Grill the shrimp over moderately high heat, turning once, until white throughout, about 4 minutes. Transfer the grilled shrimp to plates. Squeeze the lemon halves over the shrimp, drizzle with olive oil, season lightly with salt and pepper and serve at once. —*Neil Perry*
WINE Tart, citrusy Riesling.

Spicy Shrimp in Chile Sauce

 TOTAL: 30 MIN
4 SERVINGS ●

2 tablespoons sugar
3 tablespoons water
2 tablespoons canola oil
1 small red onion, cut lengthwise into ½-inch wedges
3 medium garlic cloves, very finely chopped
1½ pounds shelled and deveined large shrimp
2 serrano chiles, seeded and very finely chopped
1½ tablespoons Asian fish sauce
1½ teaspoons freshly ground black pepper
4 scallions, cut into 3-inch lengths
2 tablespoons coconut milk mixed with 2 tablespoons water
Steamed rice, for serving

1. In a small skillet, mix the sugar with 1 tablespoon of the water and cook over high heat, stirring, until the sugar is completely dissolved. Cook without stirring until the mixture becomes a deep amber caramel, 2 to 3 minutes. Remove from the heat and carefully stir in the remaining 2 tablespoons of water. Transfer the caramel to a very small heatproof bowl.
2. Heat a wok over high heat. Add the canola oil and heat until just beginning to smoke. Add the onion wedges and chopped garlic and stir-fry until the onions and garlic are just softened, about 1 minute. Add the shrimp and stir-fry for 1 minute. Add the chopped serrano chiles, fish sauce, black pepper, scallion pieces and caramel and cook over moderate heat, stirring occasionally, until the shrimp are pink and curled, about 5 minutes. Stir in the diluted coconut milk, bring to a boil and simmer until the liquid is slightly reduced, about 1 minute. Serve immediately, with steamed rice.
—*Eric Banh and Sophie Banh*
WINE Tart, citrusy Riesling.

Shrimp with Green Beans and Toasted Coconut

TOTAL: 40 MIN
4 SERVINGS

F&W's Marcia Kiesel seasons shrimp, crunchy green beans and smooth coconut milk with a garam masala spice mixture that blends the deep, fragrant flavors of cloves, coriander and cumin seeds.

- ½ pound slender green beans
- ½ cup shredded unsweetened coconut
- 2 tablespoons vegetable oil
- 1 small onion, thinly sliced
- 1 teaspoon garam masala
- 1 Thai chile, minced
- 1 pound medium shrimp—shelled, deveined and halved lengthwise
- Salt and freshly ground pepper
- 2 tablespoons unsweetened coconut milk
- 1 tablespoon soy sauce
- ¼ cup cilantro leaves
- Steamed rice, for serving

1. Preheat the oven to 350°. Bring a medium saucepan of salted water to a boil. Add the green beans and cook until just tender, about 2 minutes. Drain and spread out on a large plate to cool to room temperature.
2. Spread the coconut on a baking sheet and bake until golden, about 3 minutes. Transfer to a plate and let cool.
3. In a large skillet, heat the vegetable oil. Add the onion and cook over moderate heat, stirring occasionally, until softened, about 7 minutes. Add the garam masala and chile and cook until fragrant, about 2 minutes. Add the shrimp, season with salt and pepper and cook, stirring, until the shrimp are just white throughout, about 3 minutes. Stir in the green beans and cook to heat through, about 1 minute. Stir in the coconut milk and soy sauce, then fold in the toasted coconut. Transfer to plates, garnish with the cilantro and serve with steamed rice. —*Marcia Kiesel*
WINE Vivid, lightly sweet Riesling.

Chicken Breasts with Leeks and Pine Nuts

TOTAL: 45 MIN
4 SERVINGS ●

Cooked until they melt into the sauce, these leeks are delicious with chicken, though pork chops or a pork tenderloin would also work well here.

- 3 tablespoons pine nuts
- 2 tablespoons extra-virgin olive oil
- Four 6-ounce chicken breast halves with skin
- Salt and freshly ground pepper
- 2 medium leeks, white and tender green parts only, halved lengthwise and sliced crosswise ½ inch thick
- 2 medium shallots, thinly sliced
- 1 cup dry white wine
- 1½ cups chicken stock
- 4 tablespoons cold unsalted butter, cut into tablespoons

1. Preheat the oven to 300°. In a skillet, toast the pine nuts over moderately high heat, stirring, until golden brown, 2 minutes. Transfer to a small plate.
2. In the same skillet, heat the oil. Season the chicken breasts with salt and pepper and add them to the skillet skin side down. Cook, turning once and pressing with a spatula, until browned on both sides, about 6 minutes. Transfer to a large rimmed baking sheet and bake in the oven until just white throughout, about 20 minutes.
3. Meanwhile, add the leeks and shallots to the skillet and cook over moderately low heat, stirring, until softened, 7 minutes. Add the wine, increase the heat to high and boil until reduced by half, about 3 minutes. Add the stock and boil until reduced to ½ cup, about 10 minutes. Off the heat, swirl in the butter 1 tablespoon at a time. Season the sauce with salt and pepper. Transfer the chicken to plates. Pour the sauce over, garnish with the pine nuts and serve. —*Marcia Kiesel*
WINE Ripe, luxurious Chardonnay.

Chicken Cutlets with Green Olive and Currant Pan Sauce

TOTAL: 25 MIN
4 SERVINGS ●

Chicken cutlets get a flavor boost from a simple sauce of salty olives, tangy capers and sweet currants.

- 2 tablespoons extra-virgin olive oil
- Eight ⅓-inch-thick chicken cutlets (2 pounds)
- Kosher salt and freshly ground pepper
- 1 small shallot, minced
- 1½ cups chicken stock or low-sodium broth
- 1 teaspoon Dijon mustard
- ¾ cup pitted green Picholine olives, halved lengthwise
- 2½ tablespoons dried currants
- 2 tablespoons capers, drained
- 1 tablespoon cold unsalted butter

1. In a very large skillet, heat the oil until shimmering. Lightly season the chicken cutlets with salt and pepper. Add half of the cutlets to the skillet and cook over high heat, turning once, until lightly browned outside and white throughout, about 4 minutes. Transfer the cutlets to a plate. Repeat with the remaining cutlets.
2. Add the minced shallot to the skillet and cook over moderate heat until fragrant, about 30 seconds. Add the chicken stock and cook for 30 seconds, scraping up the browned bits. Whisk in the mustard and simmer until the stock has reduced by half, about 3 minutes. Add the olives, currants and capers and simmer over moderately low heat for 1 minute. Return the chicken and any accumulated juices to the skillet and simmer just until warmed through, about 1 minute.
3. Transfer the chicken to plates. Off the heat, whisk the butter into the sauce until incorporated. Spoon the olive-currant sauce over the chicken cutlets and serve at once. —*Melissa Rubel*
SERVE WITH Couscous.
WINE Juicy, fresh Dolcetto.

CHICKEN WITH GREEN OLIVES AND CURRANTS

CHICKEN WITH CATALAN PICADA

Chicken with Catalan Picada

ACTIVE: 40 MIN; TOTAL: 1 HR 25 MIN
4 SERVINGS ●

This Catalan dish made with chocolate and spices is reminiscent of Mexican mole, says Janet Mendel, a food and travel writer based in Spain. "But without the spiciness of the chiles, it's much easier to pair with wine." The sauce is thickened with *picada*, traditionally a blend of toasted nuts, herbs and garlic.

- 4 whole chicken legs, split into legs and thighs (2½ pounds)
- Salt and freshly ground pepper
- 2½ tablespoons extra-virgin olive oil
- 1 medium onion, finely chopped
- One 14-ounce can whole tomatoes, drained and finely chopped
- 1½ cups low-sodium chicken broth
- ¼ cup oloroso sherry
- 1 bay leaf
- One 3-inch strip of orange zest
- ¼ teaspoon thyme leaves
- 1 slice of peasant bread, crusts removed and bread cut into ½-inch cubes (½ cup)
- ¼ cup slivered almonds
- 3 garlic cloves, coarsely chopped
- 1 ounce bittersweet chocolate, chopped
- ¼ cup chopped parsley
- ⅛ teaspoon cinnamon
- Large pinch of saffron threads
- Small pinch each of aniseeds and ground cloves

1. Season the chicken pieces with salt and pepper. In a large skillet, heat 2 tablespoons of the olive oil. Add the chicken pieces skin side down and cook over moderately high heat until the pieces are browned, about 4 minutes per side. Transfer the chicken to a plate.

2. Add the onion to the skillet and cook over moderate heat until it is softened, 5 minutes. Add the tomatoes and cook over moderately high heat until very thick, 5 minutes. Add the broth, sherry, bay leaf, orange zest and thyme and bring to a boil. Add the chicken, cover and simmer over low heat for 30 minutes, turning once.

3. Meanwhile, preheat the oven to 350°. Toast the bread and almonds on a baking sheet for about 8 minutes.

4. In a skillet, heat the remaining ½ tablespoon of oil. Add the garlic and cook over moderate heat until golden, 3 minutes. Transfer to a food processor with the bread and almonds, the chocolate, parsley, cinnamon, saffron, aniseeds and cloves. Process the mixture to a paste.

5. Stir the *picada* into the sauce and simmer over low heat for 15 minutes. Discard the bay leaf and orange zest, season with salt and pepper and serve.
—*Janet Mendel*

WINE Juicy, spicy Grenache.

Sweet-and-Spicy Chicken Curry

TOTAL: 1 HR

4 SERVINGS ●

This is Australian chef Neil Perry's take on a rich, nuanced Malaysian curry that he calls Chicken Kapitan. Because he makes the recipe with plenty of fresh and dried chiles and coconut milk, it's sweet, spicy and altogether sublime, especially when topped with a mound of crispy fried shallots.

- 8 fresh long red chiles, such as Holland, seeded and coarsely chopped
- 5 small dried red chiles, such as *chiles de árbol,* seeded
- 2 stalks of fresh lemongrass, tender inner white bulbs only, thinly sliced
- 3 garlic cloves, coarsely chopped
- 3 small shallots, coarsely chopped, plus 4 medium shallots, thinly sliced
- 1 tablespoon water
- ½ cup plus 1 tablespoon vegetable oil
- 4 whole chicken legs, split into legs and thighs (2½ pounds)

Kosher salt

One 14-ounce can unsweetened coconut milk

- 2 tablespoons fresh lemon juice

Freshly ground pepper

TECHNIQUE

frying leeks and garlic

Fried sliced leeks or garlic are tasty, crispy garnishes. To make them, follow the technique for the shallots in the Sweet-and-Spicy Chicken Curry recipe above, frying until golden brown.

1. In a food processor, combine the fresh and dried red chiles, lemongrass, garlic, coarsely chopped shallots and water and process to a fine paste.

2. In a large, deep skillet, heat 3 tablespoons of the oil. Season the chicken with salt and cook over moderately high heat, turning once, until browned on both sides, about 10 minutes. Transfer to a plate.

3. Reduce the heat to moderate and add the chile paste. Cook, stirring constantly, until the paste begins to stick to the bottom of the pan and brown, about 7 minutes. Stir in the coconut milk and return the chicken to the skillet. Cover partially and simmer over moderately low heat until the chicken is cooked through and the sauce has thickened, about 25 minutes.

4. Meanwhile, in a medium skillet, heat the remaining 6 tablespoons of oil. Add the sliced shallots and fry over moderate heat, stirring occasionally, until golden brown, about 10 minutes. Using a slotted spoon, transfer to paper towels to drain.

5. Transfer the chicken to plates. Add the lemon juice to the sauce and season with salt and pepper. Spoon the sauce over the chicken, sprinkle with the fried shallots and serve. —*Neil Perry*

SERVE WITH Steamed white rice.

WINE Fruity, low-oak Chardonnay.

Pan-Seared Chicken Breasts with Jamaican Curry

TOTAL: 45 MIN PLUS OVERNIGHT MARINATING

4 SERVINGS ●

CHICKEN

- 2 teaspoons vegetable oil
- 1 scallion, minced
- 2 teaspoons curry powder
- 2 teaspoons minced fresh ginger
- ½ teaspoon ground allspice
- ½ teaspoon Scotch bonnet hot sauce (see Note)

Four 6-ounce boneless chicken breast halves with skin

CURRY

Salt and freshly ground pepper

- 2 tablespoons vegetable oil
- 1 medium onion, thinly sliced
- 1 scallion, thinly sliced
- 1 teaspoon curry powder
- 2 teaspoons minced fresh ginger
- ¼ teaspoon ground allspice
- ½ teaspoon Scotch bonnet hot sauce

1½ cups water

- 1 tablespoon unsalted butter

Caribbean-Style Sliced Salad (p. 340), for serving

1. MARINATE THE CHICKEN: In a shallow dish, combine the oil with the scallion, curry powder, ginger, allspice and hot sauce. Add the chicken breasts and turn to coat. Cover and refrigerate overnight.

2. MAKE THE CURRY: Remove the chicken from the marinade and season with salt and pepper. In a large skillet, heat the oil. Cook the chicken skin side down over moderately high heat until the skin browns, 2 minutes. Reduce the heat to moderate; cook until the skin is crisp, 4 minutes longer. Reduce the heat to low, turn the chicken and cook until white throughout, 7 minutes. Transfer the chicken to a platter.

3. Add the onion to the skillet and cook over moderate heat, stirring occasionally, until softened, 6 minutes. Stir in the scallion, curry, ginger, allspice and hot sauce and cook, stirring, until fragrant, 5 minutes. Add the water and bring to a boil over high heat, scraping up the browned bits on the bottom of the pan. Cook until the sauce has reduced to about ½ cup, 5 minutes.

4. Return the chicken to the skillet skin side up and simmer for 2 minutes, then transfer to plates. Stir the butter into the sauce; season with salt and pepper. Pour the curry sauce over the chicken and serve with the sliced salad. —*Marcia Kiesel*

NOTE Scotch bonnet hot sauce is available online at hotsauce.com.

WINE Fruity, soft Chenin Blanc.

SWEET-AND-SPICY CHICKEN CURRY

Braised Chicken with Oaxacan Chocolate Mole Sauce

ACTIVE: 1 HR 15 MIN;

TOTAL: 3 HR 15 MIN

10 SERVINGS ●

- 5 ancho chiles
- 3 dried New Mexico or *guajillo* chiles, stemmed and seeded
- 2 dried *chiles negros* (see Note), stemmed and seeded
- ⅓ cup sesame seeds, plus 1 tablespoon for garnish
- ¾ teaspoon anise seeds
- ½ teaspoon cumin seeds
- ½ teaspoon coriander seeds
- 2 cloves
- 12 black peppercorns
- One ½-inch cinnamon stick
- 5 tablespoons lard or vegetable shortening
- 2½ tablespoons raisins
- 20 whole almonds
- ⅓ cup raw pumpkin seeds
- 1 corn tortilla, quartered
- 5 medium plum tomatoes
- 5 garlic cloves, unpeeled
- 1 small onion, quartered
- 5 cups chicken stock or low-sodium broth
- 3¼ ounces Mexican chocolate, coarsely chopped (see Note)
- Salt and freshly ground pepper
- Two 3- to 4-pound chickens, each cut into 8 pieces
- 2 tablespoons chopped cilantro

1. In a medium bowl, cover all of the chile peppers with hot water. Let them stand for 30 minutes.

2. Meanwhile, in a large skillet, combine the ⅓ cup of sesame seeds with the anise, cumin and coriander seeds, the cloves, the peppercorns and the cinnamon stick. Toast over moderately low heat, stirring, until fragrant, about 2 minutes. Transfer the seeds and spices to a spice grinder and let cool completely, then grind them to a fine powder.

3. In the same skillet, melt 1 tablespoon of the lard. Stir in the raisins, almonds, pumpkin seeds and tortilla. Cook the mixture over moderately low heat until the almonds are toasted and the raisins are plump, about 5 minutes. Transfer the contents of the skillet to a large bowl.

4. Add the tomatoes to the skillet and cook, turning, until the skins are lightly blistered on all sides, about 12 minutes. Transfer the blistered tomatoes to the bowl. Add the garlic and onion to the skillet and cook, stirring, until lightly browned, about 8 minutes. Transfer the garlic and onions to the bowl and let cool. Empty the vegetables onto a work surface. Peel the garlic cloves and coarsely chop them along with the onions and tomatoes.

5. Melt 1 tablespoon of the lard in the skillet. Stir in the chopped vegetables and the spice powder and cook over moderately high heat until warmed through, about 3 minutes. Add the drained chiles and the chicken stock, cover partially and simmer for 1 hour. Remove from the heat. Working in batches, transfer the contents of the skillet along with the chocolate to a blender and puree until smooth. Season the mole sauce with salt and pepper.

6. Preheat the oven to 350°. Season the chicken with salt and pepper. Melt the remaining 3 tablespoons of lard in a large ovenproof skillet. Working in 2 batches, brown the chicken over high heat, turning once, about 10 minutes per batch. Pour the mole sauce over the chicken and bring to a simmer. Cover and braise in the oven until the meat is very tender, 1 hour. Transfer the chicken mole to a serving platter, garnish with the remaining 1 tablespoon of sesame seeds and the cilantro and serve.

—*Stephanie Valentine*

NOTE *Chiles negros* can be replaced with ancho chiles. Mexican chocolate can be found at grocery stores like Whole Foods, and both the chiles and the chocolate can be purchased online at mexgrocer.com.

MAKE AHEAD The Oaxacan mole sauce can be refrigerated for 2 weeks and frozen for 1 month. The braised chicken and mole sauce can be refrigerated for 4 days.

WINE Round, deep-flavored Syrah.

Lemongrass Chicken

TOTAL: 30 MIN

4 SERVINGS ●

- 2 tablespoons Asian fish sauce
- 3 garlic cloves, crushed
- 1 tablespoon mild curry powder
- ½ teaspoon kosher salt
- 2 tablespoons plus 1½ teaspoons sugar
- 1½ pounds skinless, boneless chicken thighs, cut into 1½-inch pieces
- 3 tablespoons water
- 3 tablespoons canola oil
- 2 fresh lemongrass stalks, tender inner white bulbs only, minced
- 1 large shallot, thinly sliced
- 3 serrano chiles, seeded and minced
- 5 cilantro sprigs
- Steamed rice, for serving

1. In a bowl, combine the fish sauce, garlic, curry powder, salt and 1½ teaspoons of the sugar. Add the chicken to coat.

2. In a small skillet, mix the remaining 2 tablespoons of sugar with 1 tablespoon of the water; cook over high heat, stirring, until the sugar is dissolved. Cook without stirring until a deep amber caramel forms, 2 to 3 minutes. Remove from the heat and stir in the remaining 2 tablespoons of water. Transfer to a very small heatproof bowl.

3. Heat a wok over high heat. Add the oil and heat until shimmering. Add the lemongrass, shallot and chiles and stir-fry until fragrant, about 1 minute. Add the chicken and caramel and stir-fry over moderate heat until the chicken is cooked through and the sauce is slightly thickened, about 8 minutes. Transfer to a bowl and top with the cilantro. Serve with rice.

—*Eric Banh and Sophie Banh*

WINE Fruity, light-bodied Beaujolais.

Lemon-Brined Fried Chicken

TOTAL: 1 HR 30 MIN PLUS OVERNIGHT MARINATING

8 SERVINGS ●

To make his delectably crisp chicken, star chef Thomas Keller soaks it in a lemony brine, then fries it. It's one of the most popular dishes at Ad Hoc, his restaurant in Yountville, California, where it's served every other Monday. "Fried Chicken Night happens twice a month," Keller says, "so people have a wonderful sense of anticipation."

- 1 gallon cold water
- 1 cup plus 2 teaspoons kosher salt
- ¼ cup plus 2 tablespoons honey
- 12 bay leaves
- 1 head of unpeeled garlic, smashed
- 2 tablespoons black peppercorns
- 3 large rosemary sprigs
- 1 small bunch of thyme
- 1 small bunch of parsley

Finely grated zest and juice of 2 lemons

Two 3-pound chickens

- 3 cups all-purpose flour
- 2 tablespoons garlic powder
- 2 tablespoons onion powder
- 2 teaspoons cayenne pepper
- 2 cups buttermilk

Vegetable oil, for frying

Rosemary and thyme sprigs, for garnish

1. In a very large pot, combine 1 quart of the water with 1 cup of the salt and the honey, bay leaves, garlic, peppercorns, rosemary, thyme and parsley. Add the lemon zest, juice and halves and bring to a simmer, stirring until the salt is dissolved. Let cool, then stir in the remaining 3 quarts of cold water. Submerge the chickens in the marinade and refrigerate overnight.
2. Drain the chickens and pat dry; cut each bird into 8 pieces, keeping the breast meat on the bone.
3. In a large bowl, combine the flour, garlic powder, onion powder, cayenne and the remaining 2 teaspoons of salt. Put the

buttermilk in a large, shallow bowl. Working with a few pieces at a time, dip the chicken in the buttermilk, then dredge in the flour mixture, pressing so it adheres. Transfer the chicken to a wax paper–lined baking sheet.
4. In a very large, deep skillet, heat 1 inch of oil to 330°. Fry the chicken in 2 or 3 batches over moderate heat, turning once, until golden and crunchy and an instant-read thermometer inserted in the thickest part of each piece registers 160°, about 20 minutes. Drain on paper towels; keep warm in a low oven while you fry the remaining pieces. Transfer to a platter, garnish with the herb sprigs and serve hot or at room temperature. —*Thomas Keller*
WINE Deep, velvety Merlot.

Crispy Turkey Cutlets with Walnut-Sage Sauce

TOTAL: 30 MIN
4 SERVINGS

This fantastic sauce, made with walnuts, sage, garlic and olive oil, would be good on almost anything—it could even be used as a dip or tossed into pasta.

- 1¼ cups walnuts (4½ ounces)
- ¾ cup dried bread crumbs
- ¾ cup freshly grated Parmigiano-Reggiano cheese

Kosher salt and freshly ground black pepper

- 8 medium sage leaves, coarsely chopped
- 1 garlic clove, peeled
- 1 tablespoon unsalted butter, softened
- ⅓ cup extra-virgin olive oil, plus 6 tablespoons for frying
- ½ cup all-purpose flour
- 2 large eggs, beaten

Eight ¼-inch-thick turkey cutlets (1½ pounds)

1. In a food processor, combine ¾ cup of the walnuts with the bread crumbs and Parmigiano-Reggiano. Pulse until the

walnuts are finely ground. Transfer the mixture to a shallow bowl and season with kosher salt and black pepper.
2. Wipe out the bowl of the food processor. Add the remaining ½ cup of walnuts along with the sage and garlic and pulse until the nuts are coarsely chopped. Add the softened butter and ⅓ cup of the olive oil and process until the walnuts are finely chopped and the butter is completely incorporated. Season the sauce generously with kosher salt and black pepper and transfer to a small bowl.
3. Put the flour and eggs in 2 shallow bowls. Season the turkey cutlets with salt and pepper, then dust them with flour, tapping off the excess. Dip the cutlets in the beaten eggs, letting the excess drip back into the bowl. Dip the cutlets in the walnut-crumb mixture, pressing to help the crumbs adhere.
4. In a very large skillet, heat 3 tablespoons of the olive oil until shimmering. Add half of the cutlets and fry over moderately high heat, turning once, until golden outside and cooked through, about 3 minutes. Transfer the cutlets to a paper towel–lined plate to drain. Repeat with the remaining olive oil and cutlets. Transfer the cutlets to plates, spoon some of the walnut-sage sauce on top and serve. —*Melissa Rubel*
SERVE WITH Pasta.
WINE Fresh, lively Soave.

TECHNIQUE

making perfect chicken

For moist, flavorful, crisp-skinned roast chicken, rub the skin with ¾ teaspoon of kosher salt per pound, cover loosely and refrigerate for 12 to 48 hours. Pat dry before roasting.

Roasted Turkey with Tangerine Glaze

ACTIVE: 1 HR 45 MIN; TOTAL: 6 HR

12 SERVINGS ● ●

The fresh tangerine juice, brown sugar and sage on this gorgeous turkey give it a rich, burnished color when it comes out of the oven. Besides making the turkey look impressive, the citrus-herb glaze adds an alluring holiday flavor.

TURKEY

One 18-pound turkey, neck reserved

Salt and freshly ground
    black pepper

2 tablespoons vegetable oil,
    plus more for rubbing

2 quarts chicken stock or
    low-sodium broth

1 medium onion, coarsely chopped

1 large carrot, coarsely chopped

1 large celery rib, coarsely
    chopped

½ cup all-purpose flour

GLAZE

3 cups plus 3 tablespoons fresh
    tangerine or orange juice
    (about 6 large tangerines
    or 6 large navel oranges)

1 tablespoon finely grated
    fresh ginger

1 tablespoon light brown sugar

2 tablespoons cornstarch

1 tablespoon very finely chopped
    sage leaves

Salt

1. PREPARE THE TURKEY: Preheat the oven to 400°. Set the turkey breast side up in a large roasting pan. Fold the wing tips under the bird and season the cavity with salt and ground pepper. Rub the bird generously with vegetable oil and season with salt and ground pepper. Roast the turkey for 20 minutes.

2. In a bowl, combine 2 cups of the chicken stock with the 2 tablespoons of vegetable oil. Baste the turkey with the stock and vegetable oil mixture and scatter the chopped onion, carrot and celery around the turkey in the pan. Lower the oven temperature to 325° and roast the turkey for 3½ hours longer, basting the turkey skin with the stock mixture every 30 minutes and rotating the pan several times during the cooking, until an instant-read thermometer inserted in the inner thigh of the turkey registers 165°.

3. Meanwhile, rub the turkey neck with vegetable oil and season it with salt and black pepper. Heat a saucepan over moderately high heat. Add the turkey neck and cook until it is starting to brown on the first side, about 3 minutes. Turn the neck, lower the heat to moderate and cook until browned on the second side, 10 minutes. Pour the remaining 6 cups of stock into the saucepan and bring to a boil over high heat. Cover, reduce the heat to low and simmer, skimming frequently, for 2 hours. Remove and discard the neck; you should have about 4½ cups of stock.

4. MAKE THE GLAZE: In another saucepan, combine 3 cups of the fresh tangerine juice with the grated ginger and sugar. Bring the mixture to a boil over moderately high heat. In a small bowl, blend the cornstarch with the remaining 3 tablespoons of tangerine juice until smooth. Whisk the

cornstarch mixture into the tangerine juice mixture in the saucepan and bring the liquid to a boil, whisking constantly, until it has thickened, about 2 minutes. Take the saucepan off the heat, stir in the chopped sage leaves and season with salt; let the glaze cool.

5. When the turkey is done, remove it from the oven. Increase the oven temperature to 400°. Generously spoon half of the tangerine glaze over the turkey and roast for about 10 minutes, or until the skin starts to brown. Coat the turkey skin with the remaining tangerine glaze and bake the turkey for about 10 minutes longer, or until the skin is richly browned. Transfer the turkey to a large carving board and let rest for 15 to 25 minutes.

6. Meanwhile, set the roasting pan over 2 burners on moderately high heat. Add 1 cup of the turkey stock and boil, stirring with a sturdy wooden spoon and scraping up the browned bits. Set a mesh strainer over a medium saucepan. Carefully pour the roasting pan juices into the strainer, pressing down on the vegetables to extract as much of the pan juices as possible. Discard the vegetables.

7. Skim the fat from the pan juices, reserving ¼ cup of the fat in a small bowl and discarding the rest. Whisk the flour into the fat to make a smooth paste. Gradually whisk the flour paste into the pan juices in the saucepan and bring to a boil, whisking constantly. Simmer until the liquid is thickened, about 2 minutes, then whisk in the remaining 3½ cups of turkey stock. Simmer over moderately low heat, whisking often, until the gravy is thickened, about 10 minutes. Season with salt and pepper and transfer to a gravy boat. Carve the turkey and serve, passing the gravy.

—*Dean Fearing*

MAKE AHEAD The tangerine glaze and turkey stock can be made, cooled, covered and refrigerated for 2 days.

WINE Cherry-inflected, earthy Sangiovese.

TECHNIQUE

roasting turkey

Chef **Mark Sullivan** of San Francisco's Spruce shares his secret for a juicy turkey: He wraps the whole bird in parchment paper, then foil, and roasts it at a low temperature until it's nearly cooked; then he unwraps the turkey and browns it in a hot oven until the skin is crisp and golden.

ROASTED TURKEY WITH
TANGERINE GLAZE

Roasted Turkey with Italian Sausage Stuffing

ACTIVE: 1 HR 20 MIN;
TOTAL: 4 HR 15 MIN
12 SERVINGS

This is a marvelous turkey—simple, satisfying and completely delicious. Since F&W's Grace Parisi is a big fan of sweet Italian sausage (which was always in the rice-based stuffing she ate as a kid), she often adds it to the dressing; the fennel seed in the sausage truly elevates the dish.

- 2 loaves Italian bread (2 pounds), crusts removed and bread cut into ¾-inch cubes (20 cups)
- ¼ cup extra-virgin olive oil
- 1½ pounds sweet Italian sausage, casings removed
- 2 large onions—1 finely chopped, 1 quartered
- 1 large celery rib, finely diced
- 3 large garlic cloves, very finely chopped
- ¼ cup finely chopped sage leaves
- 4 tablespoons unsalted butter
- 6 cups turkey stock or low-sodium chicken broth

Salt and freshly ground pepper
One 18- to 20-pound turkey, rinsed and patted dry
- 2 carrots, cut into 1-inch pieces
- 3 cups water
- ¼ cup all-purpose flour

1. Preheat the oven to 375°. Spread the bread cubes in a large roasting pan and toast for 15 minutes, stirring occasionally, until dry and lightly browned.

2. In a large, deep skillet, heat the olive oil. Crumble in the sweet Italian sausage and cook over moderately high heat, breaking up the sausage meat, until it is browned and no trace of pink remains, 10 to 12 minutes. Add the chopped onion, celery and garlic and cook until softened, about 6 minutes. Stir in the chopped sage leaves and butter. Scrape the mixture into a large bowl. Add the bread cubes and toss until thoroughly combined. Stir in 2 cups of the stock and season with salt and pepper.

3. Increase the oven temperature to 450° and position a rack in the bottom of the oven. Set the turkey in the large roasting pan fitted with a shallow rack. Spoon 5 cups of the stuffing into the cavity and tie the legs together with kitchen string. Spoon the remaining stuffing into a shallow 2½-quart baking dish. Scatter the quartered onion and the carrot pieces around the turkey and add 1 cup of the turkey stock. Roast the turkey for 30 minutes. Lower the oven temperature to 375°. Roast for 3 hours longer, covering the turkey loosely with foil as the skin browns and adding 1 cup of water every 45 minutes to prevent the pan from scorching. The turkey is done when an instant-read thermometer inserted into the thickest part of the inner thigh registers 175°. Transfer the bird to a large cutting board and let it rest for 30 minutes.

4. Drizzle 1 cup of the stock over the remaining stuffing in the baking dish. Bake for 30 minutes, until the stuffing is heated through and crisp on top.

5. Meanwhile, pour the turkey pan juices from the roasting pan into a heatproof glass measuring cup. Skim off and discard the fat. In a small bowl, whisk ½ cup of the stock with the flour and reserve. Place the roasting pan over 2 burners on high heat. Pour in the remaining 1½ cups of stock, bring to a simmer and cook, stirring with a wooden spoon and scraping up any browned bits stuck to the bottom and sides of the pan. Return the reserved pan juices to the roasting pan and stir well, then carefully strain the liquid into a medium saucepan. Bring to a boil over high heat, then simmer rapidly until reduced to 4 cups, about 10 minutes. Whisk in the flour mixture and boil until the gravy is thickened and no floury taste remains, about 5 minutes. Season the gravy with salt and pepper.

6. Spoon the stuffing from the turkey cavity into a bowl. Carve the turkey and serve the stuffing and gravy alongside.
—*Grace Parisi*

MAKE AHEAD The Italian sausage stuffing can be prepared through Step 2, covered and refrigerated overnight.
WINE Intense, fruity Zinfandel.

Indian-Spiced Turkey Breast

ACTIVE: 20 MIN; TOTAL: 1 HR 45 MIN
PLUS 7 HR MARINATING
12 SERVINGS ●

Roasting a whole turkey is tricky, since the breast can dry out while the dark meat finishes cooking. To get around that problem, F&W's Melissa Rubel roasts turkey breast by itself. With the right amount of cooking, it's always juicy, especially when marinated in lemon and yogurt.

- 2 cups plain whole-milk yogurt
- 1 medium onion, coarsely chopped
- 3 large garlic cloves, peeled

One 1-inch piece of fresh ginger, peeled and thinly sliced
- ¼ cup fresh lemon juice
- 2 teaspoons ground turmeric
- 1 teaspoon ground cumin
- 1 teaspoon ground coriander
- ½ teaspoon cinnamon
- ½ teaspoon cayenne pepper
- 2 bone-in, skin-on turkey breast halves (about 3 pounds each)

Kosher salt and freshly ground black pepper
- 2 tablespoons unsalted butter, melted

1. In a food processor, puree the yogurt with the onion, garlic, ginger, lemon juice, turmeric, cumin, coriander, cinnamon and cayenne. Place the turkey breasts on a large rimmed baking sheet. Pour the yogurt marinade over the turkey and rub it over both sides and under the skin. Cover and refrigerate for at least 6 hours and up to 24 hours. Remove the turkey from the refrigerator 1 hour before roasting.

2. Preheat the oven to 475°. Transfer the turkey breasts (with any marinade that sticks to them) to a large roasting pan, skin side up. Season with salt and black pepper and drizzle the butter over the skin. Roast for 20 minutes. Reduce the oven temperature to 375° and roast for 50 minutes longer, or until an instant-read thermometer inserted in the thickest part of the breast registers 165°. Transfer to a board and let rest for 10 minutes. Carve and serve. —*Melissa Rubel*

WINE Fresh, fruity rosé.

Grilled Quail with Pine Nuts and Currants

ACTIVE: 15 MIN; TOTAL: 1 HR

8 SERVINGS ●

This elegant recipe calls for golden currants, but any kind of dried fruit, like cherries or apricots, would also be good.

- ¼ cup dried currants
- 2 tablespoons dry sherry
- 2 teaspoons sherry vinegar
- 2 bay leaves
- 2 tablespoons extra-virgin olive oil, plus more for brushing
- ¼ cup pine nuts
- 8 semi-boneless quail

Salt and freshly ground pepper

1. In a small saucepan, combine the dried currants, dry sherry, sherry vinegar and bay leaves and bring to a simmer. Remove the saucepan from the heat. Cover and let stand for 45 minutes.

2. Meanwhile, in a small skillet, heat 1 teaspoon of the olive oil. Add the pine nuts and cook over moderately low heat, stirring, until golden, about 3 minutes. Transfer to a plate to cool.

3. Light a grill. Brush the quail with olive oil and season with salt and pepper. Grill the quail over high heat, turning them once, until they are browned on the outside and cooked to medium within, about 5 minutes. Transfer the quail to a large serving platter.

4. Stir the remaining 5 teaspoons of oil and the pine nuts into the currants and season with salt and pepper. Spoon over the quail and serve. —*Octavio Becerra*

WINE Juicy, spicy Grenache.

Roasted Capon with Fig-and-Prosciutto Stuffing

ACTIVE: 1 HR; TOTAL: 4 HR

10 SERVINGS

Capon is tender, flavorful and a far more forgiving bird to cook than turkey, so it's a great holiday alternative.

STUFFING

- 1 pound whole-grain bread, cut into 1-inch cubes (13 cups)
- 1 stick unsalted butter
- 1 large onion, cut into ½-inch dice
- 2 celery ribs, cut into ¼-inch dice
- ¾ teaspoon ground fennel seeds or fennel pollen
- ¼ pound thinly sliced prosciutto, cut into ½-inch-wide strips
- 1 cup plump dried figs such as Calimyrna, cut into ½-inch pieces
- 4 large eggs
- 1 cup chicken stock or low-sodium broth
- 1 teaspoon kosher salt
- ½ teaspoon freshly ground pepper

CAPON

One 10-pound capon with neck

- 2 tablespoons unsalted butter, softened

Salt and freshly ground pepper

- 6 cups chicken stock or low-sodium broth
- ⅓ cup all-purpose flour
- 2 tablespoons Calvados or applejack

1. MAKE THE STUFFING: Preheat the oven to 350°. Bake the bread on 2 large baking sheets for 10 minutes, until dry.

2. In a skillet, melt the butter, then add the onion and celery; cook over low heat until softened, 10 minutes. Stir in the ground fennel and prosciutto and cook for 1 minute. Remove from the heat and let cool.

3. In a very large bowl, toss the bread with the prosciutto mixture and figs. In a bowl, beat the eggs, stock, salt and pepper; pour the mixture over the bread and stir well.

4. PREPARE THE CAPON: Lower the oven temperature to 325°. Cut the tips off the wings and place in a large roasting pan with the neck. Put the capon in the pan breast side down; fill the neck cavity with stuffing. Pull the skin over the stuffing; secure with a skewer. Turn the capon breast side up and fill the cavity with stuffing. Wrap any leftover stuffing in foil. Rub the butter over the capon; season with salt and pepper.

5. Roast the capon for 1½ hours, rotating the pan once. Transfer the neck and wing tips to a saucepan. Roast for about 1 hour longer, rotating the pan once. The bird is done when an instant-read thermometer inserted in the inner thigh registers 165°.

6. Meanwhile, add the stock to the saucepan and bring to a boil. Add a pinch of salt, cover and simmer over low heat for 45 minutes. Discard the neck and wing tips.

7. Remove the capon from the oven. Raise the oven temperature to 400° and cook the stuffing in the foil packet for 20 minutes.

8. With a large spoon, scoop the stuffing from both cavities into an ovenproof bowl; cover with foil and keep warm. Tilt the capon to release any juices into the roasting pan. Transfer the capon to a board to rest for up to 20 minutes before carving.

9. Pour the pan juices into a glass measuring cup and skim the fat, adding 3 tablespoons of the fat to the roasting pan (discard the rest). Set the pan over 2 burners on moderate heat and stir in the flour. Slowly whisk in the stock and Calvados and bring to a boil, whisking; whisk over low heat until no floury taste remains, 8 minutes. Add the pan juices and simmer for a few minutes. Season the gravy with salt and pepper.

10. Carve the capon and serve with the stuffing and gravy. —*Marcia Kiesel*

WINE Ripe, juicy Pinot Noir.

DUCK CONFIT WITH TURNIPS

PORK CHOP WITH SHALLOTS

Duck Confit with Turnips

ACTIVE: 30 MIN; TOTAL: 1 HR 15 MIN
4 SERVINGS

- 1 quart chicken stock
- 1 cup dry red wine
- 10 large garlic cloves, halved

Four 3-inch-long strips of orange zest

- 2 bay leaves

Eight 6-ounce confited duck legs,
    with skin (see Note)

- 1 teaspoon unsalted butter
- 2 teaspoons all-purpose flour

Salt and freshly ground pepper
Steamed baby turnips and their
    greens, for serving

1. Preheat the oven to 375°. In a saucepan, combine the stock, wine, garlic, orange zest and bay leaves and bring to a boil. Reduce to 2 cups over high heat, 30 minutes.

2. Add the reduction to a large roasting pan. Arrange the duck in the pan skin side up. Cover and braise until hot, 30 minutes.

3. Preheat the broiler. Transfer the duck to a rimmed baking sheet. Strain the braising liquid into a saucepan; press on the garlic to mash it into the sauce. Bring the sauce to a simmer. In a bowl, blend the butter with the flour; whisk the paste into the sauce. Simmer, whisking, until thickened, 3 minutes. Season with salt and pepper and keep warm, whisking occasionally.

4. Broil the duck, rotating the pan, until the skin is crisp, 4 minutes. Transfer to plates, top with the sauce and serve with turnips.
—*Marcia Kiesel*

NOTE Confited duck legs are available online from dartagnan.com.

WINE Rich, ripe Cabernet Sauvignon.

Pork Chops with Shallots

TOTAL: 35 MIN
4 SERVINGS

Four 8-ounce bone-in pork rib chops
Salt and freshly ground black pepper
All-purpose flour, for dusting

- 2 tablespoons extra-virgin olive oil
- 1 tablespoon unsalted butter

4 large shallots, sliced (1½ cups)

¼ teaspoon anise seeds

½ cup dry red wine

1 cup chicken stock

1 teaspoon very finely chopped garlic

2 teaspoons tomato paste

1. Preheat the oven to 400°. Season the pork chops with salt and black pepper and dust them lightly with flour. In a large skillet, heat the olive oil until shimmering. Add the pork chops and cook over high heat for 1 minute. Add the butter to the skillet, reduce the heat to moderately high and cook, turning once, until the chops are browned on both sides, 8 minutes. Transfer the pork to a baking sheet and bake in the oven until an instant-read thermometer inserted at the thickest point registers 145°, about 7 minutes.

2. Meanwhile, add the shallots and anise to the skillet and cook over low heat, stirring, until softened, about 8 minutes. Add the wine and reduce over moderately high heat to ¼ cup, about 2 minutes. Add the stock and reduce by half, about 5 minutes. Stir in the garlic and tomato paste and cook for 1 minute longer. Season with salt and pepper. Transfer the chops to plates and top with the sauce. —*Marcia Kiesel*

SERVE WITH Sautéed red chard.

WINE Earthy, medium-bodied Tempranillo.

Spiced Pork Tenderloin with Hazelnut Vinaigrette

ACTIVE: 40 MIN; TOTAL: 1 HR 45 MIN

PLUS OVERNIGHT MARINATING

8 SERVINGS

The rub on this pork is inspired by za'atar, a Middle Eastern spice blend that gets its pungency from ground sumac.

1 tablespoon finely chopped dried orange peel

1 tablespoon smoked paprika

1 tablespoon ground coriander

1 tablespoon ground sumac (see Note)

3 pounds pork tenderloin

3 pounds small sweet potatoes, unpeeled, quartered lengthwise

¼ cup extra-virgin olive oil

4 rosemary sprigs

Salt and freshly ground pepper

2 tablespoons unsalted butter, melted

½ cup raw hazelnuts

3 tablespoons sherry vinegar

1 tablespoon honey

2 teaspoons Dijon mustard

¼ cup hazelnut oil

¼ cup grapeseed oil

1. In a 2-gallon resealable plastic bag, combine the orange peel, smoked paprika, coriander and sumac. Add the pork tenderloin, seal the bag and turn to coat the meat thoroughly with the seasonings. Refrigerate overnight.

2. Preheat the oven to 375°. On a large rimmed baking sheet, toss the sweet potatoes with 2 tablespoons of the olive oil and the rosemary; season with salt and pepper. Roast the potatoes, turning once, until tender and lightly browned, 40 minutes. Drizzle with the melted butter; keep warm.

3. Meanwhile, in a large ovenproof skillet, heat the remaining 2 tablespoons of olive oil. Scrape most of the spices off the pork and season the meat with salt and pepper. Add the pork to the skillet and sear over moderately high heat, turning, until lightly browned all over, about 5 minutes. Transfer the skillet to the oven. Roast for about 20 minutes, until an instant-read thermometer inserted in the thickest part registers 135°. Transfer the meat to a cutting board and let stand for 10 minutes.

4. Spread the hazelnuts in a pie plate and toast until fragrant, about 12 minutes. Rub the hazelnuts together in a clean kitchen towel to remove the skins. Finely chop.

5. In a small bowl, mix the vinegar with the honey and the mustard. Whisk in the hazelnut and grapeseed oils, stir in the hazelnuts and season with salt and pepper.

6. Slice the pork on the bias. Arrange the slices on a platter along with the sweet potatoes and rosemary sprigs. Drizzle with the vinaigrette and serve.

—*Octavio Becerra*

NOTE Ground sumac is available at specialty stores and online at penzeys.com.

WINE Complex, elegant Pinot Noir.

Sausages with Grapes

 TOTAL: 40 MIN

4 SERVINGS

These plump sausages are cooked with tangy balsamic vinegar and tart grapes. Be sure not to use lean sausages; you want a little fat to help soften both the vinegar and the grapes.

2 tablespoons extra-virgin olive oil

1¼ pounds breakfast sausages or sweet Italian pork sausages

3 tablespoons water

2 medium garlic cloves, very thinly sliced

1 teaspoon chopped rosemary

1 tablespoon balsamic vinegar

½ pound red and green seedless grapes

Salt and freshly ground pepper

Crusty bread, for serving

1. In a large, deep skillet, heat the olive oil until shimmering. Add the sausages and cook over moderately high heat until they are browned on 2 sides, about 4 minutes. Cover and cook over moderate heat, turning once, until the sausages are no longer pink, about 10 minutes.

2. Add the water, sliced garlic and chopped rosemary and cook over low heat, scraping up any browned bits from the bottom of the skillet, until the garlic softens, about 5 minutes. Add the vinegar and grapes and cook over moderate heat, stirring, until the grape skins start to split, 2 minutes. Season with salt and pepper, transfer to plates and serve with crusty bread.

—*Marcia Kiesel*

WINE Intense, spicy Syrah.

8
rules for perfect pairing

F&W's **Ray Isle** simplifies the task of pairing food and drink into eight mantras.

1 *serve a dry rosé with hors d'oeuvres*
Good rosé combines the fresh acidity and light body of white wines with the fruity character of reds. This makes it the go-to wine when serving a wide range of hors d'oeuvres, from crudités to gougères.

2 *serve an unoaked white with anything you can squeeze a lemon or lime on*
White wines such as Sauvignon Blanc, Albariño and Vermentino (typically made in stainless steel tanks rather than oak barrels) have a bright, citrusy acidity that acts like a zap of lemon or lime juice to heighten flavors in everything from smoked sablefish to grilled salmon.

3 *try low-alcohol wines with spicy foods*
Alcohol accentuates the oils that make spicy food hot. So when confronted with dishes like a fiery curried chicken or Thai stir-fry, look for wines that are low in alcohol, such as off-dry German Rieslings (especially since a touch of sweetness helps counter spiciness, too).

4 *match rich red meats with tannic reds*
Tannins, the astringent compounds in red wines that help give the wine structure, are an ideal complement to luxurious meats—making brawny reds like Cabernet Sauvignon and Syrah great matches for braised duck legs or pan-seared sausages.

5 *with lighter meats, pair the wine with the sauce*

Often the chief protein in a dish—chicken or pork, say—isn't the primary flavor. Think of pork chops in a delicate white wine sauce versus pork chops in a zesty red wine sauce; in each case, the sauce dictates the pairing choice.

6 *pair earthy wines with earthy foods*

Many great pairing combinations happen when wines and foods echo one another. Earthiness is often found in reds such as Pinot Noir (particularly from Burgundy) and Nebbiolo, making them great partners for equally earthy ingredients like bison steaks or wild mushrooms.

7 *for light main courses, consider dry Champagnes*

Dry Champagnes pair with a far greater range of foods than people expect. Serve them with light main courses that are fried or salty, or that include shellfish, eggs or mushrooms.

8 *for desserts, serve a lighter wine*

When pairing desserts and dessert wines, it's easy to overwhelm the taste buds with sweetness. Instead, choose a wine that's a touch lighter and less sweet than the dessert—for instance, an effervescent Moscato d'Asti with roasted pears.

PORK WITH GRILLED VEGETABLE PISTO

Grilled Chorizo with Tangy Caramelized Onions

ACTIVE: 40 MIN; TOTAL: 1 HR 20 MIN

10 SERVINGS ●

The Spanish word *agridulce*—like the Italian *agrodolce* and the French *aigre-doux*—literally translates as "sour-sweet." That's exactly the flavor of the meltingly rich, molasses-thick onion compote slathered over the spicy sausages in this recipe. These scrumptious onions are also delicious served with grilled steak or piled onto roast beef sandwiches.

- ½ cup vegetable oil
- 4 medium onions, sliced lengthwise ⅛ inch thick
- 4 tablespoons unsalted butter
- 2 jalapeños, thinly sliced

Juice of 4 limes

Salt and freshly ground black pepper

- 4 pounds fresh chorizo sausages (see Note)

Cilantro sprigs, for garnish

1. In a large skillet, heat the vegetable oil. Add the sliced onions and cook gently over low heat, stirring occasionally, until they are evenly browned, about 1 hour. Stir in the butter, sliced jalapeños and fresh lime juice and season the mixture with salt and black pepper.

2. Light a grill. Grill the chorizo over moderately high heat, turning, until the sausages are browned all over and cooked throughout, about 15 minutes. Transfer the sausages to a platter and top with the caramelized onions. Garnish with the cilantro sprigs and serve.
—*Stephanie Valentine*

NOTE Unlike Spanish chorizo, which is usually smoked and/or dried, fresh Mexican chorizo is uncooked. It can be found at grocery stores like Whole Foods.

MAKE AHEAD The cooked onions can be refrigerated for up to 2 days. Reheat them gently before serving.

WINE Ripe, juicy Pinot Noir.

Pork with Grilled Vegetable Pisto

TOTAL: 1 HR 10 MIN PLUS 1 HR MARINATING

4 SERVINGS

Pisto is a Spanish mixture of vegetables very similar to French ratatouille or Italian *caponata*. In Rioja, a region known for great vegetables, it's served both hot (topped with a fried egg) and cold, as a salad or side dish. Here, food and travel writer Janet Mendel, who is based in Spain, grills the vegetables before simmering them into a deep-flavored *pisto*.

- ¼ cup plus 3 tablespoons extra-virgin olive oil
- 2 tablespoons fresh lemon juice
- 2 garlic cloves, very finely chopped, plus ½ head of garlic, top third sliced off and discarded
- 1 tablespoon chopped parsley

Salt and freshly ground black pepper

Eight ½-inch-thick slices of boneless pork loin

One 1¼-pound eggplant, pierced in several places with a fork

- 1 medium red onion, unpeeled
- 2 pounds tomatoes, cored
- 2 red bell peppers
- 1 green bell pepper
- 2 medium zucchini
- 1 teaspoon crumbled dried oregano
- ⅛ teaspoon cumin seeds

Pinch of crushed red pepper

1. Light a grill. In a large, shallow dish, combine 2 tablespoons of the olive oil with the fresh lemon juice, chopped garlic and parsley and a pinch each of salt and black pepper and stir. Add the pork loin slices and turn to coat the meat well. Cover and refrigerate for 1 hour.

2. Grill the eggplant, onion and garlic head cut side up over moderately high heat, turning a few times, until the vegetables are charred all over but not quite tender, about 15 minutes. Transfer the eggplant, onion and garlic head to a large, rimmed baking sheet. Grill the tomatoes, red and green bell peppers and zucchini over moderately high heat, turning frequently, until charred all over, about 5 minutes for the tomatoes and zucchini and 12 minutes for the peppers. Transfer the vegetables to the baking sheet.

3. Working over the baking sheet, peel off and discard the charred vegetable skins. Remove the seeds from the tomato and eggplant. Seed and core the peppers. Cut the tomatoes into wedges. Thinly slice the onion. Cut the eggplant, bell peppers and zucchini into ¾-inch cubes. Remove the garlic cloves from their skins and trim off any charred parts. Pour any juices on the baking sheet through a strainer set over a bowl and reserve.

4. In a large, deep skillet, heat ¼ cup of the olive oil. Add the cubed eggplant and sliced onion and cook over moderate heat for 3 minutes. Add the cubed bell peppers, peeled garlic, cubed zucchini, dried oregano, cumin seeds and crushed red pepper and cook, stirring, for 3 minutes. Add the tomato wedges and reserved strained vegetable juices and bring to a boil over high heat. Reduce the heat to medium and simmer, stirring occasionally, until most of the liquid has evaporated and the vegetables are tender, about 8 minutes. Season the *pisto* with salt and black pepper.

5. In a skillet, heat the remaining 1 tablespoon of olive oil. Scrape the garlic off the marinated pork slices; season the meat with salt and black pepper. Cook over moderately high heat until the slices are browned on 1 side, 4 minutes. Turn the pork over, reduce the heat to moderate and cook until the meat is white throughout, about 5 minutes. Spoon the *pisto* onto plates, top with the browned pork slices and serve. —*Janet Mendel*

WINE Earthy, medium-bodied Tempranillo.

Pork and Tomatillo Stew

ACTIVE: 45 MIN; TOTAL: 1 HR 20 MIN

4 SERVINGS ● ●

- 2 tablespoons vegetable oil
- 1½ pounds boneless pork loin, cut into 3-inch chunks

Salt and freshly ground pepper

- 2 large celery ribs, finely diced
- 1 small red onion, finely diced
- 1 Anaheim chile, seeded and finely diced
- 2 garlic cloves, minced
- 2 teaspoons mild chile powder
- 1 tablespoon ground cumin

Pinch of dried oregano

- 2 cups chicken stock or low-sodium broth
- 1 cup ½-inch-diced carrots

Two 6-ounce russet potatoes, peeled and cut into 1-inch dice

One 28-ounce can diced tomatoes

- 1 pound tomatillos—husked, rinsed and cut into 1-inch dice

Hot sauce

Chopped cilantro, for garnish

Corn tortilla chips, for serving

1. In a medium casserole or Dutch oven, heat the vegetable oil. Season the pork chunks with salt and pepper and cook over high heat until browned on 2 sides, about 2 minutes per side. Add the celery and onion and cook over moderate heat, stirring occasionally, until softened, about 7 minutes. Add the diced chile, garlic, chile powder, cumin and oregano and cook, stirring frequently, until fragrant, about 3 minutes. Add the chicken stock and bring to a boil. Add the carrots, potatoes, tomatoes and tomatillos, cover and simmer over low heat until the pork is cooked through, about 25 minutes.

2. Transfer the pork to a plate and shred with 2 forks. Meanwhile, simmer the stew over moderate heat until thickened, about 10 minutes. Stir the shredded pork into the stew and season with salt, pepper and hot sauce. Ladle the stew into wide, deep bowls, garnish with chopped cilantro and serve with a few tortilla chips.
—*Andrew Murray*

MAKE AHEAD The stew can be refrigerated overnight. Reheat gently.

WINE Intense, spicy Syrah.

Roasted Rack of Pork with Sausage Stuffing

ACTIVE: 1 HR 15 MIN;

TOTAL: 3 HR 15 MIN

10 SERVINGS

Chef and sausage-maker Bruce Aidells stuffs a bone-in roast with sausage, mushrooms and kale, then spit-roasts the pork in his wood-fired hearth oven. "It's like one giant stuffed pork chop," he says.

- 1 ounce dried porcini mushrooms (1 cup)
- 2 cups boiling water
- 1¼ pounds kale, stems and inner ribs discarded
- 3 tablespoons extra-virgin olive oil
- ½ pound hot Italian sausage, casings removed
- 1 medium onion, finely chopped
- 1 large leek, white and tender green parts only, finely chopped
- 6 garlic cloves, minced
- 2 tablespoons finely chopped sage
- 2 ounces dry, crustless sourdough bread, finely diced (1 cup)
- ¼ cup freshly grated Parmigiano-Reggiano cheese

Kosher salt and freshly ground pepper

- 1 large egg, beaten

One 9-rib center-cut rack of pork, chine bone removed (8 pounds)

- 1 tablespoon sweet pimentón de la Vera (smoked Spanish paprika)

1. Preheat the oven to 450°. In a heatproof bowl, cover the porcini with the boiling water and let stand until softened, about 20 minutes. Drain the mushrooms, reserving their soaking liquid, then finely chop.

2. Bring a large pot of salted water to a boil. Add the kale and boil until just softened, about 5 minutes. Drain and chop the kale; squeeze out any excess liquid.

3. Heat 1 tablespoon of the oil in a large, deep skillet. Add the sausage and cook over moderate heat, breaking it up with a spoon, until cooked through and lightly browned, about 5 minutes. Add the onion, leek and garlic, cover and cook, stirring, until the vegetables are softened, about 8 minutes. Add 1 tablespoon of the sage and the porcini and cook 2 minutes longer. Stir in the kale, bread and cheese and transfer to a bowl to cool slightly. Season with salt and pepper and stir in the egg. Moisten the stuffing with 2 tablespoons of the reserved porcini liquid.

4. Set the pork roast on a work surface, fat side up, with the bones facing you. Using a sharp knife, run the blade along the bones, partially separating the meat but leaving 1½ inches of it attached at the bottom. Slice through the middle of the pork, butterflying it but not cutting completely through. Open up the meat flap and season well with salt and pepper. Pack three-fourths of the stuffing into the slit in the roast and roll it back into shape. Pack the remaining stuffing between the rack and the meat. Cut 9 lengths of butcher's twine and tie the roast between the bones. Place the roast in a large roasting pan, fat side up.

5. In a bowl, stir the remaining 1 tablespoon of sage and 2 tablespoons of olive oil with the paprika, 1 tablespoon of salt and 2 teaspoons of pepper. Spread the paste all over the meat and roast in the lower third of the oven for 15 minutes. Reduce the oven temperature to 300° and roast for 1½ hours longer, or until an instant-read thermometer inserted in the center of the meat registers 140°. Transfer to a cutting board and let rest for 20 minutes. Remove the strings and cut the roast between the bones into chops. —*Bruce Aidells*

WINE Deep, velvety Merlot.

Herb-Crusted Pork Roast with Ginger-Fig Compote

ACTIVE: 45 MIN; TOTAL: 1 HR 35 MIN PLUS 6 HR MARINATING

6 SERVINGS ●

- 6 large garlic cloves, smashed and chopped
- 2 teaspoons chopped rosemary
- 2 teaspoons chopped thyme
- 2 teaspoons whole-grain mustard
- 1 teaspoon dried lavender
- ¼ cup plus 2 tablespoons extra-virgin olive oil

One 1½-pound boneless pork loin roast

- 1 cup water
- ¼ cup honey
- 2 tablespoons fresh lemon juice

One 1-inch piece of fresh ginger, peeled and very thinly sliced

- 6 allspice berries, cracked
- 6 black peppercorns, cracked
- 8 dried figs, left whole

Salt and freshly ground pepper

- ¼ cup raisins
- ½ cup dry red wine
- ¾ cup chicken stock or canned low-sodium broth

1. In a bowl, combine the chopped garlic, rosemary and thyme, whole-grain mustard, dried lavender and ¼ cup of the olive oil. Add the pork loin and turn to coat thoroughly with the marinade. Cover and refrigerate for at least 6 hours or overnight. Remove the pork from the refrigerator and bring the meat to room temperature before roasting.

2. In a small saucepan, combine the water, honey, fresh lemon juice, sliced ginger and cracked allspice and peppercorns and bring the mixture to a boil over high heat. Add the whole figs and cover the saucepan; reduce the heat to low and simmer until the figs are tender, about 10 minutes. Remove the saucepan from the heat and let steep, covered, for 10 minutes.

3. Preheat the oven to 400°. Scrape the garlic and herbs from the pork and set them aside. Season the pork with salt and pepper. In a medium ovenproof skillet, heat 1 tablespoon of the olive oil. Add the pork and cook over moderately high heat until browned all over, about 4 minutes per side. Transfer the skillet to the oven and roast the pork for about 20 minutes, until an instant-read thermometer inserted into the center of the meat registers 145° for medium. Transfer the pork to a cutting board and let rest for 10 minutes.

4. Heat the remaining 1 tablespoon of olive oil in the skillet. Add the reserved garlic and herbs and cook over low heat until the garlic is golden brown, about 5 minutes. Add the raisins and wine and boil over moderately high heat until the wine is reduced by half, about 3 minutes. Add the chicken broth and boil for 3 minutes. Using a slotted spoon, transfer the figs to the skillet. Simmer over moderate heat until the liquid has reduced to about ½ cup, about 4 minutes. Season with salt and pepper. Carve the pork into ½-inch slices and serve with the figs. —*Jan Birnbaum*

MAKE AHEAD The figs can be refrigerated in their liquid for up to 5 days.

WINE Rustic, peppery Malbec.

Dr Pepper–Glazed Ham with Prunes

ACTIVE: 30 MIN; TOTAL: 3 HR 45 MIN

12 SERVINGS

Most smoked hams are sold fully cooked, so "why bake them again?" asks chef and cookbook author Bruce Aidells before answering his own question: to improve the texture and add a homemade glaze—in this case, one made with Dr Pepper soda and prunes—for extra flavor. After the ham is cooked, Aidells reduces the pan juices and tosses in prunes to make a sauce. "Glazes flavor only the outside of the ham," he says. "But you can spoon pan sauces over every slice."

One 10-pound, bone-in smoked ham, skin removed and fat trimmed to ¼ inch

- 3 cups regular Dr Pepper soda (not diet)
- 2 cups water
- ½ cup pitted prunes
- ⅓ cup yellow mustard
- ⅓ cup light brown sugar
- 2 tablespoons cider vinegar
- 1½ teaspoons cornstarch mixed with 2 tablespoons of water

1. Preheat the oven to 325° and position a rack in the bottom third of the oven. Set the smoked ham in a large roasting pan. Score a ¼-inch-deep crosshatch pattern into the fat at 2-inch intervals. Pour 2 cups of the Dr Pepper and the 2 cups of water into the pan and roast the ham for about 2½ hours, until an instant-read thermometer inserted in the thickest part of the ham registers 120°. Increase the oven temperature to 425°.

2. Meanwhile, in a medium saucepan, simmer the prunes in the remaining 1 cup of Dr Pepper until they are plump and the liquid is slightly reduced, about 10 minutes. Using a slotted spoon, transfer the prunes to a small bowl and cover with plastic wrap. Whisk the mustard, brown sugar and vinegar into the liquid in the saucepan and boil until very thick and syrupy, about 5 minutes.

3. Drizzle the syrupy glaze over the ham and roast until the glaze is glossy, about 20 minutes. Carefully transfer the ham to a large carving board.

4. Pour the pan juices into the saucepan and spoon off the fat. Boil the sauce until reduced to 2 cups, 10 minutes. Whisk in the cornstarch slurry and the prunes and bring to a boil. Simmer the sauce until thickened, 2 minutes. Slice the ham and serve with the Dr Pepper sauce.
—*Bruce Aidells*

WINE Intense, fruity Zinfandel.

Green-Olive-and-Lemon-Crusted Leg of Lamb

ACTIVE: 25 MIN; TOTAL: 1 HR 45 MIN

10 SERVINGS ●

The inspiration for this roasted leg of lamb was a French dish Bruce Aidells tried during the annual sheep festival in St-Rémy, Provence. During the festival, legs of lamb are strung up and cooked over an open fire, then served with a green-olive tapenade; that tapenade became the basis for the lemon-scented crust here. "You can also use the crust as a stuffing in a boneless leg of lamb," Aidells says.

- **4 anchovy fillets**
- **4 medium garlic cloves, very thinly sliced**

Finely grated zest of 2 lemons

- **1 tablespoon chopped marjoram**
- **1 teaspoon freshly ground black pepper**
- **1 cup pitted green olives, such as Picholine**
- **⅓ cup extra-virgin olive oil**

One 7-pound bone-in leg of lamb

1. Preheat the oven to 450°. In a food processor, combine the anchovy fillets, sliced garlic, grated lemon zest, chopped marjoram and black pepper and pulse until the mixture is finely chopped. Add the green olives and pulse until they are finely chopped. With the machine running, pour the olive oil through the feed tube and process to a coarse paste.

2. Place a rack in a roasting pan and set the lamb on the rack. Slather the lamb with the olive paste and roast on the lowest rack of the oven for 20 minutes. Reduce the temperature to 350° and roast the lamb for about 1 hour and 10 minutes longer, until an instant-read thermometer inserted into the thickest part of the meat registers 125°. Transfer the lamb to a board and let rest 15 minutes before carving. Pour any accumulated juices into a bowl and serve with the lamb. —*Bruce Aidells*
WINE Firm, complex Cabernet Sauvignon.

HERB-CRUSTED PORK ROAST WITH GINGER-FIG COMPOTE

DR PEPPER—GLAZED HAM WITH PRUNES

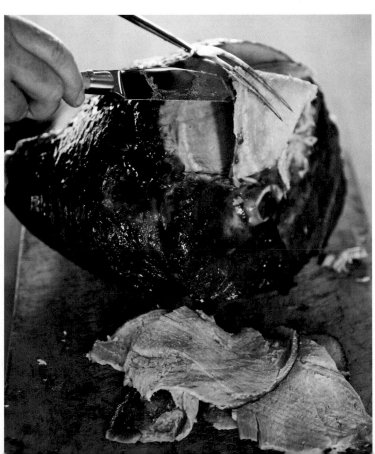

Aromatic Braised Lamb with Prunes and Pine Nuts

ACTIVE: 30 MIN; TOTAL: 2 HR 30 MIN
4 SERVINGS ●

Catalan cooking is known for its wonderful combinations of dried fruit and meat. For this rich and nutty dish, prunes and carrots mingle to create a sweet sauce that enhances the earthy lamb.

- 3 tablespoons extra-virgin olive oil
- 2 pounds boneless lamb shoulder, cut into 1½-inch cubes

Salt and freshly ground pepper

- 3 garlic cloves, minced
- 1 medium onion, finely chopped
- ½ cup dry red wine
- ½ cup water

One 1-inch strip of lemon zest, minced

Pinch of ground cloves

Pinch of ground ginger

- 1 cup pitted prunes
- 1 cup boiling water
- 2 medium carrots, thinly sliced
- ¼ cup pine nuts

1. In a large saucepan, heat the olive oil. Add half of the lamb, season with salt and pepper and cook over moderately high heat until browned on 2 sides, about 3 minutes per side. Transfer to a plate and repeat with the remaining lamb.

2. Add the garlic and onion to the saucepan and cook over moderately low heat, stirring, until softened, 5 minutes. Stir in the wine, ½ cup of water, lemon zest, cloves and ginger. Return the lamb to the saucepan and bring to a boil. Cover and simmer over low heat until very tender, about 1½ hours.

3. Meanwhile, in a heatproof bowl, cover the prunes with the boiling water. Let stand until softened, about 10 minutes. Add the prunes with their cooking liquid and the carrots to the stew. Cover and simmer until the carrots are tender, about 20 minutes.

4. In a medium skillet, cook the pine nuts over moderate heat, shaking the pan a few times, until the nuts are toasted, about 4 minutes. Let cool.

5. Season the stew with salt and pepper and spoon into bowls. Sprinkle with the toasted pine nuts and serve.
—*Janet Mendel*

WINE Juicy, spicy Grenache.

Iraqi Lamb and Eggplant Stew with Pitas

ACTIVE: 1 HR 10 MIN; TOTAL: 3 HR
4 SERVINGS ● ●

The recipe for this sweet and tangy Middle Eastern stew, with falling-apart-tender lamb, comes from Nawal Nasrallah's *Delights from the Garden of Eden: A Cookbook and a History of the Iraqi Cuisine.*

Kosher salt

- 1 large eggplant (1½ pounds), sliced crosswise ½ inch thick
- ¼ cup plus 2½ tablespoons vegetable oil
- 4 lamb shanks (about 1¼ pounds each)

Freshly ground pepper

- 1 large white onion, chopped
- ½ cup pomegranate molasses (see Note)
- ½ cup dried yellow split peas (3 ounces)
- 4 dried red chiles
- 2 teaspoons *baharat* spice blend (see Note) or garam masala
- 2 teaspoons ground coriander
- 8 small pita breads, warmed and torn into large pieces

1. In a bowl, dissolve 2 teaspoons of salt in 1 quart of water. Add the eggplant, cover with a small plate to keep the slices submerged and let soak for 30 minutes.

2. Meanwhile, in a large enameled cast-iron casserole, heat 2 tablespoons of the oil. Season the lamb with salt and pepper and cook over high heat, turning once, until well browned, about 5 minutes per side. Add the onion and cook over moderate heat, stirring, until softened, 10 minutes. Add 3 quarts of water, the pomegranate molasses, split peas, dried chiles, *baharat* and

coriander and bring to a boil. Reduce the heat to low and simmer for 45 minutes, skimming and stirring a few times.

3. Drain the eggplant and pat dry. In a large nonstick skillet, heat 1½ tablespoons of the oil. Add one-third of the eggplant and cook over moderately high heat until browned, 3 minutes per side; transfer to paper towels to drain. Brown the remaining eggplant in the 3 tablespoons of oil. Add the eggplant to the lamb and simmer over low heat, stirring, until the lamb is tender, 45 minutes.

4. Transfer the lamb to a rimmed baking sheet. Remove the meat from the bones and cut into 1-inch pieces. Boil the stew over high heat, skimming, until the liquid has reduced to 3 cups, about 40 minutes.

5. Return the lamb to the stew and season with salt and pepper. Divide the pita among 4 bowls. Ladle the stew on top and serve.
—*Nawal Nasrallah*

NOTE Pomegranate molasses is basically reduced pomegranate juice. *Baharat* is a complex spice blend typically containing cumin, coriander and paprika. Both are available at Middle Eastern groceries.

WINE Fresh, fruity rosé.

Grilled Beef with Spicy Asian Dipping Sauce

ACTIVE: 20 MIN; TOTAL: 45 MIN
4 SERVINGS ●

This simple recipe is all about the beef, says Australian chef Neil Perry, though he adds, "The sweet-salty Indonesian dipping sauce would also be fantastic with poached chicken or grilled salmon."

- 2 tablespoons peanut oil
- 1 tablespoon *kecap manis* (see Note)
- 1 pound sirloin steak, cut ¾ inch thick

Salt and freshly ground black pepper

- 3 tablespoons Asian fish sauce
- 3 tablespoons fresh lime juice
- 1 tablespoon Asian red pepper flakes or crushed red pepper

IRAQI LAMB AND EGGPLANT STEW WITH PITAS

BISON RIB EYE STEAK WITH ROASTED GARLIC

1 tablespoon dark brown sugar
2 teaspoons finely chopped cilantro
1 medium shallot, thinly sliced
½ head of green cabbage, finely shredded

1. Light a grill. In a small glass baking dish, mix the peanut oil with the *kecap manis*. Season the sirloin steak with salt and black pepper, add it to the baking dish and turn to coat. Let the meat stand at room temperature for 30 minutes.

2. In a small bowl, mix the fish sauce with the lime juice, red pepper flakes, brown sugar, cilantro and shallot.

3. Grill the steak over moderately high heat, turning once, until medium-rare, about 6 minutes. Transfer to a cutting board and let rest for 5 minutes. Thinly slice the steak across the grain. Mound the cabbage on plates, top with the sliced steak and serve the sauce on the side.
—*Neil Perry*

NOTE *Kecap manis* is a thick, slightly sweet Indonesian seasoning with a soybean base. Look for it at Asian markets or online at indomart.us.

WINE Rich, ripe Cabernet Sauvignon.

Bison Rib Eye Steaks with Roasted Garlic

ACTIVE: 30 MIN; TOTAL: 1 HR 15 MIN
4 SERVINGS

4 large heads of garlic, halved
Salt and freshly ground pepper
4 tablespoons unsalted butter
1 cup chicken stock
2 tablespoons vegetable oil
Four 9-ounce boneless bison rib eyes
½ cup dry red wine
1 cup water

1. Preheat the oven to 350°. Season the garlic with salt and pepper. In an ovenproof skillet, melt 2 tablespoons of the butter. Add the garlic cut side down, then add the stock and bring to a simmer. Cover and roast until tender, about 30 minutes.

2. Set the skillet over moderate heat. Simmer to evaporate the stock. Add 1 tablespoon of the butter; cook until the garlic is browned. Transfer the garlic to a plate.

3. In each of 2 large skillets, heat 1 tablespoon of vegetable oil. Season the bison steaks, add them to the skillets and sear over high heat for 2 minutes. Reduce the heat to moderately high and cook, turning once, until the steaks are medium-rare, about 6 minutes; transfer to plates.

4. Pour half of the wine into each skillet and boil. Scrape the juices from 1 skillet into the other; boil until reduced by half. Add the water and boil until reduced by half, 5 minutes. Off the heat, swirl in the remaining butter. Season with salt and pour over the steaks. Garnish with the garlic and serve.
—*Marcia Kiesel*

WINE Complex, elegant Pinot Noir.

Spanish-Style Beef Brisket

ACTIVE: 1 HR; TOTAL: 4 HR 30 MIN

12 SERVINGS ●

- 2 tablespoons sweet pimentón de la Vera (smoked Spanish paprika)
- Salt and freshly ground pepper
- One 6½-pound beef brisket
- 2 tablespoons extra-virgin olive oil
- 2 large onions, thinly sliced
- 6 large garlic cloves, chopped
- 2½ cups chicken stock or broth
- One 14-ounce can diced tomatoes
- 2 tablespoons sherry vinegar
- 2 teaspoons thyme leaves
- 2 bay leaves
- Large pinch of saffron threads
- 1½ cups dry sherry
- ½ cup pitted Spanish green olives

1. Preheat the oven to 325°. Mix the paprika with 1 teaspoon of salt and 2 teaspoons of pepper. Rub over the brisket. Heat the oil in a large roasting pan over 2 burners. Add the meat and cook over moderately high heat, turning once, until lightly browned on both sides, 6 minutes. Transfer to a platter.
2. Add the onions and garlic to the pan and cook over moderately low heat, stirring, until softened, about 10 minutes. Add the chicken stock, tomatoes, sherry vinegar, thyme, bay leaves, saffron and sherry and bring to a boil over high heat. Return the brisket to the pan and cover well with foil. Braise in the oven for 3 hours, or until tender, turning once and basting occasionally with pan juices. Add the olives after the first 1½ hours.
3. Transfer the meat to a platter and cover with foil. Strain the pan juices into a large saucepan, reserving the solids. Skim the juices and boil until reduced to 3 cups, about 20 minutes. Return the solids to the juices and season with salt and pepper.
4. Slice the meat across the grain and return to the pan, retaining the shape of the brisket. Spoon the juices on top, cover with foil and braise for 25 minutes. Serve the brisket in its juices. —*Bruce Aidells*
WINE Earthy, medium-bodied Tempranillo.

Mexican Shredded Beef with Red Chiles

ACTIVE: 1 HR; TOTAL: 3 HR

10 SERVINGS ●

- 4 dried New Mexico or *guajillo* chiles, stemmed and seeded
- 2 ancho chiles, seeded
- One 5-pound beef brisket with a layer of fat, cut into 3 pieces
- Salt
- 3 tablespoons vegetable oil
- 1 medium onion, sliced lengthwise ⅛ inch thick
- 4 garlic cloves, minced
- 1 teaspoon cumin seeds
- ¼ teaspoon coriander seeds
- 5 large plum tomatoes—cored, seeded and chopped
- 1 jalapeño, seeded and chopped
- One 2-inch cinnamon stick
- 2 cups chicken stock
- Freshly ground pepper
- Thinly sliced scallions, for garnish

1. In a medium bowl, cover the chiles with hot water and let stand for 30 minutes. Drain, discarding the soaking liquid.
2. Meanwhile, preheat the oven to 325°. Season the brisket with salt. In an ovenproof enameled cast-iron casserole, heat the oil. Sear the meat 1 piece at a time over high heat, turning once, until browned, 10 minutes per piece; transfer to a plate.
3. Add the onion, garlic, cumin and coriander to the casserole. Cook over high heat, stirring, until the onion is translucent, 3 minutes. Stir in the chiles, tomatoes, jalapeño and cinnamon stick. Return the meat to the casserole. Add the stock, season with salt and pepper and bring to a simmer. Cover and braise in the oven, turning the meat after 1 hour, until tender, 2 hours.
4. Discard the cinnamon. Transfer the meat to a board and let cool. Shred the meat.
5. Working in batches, transfer the contents of the casserole to a blender and puree until smooth. Strain and return to the casserole. Add the shredded meat and season with

salt and pepper. Reheat, garnish with scallions and serve. —*Stephanie Valentine*
WINE Intense, fruity Zinfandel.

Asian-Spiced Short Ribs

ACTIVE: 30 MIN; TOTAL: 4 HR 30 MIN

6 SERVINGS ●●

- Six 12-ounce bone-in beef short ribs
- Kosher salt
- Ground fennel, for dusting
- 1 cup ketchup
- 1 cup dry red wine, such as Syrah
- ⅓ cup red wine vinegar
- ½ cup unsulfured molasses
- 3 tablespoons dried onion flakes
- 2 tablespoons Asian fish sauce
- 1 tablespoon soy sauce
- 1 tablespoon garlic powder
- 1 tablespoon seeded and minced chipotle chile in adobo
- 1 teaspoon Asian sesame oil
- 3 quarts water

1. Light a grill. Preheat the oven to 325°. Season the ribs with salt and fennel. Grill over high heat, turning, until charred, about 12 minutes. Transfer to a roasting pan.
2. In a large bowl, mix the ketchup, wine, vinegar, molasses, onion flakes, fish sauce, soy sauce, garlic powder, chipotle, sesame oil and 1 tablespoon of salt. Whisk in the water. Pour the sauce over the ribs and bring to a simmer over 2 burners.
3. Cover the pan and bake, turning the ribs once, until the meat is very tender, about 2½ hours. Lower the oven temperature to 200°. Transfer the sauce to a large saucepan. Keep the ribs warm in the oven. Boil the sauce over high heat until reduced to 4 cups, about 1 hour.
4. Increase the oven temperature to 350°. Pour the sauce over the ribs and roast until the ribs are glazed, about 15 minutes. Serve the ribs on plates with their sauce. —*Jean-Georges Vongerichten*
SERVE WITH Polenta or cheese grits.
WINE Intense, spicy Syrah.

BRAISED CHICKEN WITH
OAXACAN CHOCOLATE MOLE SAUCE
(P. 312), CUMIN-SCENTED WHITE
RICE (P. 350) AND MEXICAN SHREDDED
BEEF WITH RED CHILES (P. 330)

Fried Veal Cutlets with Herb Salad

TOTAL: 30 MIN
4 SERVINGS ●

F&W's Melissa Rubel serves crisp, golden veal cutlets with a deliciously fresh and tangy salad that combines peppery watercress with a mix of parsley, tarragon and snipped chives, but any combination of herbs would be great.

- ½ cup all-purpose flour
- 2 large eggs, beaten
- 1½ cups dry bread crumbs

Kosher salt and freshly ground
    black pepper

Eight ⅛-inch-thick veal cutlets
    (1¼ pounds)

- ½ cup plus 2 teaspoons
    extra-virgin olive oil
- 2 cups watercress, stemmed
- 1 cup flat-leaf parsley leaves
- ¼ cup tarragon leaves
- ¼ cup snipped 1-inch-long chives
- 1 teaspoon red wine vinegar

1. Put the flour, beaten eggs and dry bread crumbs in 3 shallow bowls. Season the bread crumbs with salt and black pepper. Season the veal cutlets with salt and black pepper and dust them with flour, tapping off the excess. Dip the cutlets in the beaten eggs, letting excess egg drip back into the bowl, then dredge the cutlets in the bread crumbs, patting firmly to help the bread crumbs to adhere.

2. In a very large skillet, heat ¼ cup of the olive oil. Add half of the veal cutlets and fry over high heat, turning them once, until the breading is golden and the meat is cooked through, about 3 minutes. Transfer the fried cutlets to a paper towel–lined plate to drain. Repeat, heating another ¼ cup of the olive oil and frying the remaining veal cutlets.

3. In a medium bowl, toss the watercress with the parsley and tarragon leaves and the snipped chives. Add the remaining 2 teaspoons of olive oil and the red wine vinegar, season the herb salad lightly with salt and black pepper and toss well. Transfer the veal cutlets to plates, top each cutlet with some of the herb salad and serve immediately. —*Melissa Rubel*

SERVE WITH Roasted potatoes.

WINE Juicy, fresh Dolcetto.

Corzetti Pasta with Veal Ragù

ACTIVE: 30 MIN; TOTAL: 2 HR 30 MIN
6 SERVINGS ● ●

Corzetti are coin-shaped pasta dating back to the days of the Genovese Republic, when they were embossed with the family crest and served at festive meals.

- 1 ounce dried porcini mushrooms
- 3 cups hot water
- ¼ cup extra-virgin olive oil
- 1 sweet onion, cut into
    ½-inch dice
- 2 medium carrots, cut into
    ½-inch dice
- 1 medium celery rib, cut into
    ½-inch dice

Two ¾-pound veal shanks
    (about 1½ inches thick),
    meat cut into 2-inch pieces
    and bones reserved

Salt and freshly ground
    black pepper

All-purpose flour, for dusting

- 1 cup dry red wine

One 14-ounce can peeled Italian
    tomatoes, crushed by hand

- 1 marjoram sprig, plus
    1½ teaspoons chopped
    leaves
- 1 pound *corzetti* or pappardelle

Shaved Parmigiano-Reggiano
    cheese, for serving

1. In a large heatproof glass measuring cup, soak the dried porcini in the hot water until softened, about 15 minutes. Using a slotted spoon, scoop out the mushrooms and squeeze them to release excess liquid back into the cup. Chop the mushrooms. Reserve the soaking liquid.

2. Meanwhile, in a large enameled cast-iron casserole or Dutch oven, heat 2 tablespoons of the olive oil. Add the diced sweet onion, carrots and celery and cook over moderate heat, stirring frequently, until the vegetables are softened, about 6 minutes. Use a slotted spoon to transfer the softened vegetables to a plate.

3. Add the remaining 2 tablespoons of olive oil to the casserole. Season the veal shanks with salt and pepper and dust with flour. Add the veal shanks and reserved bones to the casserole and cook over moderately high heat, turning once, until browned on both sides, about 10 minutes. Add the red wine and cook, stirring with a sturdy wooden spoon and scraping up any browned bits from the bottom of the casserole, until the wine has nearly evaporated, about 5 minutes.

4. Return the softened vegetables to the casserole. Add the crushed tomatoes, marjoram sprig and chopped porcini. Slowly pour in 2 cups of the porcini soaking liquid, stopping just before you reach the grit. Season with salt and black pepper and bring to a boil over high heat. Cover the casserole and simmer over very low heat until the veal is completely tender, about 2 hours. Scoop the marrow from the bones and stir it into the ragù. Discard the bones and marjoram sprig and stir in the chopped marjoram leaves.

5. Bring a large pot of salted water to a boil over high heat. Add the *corzetti* to the boiling water, stir once or twice and cook until the pasta is just al dente. Drain the *corzetti* well and add them to the ragù. Toss gently to coat the pasta with the veal ragù. Spoon the pasta and sauce into deep bowls and serve, passing the shaved cheese at the table. —*Michela Larson*

MAKE AHEAD The veal ragù can be prepared in advance and refrigerated for up to 3 days or frozen for up to a month. Rewarm gently before adding the pasta.

WINE Cherry-inflected, earthy Sangiovese.

TAGLIATELLE WITH MUSSELS AND TARRAGON

SPAGHETTI WITH CLAMS AND GREEN BEANS

Stir-Fried Noodles with Chanterelles

TOTAL: 30 MIN
4 SERVINGS

- 8 ounces chow mein noodles
- ¼ cup canola oil
- 9 ounces chanterelles, thickly sliced (2 cups)
- Salt and freshly ground pepper
- 4 large eggs, beaten
- 2 tablespoons unsalted butter
- 1 scallion, halved lengthwise and cut crosswise into 3-inch lengths
- 1 tablespoon soy sauce
- 1 tablespoon oyster sauce
- ½ teaspoon chile oil or Chinese chile sauce

1. Bring a large pot of salted water to a boil over high heat. Add the noodles, stir once and boil until al dente. Drain and shake off the excess water.

2. Heat a wok until very hot, then add the canola oil and heat until shimmering. Add the chanterelles, season with salt and pepper and stir-fry over high heat until softened, 5 minutes. Add the eggs and stir-fry for 10 seconds. Immediately add the noodles, butter, scallion, soy sauce, oyster sauce and chile oil and continue to stir-fry until the eggs are cooked but still slightly creamy, 2 to 3 minutes. Serve.
—*Eric Banh and Sophie Banh*
WINE Complex, elegant Pinot Noir.

Tagliatelle with Mussels and Tarragon

TOTAL: 30 MIN
4 SERVINGS

This simple, strikingly black-and-white seafood pasta gets a double hit of anise flavor from Pernod and fresh tarragon.

- 2 **tablespoons extra-virgin olive oil**
- 1 **onion, cut into ¼-inch dice**
- 2 garlic cloves, minced
- 4 thyme sprigs
- ¾ cup dry white wine
- ¼ cup Pernod
- 36 mussels (about 2 pounds)
- ¾ cup heavy cream
- Kosher salt and freshly ground pepper
- ½ pound dried tagliatelle
- 1 tablespoon coarsely chopped tarragon leaves, plus a few whole leaves for garnish
- Coarse black and white salts, for garnish (see Note)

1. In a large, deep skillet, heat the olive oil. Add the onion and garlic and cook over moderate heat, stirring occasionally, until softened, about 10 minutes. Add the thyme, wine and Pernod and bring to a boil. Stir in the mussels, cover and cook over moderate heat until they open, about 3 minutes. Transfer the mussels to a bowl, discarding any that do not open.

2. Boil the liquid in the skillet over moderately high heat until reduced by half, about 2 minutes. Stir in the heavy cream and simmer just until the sauce is thick enough to coat the back of a spoon, about 3 minutes. Discard the thyme sprigs and stir in the mussels along with any accumulated juices. Season with kosher salt and ground pepper.

3. In a large pot of boiling salted water, cook the tagliatelle until al dente; drain well. Add the pasta and the chopped tarragon to the skillet; toss to coat thoroughly with the sauce. Transfer the pasta and mussels to a large bowl. Garnish with the tarragon leaves and the black and white salts and serve. —*Susan Spungen*

NOTE Black salt from Hawaii takes its glittering ebony color from purified volcanic charcoal. Its coarse texture, along with the color, makes for a beautiful garnish. Black salt is available at some specialty food shops and online at thespicehouse.com.

WINE Zesty, fresh Albariño.

Spaghetti with Clams and Green Beans

TOTAL: 25 MIN
4 SERVINGS ●

This is Australian chef and TV personality Neil Perry's variation on the Italian classic *spaghetti vongole* (pasta with clams). He adds green beans to make the dish fresher tasting, and then finishes it with a sprinkling of Parmigiano-Reggiano. As he says, "Serving cheese with seafood is not the norm in Italy, but I just love it here."

- 10 ounces green beans
- ¼ cup extra-virgin olive oil
- 2 garlic cloves, finely chopped
- ½ teaspoon crushed red pepper
- 2 large plum tomatoes (½ pound), coarsely chopped
- Kosher salt and freshly ground pepper
- ½ cup dry white wine
- 24 littleneck clams (2 pounds), scrubbed and rinsed
- 10 large basil leaves, torn
- ¾ pound spaghetti
- Freshly grated Parmigiano-Reggiano cheese, for serving (optional)

1. Bring a large pot of salted water to a boil. Add the green beans and cook until tender, about 10 minutes. Using a slotted spoon, transfer the beans to a plate. Bring the water back to a boil.

2. Meanwhile, in a large skillet, heat the olive oil. Add the garlic and crushed red pepper and cook over moderate heat until fragrant, about 1 minute. Add the tomatoes and season with salt and pepper. Cook, stirring occasionally, until the tomatoes begin to break down, about 5 minutes. Add the wine and clams and bring to a boil. Cover the skillet and simmer until the clams open, about 5 minutes. Discard any that don't open. Remove the skillet from the heat and add the green beans and basil.

3. Add the spaghetti to the boiling water and cook until al dente. Drain the pasta, reserving ¼ cup of the cooking water. Return the spaghetti to the pot and add the clam–and–green bean sauce and the reserved pasta cooking water. Toss over moderate heat until the sauce coats the spaghetti, about 1 minute. Transfer the spaghetti and clams to shallow bowls and serve, passing the grated Parmigiano-Reggiano at the table. —*Neil Perry*

WINE Tart, citrusy Riesling.

Gnocchi Gratin with Pine Nuts and Gorgonzola Dolce

ACTIVE: 1 HR 25 MIN;
TOTAL: 4 HR 30 MIN
4 TO 6 SERVINGS ● ●

F&W contributing editor Paula Wolfert usually bakes gnocchi in gratins, relieving her of the stress of last-minute cooking. Good, light potato gnocchi can take a really lush sauce such as this one from Emilia-Romagna, which is creamy and fragrant with stewed radicchio, seared pancetta, pine nuts and a mild Gorgonzola dolce.

- 2 tablespoons unsalted butter
- Cooked Potato Gnocchi (recipe follows)
- 1 tablespoon extra-virgin olive oil
- 2 ounces thinly sliced pancetta
- 2 medium garlic cloves, very finely chopped
- 1 medium head of radicchio (½ pound), thinly sliced
- ⅓ cup heavy cream
- ⅓ cup whole milk
- 4½ ounces Gorgonzola dolce, crumbled (1½ cups)
- Salt and freshly ground pepper
- ½ cup freshly grated Parmigiano-Reggiano cheese
- 3 tablespoons fresh bread crumbs
- 3 tablespoons pine nuts

1. Preheat the oven to 350°. In a large nonstick skillet, melt the butter. Add the gnocchi and cook over high heat until browned on the bottom, about 2 minutes. Transfer the browned gnocchi to a 9-by-13-inch baking dish.

2. In the same skillet, heat the olive oil. Add the sliced pancetta and cook over low heat until the fat has rendered, about 6 minutes. Add the chopped garlic and cook over moderate heat for 1 minute. Stir in the sliced radicchio, cover and cook until tender, about 4 minutes. Add the heavy cream, milk and Gorgonzola dolce and simmer over moderately low heat just until the cheese has melted, about 2 minutes. Season the sauce with salt and pepper.

3. Pour the sauce over and around the gnocchi in the baking dish. Top with the grated Parmigiano-Reggiano, fresh bread crumbs and pine nuts. Bake on the upper rack for 20 minutes, until the gratin is golden. Serve immediately.
—*Paula Wolfert*

MAKE AHEAD The gorgonzola sauce can be refrigerated overnight. Reheat very gently before pouring over the gnocchi.

WINE Cherry-inflected, earthy Sangiovese.

POTATO GNOCCHI

ACTIVE: 1 HR; TOTAL: 4 HR

4 TO 6 SERVINGS ● ● ○

According to Paula Wolfert, "You can dress up perfect gnocchi in as many ways as you can sauce pasta, garnishing them with an unheated pesto sauce as the Ligurians do, or tossing them with foaming butter and slivered sage leaves as the Piedmontese do. You can mix them with a chunky tomato sauce or smother them in a wild boar ragù. A little olive oil added to the dough makes for a silkier consistency, but it is optional."

Kosher salt

- **2 pounds medium Yukon Gold potatoes**
- **⅔ cup all-purpose flour**
- **⅓ cup cake flour**
- **1 teaspoon extra-virgin olive oil**

1. Preheat the oven to 400°. Spread a 1-inch layer of salt in a small roasting pan. Prick the potatoes all over with a fork and arrange them on the salt in a single layer. Bake until fork-tender, about 1½ hours. Remove them from the oven and slit them lengthwise to release their steam.

2. Line a large rimmed baking sheet with paper towels. As soon as the potatoes are cool enough to handle, scoop their flesh into a ricer or tamis and rice the potatoes onto the paper towels in a shallow layer. Let cool completely.

3. Working over a medium bowl, sift the all-purpose and cake flours with a large pinch of salt. Measure out 4 lightly packed cups of the riced potatoes (1 pound), and transfer the potatoes to a work surface. Sprinkle the sifted flour mixture over the potatoes and drizzle with the olive oil. Gently form the dough into a firm ball.

4. Test the gnocchi dough: Bring a small saucepan of salted water to a boil. Using your hands, form one ¾-inch round (a single *gnocco*). Boil the *gnocco* until it floats to the surface, about 1 minute. Using a slotted spoon, transfer the *gnocco* to a plate and let cool. It should be light and tender but still hold together. If the *gnocco* breaks apart in the boiling water, the dough has too little flour; add more. If the *gnocco* is tough and chewy, the dough has too much flour; cut in a little more of the reserved riced potatoes.

5. Line a baking sheet with paper towels. Divide the dough into quarters. Working with 1 piece at a time, gently roll the dough into a long rope about ½ inch wide. Using a sharp knife, cut the rope into ½-inch pieces. Roll each piece against the tines of a fork to make light ridges. Transfer the gnocchi to the towel-lined baking sheet. Repeat with the remaining dough. Let the gnocchi stand at room temperature for 1 hour to dry.

6. Bring a large pot of salted water to a boil. Fill a large bowl with ice water. Add half of the gnocchi at a time and boil over high heat until they rise to the surface, then cook for 15 seconds longer. Using a wire skimmer, transfer the gnocchi to the bowl of ice water. Drain on paper towels and pat dry. Toss with oil and refrigerate for up to 3 hours, or freeze the gnocchi on baking sheets in a single layer. Transfer them to an airtight container or resealable plastic bags and freeze for up to 6 weeks. To serve, sauté them in butter until heated through before proceeding. —*P.W.*

VARIATION To make Chestnut Gnocchi, substitute ⅓ cup chestnut flour (available at Italian markets) for the cake flour before forming the gnocchi dough.

Eggplant Ravioli with Gewürztraminer and Bacon

TOTAL: 1 HR 15 MIN

6 SERVINGS ●

F&W contributing editor Jean-Georges Vongerichten transforms Gewürztraminer, a fruity white wine, into a light syrup. After swirling it with extra-virgin olive oil, basil and bacon, he drizzles the dressing over eggplant ravioli. It would also be superb on a green salad.

- **3 Asian eggplants (1 pound), halved lengthwise**
- **1½ teaspoons olive oil, plus more for brushing**

Salt

- **½ pound lean bacon— 2 ounces cut into ½-inch-thick lardons, 6 ounces thinly sliced**
- **½ cup Gewürztraminer**
- **½ cup red wine vinegar**
- **¼ cup chopped basil stems, plus ¼ cup finely chopped basil leaves**
- **¼ cup thinly sliced green apple**
- **1 whole clove**
- **1 tablespoon finely chopped mint**
- **24 wonton wrappers**
- **1 large egg white**

1. Light a grill. Score the cut sides of the eggplants in a crosshatch pattern, slicing down to the skin but not through it. Brush the eggplants generously with olive oil and season them with salt. Grill the eggplants over high heat, turning once, until they are charred and soft, about 10 minutes. Transfer the eggplants to a baking sheet and let cool.

2. In a medium saucepan, cook the bacon lardons over moderate heat, stirring occasionally, until they are browned and crisp, about 7 minutes. Using a slotted spoon, transfer the lardons to paper towels to drain. Discard the fat and wipe out the saucepan with paper towels.

3. In the same saucepan, combine the sliced bacon, Gewürztraminer, red wine vinegar, chopped basil stems, sliced apple and clove and bring to a boil. Reduce the heat to low and simmer for 10 minutes. Strain the sauce into a small saucepan. Stir in the 1½ teaspoons of olive oil and season the sauce with salt. Keep warm.

4. Scoop the eggplant flesh into a medium bowl, leaving some of it in small chunks. Stir in the mint and season with salt.

EGGPLANT RAVIOLI WITH GEWÜRZTRAMINER

PENNE WITH CAULIFLOWER AND LEEKS

5. Set out 4 wonton wrappers on a work surface. Moisten the edges with egg white and place a rounded teaspoon of the eggplant filling on each wrapper. Fold the wontons into triangles and press to seal, releasing all of the air. Repeat with the remaining wontons and filling.

6. Bring a large pot of salted water to a boil. Cook the ravioli until tender, about 2 minutes. Drain and transfer to bowls. Drizzle the sauce on top, garnish with the lardons and chopped basil and serve.
—Jean-Georges Vongerichten
WINE Rich Alsace Gewürztraminer.

Penne with Cauliflower and Leeks

ACTIVE: 30 MIN; TOTAL: 1 HR 10 MIN
6 SERVINGS ● ● ○

This very flexible recipe can be easily adapted to include several different seasonal vegetables. In winter and spring,

Salvatore Denaro, the chef and owner of Il Bacco Felice in Foligno, Italy, might make it with the area's small violet-colored artichokes; in the fall he prefers cauliflower or broccoli. A pretty alternative is *pasta con cavolfiore e broccoli siciliani,* with equal parts cauliflower and broccoli; the dish is also quite good made with leeks alone.

⅓ **cup extra-virgin olive oil**
2 **medium leeks, white**
   and light-green parts only,
   thinly sliced crosswise
2 **garlic cloves, thinly sliced**
1 **pound cauliflower,**
   cut into 1-inch florets
1 **fresh red chile, seeded**
   and thinly sliced
1 **cup dry white wine**
½ **cup water**
8 **cherry tomatoes, quartered**
¾ **pound** *penne rigate*
Salt and freshly ground black pepper

1. In a large, deep skillet, heat the olive oil. Add the leeks and garlic and cook over low heat, stirring often, until the leeks are softened but not browned, about 10 minutes. Add the cauliflower and chile. Cover and cook over low heat, stirring occasionally, until the cauliflower is tender, about 25 minutes. Add the wine and water, cover and simmer over moderately low heat until the liquid has reduced to about ½ cup, about 12 minutes. Add the cherry tomatoes and simmer for 5 minutes longer.

2. Meanwhile, bring a large pot of salted water to a boil. Add the pasta and cook over high heat, stirring occasionally, until al dente. Drain the pasta, then toss it with the vegetables in the skillet. Season with salt and black pepper and serve.
—Salvatore Denaro
MAKE AHEAD The vegetables can be prepared up to 5 hours ahead.
WINE Fresh, lively Gavi.

slow cookers

F&W tested the latest models, then asked cookbook author and slow-cooker expert **Beth Hensperger** for smart and unexpected ways to use them, as in the risotto recipe at right.

MARATHON COOKER

All-Clad's Slow Cooker can be programmed for up to 26 hours of continual cooking—the longest of all the ones we tested—making it especially well suited for tough cuts of meat that require slow, steady heat. Because the machine also seals in moisture while cooking—this model had the least evaporation in our test—the meat won't dry out ($150; 877-812-6235 or williams-sonoma.com).

three more standouts

EASY-TO-USE COOKER

Cuisinart's dependable CSC-650 takes the guesswork out of slow cooking: When you use the timer, it always starts on high, ensuring that food reaches the temperature recommended by the USDA within 2 hours, before automatically switching to low. The dials appeal to the digital-shy, and this model is a third less expensive than others we tested ($100; 800-211-9604 or cuisinartwebstore.com).

POWERHOUSE COOKER

KitchenAid's 400-watt Slow Cooker is the most powerful of the models we tested, which means food reaches the USDA-recommended safe temperature range faster. If the temperature drops too low, an electronic sensor beeps. Plus, the machine's "reserve power" feature helps stabilize temperatures when the lid is lifted ($150; 800-541-6390 or shopkitchenaid.com).

HEALTHY COOKER

New Age guru **Dr. Andrew Weil**'s Healthy Kitchen Slow Cooker—part of his first line of cookware, developed in collaboration with Waterford Wedgwood—comes preprogrammed with temperature settings and cooking times for 40 recipes from his cookbook *The Healthy Kitchen*. Other recipes require additional programming ($150; 866-593-2540 or bloomingdales.com).

Slow-Cooker Sausage and Vegetable Risotto

ACTIVE: 25 MIN; TOTAL: 1 HR 30 MIN

6 SERVINGS

Risotto usually requires endless stirring, but slow cookers can do a lot of the work, with surprisingly good results.

4½ cups low-sodium chicken broth
¾ pound sweet Italian sausages, casings removed
3 tablespoons water
5 tablespoons unsalted butter
1 small onion, cut into ¼-inch dice
½ cup dry white wine
2 cups arborio rice (14 ounces)
1 medium zucchini, cut into ½-inch dice
1 tablespoon kosher salt
5 ounces baby spinach (5 cups)
¾ cup grated Parmigiano-Reggiano cheese, plus more for serving
Freshly ground pepper

1. Turn a 6- to 7-quart slow cooker to high. In a saucepan, bring the broth to a simmer. In a skillet, cook the sausage with the water over moderately high heat, breaking it up with a spoon until the water has evaporated and the sausage is browned, 10 minutes. Transfer the sausage to the slow cooker.

2. In the same skillet, melt 3 tablespoons of the butter. Add the onion and cook over moderate heat until translucent, 4 minutes. Add the wine and cook, scraping up any browned bits, until reduced by half, 2 minutes. Stir in the rice and cook until all of the wine has been absorbed. Transfer to the slow cooker. Add the broth, zucchini and salt; cover. Cook for 1 hour, stirring halfway through. The risotto is done when the rice is al dente and most of the liquid has been absorbed. Turn off the slow cooker.

3. Stir in the spinach, the remaining 2 tablespoons of butter and the cheese, season with pepper and serve immediately, passing additional cheese at the table.
—*Beth Hensperger*

WINE Juicy, fresh Dolcetto.

Red Wine Risotto with Mushroom "Marmalade"

TOTAL: 1 HR 45 MIN

4 SERVINGS

An intensely fruity wine like an Amarone boils down to something so rich, it's almost meaty. F&W contributing editor Jean-Georges Vongerichten reduces the Italian red with thin slices of earthy mushrooms, then swirls the purply sauce into a risotto; it would be equally delicious on polenta or even on a piece of grilled bread.

MARMALADE

3 tablespoons vegetable oil
¾ pound fresh porcini or stemmed shiitake mushrooms—½ pound cut into ½-inch dice, ¼ pound sliced ¼ inch thick
Salt and freshly ground pepper
1 medium shallot, thinly sliced
1 garlic clove, thinly sliced
2 tablespoons sugar
1 tablespoon water
¾ cup dry red wine, such as Amarone
½ cup red wine vinegar
½ tablespoon unsalted butter

RISOTTO

5 cups chicken stock
1 tablespoon extra-virgin olive oil
1 small onion, minced
1 cup arborio rice (6 ounces)
½ cup dry red wine, such as Amarone
1 tablespoon unsalted butter
Salt and freshly ground pepper
One 2-ounce piece of Parmigiano-Reggiano cheese, for shaving
2 teaspoons chopped mixed herbs, such as chives, mint and tarragon

1. MAKE THE MARMALADE: In a large non-stick skillet, heat 1 tablespoon of the vegetable oil. Add the diced mushrooms; season with salt and pepper. Cover and cook over moderate heat until tender, 5 minutes. Uncover and cook, stirring, until browned. Transfer the mushrooms to a plate.

2. In the same skillet, heat another 1 tablespoon of vegetable oil. Add the shallot and garlic and cook over low heat until softened, about 10 minutes. Remove from the heat and stir in the cooked mushrooms.

3. In a small saucepan, simmer the sugar and water over moderate heat, washing down the side of the pan with a wet pastry brush, until amber, 6 minutes. Add the wine and bring to a boil, stirring to dissolve the sugar. Add the vinegar and boil over high heat until reduced by half, 12 minutes. Stir the mixture into the skillet and cook over moderate heat until the mushrooms are glazed, 3 minutes. Season with salt.

4. In a medium skillet, heat the remaining 1 tablespoon of vegetable oil. Add the sliced mushrooms, season with salt and cook over moderate heat until tender and lightly browned, about 8 minutes. Stir the mushrooms into the marmalade and swirl in the butter. Cover and keep warm.

5. MAKE THE RISOTTO: In a medium saucepan, bring the chicken stock to a simmer; cover and keep warm over low heat. In a large saucepan, heat the olive oil. Add the onion and cook over moderate heat until softened, about 5 minutes. Stir in the rice and cook for 2 minutes. Add the wine and simmer until almost evaporated. Pour in about 1 cup of the hot stock, or enough to cover the rice. Cook, stirring constantly, until the stock has been absorbed, about 5 minutes. Repeat, adding 1 cup of stock at a time and stirring until all of the stock has been absorbed. The risotto is done when the rice is just cooked and suspended in the creamy sauce, about 25 minutes. Stir in the butter and season with salt and pepper.

6. Spoon the risotto into bowls and top with the mushroom marmalade. Shave a few slices of Parmigiano-Reggiano over the risotto, garnish with the herbs and serve.
—*Jean-Georges Vongerichten*

MAKE AHEAD The mushroom marmalade can be refrigerated for up to 3 days.

WINE Intense, fruity Zinfandel.

● HEALTHY   ● MAKE AHEAD   ● VEGETARIAN   ● STAFF FAVORITE

AUTUMN

side dishes

Radicchio Salad with Beets, Pear, Walnuts and Roquefort

ACTIVE: 20 MIN; TOTAL: 1 HR 10 MIN

4 SERVINGS ●

This is a serious autumn salad, with an abundance of sweet roasted onions, juicy pear, crisp greens and salty, pungent Roquefort cheese. But the most compelling part of the dish is the beets, which are first boiled, then roasted to deepen and intensify their flavor.

- ¾ cup walnuts
- 2 medium red onions, each cut into 6 wedges through the root ends
- ¼ cup extra-virgin olive oil, plus more for drizzling
- Kosher salt
- 4 medium beets (1¼ pounds)
- 2 teaspoons balsamic vinegar
- 1 teaspoon dark brown sugar
- 1 large firm pear such as Bosc—quartered, cored lengthwise and cut into 16 slices
- 2 tablespoons fresh lemon juice
- 1 large head of radicchio (1 pound), leaves torn into bite-size pieces
- 1 endive, cored and leaves halved crosswise
- Freshly ground pepper
- 5½ ounces Roquefort cheese, crumbled (1 cup)

1. Preheat the oven to 350°. Spread the walnuts in a pie plate and toast for 8 minutes, until fragrant. Let the walnuts cool, then coarsely chop them.

2. Increase the oven temperature to 450°. On a rimmed baking sheet, toss the onion wedges with 1 tablespoon of the olive oil and season with salt. Roast the onions for about 25 minutes, turning once, until tender and browned in spots. Let the onion wedges cool to room temperature.

3. Meanwhile, in a large saucepan, cover the beets with water and bring to a boil. Simmer the beets over moderately high heat until almost tender, about 25 minutes; drain and let cool slightly.

4. Peel the beets and cut each one into 6 wedges. Transfer the beets to a small baking dish and toss them with 1 tablespoon of the olive oil and the balsamic vinegar and brown sugar; season with salt. Roast the beets for about 15 minutes, turning once, until tender. Let the beets cool to room temperature.

5. In a small bowl, toss the sliced pear with 1 tablespoon of the lemon juice. In a large bowl, toss the radicchio and endive with the remaining 2 tablespoons of olive oil and 1 tablespoon of lemon juice; season with salt and pepper. Mound the salad on plates and top with the walnuts, onions, beets, pear and Roquefort. Drizzle with olive oil and serve. —*Neil Perry*

MAKE AHEAD The toasted nuts can be stored in an airtight container for up to 3 days. The roasted beets and onions can be refrigerated overnight. Bring to room temperature before serving.

Caribbean-Style Sliced Salad

 **TOTAL: 15 MIN**

4 SERVINGS ●

- 1 teaspoon whole-grain mustard
- 1 tablespoon white wine vinegar
- 3 tablespoons extra-virgin olive oil
- Salt and freshly ground pepper
- ½ small cabbage, thinly sliced
- 1 carrot, sliced lengthwise ⅛ inch thick on a mandoline
- 1 yellow bell pepper, thinly sliced
- 1 yellow tomato, thinly sliced
- 1 ripe green tomato, thinly sliced

1. In a small bowl, whisk the mustard with the white wine vinegar and olive oil. Season with salt and pepper.

2. Arrange the vegetables on plates. Season with salt and pepper, drizzle with the vinaigrette and serve. —*Marcia Kiesel*

Goat Cheese, Lentil and Potato Salad

 TOTAL: 35 MIN
4 SERVINGS ●

This combination of warm Yukon Gold potatoes and green lentils tossed with rich goat cheese and a lively dressing is utterly delicious. Australian chef Neil Perry warns against overcooking the lentils, which can ruin the texture; he also suggests topping the dish with a poached egg to enhance the salad's richness.

1¼ cups French green lentils (9 ounces), rinsed and drained
2 Yukon Gold potatoes (about 14 ounces), peeled and cut into ½-inch dice
3 scallions, thinly sliced
2 medium tomatoes, seeded and finely diced
½ cup finely chopped flat-leaf parsley
¼ cup finely chopped mint
1 large garlic clove, minced
½ cup extra-virgin olive oil
¼ cup fresh lemon juice
Kosher salt and freshly ground pepper
8 ounces fresh goat cheese, crumbled (1¾ cup)

1. In a large saucepan, cover the lentils with cold water and bring to a simmer. Cook over moderately low heat, stirring occasionally, until the lentils are tender, about 18 minutes. Drain the lentils well and transfer to a large bowl.

2. Meanwhile, in a medium saucepan, cover the potatoes with cold water and bring to a boil. Cook over moderately high heat until the potatoes are tender, about 10 minutes. Drain very well and add to the lentils. Add the scallions, tomatoes, parsley, mint, garlic, olive oil and lemon juice, season with salt and pepper and toss. Spoon the lentil salad onto plates and top with the goat cheese. Serve at once. —*Neil Perry*

MAKE AHEAD The cooked lentils and potatoes can be refrigerated overnight. Bring to room temperature before serving.

Mashed Potatoes with Horseradish Cream

ACTIVE: 30 MIN; TOTAL: 1 HR 20 MIN
12 SERVINGS ● ●

Everyone loves classic mashed potatoes, but to add a bit of elegance, F&W's Grace Parisi sometimes serves them with a creamy, tangy horseradish sauce.

6 pounds Yukon Gold potatoes, peeled and cut into 2-inch chunks
6 garlic cloves, peeled
14 tablespoons (7 ounces) unsalted butter, softened
Salt
½ cup crème fraîche
1½ tablespoons prepared horseradish
Freshly ground white pepper

1. Put the potatoes and garlic in a pot, cover with cold water and bring to a boil. Cook over moderate heat until the potatoes are tender, about 20 minutes. Drain the potatoes and garlic and return them to the pot. Shake the pot over moderate heat to evaporate any water. Press the potatoes and garlic through a ricer into a large bowl and stir in 12 tablespoons of the butter. Season with salt.

2. Preheat the oven to 425°. Transfer the potatoes to a 3-quart baking dish and use the back of a spoon to make indentations in the surface. Melt the remaining 2 tablespoons of butter and brush all over the surface of the potatoes.

3. Bake the potatoes for about 30 minutes, until golden on top.

4. Meanwhile, in a small saucepan, whisk the crème fraîche with the horseradish. Season with salt and white pepper and warm over moderately low heat. Transfer to a small serving bowl.

5. Serve the mashed potatoes, passing the horseradish cream on the side. —*Grace Parisi*

MAKE AHEAD The recipe can be prepared through Step 2, covered and refrigerated overnight. Bring the potatoes to room temperature before baking.

Whipped Yukon Gold Potatoes

ACTIVE: 30 MIN; TOTAL: 1 HR 10 MIN
8 SERVINGS ●

These potatoes from Thomas Keller's restaurant Ad Hoc in Yountville, California, have a wonderfully fluffy, airy texture because they're passed through a ricer or food mill. They're also rich, thanks to generous amounts of butter and cream.

4 pounds Yukon Gold potatoes, peeled and cut into 2-inch chunks
1½ sticks (6 ounces) unsalted butter, cut into small cubes
1 cup heavy cream
Salt and freshly ground white pepper
2 tablespoons snipped chives

1. Put the potato chunks in a large pot, cover with water and bring to a boil over high heat. Reduce the heat to moderate and simmer until the potatoes are tender, about 25 minutes. Drain and return the cooked potatoes to the hot pot. Cook over moderate heat for 1 minute, shaking the pot to dry the potatoes.

2. In a large saucepan, melt the butter cubes in the heavy cream. Working over the saucepan, pass the hot potatoes through a ricer or food mill. Stir with a wooden spoon until light and fluffy. Season with salt and white pepper and stir in the snipped chives. Serve immediately. —*Thomas Keller*

CURRY-ROASTED BUTTERNUT
SQUASH AND CHICKPEAS

Rioja-Style Potatoes

ACTIVE: 20 MIN; TOTAL: 1 HR

4 SERVINGS ● ●

One of the Rioja's most famous dishes contains many of the Spanish region's signature ingredients: bell peppers, potatoes and chorizo simmered in a smoky sauce thickened by the potato starch.

- 2 tablespoons extra-virgin olive oil
- 1 small onion, finely chopped
- 1½ pounds Yukon Gold potatoes, peeled and cut into 1½-inch pieces
- 1 small portobello mushroom, stemmed and cap thinly sliced
- ½ green bell pepper, diced
- 1 bay leaf
- ½ teaspoon pimentón de la Vera (smoked Spanish paprika)

Pinch of crushed red pepper

- 2 cups water
- 6 ounces dry Spanish chorizo, sliced ¼ inch thick

Salt

1. In a large skillet, heat the olive oil. Add the chopped onion and cook over moderate heat until softened, 5 minutes. Add the potatoes and portobello and stir to coat with oil. Add the green pepper, bay leaf, paprika, crushed red pepper and water and bring to a boil.

2. Cook the potatoes over low heat for 10 minutes. Add the chorizo and simmer over moderately low heat until the potatoes are tender, 20 minutes. Season with salt, discard the bay leaf and serve.
—*Janet Mendel*

Sweet Potatoes with Apple Butter

ACTIVE: 15 MIN; TOTAL: 1 HR 45 MIN

10 SERVINGS ● ●

- 4 pounds sweet potatoes
- 6 tablespoons unsalted butter, at room temperature
- ½ cup apple butter

Salt

1. Preheat the oven to 350°. Pierce the sweet potatoes all over with a fork and place on a large rimmed baking sheet. Bake for 1½ hours, or until very tender.

2. Peel the sweet potatoes and transfer to a large bowl. Mash with a potato masher until creamy, then mash in the butter and apple butter. Season with salt and serve.
—*Marcia Kiesel*

Carrots with Caraway Seeds

TOTAL: 30 MIN

8 SERVINGS ● ●

If you can't find young carrots, thinly slice full-size ones; just don't use the pre-trimmed carrots that come in a plastic bag. Unsalted butter also works in place of the goat's-milk butter.

- 1½ tablespoons caraway seeds
- 1½ pounds baby carrots without tops, unpeeled, halved lengthwise
- 3 tablespoons extra-virgin olive oil
- 2 cups carrot juice
- 3 bay leaves
- 4 tablespoons goat's-milk butter at room temperature, cut into cubes (see Note)

Salt and freshly ground pepper

1. In a large skillet, toast the caraway seeds over high heat just until fragrant, about 1 minute. Transfer to a plate.

2. In a bowl, toss the carrots with the oil. Add the carrots to the skillet and cook over high heat, stirring occasionally, until lightly charred all over, about 5 minutes. Stir in the carrot juice, bay leaves and caraway seeds. Reduce the heat to moderate and simmer until the carrots are tender and the liquid is reduced to a few tablespoons, about 10 minutes. Discard the bay leaves. Remove from the heat and stir in the butter until smooth and creamy. Season with salt and pepper and serve hot or at room temperature. —*Octavio Becerra*

NOTE Goat's-milk butter is available at health food stores, large grocery stores like Whole Foods and online at igourmet.com.

Curry-Roasted Butternut Squash and Chickpeas

ACTIVE: 30 MIN; TOTAL: 1 HR 30 MIN

12 SERVINGS ● ● ● ●

This Indian twist on traditional roasted butternut squash is supereasy: After tossing the squash and chickpeas with curry and cayenne, F&W's Melissa Rubel roasts them, then tops the dish with a cooling cilantro-spiked yogurt sauce.

- 2 large butternut squash (5½ pounds)—peeled, seeded and cut into 1-inch dice

One 19-ounce can chickpeas—drained, rinsed and dried

- ¼ cup extra-virgin olive oil
- 1 tablespoon mild curry powder
- ¼ teaspoon cayenne pepper

Kosher salt and freshly ground black pepper

- 3 cups plain whole-milk yogurt
- ¾ cup minced cilantro
- 3 tablespoons fresh lemon juice

1. Preheat the oven to 375°. In a large bowl, toss the butternut squash with the chickpeas, olive oil, curry and cayenne and season with salt and black pepper. Spread on a large rimmed baking sheet and roast for 1 hour, or until the squash is tender.

2. Meanwhile, in a medium bowl, combine the yogurt with the chopped cilantro and fresh lemon juice and season with salt and black pepper.

3. Spoon the roasted squash and chickpeas onto a large serving platter and drizzle with ½ cup of the cilantro-yogurt sauce. Serve the remaining sauce on the side.
—*Melissa Rubel*

NOTE The cilantro-yogurt sauce served with this dish is also an excellent accompaniment to the Indian-Spiced Turkey Breast (p. 316) and the Fragrant Cauliflower in Tomato Sauce (p. 350).

MAKE AHEAD The recipe can be prepared through Step 2 and refrigerated overnight. Reheat the squash and chickpeas in a 350° oven until hot.

Iceberg Wedges with Bacon and Buttermilk Dressing

ACTIVE: 45 MIN; TOTAL: 3 HR 30 MIN
8 SERVINGS

This salad is a play on the quintessential American combination of iceberg lettuce, tomato wedges and packaged bacon bits with a mayonnaise dressing. Only the iceberg lettuce wedges stay the same: The tomatoes are oven-roasted, the bacon is cut extra thick and the buttermilk dressing is spiked with chives, mint and parsley.

  4 large plum tomatoes, bottoms
     marked with an X
  ¼ cup extra-virgin olive oil
  1 teaspoon finely chopped thyme
Salt and freshly ground
     black pepper
  2 ounces brioche, cut into
     ¾-inch cubes (2 cups)
  ⅔ cup mayonnaise
  ¼ cup crème fraîche or
     sour cream
  ¼ cup buttermilk
2½ tablespoons fresh lemon juice
  1 tablespoon chopped
     flat-leaf parsley
1½ teaspoons chopped mint
  3 tablespoons snipped chives
  ½ pound thickly sliced bacon, cut
     into 2-by-½-inch pieces
  2 medium heads of iceberg lettuce,
     each cut into 4 wedges

INGREDIENT

panko

Fluffy, crisp Japanese *panko* bread crumbs are increasingly available. They add a light crunch wherever dried bread crumbs are called for. Try topping casseroles and gratins with buttered *panko* and grated cheese, as in the creamed spinach at right.

1. Preheat the oven to 275°. Prepare a bowl of ice water. In a medium pot of boiling water, blanch the scored tomatoes just until the skins loosen, about 30 seconds. Using a slotted spoon, transfer the tomatoes to the ice water to cool. Drain and peel the tomatoes, pat dry and slice them in half crosswise.

2. Arrange the tomatoes cut side up on a large nonstick baking sheet (or a baking sheet with a nonstick liner) and drizzle with 2 tablespoons of the olive oil. Sprinkle with the chopped thyme and season with salt and pepper. Roast for about 2½ hours, or until the tomatoes are very tender and slightly shrunken. Transfer the tomatoes to a plate and let cool.

3. Meanwhile, spread the brioche cubes on a small baking sheet and toast for about 15 minutes, or until golden and crisp. Let the croutons cool.

4. In a bowl, whisk the mayonnaise, crème fraîche and buttermilk until smooth. Add the lemon juice, parsley, mint and 1 tablespoon of the chives and season with salt and pepper. Refrigerate until chilled.

5. In a medium skillet, cook the bacon over moderate heat, stirring occasionally, until browned and slightly crisp, 8 to 10 minutes. Transfer to paper towels to drain.

6. Put each iceberg wedge on a plate with a tomato half and drizzle with the remaining 2 tablespoons of oil. Top with the croutons, bacon and remaining 2 tablespoons of chives and serve with buttermilk dressing. —*Thomas Keller*

Creamed Spinach with Buttery Crumbs

ACTIVE: 40 MIN; TOTAL: 1 HR 10 MIN
12 SERVINGS ●●

F&W's Grace Parisi updates classic creamed spinach by adding shiitake mushrooms and aged Gouda and covering the dish with crispy, buttery bread crumbs. She lightens the traditional recipe by using whole milk in place of heavy cream.

2¼ pounds baby spinach
  6 tablespoons unsalted butter
  ½ pound shiitake mushrooms,
     stemmed and caps cut
     into ½-inch dice
  2 medium shallots, minced
  1 teaspoon finely chopped
     thyme leaves
  3 tablespoons all-purpose flour
2½ cups whole milk
  ¾ cup finely grated aged Gouda
     cheese (about 2 ounces)
Salt and freshly ground black pepper
  1 cup *panko* bread crumbs

1. Preheat the oven to 375°. Bring 4 inches of water to a boil in a large pot over high heat. Add the baby spinach in large handfuls and cook just until wilted, about 2 minutes. Drain the spinach in a colander and cool under running water. Drain the spinach again, pressing and squeezing out as much water as possible. Transfer the well-drained spinach to a cutting board and coarsely chop it.

2. In a large, deep skillet, melt 4 tablespoons of the butter. Add the shiitake mushrooms, minced shallots and chopped thyme and cook over moderate heat, stirring, until softened and just beginning to brown, about 8 minutes. Stir in the flour and cook, stirring, just until the pan looks dry, about 2 minutes. Gradually whisk in the milk and stir until smooth and creamy. Bring to a boil over moderate heat and cook, stirring, until very thick, 2 to 3 minutes. Stir in the baby spinach and half of the grated Gouda cheese and season with salt and black pepper. Scrape the mixture into a shallow 1½-quart baking dish in an even layer.

3. In a small skillet, melt the remaining 2 tablespoons of butter. Remove from the heat and add the *panko* and the remaining grated Gouda and season with salt and black pepper. Scatter the seasoned, buttered crumbs over the spinach and bake for about 20 minutes, until the sauce is

bubbling and the crumbs are golden. Let stand for 10 minutes before serving.
—*Grace Parisi*

MAKE AHEAD The recipe can be prepared through Step 2 and refrigerated overnight. Return to room temperature before topping and baking.

Honey-Glazed Roasted Root Vegetables

ACTIVE: 25 MIN; TOTAL: 1 HR 15 MIN

12 SERVINGS ● ● ○

The secret to this sweet, slightly tangy dish: a touch of sherry vinegar in the glaze.

1¼ pounds parsnips, peeled and sliced ½ inch thick

1¼ pounds carrots, peeled and sliced ½ inch thick

One 1¼-pound celery root— peeled, quartered and sliced ½ inch thick

1¼ pounds golden beets, peeled and sliced ½ inch thick

½ cup extra-virgin olive oil

½ cup honey

6 thyme sprigs

Salt and freshly ground black pepper

2 tablespoons sherry vinegar

Preheat the oven to 425°. In a large bowl, toss the parsnips, carrots, celery root and golden beets with the oil, honey and thyme sprigs and season with salt and black pepper. Divide the root vegetable mixture between 2 large, sturdy rimmed baking sheets. Cover both sheets with foil and roast for 40 minutes, rotating the pans from top to bottom and back to front halfway through, until the vegetables are tender. Remove the foil and roast for 10 minutes longer, until glazed. Return them to the bowl, stir in the vinegar and season with salt and pepper. Serve right away.
—*Grace Parisi*

MAKE AHEAD The vegetables can be cooked early in the day and kept at room temperature before rewarming.

ICEBERG WEDGES WITH BACON AND BUTTERMILK DRESSING

GARLIC-PARMIGIANO BROCCOLI (P. 349), HONEY-GLAZED VEGETABLES

Creamed Onions with Thyme and Sage

ACTIVE: 25 MIN; TOTAL: 1 HR

12 SERVINGS ●●○

- 2 tablespoons unsalted butter
- 4 large onions (about 2 pounds), cut into 1-inch dice
- 1½ teaspoons minced thyme
- 1½ teaspoons minced sage
- ½ teaspoon freshly grated nutmeg
- ½ teaspoon freshly ground white pepper
- 1½ cups heavy cream
- Salt

In a large skillet, melt the butter. Add the onions and cook over moderately low heat, stirring, until softened, about 30 minutes. Add the thyme, sage, nutmeg and white pepper and cook, stirring, for 2 minutes. Add the cream and bring to a boil. Simmer over low heat, stirring occasionally, until thickened, about 5 minutes. Season with salt, transfer to a bowl and serve. —*Dean Fearing*

MAKE AHEAD The onions can be refrigerated for up to 2 days. Reheat gently.

Green Beans with Shallots and Walnuts

 TOTAL: 30 MIN

10 SERVINGS ●●○

- 2½ pounds green beans, cut into 2-inch lengths
- 2 large shallots, thinly sliced
- 3 tablespoons extra-virgin olive oil
- 1 tablespoon fresh lemon juice
- ½ cup chopped toasted walnuts
- Salt and freshly ground pepper

In a large pot of boiling salted water, blanch the beans until bright green, about 3 minutes; drain and pat dry. In a very large, deep skillet, cook the shallots in the olive oil over moderate heat until they are softened, about 5 minutes. Add the beans and cook, tossing, until heated through. Add the lemon juice and walnuts, season with salt and pepper and serve. —*Marcia Kiesel*

Mushroom-Shallot Ragout

TOTAL: 1 HR 15 MIN

4 SERVINGS ●●○

- ½ ounce dried porcini mushrooms (½ cup)
- ½ cup boiling water
- ½ pound large white mushroom caps, cut into eighths
- 1 tablespoon fresh lemon juice
- 3½ tablespoons unsalted butter, ½ tablespoon softened
- 2 tablespoons extra-virgin olive oil
- Salt and freshly ground pepper
- 1 pound chanterelle mushrooms, sliced ½ inch thick
- 2 large shallots, thinly sliced
- 1½ cups mushroom broth or water
- 1 tablespoon all-purpose flour
- 1 garlic clove, minced
- 1 teaspoon chopped thyme
- Soft polenta, for serving

1. In a small heatproof bowl, cover the dried porcini mushrooms with the boiling water. Let stand until softened, 15 minutes.

2. Meanwhile, in a medium bowl, toss the mushroom caps with 2 teaspoons of the lemon juice. In a large skillet, melt 1 tablespoon of butter in 1 tablespoon of the oil until sizzling. Add the mushroom caps and season with salt and pepper. Cover and cook over moderate heat until the liquid released from the mushrooms has evaporated, about 6 minutes. Uncover and cook, stirring occasionally, until browned, about 4 minutes. Transfer to a plate.

3. In the same skillet, melt 2 tablespoons of the butter in the remaining 1 tablespoon of oil. Add the chanterelles and season with salt and pepper. Cover and cook over moderate heat until the mushrooms are swimming in liquid, about 5 minutes. Uncover and cook over moderately high heat until the liquid has evaporated, about 3 minutes. Continue to cook, stirring occasionally, until browned, about 8 minutes. Add the shallots and cook over moderate heat, stirring, until softened, about 4 minutes.

4. With a slotted spoon, transfer the porcini to a board. Chop and add to the chanterelles along with the soaking liquid, stopping before the grit. Add the mushroom broth and caps and simmer over moderate heat until the porcini are soft, 4 minutes.

5. In a small bowl, blend the softened butter with the flour to a smooth paste. Stir in ⅓ cup of the ragout liquid to dissolve the paste, then whisk the mixture into the ragout. Add the garlic, thyme and the remaining 1 teaspoon of lemon juice and simmer over low heat, stirring occasionally, until thickened and glossy, about 4 minutes. Season with salt and pepper and serve with soft polenta. —*Marcia Kiesel*

Green Beans and Salsify with Country Ham and Pecans

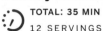 TOTAL: 35 MIN

12 SERVINGS

- 2 pounds green beans, trimmed
- ½ lemon
- 1 pound salsify
- 3 tablespoons vegetable oil
- ¾ cup pecan halves
- 4 ounces country ham, cut into 2-by-¼-inch strips
- ½ tablespoon pure maple syrup
- Salt and freshly ground pepper

1. In a large pot of boiling, salted water, cook the beans until tender, 7 minutes. Transfer to a baking sheet. Keep the water boiling.

2. Squeeze the lemon into a bowl of water. Peel the salsify, slice on the diagonal ½ inch thick and transfer to the lemon water. Drain and add to the boiling water. Cook until just tender, 4 minutes, then drain and pat dry.

3. In a large, deep skillet, heat the oil. Add the pecans and salsify and cook over high heat until browned on the bottom, about 4 minutes. Add the ham, reduce the heat to moderate and cook, stirring, until heated through, 1 minute. Add the beans and cook, stirring, until hot, 3 minutes. Stir in the maple syrup, season with salt and pepper and serve at once. —*Dean Fearing*

Chef Dean Fearing carves holiday turkey.

BRUSSELS SPROUTS WITH CRANBERRY BROWN BUTTER

Smoky Kale and Olives

 TOTAL: 30 MIN

10 SERVINGS ● ●

This Spanish-inspired side dish made with kale and smoky paprika uses very few ingredients but tastes infinitely complex.

- **4 pounds kale, stems discarded**
- **½ cup extra-virgin olive oil**
- **2 teaspoons sweet smoked paprika**
- **½ cup chopped kalamata olives**
- **Salt and freshly ground pepper**

Bring a large pot of water to a boil over high heat. Add the kale and blanch until tender, about 5 minutes; drain well, transfer to a board and chop. In a large, deep skillet, warm the olive oil with the sweet smoked paprika over moderate heat. Add the blanched, chopped kale and cook, tossing, until the kale is heated through. Add the chopped kalamata olives, season with salt and pepper and serve.
—*Marcia Kiesel*

Roasted Brussels Sprouts with Cranberry Brown Butter

ACTIVE: 40 MIN; TOTAL: 1 HR

12 SERVINGS ●

Dallas chef Dean Fearing tops brussels sprouts with a cranberry-maple-butter sauce. "This dish turns a non–brussels sprouts lover to the other side," he says.

- **4 pounds brussels sprouts, halved lengthwise**
- **6 tablespoons extra-virgin olive oil**
- **Kosher salt and freshly ground pepper**
- **½ pound fresh or thawed frozen cranberries**
- **3 tablespoons pure maple syrup**
- **1 tablespoon finely grated fresh ginger**
- **1½ teaspoons finely grated orange zest**
- **2 sticks (½ pound) unsalted butter**
- **1 large shallot, minced**
- **1 teaspoon chopped thyme**

1. Preheat the oven to 400°. On 2 large rimmed baking sheets, toss the brussels sprouts with the oil and season with salt and pepper. Roast for about 40 minutes, stirring halfway through, until the sprouts are tender and browned in spots.

2. Meanwhile, in a small saucepan, combine the cranberries, maple syrup, ginger and orange zest. Cook over moderately low heat, stirring, until the cranberries break down and thicken, about 10 minutes.

3. In a medium skillet, cook the butter over moderately high heat until deep golden, about 4 minutes. Remove from the heat, add the shallot and thyme and stir into the cranberry sauce. Transfer the cranberry butter to a bowl, add the brussels sprouts and toss. Season with salt and serve.
—*Dean Fearing*

MAKE AHEAD The cranberry brown butter can be covered and refrigerated for up to 3 days. Reheat gently.

Sautéed Brussels Sprouts and Squash with Fried Sage

TOTAL: 45 MIN
8 SERVINGS ● ●

The combination of brussels sprouts and butternut squash, which generally stand on their own as side dishes, is unusual and super-autumnal. The brussels sprouts are savory, the chunks of squash are tender and sweet and the fried sage leaves are pungent and crunchy.

¼ cup plus 2 tablespoons
    extra-virgin olive oil
16 large sage leaves
Salt and freshly ground pepper
2 pounds brussels sprouts,
    trimmed and separated
    into individual leaves
1 medium butternut squash
    (1½ pounds), peeled and
    cut into ¾-inch cubes
4 tablespoons unsalted butter
1 tablespoon snipped chives

1. In a small skillet, heat ¼ cup of the oil. Add the sage and fry over high heat until deep green and translucent, about 1 minute. Transfer to a paper towel–lined plate to cool. Season with salt and pepper.

2. Bring a medium saucepan of salted water to a boil over high heat. Fill a large bowl with ice water. Blanch the brussels sprout leaves in the boiling water until tender, about 2 minutes. Using a slotted spoon, transfer the leaves to the ice water to cool. Drain and pat dry.

3. Heat the remaining 2 tablespoons of oil in a large, deep skillet. Add the squash and cook over moderate heat, stirring occasionally, until lightly browned in spots, about 8 minutes. Add the butter and continue cooking until the squash is tender, about 7 minutes longer. Add the brussels sprout leaves, season with salt and pepper and cook until heated through, about 3 minutes. Transfer to a bowl, scatter the fried sage and chives on top and serve. —*Thomas Keller*

Caramelized Broccoli with Garlic

ACTIVE: 15 MIN; TOTAL: 35 MIN
4 SERVINGS ● ● ●

David Gingrass, chef-owner of Two restaurant in San Francisco, swears broccoli haters will love the polarizing green vegetable when it's prepared this way: slowly caramelized to bring out its sweetness, then enlivened with a squeeze of lemon and a pinch of crushed red pepper.

3 tablespoons extra-virgin olive oil
2 medium heads of broccoli
    (1¼ pounds total), stems
    peeled and heads halved
    lengthwise
½ cup water
3 medium garlic cloves,
    very thinly sliced
Pinch of crushed red pepper
Salt and freshly ground
    black pepper
2 tablespoons fresh lemon juice

In a large, deep skillet, heat 2 tablespoons of the olive oil. Add the broccoli cut side down, cover and cook over moderate heat until richly browned on the bottom, about 8 minutes. Pour in the water, cover and cook until the broccoli is just tender and the water has evaporated, about 7 minutes. Add the remaining 1 tablespoon of olive oil along with the sliced garlic and the crushed red pepper and cook uncovered, stirring a few times, until the garlic is golden brown, about 3 minutes. Season the broccoli with salt and black pepper, drizzle with the fresh lemon juice and serve. —*David Gingrass*

Roasted Garlic-Parmigiano Broccoli

TOTAL: 30 MIN
12 SERVINGS ● ●

Roasting broccoli makes it sweet; topping it with lots of grated Parmigiano-Reggiano cheese and broiling it makes it addictively crispy and almost nutty tasting.

1 stick unsalted butter, softened
2 large garlic cloves,
    very thinly sliced
¾ cup freshly grated
    Parmigiano-Reggiano cheese
Salt and freshly ground pepper
4 pounds broccoli, cut into
    long spears and stems peeled
¼ cup plus 2 tablespoons
    extra-virgin olive oil

1. Preheat the oven to 425°. Position racks in the upper and lower thirds of the oven. In a food processor, pulse the butter with the garlic and cheese until smooth. Scrape the garlic-cheese butter into a small bowl and season lightly with salt and pepper.

2. In a large bowl, toss the broccoli with the olive oil and season with salt and pepper. Spread on 2 large rimmed baking sheets and roast for 10 to 15 minutes, stirring once and shifting the pans from top to bottom and front to back halfway through, until the broccoli is crisp-tender and browned on the bottom.

3. Preheat the broiler. Return the broccoli spears to the bowl and toss with the garlic-cheese butter. Transfer the broccoli to the baking sheets, scraping all of the butter in the bowl onto the spears. Broil one pan at a time 6 inches from the heat for 2 to 3 minutes, until the butter is golden in spots. Transfer the roasted broccoli to a platter and serve. —*Grace Parisi*

TECHNIQUE

roasting cauliflower

The roasted broccoli recipe above is also wonderful when made with cauliflower florets. If you prefer, substitute grated Manchego for the Parmigiano-Reggiano cheese.

Fragrant Cauliflower in Tomato Sauce

ACTIVE: 20 MIN; TOTAL: 50 MIN

12 SERVINGS ● ● ●

It takes only a few minutes to get this richly flavored, saucy cauliflower dish simmering on the stove. Consider buying precut cauliflower florets to make it even quicker.

- 6 tablespoons unsalted butter
- 2 heads cauliflower (4 pounds), cut into 1½-inch florets
- 2 medium onions, halved lengthwise and thinly sliced crosswise

Salt and freshly ground
    black pepper
- 1 teaspoon turmeric
- ½ teaspoon cumin seeds
- ½ teaspoon cayenne pepper

One 4-inch cinnamon stick
- 2 cups tomato puree
- 1 cup water
- 1½ cups frozen baby peas

1. In a very large, deep skillet, melt the butter. Add the cauliflower and cook over moderately high heat until browned in spots, about 5 minutes. Add the onions, season with salt and black pepper and cook until the onions are softened, about 2 minutes. Stir in the turmeric, cumin seeds, cayenne and cinnamon stick and cook until fragrant, about 1 minute. Add the tomato puree and the water and bring to a simmer. Cover and cook over moderately low heat until the cauliflower is tender, about 15 minutes.

2. Stir the frozen peas into the cauliflower mixture and simmer uncovered over moderate heat until the sauce is thick, about 5 minutes. Remove and discard the cinnamon stick, then season the cauliflower with salt and black pepper. Transfer the cauliflower to a bowl and serve hot or warm. —*Melissa Rubel*

MAKE AHEAD The Fragrant Cauliflower in Tomato Sauce can be refrigerated overnight. Rewarm over moderate heat.

Cauliflower Pilaf

ACTIVE: 45 MIN; TOTAL: 1 HR 30 MIN

8 SERVINGS ●

This aromatic side dish was born out of an argument between chef and cookbook author Bruce Aidells and his wife, Nancy Oakes, executive chef of San Francisco's Boulevard: Could an entire head of cauliflower be filled with rice, like dolma, the Middle Eastern family of stuffed dishes? "Nancy thought it could be done; I didn't," Aidells says. He turns the idea of dolma inside out by topping a rice casserole with cauliflower florets. "I'm the lazy, more practical cook. That's why Nancy has the big fancy restaurant."

- 2 heads of cauliflower, cored (about 5 pounds total)
- ¼ cup extra-virgin olive oil

Salt and freshly ground pepper
- ½ cup pine nuts
- 1 large onion, finely chopped
- 1 teaspoon ground turmeric
- 1½ cups basmati rice
- 2½ cups low-sodium chicken broth
- ½ cup dried currants
- ¼ cup chopped cilantro
- 3 tablespoons unsalted butter, melted
- ½ teaspoon pimentón de la Vera (smoked Spanish paprika)

1. Preheat the oven to 425°. Separate 1 head of cauliflower into 2-inch florets and the other into 1-inch florets. On a large rimmed baking sheet, toss the 1-inch florets with 3 tablespoons of the oil and season with salt and pepper. Roast the cauliflower for about 15 minutes, stirring occasionally, until golden in spots and tender.

2. Meanwhile, bring a pot of salted water to a boil. Add the 2-inch cauliflower florets and cook until tender, about 15 minutes. Drain and pat dry.

3. Spread the pine nuts in a pie plate and toast until golden, about 5 minutes.

4. In a large, deep skillet, heat the remaining 1 tablespoon of olive oil. Add the onion and cook over moderate heat, stirring occasionally, until softened and just beginning to brown, about 10 minutes. Add the turmeric and rice and stir to coat. Stir in the chicken broth and ½ teaspoon of salt and bring to a boil. Cover tightly and cook over low heat until the broth is absorbed and the rice is tender, about 20 minutes.

5. Transfer the rice to a large bowl. Fold in the roasted cauliflower, toasted pine nuts, currants and cilantro. Spoon the rice into a 2½- to 3-quart soufflé dish and press lightly on the top. Arrange the boiled cauliflower florets on top.

6. In a small bowl, combine the melted butter and paprika. Brush half of the butter mixture over the cauliflower and bake for about 15 minutes, until heated through.

7. Preheat the broiler. Brush the cauliflower with the remaining butter and broil about 6 inches from the heat until lightly browned, about 5 minutes. Serve hot or warm.

—*Bruce Aidells*

Cumin-Scented White Rice

ACTIVE: 10 MIN; TOTAL: 40 MIN

10 SERVINGS ●

For such a simple dish, this fragrant white rice is ridiculously good. Stirred in a thin layer of pork fat and simmered with cumin seeds and bay leaves, the grains take on an alluring smoky-sweet flavor and a nutty texture. Serve with either chili or mole.

- 3 tablespoons lard or vegetable shortening
- 1 garlic clove, minced
- ½ small onion, diced
- 1 teaspoon cumin seeds
- 2 bay leaves
- 2 cups long-grain white rice
- 2½ cups water
- 1 teaspoon salt

Heat the lard in a saucepan. Add the garlic and onion and cook over moderate heat, stirring occasionally, until the vegetables are translucent, about 5 minutes. Stir in the cumin and bay leaves and cook until the cumin is fragrant, about 2 minutes. Add the rice, stirring to coat with the lard. Add the water and salt; bring to a simmer. Cover and cook over low heat for 18 minutes. Remove from the heat and let stand, covered, for 10 minutes. Fluff the rice with a fork, discard the bay leaves and serve. —Stephanie Valentine

Toasted-Coconut Basmati Rice

TOTAL: 25 MIN
12 SERVINGS ● ●

To make this recipe easier, buy steamed basmati rice from an Indian restaurant.

4½ cups water
 4 ounces basmati rice (2¼ cups)
 1 tablespoon kosher salt
 3 cardamom pods, gently crushed
 ¾ cup slivered almonds
 ¾ cup shredded unsweetened
   coconut

1. In a large saucepan, bring the water to a boil. Stir in the rice, salt and cardamom pods and cover. Reduce the heat to low and cook for 15 minutes without removing the lid. Remove the saucepan from the heat and let stand, covered, for 5 minutes.

2. Meanwhile, in a medium skillet, toast the almonds over moderate heat, stirring, until golden, about 5 minutes. Transfer to a plate to cool. In the same skillet, toast the coconut until golden, about 4 minutes. Transfer to the plate with the almonds.

3. Using a fork, fluff the rice. Remove the cardamom pods. Stir the toasted almonds and coconut into the rice and serve. —Melissa Rubel

Tortilla–Corn Bread Dressing

ACTIVE: 1 HR 30 MIN;
TOTAL: 3 HR 30 MIN
12 SERVINGS ● ●

"My sister Amy Reisner will not come over for Thanksgiving unless I serve my tortilla dressing," says Dallas chef Dean Fearing. His delicious twist on corn bread stuffing is a kind of Thanksgiving *chilaquiles,*

combining crispy fried tortilla strips with crumbled corn bread, jalapeño and cilantro. "If I didn't serve tortilla dressing at Thanksgiving, it would be like a birthday party without the cake," he says.

Vegetable oil, for frying
Fourteen 6-inch corn tortillas, halved
   and cut into ¼-inch strips
 6 cups crumbled Skillet Corn
   Bread (p. 354) or store-bought
   corn bread
 2 tablespoons extra-virgin olive oil,
   plus more for the baking dish
 1 large onion, cut into ¼-inch dice
 2 celery ribs, cut into ¼-inch dice
 2 garlic cloves, minced
 1 large jalapeño, seeded
   and very finely chopped
 1 tablespoon very finely
   chopped cilantro
 2 teaspoons finely chopped sage
 2 teaspoons finely chopped thyme
 2 teaspoons chile powder
 1 quart Tortilla Broth
   (recipe follows)
Kosher salt

1. In a large saucepan, heat 2 inches of vegetable oil to 350°. Working in batches, fry the tortilla strips over moderately high heat, stirring a few times, until golden and crisp, 3 minutes. Using a slotted spoon, transfer to paper towels to drain. Put the strips in a bowl and add the Skillet Corn Bread.

2. In a large, deep skillet, heat the 2 tablespoons of olive oil. Add the onion and celery and cook over moderate heat, stirring, until softened, about 6 minutes. Add the garlic and jalapeño and cook until fragrant, about 1 minute. Stir in the cilantro, sage, thyme and chile powder and cook until the chile powder is fragrant, about 1 minute.

3. Add the Tortilla Broth to the skillet and bring to a simmer over moderate heat. Pour the mixture over the tortilla strips and corn bread, season with salt and toss gently to coat. Let stand until the broth has been absorbed, about 30 minutes.

4. Preheat the oven to 350°. Lightly oil a 9-by-13-inch baking dish. Transfer the dressing to the prepared dish and cover with foil. Bake for about 20 minutes, until heated through. Uncover and bake for about 15 minutes longer, until the top begins to brown. Serve. —Dean Fearing

MAKE AHEAD The unbaked dressing can be refrigerated for up to 2 days. Bring to room temperature before baking.

TORTILLA BROTH

ACTIVE: 20 MIN; TOTAL: 50 MIN
MAKES 1 QUART ●

This key component of the tortilla dressing, prepared with garlic-infused corn tortillas and tomatoes, also makes a delicious soup topped with chicken (or leftover turkey) and torn-up fried tortillas.

 3 tablespoons vegetable oil
Two 6-inch corn tortillas, chopped
 3 garlic cloves, peeled
 1 medium onion, minced
 1 cup canned tomato puree
 5 cups chicken stock
 1 tablespoon chile powder
 1 bay leaf
 ½ tablespoon ground cumin
Pinch of cayenne pepper
Salt

1. In a large saucepan, heat the oil. Add the chopped tortillas and garlic and cook over moderately high heat, stirring occasionally, until the tortillas are crisp and the garlic is browned, about 3 minutes.

2. Add the minced onion to the saucepan along with the tomato puree and bring to a boil. Add the stock, chile powder, bay leaf and cumin and bring to a boil. Simmer over low heat until reduced to 1 quart, about 30 minutes. Discard the bay leaf.

3. Working in batches, puree the mixture in a blender. Add a pinch of cayenne and season with salt. —D.F.

MAKE AHEAD The Tortilla Broth can be made ahead and refrigerated for up to 3 days or frozen for 1 month.

perfect tomato sauce

The secret to excellent tomato sauce? The trick is starting with superlative whole (not crushed) tomatoes and simmering them with whole (not chopped) garlic cloves. The result: a classic marinara that can quickly be spun into all sorts of variations. —*Grace Parisi*

Classic Marinara Sauce

⏱ **ACTIVE: 10 MIN; TOTAL: 40 MIN**
MAKES 3 CUPS (ENOUGH FOR 1 POUND OF PASTA) ● ● ○

- ¼ cup extra-virgin olive oil
- 3 garlic cloves, peeled
- 1 tablespoon tomato paste

One 35-ounce can whole peeled Italian tomatoes with their juices, crushed by hand

Pinch of sugar

- 2 basil sprigs

Salt and freshly ground pepper

In a large saucepan, heat the olive oil. Add the garlic cloves and cook over moderate heat, stirring occasionally, until golden, about 5 minutes. Add the tomato paste and cook, stirring, for 1 minute. Add the crushed canned tomatoes with their juices. Stir in the sugar and basil sprigs, season with salt and pepper and bring to a boil. Simmer the sauce over low heat, stirring occasionally, until it has thickened and is reduced to 3 cups, about 30 minutes. Taste and season again with salt and pepper. Remove and discard the basil sprigs and garlic cloves and serve. —*G.P.*

MAKE AHEAD The Classic Marinara Sauce can be refrigerated for up to 3 days.

---

three more fantastic sauces

1 All'Amatriciana Sauce
This spicy, pancetta-studded sauce is great with shellfish and bucatini, the hollow, spaghetti-like pasta.

Slice 3 ounces of pancetta ¼ inch thick, then cut the slices into ¼-inch dice. Sauté the diced pancetta and ½ teaspoon of crushed red pepper with the garlic.

2 Puttanesca Sauce
The combination of anchovies, olives and capers gives this Neapolitan-style sauce a robust flavor.

Sauté 6 anchovy fillets and ¼ teaspoon of crushed red pepper with the garlic; add ¼ cup of chopped kalamata olives and 2 tablespoons of drained capers with the basil.

3 Vodka Sauce
Vodka enhances the flavors in this popular Italian American sauce.

Sauté 2 ounces of diced pancetta and ¼ teaspoon of crushed red pepper with the garlic; deglaze with ¼ cup of vodka; stir in ¼ cup of heavy cream after discarding the basil and garlic; simmer for 5 minutes.

Skillet Corn Bread

ACTIVE: 10 MIN; TOTAL: 30 MIN
MAKES ONE 9-INCH CORN
BREAD OR 8 CUPS CRUMBLED
CORN BREAD ● ● ○

- 1½ tablespoons vegetable oil
- ¾ cup all-purpose flour
- 3 tablespoons sugar
- 1 tablespoon baking powder
- 1 teaspoon salt
- 1¼ cups cornmeal, preferably stone-ground
- 1 cup milk
- 2 large eggs, lightly beaten
- 3 tablespoons unsalted butter, melted

1. Preheat the oven to 425°. Warm a 9-inch cast-iron skillet over moderate heat. Add the oil and heat.

2. Meanwhile, in a bowl, sift the flour with the sugar, baking powder and salt. Stir in the cornmeal. Add the milk and eggs and stir lightly. Add the butter and stir just until blended. Scrape the batter into the hot skillet; the oil should bubble. Transfer to the oven and bake for about 18 minutes, or until the center springs back when gently pressed. Turn the corn bread out onto a rack to cool. —*Grace Parisi*

MAKE AHEAD The unmolded corn bread can stand at room temperature for 2 days.

TECHNIQUE

toasting grains

Toasting grains like farro, barley or millet in a dry pan until fragrant (as for the wheat berries at right) gives them a deeper flavor. It also speeds the cooking and helps keep the grains' texture fluffy once liquid is added. This technique is also known as parching.

Oven Fries with Roasted Garlic

ACTIVE: 20 MIN; TOTAL: 50 MIN
6 SERVINGS ● ● ●

- 3 large Yukon Gold potatoes (1¾ pounds), halved lengthwise and cut into ½-inch-thick wedges
- 8 unpeeled garlic cloves
- 3 tablespoons extra-virgin olive oil
- Salt and freshly ground pepper
- 2 teaspoons chopped thyme
- ¼ cup parsley leaves

Preheat the oven to 425°. On a large rimmed baking sheet, toss the potatoes and garlic cloves with the olive oil. Spread the potatoes in an even layer cut side down. Season with salt and pepper and sprinkle with the chopped thyme. Bake for about 30 minutes, or until the potatoes are browned on the bottom and very crisp. Peel the garlic cloves. Transfer the potatoes and garlic to a platter, sprinkle with the parsley leaves and serve.
—*Jan Birnbaum*

Toasted Wheat Berries with Pancetta and Roasted Apples

ACTIVE: 40 MIN; TOTAL: 3 HR 30 MIN
8 SERVINGS

Nutty-flavored wheat berries (whole, unhulled wheat kernels) are particularly delicious in this recipe, combined with crispy pancetta, sweet-tart oven-roasted apples and a syrupy reduction of apple cider and cider vinegar.

- 1½ cups wheat berries
- 12 cups water
- ½ pound thinly sliced pancetta
- 5 Fuji apples—peeled, halved, cored and cut into 8 wedges each (2½ pounds)
- 2 tablespoons extra-virgin olive oil
- 3 medium shallots, very thinly sliced
- 3 medium garlic cloves, very thinly sliced
- 2 cups fresh apple cider

- 1 tablespoon cider vinegar
- 2 tablespoons unsalted butter
- Salt and freshly ground black pepper
- ½ cup flat-leaf parsley leaves

1. Preheat the oven to 350°. In a large saucepan, toast the wheat berries over moderate heat, stirring constantly, until they are fragrant, 5 minutes. Add 6 cups of water and bring to a boil. Remove from the heat, cover the pot and let the wheat berries sit off the heat for 1 hour.

2. Meanwhile, arrange the pancetta slices in a single layer on a large rimmed baking sheet. Bake for 20 minutes, until the slices are browned and crisp. Using tongs, transfer the crispy pancetta to a plate to cool, first shaking the slices over the baking sheet to release any excess fat onto the baking sheet.

3. Toss the apple wedges with the pancetta fat in the baking sheet and arrange them on the baking sheet in a single layer. Bake the apples for about 1½ hours, turning once, until tender.

4. Meanwhile, drain the wheat berries. Heat the olive oil in the saucepan. Add the sliced shallots and garlic and cook over moderate heat, stirring, until softened, about 3 minutes. Add the drained wheat berries and remaining 6 cups of water and bring to a boil over high heat. Reduce the heat to low, cover and simmer until the wheat berries are tender, about 45 minutes.

5. While the wheat berries simmer, combine the apple cider and cider vinegar in a large saucepan and bring to a boil over high heat. Boil until reduced to a syrup, about 15 minutes. Remove from the heat and swirl in the butter.

6. Drain the wheat berries and transfer them to a large serving bowl. Scrape in the reduced apple cider mixture and toss well. Chop the crisped pancetta and fold it in along with the roasted apple wedges. Season with salt and black pepper, garnish with parsley and serve. —*Octavio Becerra*

OVEN FRIES WITH ROASTED GARLIC

BUTTERNUT SQUASH BREAD PUDDING

MAKE AHEAD The crisped pancetta can be stored at room temperature for up to 4 hours. The roasted apples can be stored at room temperature for up to 3 hours; rewarm in the oven before proceeding.

Butternut Squash Bread Pudding

ACTIVE: 40 MIN; TOTAL: 2 HR 15 MIN

10 SERVINGS ● ○

This savory bread pudding, loaded with sweet butternut squash, is based on a recipe that meat master Bruce Aidells's wife, Nancy Oakes, created at her San Francisco restaurant, Boulevard. Aidells bakes the pudding in individual ramekins, which makes for a very elegant presentation. It's great with his Dr Pepper–Glazed Ham with Prunes (p. 326).

- 2 **medium butternut squash (about 1½ pounds each)—halved lengthwise, seeded and peeled**
- 2 **tablespoons unsalted butter, melted**
- 2 **tablespoons extra-virgin olive oil**
- **Salt**
- **Pinch of freshly grated nutmeg**
- **Pinch of cinnamon**
- 2 **tablespoons pure maple syrup**
- 3 **cups half-and-half**
- 6 **large eggs, beaten**
- ½ **cup freshly grated Parmigiano-Reggiano cheese**
- **Freshly ground pepper**
- 1½ **baguettes, crusts trimmed and bread cut into ½-inch cubes (8 cups)**

1. Preheat the oven to 400°. Butter a shallow 3-quart baking dish. Thinly slice the bulbous parts of the squash into crescents and arrange them in a single layer on a rimmed baking sheet. Cut the necks of the squash into ½-inch cubes and spread them on another baking sheet.

2. In a small bowl, combine the butter and olive oil. Lightly brush the squash crescents with the butter mixture and season with salt. Drizzle the remaining butter over the diced squash and sprinkle with salt, nutmeg and cinnamon. Roast the squash for about 10 minutes, turning once, until softened and lightly browned in spots. Drizzle with the maple syrup and roast for about 5 minutes longer. Let cool.

3. In a bowl, whisk the half-and-half with the eggs, grated cheese and a pinch each of salt and pepper. Add the bread and squash cubes; toss gently. Spoon the mixture into the prepared baking dish and arrange the squash crescents on top. Bake the bread pudding for 1 hour, until the top is golden in spots and the center is firm. Let cool for 15 minutes before serving.
—*Bruce Aidells*

MAKE AHEAD The bread pudding can be refrigerated overnight. Rewarm at 350°.

●HEALTHY ●MAKE AHEAD ·VEGETARIAN ●STAFF FAVORITE

For Thanksgiving, F&W's Melissa Rubel serves Indian-Spiced Turkey Breast (p. 316) and Pumpkin and Yellow Split Pea Soup (p. 288).

Creamy Refried Beans

ACTIVE: 45 MIN; TOTAL: 1 HR 30 MIN
PLUS 2 DAYS SOAKING AND RESTING
10 SERVINGS ● ●

This sublimely silken puree, gently infused with oregano and black pepper, bears blessed little resemblance to the version that comes out of a can. Letting the cooked whole pinto beans soak overnight before frying them makes the resulting puree that much softer and smoother.

1 pound dried pinto beans,
   soaked overnight in water
   and drained
1 small onion, halved
1 small head of garlic, halved
2 oregano sprigs
¼ cup lard or vegetable
   shortening
Salt and freshly ground
   black pepper

1. In a large pot, combine the pinto beans, halved onion and garlic and oregano sprigs. Add cold water to cover by 2 inches and bring to a boil over high heat. Reduce the heat to low and simmer until the pinto beans are completely tender, about 45 minutes. Let the beans cool to room temperature. Remove and discard the onion, garlic and oregano. Refrigerate the beans in their cooking liquid overnight.

2. Drain the beans, reserving 1 cup of their cooking liquid. Working in batches, puree the pinto beans in a food processor, adding some of the reserved cooking liquid if necessary to achieve a smooth puree.

3. In a large saucepan, heat the lard over moderate heat. Add the pureed beans and their reserved liquid and cook over moderate heat, stirring frequently, until the puree thickens, about 20 minutes. Season the puree with salt and black pepper and serve the refried beans immediately.
—*Stephanie Valentine*

MAKE AHEAD The refried beans can be made in advance, covered and refrigerated for up to 3 days.

Avocado Relish with Caramelized Onions

 TOTAL: 35 MIN
12 SERVINGS ● ● ○

Dean Fearing, chef at Fearing's in the Dallas Ritz-Carlton, serves this chunky avocado and sweet onion condiment with turkey as a creamy, unexpected alternative to cranberry sauce at Thanksgiving dinner. Fearing likes the Southwestern richness the relish adds to turkey, particularly the lean breast meat; it's also terrific served along with his delicious Tortilla–Corn Bread Dressing (p. 351).

1 tablespoon vegetable oil
1 medium onion, cut into
   ¾-inch dice
Salt
Juice of 2 limes
2 medium garlic cloves,
   very finely chopped
1 red bell pepper, cut into
   ¾-inch dice
1 jalapeño, seeded and very
   finely chopped
4 large Hass avocados,
   cut into ¾-inch dice
1 tablespoon slivered
   basil leaves

1. In a medium skillet, heat the vegetable oil. Add the diced onion, season with salt and cook over moderate heat, stirring occasionally, until richly browned, about 10 minutes; let cool.

2. In a large bowl, combine the sautéed onion with the fresh lime juice, chopped garlic, diced red bell pepper and chopped jalapeño. Gently fold in the diced Hass avocado and slivered basil. Season with salt and serve the avocado relish at room temperature. —*Dean Fearing*

MAKE AHEAD The Avocado Relish with Caramelized Onions can be refrigerated overnight; press plastic wrap directly onto the relish to keep the avocado from discoloring. Bring the relish to room temperature before serving.

Cranberry Sauce with Spiced Pumpkin Seeds

TOTAL: 30 MIN
MAKES 5 CUPS ● ● ○

F&W's Marcia Kiesel adds delightful crunch and nutty flavor to traditional cranberry sauce by folding in pumpkin seeds roasted with cumin and paprika.

1½ pounds fresh or
   frozen cranberries
2 cups sugar
1½ cups water
Pinch of ground cinnamon
¾ cup raw pumpkin seeds
1 teaspoon vegetable oil
½ teaspoon sweet paprika
¼ teaspoon ground cumin
Salt and freshly ground
   black pepper

1. Preheat the oven to 350°. In a medium saucepan, combine the cranberries, sugar and water and bring to a boil over high heat, stirring to dissolve the sugar. Continue to boil, stirring occasionally, until the cranberries pop, about 10 minutes. Remove the saucepan from the heat and let the cranberry sauce cool until it is just warm; stir in the ground cinnamon.

2. On a large rimmed baking sheet, toss the raw pumpkin seeds with the vegetable oil. In a small bowl, whisk together the sweet paprika and ground cumin; toss the spice mixture with the pumpkin seeds. Spread the seeds in an even layer on the baking sheet and sprinkle with salt and black pepper. Bake for about 8 minutes, until the seeds are lightly browned. Let them cool completely. Just before serving, stir the spice-roasted pumpkin seeds into the cranberry sauce and serve.
—*Marcia Kiesel*

MAKE AHEAD The cranberry sauce can be refrigerated for up to 1 week. The pumpkin seeds can be roasted up to 1 day ahead; store in an airtight container. Bring the cranberry sauce to room temperature and fold in the seeds just before serving.

desserts & brunch

desserts

Moscato-Roasted Pears and Cider-Poached Apples

TOTAL: 1 HR

4 SERVINGS ●

4 semiripe Bartlett pears

Confectioners' sugar, for dusting

2 tablespoons unsalted butter

¾ cup Moscato d'Asti

½ cup Poire Williams

½ cup fresh apple cider

1 large Fuji apple, cored and sliced ⅛ inch thick

Cinnamon, for dusting

Sweetened whipped cream, for serving

1. Preheat the oven to 400°. Quarter and core the pears and place them in a large bowl; dust the pears generously with confectioners' sugar. In a large ovenproof nonstick skillet, melt the butter. Add the sugar-dusted pear quarters to the skillet cut side down and cook them over high heat until their cut sides are richly browned, about 10 minutes.

2. Turn the pears skin side down. Pour in the Moscato d'Asti. Transfer the skillet to the oven and roast until the pears are tender and the Moscato has reduced to a syrup, about 18 minutes. Transfer the pears to a large platter.

3. Add the Poire Williams to the skillet and boil for about 3 minutes, stirring with a sturdy wooden spoon and scraping up any browned bits from the bottom. Add the cider and bring to a boil. Add the apple slices, cover and simmer over low heat, turning once, until the apple slices are translucent, about 5 minutes. Uncover and simmer until the cider has reduced to a syrup. Spoon the apples into shallow bowls and top them with the pear wedges. Dust with cinnamon and serve with whipped cream. —*Marcia Kiesel*

Blackberry and Apple Crisp with Nut Topping

ACTIVE: 15 MIN; TOTAL: 1 HR

6 SERVINGS ● ● ○

Andrew Murray, winemaker and owner of an eponymous vineyard in Los Olivos, California, makes the topping for this easy dessert extra-crunchy by using a combination of oats and nuts. In summer, in place of the blackberries, Murray substitutes huckleberries, which he picks with his kids during their family vacations in Idaho.

3 Fuji apples—peeled, cored and sliced ¼ inch thick

1½ cups fresh or frozen blackberries

¼ cup granulated sugar

½ cup plus 2 tablespoons all-purpose flour

⅓ cup rolled oats

⅓ cup whole almonds and pecans, coarsely chopped

3 tablespoons light brown sugar

½ teaspoon cinnamon

3 tablespoons butter, softened

1. Preheat the oven to 350°. Oil an 8-by-8-inch glass baking dish. In a large bowl, toss the sliced apples with the blackberries, granulated sugar and 2 tablespoons of the flour. Scrape the filling into the prepared baking dish.

2. In another large bowl, toss the rolled oats with the remaining ½ cup of flour and the chopped nuts, brown sugar and cinnamon. Add the butter and rub it in thoroughly. Sprinkle the topping over the filling and bake for 35 minutes, until the filling is bubbling and the topping is browned. Let cool for 10 minutes before serving. —*Andrew Murray*

MAKE AHEAD The crisp can be made up to 4 hours ahead.

MOSCATO-ROASTED PEARS AND
CIDER-POACHED APPLES

Texas State Fair Pecan Pie

ACTIVE: 40 MIN; TOTAL: 3 HR 30 MIN
PLUS COOLING

MAKES ONE 10-INCH PIE ● ●

PIE SHELL

- 2 cups all-purpose flour
- 1 tablespoon granulated sugar
- 1 teaspoon salt
- 1 stick plus 4 tablespoons unsalted butter, cut into ½-inch dice
- ¼ cup plus 1 tablespoon ice water

FILLING

- 1½ cups pecan halves (5½ ounces)
- 1½ sticks cold unsalted butter
- 1½ cups dark brown sugar
- ¾ cup granulated sugar
- ½ cup light corn syrup
- 3 tablespoons whole milk
- 2 tablespoons all-purpose flour
- ½ vanilla bean, split, seeds scraped
- ½ teaspoon salt
- 4 large eggs

Unsweetened whipped cream or vanilla ice cream, for serving

1. MAKE THE PIE SHELL: In a food processor, pulse the flour with the sugar and salt. Add the butter and pulse until it is the size of small peas. Add the ice water and pulse until evenly moistened. Knead on a floured surface 2 or 3 times. Form into a disk, wrap in plastic and refrigerate until firm, 1 hour.
2. Preheat the oven to 350°. On a floured surface, roll out the pastry ⅛ inch thick; transfer to a deep 10-inch glass pie plate and trim the overhang to ½ inch. Fold the edge under and crimp the edges. Prick the bottom with a fork. Freeze for 30 minutes.
3. Line the shell with parchment and fill with pie weights. Bake for 25 minutes, or until lightly browned at the edge. Remove the paper and weights and bake for 15 minutes, or until lightly golden. Leave the oven on.
4. MEANWHILE, MAKE THE FILLING: In a pie plate, toast the pecans for 8 minutes, or until lightly browned. Let cool.
5. In a medium saucepan, melt the butter. Add the brown sugar, granulated sugar, corn syrup, milk, flour, vanilla seeds and salt. Cook over moderate heat just until the mixture comes to a boil. Remove from the heat and let stand for 5 minutes.
6. In a bowl, lightly beat the eggs. Gradually whisk in the hot sugar mixture. Spread the pecans in the pie shell and pour the filling on top. Bake for 45 minutes, or until the center is barely set and the crust is golden brown. Cool on a rack. Serve with whipped cream or ice cream. —*Dean Fearing*

Grandma Zerr's Apricot Kuchen

ACTIVE: 1 HR 30 MIN; TOTAL: 3 HR
30 MIN PLUS OVERNIGHT CHILLING

MAKES FOUR 9-INCH KUCHENS ● ●

DOUGH

- 1¼ cups whole milk
- 1 envelope active dry yeast
- 1 large egg
- 4 cups all-purpose flour, plus more for rolling
- ⅓ cup sugar
- 1 teaspoon salt
- 1½ sticks unsalted butter, softened

PASTRY CREAM

- ¼ cup all-purpose flour
- ½ cup sugar
- 1½ cups whole milk
- 2 large eggs
- 1 teaspoon pure vanilla extract
- 1 pound dried Turkish apricots— soaked in boiling water for 1 hour, drained and patted dry

TOPPING

- ¾ cup sugar
- 3 tablespoons all-purpose flour
- 3 tablespoons unsalted butter, softened

Pinch of cinnamon

INGREDIENT

fresh fruit all year long

Long after the growing season, these three packaged foods capture the harvest's best fruit in various ways: preserved, pureed and frozen.

FRUIT MUSTARD
Ingrid Oswald blends mustard with fruit and spirits—strawberries and vodka, figs and grappa—in a single tangy condiment (formaggiokitchen.com).

FRUIT PUREE
Favored by mixologists, Funkin fruit purees come in 21 flavors and are great in cocktails, smoothies and salad dressings—or over ice cream (funkin.co.uk).

FROZEN FRUIT
Stahlbush Island Farms' quick-frozen fruits and vegetables, like cranberries from Oregon's Willamette Valley, are sustainably grown (stahlbush.com).

1. MAKE THE DOUGH: Heat the milk to 110° and transfer it to a bowl. Stir in the yeast and let stand 5 minutes. Stir in the egg. In a standing mixer fitted with a dough hook, mix the 4 cups of flour with the sugar and salt; add the warm milk mixture and knead at medium-low speed until a stiff dough forms, 3 minutes. Add the butter and knead at medium speed until the dough is silky and soft, 5 minutes. Transfer to a buttered bowl, cover and refrigerate overnight.

2. MEANWHILE, MAKE THE PASTRY CREAM: In a medium bowl, whisk the flour with ¼ cup of the sugar and ¼ cup of the milk. Whisk in the eggs and vanilla. In a saucepan, heat the remaining 1¼ cups of milk and ¼ cup of sugar over moderate heat until the sugar dissolves. Gradually whisk the hot milk into the egg mixture, then cook the mixture in the saucepan over moderate heat, whisking, until thickened and no floury taste remains, 4 minutes. Transfer to a bowl; lay plastic wrap directly onto the surface. Refrigerate overnight.

3. Butter four 9-inch pie plates. Divide the dough into 4 and flatten into disks. On a floured surface, roll each disk of dough to a 9½-inch round. Place each in a pie plate, making sure the dough doesn't extend past the rims. Cover the pie plates with plastic wrap and let stand at room temperature until the dough has risen slightly, 1 hour.

4. Preheat the oven to 350° and set racks in the upper and lower thirds. Lightly press the dough to deflate it. Arrange the apricots on the bottom in a single layer. Spread the pastry cream evenly over them.

5. MAKE THE TOPPING: In a medium bowl, rub the sugar with the flour and butter until the texture is sandy. Sprinkle over the pastry cream and dust lightly with cinnamon. Bake the *kuchens* for 40 minutes, until the crusts are deeply golden. Cool on a rack before serving. —*Nancy Olson*

MAKE AHEAD The baked *kuchens* can be wrapped in foil and frozen for up to 1 month. Rewarm before serving.

TEXAS STATE FAIR PECAN PIE

GRANDMA ZERR'S APRICOT KUCHEN

TORTA DELLA NONNA

CANTUCCI DI PRATO

Torta della Nonna

ACTIVE: 30 MIN; TOTAL: 2 HR

8 SERVINGS ● ●

PASTRY

3 cups all-purpose flour

½ cup sugar

1 teaspoon baking powder

Finely grated zest of 1 lemon

¼ teaspoon salt

1 stick plus 6 tablespoons unsalted butter (7 ounces), softened

2 large eggs

4 large egg yolks

PASTRY CREAM

2 cups milk

½ cup sugar

½ vanilla bean, scraped

Two 2-by-1-inch strips of lemon zest

5 large egg yolks

⅓ cup all-purpose flour

Toasted pine nuts and fresh berries, for serving

1. MAKE THE PASTRY: In a food processor, combine the flour, sugar, baking powder, lemon zest and salt. Add the butter in clumps and pulse until the mixture resembles coarse meal. Add the whole eggs and egg yolks and pulse a few times, until the dough just comes together. Turn the pastry dough out onto a lightly floured work surface and knead it 2 or 3 times, just until it comes together. Divide the pastry dough into 2 pieces, 1 slightly smaller than the other. Pat the pastry dough into disks, wrap each disk in plastic and refrigerate for at least 30 minutes.

2. MEANWHILE, MAKE THE PASTRY CREAM: In a medium saucepan, heat the milk with ¼ cup of the sugar, the vanilla bean and seeds and the lemon zest until hot. In a medium bowl, whisk the egg yolks with the remaining ¼ cup of sugar until blended. Stir in the flour until incorporated. Whisk in the hot milk in a thin stream.

3. Set a fine-mesh strainer over another medium bowl. Pour the pastry cream mixture into the medium saucepan and cook over moderate heat, whisking, until it is thick and bubbling, about 2 minutes. Immediately strain the pastry cream into the bowl, scraping the strainer with a rubber spatula. Press a sheet of plastic wrap directly onto the surface of the pastry cream in the bowl and refrigerate until chilled, about 1 to 2 hours.

4. Preheat the oven to 350°. Butter and flour a 10-inch fluted tart pan with a removable bottom. On a lightly floured work surface, roll out the larger disk of pastry to an ⅛-inch-thick round. Ease the pastry into the tart pan, pressing the dough into the corners. Don't trim the overhang.

5. Spread the chilled pastry cream in the tart shell in an even layer. Roll out the remaining pastry disk to an ⅛-inch-thick round and set it over the tart; gently press

out any air bubbles. Carefully roll the rolling pin over the tart pan rim to cut off the overhanging dough. Gently press the edge together to seal the tart.

6. Bake the tart in the lower third of the oven for about 40 minutes, until the crust is golden brown; rotate the tart pan halfway through baking. Let the tart cool completely in the pan. Unmold the tart and transfer it to a large serving plate. Sprinkle the tart with toasted pine nuts, cut into wedges and serve with fresh berries.
—*Joe Sponzo*

MAKE AHEAD The tart can be made earlier in the day.

Cantucci di Prato

ACTIVE: 30; TOTAL: 1 HR 30 MIN
MAKES ABOUT 72 BISCOTTI ● ● ○ ○

In Tuscany, *cantucci di Prato*—miniature anise-flavored almond biscotti—are traditionally served at the end of a meal with a glass of Tuscan dessert wine, vin santo, for dipping.

- 3 cups all-purpose flour
- 1 cup granulated sugar, plus more for sprinkling
- 1 cup whole almonds
- 2 teaspoons baking powder
- 2 teaspoons anise seeds

Finely grated zest of 1 lemon
- ¼ teaspoon salt
- 3 large eggs
- 2 large egg yolks
- 2 teaspoons vin santo or other sweet wine
- 1 large egg white, lightly beaten

1. Preheat the oven to 350°. Line a baking sheet with parchment paper. In the bowl of a standing mixer fitted with a paddle, combine the flour with the 1 cup of granulated sugar and the almonds, baking powder, anise seeds, lemon zest and salt. Add the whole eggs, egg yolks and vin santo and beat at low speed until a stiff, crumbly, slightly sticky dough forms.

2. Turn the dough onto a lightly floured work surface and knead it 2 or 3 times, until it just comes together. Divide the dough into 3 equal pieces and form each one into a 12-by-1½-inch log. Transfer the logs to the prepared baking sheet. Brush the tops of the logs with the egg white and sprinkle lightly with sugar. Bake the logs in the center of the oven for 25 minutes, or until they are lightly browned and slightly firm. Let the logs cool for 30 minutes on the baking sheet, then transfer them to a cutting board.

3. Line 2 baking sheets with parchment paper. While the logs are still warm, cut them into ⅓-inch slices with a serrated knife. Arrange the *cantucci* on the baking sheets cut side down and bake, turning once, until golden, about 25 minutes.
—*Joe Sponzo*

MAKE AHEAD Once fully cooled, the *cantucci* can be stored in an airtight container for up to 1 week.

Umbrian Apple-Walnut Roll-Ups

ACTIVE: 50 MIN; TOTAL: 2 HR
6 TO 8 SERVINGS ● ○

This is the only dessert ever served at Il Bacco Felice, a tiny trattoria in the Umbrian town of Foligno. Like many wine enthusiasts, chef-owner Salvatore Denaro has little patience with sweets. Called *la rocciata* (roughly meaning "the round dessert" in Italian), this classic Umbrian pastry is similar to a strudel. It's made from a type of *pastafrolla* (a rich short pastry) and rolled around a delicious filling of apples and walnuts.

- ¼ cup extra-virgin olive oil
- 2 tablespoons dry white wine
- 2 cups all-purpose flour
- ¼ cup sugar

Pinch of salt
- 4 large egg yolks
- 4 tablespoons cold unsalted butter, cut into small pieces

- 2 medium-firm, tart-sweet apples such as Staymans, Winesaps or Granny Smiths— peeled, cored and coarsely chopped (2 cups)
- 1 cup coarsely chopped walnuts
- ¼ cup sugar
- ½ cup golden raisins
- ¼ cup pine nuts
- 1 teaspoon cinnamon
- 2 tablespoons anisette or Sambuca
- 1 large egg, beaten

1. In a small bowl, mix the olive oil with the wine. In a food processor, pulse the flour with the sugar and salt. Add the egg yolks 1 at a time, pulsing to blend between additions. Add the butter and pulse until it is in tiny pieces. With the machine on, add the oil mixture and pulse until a dough forms. Turn the dough out onto a lightly floured work surface and knead until smooth, about 2 minutes. Flatten the dough into a disk, wrap in plastic and refrigerate for 1 hour.

2. Preheat the oven to 350°. In a large bowl, toss the chopped apples with the chopped walnuts, sugar, raisins, pine nuts, cinnamon and anisette.

3. Divide the dough into 4 equal pieces. Roll each piece between wax paper to form a 12-by-8-inch rectangle. Stack the rectangles between layers of wax paper and refrigerate them for about 10 minutes, until they are chilled.

4. Return the rectangles to a lightly floured surface. Spoon 1 cup of the apple filling onto each rectangle in a thick stripe about ½ inch from a long edge. Roll up the pastry to enclose the filling, pressing the seams to seal. Transfer to a large cookie sheet seam side down and brush the tops with beaten egg. Bake until golden brown, about 35 minutes. Let cool until warm, then cut in half and serve. —*Salvatore Denaro*

MAKE AHEAD The uncooked, unrolled dough can be wrapped in plastic and frozen for up to 1 month.

Cocoa Tuiles with Nuts

ACTIVE: 20 MIN; TOTAL: 1 HR

MAKES ABOUT 42 COOKIES ● ○

- ¼ cup hazelnuts, coarsely chopped
- ¼ cup raw pistachios, coarsely chopped
- ¼ cup slivered almonds
- ¼ cup pine nuts
- 4 tablespoons unsalted butter, melted and still warm
- ½ cup sugar
- ¼ cup unsweetened cocoa powder (not Dutch-process)
- ⅛ teaspoon salt
- 2 large egg whites
- 1 tablespoon plus 1 teaspoon all-purpose flour
- 2 teaspoons freshly grated Parmigiano-Reggiano cheese

1. Preheat the oven to 350°. Line 3 large baking sheets with silicone liners or lightly buttered aluminum foil (press out any wrinkles). In a medium bowl, mix the hazelnuts, pistachios, almonds and pine nuts.
2. In another medium bowl, whisk the melted butter with the sugar, cocoa powder and salt. Add the egg whites and whisk until smooth, then whisk in the flour and the grated Parmigiano-Reggiano.
3. Spoon level teaspoons of the batter onto the baking sheets about 3 inches apart. Using the back of a spoon, flatten the batter into 2½-inch rounds. Sprinkle each round with 1 teaspoon of the nuts.
4. Bake 1 sheet of cookies at a time for about 12 minutes, until just firm. Let the cookies cool on the baking sheet for 1 minute, then transfer a wire rack. To make curved cookies, carefully drape the hot cookies over a rolling pin and let cool until hardened, about 2 minutes. Bake the remaining cookies and let cool completely before serving. —*Alice Medrich*

MAKE AHEAD The cocoa tuiles can be stored in an airtight container at room temperature for up to 3 days.

Dulce de Leche Crispies

ACTIVE: 20 MIN; TOTAL: 50 MIN

MAKES 24 CRISPIES ● ● ○

For a grown-up twist on the classic Rice Krispies Treats, F&W's Marcia Kiesel ingeniously swaps out marshmallows for the Latin American dessert sauce dulce de leche, then adds even more crunch with sliced almonds. This dessert is caramelly, nutty and amazingly crispy.

- ¾ cup crispy rice cereal
- 1½ teaspoons vegetable oil, plus more for coating
- 3½ ounces blanched sliced almonds (1¼ cups)
- 5 tablespoons dulce de leche at room temperature, plus more for topping

Salt

1. Preheat the oven to 350°. In a small bowl, toss the rice with 1 teaspoon of the vegetable oil. Spread the oiled rice in an even layer on a large nonstick rimmed baking sheet. Bake until the rice is very crisp, about 10 minutes. Transfer to a plate and let cool to room temperature.
2. In a large bowl, mix the sliced almonds with the toasted rice. Using a rubber spatula, blend in the 5 tablespoons of dulce de leche and the remaining ½ teaspoon of oil, stirring well to coat the rice and almonds thoroughly.
3. Lightly oil 2 large nonstick rimmed baking sheets. Scoop rounded tablespoons of the rice-almond mixture onto the pan and gently flatten them into 2½-inch-wide disks. Lightly sprinkle the crispies with salt. Bake until they are lightly browned, about 15 minutes.
4. Let the dulce de leche crispies cool on the baking sheets for 1 minute. Using a spatula, carefully transfer them to a platter to cool completely. Dollop each one with ¼ teaspoon of the remaining dulce de leche and serve. —*Marcia Kiesel*

MAKE AHEAD The crispies can be stored in an airtight container overnight.

Crispy Meringue-Topped Blondies

ACTIVE: 30 MIN; TOTAL: 1 HR

MAKES 24 SQUARES ● ○

- 1 stick unsalted butter, softened
- 2½ cups light brown sugar (1 pound)
- 3 large eggs, separated
- 1 teaspoon pure vanilla extract
- 2 cups all-purpose flour
- 1 teaspoon baking soda
- 1 teaspoon baking powder
- ½ teaspoon salt
- 1 cup semisweet chocolate chips (6 ounces)
- 1 cup salted toasted pecans (4 ounces), coarsely chopped

1. Preheat the oven to 350°. Butter a 10½-by-15½-inch jelly roll pan. In a large bowl, using an electric mixer, beat the softened butter with 1 cup of the light brown sugar at medium-low speed until light and fluffy, 2 to 3 minutes. Add the egg yolks and vanilla extract and beat until combined. In a medium bowl, whisk the flour with the baking soda, baking powder and salt. Beat the dry ingredients into the wet ingredients just until moist crumbs form. Add the chocolate chips and toasted pecans and stir with a wooden spoon until they are evenly distributed.
2. Scrape the mixture into the prepared pan and press to form an even layer. In a clean bowl, beat the egg whites at medium speed until soft peaks form. Increase the speed to medium-high and beat in the remaining 1½ cups of brown sugar, a small handful at a time, until the meringue is soft and glossy, about 7 minutes. Spread the meringue all over the dough and bake for about 25 minutes, until the meringue top is golden and crisp. Let cool completely before cutting into squares.
—*Nancy Olson*

MAKE AHEAD The squares can be stored at room temperature for up to 2 days.

Chai-Spiced Caramel Fondue

ACTIVE: 15 MIN; TOTAL: 45 MIN
12 SERVINGS ● ●

This luscious, golden dessert fondue laced with warming spices like ginger and cardamom is perfect after a heavy holiday meal. Dip anything you like in it, from apple and pineapple slices to gingersnap cookies. The fondue can also be made ahead and served at room temperature, which simplifies things for the busy cook around holiday time.

2½ cups sugar

6 tablespoons water

1½ cups heavy cream

2 tablespoons unsalted butter

1½ teaspoons ground cardamom

1 teaspoon ground ginger

½ teaspoon cinnamon

½ teaspoon kosher salt

½ teaspoon freshly ground
   black pepper

¼ teaspoon ground cloves

⅛ teaspoon freshly grated nutmeg

In a medium saucepan, combine the sugar and water. Using a wet pastry brush, wash down the side of the saucepan to remove any sugar crystals. Cook over moderately high heat without stirring until an amber caramel forms, about 8 minutes. Remove the saucepan from the heat and carefully stir in the heavy cream and butter until smooth. Stir in the cardamom, ginger, cinnamon, salt, black pepper, cloves and nutmeg. Return the saucepan to the heat and cook for 1 minute, stirring until the caramel is smooth. Transfer the caramel to a bowl and let cool for about 30 minutes before serving. Serve the caramel fondue warm or at room temperature.
—*Melissa Rubel*

SERVE WITH Sliced apples, pears, bananas, dried figs, cubes of pound cake, gingersnaps and graham crackers, for dipping.
MAKE AHEAD The caramel fondue can be refrigerated for up to 3 days. Reheat gently before serving.

Apple Cake with Toffee Crust

ACTIVE: 1 HR; TOTAL: 1 HR 45 MIN
PLUS 2 HR COOLING
10 TO 12 SERVINGS ● ● ●

When pastry chef Lara Atkins of the Kitchen Table Bistro in Richmond, Vermont, was little, her mother made this cake for her bridge club. Atkins remembers how she and her brothers would have to wait for their slices until all the ladies of the club had served themselves. Atkins now makes the cake for her son, who never has to wait for his piece.

CAKE

3 cups all-purpose flour

1 teaspoon salt

1 teaspoon baking soda

1¼ cups vegetable oil

2 cups granulated sugar

3 large eggs

2 large Granny Smith apples—
   peeled, cored and cut into
   ½-inch dice

1 stick unsalted butter

¼ cup heavy cream

1 cup light brown sugar

1 teaspoon pure vanilla extract

TOFFEE SAUCE

1½ cups granulated sugar

½ cup water

¾ cup plus 2 tablespoons
   heavy cream

2 tablespoons unsalted butter

1 tablespoon brandy

CARAMELIZED APPLES

2 tablespoons unsalted butter

2 tablespoons light brown sugar

3 large Granny Smith apples—
   peeled, cored and cut into
   8 wedges each

⅛ teaspoon cinnamon

2 tablespoons water

Vanilla ice cream, for serving

1. MAKE THE CAKE: Preheat the oven to 325°. Butter and flour a 9-inch springform tube pan. In a bowl, whisk the flour with the salt and baking soda. In a large bowl, whisk the oil with the granulated sugar. Whisk in the eggs 1 at a time. Whisk in the dry ingredients until smooth. Fold in the apples. Scrape into the pan and bake in the lower third of the oven for 1 hour and 15 minutes, or until a toothpick inserted in the center comes out clean. Let cool slightly.

2. Meanwhile, in a medium saucepan, bring the butter, cream and brown sugar to a boil over moderate heat, stirring. Remove from the heat and stir in the vanilla.

3. Place the warm cake (still in its pan) on a rimmed baking sheet. Pour the hot glaze over the cake; let it seep in, poking lightly with a toothpick. Let cool for 2 hours. Invert the cake onto a plate and invert again onto another plate, right side up.

4. MEANWHILE, MAKE THE TOFFEE SAUCE: In a medium saucepan, combine the sugar and water and bring to a boil over high heat, stirring until the sugar dissolves. Using a moistened pastry brush, wash down any sugar crystals on the side of the pan. Cook without stirring to a medium-amber caramel, about 5 minutes. Remove from the heat and stir in the cream and butter. Simmer the sauce over moderate heat for 2 minutes, then remove from the heat and stir in the brandy. Pour the sauce into a pitcher.

5. MAKE THE CARAMELIZED APPLES: In a large skillet, melt the butter and brown sugar. Add the apples and cinnamon and cook over moderately high heat, turning the apples once or twice, until tender and caramelized, about 10 minutes. Add the water to dissolve the caramel in the skillet, then transfer the apples to a plate.

6. Slice the cake and serve with the apples, toffee sauce and ice cream. —*Lara Atkins*
MAKE AHEAD The unmolded cake can be stored in an airtight container overnight at room temperature. The toffee sauce can be refrigerated for up to 1 week; reheat gently before serving. The apples can be made up to 2 hours ahead and kept at room temperature.

Olive Oil and Sauternes Cake with Roasted Pears

ACTIVE: 35 MIN; TOTAL: 1 HR 30 MIN
PLUS COOLING

8 SERVINGS ● ● ○

Australian chef and television personality Neil Perry uses Sauternes in every component of this dessert. He also adds olive oil to the batter, which creates a delightfully moist crumb.

CAKE

- ¾ cup pure olive oil, plus more for the pan
- ½ cup sugar
- 2 large eggs
- ½ cup Sauternes
- ⅓ cup whole milk
- 2 tablespoons finely grated lemon zest
- 1½ cups all-purpose flour
- 2½ teaspoons baking powder
- ¾ teaspoon salt

ROASTED PEARS

- 4 firm pears, such as Bosc (2 pounds), quartered lengthwise and cored
- ⅓ cup Sauternes
- 2 tablespoons pure olive oil
- 2 tablespoons sugar

SAUTERNES SYRUP

- ½ cup sugar
- 2 tablespoons water
- ½ cup Sauternes

SUPERFAST

sauternes syrup

For a really elegant dessert, make the Sauternes syrup in the recipe above and spoon it on top of vanilla ice cream or pieces of pound cake—or just serve the syrup over slices of ripe pear.

1. MAKE THE CAKE: Preheat the oven to 350°. Lightly oil a 10-by-5-inch loaf pan with olive oil. In the large bowl of an electric standing mixer fitted with a whip attachment, beat the sugar and eggs at medium speed until pale yellow and fluffy, about 2 minutes. Add the ¾ cup of olive oil along with the Sauternes, milk and lemon zest and beat at low speed until blended. Beat in the flour, baking powder and salt. Scrape the batter into the prepared loaf pan and bake the cake for about 50 minutes, or until it is golden on top and a toothpick inserted in the center comes out clean. Cool on a rack for 30 minutes, then unmold onto the rack to cool completely.

2. MEANWHILE, PREPARE THE PEARS: In an 8-by-11-inch baking dish, toss the cored, quartered pears with the Sauternes, olive oil and sugar. Roast in the oven along with the cake for about 40 minutes, until the pears are tender and their edges have begun to brown. Remove the pan from the oven and let the pears stand until cool, about 1 hour.

3. MAKE THE SYRUP: In a small saucepan, combine the sugar with the water and bring to a boil over moderate heat, stirring until the sugar dissolves. Continue to cook without stirring until an amber caramel forms, about 7 minutes. Remove the saucepan from the heat, carefully stir the Sauternes into the caramel and continue to stir until smooth. Scrape the mixture into a heatproof measuring cup and set aside to cool.

4. Slice the cake and serve with the roasted pears and a drizzle of the syrup.
—*Neil Perry*

SERVE WITH Freshly whipped unsweetened cream.

MAKE AHEAD The olive oil cake and roasted pears can be made earlier in the day and kept at room temperature. The Sauternes syrup can be covered and refrigerated for up to 3 days; bring to room temperature before serving.

Cranberry Streusel Cake

ACTIVE: 45 MIN; TOTAL: 2 HR 30 MIN

8 SERVINGS ● ● ○

Cranberries usually appear on the holiday table as a condiment, but here they flavor a delicious cake, topped with a crumbly, buttery oat streusel.

BATTER

- 1 cup all-purpose flour
- ½ cup plus 2 tablespoons granulated sugar
- ¾ teaspoon baking powder
- ¼ teaspoon baking soda
- ¼ teaspoon salt
- 1 stick unsalted butter, cubed and chilled
- 3 large egg yolks
- ½ cup sour cream
- 1 teaspoon pure vanilla extract

FILLING AND TOPPING

- 2½ cups fresh or frozen cranberries (10 ounces)
- 2 teaspoons fresh lime juice
- 1 teaspoon freshly grated lime zest
- ¼ cup granulated sugar
- 2 tablespoons cornstarch
- 1 teaspoon pure vanilla extract

Pinch of salt

- ¼ teaspoon freshly ground black pepper
- ¾ teaspoon cinnamon
- ½ cup all-purpose flour
- ½ cup rolled oats
- ½ cup light brown sugar
- 1 stick unsalted butter, cubed and chilled

1. MAKE THE BATTER: Preheat the oven to 350°. Butter and flour a 9-inch-round springform cake pan. In a bowl, whisk together the flour, sugar, baking powder, baking soda and salt. Using an electric mixer at low speed, beat in the butter until it looks like coarse meal. In a bowl, whisk the egg yolks with the sour cream and vanilla. Beat the egg mixture into the dry ingredients at medium-low speed just until incorporated, 1 minute. Scrape the batter into the pan.

2. MAKE THE FILLING AND TOPPING: In a medium bowl, stir the cranberries with the lime juice, zest, granulated sugar, cornstarch, vanilla, salt, black pepper and ¼ teaspoon of the cinnamon. Spoon the mixture over the cake batter.

3. In another bowl, mix together the flour, rolled oats and light brown sugar, then stir in the remaining ½ teaspoon of cinnamon. Using a pastry blender or 2 knives, cut in the chilled butter until it resembles coarse meal. Sprinkle the topping over the cranberries and bake the streusel cake for about 1½ hours, until the fruit is bubbling. Let the cake cool completely, then remove the ring; slice into wedges and serve.
—*Nancy Olson*

MAKE AHEAD The Cranberry Streusel Cake can be kept covered at room temperature for up to 2 days.

Crunchy Milk Chocolate–Peanut Butter Layer Cake

ACTIVE: 1 HR 45 MIN; TOTAL 4 HR
16 SERVINGS ● ● ●

The genius of this layer cake is its extraordinarily crunchy filling, made with almonds, salted peanuts, creamy peanut butter, chocolate and Rice Krispies. The silky milk-chocolate ganache frosting almost pushes the recipe over the top.

CAKE

- 2 cups plus 2 tablespoons granulated sugar
- 1¾ cups all-purpose flour
- ¾ cup plus 2 tablespoons unsweetened cocoa powder
- 1½ teaspoons baking powder
- 1½ teaspoons baking soda
- 1½ teaspoons salt
- 2 large eggs
- 1 cup milk
- ½ cup vegetable oil
- 1 tablespoon pure vanilla extract
- ¾ cup plus 2 tablespoons boiling water

FILLING

- ⅓ cup sliced almonds
- ½ cup confectioners' sugar
- 2 large egg whites
- 1 tablespoon granulated sugar
- ½ cup salted roasted peanuts, coarsely chopped
- 1 cup creamy peanut butter
- 2 tablespoons unsalted butter, softened
- 3 ounces milk chocolate, coarsely chopped
- 1 cup Rice Krispies

GANACHE

- 1¼ pounds milk chocolate, coarsely chopped
- 1¾ cups plus 2 tablespoons heavy cream, warmed

1. MAKE THE CAKE: Preheat the oven to 350°. Butter and flour a 9-by-13-inch cake pan. In a large bowl, whisk the granulated sugar with the flour, cocoa powder, baking powder, baking soda and salt. In a medium bowl, whisk the eggs, milk, vegetable oil and vanilla. Whisk the wet ingredients into the dry ingredients, then whisk in the boiling water. Pour the batter (it will be thin) into the prepared cake pan and bake for about 50 minutes, until a toothpick inserted in the center of the cake comes out clean. Transfer the cake to a cooling rack and let cool in the pan.

2. Slide a knife or offset spatula around the sides of the cake; invert the cake onto a work surface. Working carefully, use a long, serrated knife to slice the cake in half horizontally to form 2 layers. Reduce the oven temperature to 325°.

3. MAKE THE FILLING: Trace a 9-by-13-inch rectangle onto a sheet of parchment paper and lay it on a large baking sheet. In a food processor, pulse the sliced almonds with the confectioners' sugar until they're finely ground. In a large bowl of an electric standing mixer fitted with the whip attachment, beat the egg whites at medium speed until soft peaks form.

With the mixer running, gradually pour in the granulated sugar and continue to beat at medium speed until the egg whites form a stiff, glossy meringue, about 2 minutes. Using a rubber spatula, gently fold the chopped almond mixture into the whites until combined. Spread the meringue on the parchment paper to fill the rectangle. Sprinkle the chopped peanuts on top of the meringue. Bake for about 20 minutes, until lightly browned and firm. Transfer the pan to a wire rack and let the meringue cool completely.

4. In a medium heatproof bowl set over a saucepan of simmering water, combine the peanut butter with the butter and milk chocolate and cook, stirring constantly, until the mixture is completely smooth and melted. Take the bowl off the heat and fold in the Rice Krispies. Spread the mixture evenly all over the top of the meringue rectangle. Transfer to the freezer and let cool completely.

5. MAKE THE GANACHE: In a medium heatproof bowl set over a saucepan of simmering water, melt the chocolate, stirring occasionally, until smooth. Whisk in the cream until smooth. Take the bowl off the heat and refrigerate the ganache for 1 hour, whisking occasionally, until it is thick enough to spread.

6. ASSEMBLE THE CAKE: Place the bottom cake layer cut side up on a large board for serving. Spread one-third of the ganache evenly over the cake. Invert the meringue filling onto the cake and peel off the paper. Spread half of the remaining ganache over the filling, then top with the second cake layer. Refrigerate until firm, at least 1 hour. Using a serrated knife, trim the edges. Spread the remaining ganache over the top and sides of the cake and refrigerate to set. Cut the cake into slices, transfer to plates and serve immediately.
—*Nancy Olson*

MAKE AHEAD The cake can be covered and refrigerated for up to 4 days.

PUMPKIN CAKE WITH
CARAMEL–CREAM CHEESE FROSTING

Pumpkin Cake with Caramel– Cream Cheese Frosting

ACTIVE: 1 HR; TOTAL: 2 HR PLUS
8 HR CHILLING

12 SERVINGS ● ●

In this fun variation on traditional pumpkin pie, a dense, moist pumpkin cake spiced with ginger, cinnamon, nutmeg and cloves is frosted with a slightly tangy, super-caramelly frosting. It's equally good served cold or at room temperature.

FROSTING

- 1 cup sugar
- ½ cup water
- ½ vanilla bean, split and seeds scraped
- 1½ sticks (6 ounces) unsalted butter, softened
- 2 tablespoons heavy cream
- 1 pound cream cheese, cut into 2-inch cubes

CAKE

- 2 cups all-purpose flour
- 2¼ teaspoons baking powder
- 1 teaspoon salt
- 1 teaspoon cinnamon
- 1 teaspoon ground ginger
- ¾ teaspoon baking soda
- ½ teaspoon freshly grated nutmeg
- ¼ teaspoon ground cloves
- 1¼ cups light brown sugar
- 4 large eggs
- ¾ cup vegetable oil
- One 15-ounce can pumpkin puree
- ½ cup whole milk

1. MAKE THE FROSTING: In a medium saucepan, combine the sugar, water, and vanilla bean and seeds. Cook over high heat, stirring, until the sugar is dissolved. Using a wet pastry brush, wash down any crystals from the side of the pan. Cook over moderate heat without stirring until a medium-dark amber caramel forms, about 9 minutes. Remove from the heat and immediately stir in the butter and heavy cream. (Don't worry if the butter separates.) Discard the vanilla bean.

2. Transfer the caramel to the large bowl of a standing mixer fitted with a whisk and beat at low speed until the caramel cools slightly and comes together, about 5 minutes. With the machine running, beat in the cream cheese, adding 1 cube at a time and beating well between additions, until the frosting is smooth and silky. Scrape the frosting into a medium bowl, cover with plastic wrap and refrigerate until very firm, at least 6 hours.

3. MEANWHILE, MAKE THE CAKE: Preheat the oven to 350°. Butter and flour two 8-inch round cake pans. In a medium bowl, whisk the flour with the baking powder, salt, cinnamon, ginger, baking soda, nutmeg and cloves until the ingredients are well combined.

4. In the large bowl of an electric standing mixer fitted with the whip attachment, beat the brown sugar and eggs at medium-high speed until fluffy, 3 minutes. Beat in the oil until smoothly combined, then beat in the pumpkin puree. Alternately add the dry ingredients and the milk in 3 batches, beating well between additions.

5. Pour the batter into the prepared cake pans and smooth the tops with a rubber spatula. Bake the cakes for 40 to 45 minutes, until a toothpick inserted in the center of the cake comes out clean. Let the cakes cool on a rack for 20 minutes. Run a knife or offset spatula around the edges to loosen the cakes, then invert them onto a wire rack to cool completely.

6. Place 1 layer on a plate and spread with 1 cup of the frosting. Top with the second layer and frost the top and side. Refrigerate the cake for 2 hours before serving. —*Grace Parisi*

NOTE The frosted pumpkin cake can be garnished with white currants and candied pecans if desired.

MAKE AHEAD The frosted pumpkin cake can be refrigerated in an airtight container for up to 2 days. Serve cold or at room temperature.

Slow-Cooker Sour Cream Cheesecake

ACTIVE: 20 MIN; TOTAL: 4 HR 15 MIN
PLUS 4 HR CHILLING

6 SERVINGS ● ● ●

- ¾ cup graham cracker crumbs
- 2½ tablespoons unsalted butter, melted
- ¼ teaspoon cinnamon
- ⅔ cup plus 1 tablespoon sugar
- Salt
- 12 ounces cream cheese, at room temperature
- 1 tablespoon all-purpose flour
- 2 large eggs
- 1 teaspoon pure almond extract
- 1 cup sour cream

1. In a bowl, mix the crumbs with the butter, cinnamon, 1 tablespoon of the sugar and a pinch of salt. Press the crumbs over the bottom and 1 inch up the side of a 6-inch springform pan that's 3 inches deep.

2. In a standing mixer fitted with a paddle, combine the cream cheese with the flour, the remaining ⅔ cup of sugar and ¼ teaspoon of salt. Beat at medium-high speed until smooth, 2 minutes. Scrape down the bowl; add the eggs and the almond extract. Beat at medium speed until blended. Add the sour cream and beat until smooth. Pour the batter into the springform pan.

3. Fill a 6- to 7-quart round or oval slow cooker with ½ inch of water and position a rack in the bottom. Set the cheesecake on the rack. Cover the slow cooker with a triple layer of paper towels and the lid. Turn the cooker to high and cook for 2 hours without peeking. Turn off the heat and let stand until the slow cooker has cooled, 1 hour.

4. Remove the lid and paper towels and transfer the cake to a rack to cool for about 1 hour. Cover with plastic and refrigerate until chilled, at least 4 hours.

5. Heat a thin-bladed knife under hot water; dry it and run it around the edge of the cake. Release the spring, lift the cake out, slice and serve. —*Beth Hensperger*

Gingerbread with Quark Cheesecake

ACTIVE: 1 HR; TOTAL: 3 HR 30 MIN PLUS OVERNIGHT CHILLING

8 SERVINGS ● ●○

This clever recipe combines two cakes in one: gingerbread and cheesecake. The cheesecake is light and creamy, with a pleasant tang from quark, while the gingerbread is moist and delicately spiced with cinnamon, nutmeg and ginger.

CHEESECAKE

- 6 ounces cream cheese, softened
- ¼ cup plus 2 tablespoons granulated sugar
- 12 ounces quark or Greek-style whole-milk yogurt (1½ cups; see Note)
- 1 large egg
- 3 large egg yolks
- 1 tablespoon Cointreau or other orange brandy

GINGERBREAD

- ½ cup plus ⅓ cup all-purpose flour
- 1¼ teaspoons baking powder
- ¾ teaspoon ground ginger
- ¼ teaspoon cinnamon
- ⅛ teaspoon freshly ground white pepper
- ⅛ teaspoon freshly grated nutmeg

TECHNIQUE

candying kumquats

Bring 1 cup of water and 2 cups of sugar to a boil, stirring. Add 1 pound of thinly sliced kumquats; simmer until translucent, 15 minutes. Cool in the syrup, transfer to a jar and refrigerate.

- ⅛ teaspoon salt
- ½ cup light brown sugar
- 1 large egg
- 1 large egg yolk
- 6 tablespoons unsalted butter, softened
- ¼ cup whole milk
- 1 tablespoon unsulfured molasses
- 1½ teaspoons finely grated fresh ginger
- 1 teaspoon pure vanilla extract

Candied kumquats in syrup, sliced, for garnish (see Note)

1. Preheat the oven to 275°. Spray a 6-inch springform pan with vegetable oil spray. Wrap the outside of the pan tightly with foil and set it in a small roasting pan.

2. MAKE THE CHEESECAKE: In a medium bowl, using an electric mixer, beat the cream cheese and sugar at medium speed until smooth. Add the quark and beat just until blended. Add the egg and egg yolks 1 at a time, beating well between additions. Beat in the Cointreau. Pour the mixture into the prepared pan.

3. Add enough hot water to the roasting pan to reach halfway up the side of the springform pan. Bake for about 1 hour and 15 minutes, until the cheesecake is slightly jiggly in the center and set around the edge. Remove it from the water bath and run a knife around the edge of the cake to allow it to settle in the pan as it cools. Cover and refrigerate overnight.

4. MAKE THE GINGERBREAD: Preheat the oven to 350°. Butter and flour a 6-inch cake pan. In a small bowl, whisk the flour with the baking powder, ground spices and salt. In a medium bowl, using an electric mixer, beat the brown sugar with the egg and egg yolk at medium-high speed until light and fluffy. In a microwave-safe bowl, melt the butter in the milk. Stir in the molasses, fresh ginger and vanilla. In 3 alternating additions, beat the dry and wet ingredients into the egg mixture.

5. Scrape the batter into the prepared pan and bake in the lower third of the oven for 35 to 40 minutes, until springy. Let the gingerbread cake cool in the pan for 20 minutes, then turn it out onto a rack. Turn it right side up and let cool completely.

6. Using a serrated knife, carefully slice the rounded top off of the gingerbread cake to make it level. Invert the cake (cut side down) onto the cheesecake. Place a plate over the cake pan. Holding both the plate and pan, swiftly invert the entire cake onto the plate. Remove the ring, then carefully lift off the pan bottom. Garnish with the kumquat slices and serve chilled. —*Nancy Olson*

NOTE Quark is a soft, unripened cow's-milk cheese with a texture similar to sour cream. It is native to Germany and Austria (where it is called *topfen*) but is also made in America. Look for quark in tubs in the refrigerator case of specialty food stores, or buy it online at igourmet.com. Kumquats are orange citrus fruits the size and shape of grape tomatoes, with thin rinds and very little juice. They are in season in the winter and can be found in many produce markets. They can be eaten raw but are more often candied. Sliced candied kumquats in syrup are available in jars in specialty food stores, or you can make your own (see Candying Kumquats, at left).

MAKE AHEAD The finished cake can be refrigerated in an airtight container for up to 2 days.

Bittersweet Chocolate Mousse

TOTAL: 30 MIN PLUS 3 HR CHILLING

8 SERVINGS ● ●○

Dave Cruz, chef de cuisine at Ad Hoc, Thomas Keller's family-style restaurant in Yountville, California, created this chocolate mousse as a refined homage to the creamy chocolate pudding he loved as a child. At the restaurant he serves it unadorned, but it can also be garnished with giant curls of bittersweet chocolate made with a vegetable peeler, which dress up the mousse and add texture, too.

- 9 ounces bittersweet chocolate, finely chopped
- 4½ tablespoons unsalted butter, cut into small cubes
- 2 tablespoons strong-brewed espresso
- 6 large eggs, separated
- 2 tablespoons sugar
- 2 cups heavy cream, chilled

Bittersweet chocolate shavings, for garnish

1. In the top of a double boiler, or in a heat-proof bowl set over a saucepan of simmering water, combine the chopped chocolate, butter and espresso and cook over moderately low heat, stirring, until the chocolate is melted. Remove the double boiler top from the heat and let the chocolate cool until the mixture registers 75° on an instant-read thermometer. Beat in the egg yolks until incorporated.

2. In the large bowl of an electric standing mixer fitted with a whip attachment, beat the egg whites at medium-high speed until very soft peaks form. With the mixer running, gradually add the sugar and beat until the whites form a slightly firm and glossy meringue.

3. In another bowl of an electric mixer, beat the heavy cream until firm. Gently fold half of the whipped cream into the chocolate mixture, then fold in half of the beaten egg whites until no streaks remain. Repeat with the remaining beaten egg whites and whipped cream until all the ingredients are smoothly combined.

4. Spoon the mousse into glasses and refrigerate until chilled, at least 3 hours. Garnish the glasses with the chocolate shavings and serve. —*Dave Cruz*

MAKE AHEAD The mousse can be refrigerated for up to 2 days. Let chill before covering the bowl with plastic wrap to avoid condensation.

GINGERBREAD WITH QUARK CHEESECAKE

BITTERSWEET CHOCOLATE MOUSSE

PUMPKIN PUDDING WITH
MILE-HIGH MERINGUE

Pumpkin Puddings with Mile-High Meringue

ACTIVE: 40 MIN; TOTAL: 1 HR 40 MIN
PLUS 1 HR 30 MIN CHILLING
12 SERVINGS ● ○ ○

Chef Dean Fearing and pastry chef Jill Bates collaborated at Fearing's eponymous Dallas restaurant on these spiced pumpkin puddings covered with meringue swirls. "The meringue is what all Southerners love about their pies, whether they're coconut, chocolate or banana," Fearing says.

2½ cups sugar
3 tablespoons water
2 cups heavy cream
1 cup whole milk
One 15-ounce can unsweetened
    pumpkin puree
8 large eggs, 6 separated
1½ teaspoons cinnamon
½ teaspoon ground ginger
¼ teaspoon freshly grated nutmeg
⅛ teaspoon ground cloves
Pinch of freshly ground pepper
Salt
1 vanilla bean, split, seeds scraped

1. Preheat the oven to 350°. In a medium saucepan, mix 1 cup of the sugar with the water. Using a wet pastry brush, wash down the pan's side to remove any sugar. Cook without stirring over moderately high heat until an amber caramel forms, about 8 minutes. Off the heat, stir in the cream and milk. Cook the caramel over moderate heat, stirring, until smooth, about 1 minute.

2. In a medium bowl, whisk the pumpkin puree with the 6 egg yolks and 2 whole eggs. Add the cinnamon, ginger, nutmeg, cloves, pepper and a pinch of salt. Gradually whisk in the hot caramel cream.

3. Pour the pudding into twelve ¾-cup ramekins set in a roasting pan. Pour enough hot water into the roasting pan to reach halfway up the sides of the ramekins. Cover the pan with foil and cut 4 small slits in the top. Bake the puddings for about 40 minutes, or until the centers are just set.

Remove the puddings from the water bath. Let cool on a wire rack, then refrigerate until completely chilled, at least 1½ hours.

4. Preheat the broiler. In a large bowl set over a pot of simmering water, whip the 6 egg whites with the remaining 1½ cups of sugar, the vanilla seeds and a pinch of salt. Whip until the sugar has dissolved, 3 minutes. Remove the bowl from the water bath. Beat the whites until stiff, glossy peaks form, 6 minutes. Spread the meringue in swirls over the puddings. Broil 4 inches from the heat for 2 minutes, until golden, and serve. —*Dean Fearing and Jill Bates*

MAKE AHEAD The puddings can be refrigerated for 1 day. They can be topped with the meringue and broiled 2 hours before serving; keep at room temperature.

Date Cake with Pistachio Lebneh

ACTIVE: 30 MIN; TOTAL: 1 HR 50 MIN
8 SERVINGS ● ○ ○

This elegant but incredibly simple cake is rich, dense and buttery, flavored with vanilla and sweet Deglet Noor dates and topped with a tangy-crunchy mix of pistachios and *lebneh* (a yogurtlike Lebanese fresh cheese). Medjool dates can be substituted for the Deglet Noors.

2 sticks unsalted butter
    (½ pound), plus more
    for the pan
½ vanilla bean, split lengthwise,
    seeds scraped
1⅓ cups confectioners' sugar
⅓ cup all-purpose flour
9 ounces pitted Deglet Noor
    dates, cut into ½-inch
    pieces (1½ cups)
5 large egg whites, at room
    temperature
3 tablespoons granulated sugar
¾ cup *lebneh* or any
    Greek-style strained yogurt
½ cup unsalted roasted
    pistachios, coarsely chopped

1. Preheat the oven to 350°. Butter a 10-inch round cake pan, line the bottom with a round of parchment paper and butter the parchment paper.

2. In a small saucepan, melt the 2 sticks of butter with the vanilla bean and seeds. Cook over moderate heat until the milk solids begin to brown and the butter has a nutty aroma, about 8 minutes. Pour into a heatproof bowl. Remove the vanilla bean and save it for another use.

3. In a medium bowl, whisk the confectioners' sugar with the flour, then fold in the date pieces. In the large bowl of an electric standing mixer, beat the egg whites at medium-high speed until soft peaks form. Gradually add the granulated sugar and beat at high speed until the whites form a stiff and glossy meringue. Using a rubber spatula, gently fold the dry ingredients into the egg whites, working quickly to keep the whites from deflating. Drizzle one-third of the vanilla–brown butter mixture against the inside of the mixing bowl and fold it into the egg whites until well combined. Fold in the remaining vanilla–brown butter mixture in 2 additions. Scrape the cake batter into the cake pan and gently smooth the surface with the rubber spatula. Bake the date cake for about 50 minutes, or until the cake is golden on top and feels firm to the touch. (The cake will rise, then fall when it's done.) Transfer the cake pan to a wire rack and let cool for 30 minutes. Run the tip of a sharp-bladed knife or offset spatula around the edge of the pan to loosen the cake, then invert it onto a large serving plate.

4. In a small bowl, stir together the *lebneh* and the chopped roasted pistachios. Slice the date cake into 8 wedges, transfer to dessert plates and garnish each slice with a dollop of the pistachio *lebneh*.
—*Octavio Becerra*

MAKE AHEAD The date cake can be baked earlier the same day and stored at room temperature.

Chestnut-Chocolate Mousse

ACTIVE: 30 MIN; TOTAL: 2 HR 30 MIN

10 SERVINGS ● ●

F&W's Marcia Kiesel uses vacuum-packed roasted chestnuts to add a sophisticated flavor to a luxe chocolate mousse.

- 4 ounces semisweet chocolate, chopped
- 4 ounces bittersweet chocolate, chopped
- 2 cups heavy cream, chilled
- 1 cup vacuum-packed roasted chestnuts, chopped

Salt

- 4 large egg whites
- ¼ cup plus 2 tablespoons sugar

Unsweetened whipped cream and crushed chocolate-covered espresso beans, for serving

1. In a small heatproof glass bowl, microwave the chocolates at 20-second intervals, stirring a few times after each interval, until the chocolate is melted and smooth. Let the chocolate cool until it is just warm to the touch.

2. In a large stainless steel bowl, use a whisk or handheld electric mixer to beat the cream until soft peaks form. Use a rubber spatula to fold in the melted, cooled chocolate, chopped roasted chestnuts and a pinch of salt.

3. In a large stainless steel or copper bowl, use an electric mixer to beat the egg whites to very soft peaks. While beating, gradually pour in the sugar and beat until firm, glossy peaks form, about 2 minutes. Stir one-third of the beaten whites into the chocolate mixture, then gently fold in the remaining whites, working quickly so that the whites do not deflate.

4. Spoon the mousse into ten ⅔-cup ramekins. Cover and refrigerate until firm, at least 2 hours. Serve each mousse with a dollop of whipped cream and crushed chocolate-covered espresso beans.
—*Marcia Kiesel*

Caramel–Passion Fruit Sundaes

ACTIVE: 25 MIN; TOTAL: 2 HR

4 SERVINGS ●

To make these layered, free-form sundaes quickly, use store-bought caramel or butterscotch sauce. As a variation, substitute ginger cookies for the chocolate wafers.

CARAMEL SAUCE

- 2 cups sugar
- ½ cup water
- 1 cup heavy cream
- 4 tablespoons unsalted butter
- ½ vanilla bean, split, seeds scraped

SUNDAES

- 24 chocolate wafer cookies, crushed (5 ounces)
- 1 pint passion fruit sorbet, softened slightly
- 1 pint vanilla ice cream, softened slightly

1. MAKE THE CARAMEL SAUCE: In a saucepan, stir the sugar with the water; bring to a boil over high heat. Using a wet pastry brush, wash down any sugar crystals from the side of the pan. Cook without stirring until a deep amber caramel forms, 8 minutes. Remove the saucepan from the heat; carefully whisk in the heavy cream, butter and vanilla bean and seeds. Carefully scrape the caramel sauce into a heatproof glass jar; let cool to room temperature. Discard the vanilla bean.

2. ASSEMBLE THE SUNDAES: Spoon 2 tablespoons of the cookie crumbs into each of 4 tall 10-ounce glasses. For each sundae, top the crumbs with a ¼-cup scoop of the passion fruit sorbet, 2 tablespoons of the caramel sauce and a ¼-cup scoop of the vanilla ice cream. Repeat the layering once more, starting with the cookie crumbs. Sprinkle 1 tablespoon of the crumbs over each sundae and serve at once. —*Susan Spungen*

MAKE AHEAD The caramel sauce can be refrigerated in an airtight container for up to 2 weeks. Rewarm before serving.

brunch

Buttery Buttermilk Biscuits

TOTAL: 30 MIN

MAKES 15 BISCUITS ● ● ●

When she was growing up, Alabama fashion designer Natalie Chanin ate homemade biscuits every day. "Now, I suppose, people don't make them from scratch as much," she says. "They seem like some kind of luxury." In truth, Chanin's light, flaky biscuits are surprisingly easy to prepare—just don't overwork the dough or the biscuits will get tough.

- 2 cups all-purpose flour, plus more for rolling
- 2 teaspoons baking powder
- 1 teaspoon salt
- 1 stick plus 2 tablespoons unsalted butter—1 stick cut into cubes and chilled, 2 tablespoons melted
- ¾ cup buttermilk

1. Preheat the oven to 425°. In a large bowl, combine the 2 cups of flour with the baking powder and salt. Using a pastry blender or 2 knives, cut in the cubed butter until the mixture resembles coarse meal. Add the buttermilk and stir with a fork or wooden spoon until a soft dough forms. Turn the dough out onto a lightly floured work surface and knead 2 or 3 times, just until it comes together.

2. Using a lightly floured rolling pin, roll out the dough ½ inch thick. Using a lightly floured 2¼-inch round cutter, stamp out biscuits as close together as possible. Pat the dough scraps together and stamp out more biscuits. Transfer the biscuits to a large baking sheet. Bake for about 20 minutes, until the biscuits are risen and golden. Brush the hot biscuits with the melted butter and serve them hot or at room temperature. —*Natalie Chanin*

MAKE AHEAD The biscuits can be kept in an airtight container for up to 4 hours. Serve at room temperature or briefly reheat in a low oven before serving.

CHESTNUT–CHOCOLATE MOUSSE

CARAMEL—PASSION FRUIT SUNDAES

Flaky Biscuits with Sea Salt

TOTAL: 40 MIN

MAKES 15 BISCUITS ● ●

To make her biscuits exquisitely flaky and delicious, F&W's Grace Parisi always does two things: She uses lots of cold butter and she chills the dough before baking it. Try the Sweet Lemon-Poppy variation, too—they are wonderful warm for breakfast, slathered with lots of strawberry or raspberry jam.

2¼ cups all-purpose flour

2 teaspoons baking powder

½ teaspoon baking soda

1 teaspoon fine salt

1½ sticks unsalted butter—
   10 tablespoons cut
   into ½-inch cubes and
   chilled, 2 tablespoons melted

1 cup buttermilk, chilled

Flaky salt, such as Maldon,
   for sprinkling

1. Preheat the oven to 425° and position a rack in the lower third of the oven. In a large, shallow bowl, whisk the flour, baking powder, baking soda and fine salt. Add the chilled butter and use a pastry blender or 2 knives to cut the butter into the flour until it is the size of small peas. Stir in the chilled buttermilk just until the dough is moistened. Lightly dust a work surface with flour. Turn the dough out onto the work surface and knead 2 or 3 times, just until it comes together. Pat the dough into a ½-inch-thick disk.

2. Using a floured 2¼-inch round cookie cutter, stamp out biscuit rounds from the disk of dough, cutting them out as closely together as possible. Gather the scraps and knead them together 2 or 3 times, then flatten the dough and stamp out more biscuit rounds. Pat the remaining scraps together and gently press them into 1 last biscuit.

3. Transfer the biscuits to a large baking sheet and brush the tops with the melted butter. Lightly sprinkle the biscuits with a few grains of flaky salt and chill until firm, about 10 minutes.

4. Bake the biscuits for 20 minutes, or until golden. Let the biscuits cool slightly on the baking sheet before serving.
—*Grace Parisi*

VARIATION To make Sweet Lemon-Poppy biscuits, follow the recipe at left, making the following changes: Whisk ¼ cup of sugar with the dry ingredients. Stir in the grated zest of 1 lemon and 1 tablespoon of poppy seeds just before adding the buttermilk. Sprinkle each biscuit with a pinch of sugar instead of flaky salt.

MAKE AHEAD Freeze unbaked biscuits in a single layer and transfer to a resealable plastic bag for up to 1 month. Bake straight from the freezer, adding a few minutes to the cooking time.

Gruyère Soufflés

TOTAL: 45 MIN
7 SERVINGS •

- 4 tablespoons unsalted butter, plus softened butter for brushing
- ¼ cup freshly grated Parmigiano-Reggiano cheese
- 6 tablespoons all-purpose flour
- 1½ cups milk
- ¾ teaspoon salt
- ¼ teaspoon cayenne
- 6 large eggs, separated
- 8 ounces coarsely shredded

Gruyère cheese (2 packed cups)
- ½ teaspoon cream of tartar

1. Preheat the oven to 400°; brush seven 1-cup ramekins with butter. Coat them with 2 tablespoons of the Parmigiano-Reggiano and set on a baking sheet.

2. In a saucepan, melt the 4 tablespoons of butter. Whisk in the flour and cook over moderate heat for 1 minute. Whisk in the milk; cook over moderately low heat until smooth and very thick, about 2 minutes. Stir in the salt and cayenne. Off the heat, whisk in the egg yolks. Let cool slightly.

Transfer to a bowl and stir in the Gruyère.

3. In a mixer, beat the egg whites with the cream of tartar at medium-high speed until frothy. Increase the speed to high and beat until firm peaks form. With a rubber spatula, fold the egg whites into the soufflé base.

4. Fill the ramekins to ½ inch below the rims. Run your thumb inside the rim of each ramekin to help the soufflés rise evenly. Sprinkle with the remaining Parmigiano-Reggiano and bake in the bottom third of the oven until puffed and golden brown, about 20 minutes. Serve at once. —*Grace Parisi*

an italian-style breakfast

ESPRESSO The compact Nespresso Lattissima machine, a collaboration between Nestlé Nespresso and De'Longhi, produces frothy cappuccino and balanced espresso (from $699; nespresso.com).

JAM Luxardo, known for its liqueur distilled from real *marasca* cherries from Padua, has made an easy transition—maraschino cherry jam. Its superconcentrated version is nicely sweet and tart ($20 for 13 oz; markethallfoods.com).

BUTTER Casa Madaio's superbly creamy butter, with a slightly pungent tang, is made with buffalo milk from small farms in Campania ($13 for 9 oz; formaggiokitchen.com).

PASTRY Sfoglia D'Oro's newly imported *sfogliatini* from Tuscany are lightly topped with sugar and are irresistibly flaky ($4.60 for 8 oz; Buon'Italia; 212-633-9090).

Sommelier Eric Zillier (center) of New York City's Alto presides over an Italian wine–tasting party.

wine pairings

champagne & sparkling wines

Champagne, which is produced only in the Champagne region of France, is the greatest sparkling wine in the world—it's effervescent and lively, at the same time offering tremendous complexity and finesse. Champagnes are usually a blend of grapes, typically Pinot Noir and Chardonnay, often with a touch of Pinot Meunier as well. They range from dry (brut) to mildly sweet (demi-sec) to very sweet (doux). Different producers, or "houses," have different styles, too, ranging from light and delicate to rich and full-flavored. Many other countries also make sparkling wines. Those from North America tend to be more fruit-forward than most Champagnes. Cava, an inexpensive sparkler from Spain, often has an earthy character. Italy's Prosecco is also affordable, and popular for its engaging foaminess and hint of sweetness on the finish. Sparkling wines make great aperitifs, but they're also good throughout the meal, especially with shellfish and salty or spicy dishes.

DRY, LIGHT CHAMPAGNE
Larmandier-Bernier Blanc de Blancs Premier Cru (France)
Nicolas Feuillatte Brut (France)
Taittinger Brut La Française (France)
PAIRINGS
- Herbed Crème Fraîche Dip with Crudités, p. 15
- Potato Pancakes with Smoked Salmon, Caviar and Dill Cream, p. 211
- Winter Squash and Gouda Croquettes, p. 294

DRY, RICH CHAMPAGNE
Bollinger Brut Special Cuvée (France)
Pol Roger Brut Global (France)
Veuve Clicquot Brut Yellow Label (France)
PAIRINGS
- Eggs with Brown Butter and Salmon Caviar, p. 14
- Warm Leek and Goat Cheese Dip, p. 15
- Steamed Dungeness Crab with Meyer Lemon Aioli, p. 35

DRY, FRUITY SPARKLING WINE
Domaine Ste. Michelle Cuvée Brut (Washington State)
Gloria Ferrer Sonoma Brut (California)
Nino Franco Prosecco Rustico (Italy)
PAIRINGS
- Cheese Crisps, p. 27
- Redfish on the Half Shell, p. 34
- Creamy Risotto with Edamame, p. 172

DRY, EARTHY SPARKLING WINE
Jaume Serra Cristalino Brut NV (Spain)
Raventós i Blanc L'Hereu Brut (Spain)
Segura Viudas Brut Reserva (Spain)
PAIRINGS
- Chicken Liver Pâté with Pistachios, p. 14
- Piadina with Ricotta, Prosciutto and Arugula, p. 225
- Cod with Ham Powder and Garlic Wafers, p. 232
- Loh Shi Fun, p. 256
- Texas Smoked Salmon Tartare, p. 286

whites

ALBARIÑO & VINHO VERDE
The Albariño grape produces Spain's best white wines, fresh, lively bottlings that pair especially well with seafood—no surprise, as Albariño is grown in Galicia, where the fishing industry drives the economy. Mostly made in stainless steel tanks without oak, Albariño has crisp flavors that suggest grapefruit and other citrus fruits, with a light mineral edge. Vinho Verde, or "green wine," from northern Portugal, often blends the Albariño grape (called Alvarinho there) with local varieties Loureiro and Trajadura. Bottled so young that it often has a lightly spritzy quality, Vinho Verde has a razor-sharp acidity and ocean freshness; it too is an ideal match for raw shellfish.

ZESTY, FRESH ALBARIÑO/VINHO VERDE
Burgáns Albariño (Spain)
Casal Garcia Vinho Verde (Portugal)
Vionta Albariño (Spain)

PAIRINGS
- Greek Salad Skewers with Anchovy Aioli, p. 24
- Carolina Gold Pilau with Shrimp, p. 65
- Lemony Asparagus Soup, p. 117
- Halibut with Avocado Mash and Green Papaya Slaw, p. 231
- Nantucket Clambake, p. 237
- Stuffed Fried Sardines, p. 294
- Galician Fish Stew, p. 305
- Pan-Glazed Salmon with Oyster Sauce, p. 305
- Tagliatelle with Mussels and Tarragon, p. 334

CHARDONNAY & WHITE BURGUNDY

Chardonnay is grown in almost every wine-producing country in the world, and it's used to create wines in a wide range of styles. It is originally from France's Burgundy region, where the best white Burgundies are powerful and rich, with complex fruit flavors and notes of earth and minerals. More affordable Chardonnays from Burgundy—for instance, those simply labeled Bourgogne Blanc—are crisp and lively, with apple and lemon flavors. Chardonnays from America, Australia and Chile tend to be ripe and full-bodied, even buttery, with higher alcohol levels and vanilla notes from oak aging. Recently, however, more and more wine regions have been experimenting with fruity, fresh Chardonnays produced with very little or even no oak aging. Pair Chardonnays in the leaner Burgundian style with roasted chicken or seafood; the more voluptuous New World Chardonnays pair well with pasta dishes made with cream or cheese, with lobster or other rich seafood and with Asian dishes that include coconut milk.

RICH, COMPLEX WHITE BURGUNDY

Domaine Bouchard Père & Fils Beaune du Château Premier Cru (France)
Joseph Drouhin Beaune Clos des Mouches Blanc Premier Cru (France)
Vincent Girardin Rully Vieilles Vignes (France)

PAIRINGS
- Chicken Soup with Rosemary Matzo Balls, p. 11
- Chilled Shrimp with Remoulade, p. 18
- Marinated Fish with Salmoriglio Sauce, p. 237

LIGHT, CRISP WHITE BURGUNDY

Domaine Jean-Claude Thévenet Mâcon-Pierreclos (France)
Jean-Marc Brocard Domaine Sainte Claire Chablis (France)
Louis Latour Mâcon-Lugny (France)

PAIRINGS
- Supercrispy Pan-Fried Chicken, p. 36
- Thai Chicken Stew with Potato-Chive Dumplings, p. 42
- Mirin-Glazed Halibut, p. 140
- Chicken in Tarragon-Mustard Cream Sauce, p. 153

RIPE, LUXURIOUS CHARDONNAY

Beringer Napa Valley (California)
Hess Monterey (California)
Rosemount Estate Show Reserve Hunter Valley (Australia)

PAIRINGS
- Chestnut and Celery Root Soup, p. 12
- Mini Brioche Lobster Rolls, p. 14
- King Crab and Avocado Shooters, p. 124
- Bacon-Wrapped Shrimp with Passion Fruit Mustard, p. 146
- Shrimp Boil Hobo Packs, p. 146
- Sunchoke and Cauliflower Soup, p. 207
- Corn and Bacon Soup with Jalapeño Crema, p. 210
- Seared Scallops with Sweet Corn Pudding, p. 231
- Fish Curry with Tamarind, p. 234
- Creamy Chicken Soup with Baby Peas and Carrots, p. 288
- Halibut with Lemon Oil and Sautéed Escarole, p. 307
- Chicken Breasts with Leeks and Pine Nuts, p. 308

FRUITY, LOW-OAK CHARDONNAY

Chehalem Inox (Oregon)
Foxglove Edna Valley (California)
Kim Crawford Marlborough Unoaked (New Zealand)

PAIRINGS
- Three-Cheese Mini Macs, p. 17
- Poached Salmon Salad with Lettuce and Asparagus, p. 132
- Bagna Cauda Salad Sandwiches, p. 225
- Chicken Noodle Stir-Fry, p. 256
- Spicy Onion-Garlic Soup with Poached Eggs, p. 287
- Smoked Mozzarella Spread, p. 293
- Sweet-and-Spicy Chicken Curry, p. 310

CHENIN BLANC

Chenin Blanc is the star of France's Loire region, where it's used for complex Vouvrays and Savennières. Chenin has also proved to be at home in parts of California (particularly the little-known Clarksburg region), in Washington State and in South Africa, which produces some of the best-value white wines around—tart, medium-bodied whites with flavors of apple and peach. The more affordable South African, Californian and Washington versions are good with light fish or simple poultry dishes.

FRUITY, SOFT CHENIN BLANC
Hogue (Washington State)
Indaba (South Africa)
Man Vintners (South Africa)
PAIRINGS
- Battered Cod with Marie Rose Sauce, p. 32
- Pasta Shells with Artichoke Cream, p. 61
- Summertime Ribollita, p. 208
- Corn and Shiitake Fritters, p. 212
- Pan-Seared Chicken Breasts with Jamaican Curry, p. 310

COMPLEX, AROMATIC CHENIN BLANC
Château d'Epiré Savennières (France)
Marc Brédif Vouvray (France)
PAIRINGS
- Caramelized Onion and Toasted Bread Soup, p. 10
- Prosciutto-Wrapped Halibut with Asparagus Sauce, p. 140
- Grilled Shrimp with Orange Aioli, p. 238

GEWÜRZTRAMINER
One of the most easily identifiable grapes—the flamboyant aroma recalls roses, lychee nuts and spices such as clove and allspice—Gewürztraminer reaches its peak in France's Alsace region, producing luxuriant, full-bodied wines ranging from dry to quite sweet, with flavors of apricot, apple and baking spices. Gewürztraminer pairs well with classic Alsace cuisine—a rich tarte flambée made with ham and Gruyère, for instance. American Gewürztraminers tend to be less dense and unctuous, though they typically have a touch of sweetness on the finish and a delicate spiciness. Pair them with Asian food of all kinds.

RICH ALSACE GEWÜRZTRAMINER
Domaine Marcel Deiss Bergheim (France)
Trimbach (France)
PAIRINGS
- Ginger Beef and Pork Toasts, p. 22
- Mahimahi Coconut Curry Stew with Carrots, p. 140
- Eggplant Ravioli with Gewürztraminer and Bacon, p. 336

SPICY AMERICAN GEWÜRZTRAMINER
Canoe Ridge Vineyard (Washington State)
Navarro Vineyards (California)
PAIRINGS
- Curried Mussels in White Ale, p. 146
- Cajun-Spiced Shrimp and Corn Salad, p. 222
- Indian Pulled-Chicken Sandwiches, p. 228

GRÜNER VELTLINER
Grüner Veltliner, from Austria, has recently become a darling of top American sommeliers, after decades of near obscurity in the United States. A refreshing, medium-bodied, peppery white wine with stone fruit flavors, it goes with everything from green salads to cold poached salmon to roasted chicken. The best Grüners can be quite expensive and have enormous aging potential.

PEPPERY, REFRESHING GRÜNER VELTLINER
Weingut Hofer (Austria)
Schloss Gobelsburg (Austria)
PAIRINGS
- Asparagus Egg Drop Soup, p. 117
- Sea Bass with Popcorn Ponzu, p. 142
- Sichuan Peppercorn Shrimp, p. 147
- Farfalle with Yogurt and Zucchini, p. 170
- Tuna Salad with Fennel, Cucumber and Tarragon, p. 222

PINOT BLANC & PINOT BIANCO
These are two names for the same grape; the first one is French and the second Italian. The French versions, from Alsace, are musky and creamy-textured; those from Italy have zippier acidity, with pear or even soft citrus flavors. American Pinot Blancs are usually made in the French style, as the name suggests. Pour Pinot Blancs with cheese-based dishes; Pinot Biancos go nicely with light foods like chicken breasts or flaky white fish in a simple sauce.

ZIPPY, FRESH PINOT BIANCO
St. Michael-Eppan (Italy)
Tiefenbrunner (Italy)
PAIRINGS
- Lemony Artichoke and Potato Soup, p. 116
- Chinese Chicken Salad, p. 132
- Grilled Chicken Sandwiches with Mozzarella, Tomato and Basil, p. 228

CREAMY, SUPPLE PINOT BLANC
Hugel & Fils (France)
Robert Sinskey Vineyards (California)
PAIRINGS
- Oyster Tartlets, p. 18
- Crispy Potato Latkes, p. 19
- Halibut with Tartar-Style Dressing, p. 141

PINOT GRIS & PINOT GRIGIO

Pinot Gris (from France's Alsace) and Pinot Grigio (from Italy) are the same grape variety. Italian Pinots (and others modeled on them) tend to be light, simple wines with suggestions of peach and melon. These crisp, fresh whites are ideal as an aperitif or with light seafood or chicken breast dishes. Bottlings from Alsace are richer, with strong notes of almonds, spice and sometimes honey. American versions, mainly from Oregon, often tend more toward the Alsace style, and thus are mostly labeled Pinot Gris. They go well with creamy pastas or smoked foods.

LIGHT, FRESH PINOT GRIGIO

Marco Felluga (Italy)

Meridian (California)

Peter Zemmer (Italy)

PAIRINGS

- Chicory Salad with Quince and Pecans, p. 24
- Stir-Fried Tofu with Bok Choy, p. 130
- Grilled Seafood Kebabs and Orecchiette, p. 138
- Stir-Fried Chicken with Bok Choy, p. 151
- Lemongrass Salad with Chinese Sausage, p. 220
- Sweet-and-Sour Eggplant with Ricotta Salata, p. 230
- Miso Soup with Shrimp and Tofu, p. 291

FULL-BODIED, RICH PINOT GRIS

Benton-Lane (Oregon)

Domaine Weinbach (France)

Domaines Schlumberger Les Princes Abbés (France)

King Estate (Oregon)

PAIRINGS

- Mustard-and-Coriander-Crusted Salmon, p. 144
- Smoked Chicken Pizza with Red Pepper Pesto, p. 156
- Two-Corn Crêpes, p. 212
- Knuckle Sandwich, p. 227
- Pumpkin and Yellow Split Pea Soup, p. 288

RIESLING

Riesling is one of the great white grapes, and the style of the wines it produces varies dramatically by region. German Rieslings balance impressive acidity with apple and citrus fruit flavors, and range from dry and refreshing to sweet and unctuous. Alsace and Austrian Rieslings are higher in alcohol, which makes them more full-bodied, but they are quite dry, full of mineral notes. Australia's Rieslings (the best are from the Clare Valley) are zippy and full of lime and other citrus flavors. Those from Washington State tend to split the difference, offering juicy, appley fruit and lively acidity, with a hint of sweetness. Rieslings are extraordinarily versatile with food. In general, pair lighter, crisper Rieslings with delicate (or raw) fish; more substantial Rieslings are good with Asian food, chicken, salmon and tuna.

TART, CITRUSY RIESLING

Banrock Station (Australia)

Knappstein Clare Valley (Australia)

Penfolds Eden Valley Reserve (Australia)

PAIRINGS

- Whole Wheat Linguine with Manila Clams, p. 64
- Asian Chicken Noodle Soup, p. 116
- Spicy Vietnamese Chicken Sandwiches, p. 133
- Grilled Mahimahi with Tomatoes Two Ways, p. 139
- Grilled Shrimp Summer Rolls, p. 212
- Asian Shrimp and Cabbage Salad, p. 222
- Shrimp Fried Rice, p. 252
- Lemony Herb-Grilled Jumbo Shrimp, p. 307
- Spicy Shrimp in Chile Sauce, p. 307
- Spaghetti with Clams and Green Beans, p. 335

VIVID, LIGHTLY SWEET RIESLING

Columbia Winery Cellarmaster's (Washington State)

J. Lohr Estates Bay Mist (California)

Weingut Selbach-Oster Estate (Germany)

PAIRINGS

- Spicy Red Curry Chicken, p. 151
- Steamed Fish with Mushrooms and Noodles, p. 304
- Shrimp with Green Beans and Toasted Coconut, p. 308

FULL-BODIED, MINERALLY RIESLING

Domaine Marc Kreydenweiss Andlau (France)

Dr. Konstantin Frank (New York State)

Hiedler Heiligenstein (Austria)

PAIRINGS

- Dan Dan Noodles, p. 20
- Green-Chile Chicken Thighs with Arugula Salad, p. 36
- Ginger Duck Salad with Green Tea Dressing, p. 39

SAUVIGNON BLANC

Sauvignon's herbal scent and tart, citrus-driven flavors make it instantly identifiable. The best regions for Sauvignon are the Loire Valley in France, where it takes on a firm, minerally depth; New Zealand, where it recalls the tartness of gooseberries and, sometimes, an almost green, jalapeño-like note; California, where it pairs crisp grassiness and a melon-like flavor; and South Africa, particularly the Cape region, where it combines the minerality of France with the rounder fruit of California. Sauvignon Blanc teams well with light fish, shellfish, salads and green vegetables, and it's a perfect aperitif, too.

LIVELY, TART SAUVIGNON BLANC
Geyser Peak Winery (California)
Pomelo (California)
Westerly Vineyards (California)
PAIRINGS
- Green Salad with Goat Cheese and Pistachios, p. 25
- Sizzled Clams with Udon Noodles and Watercress, p. 63
- Egg White Soufflés with Ratatouille, p. 118
- Fromage Fort, p. 119
- Blood Orange–Scallop Ceviche, p. 123
- Lemony Shrimp Salad, p. 130
- Wild Striped Bass with Scallions and Herb Salad, p. 142
- Grilled Scallops with Parsley Salad, p. 145
- Zesty Braised Chicken with Lemon and Capers, p. 154
- Summer Squash and Tomato Tart, p. 214
- Grilled Squid with Miner's Lettuce Salad, p. 221
- Green Salad with Tangy Mustard Vinaigrette, p. 296
- Potato Chips with Chèvre, Pepper Jelly and Bacon, p. 296
- Crunchy Vietnamese Chicken Salad, p. 302

MINERALLY, COMPLEX SAUVIGNON BLANC
Craggy Range Winery (New Zealand)
Henri Bourgeois Sancerre (France)
Santa Rita Reserva (Chile)
PAIRINGS
- Watercress Salad with Beets and Garlic Crostini, p. 22
- Fallen Polenta and Goat Cheese Soufflé with Mixed Salad, p. 117
- Smoked Sablefish and Potato Salad with Capers, p. 287

SOAVE, VERDICCHIO & GAVI
These three light, usually inexpensive wines from Italy all match well with a wide range of foods. Soave, mostly made from the Garganega grape, is a fruity white that often has an almond note. Verdicchio, made from the grape of the same name, has a lemony zestiness. Gavi, made from a grape called Cortese, is typically tart, with an aroma that suggests fresh limes. All pair well with herby pasta sauces like pesto, white fish or vegetable dishes.

FRESH, LIVELY SOAVE OR SIMILAR ITALIAN WHITE
Banfi Principessa Gavi (Italy)
Inama Soave Classico (Italy)
Villa Bucci Verdicchio (Italy)
PAIRINGS
- Spinach and Egg-Drop Pasta Soup, p. 12
- Bagel Chips with Ricotta, Chive Puree and Prosciutto, p. 17
- Scallop Fritters, p. 122
- Swordfish Spiedini, p. 135
- Grilled Vegetable Bruschetta, p. 216
- Rock Shrimp Poke with Ginger Soy Sauce and Hijiki, p. 238
- Vitello Tonnato, p. 248
- Cold Peanut Noodles with Tofu and Red Peppers, p. 257
- Chicory and Endive Salad with Spiced Pistachios, p. 297
- Crispy Turkey Cutlets with Walnut-Sage Sauce, p. 313
- Penne with Cauliflower and Leeks, p. 337

VERMENTINO
An up-and-coming white grape from the coastal regions of Italy, Vermentino marries vivacious acidity with stony minerality. The best Vermentinos come from very different parts of Italy—from Liguria in the north and from the island of Sardinia, off the central west coast. Drink Vermentino with seafood dishes of all kinds.

FRESH, MINERALLY VERMENTINO
Antinori (Italy)
Argiolas Costamolino (Italy)
Sella & Mosca La Cala (Italy)
PAIRINGS
- Green Salad with Nutty Vinaigrette, p. 27
- Salt-Baked Branzino with Citrus, Fennel and Herbs, p. 32
- Vegetable and Chicken Stir-Fry, p. 39
- Striped Bass with Spiced Vegetables, p. 141
- Crispy Tuna with Tuna-Caper Sauce, p. 142
- Broken Pappardelle with Shrimp and Zucchini, p. 170
- Orecchiette with Grilled Squid, Arugula and Chickpeas, p. 171
- Vegetable Soup with Fennel, Herbs and Parmesan, p. 207
- Smoked Trout Salad with Apple and Manchego, p. 221
- Tuna, Olive and Bread Salad, p. 224
- Baked Sole with Pecorino and Butter, p. 230
- Shellfish Paella with Fregola, p. 250
- Orecchiette with Pistachio Pesto, p. 257

VIOGNIER

Viogniers are seductive white wines, lush with peach and honeysuckle scents, a round, mouth-filling texture and little acidity. The Condrieu region in France's Rhône Valley produces the world's greatest Viogniers, and they can often be quite expensive; California and occasionally Australia have also had success with this grape. Viognier pairs well with grilled seafood; it's also a good match for most foods flavored with fruit salsas.

LUSH, FRAGRANT VIOGNIER
Cave Yves Cuilleron Condrieu (France)
Cono Sur (Chile)
Qupé Ibarra-Young Vineyard (California)
PAIRINGS
- Butternut Squash Soup with Smoked Cheddar, p. 12
- Pork and Wild Mushroom Daube, p. 44
- Crispy Tofu with Noodles, p. 64
- Chicken Liver Pâté, p. 121
- Seared Scallops with Cauliflower and Capers, p. 145
- Gingered Butternut Squash Soup, p. 288
- Mussel and Spinach Bisque, p. 290
- Spice-Crusted Tuna with Thai Snow Pea Salad, p. 302

rosés

Rosé—that is, dry rosé—may be the world's most underrated wine. Combining the light, lively freshness of white wines with the fruit and depth of reds, good rosés pair well with a remarkable range of foods, from delicate fish like sole to meats such as pork and veal. They also complement a range of ethnic cuisines—Chinese, Thai, Mexican and Greek. The best rosés, from southern France, are typically blends of grapes such as Syrah, Grenache, Cinsaut and Mourvèdre. Italy, Greece and Spain also produce terrific, refreshing rosés. American and Australian rosés, which tend to be fruitier and heavier, can also be very good.

FRESH, FRUITY ROSÉ
Château Routas Rouvière (France)
Crios de Susana Balbo (Argentina)
SoloRosa (California)
PAIRINGS
- Pimento Cheese, p. 17
- Ricotta-Stuffed Arancini, p. 18
- Italian Tuna, Olive and Tangerine Salad, p. 24

- White Rice with Wild Mushrooms and Merguez, p. 64
- Two-Cheese Enchiladas, p. 118
- Crispy Turkey Kathi Rolls, p. 121
- Deviled Ham Salad on Marbled Rye Bread, p. 133
- Swordfish in Creamy Tomato Sauce, p. 138
- Swordfish Steaks with Smoky Tomato Ketchup, p. 138
- Pan-Roasted Salmon with Tomato Vinaigrette, p. 145
- Crispy Pan-Fried Shrimp and Chorizo Fideo Cakes, p. 148
- Sautéed Chicken with Olives and Roasted Lemons, p. 149
- Grilled Garlic Chicken with Salsa Verde, p. 152
- Penne with Salmon Puttanesca, p. 170
- Italian Tuna Melts, p. 225
- Soft-Shell Crab Sandwiches with Pancetta, p. 226
- Baked Eggplant Marinara with Basil, p. 230
- Tuna with Provençal Vegetables, p. 233
- Grilled Trout with Smoky Tomatillo Sauce, p. 234
- Saffron Risotto with Mussels and Bottarga, p. 252
- Creamy Anchoïade with Crudités, p. 286
- Classic Deviled Eggs, p. 287
- Roquefort Gougères, p. 296
- Roasted Beet Salad with Lemon Crème Fraîche, p. 297
- Indian-Spiced Turkey Breast, p. 316
- Iraqi Lamb and Eggplant Stew with Pitas, p. 328

reds

BARBERA

Barbera, which grows primarily in Italy's Piedmont region, mostly produces medium-bodied wines with firm acidity and flavors suggesting red cherries with a touch of spice. (Barrel-aged versions tend to be more full-bodied, and more expensive.) A great wine for pastas with meat- or tomato-based sauces, Barbera is also good with game and hard cheeses.

BRIGHT, TART BARBERA
Coppo Camp du Rouss Barbera d'Asti (Italy)
Michele Chiarlo Barbera d'Asti (Italy)
Renwood Barbera Sierra Series (California)
PAIRINGS
- Grilled Capon with Salsa Verde, p. 41
- Buckwheat Crêpes with Roast Veal and Parmesan, p. 67
- Grilled Lamb Shwarma, p. 162
- Rosemary Lamb Chops, p. 164
- Linguine with Spicy Sausage and Scallion Sauce, p. 172
- Ham-and-Cheese-Stuffed Veal Chops, p. 248
- Lattice-Crusted Minestrone Pot Pies, p. 293

BEAUJOLAIS & GAMAY

Gamay, the grape of France's Beaujolais region, makes wines that embody everything that region is known for: light, fruity, easy-to-drink reds, ideal for a party or a picnic. Typically they are not aged in oak barrels and are released early (Beaujolais Nouveau, which appears on shelves little more than a month after the grapes are harvested, is the extreme example). Little Gamay is grown outside of Beaujolais, but what has been planted pairs well with the same foods as Beaujolais: light chicken dishes, salads, cheeses and charcuterie.

FRUITY, LIGHT-BODIED BEAUJOLAIS/GAMAY

Château Thivin Côte de Brouilly (France)
Georges Duboeuf Beaujolais-Villages (France)
Marcel Lapierre Morgon (France)

PAIRINGS

- Caramelized Onion Tart with Whole Wheat Crust, p. 20
- Roasted Salmon with Tomato Jam, p. 35
- Sherry-Braised Short Ribs, p. 57
- Meatballs with Tomato Sauce, p. 60
- Barbecued Salmon Sandwiches, p. 135
- Chicken with Carrots and Olives, p. 153
- Grilled Pork Chops with Anchovies and Swiss Chard, p. 244
- Lemongrass Chicken, p. 312

CABERNET SAUVIGNON

Arguably the most significant red wine grape, Cabernet Sauvignon has traveled far beyond its origins in France's Bordeaux—it's now widely planted in almost every wine-producing country. Depending on climate, Cabernet can make either firm, tannic wines that recall red currants with a touch of tobacco or green bell pepper (colder climates) or softer wines that recall ripe black currants or black cherries (warmer climates). It almost always has substantial tannins, which help great Cabernets age for many years. The classic pairing with Cabernet is lamb, but it goes well with almost any meat—beef, pork, venison, even rabbit.

FIRM, COMPLEX CABERNET SAUVIGNON

Château Meyney (France)
Concha y Toro Don Melchor (Chile)
Ladera Howell Mountain (California)

PAIRINGS

- Rack of Lamb with Rosemary Butter, p. 48
- Bone-In Rib Eye Steaks with Chanterelles, p. 53
- Asian Baby Back Ribs, p. 158
- Rack of Lamb with Coconut-Mint Sauce and Peas, p. 161
- Green-Olive-and-Lemon-Crusted Leg of Lamb, p. 327

RICH, RIPE CABERNET SAUVIGNON

Joel Gott Blend No. 815 (California)
Justin Vineyards & Winery (California)
Paringa (Australia)

PAIRINGS

- Grilled Strip Steaks with Sweet Potato Hash Browns, p. 50
- Herb-Crusted Leg of Lamb, p. 164
- Grilled Hanger Steak with Bacon Chimichurri, p. 166
- Duck Confit with Turnips, p. 318
- Grilled Beef with Spicy Asian Dipping Sauce, p. 328

DOLCETTO

Though Dolcetto means "little sweet one," wines from this Italian grape are dry, grapey, tart, simple reds distinguished by their vibrant purple color and ebullient berry juiciness. Dolcettos should be drunk young, with antipasti, pastas with meat sauces or roasted poultry of any kind.

JUICY, FRESH DOLCETTO

Beni di Batasiolo Dolcetto d'Alba (Italy)
Parusso Dolcetto d'Alba Piani Noce (Italy)
Vietti Dolcetto d'Alba Tre Vigne (Italy)

PAIRINGS

- Crispy Frico with Soppressata, p. 27
- Lasagna-Style Baked Pennette with Meat Sauce, p. 63
- Mini Turkey Meat Loaves with Red Pepper Sauce, p. 158
- Seared Chicken Liver Salad, p. 220
- Crispy Pork Milanese, p. 247
- Chicken Cutlets with Green Olive Pan Sauce, p. 308
- Fried Veal Cutlets with Herb Salad, p. 332
- Slow-Cooker Sausage and Vegetable Risotto, p. 339

GRENACHE

When made well, Grenache produces full-bodied, high-alcohol red wines that tend to be low in acidity and full of black cherry and raspberry flavors. Grenache is often blended with other grapes to make dark, powerful reds in regions such as France's Châteauneuf-du-Pape or Spain's Rioja and Priorato. On its own in Australia and the United States, it can produce deeply fruity, juicy wines that go perfectly with grilled meats, sausages and highly spiced dishes.

seasonal pairing menus

winter

Eggs with Brown Butter
and Salmon Caviar
P. 14

Chicory Salad with
Quince and Pecans
P. 24

Dry, rich Champagne

Slow-Roasted Pork
P. 48

Creamy Potatoes
with Bacon
P. 79

Braised Red Cabbage
P. 76

Maple-Glazed Root
Vegetables
P. 78

Intense, fruity Zinfandel

Sticky Toffee Pudding
P. 96

spring

Fromage Fort
P. 119

Lemony Asparagus Soup
P. 117

Zesty, fresh Albariño

Herb-Crusted
Leg of Lamb
P. 164

Sage Polenta
P. 182

Cannellini and Green
Bean Salad
P. 176

Chilean Tomato
and Onion Salad
P. 176

Rich, ripe Cabernet Sauvignon

Strawberry Shortcakes with
Meyer Lemon Cream
P. 198

summer

Corn and Shiitake Fritters
P. 212

Watermelon Gazpacho
P. 208

Fruity, soft Chenin Blanc

Double-Decker Burgers
with Goat Cheese
P. 249

Potato Salad
with Bacon and
Barbecue Sauce
P. 264

Grilled Vegetable Salad
P. 259

Bread-and-Butter
Pickles
P. 264

Lively, fruity Merlot

Peach-Raspberry Pie
P. 275

autumn

Cashews with Crispy Sage
P. 300

Pumpkin and Yellow
Split Pea Soup
P. 288

Full-bodied, rich Pinot Gris

Chicken Breasts with
Leeks and Pine Nuts
P. 308

Whipped Potatoes
P. 341

Caramelized Broccoli
P. 349

Green Salad with Tangy
Mustard Vinaigrette
P. 296

Ripe, luxurious Chardonnay

Apple Cake with
Toffee Crust
P. 366

JUICY, SPICY GRENACHE
Beckmen Vineyards Estate (California)
Bodegas Zabrin Garnacha de Fuego (Spain)
Yalumba Bush Vine (Australia)
PAIRINGS
- Sicilian-Style Meatballs, p. 60
- Berber-Spiced Chicken Breasts, p. 152
- Tandoori Leg of Lamb, p. 164
- Eggplant Caponatina, p. 214
- Lamb Chops and Ragù with Malloreddus, p. 251
- Spaghettini with Eggplant and Fried Capers, p. 257
- Chicken with Catalan Picada, p. 309
- Grilled Quail with Pine Nuts and Currants, p. 317
- Aromatic Braised Lamb with Prunes and Pine Nuts, p. 328

MALBEC
Originally used as a blending grape in France's Bordeaux region, Malbec has found its true home in Argentina's Mendoza region. There, it produces darkly fruity wines with hints of black pepper and leather—like a traditional rustic country red, but with riper, fuller fruit. Malbecs are often very affordable, too, and go wonderfully with steaks and roasts, hearty stews and grilled sausages.

RUSTIC, PEPPERY MALBEC
Bodega Catena Zapata (Argentina)
Bodega Norton (Argentina)
Mendel (Argentina)
PAIRINGS
- Chicken and Cheese Enchiladas Verdes, p. 40
- Horseradish-and-Herb-Crusted Beef Rib Roast, p. 54
- Adobo-Rubbed Beef Tenderloin, p. 56
- Sweet and Savory Pork Empanadas, p. 122
- Soft Pork Tacos with Spicy Black Beans, p. 134
- Brazilian Beer–Marinated Chicken, p. 152
- Missouri Baby Back Ribs with Apple Slaw, p. 159
- Roast Pork Shoulder with Fennel and Potatoes, p. 161
- Four-Pepper Steak au Poivre, p. 166
- Grilled Steaks with Ancho Mole Sauce, p. 166
- Easy Chicken Fajitas, p. 228
- Smoky Strip Steaks with Chimichurri Sauce, p. 247
- Pork and Pink Bean Soup, p. 290
- Herb-Crusted Pork Roast with Ginger-Fig Compote, p. 326

MERLOT
The most widely planted grape in France's Bordeaux region isn't Cabernet Sauvignon; it's Merlot. That's because Merlot blends so well with other grapes, and also because Merlot's gentle succulence and plummy flavors have gained favor as worldwide tastes have shifted toward fruitier, easier-drinking wines. Good Merlots are made in France, Italy, Chile, the United States and Australia, and all of them tend to share supple, velvety tannins and round black cherry or plum flavors. Merlot pairs beautifully with many foods—try it with pâtés or other charcuterie, pork or veal roasts, rich, cheesy gratins and even hamburgers.

LIVELY, FRUITY MERLOT
Columbia Crest Grand Estates (Washington State)
Francis Coppola Diamond Collection (California)
Hardys Stamp of Australia (Australia)
PAIRINGS
- Eggplant Caponata Crostini, p. 22
- Cheddar-and-Cayenne Crackers, p. 27
- Pork-and-Ricotta Meatballs in Tomato Sauce, p. 47
- All-American Hamburgers with Red Onion Compote, p. 50

DEEP, VELVETY MERLOT
Avignonesi Desiderio (Italy)
L'Ecole No 41 (Washington State)
Pride Mountain Vineyards (California)
PAIRINGS
- Beef Brisket Pot Roast, p. 56
- Lemon-Brined Fried Chicken, p. 313
- Roasted Rack of Pork with Sausage Stuffing, p. 324

NEBBIOLO, BAROLO & BARBARESCO
Nebbiolo is the greatest grape of Italy's Piedmont. And if you ask a farmer, it is unquestionably one of the most difficult to grow. Certainly it is formidable, with fierce tannins and acidity, but it is also gloriously scented—"tar and roses" is the classic description—and has a supple, evocative flavor that lingers on the tongue. Those flavors are more substantial and emphatic in Barolos and more delicate and filigreed in Barbarescos, the two primary wines from Piedmont. Pour good Nebbiolo with foods such as braised short ribs, beef roasts, bollito misto and anything that involves truffles.

COMPLEX, AROMATIC NEBBIOLO
Pio Cesare Barolo (Italy)
Produttori del Barbaresco Barbaresco (Italy)
Prunotto Barolo (Italy)

wine pairings

PAIRINGS
- Slow-Braised Osso Buco, p. 59
- Stir-Fried Pork Belly with Kimchi, p. 160
- Pappardelle with Milk-Roasted Baby Goat Ragù, p. 255

PINOT NOIR & RED BURGUNDY

Pinot Noir probably inspires more rhapsodies—and disappointments—among wine lovers than any other grape. When it's good, it's ethereally aromatic, with flavors ranging from ripe red berries to sweet black cherries, and tannins that are firm but never obtrusive. (When bad, unfortunately, it's acidic, raspy and bland.) The greatest Pinot Noirs come from France's Burgundy region, age-worthy wines that are usually quite expensive. More affordable and typically more fruit-forward Pinots can be found from California and Oregon as well as New Zealand, Chile and Australia. Pinot Noir pairs well with a wide range of foods—fruitier versions make a great match with salmon or other fatty fish, roasted chicken or pasta dishes; bigger, more tannic Pinots are ideal with duck and other game birds, casseroles or, of course, stews such as beef bourguignon.

COMPLEX, ELEGANT PINOT NOIR
Faiveley Nuits-St-Georges (France)
Felton Road Central Otago (New Zealand)
Merry Edwards Klopp Ranch (California)
PAIRINGS
- Cornish Hens with Porcini-Rice Stuffing, p. 238
- Crispy Twice-Fried Chicken, p. 242
- Spiced Pork Tenderloin with Hazelnut Vinaigrette, p. 319
- Bison Rib Eye Steaks with Roasted Garlic, p. 329
- Stir-Fried Noodles with Chanterelles, p. 334

RIPE, JUICY PINOT NOIR
A to Z (Oregon)
Au Bon Climat Santa Barbara County (California)
DeLoach Russian River Valley (California)
PAIRINGS
- Malabar Spice–Crusted Hanger Steaks, p. 53
- Salmon Steaks with Soy-Maple Glaze, p. 144
- Cornish Hens with Challah Stuffing, p. 154
- Rosemary-Grilled Chicken with Mushroom Sauce, p. 241
- Mushroom Barley Soup with Mini Meatballs, p. 290
- Grilled Beef Rolls, p. 304
- Salmon with Tomato-Braised Chickpeas, p. 305
- Roasted Capon with Fig-and-Prosciutto Stuffing, p. 317
- Grilled Chorizo with Tangy Caramelized Onions, p. 323

RIOJA & TEMPRANILLO

Tempranillo, the top red grape of Spain, is best known as the main component in red Rioja, where it contributes earthy cherry flavors and firm structure. It is also used in almost every other region of Spain, and generally produces medium-bodied, firm reds suitable for meat dishes of all kinds, particularly lamb.

EARTHY, MEDIUM-BODIED TEMPRANILLO
Cuné Viña Real Reserva (Spain)
Finca Allende Rioja (Spain)
Marqués de Cáceres Rioja Crianza (Spain)
PAIRINGS
- Spanish Devils, p. 17
- Stir-Fried Chicken in Lettuce Leaves, p. 149
- Almond Skordalia, p. 173
- Fennel Slaw with Bresaola and Walnut Pesto, p. 221
- Milk-Braised Pork Tenderloin with Spinach, p. 247
- Pork Chops with Shallots, p. 318
- Pork with Grilled Vegetable Pisto, p. 323
- Spanish-Style Beef Brisket, p. 330

SANGIOVESE

Sangiovese is primarily known for the principal role it plays in Tuscan wines such as Chianti, Brunello and Carmignano, though these days more and more of it is also being grown in the United States and Australia. Italian Sangioveses have vibrant acidity and substantial tannins, along with fresh cherry fruit and herbal scents. New World versions tend toward softer acidity and fleshier fruit. Pair Sangioveses with rare steaks, roasted game birds (or wild boar), rich chicken or mushroom dishes or anything with tomato sauce.

CHERRY-INFLECTED, EARTHY SANGIOVESE
Castello Banfi Col di Sasso (Italy)
Castello di Monsanto Chianti Classico Riserva (Italy)
Di Majo Norante (Italy)
PAIRINGS
- Passatelli in Brodo, p. 10
- Basque Chicken with Sweet Peppers and Tomatoes, p. 41
- Tuscan Pork Stew with Polenta, p. 46
- Grilled Meatballs with Scallion and Cheese Salad, p. 59
- Ham, Soppressata and Two-Cheese Stromboli, p. 67
- Chicken Saltimbocca, p. 154
- T-Bone Fiorentina with Sautéed Spinach, p. 168
- Tuscan-Style Veal Chops, p. 168
- Creamy Sun-Dried Tomato Soup with Panini, p. 206

- Pappa al Pomodoro, p. 206
- Chicken alla Diavola, p. 241
- Bucatini with Sausage and Peas, p. 253
- Malay Gnocchi with Shredded Pork Sauce, p. 253
- Roasted Turkey with Tangerine Glaze, p. 314
- Corzetti Pasta with Veal Ragù, p. 332
- Gnocchi Gratin with Pine Nuts and Gorgonzola, p. 335

SYRAH & SHIRAZ

Probably no other grape scores higher on the intensity meter than Syrah. It's the marquee grape of France's Rhône Valley, where it makes smoky, powerful reds with hints of black pepper. It has also become the signature grape of Australia, where it's known as Shiraz, and typically produces fruitier, less tannic wines marked by sweet blackberry flavors. American Syrahs lean more toward the Australian mold, thanks to California's similarly moderate weather; there are a few very good, earthy Syrahs coming from South Africa, too. Barbecued foods with a smoky char pair nicely with Syrah, as do lamb, venison and game birds.

INTENSE, SPICY SYRAH

Alain Graillot Crozes-Hermitage (France)
E. Guigal Hermitage (France)
K Vintners Milbrandt (Washington State)
PAIRINGS
- Red Wine–Braised Lamb Shanks, p. 48
- Beef Stew in Red Wine Sauce, p. 169
- Slow-Roasted Pork Belly with Eggplant, p. 244
- Roast Pork Loin with Saba, p. 245
- Sausages with Grapes, p. 319
- Pork and Tomatillo Stew, p. 324
- Asian-Spiced Short Ribs, p. 330

ROUND, DEEP-FLAVORED SHIRAZ OR SYRAH

d'Arenberg The Footbolt (Australia)
Stolpman Estate (California)
Torbreck Woodcutters (Australia)
PAIRINGS
- Asian-Glazed Pork Shoulder, p. 42
- Rack of Lamb with Arugula Pesto, p. 162
- Braised Chicken with Oaxacan Chocolate Mole, p. 312

FRUITY, LUSCIOUS SHIRAZ

Banrock Station (Australia)
Jacob's Creek (Australia)
Porcupine Ridge (South Africa)

PAIRINGS
- Red Wine–Braised Chuck Roast, p. 56
- Pork Fried Rice, p. 65
- Chicken with Coconut-Caramel Sauce and Citrus Salad, p. 151
- Tex-Mex Porterhouse Steaks, p. 165

ZINFANDEL

Though Zinfandel is descended from the Croatian grape Crljenak, the wine it produces is entirely Californian in character. The California wine country's warm, easygoing weather gives Zinfandel a jammy, juicy fruitiness (except when it's made into dull, lightly sweet white Zinfandel). Typically high in both alcohol and flavor—boysenberries with a touch of brambly spiciness—Zinfandel is the perfect cookout wine, great with grilled burgers, sausages or chicken, or even chips and dip.

INTENSE, FRUITY ZINFANDEL

Bogle Vineyards Old Vine (California)
Dashe Dry Creek Valley (California)
Hartford Russian River Valley (California)
PAIRINGS
- Red Curry Buffalo Wings, p. 20
- Baked Beans with Pork Belly and Quince, p. 46
- Slow-Roasted Pork, p. 48
- Thai Grilled Beef Salad, p. 51
- Pepper-Crusted Prime Rib Roast, p. 54
- Spicy Beef Chili, p. 60
- Dry-Rubbed Salmon Tacos, p. 135
- Chile-Chicken Sauté, p. 148
- Chipotle Chilaquiles, p. 148
- Smoky Barbecued Chicken, p. 157
- Pork and Bacon Kebabs, p. 159
- Double-Pork, Double-Cheese Burgers, p. 160
- Barbecued Brisket and Burnt Ends, p. 165
- Bucatini with Pancetta, Pecorino and Pepper, p. 172
- Chicken Quesadillas with Blue Cheese and Caramelized Onions, p. 227
- Caribbean Jerk Chicken, p. 242
- Grilled Steaks with Sweet-Spicy Hoisin Sauce, p. 248
- Grilled Pork and Onion Tacos, p. 304
- Roasted Turkey with Italian Sausage Stuffing, p. 316
- Dr Pepper–Glazed Ham with Prunes, p. 326
- Mexican Shredded Beef with Red Chiles, p. 330
- Red Wine Risotto with Mushroom "Marmalade," p. 339

recipe index

a

almonds
Almond and Cream Spiced Buns, 200, **200**
Almond Ice Milk, 271
Almond-Plum Cake with Crème Fraîche, 271
Almond Skordalia, 173
Asian Bar Mix, 300, **301**
Bacon Baklava, 101
Blackberry and Apple Crisp with Nut Topping, 358
Cantucci di Prato, **362,** 363
Chunky Granola, 110
Cocoa Tuiles with Nuts, 364, **365**
Crunchy Milk Chocolate–Peanut Butter Layer Cake, 369
Dulce de Leche Crispies, 364
Frasca's Gorp, 110, **111**
Grilled Cauliflower Salad with Raisin-Almond Dressing, 71
Lebanese Rice Pudding with Cinnamon and Caraway, 95
Toasted-Coconut Basmati Rice, 351

anchovies
Bagna Cauda Salad Sandwiches, 225
Creamy Anchoïade with Crudités, 286
Crunchy Cabbage Salad, 68
Greek Salad Skewers with Anchovy Aioli, 24, **25**
Grilled Pork Chops with Anchovies and Swiss Chard, 244, **244**
Grilled Squid with Miner's Lettuce Salad and Green Sauce, 221
Puttanesca Sauce, 353

appetizers. *See* **starters**

apples + apple juice
Apple Cake with Toffee Crust, 366, **367**

Apple Pie Granita, **278,** 279
Blackberry and Apple Crisp with Nut Topping, 358
Butternut Squash Soup with Apple and Smoked Cheddar, 12
Missouri Baby Back Ribs with Apple Slaw, 159
Moscato-Roasted Pears and Cider-Poached Apples, 358, **359**
Potato-Apple "Risotto," 57
Smoked Trout Salad with Apple and Manchego, 221
Toasted Wheat Berries with Pancetta and Roasted Apples, 354
Umbrian Apple-Walnut Roll-Ups, 363
Applesauce–Chocolate Chip Bundt Cake, 91

apricots
Apricot Pâtes de Fruits, 104
Dried Fruit Compote in Spiced Syrup, 107
Grandma Zerr's Apricot Kuchen, 360, **361**
Peach-Apricot Cobbler with Almond Ice Milk, 271

artichokes
Fried Baby Artichokes, 23, **23**
Italian Tuna Melts, 225
Lemony Artichoke and Potato Soup, 116
Pasta Shells with Artichoke Cream and Smoked Chicken, 61, **61**
Seared Chicken Liver Salad, 220

arugula
Arugula Salad with Ricotta Salata, 174
Fallen Polenta and Goat Cheese Soufflé with Mixed Salad, 117
Green-Chile Chicken Thighs with Arugula Salad, 36
Grilled Eggplant Salad, 179

Grilled Seafood Kebabs and Orecchiette with Arugula, 138, **139**
Orecchiette with Grilled Squid, Arugula and Chickpeas, 171
Orecchiette with Sautéed Greens and Scallion Sauce, 180, **181**
Piadina with Ricotta, Prosciutto and Arugula, **224,** 225
Rack of Lamb with Arugula Pesto, 162, **163**
Roasted Carrot and Beet Salad with Oranges and Arugula, 70
Salad of Bitter Greens with Balsamic-Glazed Prosciutto, 259
Watermelon and Arugula Salad with Walnuts, 258

asparagus
Asparagus Egg Drop Soup, 117
Asparagus with Poached Eggs and Citrus-Ginger Vinaigrette, 202
Broken Pappardelle with Shrimp and Zucchini, 170
Herbed Crème Fraîche Dip with Crudités, 15
Lemony Asparagus Soup, 117
Poached Salmon Salad with Lettuce and Asparagus, 132
Prosciutto-Wrapped Halibut with Asparagus Sauce, 140
Ten-Vegetable Salad with Lemon Vinaigrette, 174

avocados
Avocado Relish with Caramelized Onions, 357
Citrus and Avocado Salad with Honey Vinaigrette, 70
Dry-Rubbed Salmon Tacos with Tomatillo-Avocado Slaw, 135
Halibut with Avocado Mash and Green Papaya Slaw, 231
King Crab and Avocado Shooters, 124, **124**

b

bacon. *See also* **pancetta**

Bacon Baklava, 101

Bacon, Cheese and Egg Sandwiches with
Hollandaise, 203, **203**

Bacon Fried Rice, 184

Bacon-Wrapped Shrimp with Passion
Fruit Mustard, 146, **147**

BLT, Fried Egg and Cheese Sandwich,
282, **282**

Corn and Bacon Soup with Jalapeño
Crema, 210, **210**

Creamy Potatoes with Bacon, **55,** 79

Double-Pork, Double-Cheese Burgers,
160, **160**

Eggplant Ravioli with Gewürztraminer
and Bacon, 336, **337**

Grilled Hanger Steak with Bacon
Chimichurri, 166, **167**

Iceberg Wedges with Bacon and
Buttermilk Dressing, 344, **345**

Pork and Bacon Kebabs, 159

Pork and Pink Bean Soup with Corn
Muffin Croutons, 290, **291**

Potato Chips with Chèvre, Pepper Jelly
and Bacon, 296

Potato Salad with Bacon and Barbecue
Sauce, 264

Bagel Chips with Ricotta, Chive Puree
and Prosciutto, 17

bananas

Père Roux's Cake, **89,** 92

Barbecue Sauce, Kansas City–Style, 157

barley

Mushroom Barley Soup with Mini
Meatballs, 290

basil

Baked Eggplant Marinara with Basil, 230

Broken Lasagna with Walnut Pesto,
76, **77**

Cucumber-Basil Martini, 216

Grilled Vegetable Bruschetta, 216

Perfect Pizza Margherita, **136,** 137

Salsa Verde, 41

Thai-Basil Sangria, 218, **219**

beans. *See also* **green beans**

Baked Beans with Pork Belly and
Quince, 46

Cannellini and Green Bean Salad,
176, **177**

Creamy Refried Beans, 357

Creamy Risotto with Edamame, 172

Crisp Salami Cocktail Mix, 28

Curry-Roasted Butternut Squash and
Chickpeas, **342,** 343

Farinata, 224

Gazpacho Salad, 175

Grandma Kirk's Baked Beans, 185

Grilled Fava Bean Pods with Chile and
Lemon, 185

Lattice-Crusted Minestrone Pot Pies,
292, 293

Orecchiette with Grilled Squid, Arugula
and Chickpeas, 171

Pork and Pink Bean Soup with Corn
Muffin Croutons, 290, **291**

Rosemary Lamb Chops, 164

Salmon with Tomato-Braised Chickpeas
and Herbed Yogurt, 305

Sautéed Chickpeas with Ham and Kale,
86, 87

Soft Pork Tacos with Spicy Black Beans,
134, **134**

Spicy Beef Chili, 60

Summertime Ribollita, 208

Sweet-and-Sour Pickles, 189

Thin-Sliced Beans with Citrus Zest and
Chives, 76, **77**

Wax Bean and Cherry Tomato Salad with
Goat Cheese, 176

beef

Adobo-Rubbed Beef Tenderloin, 56

All-American Hamburgers with Red
Onion Compote, 50, **51**

All-Time-Favorite Hamburger, 249

Asian-Spiced Short Ribs, 330

Barbecued Brisket and Burnt Ends, 165

Beef Brisket Pot Roast, 56

Beef Stew in Red Wine Sauce, **168,** 169

Bone-In Rib Eye Steaks with
Chanterelles, 53

Chorizo-Olive Burgers with Fried
Egg, 249

Double-Decker Burgers with Goat
Cheese, 249

Fennel Slaw with Bresaola and Walnut
Pesto, 221

Flatiron Steak Salad with Thai
Dressing, 132

Four-Pepper Steak au Poivre, 166

Ginger Beef and Pork Toasts, 22

Grilled Beef Rolls, 304

Grilled Beef with Spicy Asian Dipping
Sauce, 328

Grilled Hanger Steak with Bacon
Chimichurri, 166, **167**

Grilled Steaks with Ancho Mole
Sauce, 166

Grilled Steaks with Sweet-Spicy Hoisin
Sauce, 248

Grilled Strip Steaks with Sweet Potato
Hash Browns, 50, **51**

Horseradish-and-Herb-Crusted Beef Rib
Roast, 54, **55**

Malabar Spice–Crusted Hanger Steaks
with Gingered Carrot Puree, 53

Meatballs with Tomato Sauce, 60

Mexican Shredded Beef with Red Chiles,
330, **331**

Mushroom Barley Soup with Mini
Meatballs, 290

Pepper-Crusted Prime Rib Roast with
Mushroom-Armagnac Sauce, 54

Pimiento Cheese–Stuffed Burgers, 249

Red Wine–Braised Chuck Roast, 56

Sherry-Braised Short Ribs with Potato-
Apple "Risotto," 57

Sicilian-Style Meatballs, 60, **61**

Smoky Strip Steaks with Chimichurri
Sauce, **246,** 247

Spanish-Style Beef Brisket, 330

Spicy Beef Chili, 60

T-Bone Fiorentina with Sautéed
Spinach, 168

Tex-Mex Porterhouse Steaks, 165

Thai Grilled Beef Salad, 51

beets

Beet and Cheddar Risotto, 263

recipe index

Honey-Glazed Roasted Root Vegetables, 345, **345**

Radicchio Salad with Beets, Pear, Walnuts and Roquefort, 340

Roasted Beet Salad with Lemon Crème Fraîche, 297

Roasted Carrot and Beet Salad with Oranges and Arugula, 70

Root Vegetable, Pear and Chestnut Ragout, 68, **69**

Watercress Salad with Beets and Roasted-Garlic Crostini, 22

Bellinis, Virgin Strawberry, 125

berries. *See specific berries*

biscuits

Buttery Buttermilk Biscuits, 376

Flaky Biscuits with Sea Salt, 377

Sweet Lemon-Poppy Biscuits, 377

Bison Rib Eye Steaks with Roasted Garlic, 329, **329**

Blackberry and Apple Crisp with Nut Topping, 358

Blondies, Crispy Meringue-Topped, 364

blueberries

Blueberry-Lemon Parfaits, 276, **277**

Blueberry Muffins with Crumb Topping, 108, **109**

Blueberry Pie, 275

blue cheese

Blue Cheese Dressing, 187

Caramelized Onion Tart with Whole Wheat Crust, 20

Chicken Quesadillas with Blue Cheese and Caramelized Onions, 227

Chicory Salad with Quince and Pecans, 24, **25**

Creamy Blue Cheese Dip, 24

Double-Pork, Double-Cheese Burgers, 160, **160**

Gnocchi Gratin with Pine Nuts and Gorgonzola Dolce, 335

Radicchio Salad with Beets, Pear, Walnuts and Roquefort, 340

Roquefort Gougères, 296

Bluefish, Smoked, Pâté, 211

bok choy

Chinese Chicken Salad, 132

Crispy Tofu with Noodles, 64

Stir-Fried Bok Choy with Miso, 74

Stir-Fried Chicken with Bok Choy, **150,** 151

Stir-Fried Tofu with Bok Choy, 130

Thai Chicken Stew with Potato-Chive Dumplings, 42, **43**

Brandied Peaches, 280

Branzino, Salt-Baked, with Citrus, Fennel and Herbs, 32, **33**

bread dressings and stuffings

Oyster Dressing "Grand-Mère," 84

Roasted Capon with Fig-and-Prosciutto Stuffing, 317

Roasted Turkey with Italian Sausage Stuffing, 316

Tortilla–Corn Bread Dressing, 351

bread puddings

Butternut Squash Bread Pudding, 355, **355**

Kabocha Bread Pudding with Pisco-Soaked Prunes, 99

breads. *See also* **tortillas**

Bread Salad with Tomatoes and Olives, 262

Breadstick Twists, 300

Buttery Buttermilk Biscuits, 376

Caramelized Onion and Toasted Bread Soup, 10

Corn Bread with Scallions, 85

Flaky Biscuits with Sea Salt, 377

Honey Spelt Bread, 108

Pappa al Pomodoro, 206

Pat's Popovers, 110

Raisin Rye Bread, 108

Skillet Corn Bread, 354

Sweet Lemon-Poppy Biscuits, 377

Syrian Pita Bread, 163

Tomato and Bread Salad with Watercress Salsa Verde, 261

Tuna, Olive and Bread Salad, 224, **224**

Turkish Ridged Flat Bread, 184

broccoli

Bay-Steamed Broccoli, 74

Broccoli and Wild Mushroom Casserole, 74

Broccoli-Cheddar Gratin with Chipotle, 75

Broccoli with Cheddar Cheese "Dunk," 269

Broccoli with Garlicky Tapenade, 267

Caramelized Broccoli with Garlic, 349

Roasted Garlic-Parmigiano Broccoli, **345,** 349

Vegetable and Chicken Stir-Fry, 39

broccoli rabe

Broccoli Rabe with Garlic and Red Pepper, 75

Savory Baked Carrot and Broccoli Rabe Terrine, 266

brownies

Gooey Walnut Brownies, 280

Mascarpone-Swirled Brownies with Nutty Caramel Corn, 192

Salted Fudge Brownies, 101

brunch dishes

Asparagus with Poached Eggs and Citrus-Ginger Vinaigrette, 202

Bacon, Cheese and Egg Sandwiches with Hollandaise, 203, **203**

Baked Eggs with Chorizo and Potatoes, 112, **113**

BLT, Fried Egg and Cheese Sandwich, 282, **282**

Blueberry Muffins with Crumb Topping, 108, **109**

Buttery Buttermilk Biscuits, 376

Chanterelle Omelets with Fines Herbes Sauce, 281

Chunky Granola, 110

Cranberry-Walnut Power Bars, 110

Flaky Biscuits with Sea Salt, 377

Frasca's Gorp, 110, **111**

Granola with Maple-Glazed Walnuts, 109

Gruyère Soufflés, 378, **379**

Honey Spelt Bread, 108

Meyer Lemon Marmalade, 109

Over-the-Top Mushroom Quiche, 282, **282**

Pat's Popovers, 110

Poached Eggs with Chicken Hash, 201

Potato Frittata with Prosciutto and Gruyère, 111, **111**

Raisin Rye Bread, 108

Smoked Salmon Panini, 202, **203**

Spicy Indian-Style Scrambled
Eggs, 201

Strawberry Preserves, 281

Sweet Lemon-Poppy Biscuits, 377

Yukon Gold Potato, Leek and Fromage
Blanc Frittata, 112

Bruschetta, Grilled Vegetable, 216

brussels sprouts

Brussels Sprouts with Cranberries, 188

Roasted Brussels Sprouts with Cranberry
Brown Butter, 348, **348**

Sautéed Brussels Sprouts and Squash
with Fried Sage, 349

Buckwheat Crêpes with Roast Veal
and Parmesan, 67

burgers

All-American Hamburgers with Red
Onion Compote, 50, **51**

All-Time-Favorite Hamburger, 249

Chorizo-Olive Burgers with Fried
Egg, 249

Double-Decker Burgers with Goat
Cheese, 249

Double-Pork, Double-Cheese Burgers,
160, **160**

Pimiento Cheese–Stuffed Burgers, 249

buttermilk

Buttermilk Dressing, 187

Buttery Buttermilk Biscuits, 376

butternut squash

Butternut Squash Bread Pudding,
355, **355**

Butternut Squash Soup with Apple and
Smoked Cheddar, 12

Butternut Squash with Homemade
Harissa, 78

Curry-Roasted Butternut Squash and
Chickpeas, **342, 343**

Gingered Butternut Squash Soup with
Spicy Pecan Cream, 288, **289**

Lattice-Crusted Minestrone Pot Pies,
292, 293

Sautéed Brussels Sprouts and Squash
with Fried Sage, 349

Butterscotch Pudding, Rich and Creamy,
96, **97**

C

cabbage. *See also* **bok choy**

Asian Shrimp and Cabbage Salad,
222, **223**

Asian-Style Spicy Coleslaw, 264, **265**

Braised Red Cabbage, 76

Caribbean-Style Sliced Salad, 340

Chowchow, 266

Crunchy Cabbage Salad, 68

Crunchy Vietnamese Chicken
Salad, 302

Dry-Rubbed Salmon Tacos with
Tomatillo-Avocado Slaw, 135

Fennel Slaw with Bresaola and Walnut
Pesto, 221

Missouri Baby Back Ribs with Apple
Slaw, 159

Shredded Green Cabbage Salad with
Lemon and Garlic, 71

Caipirinha, Grilled-Lime, 128

cakes

Almond-Plum Cake with Crème
Fraîche, 271

Apple Cake with Toffee Crust, 366, **367**

Applesauce–Chocolate Chip Bundt
Cake, 91

Cardamom Spiced Crumb Cake, 93

Cranberry Streusel Cake, 368

Crunchy Milk Chocolate–Peanut Butter
Layer Cake, 369

Date Cake with Pistachio Lebneh, 375

Double-Chocolate Layer Cake, 190, **191**

Feta Cheesecake and Wine-Poached
Dates, 94

Gingerbread with Quark Cheesecake,
372, **373**

Grandma Zerr's Apricot Kuchen,
360, **361**

Jacques Pépin's Favorite Pound Cake,
90, **90**

Lane Cake, 92

Lemon Cake with Crackly Caramel Glaze,
196, 197

Lemon Pudding Cakes, 198, **199**

Malt-Ball Cake, 194

Olive Oil and Sauternes Cake with
Roasted Pears, 368

Père Roux's Cake, **89,** 92

Pumpkin Cake with Caramel–Cream
Cheese Frosting, **370,** 371

Pumpkin Cheesecake, 95

Slow-Cooker Sour Cream
Cheesecake, 371

Sticky Toffee Pudding, 96

Strawberry Shortcakes with Meyer
Lemon Cream, 198, **199**

Syrian Walnut-Semolina Cake with Figs
and Chocolate, 194

Walnut Cake with Cinnamon Glaze, 94

Yellow Layer Cake with Vanilla
Frosting, 195

Zucchini Cupcakes with Cream Cheese
Frosting, 273

candy

Apricot Pâtes de Fruits, 104

Best-Ever Nut Brittle, 102

Coffee-Rum Truffettes, 102

Raspberry Pâtes de Fruits, 107

capers

Eggplant Caponatina, 214

Grilled Squid with Miner's Lettuce Salad
and Green Sauce, 221

Smoked Sablefish and Potato Salad with
Capers and Onions, 287

Spaghettini with Eggplant and Fried
Capers, 257

capon

Grilled Capon with Salsa Verde, 41

Roasted Capon with Fig-and-Prosciutto
Stuffing, 317

Caponata, Eggplant, Crostini, 22, **23**

Caponatina, Eggplant, 214

caramel

Caramel–Passion Fruit Sundaes,
376, **377**

Chai-Spiced Caramel Fondue, 366

Crème Caramel, 276

Lemon Cake with Crackly Caramel Glaze,
196, 197

Nutty Caramel Corn, 192

Pumpkin Cake with Caramel–Cream
Cheese Frosting, **370,** 371

recipe index

Cardamom Spiced Crumb Cake, 93

carrots

Baby Root Vegetable Stew with Black Tea Prunes, 79

Carrots with Caraway Seeds, 343

Chicken with Carrots and Olives, 153

Chopped Salad with Apple Vinaigrette, 175

Creamy Chicken Soup with Baby Peas and Carrots, 288

Honey-Glazed Roasted Root Vegetables, 345, **345**

Mahimahi Coconut Curry Stew with Carrots and Fennel, 140

Malabar Spice–Crusted Hanger Steaks with Gingered Carrot Puree, 53

Maple-Glazed Root Vegetables, 78

Minty Peas and Carrots, 74

Roasted Carrot and Beet Salad with Oranges and Arugula, 70

Roasted Red Curry Carrots with Ginger and Garlic, 73

Savory Baked Carrot and Broccoli Rabe Terrine, 266

Ten-Vegetable Salad with Lemon Vinaigrette, 174

Vegetable Salad with Curry Vinaigrette and Fresh Mozzarella, 70

Vegetables à la Grecque, 87

cashews

Best-Ever Nut Brittle, 102

Cashews with Crispy Sage and Garlic, 300, **301**

Rosemary-Maple Cashews, 28

cauliflower

Cauliflower Pilaf, 350

Fragrant Cauliflower in Tomato Sauce, 350

Grilled Cauliflower Salad with Raisin-Almond Dressing, 71

Hot, Buttered Cauliflower Puree, 73

Penne with Cauliflower and Leeks, 337, **337**

Roasted Cauliflower with Ajvar Dressing, 73

Roasted Cauliflower with Green Olives and Pine Nuts, 73

Seared Scallops with Cauliflower, Capers and Raisins, **144,** 145

Striped Bass with Spiced Vegetables and Cilantro Dressing, 141

Sunchoke and Cauliflower Soup, 207

celery root

Chestnut and Celery Root Soup with Chorizo and Scallops, 12

Chopped Salad with Apple Vinaigrette, 175

Honey-Glazed Roasted Root Vegetables, 345, **345**

Root Vegetable, Pear and Chestnut Ragout, 68, **69**

Chai-Spiced Caramel Fondue, 366

Champagne Mojitos, 29

chard

Galician Fish Stew, 305

Grilled Pork Chops with Anchovies and Swiss Chard, 244, **244**

Orecchiette with Sautéed Greens and Scallion Sauce, 180, **181**

Summertime Ribollita, 208

Swiss Chard Soufflé, 267

Swiss Chard with Poblanos and Hominy, 75

cheddar cheese

Beet and Cheddar Risotto, 263

Broccoli and Wild Mushroom Casserole, 74

Broccoli-Cheddar Gratin with Chipotle, 75

Broccoli with Cheddar Cheese "Dunk," 269

Butternut Squash Soup with Apple and Smoked Cheddar, 12

Cheddar-and-Cayenne Crackers, 27

Cheese Crisps, 27

Cheesy Grits Casserole, 85

Chicken and Cheese Enchiladas Verdes, 40, **40**

Pimento Cheese, 17

Three-Cheese Mini Macs, **16,** 17

cheese. *See also* **blue cheese; cheddar cheese; cream cheese; goat cheese; Parmesan cheese; ricotta cheese**

Arugula Salad with Ricotta Salata, 174

Bacon, Cheese and Egg Sandwiches with Hollandaise, 203, **203**

Baked Eggplant Marinara with Basil, 230

Baked Sole with Pecorino and Butter, 230

BLT, Fried Egg and Cheese Sandwich, 282, **282**

Bucatini with Pancetta, Pecorino and Pepper, 172

Chicken and Cheese Enchiladas Verdes, 40, **40**

Chopped Salad with Apple Vinaigrette, 175

Classic Tiramisù, **98,** 99

Creamed Spinach with Buttery Crumbs, 344

Creamy Pear, Mascarpone and Pecorino Farfalle, 180

Creamy Risotto with Edamame, 172

Creamy Sun-Dried Tomato Soup with Cheese Panini, 206

Crispy Frico with Soppressata, 27

Double-Pork, Double-Cheese Burgers, 160, **160**

Feta Cheesecake and Wine-Poached Dates, 94

Fettuccine with Escarole and Brie, 182, **183**

Four Cheese–Stuffed Portobellos, 269

Fromage Fort, 119, **119**

Greek Salad Skewers with Anchovy Aioli, 24, **25**

Greek Salad with Feta Mousse, 214, **215**

Green-Chile Chicken Thighs with Arugula Salad, 36

Grilled Chicken Sandwiches with Mozzarella, Tomato and Basil, 228, **229**

Grilled-Pepper Salad with Currants, Capers and Feta, 178

Gruyère Soufflés, 378, **379**

Ham-and-Cheese-Stuffed Veal Chops, 248

Ham, Soppressata and Two-Cheese Strombolis, **13,** 67

Italian Tuna Melts, 225

Mascarpone-Swirled Brownies, 192

Mixed Grilled Vegetables with Fontina
Fonduta, 259

Over-the-Top Mushroom Quiche,
282, **282**

Perfect Pizza Margherita, **136,** 137

Potato Frittata with Prosciutto and
Gruyère, 111, **111**

Smoked Chicken Pizza with Red Pepper
Pesto, 156

Smoked Mozzarella Spread, 293

Smoked Salmon Panini, 202, **203**

Smoked Trout Salad with Apple and
Manchego, 221

Spanish Devils, 17

Sweet-and-Sour Eggplant with Ricotta
Salata, 230

Three-Cheese Mini Macs, **16,** 17

Two-Cheese Enchiladas, 118

Tzatziki Dressing, 187

Vegetable Salad with Curry Vinaigrette
and Fresh Mozzarella, 70

Winter Squash and Gouda
Croquettes, 294

Yukon Gold Potato, Leek and Fromage
Blanc Frittata, 112

cheesecakes

Feta Cheesecake and Wine-Poached
Dates, 94

Gingerbread with Quark Cheesecake,
372, **373**

Pumpkin Cheesecake, 95

Slow-Cooker Sour Cream
Cheesecake, 371

cherries

Granola with Maple-Glazed
Walnuts, 109

Sour Cherry Pie, 275

Sour Cherry Turnovers, 270

chestnuts

Chestnut and Celery Root Soup with
Chorizo and Scallops, 12

Chestnut-Chocolate Mousse, 376, **377**

Root Vegetable, Pear and Chestnut
Ragout, 68, **69**

Sweet Potato Gnocchi with Salsify,
Chestnuts and Ham, 80

chicken

Asian Chicken Noodle Soup, 116

Basque Chicken with Sweet Peppers and
Tomatoes, **40,** 41

Berber-Spiced Chicken Breasts, 152

Braised Chicken with Oaxacan Chocolate
Mole Sauce, 312

Brazilian Beer–Marinated Chicken, 152

Caribbean Jerk Chicken, 242

Chicken alla Diavola, 241

Chicken and Cheese Enchiladas
Verdes, 40, **40**

Chicken Breasts with Leeks and Pine
Nuts, 308

Chicken Cutlets with Green Olive and
Currant Pan Sauce, 308, **309**

Chicken in Tarragon-Mustard Cream
Sauce, 153

Chicken Liver Pâté, 121

Chicken Liver Pâté with Pistachios,
14, **15**

Chicken Noodle Stir-Fry, 256

Chicken Quesadillas with Blue Cheese
and Caramelized Onions, 227

Chicken Saltimbocca, 154

Chicken Soup with Rosemary Matzo
Balls, 11

Chicken with Carrots and Olives, 153

Chicken with Catalan Picada,
309, **309**

Chicken with Coconut-Caramel Sauce
and Citrus Salad, 151

Chile-Chicken Sauté, 148

Chinese Chicken Salad, 132

Chipotle Chilaquiles, 148

Creamy Chicken Soup with Baby Peas
and Carrots, 288

Crispy Twice-Fried Chicken, 242

Crunchy Vietnamese Chicken Salad, 302

Easy Chicken Fajitas, 228

Green-Chile Chicken Thighs with Arugula
Salad, 36

Grilled Chicken Sandwiches with
Mozzarella, Tomato and Basil,
228, **229**

Grilled Garlic Chicken with Salsa
Verde, 152

Indian Pulled-Chicken Sandwiches, 228

Lemon-Brined Fried Chicken, 313

Lemongrass Chicken, 312

Pan-Seared Chicken Breasts with
Jamaican Curry, 310

Pasta Shells with Artichoke Cream and
Smoked Chicken, 61, **61**

Poached Eggs with Chicken Hash, 201

Red Curry Buffalo Wings, 20

Rosemary-Grilled Chicken with
Mushroom Sauce, 241

Sautéed Chicken with Olives, Capers and
Roasted Lemons, 149

Seared Chicken Liver Salad, 220

Smoked Chicken Pizza with Red Pepper
Pesto, 156

Smoky Barbecued Chicken, 157

Spicy Red Curry Chicken, 151

Spicy Vietnamese Chicken
Sandwiches, 133

Stir-Fried Chicken in Lettuce Leaves, 149

Stir-Fried Chicken with Bok Choy,
150, 151

Supercrispy Pan-Fried Chicken, 36, **37**

Sweet-and-Spicy Chicken Curry,
310, **311**

Thai Chicken Stew with Potato-Chive
Dumplings, 42, **43**

Vegetable and Chicken Stir-Fry, 39

Zesty Braised Chicken with Lemon and
Capers, 154, **155**

chickpeas

Crisp Salami Cocktail Mix, 28

Curry-Roasted Butternut Squash and
Chickpeas, **342,** 343

Farinata, 224

Orecchiette with Grilled Squid, Arugula
and Chickpeas, 171

Salmon with Tomato-Braised Chickpeas
and Herbed Yogurt, 305

Sautéed Chickpeas with Ham and Kale,
86, 87

Chicory and Endive Salad with
Spiced Pistachios, 297

Chicory Salad with Quince and
Pecans, 24, **25**

Chilaquiles, Chipotle, 148

recipe index

chiles

Adobo-Rubbed Beef Tenderloin, 56

Braised Chicken with Oaxacan Chocolate
Mole Sauce, 312

Broccoli-Cheddar Gratin with
Chipotle, 75

Caribbean Jerk Chicken, 242

Chile-Chicken Sauté, 148

Chipotle Chilaquiles, 148

Corn and Bacon Soup with Jalapeño
Crema, 210, **210**

Fish Curry with Tamarind, 234, **235**

Grilled Chile Relish, 249

Grilled Trout with Smoky Tomatillo Sauce
and Cucumber Salad, 234, **235**

Mexican Shredded Beef with Red Chiles,
330, **331**

Pan-Seared Chicken Breasts with
Jamaican Curry, 310

Salsa Roja, 118

Spicy Indian-Style Scrambled Eggs, 201

Sweet-and-Spicy Chicken Curry,
310, **311**

Swiss Chard with Poblanos and
Hominy, 75

chili

Mexican Shredded Beef with Red Chiles,
330, **331**

Spicy Beef Chili, 60

chocolate

Applesauce–Chocolate Chip Bundt
Cake, 91

Bittersweet Chocolate Mousse,
372, **373**

Braised Chicken with Oaxacan Chocolate
Mole Sauce, 312

Chestnut-Chocolate Mousse, 376, **377**

Chocolate-Oatmeal Carmelitas, 192

Chocolate Tartlets with Candied
Grapefruit Peel, 193

Cocoa Nib–Chocolate Chip Cookies,
103, **103**

Cocoa Tuiles with Nuts, 364, **365**

Coffee-Rum Truffettes, 102

Cream Puffs with Chocolate Sauce,
104, **105**

Crispy Meringue-Topped Blondies, 364

Crunchy Milk Chocolate–Peanut Butter
Layer Cake, 369

Double-Chocolate Layer Cake, 190, **191**

Espresso-Chocolate Semifreddo, 279

Frasca's Gorp, 110, **111**

Gianduja Mousse, 96

Gooey Walnut Brownies, 280

Grilled Steaks with Ancho Mole Sauce, 166

Malt-Ball Cake, 194

Mascarpone-Swirled Brownies with Nutty
Caramel Corn, 192

Rich Baked Chocolate Puddings, 100

Salted Fudge Brownies, 101

Spotted Porcupine Cookies, 280

Superrich Hot Chocolate with Coconut
Cream, 104

Syrian Walnut-Semolina Cake with Figs
and Chocolate, 194

Warm Churros and Hot Chocolate,
106, 107

chorizo

Baked Eggs with Chorizo and Potatoes,
112, **113**

Chestnut and Celery Root Soup with
Chorizo and Scallops, 12

Chorizo-Olive Burgers with Fried
Egg, 249

Crispy Pan-Fried Shrimp and Chorizo
Fideo Cakes, 148

Grilled Chorizo with Tangy Caramelized
Onions, 323

Nantucket Clambake, **236,** 237

Rioja-Style Potatoes, 343

Spanish Devils, 17

Chowchow, 266

Churros, Cinnamon, and Chilled Peaches
with Arborio Rice Pudding, **272,** 273

Churros, Warm, and Hot Chocolate,
106, 107

Cilantro Dressing, 141

clams

Cod with Ham Powder and Garlic Wafers,
232, **232**

Nantucket Clambake, **236,** 237

Shellfish Paella with Fregola, **250,** 251

Sizzled Clams with Udon Noodles and
Watercress, 63

Spaghetti with Clams and Green Beans,
334, 335

Whole Wheat Linguine with Manila Clams
and Baby Fennel, 64

coconut

Chicken with Coconut-Caramel Sauce
and Citrus Salad, 151

Coconut-Raspberry Thumbprints,
103, **103**

Fish Curry with Tamarind, 234, **235**

Frasca's Gorp, 110, **111**

Lane Cake, 92

Mahimahi Coconut Curry Stew with
Carrots and Fennel, 140

Rack of Lamb with Coconut-Mint Sauce
and Glazed Peas, 161

Shrimp with Green Beans and Toasted
Coconut, 308

Spicy Red Curry Chicken, 151

Superrich Hot Chocolate with Coconut
Cream, 104

Sweet-and-Spicy Chicken Curry,
310, **311**

Toasted-Coconut Basmati Rice, 351

cod

Battered Cod with Marie Rose Sauce, 32

Cod with Ham Powder and Garlic Wafers,
232, **232**

condiments. *See also* **sauces**

All-American Burgers with Red Onion
Compote, 50, **51**

Avocado Relish with Caramelized
Onions, 357

Bitter Orange Compote, 294

Brandied Peaches, 280

Bread-and-Butter Pickles, 264

Chowchow, 266

Golden Yellow Mustard, 188

Grilled Chile Relish, 249

Lemon-Dijon Mayonnaise, 188

Meyer Lemon Marmalade, 109

Pickled Pearl Onions, **30,** 31

Quick Kimchi Cucumbers, 189

Strawberry Preserves, 281

Superfast Salt-and-Sugar Pickles, 189

Sweet-and-Sour Pickles, 189

Sweet-and-Spicy Ketchup, 188

cookies + bars

Cantucci di Prato, **362,** 363

Cartellata Cookies, 100

Chocolate-Oatmeal Carmelitas, 192

Cocoa Nib–Chocolate Chip Cookies, 103, **103**

Cocoa Tuiles with Nuts, 364, **365**

Coconut-Raspberry Thumbprints, 103, **103**

Cranberry-Walnut Power Bars, 110

Crispy Meringue-Topped Blondies, 364

Double-Ginger Sugar Cookies, 102, **103**

Dulce de Leche Crispies, 364

Gooey Walnut Brownies, 280

Hazelnut-Nutella Sandwich Cookies, 103, **103**

Mascarpone-Swirled Brownies with Nutty Caramel Corn, 192

Pecan Sandies, 102, **103**

Salted Fudge Brownies, 101

Spotted Porcupine Cookies, 280

corn

Cajun-Spiced Shrimp and Corn Salad, 222

Corn and Bacon Soup with Jalapeño Crema, 210, **210**

Corn and Shiitake Fritters, 212, **213**

Creamy Grits, 85

Fresh Corn Risotto, 262

Grilled Vegetable Salad, 259

Knuckle Sandwich, **226,** 227

Nantucket Clambake, **236,** 237

Raw Corn and Radish Salad with Spicy Lime Dressing, 258

Seared Scallops with Basil, Anchovy and Sweet Corn Pudding, 231

Shrimp Boil Hobo Packs, 146, **147**

Sweet-and-Sour Pickles, 189

Two-Corn Crêpes, 212

corn bread

Corn Bread with Scallions, 85

Skillet Corn Bread, 354

Tortilla–Corn Bread Dressing, 351

Cornish Hens with Challah Stuffing, 154

Cornish Hens with Porcini-Rice Stuffing, 238

crab

Cucumber-Grapefruit Crab Salad, **124,** 125

King Crab and Avocado Shooters, 124, **124**

Soft-Shell Crab Sandwiches with Pancetta and Remoulade, 226, **226**

Steamed Dungeness Crab with Meyer Lemon Aioli, 35

Summer Melon Soup with Crab, 211

crackers

Cheddar-and-Cayenne Crackers, 27

Cheese Crisps, 27

cranberries

Brussels Sprouts with Cranberries, 188

Cranberry Sauce with Spiced Pumpkin Seeds, 357

Cranberry Streusel Cake, 368

Cranberry-Walnut Power Bars, 110

Granola with Maple-Glazed Walnuts, 109

Roasted Brussels Sprouts with Cranberry Brown Butter, 348, **348**

cream cheese

Feta Cheesecake and Wine-Poached Dates, 94

Gingerbread with Quark Cheesecake, 372, **373**

Pumpkin Cake with Caramel–Cream Cheese Frosting, **370,** 371

Pumpkin Cheesecake, 95

Slow-Cooker Sour Cream Cheesecake, 371

Zucchini Cupcakes with Cream Cheese Frosting, 273

Cream Puffs with Chocolate Sauce, 104, **105**

Crème Caramel, 276

Crème Fraîche Dip, Herbed, with Crudités, 15

crêpes

Buckwheat Crêpes with Roast Veal and Parmesan, 67

Crêpes with Strawberries and Muscat-Yogurt Sauce, **200,** 201

Two-Corn Crêpes, 212

Croquettes, Winter Squash and Gouda, 294

crostini

Eggplant Caponata Crostini, 22, **23**

Watercress Salad with Beets and Roasted-Garlic Crostini, 22

cucumbers

Bread-and-Butter Pickles, 264

Chopped Salad with Apple Vinaigrette, 175

Cucumber-Basil Martini, 216

Cucumber-Grapefruit Crab Salad, **124,** 125

Gazpacho Salad, 175

Greek Salad Skewers with Anchovy Aioli, 24, **25**

Grilled Trout with Smoky Tomatillo Sauce and Cucumber Salad, 234, **235**

Quick Kimchi Cucumbers, 189

Superfast Salt-and-Sugar Pickles, 189

Ten-Vegetable Salad with Lemon Vinaigrette, 174

Tomato, Cucumber and Onion Salad, 261

Tuna Salad with Fennel, Cucumber and Tarragon, 222

Watermelon Gazpacho, 208, **209**

Cupcakes, Zucchini, with Cream Cheese Frosting, 273

currants

Chicken Cutlets with Green Olive and Currant Pan Sauce, 308, **309**

Grilled Quail with Pine Nuts and Currants, 317

curried dishes

Curried Mussels in White Ale, 146

Curry-Roasted Butternut Squash and Chickpeas, **342,** 343

Fish Curry with Tamarind, 234, **235**

Indian Rub, 38

Mahimahi Coconut Curry Stew with Carrots and Fennel, 140

Pan-Seared Chicken Breasts with Jamaican Curry, 310

Red Curry Buffalo Wings, 20

Roasted Red Curry Carrots with Ginger and Garlic, 73

Spicy Red Curry Chicken, 151

Sweet-and-Spicy Chicken Curry, 310, **311**

Vegetable Salad with Curry Vinaigrette and Fresh Mozzarella, 70

recipe index

d

dates

Bacon Baklava, 101

Date Cake with Pistachio Lebneh, 375

Feta Cheesecake and Wine-Poached Dates, 94

Mint-and-Date Dipping Sauce, **120,** 121

Spanish Devils, 17

Sticky Toffee Pudding, 96

desserts. *See also* **cakes; cookies + bars; pies**

Almond and Cream Spiced Buns, 200, **200**

Apple Pie Granita, **278,** 279

Apricot Pâtes de Fruits, 104

Bacon Baklava, 101

Best-Ever Nut Brittle, 102

Bittersweet Chocolate Mousse, 372, **373**

Blackberry and Apple Crisp with Nut Topping, 358

Blanco y Negro, 279

Blood Orange Granita with Vanilla Ice Cream, 100

Blueberry-Lemon Parfaits, 276, **277**

Brandied Peaches, 280

Brûléed Key Lime Tarts, 90, **90**

Caramel–Passion Fruit Sundaes, 376, **377**

Chai-Spiced Caramel Fondue, 366

Chestnut-Chocolate Mousse, 376, **377**

Chilled Peaches with Arborio Rice Pudding and Cinnamon Churros, **272,** 273

Chocolate Tartlets with Candied Grapefruit Peel, 193

Classic Tiramisù, **98,** 99

Coffee-Rum Truffettes, 102

Cream Puffs with Chocolate Sauce, 104, **105**

Creamy Rose Panna Cotta, 276, **277**

Crème Caramel, 276

Crêpes with Strawberries and Muscat-Yogurt Sauce, **200,** 201

Dried Fruit Compote in Spiced Syrup, 107

Dulce de Leche Napoleons, 192

Easy Vanilla Bean Panna Cotta, 195

Espresso-Chocolate Semifreddo, 279

Gianduja Mousse, 96

Grandma Zerr's Apricot Kuchen, 360, **361**

Honey-Lemon Curd with Crème Fraîche, 101

Kabocha Bread Pudding with Pisco-Soaked Prunes, 99

Lebanese Rice Pudding with Cinnamon and Caraway, 95

Lemon Pudding Cakes, 198, **199**

Lemon-Ricotta Puddings, 198

Moscato-Roasted Pears and Cider-Poached Apples, 358, **359**

Nutty Caramel Corn, 192

Peach-Apricot Cobbler with Almond Ice Milk, 271

Poached Pear and Brown Butter Tart, 88, **89**

Pumpkin Puddings with Mile-High Meringue, **374,** 375

Raspberry Pâtes de Fruits, 107

Rich and Creamy Butterscotch Pudding, 96, **97**

Rich Baked Chocolate Puddings, 100

Ricotta with Berries and Bitter Honey, 277

Sour Cherry Turnovers, 270

Sticky Toffee Pudding, 96

Strawberry Shortcakes with Meyer Lemon Cream, 198, **199**

Superrich Hot Chocolate with Coconut Cream, 104

Torta della Nonna, 362, **362**

Umbrian Apple-Walnut Roll-Ups, 363

Vanilla Tapioca Pudding, 197

Warm Churros and Hot Chocolate, **106,** 107

dips + spreads

Chai-Spiced Caramel Fondue, 366

Chicken Liver Pâté, 121

Chicken Liver Pâté with Pistachios, 14, **15**

Creamy Anchoïade with Crudités, 286

Fromage Fort, 119, **119**

Greek Salad Skewers with Anchovy Aioli, 24, **25**

Herbed Crème Fraîche Dip with Crudités, 15

Mint-and-Date Dipping Sauce, **120,** 121

Pimiento Cheese, 17

Red Pepper and Walnut Dip, 125

Smoked Bluefish Pâté, 211

Smoked Mozzarella Spread, 293

Warm Leek and Goat Cheese Dip, 15

dressings + stuffings

Cornish Hens with Porcini-Rice Stuffing, 238

Oyster Dressing "Grand-Mère," 84

Roasted Capon with Fig-and-Prosciutto Stuffing, 317

Roasted Rack of Pork with Sausage Stuffing, 324

Roasted Turkey with Italian Sausage Stuffing, 316

Tortilla–Corn Bread Dressing, 351

drinks

Blood Orange Margaritas, 301

Bluegrass Cobbler, 28

Brewsky Sangria, 299

Champagne Mojitos, 29

Cucumber-Basil Martini, 216

Frost Nip, 29

Ginger Margarita, 128

Grilled-Lime Caipirinha, 128

Hot Spiced Wine, 29

Key Lime Pisco Sour, 217

Le Demon Vert, 29

Mango–Rose Water Cocktail, 301

Middle Eastern Yogurt Coolers, 28

Mock Gin, **30,** 31

O-Hurricane Cocktail, 128, **129**

Paprika Punch, 31

Pisco Cup, 217

Pisco Smash, 217

Pomelo-Mint Mojito, 128

Prosecco-Saba Cocktail, 218

Sangria Flora, 299

Santa's Little Helper, 29

Sticky Toffee Pudding Eggnog, 31

Superrich Hot Chocolate with Coconut
Cream, 104
Sweet-Tart Tarragon Lemonade, 218
Thai-Basil Sangria, 218, **219**
The Thoroughbred, 29
Tuscan Sangria, **298,** 299
Vino Francesca, 299
Virgin Strawberry Bellinis, 125
Warm Churros and Hot Chocolate,
106, 107

duck
Duck Confit with Turnips, 318, **318**
Ginger Duck Salad with Green Tea
Dressing, 39

dulce de leche
Chocolate-Oatmeal Carmelitas, 192
Dulce de Leche Crispies, 364
Dulce de Leche Napoleons, 192

Edamame, Creamy Risotto with, 172
Eggnog, Sticky Toffee Pudding, 31

eggplant
Baked Eggplant Marinara with Basil, 230
Eggplant Caponata Crostini, 22, **23**
Eggplant Caponatina, 214
Eggplant Ravioli with Gewürztraminer
and Bacon, 336, **337**
Egg White Soufflés with Ratatouille,
118, **119**
Grilled Eggplant Salad, 179
Grilled Vegetable Salad, 259
Iraqi Lamb and Eggplant Stew with Pitas,
328, **329**
Pork with Grilled Vegetable Pisto,
322, 323
Slow-Roasted Pork Belly with Eggplant
and Pickled Fennel, 244, **244**
Spaghettini with Eggplant and Fried
Capers, 257
Sweet-and-Sour Eggplant with Ricotta
Salata, 230

eggs
Asparagus Egg Drop Soup, 117

Asparagus with Poached Eggs and
Citrus-Ginger Vinaigrette, 202
Bacon, Cheese and Egg Sandwiches with
Hollandaise, 203, **203**
Bacon Fried Rice, 184
Bagna Cauda Salad Sandwiches, 225
Baked Eggs with Chorizo and Potatoes,
112, **113**
BLT, Fried Egg and Cheese Sandwich,
282, **282**
Chanterelle Omelets with Fines Herbes
Sauce, 281
Chorizo-Olive Burgers with Fried Egg, 249
Classic Deviled Eggs, 287
Eggs with Brown Butter and Salmon
Caviar, 14
Egg White Soufflés with Ratatouille,
118, **119**
Fallen Polenta and Goat Cheese Soufflé
with Mixed Salad, 117
Gruyère Soufflés, 378, **379**
Loh Shi Fun, 256
Poached Eggs with Chicken Hash, 201
Potato Frittata with Prosciutto and
Gruyère, 111, **111**
Spicy Indian-Style Scrambled Eggs, 201
Spicy Onion-Garlic Soup with Poached
Eggs, 287
Spinach and Egg-Drop Pasta Soup,
12, **13**
Swiss Chard Soufflé, 267
Yukon Gold Potato, Leek and Fromage
Blanc Frittata, 112
Empanadas, Sweet and Savory Pork, 122

enchiladas
Chicken and Cheese Enchiladas
Verdes, 40, **40**
Two-Cheese Enchiladas, 118

endive
Chicory and Endive Salad with Spiced
Pistachios, 297
Endive, Radish and Lemon Salad, 174

escarole
Fettuccine with Escarole and Brie,
182, **183**
Halibut with Lemon Oil and Sautéed
Escarole, 307

espresso
Blanco y Negro, 279
Classic Tiramisù, **98,** 99
Coffee-Rum Truffettes, 102
Espresso-Chocolate Semifreddo, 279

Fajitas, Easy Chicken, 228
Farinata, 224

fennel
Fennel Salad with Tarragon and Creamy
Tapenade, 258
Fennel Slaw with Bresaola and Walnut
Pesto, 221
Grilled Scallops with Parsley Salad, 145
Grilled Vegetable Salad, 259
Mahimahi Coconut Curry Stew with
Carrots and Fennel, 140
Roast Pork Shoulder with Fennel and
Potatoes, **160,** 161
Slow-Roasted Pork Belly with Eggplant
and Pickled Fennel, 244, **244**
Ten-Vegetable Salad with Lemon
Vinaigrette, 174
Tuna Salad with Fennel, Cucumber and
Tarragon, 222
Vegetable Soup with Fennel, Herbs and
Parmesan Broth, 207
Whole Wheat Linguine with Manila Clams
and Baby Fennel, 64

feta cheese
Chopped Salad with Apple
Vinaigrette, 175
Feta Cheesecake and Wine-Poached
Dates, 94
Greek Salad Skewers with Anchovy Aioli,
24, **25**
Greek Salad with Feta Mousse, 214, **215**
Grilled-Pepper Salad with Currants,
Capers and Feta, 178
Tzatziki Dressing, 187

figs
Herb-Crusted Pork Roast with Ginger-Fig
Compote, 326, **327**

Roasted Capon with Fig-and-Prosciutto Stuffing, 317

Syrian Walnut-Semolina Cake with Figs and Chocolate, 194

fish. *See also* **anchovies; halibut; salmon; tuna**

Baked Sole with Pecorino and Butter, 230

Battered Cod with Marie Rose Sauce, 32

Cod with Ham Powder and Garlic Wafers, 232, **232**

Fish Curry with Tamarind, 234, **235**

Galician Fish Stew, 305

Grilled Mahimahi with Tomatoes Two Ways, 139

Grilled Trout with Smoky Tomatillo Sauce and Cucumber Salad, 234, **235**

Mahimahi Coconut Curry Stew with Carrots and Fennel, 140

Marinated Fish with Salmoriglio Sauce, 237

Redfish on the Half Shell, 34, **34**

Salt-Baked Branzino with Citrus, Fennel and Herbs, 32, **33**

Sea Bass with Popcorn Ponzu, 142

Shellfish Paella with Fregola, **250,** 251

Smoked Bluefish Pâté, 211

Smoked Sablefish and Potato Salad with Capers and Onions, 287

Smoked Trout Salad with Apple and Manchego, 221

Steamed Fish with Mushrooms and Noodles, 304

Striped Bass with Spiced Vegetables and Cilantro Dressing, 141

Stuffed Fried Sardines, 294, **295**

Swordfish in Creamy Tomato Sauce, 138, **139**

Swordfish Spiedini, 135

Swordfish Steaks with Smoky Tomato Ketchup, 138

Wild Striped Bass with Scallions and Herb Salad, 142, **143**

Fondue, Chai-Spiced Caramel, 366

Fontina cheese

Creamy Sun-Dried Tomato Soup with Cheese Panini, 206

Mixed Grilled Vegetables with Fontina Fonduta, 259

Spanish Devils, 17

frittatas

Potato Frittata with Prosciutto and Gruyère, 111, **111**

Yukon Gold Potato, Leek and Fromage Blanc Frittata, 112

fritters

Corn and Shiitake Fritters, 212, **213**

Scallop Fritters, 122

fruit. *See also specific fruits*

Dried Fruit Compote in Spiced Syrup, 107

g

garlic

Bison Rib Eye Steaks with Roasted Garlic, 329, **329**

Braised Green Beans with Tomatoes and Garlic, 76

Broccoli Rabe with Garlic and Red Pepper, 75

Caramelized Broccoli with Garlic, 349

Cashews with Crispy Sage and Garlic, 300, **301**

Creamy Anchoïade with Crudités, 286

Garlic Wafers, 233

Grilled Romaine Salad with Roasted Garlic Dressing, 178

Oven Fries with Roasted Garlic, 354, **355**

Roasted Garlic-Parmigiano Broccoli, **345,** 349

Spicy Onion-Garlic Soup with Poached Eggs, 287

Watercress Salad with Beets and Roasted-Garlic Crostini, 22

Gazpacho, Watermelon, 208, **209**

Gazpacho Salad, 175

Gianduja Mousse, 96

ginger

Double-Ginger Sugar Cookies, 102, **103**

Ginger Beef and Pork Toasts, 22

Gingerbread with Quark Cheesecake, 372, **373**

Ginger Dressing, 187

Ginger Duck Salad with Green Tea Dressing, 39

Gingered Butternut Squash Soup with Spicy Pecan Cream, 288, **289**

Ginger Margarita, 128

Ginger Rice, 183

Herb-Crusted Pork Roast with Ginger-Fig Compote, 326, **327**

Malabar Spice–Crusted Hanger Steaks with Gingered Carrot Puree, 53

Roasted Red Curry Carrots with Ginger and Garlic, 73

gnocchi

Gnocchi Gratin with Pine Nuts and Gorgonzola Dolce, 335

Gnocchi Parisienne, 182, **183**

Malay Gnocchi with Shredded Pork Sauce, 253

Potato Gnocchi, 336

Sweet Potato Gnocchi with Salsify, Chestnuts and Ham, 80

goat

Pappardelle with Milk-Roasted Baby Goat Ragù, **254,** 255

goat cheese

Double-Decker Burgers with Goat Cheese, 249

Fallen Polenta and Goat Cheese Soufflé with Mixed Salad, 117

Goat Cheese–Garlic Toasts, 211

Goat Cheese, Lentil and Potato Salad, 341

Green Salad with Goat Cheese and Pistachios, 25

Potato Chips with Chèvre, Pepper Jelly and Bacon, 296

Smoked Chicken Pizza with Red Pepper Pesto, 156

Summer Squash and Tomato Tart, 214

Warm Leek and Goat Cheese Dip, 15

Wax Bean and Cherry Tomato Salad with Goat Cheese, 176

Gorp, Frasca's, 110, **111**

Gouda cheese

Creamed Spinach with Buttery Crumbs, 344

Winter Squash and Gouda
Croquettes, 294

Gougères, Roquefort, 296

granita

Apple Pie Granita, **278**, 279

Blood Orange Granita with Vanilla Ice
Cream, 100

Granola, Chunky, 110

Granola with Maple-Glazed Walnuts, 109

grapefruit + grapefruit juice

Candied Grapefruit Peel, 193

Chicken with Coconut-Caramel Sauce
and Citrus Salad, 151

Citrus and Avocado Salad with Honey
Vinaigrette, 70

Cucumber-Grapefruit Crab Salad,
124, 125

Grilled Scallops with Parsley Salad, 145

grapes

Chopped Salad with Apple Vinaigrette, 175

Pisco Smash, 217

Sausages with Grapes, 319

green beans

Braised Green Beans with Tomatoes
and Garlic, 76

Cannellini and Green Bean Salad,
176, **177**

Gazpacho Salad, 175

Green Beans and Salsify with Country
Ham and Pecans, 346, **347**

Green Beans with Shallots and
Walnuts, 346

Green Beans with Soffritto and Country
Ham, **268,** 269

Shrimp with Green Beans and Toasted
Coconut, 308

Spaghetti with Clams and Green Beans,
334, 335

Striped Bass with Spiced Vegetables and
Cilantro Dressing, 141

Summertime Ribollita, 208

Thin-Sliced Beans with Citrus Zest and
Chives, 76, **77**

Vegetable Salad with Curry Vinaigrette
and Fresh Mozzarella, 70

Warm Summer Vegetable Salad with
Brown Butter Dressing, **260,** 261

greens. *See also* **arugula; cabbage; chard;
kale; spinach; watercress**

Bagna Cauda Salad Sandwiches, 225

Beet and Cheddar Risotto, 263

Chicory and Endive Salad with Spiced
Pistachios, 297

Chicory Salad with Quince and Pecans,
24, **25**

Chinese Chicken Salad, 132

Chopped Salad with Apple
Vinaigrette, 175

Crunchy Salad and Buttermilk
Dressing, 187

Endive, Radish and Lemon Salad, 174

Fallen Polenta and Goat Cheese Soufflé
with Mixed Salad, 117

Fettuccine with Escarole and Brie,
182, **183**

Flatiron Steak Salad with Thai
Dressing, 132

Ginger Duck Salad with Green Tea
Dressing, 39

Green Salad with Goat Cheese and
Pistachios, 25

Green Salad with Nutty Vinaigrette,
26, 27

Green Salad with Tangy Mustard
Vinaigrette, 296

Grilled Romaine Salad with Roasted
Garlic Dressing, 178

Grilled Squid with Miner's Lettuce Salad
and Green Sauce, 221

Halibut with Lemon Oil and Sautéed
Escarole, 307

Iceberg Wedges with Bacon and
Buttermilk Dressing, 344, **345**

Leafy Salad and Dijon Vinaigrette, 187

Lemony Shrimp Salad, 130, **131**

Poached Salmon Salad with Lettuce and
Asparagus, 132

Radicchio Salad with Beets, Pear,
Walnuts and Roquefort, 340

Salad of Bitter Greens with Balsamic-
Glazed Prosciutto, 259

Seared Chicken Liver Salad, 220

Smoked Trout Salad with Apple and
Manchego, 221

Stir-Fried Chicken in Lettuce
Leaves, 149

Ten-Vegetable Salad with Lemon
Vinaigrette, 174

grits

Cheesy Grits Casserole, 85

Creamy Grits, 85

Gruyère cheese

Bacon, Cheese and Egg Sandwiches with
Hollandaise, 203, **203**

Four Cheese–Stuffed Portobellos, 269

Gruyère Soufflés, 378, **379**

Potato Frittata with Prosciutto and
Gruyère, 111, **111**

Smoked Salmon Panini, 202, **203**

h

halibut

Galician Fish Stew, 305

Halibut with Avocado Mash and Green
Papaya Slaw, 231

Halibut with Lemon Oil and Sautéed
Escarole, 307

Halibut with Tartar-Style Dressing, 141

Mirin-Glazed Halibut, 140

Prosciutto-Wrapped Halibut with
Asparagus Sauce, 140

ham. *See also* **prosciutto**

Deviled Ham Salad on Marbled Rye
Bread, 133

Dr Pepper–Glazed Ham with Prunes,
326, **327**

Green Beans and Salsify with Country
Ham and Pecans, 346, **347**

Green Beans with Soffritto and Country
Ham, **268,** 269

Ham-and-Cheese-Stuffed Veal
Chops, 248

Ham Hock Stock, 159

Ham Powder, 233

Ham, Soppressata and Two-Cheese
Strombolis, **13,** 67

Sautéed Chickpeas with Ham and Kale,
86, 87

recite index

Sweet Potato Gnocchi with Salsify,
Chestnuts and Ham, 80
Warm Lentil and Ham Salad, **178,** 179
Hash, Chicken, Poached Eggs with, 201
hazelnuts
Cocoa Tuiles with Nuts, 364, **365**
Hazelnut-Nutella Sandwich Cookies,
102, **103**
Spiced Pork Tenderloin with Hazelnut
Vinaigrette, 319
herbs. *See also specific herbs*
Chanterelle Omelets with Fines Herbes
Sauce, 281
Fried Veal Cutlets with Herb Salad, 332
Herb Vinaigrette, 187
Wild Striped Bass with Scallions and
Herb Salad, 142, **143**
Hollandaise Sauce, Classic, 203
Hominy and Poblanos, Swiss Chard with, 75
honey
Honey-Glazed Roasted Root Vegetables,
345, **345**
Honey-Lemon Curd with Crème
Fraîche, 101
Honey Spelt Bread, 108
Ricotta with Berries and Bitter
Honey, 277
hors d'oeuvres. *See* **starters**
horseradish
Horseradish-and-Herb-Crusted Beef Rib
Roast, 54, **55**
Mashed Potatoes with Horseradish
Cream, 341

k

kale
Braised Kale, **55,** 77
Lattice-Crusted Minestrone Pot Pies,
292, 293
Roasted Rack of Pork with Sausage
Stuffing, 324
Sautéed Chickpeas with Ham and Kale,
86, 87
Smoky Kale and Olives, 348

ketchup
Sweet-and-Spicy Ketchup, 188
Swordfish Steaks with Smoky Tomato
Ketchup, 138
Kimchi, Stir-Fried Pork Belly with, 160
Kimchi Cucumbers, Quick, 189
Kumquats, candying, 372

l

lamb
Aromatic Braised Lamb with Prunes and
Pine Nuts, 328
Green-Olive-and-Lemon-Crusted
Leg of Lamb, 327
Grilled Lamb Shwarma, 162, **163**
Grilled Meatballs with Scallion and
Shaved Cheese Salad, **58,** 59
Herb-Crusted Leg of Lamb, 164
Iraqi Lamb and Eggplant Stew with Pitas,
328, **329**
Lamb Chops and Ragù with
Malloreddus, 251
Lasagna-Style Baked Pennette with Meat
Sauce, **62,** 63
Rack of Lamb with Arugula Pesto,
162, **163**
Rack of Lamb with Coconut-Mint Sauce
and Glazed Peas, 161
Rack of Lamb with Rosemary Butter,
48, **49**
Red Wine–Braised Lamb Shanks, 48
Rosemary Lamb Chops, 164
Tandoori Leg of Lamb, 164
lamb sausages
Rice Salad with Merguez and Preserved
Lemon Dressing, 262, **263**
White Rice with Wild Mushrooms and
Merguez, 64
Lasagna-Style Baked Pennette with Meat
Sauce, **62,** 63
Latkes, Crispy Potato, 19, **19**
leeks
Chicken Breasts with Leeks and Pine
Nuts, 308

Fusilli with Creamy Leek Sauce, 180
Warm Leek and Goat Cheese Dip, 15
Warm Summer Vegetable Salad with
Brown Butter Dressing, **260,** 261
legumes. *See also* **beans**
Goat Cheese, Lentil and Potato
Salad, 341
Pumpkin and Yellow Split Pea Soup, 288
Warm Lentil and Ham Salad, **178,** 179
Lemongrass Chicken, 312
Lemongrass Salad with Chinese Sausage
and Mango, 220
lemons + lemon juice
Blueberry-Lemon Parfaits, 276, **277**
Endive, Radish and Lemon Salad, 174
Honey-Lemon Curd with Crème
Fraîche, 101
Lemon Cake with Crackly Caramel Glaze
and Lime-Yogurt Mousse, **196,** 197
Lemon Chess Pie, 91
Lemon-Dijon Mayonnaise, 188
Lemon Pudding Cakes, 198, **199**
Lemon-Ricotta Puddings, 198
Lemon Vinaigrette, 187
Lemony Artichoke and Potato Soup, 116
Lemony Asparagus Soup, 117
Meyer Lemon Marmalade, 109
Sautéed Chicken with Olives, Capers and
Roasted Lemons, 149
Steamed Dungeness Crab with Meyer
Lemon Aioli, 35
Strawberry Shortcakes with Meyer
Lemon Cream, 198, **199**
Sweet Lemon-Poppy Biscuits, 377
Sweet-Tart Tarragon Lemonade, 218
lentils
Goat Cheese, Lentil and Potato
Salad, 341
Warm Lentil and Ham Salad, **178,** 179
lettuce
Chopped Salad with Apple Vinaigrette, 175
Flatiron Steak Salad with Thai
Dressing, 132
Grilled Romaine Salad with Roasted
Garlic Dressing, 178
Grilled Squid with Miner's Lettuce Salad
and Green Sauce, 221

Iceberg Wedges with Bacon and
Buttermilk Dressing, 344, **345**

Leafy Salad and Dijon Vinaigrette, 187

Lemony Shrimp Salad, 130, **131**

Poached Salmon Salad with Lettuce and
Asparagus, 132

Seared Chicken Liver Salad, 220

Ten-Vegetable Salad with Lemon
Vinaigrette, 174

limes + lime juice

Brûléed Key Lime Tarts, 90, **90**

Grilled-Lime Caipirinha, 128

Key Lime Pisco Sour, 217

Lime-Yogurt Mousse, 197

liver

Chicken Liver Pâté, 121

Chicken Liver Pâté with Pistachios,
14, **15**

Seared Chicken Liver Salad, 220

lobster

Knuckle Sandwich, **226**, 227

Mini Brioche Lobster Rolls, 14, **15**

Nantucket Clambake, **236**, 237

mahimahi

Grilled Mahimahi with Tomatoes
Two Ways, 139

Mahimahi Coconut Curry Stew with
Carrots and Fennel, 140

Malt-Ball Cake, 194

Manchego cheese

Four Cheese–Stuffed Portobellos, 269

Smoked Chicken Pizza with Red Pepper
Pesto, 156

Smoked Trout Salad with Apple and
Manchego, 221

mango

Lemongrass Salad with Chinese Sausage
and Mango, 220

Mango–Rose Water Cocktail, 301

maple syrup

Granola with Maple-Glazed Walnuts, 109

Maple-Glazed Root Vegetables, 78

Rosemary-Maple Cashews, 28

Salmon Steaks with Soy-Maple Glaze,
144, **144**

margaritas

Blood Orange Margaritas, 301

Ginger Margarita, 128

marinades

Greek Marinade, 240

Peruvian Marinade, 240

Vietnamese Marinade, 240

Marmalade, Meyer Lemon, 109

Martini, Cucumber-Basil, 216

mascarpone cheese

Classic Tiramisù, **98**, 99

Creamy Pear, Mascarpone and Pecorino
Farfalle, 180

Mascarpone-Swirled Brownies with Nutty
Caramel Corn, 192

Matzo Balls, Rosemary, Chicken
Soup with, 11

mayonnaise

Greek Salad Skewers with Anchovy Aioli,
24, **25**

Grilled Shrimp with Orange Aioli, 238

Lemon-Dijon Mayonnaise, 188

meatballs

Grilled Meatballs with Scallion and
Shaved Cheese Salad, **58**, 59

Meatballs with Tomato Sauce, 60

Mushroom Barley Soup with Mini
Meatballs, 290

Pork-and-Ricotta Meatballs in Tomato
Sauce, 47

Sicilian-Style Meatballs, 60, **61**

Meat Loaves, Mini Turkey, with Red Pepper
Sauce, 158

melon

Summer Melon Soup with Crab, 211

Superfast Salt-and-Sugar Pickles, 189

Sweet-and-Sour Pickles, 189

Watermelon and Arugula Salad with
Walnuts, 258

Watermelon Gazpacho, 208, **209**

Milk, Almond Ice, 271

mint

Champagne Mojitos, 29

Cilantro Dressing, 141

Grilled Squid with Miner's Lettuce Salad
and Green Sauce, 221

Mint-and-Date Dipping Sauce, **120**, 121

Minty Peas and Carrots, 74

Pomelo-Mint Mojito, 128

Rack of Lamb with Coconut-Mint Sauce
and Glazed Peas, 161

Mirin-Glazed Halibut, 140

miso

Miso Dressing, 187

Miso Soup with Shrimp and Tofu,
291, **291**

Stir-Fried Bok Choy with Miso, 74

mojitos

Champagne Mojitos, 29

Pomelo-Mint Mojitos, 128

Monterey Jack cheese

BLT, Fried Egg and Cheese Sandwich,
282, **282**

Two-Cheese Enchiladas, 118

mousse

Bittersweet Chocolate Mousse, 372, **373**

Chestnut-Chocolate Mousse, 376, **377**

Gianduja Mousse, 96

Lime-Yogurt Mousse, 197

mozzarella cheese

Baked Eggplant Marinara with
Basil, 230

Four Cheese–Stuffed Portobellos, 269

Grilled Chicken Sandwiches with
Mozzarella, Tomato and Basil,
228, **229**

Ham, Soppressata and Two-Cheese
Strombolis, **13**, 67

Perfect Pizza Margherita, **136**, 137

Smoked Mozzarella Spread, 293

Vegetable Salad with Curry Vinaigrette
and Fresh Mozzarella, 70

Muffins, Blueberry, with Crumb Topping,
108, **109**

mushrooms

Bone-In Rib Eye Steaks with
Chanterelles, 53

Broccoli and Wild Mushroom
Casserole, 74

Chanterelle Omelets with Fines Herbes
Sauce, 281

recipe index

Chicken in Tarragon-Mustard Cream Sauce, 153

Corn and Shiitake Fritters, 212, **213**

Cornish Hens with Porcini-Rice Stuffing, 238

Creamed Spinach with Buttery Crumbs, 344

Crispy Tofu with Noodles, 64

Four Cheese–Stuffed Portobellos, 269

Loh Shi Fun, 256

Mixed Grilled Vegetables with Fontina Fonduta, 259

Mushroom Barley Soup with Mini Meatballs, 290

Mushroom-Shallot Ragout, 346

Over-the-Top Mushroom Quiche, 282, **282**

Panko-Crusted Mushrooms, 158

Pepper-Crusted Prime Rib Roast with Mushroom-Armagnac Sauce, 54

Pork and Wild Mushroom Daube, 44, **45**

Red Wine Risotto with Mushroom "Marmalade," 339

Roasted Rack of Pork with Sausage Stuffing, 324

Rosemary-Grilled Chicken with Mushroom Sauce, 241

Spicy Red Curry Chicken, 151

Steamed Fish with Mushrooms and Noodles, 304

Stir-Fried Noodles with Chanterelles, 334

Ten-Vegetable Salad with Lemon Vinaigrette, 174

Vegetables à la Grecque, 87

White Rice with Wild Mushrooms and Merguez, 64

mussels

Curried Mussels in White Ale, 146

Mussel and Spinach Bisque, 290

Saffron Risotto with Mussels and Bottarga, 252

Shellfish Paella with Fregola, **250,** 251

Shrimp Boil Hobo Packs, 146, **147**

Tagliatelle with Mussels and Tarragon, 334, **334**

mustard

Dijon Vinaigrette, 187

Golden Yellow Mustard, 188

Mustard-and-Coriander-Crusted Salmon, 144

n

noodles

Asian Chicken Noodle Soup, 116

Chicken Noodle Stir-Fry, 256

Cold Peanut Noodles with Tofu and Red Peppers, 257

Crispy Tofu with Noodles, 64

Dan Dan Noodles, 20

Grilled Shrimp Summer Rolls, 212, **213**

Loh Shi Fun, 256

Roasted Salmon with Tomato Jam, **34,** 35

Sizzled Clams with Udon Noodles and Watercress, 63

Steamed Fish with Mushrooms and Noodles, 304

Stir-Fried Noodles with Chanterelles, 334

nuts. *See also* **almonds; peanuts; pecans; pistachios; walnuts**

Best-Ever Nut Brittle, 102

Cashews with Crispy Sage and Garlic, 300, **301**

Chestnut and Celery Root Soup with Chorizo and Scallops, 12

Chestnut-Chocolate Mousse, 376, **377**

Cocoa Tuiles with Nuts, 364, **365**

Crisp Salami Cocktail Mix, 28

Grilled Quail with Pine Nuts and Currants, 317

Lebanese Rice Pudding with Cinnamon and Caraway, 95

Nutty Caramel Corn, 192

Root Vegetable, Pear and Chestnut Ragout, 68, **69**

Rosemary-Maple Cashews, 28

Spiced Pork Tenderloin with Hazelnut Vinaigrette, 319

Sweet Potato Gnocchi with Salsify, Chestnuts and Ham, 80

Torta della Nonna, 362, **362**

O

oats

Chocolate-Oatmeal Carmelitas, 192

Chunky Granola, 110

Cranberry-Walnut Power Bars, 110

Granola with Maple-Glazed Walnuts, 109

olives

Bread Salad with Tomatoes and Olives, 262

Broccoli with Garlicky Tapenade, 267

Cannellini and Green Bean Salad, 176, **177**

Chicken Cutlets with Green Olive and Currant Pan Sauce, 308, **309**

Chicken with Carrots and Olives, 153

Chorizo-Olive Burgers with Fried Egg, 249

Eggplant Caponatina, 214

Greek Salad with Feta Mousse, 214, **215**

Green-Olive-and-Lemon-Crusted Leg of Lamb, 327

Italian Tuna, Green Olive and Tangerine Salad on Grilled Bread, 24

Italian Tuna Melts, 225

Penne with Salmon Puttanesca, 170, **171**

Puttanesca Sauce, 353

Roasted Cauliflower with Green Olives and Pine Nuts, 73

Sautéed Chicken with Olives, Capers and Roasted Lemons, 149

Smoky Kale and Olives, 348

Tuna, Olive and Bread Salad, 224, **224**

Omelets, Chanterelle, with Fines Herbes Sauce, 281

onions

All-American Hamburgers with Red Onion Compote, 50, **51**

Avocado Relish with Caramelized Onions, 357

Caramelized Onion and Toasted Bread
  Soup, 10
Caramelized Onion Tart with Whole
  Wheat Crust, 20
Chicken Quesadillas with Blue Cheese
  and Caramelized Onions, 227
Chilean Tomato and Onion Salad, 176
Creamed Onions with Thyme and
  Sage, 346
Grilled Chorizo with Tangy Caramelized
  Onions, 323
Pickled Pearl Onions, **30,** 31
Spicy Onion-Garlic Soup with Poached
  Eggs, 287

oranges + orange juice
Bitter Orange Compote, 294
Blood Orange Granita with Vanilla Ice
  Cream, 100
Blood Orange Margaritas, 301
Blood Orange–Scallop Ceviche,
  123, **123**
Citrus and Avocado Salad with Honey
  Vinaigrette, 70
Grilled Shrimp with Orange Aioli, 238
Roasted Carrot and Beet Salad with
  Oranges and Arugula, 70
Roasted Turkey with Tangerine Glaze,
  314, **315**
Osso Buco, Slow-Braised, 59
Oyster Dressing "Grand-Mère," 84
Oyster Tartlets, 18

Paella, Shellfish, with Fregola, **250,** 251
pancakes. *See also* **crêpes**
Crispy Potato Latkes, 19, **19**
Potato Pancakes with Smoked Salmon,
  Caviar and Dill Cream, **210,** 211
pancetta
All'Amatriciana Sauce, 353
Bucatini with Pancetta, Pecorino and
  Pepper, 172
Soft-Shell Crab Sandwiches with
  Pancetta and Remoulade, 226, **226**

Toasted Wheat Berries with Pancetta and
  Roasted Apples, 354
panna cotta
Creamy Rose Panna Cotta, 276, **277**
Easy Vanilla Bean Panna Cotta, 195
Papaya, Green, Slaw and Avocado
  Mash, Halibut with, 231
Parmesan cheese
Buckwheat Crêpes with Roast Veal and
  Parmesan, 67
Chipotle Chilaquiles, 148
Crispy Frico with Soppressata, 27
Crispy Pork Milanese, 247
Farfalle with Yogurt and Zucchini,
  170, **171**
Grilled Meatballs with Scallion and
  Shaved Cheese Salad, **58,** 59
Grilled Vegetable Bruschetta, 216
Roasted Garlic-Parmigiano Broccoli,
  345, 349
Three-Cheese Mini Macs, **16,** 17
Vegetable Soup with Fennel, Herbs and
  Parmesan Broth, 207
parsley
Chanterelle Omelets with Fines Herbes
  Sauce, 281
Fried Veal Cutlets with Herb Salad, 332
Grilled Garlic Chicken with Salsa
  Verde, 152
Grilled Hanger Steak with Bacon
  Chimichurri, 166, **167**
Grilled Scallops with Parsley Salad, 145
Grilled Squid with Miner's Lettuce Salad
  and Green Sauce, 221
Lemony Rice-Parsley Salad, 262, **263**
Salsa Verde, 41
passion fruit
Bacon-Wrapped Shrimp with Passion
  Fruit Mustard, 146, **147**
Caramel–Passion Fruit Sundaes, 376, **377**
pasta. *See also* **noodles**
Broken Lasagna with Walnut Pesto,
  76, **77**
Broken Pappardelle with Shrimp and
  Zucchini, 170
Bucatini with Pancetta, Pecorino
  and Pepper, 172

Bucatini with Sausage and Peas, 253
Corzetti Pasta with Veal Ragù,
  332, **333**
Creamy Pear, Mascarpone and Pecorino
  Farfalle, 180
Crispy Pan-Fried Shrimp and Chorizo
  Fideo Cakes, 148
Eggplant Ravioli with Gewürztraminer
  and Bacon, 336, **337**
E.J.'s Vegetable Noodle Soup, 207
Farfalle with Yogurt and Zucchini,
  170, **171**
Fettuccine with Escarole and Brie,
  182, **183**
Fusilli with Creamy Leek Sauce, 180
Gnocchi Gratin with Pine Nuts and
  Gorgonzola Dolce, 335
Gnocchi Parisienne, 182, **183**
Grilled Seafood Kebabs and Orecchiette
  with Arugula, 138, **139**
Homemade Pappardelle, 255
Lamb Chops and Ragù with
  Malloreddus, 251
Lasagna-Style Baked Pennette with Meat
  Sauce, **62,** 63
Linguine with Spicy Sausage and Scallion
  Sauce, 172
Orecchiette with Grilled Squid, Arugula
  and Chickpeas, 171
Orecchiette with Pistachio Pesto, 257
Orecchiette with Sautéed Greens and
  Scallion Sauce, 180, **181**
Pappardelle with Milk-Roasted Baby Goat
  Ragù, **254,** 255
Pasta Shells with Artichoke Cream and
  Smoked Chicken, 61, **61**
Penne with Cauliflower and Leeks,
  337, **337**
Penne with Salmon Puttanesca, 170, **171**
Potato Gnocchi, 336
Shellfish Paella with Fregola, **250,** 251
Spaghettini with Eggplant and Fried
  Capers, 257
Spaghetti with Clams and Green Beans,
  334, 335
Spinach and Egg-Drop Pasta Soup,
  12, **13**

recipe index

Spinach and Ricotta Pappardelle, 179

Sweet Potato Gnocchi with Salsify, Chestnuts and Ham, 80

Tagliatelle with Mussels and Tarragon, 334, **334**

Three-Cheese Mini Macs, **16,** 17

Whole Wheat Linguine with Manila Clams and Baby Fennel, 64

Pastry Shell, Buttery, 283

peaches

Brandied Peaches, 280

Chilled Peaches with Arborio Rice Pudding and Cinnamon Churros, **272,** 273

Peach-Apricot Cobbler with Almond Ice Milk, 271

Peach-Raspberry Pie, 275

peanut butter

Asian-Style Spicy Coleslaw, 264, **265**

Cold Peanut Noodles with Tofu and Red Peppers, 257

Crunchy Milk Chocolate–Peanut Butter Layer Cake, 369

peanuts

Asian Bar Mix, 300, **301**

Best-Ever Nut Brittle, 102

Crunchy Milk Chocolate–Peanut Butter Layer Cake, 369

Frasca's Gorp, 110, **111**

Nutty Caramel Corn, 192

pears

Creamy Pear, Mascarpone and Pecorino Farfalle, 180

Moscato-Roasted Pears and Cider-Poached Apples, 358, **359**

Olive Oil and Sauternes Cake with Roasted Pears, 368

Poached Pear and Brown Butter Tart, 88, **89**

Radicchio Salad with Beets, Pear, Walnuts and Roquefort, 340

Root Vegetable, Pear and Chestnut Ragout, 68, **69**

peas

Bucatini with Sausage and Peas, 253

Creamy Chicken Soup with Baby Peas and Carrots, 288

Minty Peas and Carrots, 74

Rack of Lamb with Coconut-Mint Sauce and Glazed Peas, 161

Rosemary Lamb Chops, 164

Spice-Crusted Tuna with Thai Snow Pea Salad, 302, **303**

Spicy Red Curry Chicken, 151

Stir-Fried Chicken with Bok Choy, **150,** 151

Ten-Vegetable Salad with Lemon Vinaigrette, 174

Vegetable and Chicken Stir-Fry, 39

Vegetable Salad with Curry Vinaigrette and Fresh Mozzarella, 70

pecans

Best-Ever Nut Brittle, 102

Blackberry and Apple Crisp with Nut Topping, 358

Cardamom Spiced Crumb Cake, 93

Chicory Salad with Quince and Pecans, 24, **25**

Chocolate-Oatmeal Carmelitas, 192

Crispy Meringue-Topped Blondies, 364

Gingered Butternut Squash Soup with Spicy Pecan Cream, 288, **289**

Green Beans and Salsify with Country Ham and Pecans, 346, **347**

Lane Cake, 92

Pecan Sandies, 102, **103**

Spiced Pecans, 28

Sweet Potato Casserole, 82

Texas State Fair Pecan Pie, 360, **361**

pecorino cheese

Baked Sole with Pecorino and Butter, 230

Bucatini with Pancetta, Pecorino and Pepper, 172

Creamy Pear, Mascarpone and Pecorino Farfalle, 180

Ham-and-Cheese-Stuffed Veal Chops, 248

peppercorns

Four-Pepper Steak au Poivre, 166

Pepper-Crusted Prime Rib Roast with Mushroom-Armagnac Sauce, 54

Sichuan Peppercorn Shrimp, 147

peppers. *See also* **chiles**

Basque Chicken with Sweet Peppers and Tomatoes, **40,** 41

Chowchow, 266

Cold Peanut Noodles with Tofu and Red Peppers, 257

Easy Chicken Fajitas, 228

Egg White Soufflés with Ratatouille, 118, **119**

Grilled Lamb Shwarma, 162, **163**

Grilled-Pepper Salad with Currants, Capers and Feta, 178

Grilled Vegetable Bruschetta, 216

Grilled Vegetable Salad, 259

Mini Turkey Meat Loaves with Red Pepper Sauce, 158

Pimiento Cheese, 17

Pork with Grilled Vegetable Pisto, **322,** 323

Red Pepper and Walnut Dip, 125

Smoked Chicken Pizza with Red Pepper Pesto, 156

Spicy Zhoug, 173

Tuna with Provençal Vegetables, **232,** 233

pesto

Broken Lasagna with Walnut Pesto, 76, **77**

Fennel Slaw with Bresaola and Walnut Pesto, 221

Orecchiette with Pistachio Pesto, 257

Rack of Lamb with Arugula Pesto, 162, **163**

Smoked Chicken Pizza with Red Pepper Pesto, 156

Pickled Pearl Onions, **30,** 31

pickles

Bread-and-Butter Pickles, 264

Quick Kimchi Cucumbers, 189

Superfast Salt-and-Sugar Pickles, 189

Sweet-and-Sour Pickles, 189

Pie Dough, Flaky, 275

pies

Blueberry Pie, 275

Deep-Dish Strawberry-Rhubarb Pie, **274,** 275

Lemon Chess Pie, 91

Peach-Raspberry Pie, 275

Sour Cherry Pie, 275

Texas State Fair Pecan Pie, 360, **361**

Pimento Cheese, 17

pine nuts

Cocoa Tuiles with Nuts, 364, **365**

Grilled Quail with Pine Nuts and
Currants, 317

Lebanese Rice Pudding with Cinnamon
and Caraway, 95

Torta della Nonna, 362, **362**

pisco

Key Lime Pisco Sour, 217

Pisco Cup, 217

Pisco Smash, 217

pistachios

Best-Ever Nut Brittle, 102

Chicken Liver Pâté with Pistachios,
14, **15**

Chicory and Endive Salad with Spiced
Pistachios, 297

Cocoa Tuiles with Nuts, 364, **365**

Crisp Salami Cocktail Mix, 28

Date Cake with Pistachio Lebneh, 375

Green Salad with Goat Cheese and
Pistachios, 25

Orecchiette with Pistachio Pesto, 257

Pita Bread, Syrian, 163

pizza

Perfect Pizza Margherita, **136,** 137

Smoked Chicken Pizza with Red Pepper
Pesto, 156

plums

Almond-Plum Cake with Crème
Fraîche, 271

polenta

Fallen Polenta and Goat Cheese Soufflé
with Mixed Salad, 117

Sage Polenta, 182

Tuscan Pork Stew with Polenta, 46

Pomelo-Mint Mojito, 128

popcorn

Indian Popcorn, 300, **301**

Nutty Caramel Corn, 192

Sea Bass with Popcorn
Ponzu, 142

Popovers, Pat's, 110

pork. *See also* **bacon; ham; pork sausages**

Asian Baby Back Ribs with Panko-
Crusted Mushrooms, 158

Asian-Glazed Pork Shoulder, 42

Baked Beans with Pork Belly and
Quince, 46

Crispy Pork Milanese, 247

Double-Pork, Double-Cheese Burgers,
160, **160**

Ginger Beef and Pork Toasts, 22

Grilled Pork and Onion Tacos, 304

Grilled Pork Chops with Anchovies and
Swiss Chard, 244, **244**

Herb-Crusted Pork Roast with Ginger-Fig
Compote, 326, **327**

Loh Shi Fun, 256

Malay Gnocchi with Shredded Pork
Sauce, 253

Meatballs with Tomato Sauce, 60

Milk-Braised Pork Tenderloin with
Spinach and Strawberry Salad, 247

Missouri Baby Back Ribs with Apple
Slaw, 159

Pork and Bacon Kebabs, 159

Pork-and-Ricotta Meatballs in Tomato
Sauce, 47

Pork and Tomatillo Stew, 324, **325**

Pork and Wild Mushroom Daube, 44, **45**

Pork Chops with Shallots, 318, **318**

Pork Fried Rice, 65

Pork with Grilled Vegetable Pisto,
322, 323

Roasted Rack of Pork with Sausage
Stuffing, 324

Roast Pork Loin with Saba, 245

Roast Pork Shoulder with Fennel and
Potatoes, **160,** 161

Slow-Roasted Pork, 48

Slow-Roasted Pork Belly with Eggplant
and Pickled Fennel, 244, **244**

Soft Pork Tacos with Spicy Black Beans,
134, **134**

Spiced Pork Tenderloin with Hazelnut
Vinaigrette, 319

Stir-Fried Pork Belly with Kimchi, 160

Sweet and Savory Pork Empanadas, 122

Tuscan Pork Stew with Polenta, 46

pork sausages. *See also* **chorizo**

Bucatini with Sausage and Peas, 253

Crisp Salami Cocktail Mix, 28

Lemongrass Salad with Chinese Sausage
and Mango, 220

Linguine with Spicy Sausage and Scallion
Sauce, 172

Loh Shi Fun, 256

Roasted Rack of Pork with Sausage
Stuffing, 324

Roasted Turkey with Italian Sausage
Stuffing, 316

Sausages with Grapes, 319

Shrimp Boil Hobo Packs, 146, **147**

Slow-Cooker Sausage and Vegetable
Risotto, 339

Spicy Beef Chili, 60

potatoes. *See also* **sweet potatoes**

Almond Skordalia, 173

Baked Eggs with Chorizo and Potatoes,
112, **113**

Coal-Roasted Potatoes, 79

Creamy Potatoes with Bacon, **55,** 79

Crispy, Creamy Potato Puffs, 184

Crispy Potato Latkes, 19, **19**

Gnocchi Gratin with Pine Nuts and
Gorgonzola Dolce, 335

Goat Cheese, Lentil and Potato
Salad, 341

Japanese Frites, 80, **81**

Lemony Artichoke and Potato Soup, 116

Mashed Potatoes with Horseradish
Cream, 341

Oven Fries with Roasted Garlic, 354, **355**

Potato-Apple "Risotto," 57

Potato Chips with Chèvre, Pepper Jelly
and Bacon, 296

Potato Frittata with Prosciutto and
Gruyère, 111, **111**

Potato Gnocchi, 336

Potato Pancakes with Smoked Salmon,
Caviar and Dill Cream, **210,** 211

Potato Salad with Bacon and Barbecue
Sauce, 264

Rioja-Style Potatoes, 343

Roast Pork Shoulder with Fennel and
Potatoes, **160,** 161

Smoked Sablefish and Potato Salad with
Capers and Onions, 287

Thai Chicken Stew with Potato-Chive
Dumplings, 42, **43**

Two-Corn Crêpes, 212

Whipped Yukon Gold Potatoes, 341

Yukon Gold Potato, Leek and Fromage
Blanc Frittata, 112

Pot Pies, Lattice-Crusted Minestrone,
292, 293

poultry. *See also* **chicken; turkey**
Cornish Hens with Challah
Stuffing, 154

Cornish Hens with Porcini-Rice
Stuffing, 238

Duck Confit with Turnips, 318, **318**

Ginger Duck Salad with Green Tea
Dressing, 39

Grilled Capon with Salsa Verde, 41

Grilled Quail with Pine Nuts and
Currants, 317

Roasted Capon with Fig-and-Prosciutto
Stuffing, 317

prosciutto
Bagel Chips with Ricotta, Chive Puree
and Prosciutto, 17

Chicken Saltimbocca, 154

Piadina with Ricotta, Prosciutto and
Arugula, **224,** 225

Potato Frittata with Prosciutto and
Gruyère, 111, **111**

Prosciutto-Wrapped Halibut with
Asparagus Sauce, 140

Roasted Capon with Fig-and-Prosciutto
Stuffing, 317

Salad of Bitter Greens with Balsamic-
Glazed Prosciutto, 259

Prosecco-Saba Cocktail, 218

prunes
Aromatic Braised Lamb with Prunes and
Pine Nuts, 328

Baby Root Vegetable Stew with Black Tea
Prunes, 79

Dried Fruit Compote in Spiced
Syrup, 107

Dr Pepper–Glazed Ham with Prunes,
326, **327**

Kabocha Bread Pudding with Pisco-
Soaked Prunes, 99

Pudding Cakes, Lemon, 198, **199**

puddings
Butternut Squash Bread Pudding,
355, **355**

Chilled Peaches with Arborio Rice
Pudding and Cinnamon Churros,
272, 273

Kabocha Bread Pudding with Pisco-
Soaked Prunes, 99

Lebanese Rice Pudding with Cinnamon
and Caraway, 95

Lemon-Ricotta Puddings, 198

Pumpkin Puddings with Mile-High
Meringue, **374,** 375

Rich and Creamy Butterscotch Pudding,
96, **97**

Rich Baked Chocolate Puddings, 100

Sticky Toffee Pudding, 96

Vanilla Tapioca Pudding, 197

pumpkin
Pumpkin and Yellow Split Pea Soup, 288

Pumpkin Cake with Caramel–Cream
Cheese Frosting, **370,** 371

Pumpkin Cheesecake, 95

Pumpkin Puddings with Mile-High
Meringue, **374,** 375

pumpkin seeds
Cranberry Sauce with Spiced Pumpkin
Seeds, 357

Toasted Pumpkin Seeds, 301, **301**

q

Quail, Grilled, with Pine Nuts and
Currants, 317

Quark Cheesecake, Gingerbread with,
372, **373**

Quesadillas, Chicken, with Blue Cheese and
Caramelized Onions, 227

Quiche, Over-the-Top Mushroom, 282, **282**

quince
Baked Beans with Pork Belly and
Quince, 46

Chicory Salad with Quince and Pecans,
24, **25**

r

radicchio
Radicchio Salad with Beets, Pear,
Walnuts and Roquefort, 340

Salad of Bitter Greens with Balsamic-
Glazed Prosciutto, 259

radishes
Baby Root Vegetable Stew with Black Tea
Prunes, 79

Endive, Radish and Lemon Salad, 174

Herbed Crème Fraîche Dip with
Crudités, 15

Raw Corn and Radish Salad with Spicy
Lime Dressing, 258

Superfast Salt-and-Sugar Pickles, 189

Ten-Vegetable Salad with Lemon
Vinaigrette, 174

Warm Summer Vegetable Salad with
Brown Butter Dressing, **260,** 261

raisins
Frasca's Gorp, 110, **111**

Granola with Maple-Glazed Walnuts, 109

Grilled Cauliflower Salad with Raisin-
Almond Dressing, 71

Lane Cake, 92

Raisin Rye Bread, 108

raspberries
Peach-Raspberry Pie, 275

Raspberry Pâtes de Fruits, 107

Ricotta with Berries and Bitter
Honey, 277

Ratatouille, Egg White Soufflés
with, 118, **119**

Redfish on the Half Shell, 34, **34**

relish
Avocado Relish with Caramelized Onions,
357

Chowchow, 266

Grilled Chile Relish, 249

Remoulade, Chilled Shrimp with, 18

Remoulade, Tahini, 173

rhubarb

Deep-Dish Strawberry-Rhubarb Pie, **274,** 275

rice *See also* **risotto**

Bacon Fried Rice, 184

Carolina Gold Pilau with Shrimp, 65

Cauliflower Pilaf, 350

Chilled Peaches with Arborio Rice Pudding and Cinnamon Churros, **272,** 273

Cornish Hens with Porcini-Rice Stuffing, 238

Cumin-Scented White Rice, 350

Ginger Rice, 183

Golden Persian Rice, 82, **83**

Lebanese Rice Pudding with Cinnamon and Caraway, 95

Lemony Rice-Parsley Salad, 262, **263**

Pork Fried Rice, 65

Rice Salad with Merguez and Preserved Lemon Dressing, 262, **263**

Ricotta-Stuffed Arancini, 18

Shrimp Fried Rice, 252

Toasted-Coconut Basmati Rice, 351

White Rice with Wild Mushrooms and Merguez, 64

ricotta cheese

Bagel Chips with Ricotta, Chive Puree and Prosciutto, 17

Lemon-Ricotta Puddings, 198

Piadina with Ricotta, Prosciutto and Arugula, **224,** 225

Pork-and-Ricotta Meatballs in Tomato Sauce, 47

Ricotta-Stuffed Arancini, 18

Ricotta with Berries and Bitter Honey, 277

Spinach and Ricotta Pappardelle, 179

ricotta salata cheese

Arugula Salad with Ricotta Salata, 174

Sweet-and-Sour Eggplant with Ricotta Salata, 230

risotto

Beet and Cheddar Risotto, 263

Creamy Risotto with Edamame, 172

Creamy Saffron Risotto, 84

Fresh Corn Risotto, 262

Red Wine Risotto with Mushroom "Marmalade," 339

Saffron Risotto with Mussels and Bottarga, 252

Slow-Cooker Sausage and Vegetable Risotto, 339

rubs. *See* **spice rubs**

Rye Bread, Raisin, 108

S

Sablefish, Smoked, and Potato Salad with Capers and Onions, 287

Saffron Risotto, Creamy, 84

Saffron Risotto with Mussels and Bottarga, 252

Sage Polenta, 182

salad dressings

Blue Cheese Dressing, 187

Buttermilk Dressing, 187

Cilantro Dressing, 141

Dijon Vinaigrette, 187

Ginger Dressing, 187

Herb Vinaigrette, 187

Lemon Vinaigrette, 187

Miso Dressing, 187

Sesame Dressing, 187

Tzatziki Dressing, 187

salads (first course)

Chicory and Endive Salad with Spiced Pistachios, 297

Chicory Salad with Quince and Pecans, 24, **25**

Cucumber-Grapefruit Crab Salad, **124,** 125

Greek Salad with Feta Mousse, 214, **215**

Green Salad with Goat Cheese and Pistachios, 25

Green Salad with Nutty Vinaigrette, **26,** 27

Green Salad with Tangy Mustard Vinaigrette, 296

Italian Tuna, Green Olive and Tangerine Salad on Grilled Bread, 24

Roasted Beet Salad with Lemon Crème Fraîche, 297

Smoked Sablefish and Potato Salad with Capers and Onions, 287

Watercress Salad with Beets and Roasted-Garlic Crostini, 22

salads (main course)

Asian Shrimp and Cabbage Salad, 222, **223**

Cajun-Spiced Shrimp and Corn Salad, 222

Chinese Chicken Salad, 132

Crunchy Vietnamese Chicken Salad, 302

Fennel Slaw with Bresaola and Walnut Pesto, 221

Flatiron Steak Salad with Thai Dressing, 132

Ginger Duck Salad with Green Tea Dressing, 39

Grilled Squid with Miner's Lettuce Salad and Green Sauce, 221

Lemongrass Salad with Chinese Sausage and Mango, 220

Lemony Shrimp Salad, 130, **131**

Poached Salmon Salad with Lettuce and Asparagus, 132

Seared Chicken Liver Salad, 220

Smoked Trout Salad with Apple and Manchego, 221

Thai Grilled Beef Salad, 51

Tuna, Olive and Bread Salad, 224, **224**

Tuna Salad with Fennel, Cucumber and Tarragon, 222

salads (side)

Arugula Salad with Ricotta Salata, 174

Asian-Style Spicy Coleslaw, 264, **265**

Bread Salad with Tomatoes and Olives, 262

Cannellini and Green Bean Salad, 176, **177**

Caribbean-Style Sliced Salad, 340

Chilean Tomato and Onion Salad, 176

Chopped Salad with Apple Vinaigrette, 175

Citrus and Avocado Salad with Honey Vinaigrette, 70

Crunchy Cabbage Salad, 68

recite index

Crunchy Salad and Buttermilk
Dressing, 187

Endive, Radish and Lemon Salad, 174

Fennel Salad with Tarragon and Creamy
Tapenade, 258

Gazpacho Salad, 175

Goat Cheese, Lentil and Potato
Salad, 341

Grilled Cauliflower Salad with Raisin-
Almond Dressing, 71

Grilled Eggplant Salad, 179

Grilled-Pepper Salad with Currants,
Capers and Feta, 178

Grilled Romaine Salad with Roasted
Garlic Dressing, 178

Grilled Vegetable Salad, 259

Iceberg Wedges with Bacon and
Buttermilk Dressing, 344, **345**

Leafy Salad and Dijon Vinaigrette, 187

Lemony Rice-Parsley Salad, 262, **263**

Peppery Salad and Ginger Dressing,
186, 187

Potato Salad with Bacon and Barbecue
Sauce, 264

Radicchio Salad with Beets, Pear,
Walnuts and Roquefort, 340

Raw Corn and Radish Salad with Spicy
Lime Dressing, 258

Rice Salad with Merguez and Preserved
Lemon Dressing, 262, **263**

Roasted Carrot and Beet Salad with
Oranges and Arugula, 70

Salad of Bitter Greens with Balsamic-
Glazed Prosciutto, 259

Shredded Green Cabbage Salad with
Lemon and Garlic, 71

Ten-Vegetable Salad with Lemon
Vinaigrette, 174

Tomato and Bread Salad with Watercress
Salsa Verde, 261

Tomato, Cucumber and Onion
Salad, 261

Vegetable Salad with Curry Vinaigrette
and Fresh Mozzarella, 70

Warm Lentil and Ham Salad, **178,** 179

Warm Summer Vegetable Salad with
Brown Butter Dressing, **260,** 261

Watermelon and Arugula Salad with
Walnuts, 258

Wax Bean and Cherry Tomato Salad with
Goat Cheese, 176

Salami, Crisp, Cocktail Mix, 28

salmon

Barbecued Salmon Sandwiches,
134, 135

Dry-Rubbed Salmon Tacos with
Tomatillo-Avocado Slaw, 135

Eggs with Brown Butter and Salmon
Caviar, 14

Mustard-and-Coriander-Crusted
Salmon, 144

Pan-Glazed Salmon with Oyster Sauce
and Basil, 305

Pan-Roasted Salmon with Tomato
Vinaigrette, 145

Penne with Salmon Puttanesca, 170, **171**

Poached Salmon Salad with Lettuce and
Asparagus, 132

Potato Pancakes with Smoked Salmon,
Caviar and Dill Cream, **210,** 211

Roasted Salmon with Tomato Jam,
34, 35

Salmon Steaks with Soy-Maple Glaze,
144, **144**

Salmon with Tomato-Braised Chickpeas
and Herbed Yogurt, 305

Smoked Salmon Panini, 202, **203**

Texas Smoked Salmon Tartare, 286

salsas

Green Tomato Salsa, 242

Grilled Garlic Chicken with Salsa
Verde, 152

Salsa Roja, 118

Salsa Verde, 41,

Tomato and Bread Salad with Watercress
Salsa Verde, 261

salsify

Green Beans and Salsify with Country
Ham and Pecans, 346, **347**

Sweet Potato Gnocchi with Salsify,
Chestnuts and Ham, 80

sandwiches. *See also* **burgers**

Bacon, Cheese and Egg Sandwiches with
Hollandaise, 203, **203**

Bagna Cauda Salad Sandwiches, 225

Barbecued Salmon Sandwiches,
134, 135

BLT, Fried Egg and Cheese Sandwich,
282, **282**

Creamy Sun-Dried Tomato Soup with
Cheese Panini, 206

Deviled Ham Salad on Marbled Rye
Bread, 133

Grilled Chicken Sandwiches with
Mozzarella, Tomato and Basil,
228, **229**

Indian Pulled-Chicken Sandwiches, 228

Italian Tuna Melts, 225

Knuckle Sandwich, **226,** 227

Mini Brioche Lobster Rolls, 14, **15**

Piadina with Ricotta, Prosciutto and
Arugula, **224,** 225

Smoked Salmon Panini, 202, **203**

Soft-Shell Crab Sandwiches with
Pancetta and Remoulade, 226, **226**

Spicy Vietnamese Chicken
Sandwiches, 133

sangria

Brewsky Sangria, 299

Sangria Flora, 299

Thai-Basil Sangria, 218, **219**

Tuscan Sangria, **298,** 299

Vino Francesca, 299

Sardines, Stuffed Fried, 294, **295**

sauces. *See also* **salsas**

All'Amatriciana Sauce, 353

Almond Skordalia, 173

Caramel Sauce, 376

Chilled Shrimp with Remoulade, 18

Cilantro Dressing, 141

Classic Hollandaise Sauce, 203

Classic Marinara Sauce, **352,** 353

Cranberry Sauce with Spiced Pumpkin
Seeds, 357

Greek Salad Skewers with Anchovy Aioli,
24, **25**

Grilled Garlic Chicken with Salsa
Verde, 152

Grilled Shrimp with Orange Aioli, 238

Grilled Squid with Miner's Lettuce Salad
and Green Sauce, 221

Kansas City–Style Barbecue Sauce, 157

Lemon-Dijon Mayonnaise, 188

Mint-and-Date Dipping Sauce, **120,** 121

Puttanesca Sauce, 353

Salsa Roja, 118

Salsa Verde, 41

Spicy Zhoug, 173

Tahini Remoulade, 173

Toffee Sauce, 366

Vodka Sauce, 353

Yogurt-Tahini Sauce, 162

sausages. *See also* **pork sausages**

Rice Salad with Merguez and Preserved Lemon Dressing, 262, **263**

White Rice with Wild Mushrooms and Merguez, 64

scallions

Corn Bread with Scallions, 85

Grilled Meatballs with Scallion and Shaved Cheese Salad, **58,** 59

Linguine with Spicy Sausage and Scallion Sauce, 172

Orecchiette with Sautéed Greens and Scallion Sauce, 180, **181**

Wild Striped Bass with Scallions and Herb Salad, 142, **143**

scallops

Blood Orange–Scallop Ceviche, 123, **123**

Chestnut and Celery Root Soup with Chorizo and Scallops, 12

Grilled Scallops with Parsley Salad, 145

Grilled Seafood Kebabs and Orecchiette with Arugula, 138, **139**

Scallop Fritters, 122

Seared Scallops with Basil, Anchovy and Sweet Corn Pudding, 231

Seared Scallops with Cauliflower, Capers and Raisins, **144,** 145

sea bass

Salt-Baked Branzino with Citrus, Fennel and Herbs, 32, **33**

Sea Bass with Popcorn Ponzu, 142

seafood. *See* **fish; shellfish**

Semolina-Walnut Cake, Syrian, with Figs and Chocolate, 194

Sesame Dressing, 187

Shallots, Pork Chops with, 318, **318**

shellfish. *See also* **shrimp**

Blood Orange–Scallop Ceviche, 123, **123**

Chestnut and Celery Root Soup with Chorizo and Scallops, 12

Cod with Ham Powder and Garlic Wafers, 232, **232**

Cucumber-Grapefruit Crab Salad, **124,** 125

Curried Mussels in White Ale, 146

Grilled Scallops with Parsley Salad, 145

Grilled Seafood Kebabs and Orecchiette with Arugula, 138, **139**

Grilled Squid with Miner's Lettuce Salad and Green Sauce, 221

King Crab and Avocado Shooters, 124, **124**

Knuckle Sandwich, **226,** 227

Mini Brioche Lobster Rolls, 14, **15**

Mussel and Spinach Bisque, 290

Nantucket Clambake, **236,** 237

Orecchiette with Grilled Squid, Arugula and Chickpeas, 171

Oyster Dressing "Grand-Mère," 84

Oyster Tartlets, 18

Saffron Risotto with Mussels and Bottarga, 252

Scallop Fritters, 122

Seared Scallops with Basil, Anchovy and Sweet Corn Pudding, 231

Seared Scallops with Cauliflower, Capers and Raisins, **144,** 145

Shellfish Paella with Fregola, **250,** 251

Shrimp Boil Hobo Packs, 146, **147**

Sizzled Clams with Udon Noodles and Watercress, 63

Soft-Shell Crab Sandwiches with Pancetta and Remoulade, 226, **226**

Spaghetti with Clams and Green Beans, **334,** 335

Steamed Dungeness Crab with Meyer Lemon Aioli, 35

Summer Melon Soup with Crab, 211

Tagliatelle with Mussels and Tarragon, 334, **334**

Whole Wheat Linguine with Manila Clams and Baby Fennel, 64

Shortcakes, Strawberry, with Meyer Lemon Cream, 198, **199**

shrimp

Asian Shrimp and Cabbage Salad, 222, **223**

Bacon-Wrapped Shrimp with Passion Fruit Mustard, 146, **147**

Broken Pappardelle with Shrimp and Zucchini, 170

Cajun-Spiced Shrimp and Corn Salad, 222

Carolina Gold Pilau with Shrimp, 65

Chilled Shrimp with Remoulade, 18

Crispy Pan-Fried Shrimp and Chorizo Fideo Cakes, 148

Grilled Seafood Kebabs and Orecchiette with Arugula, 138, **139**

Grilled Shrimp Summer Rolls, 212, **213**

Grilled Shrimp with Orange Aioli, 238, **239**

Lemony Herb-Grilled Jumbo Shrimp, 307

Lemony Shrimp Salad, 130, **131**

Miso Soup with Shrimp and Tofu, 291, **291**

Rock Shrimp Poke with Ginger Soy Sauce and Hijiki, 238, **239**

Shellfish Paella with Fregola, **250,** 251

Shrimp Boil Hobo Packs, 146, **147**

Shrimp Fried Rice, 252

Shrimp with Green Beans and Toasted Coconut, 308

Sichuan Peppercorn Shrimp, 147

Spicy Shrimp in Chile Sauce, **306,** 307

slaws

Asian-Style Spicy Coleslaw, 264, **265**

Dry-Rubbed Salmon Tacos with Tomatillo-Avocado Slaw, 135

Fennel Slaw with Bresaola and Walnut Pesto, 221

Halibut with Avocado Mash and Green Papaya Slaw, 231

Missouri Baby Back Ribs with Apple Slaw, 159

Sole, Baked, with Pecorino and Butter, 230

soppressata

Crispy Frico with Soppressata, 27

Ham, Soppressata and Two-Cheese Strombolis, **13,** 67

recipe index

soufflés

Egg White Soufflés with Ratatouille, 118, **119**

Fallen Polenta and Goat Cheese Soufflé with Mixed Salad, 117

Gruyère Soufflés, 378, **379**

Swiss Chard Soufflé, 267

soups. *See also* **stews**

Asian Chicken Noodle Soup, 116

Asparagus Egg Drop Soup, 117

Butternut Squash Soup with Apple and Smoked Cheddar, 12

Caramelized Onion and Toasted Bread Soup, 10

Chestnut and Celery Root Soup with Chorizo and Scallops, 12

Chicken Soup with Rosemary Matzo Balls, 11

Corn and Bacon Soup with Jalapeño Crema, 210, **210**

Creamy Chicken Soup with Baby Peas and Carrots, 288

Creamy Sun-Dried Tomato Soup with Cheese Panini, 206

E.J.'s Vegetable Noodle Soup, 207

Gingered Butternut Squash Soup with Spicy Pecan Cream, 288, **289**

Lattice-Crusted Minestrone Pot Pies, **292**, 293

Lemony Artichoke and Potato Soup, 116

Lemony Asparagus Soup, 117

Miso Soup with Shrimp and Tofu, 291, **291**

Mushroom Barley Soup with Mini Meatballs, 290

Mussel and Spinach Bisque, 290

Pappa al Pomodoro, 206

Passatelli in Brodo, 10

Pork and Pink Bean Soup with Corn Muffin Croutons, 290, **291**

Pumpkin and Yellow Split Pea Soup, 288

Spicy Onion-Garlic Soup with Poached Eggs, 287

Spinach and Egg-Drop Pasta Soup, 12, **13**

Summer Melon Soup with Crab, 211

Summertime Ribollita, 208

Sunchoke and Cauliflower Soup, 207

Tortilla Broth, 351

Vegetable Soup with Fennel, Herbs and Parmesan Broth, 207

Watermelon Gazpacho, 208, **209**

Spelt Bread, Honey, 108

spice rubs

Indian Rub, 38

Jamaican Rub, 38

Spanish Rub, 38

spinach

Creamed Spinach with Buttery Crumbs, 344

Milk-Braised Pork Tenderloin with Spinach and Strawberry Salad, 247

Mussel and Spinach Bisque, 290

Sautéed Chicken with Olives, Capers and Roasted Lemons, 149

Slow-Cooker Sausage and Vegetable Risotto, 339

Spinach and Egg-Drop Pasta Soup, 12, **13**

Spinach and Ricotta Pappardelle, 179

T-Bone Fiorentina with Sautéed Spinach, 168

Split Pea, Yellow, and Pumpkin Soup, 288

squash. *See also* **pumpkin; zucchini**

Butternut Squash Bread Pudding, 355, **355**

Butternut Squash Soup with Apple and Smoked Cheddar, 12

Butternut Squash with Homemade Harissa, 78

Curry-Roasted Butternut Squash and Chickpeas, **342**, 343

Egg White Soufflés with Ratatouille, 118, **119**

Gingered Butternut Squash Soup with Spicy Pecan Cream, 288, **289**

Grilled Vegetable Bruschetta, 216

Grilled Vegetable Salad, 259

Kabocha Bread Pudding with Pisco-Soaked Prunes, 99

Lattice-Crusted Minestrone Pot Pies, **292**, 293

Mixed Grilled Vegetables with Fontina Fonduta, 259

Sautéed Brussels Sprouts and Squash with Fried Sage, 349

Summer Squash and Tomato Tart, 214

Summertime Ribollita, 208

Winter Squash and Gouda Croquettes, 294

squid

Grilled Squid with Miner's Lettuce Salad and Green Sauce, 221

Orecchiette with Grilled Squid, Arugula and Chickpeas, 171

Shellfish Paella with Fregola, **250,** 251

starters. *See also* **salads (first course); soups**

Asian Bar Mix, 300, **301**

Bagel Chips with Ricotta, Chive Puree and Prosciutto, 17

Blood Orange–Scallop Ceviche, 123, **123**

Breadstick Twists, 300

Caramelized Onion Tart with Whole Wheat Crust, 20

Cashews with Crispy Sage and Garlic, 300, **301**

Cheddar-and-Cayenne Crackers, 27

Cheese Crisps, 27

Chicken Liver Pâté, 121

Chicken Liver Pâté with Pistachios, 14, **15**

Chilled Shrimp with Remoulade, 18

Classic Deviled Eggs, 287

Corn and Shiitake Fritters, 212, **213**

Creamy Anchoïade with Crudités, 286

Crisp Salami Cocktail Mix, 28

Crispy Frico with Soppressata, 27

Crispy Potato Latkes, 19, **19**

Crispy Turkey Kathi Rolls with Mint-and-Date Dipping Sauce, **120,** 121

Dan Dan Noodles, 20

Eggplant Caponata Crostini, 22, **23**

Eggplant Caponatina, 214

Eggs with Brown Butter and Salmon Caviar, 14

Egg White Soufflés with Ratatouille, 118, **119**

Fallen Polenta and Goat Cheese Soufflé with Mixed Salad, 117

Fried Baby Artichokes, 23, **23**

Fromage Fort, 119, **119**

Ginger Beef and Pork Toasts, 22

Goat Cheese–Garlic Toasts, 211

Greek Salad Skewers with Anchovy Aioli, 24, **25**

Grilled Shrimp Summer Rolls, 212, **213**

Grilled Vegetable Bruschetta, 216

Herbed Crème Fraîche Dip with Crudités, 15

Indian Popcorn, 300, **301**

King Crab and Avocado Shooters, 124, **124**

Lattice-Crusted Minestrone Pot Pies, **292,** 293

Mini Brioche Lobster Rolls, 14, **15**

Oyster Tartlets, 18

Pimiento Cheese, 17

Potato Chips with Chèvre, Pepper Jelly and Bacon, 296

Potato Pancakes with Smoked Salmon, Caviar and Dill Cream, **210,** 211

Red Curry Buffalo Wings, 20

Red Pepper and Walnut Dip, 125

Ricotta-Stuffed Arancini, 18

Roquefort Gougères, 296

Rosemary-Maple Cashews, 28

Scallop Fritters, 122

Smoked Bluefish Pâté, 211

Smoked Mozzarella Spread, 293

Spanish Devils, 17

Spiced Pecans, 28

Stuffed Fried Sardines, 294, **295**

Summer Squash and Tomato Tart, 214

Sweet and Savory Pork Empanadas, 122

Texas Smoked Salmon Tartare, 286

Three-Cheese Mini Macs, **16,** 17

Toasted Pumpkin Seeds, 301, **301**

Two-Cheese Enchiladas, 118

Two-Corn Crêpes, 212

Warm Leek and Goat Cheese Dip, 15

Winter Squash and Gouda Croquettes, 294

stews

Aromatic Braised Lamb with Prunes and Pine Nuts, 328

Baby Root Vegetable Stew with Black Tea Prunes, 79

Beef Stew in Red Wine Sauce, **168,** 169

Galician Fish Stew, 305

Iraqi Lamb and Eggplant Stew with Pitas, 328, **329**

Mahimahi Coconut Curry Stew with Carrots and Fennel, 140

Pork and Tomatillo Stew, 324, **325**

Pork and Wild Mushroom Daube, 44, **45**

Thai Chicken Stew with Potato-Chive Dumplings, 42, **43**

Tuscan Pork Stew with Polenta, 46

Sticky Toffee Pudding, 96

Sticky Toffee Pudding Eggnog, 31

Stock, Ham Hock, 159

strawberries

Crêpes with Strawberries and Muscat-Yogurt Sauce, **200,** 201

Deep-Dish Strawberry-Rhubarb Pie, **274,** 275

Milk-Braised Pork Tenderloin with Spinach and Strawberry Salad, 247

Ricotta with Berries and Bitter Honey, 277

Strawberry Preserves, 281

Strawberry Shortcakes with Meyer Lemon Cream, 198, **199**

Virgin Strawberry Bellinis, 125

striped bass

Striped Bass with Spiced Vegetables and Cilantro Dressing, 141

Wild Striped Bass with Scallions and Herb Salad, 142, **143**

Strombolis, Ham, Soppressata and Two-Cheese, **13,** 67

stuffing. *See* **dressings + stuffings**

Summer Rolls, Grilled Shrimp, 212, **213**

Sunchoke and Cauliflower Soup, 207

sweet potatoes

Grilled Strip Steaks with Sweet Potato Hash Browns, 50, **51**

Japanese Frites, 80, **81**

Spiced Pork Tenderloin with Hazelnut Vinaigrette, 319

Sweet Potato Casserole, 82

Sweet Potatoes with Apple Butter, 343

Sweet Potato Gnocchi with Salsify, Chestnuts and Ham, 80

Winter Squash and Gouda Croquettes, 294

Swiss chard. *See* **chard**

swordfish

Swordfish in Creamy Tomato Sauce, 138, **139**

Swordfish Spiedini, 135

Swordfish Steaks with Smoky Tomato Ketchup, 138

t

tacos

Dry-Rubbed Salmon Tacos with Tomatillo-Avocado Slaw, 135

Grilled Pork and Onion Tacos, 304

Soft Pork Tacos with Spicy Black Beans, 134, **134**

tahini

Tahini Remoulade, 173

Yogurt-Tahini Sauce, 162

Tamarind, Fish Curry with, 234, **235**

tangerines

Italian Tuna, Green Olive and Tangerine Salad on Grilled Bread, 24

Roasted Turkey with Tangerine Glaze, 314, **315**

Tapioca Pudding, Vanilla, 197

tarts

Brûléed Key Lime Tarts, 90, **90**

Caramelized Onion Tart with Whole Wheat Crust, 20

Chocolate Tartlets with Candied Grapefruit Peel, 193

Oyster Tartlets, 18

Poached Pear and Brown Butter Tart, 88, **89**

Summer Squash and Tomato Tart, 214

Torta della Nonna, 362, **362**

Tiramisù, Classic, **98,** 99

Toffee Crust, Apple Cake with, 366

tofu

Cold Peanut Noodles with Tofu and Red Peppers, 257

Crispy Tofu with Noodles, 64

Miso Soup with Shrimp and Tofu, 291, **291**

Stir-Fried Tofu with Bok Choy, 130

tomatillos

Chicken and Cheese Enchiladas Verdes, 40, **40**

Dry-Rubbed Salmon Tacos with Tomatillo-Avocado Slaw, 135

Grilled Trout with Smoky Tomatillo Sauce and Cucumber Salad, 234, **235**

Pork and Tomatillo Stew, 324, **325**

tomatoes

All'Amatriciana Sauce, 353

Basque Chicken with Sweet Peppers and Tomatoes, **40,** 41

Braised Green Beans with Tomatoes and Garlic, 76

Bread Salad with Tomatoes and Olives, 262

Chilean Tomato and Onion Salad, 176

Chipotle Chilaquiles, 148

Chowchow, 266

Classic Marinara Sauce, **352,** 353

Creamy Sun-Dried Tomato Soup with Cheese Panini, 206

Fragrant Cauliflower in Tomato Sauce, 350

Gazpacho Salad, 175

Greek Salad Skewers with Anchovy Aioli, 24, **25**

Greek Salad with Feta Mousse, 214, **215**

Green Tomato Salsa, 242

Grilled Chicken Sandwiches with Mozzarella, Tomato and Basil, 228, **229**

Grilled Mahimahi with Tomatoes Two Ways, 139

Kansas City–Style Barbecue Sauce, 157

Knuckle Sandwich, **226,** 227

Meatballs with Tomato Sauce, 60

Pan-Roasted Salmon with Tomato Vinaigrette, 145

Pappa al Pomodoro, 206

Penne with Salmon Puttanesca, 170, **171**

Perfect Pizza Margherita, **136,** 137

Pork-and-Ricotta Meatballs in Tomato Sauce, 47

Puttanesca Sauce, 353

Roasted Salmon with Tomato Jam, **34,** 35

Salmon with Tomato-Braised Chickpeas and Herbed Yogurt, 305

Sicilian-Style Meatballs, 60, **61**

Summer Squash and Tomato Tart, 214

Summertime Ribollita, 208

Sweet-and-Sour Eggplant with Ricotta Salata, 230

Sweet-and-Spicy Ketchup, 188

Swordfish in Creamy Tomato Sauce, 138, **139**

Swordfish Steaks with Smoky Tomato Ketchup, 138

Tomato and Bread Salad with Watercress Salsa Verde, 261

Tomato, Cucumber and Onion Salad, 261

Vodka Sauce, 353

Watermelon Gazpacho, 208, **209**

Wax Bean and Cherry Tomato Salad with Goat Cheese, 176

tortillas

Chicken and Cheese Enchiladas Verdes, 40, **40**

Chicken Quesadillas with Blue Cheese and Caramelized Onions, 227

Chipotle Chilaquiles, 148

Crispy Turkey Kathi Rolls with Mint-and-Date Dipping Sauce, **120,** 121

Dry-Rubbed Salmon Tacos with Tomatillo-Avocado Slaw, 135

Easy Chicken Fajitas, 228

Grilled Pork and Onion Tacos, 304

Soft Pork Tacos with Spicy Black Beans, 134, **134**

Texas Smoked Salmon Tartare, 286

Tortilla Broth, 351

Tortilla–Corn Bread Dressing, 351

Two-Cheese Enchiladas, 118

trout

Grilled Trout with Smoky Tomatillo Sauce and Cucumber Salad, 234, **235**

Smoked Trout Salad with Apple and Manchego, 221

Truffettes, Coffee-Rum, 102

tuna

Crispy Tuna with Tuna-Caper Sauce, 142

Italian Tuna, Green Olive and Tangerine Salad on Grilled Bread, 24

Italian Tuna Melts, 225

Spice-Crusted Tuna with Thai Snow Pea Salad, 302, **303**

Tuna, Olive and Bread Salad, 224, **224**

Tuna Salad with Fennel, Cucumber and Tarragon, 222

Tuna with Provençal Vegetables, **232,** 233

Vitello Tonnato, 248

turkey

Crispy Turkey Cutlets with Walnut-Sage Sauce, 313

Crispy Turkey Kathi Rolls with Mint-and-Date Dipping Sauce, **120,** 121

Indian-Spiced Turkey Breast, 316

Mini Turkey Meat Loaves with Red Pepper Sauce, 158

Roasted Turkey with Italian Sausage Stuffing, 316

Roasted Turkey with Tangerine Glaze, 314, **315**

turnips

Duck Confit with Turnips, 318, **318**

Maple-Glazed Root Vegetables, 78

Root Vegetable, Pear and Chestnut Ragout, 68, **69**

Tzatziki Dressing, 187

Vanilla Bean Panna Cotta, Easy, 195

Vanilla Tapioca Pudding, 197

veal

Buckwheat Crêpes with Roast Veal and Parmesan, 67

Corzetti Pasta with Veal Ragù, 332, **333**

Fried Veal Cutlets with Herb Salad, 332

Grilled Meatballs with Scallion and Shaved Cheese Salad, **58,** 59

Ham-and-Cheese-Stuffed Veal Chops, 248

Lasagna-Style Baked Pennette with Meat Sauce, **62,** 63

Meatballs with Tomato Sauce, 60

Slow-Braised Osso Buco, 59

Tuscan-Style Veal Chops, 168, **168**

Vitello Tonnato, 248

vegetables. *See also specific vegetables*

Baby Root Vegetable Stew with Black Tea Prunes, 79

Creamy Anchoïade with Crudités, 286

E.J.'s Vegetable Noodle Soup, 207

Grilled Vegetable Bruschetta, 216

Grilled Vegetable Salad, 259

Honey-Glazed Roasted Root Vegetables, 345, **345**

Maple-Glazed Root Vegetables, 78

Mixed Grilled Vegetables with Fontina Fonduta, 259

Pork with Grilled Vegetable Pisto, **322,** 323

Root Vegetable, Pear and Chestnut Ragout, 68, **69**

Striped Bass with Spiced Vegetables and Cilantro Dressing, 141

Ten-Vegetable Salad with Lemon Vinaigrette, 174

Tuna with Provençal Vegetables, **232,** 233

Vegetable and Chicken Stir-Fry, 39

Vegetable Salad with Curry Vinaigrette and Fresh Mozzarella, 70

Vegetables à la Grecque, 87

Vegetable Soup with Fennel, Herbs and Parmesan Broth, 207

Warm Summer Vegetable Salad with Brown Butter Dressing, **260,** 261

vinaigrettes

Dijon Vinaigrette, 187

Herb Vinaigrette, 187

Lemon Vinaigrette, 187

Vodka Sauce, 353

walnuts

Broken Lasagna with Walnut Pesto, 76, **77**

Cranberry-Walnut Power Bars, 110

Crispy Turkey Cutlets with Walnut-Sage Sauce, 313

Fennel Slaw with Bresaola and Walnut Pesto, 221

Gooey Walnut Brownies, 280

Granola with Maple-Glazed Walnuts, 109

Green Beans with Shallots and Walnuts, 346

Lebanese Rice Pudding with Cinnamon and Caraway, 95

Radicchio Salad with Beets, Pear, Walnuts and Roquefort, 340

Red Pepper and Walnut Dip, 125

Roasted Carrot and Beet Salad with Oranges and Arugula, 70

Syrian Walnut-Semolina Cake with Figs and Chocolate, 194

Umbrian Apple-Walnut Roll-Ups, 363

Walnut Cake with Cinnamon Glaze, 94

Watermelon and Arugula Salad with Walnuts, 258

Zucchini Cupcakes with Cream Cheese Frosting, 273

watercress

Broken Lasagna with Walnut Pesto, 76, **77**

Citrus and Avocado Salad with Honey Vinaigrette, 70

Fried Veal Cutlets with Herb Salad, 332

Mustard-and-Coriander-Crusted Salmon, 144

Sizzled Clams with Udon Noodles and Watercress, 63

Tomato and Bread Salad with Watercress Salsa Verde, 261

Watercress Salad with Beets and Roasted-Garlic Crostini, 22

watermelon

Superfast Salt-and-Sugar Pickles, 189

Sweet-and-Sour Pickles, 189

Watermelon and Arugula Salad with Walnuts, 258

Watermelon Gazpacho, 208, **209**

Wheat Berries, Toasted, with Pancetta and Roasted Apples, 354

yogurt

Crêpes with Strawberries and Muscat-Yogurt Sauce, **200,** 201

Farfalle with Yogurt and Zucchini, 170, **171**

Gingerbread with Quark Cheesecake, 372, **373**

Lime-Yogurt Mousse, 197

Middle Eastern Yogurt Coolers, 28

Salmon with Tomato-Braised Chickpeas and Herbed Yogurt, 305

Tahini Remoulade, 173

Yogurt-Tahini Sauce, 162

Zhoug, Spicy, 173

zucchini

Broken Pappardelle with Shrimp and Zucchini, 170

Egg White Soufflés with Ratatouille, 118, **119**

Farfalle with Yogurt and Zucchini, 170, **171**

Grilled Vegetable Bruschetta, 216

Grilled Vegetable Salad, 259

Mixed Grilled Vegetables with Fontina Fonduta, 259

Pork with Grilled Vegetable Pisto, **322,** 323

Tuna with Provençal Vegetables, **232,** 233

Zucchini Cupcakes with Cream Cheese Frosting, 273

contributors

Tony Abou-Ganim, a mixologist who has appeared on the Fine Living Network and *Iron Chef America,* is currently writing his first book, *The Modern Mixologist.*

Carina Ahlin is the pastry chef at Aquavit in New York City.

Bruce Aidells is a chef, cookbook author and the founder of Aidells Sausage Company.

Ted Allen, the host of the PBS series *Uncorked: Wine Made Simple,* is a frequent judge on Food Network's *Iron Chef America* and Bravo's *Top Chef.* He is also the author of *The Food You Want to Eat: 100 Smart, Simple Recipes.*

Nate Appleman is the executive chef and co-owner of A16 and SPQR in San Francisco.

Cathal Armstrong, an F&W Best New Chef 2006, is the chef and owner of Restaurant Eve, The Majestic and Eamonn's A Dublin Chipper, all in Old Town Alexandria, Virginia.

Elena Arzak and **Juan Mari Arzak** are the father-and-daughter chefs at Restaurante Arzak in San Sebastian, Spain.

Periel Aschenbrand, an Israeli-American writer, is the author of *The Only Bush I Trust Is My Own* and founder of the T-shirt company Body as Billboard.

Lara Atkins is the pastry chef and co-owner of the Kitchen Table Bistro in Richmond, Vermont.

Eric Banh and **Sophie Banh** are siblings, co-chefs and co-owners of Monsoon in Seattle.

Dan Barber, an F&W Best New Chef 2002, is the chef and co-owner of Blue Hill in New York City and Blue Hill at Stone Barns in Pocantico Hills, New York.

Paul Bartolotta is chef and co-owner of four Bartolotta restaurants in the Milwaukee area. He is also the chef and a partner at Bartolotta Ristorante di Mare in the Wynn Las Vegas.

Lidia Bastianich, the chef and owner of six restaurants, hosts the PBS series *Lidia's Italy* and is the author of numerous cookbooks, including *Lidia's Family Table.*

Mario Batali is the chef and co-owner of 11 restaurants in New York City, Las Vegas and Los Angeles, as well as the co-owner of Italian Wine Merchants. He is the author of several cookbooks, including *Mario Tailgates NASCAR Style.*

Jill Bates is the pastry chef at Fearing's in the Dallas Ritz-Carlton.

Rick Bayless, an F&W Best New Chef 1988, is the chef and owner of Frontera Grill and Topolobampo in Chicago, the host of the PBS series *Mexico—One Plate at a Time* and the author of numerous cookbooks, including *Mexican Everyday.*

Octavio Becerra is the chef and owner of Palate Food + Wine, a restaurant and store in Glendale, California.

Pat Berrigan is the father-in-law of New Orleans chef John Besh.

John Besh, an F&W Best New Chef 1999, is the executive chef and co-owner of Restaurant August and co-owner of Lüke and Besh Steak, all in New Orleans, and La Provence in Lacombe, Louisiana.

Chris Beveridge was a bartender at 12 Baltimore in Kansas City, Missouri.

Chris Beverly is the bartender at Shinsei in Dallas.

Nichole Birdsall is a winemaker for Bonterra Vineyards and Fetzer Vineyards, both in Mendocino County, California, and makes organic wines for Bonterra as well as Five Hills Blue and Full Circle.

Jan Birnbaum is the chef and co-proprietor of the Epic Roasthouse in San Francisco.

Elena Bisestri, a native of Milan, is the executive chef at Palma in New York City.

April Bloomfield, an F&W Best New Chef 2007, is the executive chef and co-owner of the Spotted Pig in New York City.

Jimmy Bradley is the chef and owner of the Red Cat and The Harrison in New York City and author of *The Red Cat Cookbook.*

Gabriel Bremer, an F&W Best New Chef 2007, is the executive chef and co-owner of Salts in Cambridge, Massachusetts.

Yves Camdeborde is the owner of the Hôtel Relais Saint-Germain in Paris and the chef at the hotel's Le Comptoir and the adjacent La Crêperie du Comptoir.

Frank Castronovo is co-chef and partner at Frankies 457 and Frankies 17, both in New York City.

David Chang, an F&W Best New Chef 2006, is the chef and owner of Momofuku Noodle Bar, Momofuku Ssäm Bar and Momofuku Ko, all located in New York City.

Joanne Chang, a pastry chef, is the owner of Flour Bakery + Café, with two locations in Boston, and co-owner of Myers + Chang in Boston's South End.

Natalie Chanin owns Alabama Chanin, a line of clothing and accessories.

Melissa Clark, a freelance food writer, contributes regularly to F&W. She has written and co-authored 18 cookbooks; her most recent is *The Skinny: How to Fit into Your Little Black Dress Forever.*

Scott Conant, an F&W Best New Chef 2004, is the author of the forthcoming cookbook *Bold Italian.*

Steve Corry, an F&W Best New Chef 2007, is the executive chef and co-owner of Five Fifty-Five in Portland, Maine.

Dave Cruz is the chef de cuisine at Ad Hoc in Yountville, California.

Giada De Laurentiis is the host of Food Network's *Everyday Italian, Behind the Bash* and *Giada's Weekend Getaway* and the author of three cookbooks, including *Everyday Pasta.*

Jen Demarest is the pastry chef and a co-owner of Harvest Moon Café in Sonoma, California.

Salvatore Denaro is the chef and owner of Il Bacco Felice in Foligno, Italy.

Matthew Dillon, an F&W Best New Chef 2007, is the chef and owner of Sitka & Spruce in Seattle.

Paula Disbrowe, a food and travel writer, is the author of *Cowgirl Cuisine.*

Scott Dolich, an F&W Best New Chef 2004, is the chef and owner of Park Kitchen in Portland, Oregon.

Kristin Donnelly is an F&W editorial assistant.

Alexander Donowitz, age six, is the grand-prize winner of F&W's Ultimate Kid Cook Contest.

Elena D'Orazio, an expert on the traditional foods of Puglia, Italy, organizes cooking classes in New York City and Ostuni, Italy.

Palma D'Orazio is the owner of D'Orazio Food Events and Palma restaurant in New York City, where she also gives private cooking classes.

Erin Eastland is the executive chef at Cube Café, Cheese Bar & Marketplace in Los Angeles.

Eric Estrella is the executive pastry chef at The Café and The Greenhouse, both in the Chicago Ritz-Carlton.

Frank Falcinelli is co-chef and partner at Frankies 457 and Frankies 17, both in New York City.

Efisio Farris, the chef and owner of Arcodoro in Houston and Arcodoro & Pomodoro in Dallas, also owns GourmetSardinia, which imports traditional Sardinian foods.

Nick Fauchald is an F&W senior associate food editor.

Dean Fearing is the chef and a partner at Fearing's in the Dallas Ritz-Carlton.

Thom Fox is the executive chef at Acme Chophouse in San Francisco.

Gabriel Frasca is co-chef at Nantucket's Straight Wharf Restaurant.

Eben Freeman is the head bartender at Tailor in New York City.

Sandro Gamba, an F&W Best New Chef 2001, is the executive chef at the Four Seasons in Westlake Village, California.

Ina Garten is the host of Food Network's *Barefoot Contessa* and the author of five cookbooks, including *Barefoot Contessa At Home: Everyday Recipes You'll Make Over and Over Again.* She has a line of food products called Barefoot Contessa Pantry.

George Germon, co-chef and co-owner of Al Forno in Providence, co-authored *Cucina Simpatico* and *On Top of Spaghetti.*

Sara Kate Gillingham-Ryan is the food editor at apartmenttherapy.com and the author of *The Greyston Bakery Cookbook.*

David Gingrass is the co-chef and owner of TWO in San Francisco.

Artan Gjoni is the general manager of Norwood in New York City.

Ilan Hall is Bravo TV's season-two *Top Chef* winner.

Chris Hanna, the president of Hanna Winery in Sonoma, California, is a co-owner of Bungalow Coffee and Tea in Santa Rosa, California.

Marcella Hazan is the author of six Italian cookbooks, including *Essentials of Classic Italian Cooking* and *Marcella Cucina.*

Kate Heddings is an F&W senior editor and the editor of F&W cookbooks.

Marie Hejl, the host of the internationally syndicated *Cooking with Marie,* is the author of *Cooking with Marie: On Any Occasion!*

Beth Hensperger is the author of 18 cookbooks, including *The Bread Bible.*

Samia Hojaiban is a Lebanese home cook who lives in Meriden, Connecticut.

Jeff Hollinger, the manager of Absinthe Brasserie & Bar in San Francisco, is a co-author of *The Art of the Bar.*

Linton Hopkins is the executive chef and co-owner of Restaurant Eugene, and Holeman and Finch Public House, both in Atlanta.

Valeria Huneeus is the co-proprietor of Quintessa winery in Napa Valley and Veramonte winery in Chile.

contributors

Jeff Jackson is the executive chef at the Lodge at Torrey Pines in La Jolla, California.

Kate Jennings is the co-owner and pastry chef of La Laiterie at Farmstead and Farmstead in Providence.

Emily Kaiser is an F&W associate editor.

Gene Kato is a partner and one of the executive chefs at Japonais in Chicago, New York City and Las Vegas.

Elizabeth Katz is the executive pastry chef for B.R. Guest Restaurants in New York City.

Gavin Kaysen, an F&W Best New Chef 2007, is the chef at Café Boulud in New York City.

Thomas Keller is the executive chef and owner of several restaurants: the French Laundry, Ad Hoc, Bouchon and Bouchon Bakery in Yountville, California; Bouchon in Las Vegas; and Per Se and Bouchon Bakery in New York City. He has written several cookbooks, most recently *The Complete Keller: The French Laundry Cookbook & Bouchon.*

Marcia Kiesel is the F&W test kitchen supervisor and co-author of *The Simple Art of Vietnamese Cooking.*

Johanne Killeen, co-chef and co-owner of Al Forno in Providence, co-authored *Cucina Simpatico* and *On Top of Spaghetti.*

David Kinch is the chef and proprietor of Manresa in Los Gatos, California.

Paul Kirk is the author of *Paul Kirk's Championship Barbecue* and headmaster of his traveling School of Pitmasters.

Kate Krader is an F&W senior editor.

Roger Kugler is the sommelier at Suba in New York City.

Gray Kunz is the chef and owner of Café Gray and Grayz in New York City.

Harumi Kurihara is a Japanese television personality and author. Her most recent cookbook is *Harumi's Japanese Cooking.*

Kylie Kwong, the chef and owner of Billy Kwong in Sydney, is also the host of the television series *Kylie Kwong: Heart and Soul.* She has written several cookbooks, most recently *My China: A Feast for All the Senses.*

Emeril Lagasse is the chef and owner of 10 restaurants in New Orleans, Miami, Atlanta, Las Vegas, Gulfport, Mississippi, and Orlando, Florida. He stars on two Food Network shows—*Emeril Live* and *The Essence of Emeril*—and is the author of 12 cookbooks, most recently the children's book *Emeril's There's a Chef in My World!*

Padma Lakshmi, the host of Bravo TV's *Top Chef,* is the author of *Tangy, Tart, Hot & Sweet: A World of Recipes for Every Day* and *Easy Exotic: Low-Fat Recipes from Around the World.*

Louis Lambert is the chef and owner of Lamberts Downtown Barbecue in Austin. He also co-owns Dutch's in Fort Worth, Texas.

Viana La Place is the author of 10 cookbooks, including *My Italian Garden: More than 125 Seasonal Recipes from a Garden Inspired by Italy* and *Panini, Bruschetta, Crostini: Sandwiches, Italian Style.*

Michela Larson co-owns Rocca Kitchen & Bar in Boston.

Matt Lewis is the baker and co-owner of Baked in Brooklyn, New York.

Greg Lindgren, a mixologist, co-owns three San Francisco bars: 15 Romolo, Rosewood and Rye.

Shelley Lindgren is the wine director and co-owner of A16 and SPQR in San Francisco.

Donald Link is the executive chef and co-owner of Herbsaint and Cochon, both in New Orleans.

Brian Logsdon was the pastry chef at the Brown Hotel in Louisville, Kentucky.

Amanda Lydon, an F&W Best New Chef 2000, is co-chef at Nantucket's Straight Wharf Restaurant.

Matt Lyman is the co-executive chef and co-owner of Tender Greens in Los Angeles.

Lachlan Mackinnon Patterson, an F&W Best New Chef 2005, is the chef and co-owner of Frasca Food & Wine in Boulder, Colorado.

Pino Maffeo, an F&W Best New Chef 2006, is the executive chef and owner of Boston Public in Boston.

Lynnette Marrero is the head bartender at Freemans in New York City.

James Matusky was the bar manager at O-Bar in West Hollywood, California.

Duggan McDonnell is the mixologist and owner of Cantina in San Francisco.

Audwin McGee is an artist, builder and hunter in Tuscumbia, Alabama.

Alice Medrich is the author of six cookbooks, including *Pure Dessert.*

Janet Mendel is the author of six Spanish cookbooks, including *Cooking from the Heart of Spain: Food of La Mancha.*

Marc Meyer is the executive chef and co-owner of Five Points, Cookshop and Provence, all in New York City, and the author of *Brunch: 100 Recipes from Five Points Restaurant.*

Johnny Monis, an F&W Best New Chef 2007, is the chef and owner of Komi in Washington, DC.

Angie Mosier is a baker and food stylist in Atlanta. She founded the Blue-Eyed Daisy Bakeshop in Palmetto, Georgia.

Lynn Moulton is the pastry chef at Blu in Boston.

Andrew Murray is a winemaker and the owner of Andrew Murray Vineyards in Los Olivos, California.

David Myers, an F&W Best New Chef 2003, is the chef and co-owner of Sona, Boule and Comme Ça, all in Los Angeles.

Rita Nakouzi, the director of 4.5 Productions, consults on fashion and lifestyle trends.

Nawal Nasrallah is the author of *Delights from the Garden of Eden: A Cookbook and a History of the Iraqi Cuisine.*

Joan Nathan hosts the PBS series *Jewish Cooking in America.* She is the author of 10 cookbooks, including *Jewish Cooking in America.*

Michel Nischan is the chef and owner of Dressing Room: A Homegrown Restaurant in Westport, Connecticut, and the author of *Taste Pure and Simple* and *Homegrown Pure and Simple.*

Andy Nusser is the chef and a partner at Casa Mono in New York City.

Erik Oberholtzer is the co-executive chef and co-owner of Tender Greens in Los Angeles.

Sean O'Brien, an F&W Best New Chef 2007, is the executive chef and a partner at Myth Restaurant and Café Myth, both in San Francisco.

Nancy Olson is the pastry chef at Gramercy Tavern in New York City.

Grace Parisi is the F&W test kitchen senior associate and the author of *Get Saucy: Make Dinner a New Way Every Day with Simple Sauces, Marinades, Dressings, Glazes, Pestos, Pasta Sauces, Salsas, and More.*

Daniel Patterson, an F&W Best New Chef 1997, is the chef and owner of Coi in San Francisco and the co-author of *Aroma.*

Zak Pelaccio is the chef and owner of Fatty Crab and a consulting chef at Borough Food & Drink, both in New York City. He is also a consulting chef at Suka in London.

Jacques Pépin is an F&W contributing editor, master chef, television personality and cooking teacher. He authored the memoir *The Apprentice: My Life in the Kitchen* and 23 cookbooks, including *Chez Jacques: Traditions and Rituals of a Cook.*

Melissa Perello, an F&W Best New Chef 2004, was most recently the executive chef at the Fifth Floor in San Francisco.

Neil Perry, an Australian chef, cookbook author and TV personality, is the owner of Rockpool in Sydney and Rockpool Bar & Grill in Melbourne, Australia.

Adam Perry Lang is the chef and owner of Daisy May's BBQ USA in New York City.

Michelle Polzine is the pastry chef at Range in San Francisco.

Maricel Presilla is the chef and owner of Chucharamama and Zafra in Hoboken, New Jersey, and the Latin American grocery store Ultramarinos. She is the president of Gran Cacao and author of *The New Taste of Chocolate: A Cultural and Natural History of Chocolate with Recipes.*

Wolfgang Puck is the chef and owner of several restaurants, including Spago in Beverly Hills and Las Vegas. He owns Wolfgang Puck Worldwide, a catering and events company, and stars in Food Network's *Wolfgang Puck's Cooking Class.* He has written numerous cookbooks.

Anne Quatrano, an F&W Best New Chef 1995, is co-owner and co-chef of Bacchanalia, Floataway Café, Star Provisions, Provisions To Go and Quinones at Bacchanalia, all in Atlanta.

Steven Raichlen is the award-winning author of 26 cookbooks, including *BBQ USA: 425 Fiery Recipes from All Across America.* He hosts the PBS series *Barbecue University with Steven Raichlen* and has a line of grilling products called the Best of Barbecue.

Catherine Ralston, age 11, is a runner-up in F&W's Ultimate Kid Cook Contest.

Robert Rausch is a photographer and the creative director of GAS, a photography studio in Tuscumbia, Alabama.

Richard Reddington is the chef and owner of Redd in Yountville, California.

Billy Reid is a clothing designer based in Florence, Alabama.

E. Michael Reidt, an F&W Best New Chef 2001, is the executive chef at The Penthouse in Santa Monica, California.

Alex Roberts is the chef and owner of Restaurant Alma in Minneapolis.

Al Roker is the weatherman and a host of NBC's *The Today Show* as well as host of Food Network's *Roker on the Road.* He wrote two cookbooks, including Al Roker's *Hassle-Free Holiday Cookbook.*

Melissa Rubel is the F&W test kitchen associate and the assistant food editor for F&W cookbooks.

Gabriel Rucker, an F&W Best New Chef 2007, is the chef and owner of Le Pigeon in Portland, Oregon.

Alireza Sadeghzadeh runs the technology group of a small software firm. He lives in New York City.

Dede Sampson is a chef and food buyer for Nutrition Services at Berkeley Unified School District in California and a founding member of Locavores, a group committed to eating only foods grown or harvested within 100 miles of San Francisco.

contributors

Ian Schnoebelen, an F&W Best New Chef 2007, is the chef and co-owner of Iris in New Orleans.

Rob Schwartz is a co-author of *The Art of the Bar.*

Lisa Sewall is the pastry chef and co-owner of Lineage in Brookline, Massachusetts.

Dani Shaub, age eight, is a runner-up in F&W's Ultimate Kid Cook Contest.

Bruce Sherman, an F&W Best New Chef 2003, is the chef and a partner at North Pond in Chicago.

Hiroko Shimbo, a Japanese cooking expert, is the author of *The Sushi Experience* and *The Japanese Kitchen: 250 Recipes in a Traditional Spirit.*

Jeremy Silansky is the chef de cuisine at American Flatbread in Waitsfield, Vermont.

David Slape is the bartender at PDT in New York City.

Jeff Smith is the owner of Hourglass Vineyard in Napa Valley.

Hiro Sone, an F&W Best New Chef 1991, is the chef and co-owner of Terra in Napa Valley and Ame in San Francisco. He co-authored *Terra: Cooking from the Heart of Napa Valley.*

Ana Sortun is the chef and owner of Oleana in Cambridge, Massachusetts. She is the author of *Spice: Flavors of the Eastern Mediterranean.*

Isamu Soumi was the chef at Izakaya Ten in New York City.

Joe Sponzo is the private chef of the rock star Sting and his wife, Trudie Styler.

Susan Spungen is the former editorial director of food and entertaining at Martha Stewart Living Omnimedia. She is the author of *Recipes: A Collection for the Modern Cook.*

Sandi Stevens is a sculptor and co-owner of Cassetta Gallery in Tuscumbia, Alabama.

Frank Stitt is the chef and owner of Highlands Bar & Grill, Bottega, Bottega Café and Chez Fonfon in Birmingham, Alabama. He is the author of *Frank Stitt's Southern Table: Recipes and Gracious Traditions from Highlands Bar and Grill* and the forthcoming *Frank Stitt's Italian Table.*

Gary Sullivan is the co-owner of Rocca Kitchen & Bar in Boston.

Heidi Swanson is a San Francisco–based photographer, the author of *Cook 1.0* and *Super Natural Cooking* and the creator of the food blog 101Cookbooks.

Terry Sweetland is the private chef for the Swanson family of Swanson Vineyards in Oakville, California.

Pim Techamuanvivit has a food blog called Chez Pim.

Laurent Tourondel, an F&W Best New Chef 1998, is chef and owner of BLT Steak, with locations in New York City, Washington, DC, and San Juan, Puerto Rico, as well as several other BLT restaurants in New York City. He is the author of two cookbooks; his most recent is *Bistro Laurent Tourondel: New American Bistro Cooking.*

Ming Tsai is the chef and owner of Blue Ginger in Wellesley, Massachusetts, and the host and executive producer of the public television series *Simply Ming.*

Tina Ujlaki is the F&W executive food editor.

Tom Valenti is the chef and owner of Ouest and the forthcoming West Branch, both in New York City.

Stephanie Valentine is the chef at Oak Savanna Vineyard in Los Olivos, California.

Lionel Vatinet, a master baker, owns La Farm Bakery in Cary, North Carolina.

Paul Virant, an F&W Best New Chef 2007, is the executive chef and owner of Vie Restaurant in Western Springs, Illinois.

Jean-Georges Vongerichten, an F&W contributing editor, is the chef and co-owner of numerous restaurants around the world, including Jean Georges and Perry St. in New York City. He is the author of five cookbooks; the most recent is *Asian Flavors of Jean-Georges.*

Courtney Waddell is the F&W senior designer.

David Walzog is the executive chef at SW Steakhouse in the Wynn Las Vegas and the author of *The New American Steakhouse Cookbook.*

Paula Wolfert, an F&W contributing editor, is the author of many award-winning cookbooks, including *The Cooking of the Eastern Mediterranean, Couscous and Other Good Food from Morocco* and the recently updated *Cooking of Southwest France.*

Sarah Woodward is an English food and travel writer and author of *The Food of France.*

Takashi Yagihashi, an F&W Best New Chef 2000, is the chef and owner of Noodles by Takashi Yagihashi and the forthcoming Restaurant Takashi, both in Chicago.

Sang Yoon is the chef and owner of Father's Office in Santa Monica, California.

Andrew Zavala, age 11, is a runner-up in F&W's Ultimate Kid Cook Contest.

Andrew Zimmerman is the chef de cuisine at NoMI in Chicago.

photographers

Achilleos, Antonis 50, 84, 378

Akiko & Pierre 40 (right), 61 (bottom)

Albert Delamour/Clement USA Inc. 218

Bacon, Quentin 25 (left), 34 (top), 44 (center), 55, 66, 69, 81, 89, 90 (left), 150, 181, 191, 213 (bottom), 223, 229, 239 (top), 244 (left), 249 (left, right), 263 (left), front cover

Baigrie, James 13, 45, 62, 77 (top, bottom), 109, 111 (bottom), 136, 143, 144 (left), 168 (bottom), 171 (left), 178 (left), 183 (bottom), 199 (left, right), 235 (top), 268, 291 (top, bottom), 424

Barr, Edmund 44 (right)

Copyright © 2007 **Tom Hopkins** (From *Chez Jacques: Traditions and Rituals of a Cook* by Jacques Pépin, published by Stewart, Tabori & Chang) 168 (top)

Ferri, Fabrizio 362 (left, right)

Foley, Stephanie 306

French, Andrew flap photograph (Cowin), flap photograph (Heddings)

Gallagher, Dana 160 (right), 337 (right)

Halenda, Gregor 194, 202 (four salts)

Janisch, Frances 186, 187 (three salads and three dressings), 352, 353 (left, center and right)

Keller & Keller 327 (bottom), 355 (right)

Kernick, John 5 (summer, autumn), 26, 49, 86, 113, 120, 203 (right), 204, 246, 265, 277 (left), 289, 301 (right), 315, 342, 345 (bottom), 347, 348 (left, right), 356, 361 (top), 370, 374, 377 (left), 388 (summer), back cover (squash)

Kim, Kang 360

Kim, Yunhee 134 (right), 147 (top), 155, 263 (right), 280, back cover (chicken)

Kim-Bee, Max 6, 284, 345 (top), 373 (bottom)

Lagrange, Frédéric 4 (spring), 114, 124 (top), 177

Lung, Geoff 235 (bottom)

McEvoy, Maura 4 (winter), 8, 21, 58, 111 (top), 210 (left, right), 388 (winter)

Meppem, William 147 (bottom)

Merrell, James 23 (top, bottom), 98, 320–321, 380, 388 (autumn)

Miller, Ellie 303, 325, 329 (left), 337 (left)

Mortensen, Jens 156 (left, right), 185 (left, center, right)

Ngo, Ngoc Minh 163 (bottom)

Nilsson, Marcus 119 (bottom), 134 (left), 139 (top), 171 (right), 183 (top), 200 (bottom), 295, 309 (right), 322

Okada, Kana 15 (right), 16, 25 (right), 103 (top), 119 (top), 124 (bottom), 139 (bottom), 213 (top), 232 (left), 249 (center), 278, 282 (top, bottom), 309 (left), 318 (top, bottom), 329 (right), 359, 379

Pearson, Victoria 123 (left, right), 129, 167, back cover (O-Hurricane)

Pond, Edward 40 (left), 90 (right)

Rausch, Robert 37, 103 (bottom)

Roggiero, David 44 (left)

Rupp, Tina 15 (left), 30, 34 (bottom), 43, 51 (left, right), 61 (top), 97, 106, 131, 144 (right), 178 (right), 196, 200 (top), 203 (left), 224 (left, right), 226 (top), 232 (right), 274, 275 (left, center, right), 333, 361 (bottom), 373 (top), back cover (churros)

Schaeffer, Lucy 19 (left, right), 33, 83, 126–127, 327 (top), 355 (left)

Smith/Artisan, Eric Scott 331

Strickland, Buff 209, 219, 236

Tinslay, Petrina 311, 334 (right)

Tsay, David 160 (left), 163 (top)

Watson, Simon 250

Webber, Wendell 78, 293, 296, 298, 388 (spring)

Williams, Anna 105, 215, 226 (bottom), 239 (bottom), 244 (right), 254, 260, 272, 277 (right), 292, 301 (left), 334 (left), 365, 367, 377 (right)

All-Clad slow cooker courtesy of **All-Clad Metalcrafters** 338 (top)

KitchenAid slow cooker courtesy of **Kitchen Aid** 338 (bottom center)

Molteni stove courtesy of **Molteni by Electrolux Professional** 39

Dr. Andrew Weil's slow cooker courtesy of **Spring Switzerland** 338 (bottom right)

Cuisinart slow cooker courtesy of **Cuisinart** 338 (bottom left)